The McGraw-Hill Reader

McGraw-Hill Book Company

New York | St. Louis | San Francisco
Auckland | Bogotá | Hamburg
Johannesburg | London | Madrid
Mexico | Montreal | New Delhi
Panama | Paris | São Paulo | Singapore
Sydney | Tokyo | Toronto

GILBERT H. MULLER

The City University of New York
LaGuardia

The McGraw-Hill Reader

Second Edition

THE
McGRAW-HILL
READER

1234567890DOCDOC8987654

ISBN 0-07-043983-4

See Acknowledgments on pages 678-684.

This book was set in Palatino by Black Dot, Inc. (ECU).
The editors were Phillip A. Butcher and David Dunham;
the cover was designed by Nicholas Krenitsky;
the production supervisor was Leroy A. Young.
R. R. Donnelley & Sons Company was printer and binder.

Library of Congress Cataloging in Publication Data
Main entry under title:

The McGraw-Hill reader.

Includes index.
1. College readers. 2. English language—Rhetoric.
I. Muller, Gilbert H., date
PE1417.M44 1985 808′.0427 84-12265
ISBN 0-07-043983-4

To
Parisa and Darius
My favorite readers

Contents

3 Manners and Morals 109

4 Education 150

5 Human Development and Behavior 203

9 Literature, Media, and the Arts 431

10 Philosophy, Ethics, and Religious Thought 487

11 Mathematics, Science, and Technology 538

Contents of Essays by Rhetorical Mode

Narration

Description

Illustration

Comparison and Contrast

Analogy

Definition

Classification

Process Analysis

Causal Analysis

Argument and Persuasion

Logic

Humor, Irony, and Satire

Preface

The second edition of *The McGraw-Hill Reader*, which includes two new chapters on education and business and economics, presents classic and contemporary essays for today's college students. Addressing the growing national interest in core liberal arts programs, this text offers students and teachers a full range of prose models important to writing courses, reading sequences, and key undergraduate disciplines. All the selections, consisting of complete essays, chapters, and self-contained sections of chapters, have been selected for their significance, vitality, and technical precision. With its high caliber of material, its consistent humanistic emphases, and its clear organization, this text is lively, sophisticated, and eminently usable for college composition and reading programs.

The organization of *The McGraw-Hill Reader* is one of its most significant features. Composed of twelve chapters, each containing ten essays, the text moves from the personal to the global, embracing most modes of writing and most disciplines that college students encounter as undergraduates. Chapters 1 to 3 provide students with prose models largely of a personal, experiential, narrative, descriptive, or reflective nature—essays which enhance the acquisition of basic language skills. Following chapters cover core liberal arts disciplines, including education, the social sciences, business and economics, the humanities, and the sciences, and culminate in a final interdisciplinary chapter on civilization that is integral to the scope and method of *The McGraw-Hill Reader*. While reinforcing earlier modes of writing presented in the text, these disciplinary chapters offer prose models that provide practice in techniques of analysis, criticism, argumentation, and persuasion. As an integrated text, *The McGraw-Hill Reader* seeks to reconcile expressive and abstract varieties of thought in order to treat the total reading and writing process. An alternate table of contents, listing seven carefully selected essays in each of twelve rhetorical categories, adds to the flexibility of the text.

A second distinct advantage of *The McGraw-Hill Reader*, perhaps the primary one for teachers who prefer to create their own approaches to composition and reading courses, is the wide range of material and the varied constituencies represented in the text. The 120 essays in this book have been selected carefully to embrace a rich international assortment of authors, to achieve balance among constituencies, to cover major historical periods, and to provide prose models and styles for class analysis, discussion, and imitation. The authors in this text—whether Plato or Maya Angelou, Swift or Ruth Benedict—have high visibility as writers and thinkers of value. Some of these authors are represented by two or three essays. All the authors, writing from such vantage points as literature, journalism, anthropology, sociology, art history, biology, and philosophy, presuppose that ideas exist in the world, that we should be alert to them, and that we should be able to deal with them in our own discourse. Because the selections extend from very simple essays to the most abstract and complex modes of prose, teachers and students will be able to use *The McGraw-Hill Reader* at virtually all levels of a program. Above all, teachers can develop their own sequence of essays that will contribute not only to their students' reading and writing proficiency, but also to growing intellectual power.

The third major strength of *The McGraw-Hill Reader* is the uniform apparatus that has been designed for every essay. While there is a temptation not to include apparatus for some essays, particularly shorter, less complex ones—a temptation some leading anthologies have given in to—the premise here is that much can be learned from any well-written essay, especially if the apparatus is systematic in design. For each selection in this text there is a brief introduction. After each essay, there are ten questions organized in a common format created to reinforce essential reading, writing, and oral communication skills. These questions are organized in the following manner: questions 1 and 2, comprehension; questions 3 and 4, language and style; questions 5 to 8, compositional techniques and rhetorical strategies; question 9, discussion and prewriting; question 10, applications to writing. All specialized terms used in the questions are defined for students in the complete Glossary of Terms at the end of the text. The integrated design of these questions makes each essay—simple or complex, short or long, old or new—accessible to college students who possess mixed reading and writing abilities.

Supplementing *The McGraw-Hill Reader* is a comprehensive instructor's manual. Unlike many manuals, this one is a complete teacher's guide. *A Guide to the McGraw-Hill Reader* offers sample syllabi, well-considered strategies for teaching individual essays, sample rhetorical analyses, answers to questions, additional thought-provoking questions, comparative essay discussion formats, and tips for prewriting and guided writing activities. There is also a bibliography of criticism and research on the teaching of composition.

As teachers and students today, we might very well be inclined to agree with Dr. Johnson's definition of the essay as a "loose sally of the mind; an irregular, undigested piece; not a regular and orderly performance." There is, of course, an ideal essay lurking behind Johnson's whimsical definition. In this better sense of the essay, *The McGraw-Hill Reader* offers orderly performances. Here, there are regular prose models commensurate with our need and desire to read, write, and think well.

ACKNOWLEDGMENTS

It is a pleasure to acknowledge the support, assistance, and guidance of numerous individuals who helped to create *The McGraw-Hill Reader*. Foremost among these people are the many McGraw-Hill sales representatives who obtained teacher responses to questionnaires when the text was in its formative stages. I also want to thank the excellent McGraw-Hill family of assistants, editors, and executives who participated enthusiastically in the project from the outset and who encouraged me at every step.

The final design and content of *The McGraw-Hill Reader* reflects the expertise and advice offered by college teachers across the country who gave generously of their time when asked to respond to questionnaires submitted to them by McGraw-Hill sales representatives. These include: Howard Eitland, Boston College; Jack Williams, California State College, Stanislaus; John Gordon, Connecticut College; A. Harris Fairbanks, University of Connecticut; Scott Elledge, Cornell University; Bernard Beranek, G. F. Provost, Duquesne University; J. A. LaBashak, Edinboro State College; Robert Hogenson, Ferris State College; John McGrail, Fitchburg State College; James Fetler, Foothill College; Lynn Garrett, Louisiana State University; Gloria Conforti, Loyola University of Chicago; Florence Frank, University of Massachusetts; Robert L. Brown, University of Minnesota; Lee Nicholson, Modesto Junior College; Mary McHenry, Mount Holyoke College; Mary Wagoner, University of New Orleans; Linda Barlow, Walter Beale, Erika Lindemann, University of North Carolina;

June Verbillion, Northeastern Illinois University; Penny Hirsch, Northwestern University; David Fite, University of Santa Clara; Tony Tyler, State University College, Potsdam; and Peter DeBlois, Syracuse University.

Warm appreciation is also extended to those college and university English professors who carefully read the manuscript in part or in its entirety, and who made many constructive suggestions for improvement. I am most grateful to Lillian Gottesman, Bronx Community College; Dennis R. Gabriel, Cuyahoga Community College; John Hanes, Duquesne University; James Mauch, Foothill College; Margaret A. Strom, George Washington University; Robert J. Pelinski, University of Illinois; Eugene Hammond, University of Maryland; Robert L. Brown, University of Minnesota; Jack Wilson, Old Dominion University; David Fite, University of Santa Clara; Grayce F. Salerno, Seton Hall University; Carl Wooton, University of Southwestern Louisiana; and Susan Miller, University of Wisconsin.

Special recognition must also be given to those specialists in various liberal arts fields who provided advice: Jane S. Zembaty, Department of Philosophy, University of Dayton; Linda Davidoff, Department of Psychology, Essex Community College; Curtis Williams, Department of Biology, The State University of New York; and Diane Papalia-Finlay, Department of Psychology, University of Wisconsin.

For the second edition, I should like to thank the following reviewers for their supportive and most helpful evaluations: Kathleen Bell, University of Miami; Irene Clark, University of Southern California; Alan Golding, University of California, Los Angeles; Patricia Owen, Nassau Community College; Linda H. Peterson, Yale University; Rosentine Purnell, California State University, Northridge; Carl Quesnell, Iowa State University; and Mary Ann Wilson, Georgia State University.

Above all, I wish to thank Dr. Richard McAdams of Manhattan College for his help in designing biographical sketches and exercise materials and for his superlative work on *A Guide to the McGraw-Hill Reader*.

Finally, I am pleased to acknowledge support from the Mellon Foundation, the Graduate Center of The City University of New York, and the United States Office of Education (Title III) that enabled me to concentrate on the development of this text.

Gilbert H. Muller

The McGraw-Hill Reader

1

Personal Narrative

LANGSTON HUGHES

Salvation

James Langston Hughes (1902–1967), poet, playwright, fiction writer, biographer, and essayist, was for more than fifty years one of the most productive and significant modern American authors. In *The Weary Blues* (1926), *Simple Speaks His Mind* (1950), *The Ways of White Folks* (1940), *Selected Poems* (1959), and dozens of other books, he strove, in his own words, "to explain the Negro condition in America." This essay, from his 1940 autobiography *The Big Sea*, reflects the sharp, humorous, often bittersweet insights contained in Hughes's examination of human behavior.

1 I was saved from sin when I was going on thirteen. But not really saved. It happened like this. There was a big revival at my Auntie Reed's church. Every night for weeks there had been much preaching, singing, praying, and shouting, and some very hardened sinners had been brought to Christ, and the membership of the church had grown by leaps and bounds. Then just before the revival ended, they held a special meeting for children, "to bring the young lambs to the fold." My aunt spoke of it for days ahead. That night I was escorted to the

front row and placed on the mourners' bench with all the other young sinners, who had not yet been brought to Jesus.

My aunt told me that when you were saved you saw a light, 2
and something happened to you inside! And Jesus came into your life! And God was with you from then on! She said you could see and hear and feel Jesus in your soul. I believed her. I had heard a great many old people say the same thing and it seemed to me they ought to know. So I sat there calmly in the hot, crowded church, waiting for Jesus to come to me.

The preacher preached a wonderful rhythmical sermon, all 3
moans and shouts and lonely cries and dire pictures of hell, and then he sang a song about the ninety and nine safe in the fold, but one little lamb was left out in the cold. Then he said: "Won't you come? Won't you come to Jesus? Young lambs, won't you come?" And he held out his arms to all us young sinners there on the mourners' bench. And the little girls cried. And some of them jumped up and went to Jesus right away. But most of us just sat there.

A great many old people came and knelt around us and 4
prayed, old women with jet-black faces and braided hair, old men with work-gnarled hands. And the church sang a song about the lower lights are burning, some poor sinners to be saved. And the whole building rocked with prayer and song.

Still I kept waiting to *see* Jesus. 5

Finally all the young people had gone to the altar and were 6
saved, but one boy and me. He was a rounder's son named Westley. Westley and I were surrounded by sisters and deacons praying. It was very hot in the church, and getting late now. Finally Westley said to me in a whisper: "God damn! I'm tired o' sitting here. Let's get up and be saved." So he got up and was saved.

Then I was left all alone on the mourners' bench. My aunt 7
came and knelt at my knees and cried, while prayers and song swirled all around me in the little church. The whole congregation prayed for me alone, in a mighty wail of moans and voices. And I kept waiting serenely for Jesus, waiting, waiting—but he didn't come. I wanted to see him, but nothing happened to me. Nothing! I wanted something to happen to me, but nothing happened.

I heard the songs and the minister saying: "Why don't you 8
come? My dear child, why don't you come to Jesus? Jesus is waiting for you. He wants you. Why don't you come? Sister Reed, what is this child's name?"

"Langston," my aunt sobbed. 9

"Langston, why don't you come? Why don't you come and 10
be saved? Oh, Lamb of God! Why don't you come?"

Now it was really getting late. I began to be ashamed of 11
myself, holding everything up so long. I began to wonder what God

thought about Westley, who certainly hadn't seen Jesus either, but who was now sitting proudly on the platform, swinging his knicker-bockered legs and grinning down at me, surrounded by deacons and old women on their knees praying. God had not struck Westley dead for taking his name in vain or for lying in the temple. So I decided that maybe to save further trouble, I'd better lie, too, and say that Jesus had come, and get up and be saved.

So I got up. 12

Suddenly the whole room broke into a sea of shouting, as 13
they saw me rise. Waves of rejoicing swept the place. Women leaped in the air. My aunt threw her arms around me. The minister took me by the hand and led me to the platform.

When things quieted down, in a hushed silence, punctuated 14
by a few ecstatic "Amens," all the new young lambs were blessed in the name of God. Then joyous singing filled the room.

That night, for the last time in my life but one—for I was a big 15
boy twelve years old—I cried. I cried, in bed alone, and couldn't stop. I buried my head under the quilts, but my aunt heard me. She woke up and told my uncle I was crying because the Holy Ghost had come into my life, and because I had seen Jesus. But I was really crying because I couldn't bear to tell her that I had lied, that I had deceived everybody in the church, that I hadn't seen Jesus, and that now I didn't believe there was a Jesus any more, since he didn't come to help me.

QUESTIONS

1. How does Hughes describe the revival meeting he attended? What is the dominant impression?

2. Describe Hughes's shifting attitude toward salvation in this essay. What does he say about salvation in the last paragraph?

3. Key words and phrases in this essay relate to the religious experience. Locate five of these words and expressions and explain their connotations.

4. What is the level of language in the essay? How does Hughes employ language effectively?

5. Where is the thesis statement in the essay? How does it prepare the reader for the ironic situation that develops?

6. How much time elapses and why is this important to the effect? How does the author achieve narrative coherence?

7. Locate details and examples in the essay that are especially vivid and

interesting. Compare your list with what others have listed. What are the similarities? The differences?

8. What is the tone of the essay? What is the relationship between tone and point of view?

9. Can giving in to group pressures have lasting effects on a person? Why or why not?

10. a. Recount an event in your life during which you surrendered to group pressures.
b. Write a narrative account of the most intense religious experience in your life.
c. Narrate an episode in which you played a trick on people simply to win their approval or satisfy their expectations.

MARK TWAIN

The Mesmerizer

Mark Twain (1835–1910) was the pseudonym of Samuel Langhorne Clemens. In *The Adventures of Tom Sawyer* (1876), *Life on the Mississippi* (1883), and *The Adventures of Huckleberry Finn* (1885), Twain celebrated the challenge of the frontier experience and the promise of a new world. Adventurous, democratic, individualistic, hardheaded, and sentimental, he projected the image of the essential American, a role that did not always correspond to the bitter and tragic aspects of his later life. This selection, from Twain's autobiography, captures the young Clemens as a humorous crowd pleaser and perpetrator of hoaxes—characteristics that became central to his adult life and career.

An exciting event in our village was the arrival of the 1
mesmerizer. I think the year was 1850. As to that I am not sure but I know the month—it was May; that detail has survived the wear of fifty years. A pair of connected little incidents of that month have served to keep the memory of it green for me all this time; incidents of no consequence and not worth embalming, yet my memory has preserved them carefully and flung away things of real value to give them space and make them comfortable. The truth is, a person's memory has no more sense than

his conscience and no appreciation whatever of values and proportions. However, never mind those trifling incidents; my subject is the mesmerizer now.

He advertised his show and promised marvels. Admission as usual: 25 cents, children and negroes half price. The village had heard of mesmerism in a general way but had not encountered it yet. Not many people attended the first night but next day they had so many wonders to tell that everybody's curiosity was fired and after that for a fortnight the magician had prosperous times. I was fourteen or fifteen years old, the age at which a boy is willing to endure all things, suffer all things short of death by fire, if thereby he may be conspicuous and show off before the public; and so, when I saw the "subjects" perform their foolish antics on the platform and make the people laugh and shout and admire I had a burning desire to be a subject myself. 2

Every night for three nights I sat in the row of candidates on the platform and held the magic disk in the palm of my hand and gazed at it and tried to get sleepy, but it was a failure; I remained wide awake and had to retire defeated, like the majority. Also, I had to sit there and be gnawed with envy of Hicks, our journeyman; I had to sit there and see him scamper and jump when Simmons the enchanter exclaimed, "See the snake! See the snake!" and hear him say, "My, how beautiful!" in response to the suggestion that he was observing a splendid sunset; and so on—the whole insane business. I couldn't laugh, I couldn't applaud; it filled me with bitterness to have others do it and to have people make a hero of Hicks and crowd around him when the show was over and ask him for more and more particulars of the wonders he had seen in his visions and manifest in many ways that they were proud to be acquainted with him. Hicks—the idea! I couldn't stand it; I was getting boiled to death in my own bile. 3

On the fourth night temptation came and I was not strong enough to resist. When I had gazed at the disk a while I pretended to be sleepy and began to nod. Straightway came the professor and made passes over my head and down my body and legs and arms, finishing each pass with a snap of his fingers in the air to discharge the surplus electricity; then he began to "draw" me with the disk, holding it in his fingers and telling me I could not take my eyes off it, try as I might; so I rose slowly, bent and gazing, and following that disk all over the place, just as I had seen the others do. Then I was put through the other paces. Upon suggestion I fled from snakes, passed buckets at a fire, became excited over hot steamboat-races, made love to imaginary girls and kissed them, fished from the platform and landed mud cats that outweighed me—and so on, all the customary marvels. But not in the customary way. I was cautious at first and watchful, being afraid the professor would discover that I was an 4 imposter and drive me from the platform in disgrace; but as soon as I realized that I was not in danger, I set myself the task of terminating Hick's usefulness as a subject and of usurping his place.

It was a sufficiently easy task. Hicks was born honest, I 5
without that incumbrance—so some people said. Hicks saw what he saw and reported accordingly, I saw more than was visible and added to it such details as could help. Hicks had no imagination; I had a double supply. He was born calm, I was born excited. No vision could start a rapture in him and he was constipated as to language, anyway; but if I saw a vision I emptied the dictionary onto it and lost the remnant of my mind into the bargain.

At the end of my first half-hour Hicks was a thing of the past, 6
a fallen hero, a broken idol, and I knew it and was glad and said in my heart, "Success to crime!" Hicks could never have been mesmerized to the point where he could kiss an imaginary girl in public or a real one either, but I was competent. Whatever Hicks had failed in, I made it a point to succeed in, let the cost be what it might, physically or morally. He had shown several bad defects and I had made a note of them. For instance, if the magician asked, "What do you see?" and left him to invent a vision for himself, Hicks was dumb and blind, he couldn't see a thing nor say a word, whereas the magician soon found out that when it came to seeing visions of a stunning and marketable sort I could get along better without his help than with it.

Then there was another thing: Hicks wasn't worth a tallow 7
dip on mute mental suggestion. Whenever Simmons stood behind him and gazed at the back of his skull and tried to drive a mental suggestion into it, Hicks sat with vacant face and never suspected. If he had been noticing he could have seen by the rapt faces of the audience that something was going on behind his back that required a response. Inasmuch as I was an imposter I dreaded to have this test put upon me, for I knew the professor would be "willing" me to do something, and as I couldn't know what it was, I should be exposed and denounced. However, when my time came, I took my chance. I perceived by the tense and expectant faces of the people that Simmons was behind me willing me with all his might. I tried my best to imagine what he wanted but nothing suggested itself. I felt ashamed and miserable then. I believed that the hour of my disgrace was come and that in another moment I should go out of that place disgraced. I ought to be ashamed to confess it but my next thought was not how I could win the compassion of kindly hearts by going out humbly and in sorrow for my misdoings, but how I could go out most sensationally and spectacularly.

There was a rusty and empty old revolver lying on the table 8
among the "properties" employed in the performances. On May Day two or three weeks before there had been a celebration by the schools

and I had had a quarrel with a big boy who was the school bully and I had not come out of it with credit. That boy was now seated in the middle of the house, halfway down the main aisle. I crept stealthily and impressively toward the table, with a dark and murderous scowl on my face, copied from a popular romance, seized the revolver suddenly, flourished it, shouted the bully's name, jumped off the platform and made a rush for him and chased him out of the house before the paralyzed people could interfere to save him. There was a storm of applause, and the magician, addressing the house, said, most impressively—

"That you may know how really remarkable this is and how 9
wonderfully developed a subject we have in this boy, I assure you that without a single spoken word to guide him he has carried out what I mentally commanded him to do, to the minutest detail. I could have stopped him at a moment in his vengeful career by a mere exertion of my will, therefore the poor fellow who has escaped was at no time in danger."

So I was not in disgrace. I returned to the platform a hero and 10
happier than I have ever been in this world since. As regards mental suggestion, my fears of it were gone. I judged that in case I failed to guess what the professor might be willing me to do, I could count on putting up something that would answer just as well. I was right, and exhibitions of unspoken suggestion became a favorite with the public. Whenever I perceived that I was being willed to do something I got up and did something—anything that occurred to me—and the magician, not being a fool, always ratified it. When people asked me, "How *can* you tell what he is willing you to do?" I said, "It's just as easy," and they always said admiringly, "Well, it beats *me* how you can do it."

Hicks was weak in another detail. When the professor made 11
passes over him and said "his whole body is without sensation now—come forward and test him, ladies and gentlemen," the ladies and gentlemen always complied eagerly and stuck pins into Hicks, and if they went deep Hicks was sure to wince, then that poor professor would have to explain that Hicks "wasn't sufficiently under the influence." But I didn't wince; I only suffered and shed tears on the inside. The miseries that a conceited boy will endure to keep up his "reputation"! And so will a conceited man; I know it in my own person and have seen it in a hundred thousand others. That professor ought to have protected me and I often hoped he would, when the tests were unusually severe, but he didn't. It may be that he was deceived as well as the others, though I did not believe it nor think it possible. Those were dear good people but they must have carried simplicity and credulity to the limit. They would stick a pin in my arm and bear on it until they drove it a third of its length in, and then be

lost in wonder that by a mere exercise of will power the professor could turn my arm to iron and make it insensible to pain. Whereas it was not insensible at all; I was suffering agonies of pain.

12 After that fourth night, that proud night, that triumphant night, I was the only subject. Simmons invited no more candidates to the platform. I performed alone every night the rest of the fortnight. Up to that time a dozen wise old heads, the intellectual aristocracy of the town, had held out as implacable unbelievers. I was as hurt by this as if I were engaged in some honest occupation. There is nothing surprising about this. Human beings feel dishonor the most, sometimes, when they most deserve it. That handful of overwise old gentlemen kept on shaking their heads all the first week and saying they had seen no marvels there that could not have been produced by collusion; and they were pretty vain of their unbelief too and liked to show it and air it and be superior to the ignorant and the gullible. Particularly old Dr. Peake, who was the ringleader of the irreconcilables and very formidable; for he was an F.F.V., he was learned, white-haired and venerable, nobly and richly clad in the fashions of an earlier and a courtlier day, he was large and stately, and he not only seemed wise but was what he seemed in that regard. He had great influence and his opinion upon any matter was worth much more than that of any other person in the community. When I conquered him at last, I knew I was undisputed master of the field; and now after more than fifty years I acknowledge with a few dry old tears that I rejoiced without shame.

QUESTIONS

1. What reasons does Twain give for his triumph over Hicks?

2. Describe the persona that Twain creates for himself in the course of the narrative.

3. Twain uses abstract language in the first paragraph. Does Twain rely more on abstract or concrete language in the course of the narrative? Why?

4. Use these words in sentences: *embalming* (paragraph 1); *bile* (paragraph 3); *terminating* (paragraph 4); *incumbrance* (paragraph 5); *stealthily* (paragraph 8).

5. Why is Twain's introductory paragraph effective? In what way does the paragraph establish the tone of the essay?

6. What is the point of view in the essay? What advantage does Twain gain from his selection of point of view?

7. Cite three instances of comic techniques and effects in the essay and explain their significance.

8. What is the function of Twain's editorializing in the account?

9. Speaking of memory, Twain declares that "a person's memory has no more sense than his conscience and no appreciation whatever of values and proportions." Do you agree or disagree with this opinion? Why do you hold this view?

10. Recall a memorable event that occurred in your neighborhood when you were a child. Write a narrative essay about your role in it.

MAXINE HONG KINGSTON

The Woman Warrior

Maxine Hong Kingston (1940–) has written two books on the Chinese-American experience that have established her as a major contemporary prose stylist. *The Woman Warrior* (1976) and *China Men* (1980) are brilliant explorations of personal and ethnic consciousness. This selection from her first book is filled with the mysteries, family tales, and legends that she uses to create the tapestry of her complex cultural identity.

My American life has been such a disappointment. 1

"I got straight A's, Mama." 2

"Let me tell you a true story about a girl who saved her village." 3

I could not figure out what was my village. And it was important that I do something big and fine, or else my parents would sell me when we made our way back to China. In China there were solutions for what to do with little girls who ate up food and threw tantrums. You can't eat straight A's. 4

When one of my parents or the emigrant villagers said, "Feeding girls is feeding cowbirds," I would thrash on the floor and scream so hard I couldn't talk. I couldn't stop. 5

"What's the matter with her?" 6

"I don't know. Bad, I guess. You know how girls are. 'There's no profit in raising girls. Better to raise geese than girls.' " 7

"I would hit her if she were mine. But then there's no use wasting all that discipline on a girl. 'When you raise girls, you're raising children for strangers.' " 8

"Stop that crying!" my mother would yell. "I'm going to hit you if you don't stop. Bad girl! Stop!" I'm going to remember never to hit or to scold my children for crying, I thought, because then they will only cry more. 9

"I'm not a bad girl," I would scream. "I'm not a bad girl. I'm not a bad girl." I might as well have said, "I'm not a girl." 10

"When you were little, all you had to say was 'I'm not a bad girl,' and you could make yourself cry," my mother says, talking-story about my childhood. 11

I minded that the emigrant villagers shook their heads at my sister and me. "One girl—and another girl," they said, and made our parents ashamed to take us out together. The good part about my brothers being born was that people stopped saying, "All girls," but I learned new grievances. "Did you roll an egg on *my* face like that when *I* was born?" "Did you have a full-month party for *me*?" "Did you turn on all the lights?" "Did you send *my* picture to Grandmother?" "Why not? Because I'm a girl? Is that why not?" "Why didn't you teach me English?" "You like having me beaten up at school, don't you?" 12

"She is very mean, isn't she?" the emigrant villagers would say. 13

"Come, children. Hurry. Hurry. Who wants to go out with Great-Uncle?" On Saturday mornings, my great-uncle, the ex-river pirate, did the shopping. "Get your coats, whoever's coming." 14

"I'm coming. I'm coming. Wait for me." 15

When he heard girls' voices, he turned on us and roared, "No girls!" and left my sisters and me hanging our coats back up, not looking at one another. The boys came back with candy and new toys. When they walked through Chinatown, the people must have said, "A boy—and another boy—and another boy!" At my great-uncle's funeral I secretly tested out feeling glad that he was dead—the six-foot bearish masculinity of him. 16

I went away to college—Berkeley in the sixties—and I studied, and I marched to change the world, but I did not turn into a boy. I would have liked to bring myself back as a boy for my parents to welcome with chickens and pigs. That was for my brother, who returned alive from Vietnam. 17

If I went to Vietnam, I would not come back; females desert families. It was said, "There is an outward tendency in females," which meant that I was getting straight A's for the good of my future husband's family, not my own. I did not plan ever to have a husband. 18

I would show my mother and father and the nosey emigrant villagers that girls have no outward tendency. I stopped getting straight A's.

And all the time I was having to turn myself American- 19
feminine, or no dates.

There is a Chinese word for the female *I*—which is "slave." 20
Break the women with their own tongues!

I refused to cook. When I had to wash dishes, I would crack 21
one or two. "Bad girl," my mother yelled, and sometimes that made me gloat rather than cry. Isn't a bad girl almost a boy?

"What do you want to be when you grow up, little girl?" 22

"A lumberjack in Oregon." 23

Even now, unless I'm happy, I burn the food when I cook. I 24
do not feed people. I let the dirty dishes rot. I eat at other people's tables but won't invite them to mine, where the dishes are rotting.

If I could not-eat, perhaps I could make myself a warrior like 25
the swordswoman who drives me. I will—I must—rise and plow the fields as soon as the baby comes out.

Once I get outside the house, what bird might call me; on 26
what horse could I ride away? Marriage and childbirth strengthen the swordswoman, who is not a maid like Joan of Arc. Do the women's work; then do more work, which will become ours too. No husband of mine will say, "I could have been a drummer, but I had to think about the wife and kids. You know how it is." Nobody supports me at the expense of his own adventure. Then I get bitter: no one supports me; I am not loved enough to be supported. That I am not a burden has to compensate for the sad envy when I look at women loved enough to be supported. Even now China wraps double binds around my feet.

When urban renewal tore down my parents' laundry and 27
paved over our slum for a parking lot, I only made up gun and knife fantasies and did nothing useful.

From the fairy tales, I've learned exactly who the enemy are. I 28
easily recognize them—business-suited in their modern American executive guise, each boss two feet taller than I am and impossible to meet eye to eye.

I once worked at an art supply house that sold paints to 29
artists. "Order more of that nigger yellow, willya?" the boss told me. "Bright, isn't it? Nigger yellow."

"I don't like that word," I had to say in my bad, small- 30
person's voice that makes no impact. The boss never deigned to answer.

I also worked at a land developer's association. The building 31
industry was planning a banquet for contractors, real estate dealers, and real estate editors. "Did you know the restaurant you chose for

the banquet is being picketed by CORE and the NAACP?" I squeaked.

"Of course I know." The boss laughed. "That's why I chose 32
it."

"I refuse to type these invitations," I whispered, voice 33
unreliable.

He leaned back in his leather chair, his bossy stomach 34
opulent. He picked up his calendar and slowly circled a date. "You will be paid up to here," he said. "We'll mail you the check."

If I took the sword, which my hate must surely have forged 35
out of the air, and gutted him, I would put color and wrinkles into his shirt.

It's not just the stupid racists that I have to do something 36
about, but the tyrants who for whatever reason can deny my family food and work. My job is my own only land.

To avenge my family, I'd have to storm across China to take 37
back our farm from the Communists; I'd have to rage across the United States to take back the laundry in New York and the one in California. Nobody in history has conquered and united both North America and Asia. A descendant of eighty pole fighters, I ought to be able to set out confidently, march straight down our street, get going right now. There's work to do, ground to cover. Surely, the eighty pole fighters, though unseen would follow me and lead me and protect me, as is the wont of ancestors.

Or it may well be that they're resting happily in China, their 38
spirits dispersed among the real Chinese, and not nudging me at all with their poles. I mustn't feel bad that I haven't done as well as the swordswoman did; after all, no bird called me, no wise old people tutored me. I have no magic beads, or water gourd sight, no rabbit that will jump in the fire when I'm hungry. I dislike armies.

I've looked for the bird. I've seen clouds make pointed angel 39
wings that stream past the sunset, but they shred into clouds. Once at a beach after a long hike I saw a seagull, tiny as an insect. But when I jumped up to tell what miracle I saw, before I could get the words out I understood that the bird was insect-size because it was far away. My brain had momentarily lost its depth perception. I was that eager to find an unusual bird.

The news from China has been confusing. It also had 40
something to do with birds. I was nine years old when the letters made my parents, who are rocks, cry. My father screamed in his sleep. My mother wept and crumpled up the letters. She set fire to them page by page in the ashtray, but new letters came almost every day. The only letters they opened without fear were the ones with red borders, the holiday letters that mustn't carry bad news. The other

letters said that my uncles were made to kneel on broken glass during their trials and had confessed to being land-owners. They were all executed, and the aunt whose thumbs were twisted off drowned herself. Other aunts, mothers-in-law, and cousins disappeared; some suddenly began writing to us again from communes or from Hong Kong. They kept asking for money. The ones in communes got four ounces of fat and one cup of oil a week, they said, and had to work from 4 A.M. to 9 P.M. They had to learn to do dances waving red kerchiefs; they had to sing nonsense syllables. The communists gave axes to the old ladies and said, "Go and kill yourself. You're useless." If we overseas Chinese would just send money to the Communist bank, our relatives said, they might get a percentage of it for themselves. The aunts in Hong Kong said to send money quickly; their children were begging on the sidewalks and mean people put dirt in their bowls.

When I dream that I am wire without flesh, there is a letter on 41
blue airmail paper that floats above the night ocean between here and China. It must arrive safely or else my grandmother and I will lose each other.

My parents felt bad whether or not they sent money. Some- 42
times they got angry at their brothers and sisters for asking. And they would not simply ask but have to talk-story too. The revolutionaries had taken Fourth Aunt and Uncle's store, house, and lands. They attacked the house and killed the grandfather and oldest daughter. The grandmother escaped with the loose cash and did not return to help. Fourth Aunt picked up her sons, one under each arm, and hid in the pig house, where they slept that night in cotton clothes. The next day she found her husband, who had also miraculously escaped. The two of them collected twigs and yams to sell while their children begged. Each morning they tied the faggots on each other's back. Nobody bought from them. They ate the yams and some of the children's rice. Finally Fourth Aunt saw what was wrong. "We have to shout 'Fuel for sale' and 'Yams for sale,' " she said. "We can't just walk unobtrusively up and down the street." "You're right," said my uncle, but he was shy and walked in back of her. "Shout," my aunt ordered, but he could not. "They think we're carrying these sticks home for our own fire," she said. "Shout." They walked about miserably, silently, until sundown, neither of them able to advertise themselves. Fourth Aunt, an orphan since the age of ten, mean as my mother, threw her bundle down at his feet and scolded Fourth Uncle, "Starving to death, his wife and children starving to death, and he's too damned shy to raise his voice." She left him standing by himself and afraid to return empty-handed to her. He sat under a tree to think, when he spotted a pair of nesting doves. Dumping his bag of

yams, he climbed up and caught the birds. That was when the Communists trapped him, in the tree. They criticized him for selfishly taking food for his own family and killed him, leaving his body in the tree as an example. They took the birds to a commune kitchen to be shared.

It is confusing that my family was not the poor to be championed. They were executed like the barons in the stories, when they were not barons. It is confusing that birds tricked us. 43

What fighting and killing I have seen have not been glorious but slum grubby. I fought the most during junior high school and always cried. Fights are confusing as to who has won. The corpses I've seen had been rolled and dumped, sad little dirty bodies covered with a police khaki blanket. My mother locked her children in the house so we couldn't look at dead slum people. But at news of a body, I would find a way to get out; I had to learn about dying if I wanted to become a swordswoman. Once there was an Asian man stabbed next door, word on cloth pinned to his corpse. When the police came around asking questions, my father said, "No read Japanese. Japanese words. Me Chinese." 44

I've also looked for old people who could be my gurus. A medium with red hair told me that a girl who died in a far country follows me wherever I go. This spirit can help me if I acknowledge her, she said. Between the head line and heart line in my right palm, she said, I have the mystic cross. I could become a medium myself. I don't want to be a medium. I don't want to be a crank taking "offerings" in a wicker plate from the frightened audience, who, one after another, asked the spirits how to raise rent money, how to cure their coughs and skin diseases, how to find a job. And martial arts are for unsure little boys kicking away under fluorescent lights. 45

I live now where there are Chinese and Japanese, but no emigrants from my own village looking at me as if I had failed them. Living among one's own emigrant villagers can give a good Chinese far from China glory and a place. "That old busboy is really a swordsman," we whisper when he goes by, "He's a swordsman who's killed fifty. He has a tong ax in his closet." But I am useless, one more girl who couldn't be sold. When I visit the family now, I wrap my American successes around me like a private shawl; I *am* worthy of eating the food. From afar I can believe my family loves me fundamentally. They only say, "When fishing for treasures in the flood, be careful not to pull in girls," because that is what one says about daughters. But I watched such words come out of my own mother's and father's mouths; I looked at their ink drawing of poor people snagging their neighbor's flotage with long flood hooks and pushing the girl babies on down the river. And I had to get out of 46 hating range. I read in an anthropology book that Chinese say, "Girls are necessary too"; I have never heard the Chinese I know make this concession. Perhaps it was a saying in another village. I refuse to shy my way anymore through our Chinatown, which tasks me with the old sayings and the stories.

The swordswoman and I are not so dissimilar. May my 47
people understand the resemblance soon so that I can return to them. What we have in common are the words at our backs. The ideographs for *revenge* are "report a crime" and "report to five families." The reporting is the vengeance—not the beheading, not the gutting, but the words. And I have so many words—"chink" words and "gook" words too—that they do not fit on my skin.

QUESTIONS

1. Summarize the "autobiography" that Kingston presents of herself in this selection. What are her family and its individual members like?

2. Why has the author's American life "been such a disappointment"? What specific problems has she encountered in relation to Chinese culture *and* to American culture? What is her major problem?

3. What connotations does Kingston explore for the words *girls* and *females*? What connotations does she bring to the word *swordswoman*?

4. Locate five Chinese expressions or sayings in this selection. What is their effect on the tone of the essay?

5. The author's introductory paragraph consists of a single sentence. How effective is this strategy and why?

6. Analyze the author's presentation of chronology. List the scenes into which the action is divided. Where are there stories within stories? Why does Kingston present such a complex tapestry of chronology and events? How, finally, does the author use narration to advance expository or explanatory ends?

7. Why is characterization important to the development of Kingston's thesis? How does the author *create* vivid characters? Cite specific examples and techniques.

8. Which paragraphs comprise the conclusion? How do these paragraphs reflect some of the major motifs of the essay?

9. In *China Men*, Kingston speaks of "trying to unravel the mysteries" of her family. What mysteries does she explore here? Why has this become a preoccupation of contemporary Americans? What "mysteries" concerning your family or your origins would you like to explore?

10. a. Write an autobiographical or narrative essay tracing a particular problem that you had to face while growing up in your family.
b. Narrate an event that happened to one of your relatives or ancestors in the "old country," the nation of your family's origin.

JAMES THURBER

The Night the Bed Fell

James Thurber (1894–1961), foremost American cartoonist, playwright, and humorist, was from 1927 a lifelong contributer to *The New Yorker.* He demonstrated a distinctive talent for turning his personal experiences into comic renditions of American life in such books as *My Life and Hard Times* (1933) and *The Middle-Aged Man on the Flying Trapeze* (1935). Other significant works include *My World and Welcome to It* (1942), *Fables for Our Time* (1939), and *The Thurber Album* (1952). The comic misadventures that unfold in the following tale are typical of Thurber's approach to human behavior.

I suppose that the high-water mark of my youth in 1
Columbus, Ohio, was the night the bed fell on my father. It makes a better recitation (unless, as some friends of mine have said, one has heard it five or six times) than it does a piece of writing, for it is almost necessary to throw furniture around, shake doors, and bark like a dog, to lend the proper atmosphere and verisimilitude to what is admittedly a somewhat incredible tale. Still, it did take place.

It happened, then, that my father had decided to sleep in the 2
attic one night, to be away where he could think. My mother opposed the notion strongly because, she said, the old wooden bed up there was unsafe; it was wobbly and the heavy headboard would crash down on father's head in case the bed fell, and kill him. There was no dissuading him, however, and at a quarter past ten he closed the attic door behind him and went up the narrow twisting stairs. We later heard ominous creakings as he crawled into bed. Grandfather, who usually slept in the attic bed when he was with us, had disappeared some days before. (On these occasions he was usually gone six or eight days and returned growling and out of temper, with the news that the federal Union was run by a passel of blockheads and that the Army of the Potomac didn't have any more chance than a fiddler's bitch.)

We had visiting us at this time a nervous first cousin of mine named Briggs Beall, who believed that he was likely to cease breathing when he was asleep. It was his feeling that if he were not awakened every hour during the night, he might die of suffocation. He had been accustomed to setting an alarm clock to ring at intervals until morning, but I persuaded him to abandon this. He slept in my room and I told him that I was such a light sleeper that if anybody quit breathing in the same room with me, I would wake instantly. He tested me the first night—which I had suspected he would—by holding his breath after my regular breathing had convinced him I was asleep. I was not asleep, however, and called to him. This seemed to allay his fears a little, but he took the precaution of putting a glass of spirits of camphor on a little table at the head of his bed. In case I didn't arouse him until he was almost gone, he said, he would sniff the camphor, a powerful reviver. Briggs was not the only member of his family who had his crotchets. Old Aunt Melissa Beall (who could whistle like a man, with two fingers in her mouth) suffered under the premonition that she was destined to die on South High Street, because she had been born on South High Street and married on South High Street. Then there was Aunt Sarah Shoaf, who never went to bed at night without the fear that a burglar was going to get in and blow chloroform under her door through a tube. To avert this calamity—for she was in greater dread of anesthetics than of losing her household goods—she always piled her money, silverware, and other valuables in a neat stack just outside her bedroom, with a note reading: "This is all I have. Please take it and do not use your chloroform, as this is all I have." Aunt Gracie Shoaf also had a burglar phobia, but she met it with more fortitude. She was confident that burglars had been getting into her house every night for forty years. The fact that she never missed anything was to her no proof to the contrary. She always claimed that she scared them off before they could take anything, by throwing shoes down the hallway. When she went to bed she piled, where she could get at them handily, all the shoes there were about her house. Five minutes after she had turned off the light, she would sit up in bed and say "Hark!" Her husband, who had learned to ignore the whole situation as long ago as 1903, would either be sound asleep or pretend to be sound asleep. In either case he would not respond to her tugging and pulling, so that presently she would arise, tiptoe to the door, open it slightly and heave a shoe down the hall in one direction, and its mate down the hall in the other direction. Some nights she threw them all, some nights only a couple of pair. 3

But I am straying from the remarkable incidents that took place during the night that the bed fell on father. By midnight we were all in bed. The layout of the rooms and the disposition of their 4 occupants is important to an understanding of what later occurred. In the front room upstairs (just under father's attic bedroom) were my mother and my brother Herman, who sometimes sang in his sleep, usually "Marching Through Georgia" or "Onward, Christian Soldiers." Briggs Beall and myself were in a room adjoining this one. My brother Roy was in a room across the hall from ours. Our bull terrier, Rex, slept in the hall.

My bed was an army cot, one of those affairs which are made 5
wide enough to sleep on comfortably only by putting up, flat with the middle section, the two sides which ordinarily hang down like the sideboards of a drop-leaf table. When these sides are up, it is perilous to roll too far toward the edge, for then the cot is likely to tip completely over, bringing the whole bed down on top of one, with a tremendous banging crash. This, in fact, is precisely what happened, about two o'clock in the morning. (It was my mother who, in recalling the scene later, first referred to it as "the night the bed fell on your father.")

Always a deep sleeper, slow to arouse (I had lied to Briggs), I 6
was at first unconscious of what had happened when the iron cot rolled me onto the floor and toppled over on me. It left me still warmly bundled up and unhurt, for the bed rested above me like a canopy. Hence I did not wake up, only reached the edge of consciousness and went back. The racket, however, instantly awakened my mother, in the next room, who came to the immediate conclusion that her worst dread was realized: the big wooden bed upstairs had fallen on father. She therefore screamed, "Let's go to your poor father!" It was this shout, rather than the noise of my cot falling, that awakened Herman, in the same room with her. He thought that mother had become, for no apparent reason, hysterical. "You're all right, Mamma!" he shouted, trying to calm her. They exchanged shout for shout for perhaps ten seconds: "Let's go to your poor father!" and "You're all right!" That woke up Briggs. By this time I was conscious of what was going on, in a vague way, but did not yet realize that I was under my bed instead of on it. Briggs, awakening in the midst of loud shouts of fear and apprehension, came to the quick conclusion that he was suffocating and that we were all trying to "bring him out." With a low moan, he grasped the glass of camphor at the head of his bed and instead of sniffing it poured it over himself. The room reeked of camphor. "Ugf, ahfg," choked Briggs, like a drowning man, for he had almost succeeded in stopping his breath under the deluge of pungent spirits. He leaped out of bed and groped toward the open window, but he came up against one that was closed. With his hand, he beat out the glass, and I could hear it crash and tinkle on the alleyway below. It was at this juncture that I, in trying to get up, had the uncanny sensation of feeling my bed above

me! Foggy with sleep, I now suspected, in my turn, that the whole uproar was being made in a frantic endeavor to extricate me from what must be an unheard-of and perilous situation. "Get me out of this!" I bawled. "Get me out!" I think I had the nightmarish belief that I was entombed in a mine. "Gugh," gasped Briggs, floundering in his camphor.

By this time my mother, still shouting, pursued by Herman, 7
still shouting, was trying to open the door to the attic, in order to go up and get my father's body out of the wreckage. The door was stuck, however, and wouldn't yield. Her frantic pulls on it only added to the general banging and confusion. Roy and the dog were now up, the one shouting questions, the other barking.

Father, farthest away and soundest sleeper of all, had by this 8
time been awakened by the battering on the attic door. He decided that the house was on fire. "I'm coming, I'm coming!" he wailed in a slow, sleepy voice—it took him many minutes to regain full consciousness. My mother, still believing he was caught under the bed, detected in his "I'm coming!" the mournful, resigned note of one who is preparing to meet his Maker. "He's dying!" she shouted.

"I'm all right!" Briggs yelled to reassure her. "I'm all right!" 9
He still believed that it was his own closeness to death that was worrying mother. I found at last the light switch in my room, unlocked the door, and Briggs and I joined the others at the attic door. The dog, who never did like Briggs, jumped for him—assuming that he was the culprit in whatever was going on—and Roy had to throw Rex and hold him. We could hear father crawling out of bed upstairs. Roy pulled the attic door open, with a mighty jerk, and father came down the stairs, sleepy and irritable but safe and sound. My mother began to weep when she saw him. Rex began to howl. "What in the name of God is going on here?" asked father.

The situation was finally put together like a gigantic jig-saw 10
puzzle. Father caught a cold from prowling around in his bare feet but there were no other bad results. "I'm glad," said mother, who always looked on the bright side of things, "that your grandfather wasn't here."

QUESTIONS

1. Characterize the many participants in this human comedy. How are they similar? What is Thurber's attitude toward them?

2. Trace the sequence of events that throws the Thurber household into confusion.

3. Discuss Thurber's use of action verbs in this narrative.

4. What is the level of diction in this essay?

5. Why is Thurber's digressive technique in the early part of the article a useful strategy?

6. How important is setting in the creation of mood in this selection? How does Thurber create an effective setting? How do mood and tone reinforce each other?

7. Explore Thurber's use of transitions in the essay.

8. Explain the importance of Thurber's conclusion (paragraph 10). What does the conclusion reveal about the theme?

9. Thurber assumes a comic, mildly satirical attitude toward the eccentricity and confusion in his family. What is the value of this comic view in confronting confusing or chaotic situations?

10. Write a narrative account of an amusing moment in the life of your family.

DORIS LESSING

Being Prohibited

Doris Lessing (1919–   ), a major British novelist, was born in Kermanshah, Iran, of English parents. She moved at an early age with her parents to a large farm in Southern Rhodesia. At the age of 18, she went to Salisbury, entering quickly into the artistic and political life there. Lessing left Africa for London in 1949, and in 1950 she published her first novel, *The Grass is Singing*. Her later novels include *The Golden Notebook* (1962), *Briefing for a Descent into Hell* (1971), and the four-volume *Canopus in Argos: Archives* (1981). Lessing's short stories, many of the best drawn from her African experience, have been collected in five volumes. In "Being Prohibited," taken from her essaay collection *A Small Personal Voice* (1976), Lessing plots over a period of time her several confrontations with apartheid.

he border is Mafeking, a little dorp with nothing 1
interesting about it but its name. The train waits (or used to wait) interminably on the empty tracks, while immigration and customs officials made their leisurely

way through the coaches, and pale gritty dust settled over everything. Looking out, one saw the long stretch of windows, with the two, three, or four white faces at each; then at the extreme end, the single coach for "natives" packed tight with black humans; and, in between, two or three Indians or Coloured people on sufferance in the European coaches.

Outside, on the scintillating dust by the tracks, a crowd of ragged black children begged for *bonsellas*. One threw sandwich crusts or bits of spoiled fruit and watched them dive and fight to retrieve them from the dirt. 2

I was sixteen. I was not, as one says, politically conscious; nor did I know the score. I knew no more, in fact, than on which side my bread was buttered. But I already felt uneasy about being a member of the Herrenvolk. When the immigration official reached me, I had written on the form; *Nationality*, British, *Race*, European; and it was the first time in my life I had had to claim myself as a member of one race and disown the others. I remember distinctly that I had to suppress an impulse opposite *Race*: Human. Of course I *was* very young. 3

The immigration man had the sarcastic surliness which characterises the Afrikaans official, and he looked suspiciously at my form for a long time before saying that I was in the wrong part of the train. I did not understand him. (I forgot to mention that where the form asked, Where were you born?, I had written, Persia.) 4

"Asiatics," said he, "have to go to the back of the train; and anyway you are prohibited from entry unless you have documents proving you conform to the immigration quota for Asians." 5

"But," I said, "I am not an Asiatic." 6

The compartment had five other females in it; skirts were visibly being drawn aside. To prove my bona fides I should, of course, have exclaimed with outraged indignation at any such idea. 7

"You were born in Persia?" 8

"Yes." 9

"Then you are an Asiatic. You know the penalties for filling in the form wrongly?" 10

This particular little imbroglio involved my being taken off the train, escorted to an office, and kept under watch while they telephoned Pretoria for a ruling. 11

When next I entered the Union it was 1939. Sophistication had set in in the interval, and it took me no more than five minutes to persuade the official that one could be born in a country without being its citizen. The next two times there was no trouble at all, although my political views had in the meantime become nothing less than inflammatory: in a word, I had learned to disapprove of the colour bar. 12

This time, two weeks ago, what happened was as follows: one gets off the plane and sits for about fifteen minutes in a waiting room while they check the plane list with a list, or lists, of their own. They called my name first, and took me to an office which had two tables in it. At one sat a young man being pleasant to the genuine South African citizens. At the one where they made me sit was a man I could have sworn I had seen before. He proceeded to go through my form item by item, as follows: "You *say*, Mrs. Lessing, that, etc . . ." From time to time he let out a disbelieving laugh and exchanged ironical looks with a fellow official who was standing by. Sure enough, when he reached that point on my form when he had to say: "You *claim* that you are British; you *say* you were born in Persia," I merely said "*Yes*," and sat still while he gave me a long, exasperated stare. Then he let out an angry exclamation in Afrikaans and went next door to telephone Pretoria. Ten minutes later I was informed I must leave at once. A plane was waiting and I must enter it immediately. 13

I did so with dignity. Since then I have been unable to make up my mind whether I should have made a scene or not. I never have believed in the efficacy of dignity. 14

On the plane I wanted to sit near the window but was made to sit by myself and away from the window. I regretted infinitely that I had no accomplices hidden in the long grass by the airstrip, but, alas, I had not thought of it beforehand. 15

It was some time before it came home to me what an honour had been paid me. But now I am uneasy about the whole thing: suppose that I owe these attentions, not to my political views, but to the accident of my birthplace? 16

QUESTIONS

1. Trace the sequence of conflicts that the author has with South African apartheid. How does her attitude shift with each new confrontation? In what way does the conflict come full circle?

2. What do you learn about the author's personality and her beliefs? Cite evidence from the narrative to support your response.

3. Lessing uses several words drawn from South African dialect: *dorp* (paragraph 1); *bonsellas* (paragraph 2); *Herrenvolk* (paragraph 3) and *Afrikaans* (paragraph 4). Define each word. What do such terms contribute to the tone of the essay?

4. Analyze the imagery in the first paragraph of the essay. What mood or impression is created?

5. Trace Lessing's development of conflict in this narrative. How many episodes are there? How does the author handle the matter of time? Why does she shift tenses from present, to past, to present?

6. Lessing is especially effective in using dialogue to reveal character. Cite examples of this method and analyze the results.

7. In what way or ways does Lessing use narration to establish a definition in this essay? What is being defined? What is the implied thesis?

8. What is the effect of the rhetorical question at the end of the essay?

9. Why doesn't Lessing "make a scene" at the end of the essay? Do you think that she retains her dignity? Why or why not? What would you do in a similar situation?

10. a. Relate an experience that taught you about the meaning of the word *discrimination.*
b. Write a narrative essay about a *continuing* problem or conflict in your life. Establish at least three episodes for this narrative.

ISAAC BASHEVIS SINGER

Why the Geese Shrieked

Isaac Bashevis Singer (1904–) was born in Radzymin, Poland, and came to the United States in 1935. He became an American citizen in 1943. Singer, who writes in Yiddish, is the author of several superlative short story collections, including *Gimpel the Fool* (1957), *The Seance* (1968), and *The Spinoza of Market Street* (1961). He also has written five novels, books for children, and memoirs, notably *A Day of Pleasure* (1969) and *Lost in America* (1981). Singer received the Nobel Prize for Literature in 1975. A former rabbinical student, Singer injects elements of religion into his work, often in a comic way. "Why the Geese Shrieked" is typical of Singer's serio-comic approach to the conflicts and tribulations of this world.

In our home there was always talk about spirits of the 1
dead that possess the bodies of the living, souls reincarnated as animals, houses inhabited by hobgoblins, cellars haunted by demons. My father spoke of these things, first of all because he was interested in them, and second because in a big city children so easily go astray. They go everywhere,

see everything, read nonreligious books. It is necessary to remind them from time to time that there are still mysterious forces at work in the world.

2 One day, when I was about eight, he told us a story found in one of the holy books. If I am not mistaken, the author of that book is Rabbi Eliyahu Graidiker, or one of the other Graidiker sages. The story was about a girl possessed by four demons. It was said that they could actually be seen crawling around in her intestines, blowing up her belly, wandering from one part of her body to another, slithering into her legs. The Rabbi of Graidik had exorcised the evil spirits with the blowing of the ram's horn, with incantations, and the incense of magic herbs.

3 When my brother Joshua questioned these things, my father became very excited. He argued: "Was then the great Rabbi of Graidik, God forbid, a liar? Are all the rabbis, saints, and sages deceivers, while only atheists speak the truth? Woe is us! How can one be so blind?"

4 Suddenly the door opened, and a woman entered. She was carrying a basket with two geese in it. The woman looked frightened. Her matron's wig was tilted to one side. She smiled nervously.

5 Father never looked at strange women, because it is forbidden by Jewish law, but Mother and we children saw immediately that something had greatly upset our unexpected visitor.

6 "What is it?" Father asked, at the same time turning his back so as not to look upon her.

7 "Rabbi, I have a very unusual problem."

8 "What is it?"

9 "It's about these geese."

10 "What's the matter with them?"

11 "Dear Rabbi, the geese were slaughtered properly. Then I cut off their heads. I took out the intestines, the livers, all the other organs, but the geese keep shrieking in such a sorrowful voice . . ."

12 Upon hearing these words, my father turned pale. A dreadful fear befell me, too. But my mother came from a family of rationalists and was by nature a skeptic.

13 "Slaughtered geese don't shriek," she said.

14 "You will hear for yourself," replied the woman.

15 She took one of the geese and placed it on the table. Then she took out the second goose. The geese were headless, disemboweled—in short, ordinary dead geese.

16 A smile appeared on my mother's lips. "And *these geese* shriek?"

17 "You will soon hear."

18 The woman took one goose and hurled it against the other. At once a shriek was heard. It is not easy to describe that sound. It was

like the cackling of a goose, but in such a high, eerie pitch, with such groaning and quaking, that my limbs grew cold. I could actually feel the hairs on my earlocks pricking me. I wanted to run from the room. But where would I run? My throat constricted with fear. Then I, too, shrieked and clung to my mother's skirt, like a child of three.

Father forgot that one must avert one's eyes from a woman. 19
He ran to the table. He was no less frightened than I was. His red beard trembled. In his blue eyes could be seen a mixture of fear and vindication. For my father this was a sign that not only to the Rabbi of Graidik, but to him too, omens were sent from heaven. But perhaps this was a sign from the Evil One, from Satan himself?

"What do you say now?" asked the woman. 20

My mother was no longer smiling. In her eyes there was 21
something like sadness, and also anger.

"I cannot understand what is going on here," she said, with a 22
certain resentment.

"Do you want to hear it again?" 23

Again the woman threw one goose against the other. And 24
again the dead geese gave forth an uncanny shriek—the shriek of dumb creatures slain by the slaughterer's knife who yet retain a living force; who still have a reckoning to make with the living, an injustice to avenge. A chill crept over me. I felt as though someone had struck me with all his might.

My father's voice became hoarse. It was broken as though by 25
sobs. "Well, can anyone still doubt that there *is* a Creator?" he asked.

"Rabbi, what shall I do and where shall I go?" The woman 26
began to croon in a mournful singsong. "What has befallen me? Woe is me! What shall I do with them? Perhaps I should run to one of the Wonder Rabbis? Perhaps they were not slaughtered properly? I am afraid to take them home. I wanted to prepare them for the Sabbath meal, and now, such a calamity! Holy Rabbi, what shall I do? Must I throw them out? Someone said they must be wrapped in shrouds and buried in a grave. I am a poor woman. Two geese! They cost me a fortune!"

Father did not know what to answer. He glanced at his 27
bookcase. If there was an answer anywhere, it must be there.

Suddenly he looked angrily at my mother. "And what do you 28
say now, eh?"

Mother's face was growing sullen, smaller, sharper. In her 29
eyes could be seen indignation and also something like shame.

"I want to hear it again." Her words were half-pleading, half 30
commanding.

The woman hurled the geese against each other for the third 31
time, and for the third time the shrieks were heard. It occurred to me that such must have been the voice of the sacrificial heifer.

"Woe, woe, and still they blaspheme . . . It is written that the 32
wicked do not repent even at the very gates of hell." Father had again begun to speak. "They behold the truth with their own eyes, and they continue to deny their Maker. They are dragged into the bottomless pit and they maintain that all is nature, or accident . . ."

He looked at Mother as if to say: You take after *them*. 33

For a long time there was silence. Then the woman asked, 34
"Well, did I just imagine it?"

Suddenly my mother laughed. There was something in her 35
laughter that made us all tremble. I knew, by some sixth sense, that Mother was preparing to end the mighty drama being enacted before our eyes.

"Did you remove the windpipes?" my mother asked. 36

"The windpipes? No . . ." 37

"Take them out," said my mother, "and the geese will stop 38
shrieking."

My father became angry. "What are you babbling? What has 39
this got to do with windpipes?"

Mother took hold of one of the geese, pushed her slender 40
finger inside the body, and with all her might pulled out the thin tube that led from the neck to the lungs. Then she took the other goose and removed its windpipe also. I stood trembling, aghast at my mother's courage. Her hands had become bloodied. On her face could be seen the wrath of the rationalist whom someone has tried to frighten in broad daylight.

Father's face turned white, calm, a little disappointed. He 41
knew what had happened here: logic, cold logic, was again tearing down faith, mocking it, holding it up to ridicule and scorn.

"Now, if you please, take one goose and hurl it against the 42
other!" commanded my mother.

Everything hung in the balance. If the geese shrieked, 43
Mother would have lost all: her rationalist's daring, her skepticism, which she had inherited from her intellectual father. And I? Although I was afraid, I prayed inwardly that the geese *would* shriek, shriek so loud that people in the street would hear and come running.

But, alas, the geese were silent, silent as only two dead geese 44
without windpipes can be.

"Bring me a towel!" Mother turned to me. 45

I ran to get the towel. There were tears in my eyes. Mother 46
wiped her hands on the towel like a surgeon after a difficult operation.

"That's all it was!" she announced victoriously. 47

"Rabbi, what do you say?" asked the woman. 48

Father began to cough, to mumble. He fanned himself with 49
his skullcap.

"I have never before heard of such a thing," he said at last. 50

"Nor have I," echoed the woman. 51

"Nor have I," said my mother. "But there is always an 52
explanation. Dead geese don't shriek."

"Can I go home now and cook them?" asked the woman. 53

"Go home and cook them for the Sabbath." Mother pro- 54
nounced the decision. "Don't be afraid. They won't make a sound in your pot."

"What do you say, Rabbi?" 55

"Hmm . . . they are kosher," murmured Father. "They can 56
be eaten." He was not really convinced, but now he could not pronounce the geese unclean.

Mother went back to the kitchen. I remained with my father. 57
Suddenly he began to speak to me as though I were an adult. "Your mother takes after your grandfather, the Rabbi of Bilgoray. He is a great scholar, but a cold-blooded rationalist. People warned me before our betrothal . . ."

And then Father threw up this hands, as if to say: It is too late 58
now to call off the wedding.

QUESTIONS

1. Describe the conflict between the author's mother and father.

2. Where does Singer, as a child, stand in relation to the conflict? What do you think that he learns from this episode?

3. This essay contains strong *visual* and *auditory* imagery. Cite examples and explain how such imagery contributes to the effect of the narrative.

4. Locate and analyze examples of parallel sentence structure in paragraphs 1 and 2. What effects are achieved?

5. What is the function of the first three paragraphs? How are they connected to the body of the essay?

6. Trace Singer's development of conflict, terror, and suspense in the story he narrates. How does he handle these elements successfully?

7. What is the tone of the essay? How does Singer achieve it?

8. What do the last two paragraphs contribute to the essay?

9. Do you accept Singer's implied premise that children often get caught between the conflicting value systems of their parents? Why or why not? Can you think of an example from your personal experience?

10. Narrate a personal experience that grew out of a conflict of opinions or beliefs between parents, relatives, or friends.

Home for Christmas

Carson McCullers (1917–1967) was the author of a small but impressive body of fiction, including *The Heart Is a Lonely Hunter* (1940), *Reflections in a Golden Eye* (1941), *A Member of the Wedding* (1946), and *The Ballad of the Sad Cafe* (1951). Although she was preoccupied in her fiction with the theme of loneliness, this selection from her autobiography reveals instead the love, joy, and sense of community permeating one episode from her Georgia childhood.

Sometimes in August, weary of the vacant, broiling afternoon, my younger brother and sister and I would gather in the dense shade under the oak tree in the back yard and talk of Christmas and sing carols. Once after such a conclave, when the tunes of the carols still lingered in the heat-shimmered air, I remember climbing up into the tree-house and sitting there alone for a long time. 1

Brother called up: "What are you doing?" 2

"Thinking," I answered. 3

"What are you thinking about?" 4

"I don't know." 5

"Well, how can you be thinking when you don't know what you are thinking about?" 6

I did not want to talk with my brother. I was experiencing the first wonder about the mystery of Time. Here I was, on this August afternoon, in the tree-house, in the burnt, jaded yard, sick and tired of all our summer ways. (I had read *Little Women* for the second time, *Hans Brinker and the Silver Skates, Little Men*, and *Twenty Thousand Leagues under the Sea*. I had read movie magazines and even tried to read love stories in the *Woman's Home Companion*—I was so sick of everything.) How could it be that I was I and now was now when in four months it would be Christmas, wintertime, cold weather, twilight and the glory of the Christmas tree? I puzzled about the *now* and *later* and rubbed the inside of my elbow until there was a little roll of dirt between my forefinger and thumb. Would the *now* I of the tree-house and the August afternoon be the same *I* of winter, firelight and the Christmas tree? I wondered. 7

My brother repeated: "You say you are thinking but you don't know what you are thinking about. What are you really doing up there? Have you got some secret candy?" 8

September came, and my mother opened the cedar chest and we tried on winter coats and last year's sweaters to see if they would 9 do again. She took the three of us downtown and bought us new shoes and school clothes.

Christmas was nearer on the September Sunday that Daddy 10
rounded us up in the car and drove us out on dusty country roads to pick elderberry blooms. Daddy made wine from elderberry blossoms—it was a yellow-white wine, the color of weak winter sun. The wine was dry to the wry side—indeed, some years it turned to vinegar. The wine was served at Christmastime with slices of fruitcake when company came. On November Sundays we went to the woods with a big basket of fried chicken dinner, thermos jug and coffee-pot. We hunted partridge berries in the pine woods near our town. These scarlet berries grew hidden underneath the glossy brown pine needles that lay in a slick carpet beneath the tall wind-singing trees. The bright berries were a Christmas decoration, lasting in water through the whole season.

In December the windows downtown were filled with toys, 11
and my brother and sister and I were given two dollars apiece to buy our Christmas presents. We patronized the ten-cent stores, choosing between jackstones, pencil boxes, water colors and satin handkerchief holders. We would each buy a nickel's worth of lump milk chocolate at the candy counter to mouth as we trudged from counter to counter, choice to choice. It was exacting and final—taking several afternoons—for the dime stores would not take back or exchange.

Mother made fruitcakes, and for weeks ahead the family 12
picked out the nut meats of pecans and walnuts, careful of the bitter layer of the pecans that lined your mouth with nasty fur. At the last I was allowed to blanch the almonds, pinching the scalded nuts so that they sometimes hit the ceiling or bounced across the room. Mother cut slices of citron and crystallized pineapple, figs and dates, and candied cherries were added whole. We cut rounds of brown paper to line the pans. Usually the cakes were mixed and put into the oven when we were in school. Late in the afternoon the cakes would be finished, wrapped in white napkins on the breakfast-room table. Later they would be soaked in brandy. These fruitcakes were famous in our town, and Mother gave them often as Christmas gifts. When company came thin slices of fruitcake, wine and coffee were always served. When you held a slice of fruitcake to the window or the firelight the slice was translucent, pale citron green and yellow and red, with the glow and richness of our church windows.

Daddy was a jeweler, and his store was kept open until 13
midnight all Christmas week. I, as the eldest child, was allowed to stay up late with Mother until Daddy came home. Mother was always nervous without a "man in the house." (On those rare occasions when Daddy had to stay overnight on business in Atlanta, the

children were armed with a hammer, saw and a monkey wrench. When pressed about her anxieties Mother claimed she was afraid of "escaped convicts or crazy people." I never saw an escaped convict, but once a "crazy" person did come to see us. She was an old, old lady dressed in elegant black taffeta, my mother's second cousin once removed, and came on a tranquil Sunday morning and announced that she had always liked our house and she intended to stay with us until she died. Her sons and daughters and grandchildren gathered around to plead with her as she sat rocking in our front porch rocking chair and she left not unwillingly when they promised a car ride and ice cream.) Nothing ever happened on those evenings in Christmas week, but I felt grown, aged suddenly by trust and dignity. Mother confided in secrecy what the younger children were getting from Santa Claus. I knew where the Santa Claus things were hidden, and was appointed to see that my brother and sister did not go into the back-room closet or the wardrobe in our parents' room.

Christmas Eve was the longest day, but it was lined with the glory of tomorrow. The sitting-room smelled of floor wax and the clean, cold odor of the spruce tree. The Christmas tree stood in a corner of the front room, tall as the ceiling, majestic, undecorated. It was our family custom that the tree was not decorated until after we children were in bed on Christmas Eve night. We went to bed very early, as soon as it was winter dark. I lay in bed beside my sister and tried to keep her awake. 14

"You want to guess again about your Santa Claus?" 15

"We've already done that so much," she said. 16

My sister slept. And there again was another puzzle. How could it be that when she opened her eyes it would be Christmas while I lay awake in the dark for hours and hours? The time was the same for both of us, and yet not at all the same. What was it? How? I thought of Bethlehem and cherry candy, Jesus and skyrockets. It was dark when I awoke. We were allowed to get up on Christmas at five o'clock. Later I found out that Daddy juggled the clock Christmas Eve so that five o'clock was actually six. Anyway it was always still dark when we rushed in to dress by the kitchen stove. The rule was that we dress and eat breakfast before we could go in to the Christmas tree. On Christmas morning we always had fish roe, bacon and grits for breakfast. I grudged every mouthful—for who wanted to fill up on breakfast when there in the sitting-room was candy, at least three whole boxes? After breakfast we lined up, and carols were started. Our voices rose naked and mysterious as we filed through the door to the sitting-room. The carol, unfinished, ended in raw yells of joy. 17

The Christmas tree glittered in the glorious, candlelit room. There were bicycles and bundles wrapped in tissue paper. Our 18 stockings hanging from the mantlepiece bulged with oranges, nuts and smaller presents. The next hours were paradise. The blue dawn at the window brightened, and the candles were blown out. By nine o'clock we had ridden the wheel presents and dressed in the clothes gifts. We visited the neighborhood children and were visited in turn. Our cousins came and grown relatives from distant neighborhoods. All through the morning we ate chocolates. At two or three o'clock the Christmas dinner was served. The dining-room table had been let out with extra leaves and the very best linen was laid—satin damask with a rose design. Daddy asked the blessing, then stood up to carve the turkey. Dressing, rice and giblet gravy were served. There were cut-glass dishes of sparkling jellies and stateliness of festal wine. For dessert there was always sillabub or charlotte and fruitcake. The afternoon was almost over when dinner was done.

At twilight I sat on the front steps, jaded by too much pleasure, sick at the stomach and worn out. The boy next door skated down the street in his new Indian suit. A girl spun around on a crackling son-of-a-gun. My brother waved sparklers. Christmas was over. I thought of the monotony of Time ahead, unsolaced by the distant glow of paler festivals, the year that stretched before another Christmas—eternity. 19

QUESTIONS

1. Trace chronologically the preparations for Christmas by the McCullers family.

2. What is the author's attitude toward time? Paraphrase the last sentence of the essay.

3. This essay is rich in sensory language. Cite five words or phrases that are especially vivid and analyze their effect. To which senses does the writing appeal?

4. Define these words: *conclave* (paragraph 1); *patronized* (paragraph 11); *blanch* (paragraph 12); *tranquil* (paragraph 13); *festal* (paragraph 19). Use them in sentences of your own.

5. McCullers writes in paragraph 7 that she "was experiencing the first wonder about the mystery of Time." How does this theme serve as the organizing principle for the essay? How does the author convey the mystery of time? What is her dual attitude toward time, and how does this serve as a structuring device in the essay?

6. What principles of emphasis do you find in McCullers's treatment of chronology?

7. How and why does the author connect the many and varied details in the essay? How effective are her details in conveying a sense of the author's childhood and of her evolving personality? How is this reflected in point of view?

8. How does the conclusion relate to the rest of the essay? Do you find the conclusion effective? Why or why not?

9. Do you still look forward to special holidays or celebrations, or does the type of anticipation of which McCullers speaks exist only for children? Why do children have different perceptions of time than adults?

10. Write a narrative account of a vivid holiday event in your childhood.

DYLAN THOMAS

A Visit to Grandpa's

Dylan Thomas (1914–1953), Welsh poet and prose writer, had one of the most lyric voices in contemporary literature. Both his poetry and prose are filled with an animated primitivism, forceful sounds and rhythms, and complex patterns of symbolism and imagery. His poetry collections include *Eighteen Poems* (1934), *Twenty-five Poems* (1936), and *In Country Sleep* (1952). The following autobiographical sketch from *Portrait of the Artist as a Young Dog* (1952) contains many of his most expressive techniques.

1 In the middle of the night I woke from a dream full of whips and lariats as long as serpents, and runaway coaches on mountain passes, and wide, windy gallops over cactus fields, and I heard the old man in the next room crying, "Gee-up!" and "Whoa!" and trotting his tongue on the roof of his mouth.

2 It was the first time I had stayed in grandpa's house. The floorboards had squeaked like mice as I climbed into bed, and the mice between the walls had creaked like wood as though another visitor was walking on them. It was a mild summer night, but curtains had flapped and branches beaten against the window. I had pulled the sheets over my head, and soon was roaring and riding in a book.

"Whoa there, my beauties!" cried grandpa. His voice sound- 3
ed very young and loud, and his tongue had powerful hooves, and he made his bedroom into a great meadow. I thought I would see if he was ill, or had set his bed-clothes on fire, for my mother had said that he lit his pipe under the blankets, and had warned me to run to his help if I smelt smoke in the night. I went on tiptoe through the darkness to his bedroom door, brushing against the furniture and upsetting a candlestick with a thump. When I saw there was a light in the room I felt frightened, and as I opened the door I heard grandpa shout, "Gee-up!" as loudly as a bull with a megaphone.

He was sitting straight up in bed and rocking from side to 4
side as though the bed were on a rough road; the knotted edges of the counterpane were his reins; his invisible horses stood in a shadow beyond the bedside candle. Over a white flannel nightshirt he was wearing a red waistcoat with walnut-sized brass buttons. The over-filled bowl of his pipe smouldered among his whiskers like a little, burning hayrick on a stock. At the sight of me, his hands dropped from the reins and lay blue and quiet, the bed stopped still on a level road, he muffled his tongue into silence, and the horses drew softly up.

"Is there anything the matter, grandpa?" I asked, though the 5
clothes were not on fire. His face in the candlelight looked like a ragged quilt pinned upright on the black air and patched all over with goat-beards.

He stared at me mildly. Then he blew down his pipe, 6
scattering the sparks and making a high, wet dog-whistle of the stem, and shouted: "Ask no questions."

After a pause, he said shyly: "Do you ever have nightmares, 7
boy?"

I said: "No." 8

"Oh, yes, you do," he said. 9

I said I was woken by a voice that was shouting to horses. 10

"What did I tell you?" he said. "You eat too much. Who ever 11
heard of horses in a bedroom?"

He fumbled under his pillow, brought out a small, tinkling 12
bag, and carefully untied its strings. He put a sovereign in my hand, and said "Buy a cake." I thanked him and wished him good night.

As I closed my bedroom door, I heard his voice crying loudly 13
and gaily, "Gee-up! gee-up!" and the rocking of the travelling bed.

In the morning I woke from a dream of fiery horses on a plain 14
that was littered with furniture, and of large, cloudy men who rode six horses at a time and whipped them with burning bed-clothes. Grandpa was at breakfast, dressed in deep black. After breakfast he said, "There was a terrible loud wind last night," and sat in his

arm-chair by the hearth to make clay balls for the fire. Later in the morning he took me for a walk, through Johnstown village and into the fields on the Llanstephan road.

A man with a whippet said, "There's a nice morning, Mr 15
Thomas," and when he had gone, leanly as his dog, into the short-treed green wood he should not have entered because of the notices, grandpa said: "There, do you hear what he called you? Mister!"

We passed by small cottages, and all the men who leant on 16
the gates congratulated grandpa on the fine morning. We passed through the wood full of pigeons, and their wings broke the branches as they rushed to the tops of the trees. Among the soft, contented voices and the loud, timid flying, grandpa said, like a man calling across a field: "If you heard those old birds in the night, you'd wake me up and say there were horses in the trees."

We walked back slowly, for he was tired, and the lean man 17
stalked out of the forbidden wood with a rabbit held as gently over his arm as a girl's arm in a warm sleeve.

On the last day but one of my visit I was taken to Llanstephan 18
in a governess cart pulled by a short, weak pony. Grandpa might have been driving a bison, so tightly he held the reins, so ferociously cracked the long whip, so blasphemously shouted warning to boys who played in the road, so stoutly stood with his gaitered legs apart and cursed the demon strength and wilfulness of his tottering pony.

"Look out, boy!" he cried when we came to each corner, and 19
pulled and tugged and jerked and sweated and waved his whip like a rubber sword. And when the pony had crept miserably round each corner, grandpa turned to me with a sighing smile: "We weathered that one, boy."

When we came to Llanstephan village at the top of the hill, he 20
left the cart by the "Edwinsford Arms" and patted the pony's muzzle and gave it sugar, saying: "You're a weak little pony, Jim, to pull big men like us."

He had strong beer and I had lemonade, and he paid Mrs 21
Edwinsford with a sovereign out of the tinkling bag; she inquired after his health, and he said that Llangadock was better for the tubes. We went to look at the churchyard and the sea, and sat in the wood called the Sticks, and stood on the concert platform in the middle of the wood where visitors sang on mid-summer nights and, year by year, the innocent of the village was elected mayor. Grandpa paused at the churchyard and pointed over the iron gate at the angelic headstones and the poor wooden crosses. "There's no sense in lying there," he said.

We journeyed back furiously: Jim was a bison again. 22

I woke late on my last morning, out of dreams where the 23

Llanstephan sea carried bright sailing-boats as long as liners; and heavenly choirs in the Sticks, dressed in bards' robes and brass-buttoned waistcoats, sang in a strange Welsh to the departing sailors. Grandpa was not at breakfast; he rose early. I walked in the fields with a new sling, and shot at the Towy gulls and the rooks in the parsonage trees. A warm wind blew from the summer points of the weather; a morning mist climbed from the ground and floated among the trees and hid the noisy birds; in the mist and the wind my pebbles flew lightly up like hailstones in a world on its head. The morning passed without a bird falling.

I broke my sling and returned for the midday meal through the parson's orchard. Once, grandpa told me, the parson had bought three ducks at Carmarthen Fair and made a pond for them in the centre of the garden; but they waddled to the gutter under the crumbling doorsteps of the house, and swam and quacked there. When I reached the end of the orchard path, I looked through a hole in the hedge and saw that the parson had made a tunnel through the rockery that was between the gutter and the pond and had set up a notice in plain writing: "This way to the pond." 24

The ducks were still swimming under the steps. 25

Grandpa was not in the cottage. I went into the garden, but grandpa was not staring at the fruit-trees. I called across to a man who leant on a spade in the fields beyond the garden hedge: "Have you seen my grandpa this morning?" 26

He did not stop digging, and answered over his shoulder: "I seen him in his fancy waistcoat." 27

Griff, the barber, lived in the next cottage. I called to him through the open door: "Mr Griff, have you seen my grandpa?" 28

The barber came out in his shirtsleeves. 29

I said: "He's wearing his best waistcoat." I did not know if it was important, but grandpa wore his waistcoat only in the night. 30

"Has grandpa been to Llanstephan?" asked Mr Griff anxiously. 31

"We went there yesterday in a little trap," I said. 32

He hurried indoors and I heard him talking in Welsh, and he came out again with his white coat on, and he carried a striped and coloured walking-stick. He strode down the village street and I ran by his side. 33

When we stopped at the tailor's shop, he cried out, "Dan!" and Dan Tailor stepped from his window where he sat like an Indian priest but wearing a derby hat. "Dai Thomas has got his waistcoat on," said Mr Griff, "and he's been to Llanstephan." 34

As Dan Tailor searched for his overcoat, Mr Griff was striding on. "Will Evans," he called outside the carpenter's shop, "Dai Thomas has been to Llanstephan, and he's got his waistcoat on." 35

"I'll tell Morgan now," said the carpenter's wife out of the 36
hammering, sawing darkness of the shop.

We called at the butcher's shop and Mr Price's house, and Mr 37
Griff repeated his message like a town crier.

We gathered together in Johnstown square. Dan Tailor had 38
his bicycle, Mr Price his pony-trap. Mr Griff, the butcher, Morgan
Carpenter, and I climbed into the shaking trap, and we trotted off
towards Carmarthen town. The tailor led the way, ringing his bell as
though there were a fire or a robbery, and an old woman by the gate
of a cottage at the end of the street ran inside like a pelted hen.
Another woman waved a bright handkerchief.

"Where are we going?" I asked. 39

Grandpa's neighbours were as solemn as old men with black 40
hats and jackets on the outskirts of a fair. Mr Griff shook his head and
mourned: "I didn't expect this again from Dai Thomas."

"Not after last time," said Mr Price sadly. 41

We trotted on, we crept up Constitution Hill, we rattled down 42
into Lammas Street, and the tailor still rang his bell and a dog ran,
squealing, in front of his wheels. As we clip-clopped over the cobbles
that led down to the Towy bridge, I remembered grandpa's nightly
noisy journeys that rocked the bed and shook the walls, and I saw his
gay waistcoat in a vision and his patchwork head tufted and smiling
in the candlelight. The tailor before us turned round on his saddle,
his bicycle wobbled and skidded. "I see Dai Thomas!" he cried.

The trap rattled on to the bridge, and I saw grandpa there; the 43
buttons of his waistcoat shone in the sun, he wore his tight, black
Sunday trousers and a tall, dusty hat I had seen in a cupboard in the
attic, and he carried an ancient bag. He bowed to us. "Good morning,
Mr Price," he said, "and Mr Griff and Mr Morgan and Mr Evans." To
me, he said, "Good morning, boy."

Mr Griff pointed his coloured stick at him. 44

"And what do you think you are doing on Carmarthen bridge 45
in the middle of the afternoon," he said sternly, "with your best
waistcoat and your old hat?"

Grandpa did not answer, but inclined his face to the river 46
wind, so that his beard was set dancing and wagging as though he
talked, and watched the coracle men move, like turtles, on the shore.

Mr Griff raised his stunted barber's pole. "And where do you 47
think you are going," he said, "with your old black bag?"

Grandpa said: "I am going to Llangadock to be buried." And 48
he watched the coracle shells slip into the water lightly, and the gulls
complain over the fish-filled water as bitterly as Mr Price complained:

"But you aren't dead yet, Dai Thomas." 49

For a moment grandpa reflected, then: "There's no sense in 50
lying dead in Llanstephan," he said. "The ground is comfy in

Llangadock; you can twitch your legs without putting them in the sea."

His neighbours moved close to him. They said: "You aren't 51
dead, Mr Thomas."

"How can you be buried, then?" 52

"Nobody's going to bury you in Llanstephan." 53

"Come on home, Mr Thomas." 54

"There's strong beer for tea." 55

"And cake." 56

But grandpa stood firmly on the bridge, and clutched his bag 57
to his side, and stared at the flowing river and the sky, like a prophet who has no doubt.

QUESTIONS

1. What do we learn about Thomas's childhood, his views of himself, his attitude toward his grandfather, and his perceptions of the world?

2. Characterize the personality of Thomas's grandfather. Can we infer whether or not the grandfather will continue his journey at the end of the story? Why or why not?

3. The prose style in this narrative might be termed "poetic." How does Thomas's poetic style influence mood and tone in the essay? What are the components of his style? Isolate five instances of poetic style in the essay and explain their effects.

4. A major motif in the essay is nature imagery. Why is this motif important?

5. How does Thomas use dreams to structure and to inform the essay? In what ways are the dreams symbolic?

6. The author uses an episodic technique in the essay, yet he achieves unity and coherence in the presentation of episodes. How? How does he handle proportion?

7. Discuss point of view with regard to the author's relationship to the action and time of the story.

8. Assess the uniqueness of Thomas's conclusion.

9. Thomas presents a microcosm of Welsh society in this essay. What are its contours and cultural points of reference? How do people relate to each other within these social contexts?

10. Relate an episode or series of episodes about a memorable visit to one of your relatives or friends.

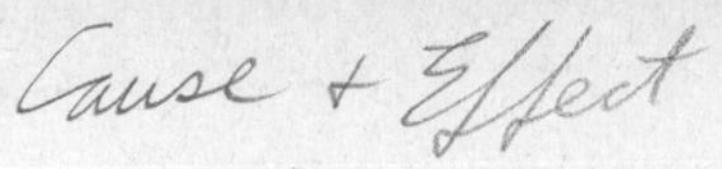

MAYA ANGELOU

The Deterioration of My Marriage

Maya Angelou (1928–   ) is an American poet, playwright, television screen writer, actress, and singer. Her autobiographical writing, notably *I Know Why the Caged Bird Sings* (1970), provides one of the fullest accounts of the black female experience in the United States. Fluent in six languages, active in artistic and political affairs, Angelou often presents autobiographical material against the backdrop of larger cultural concerns. Her account of the crisis in her marriage constitutes a chapter in *Singin' and Swingin' and Gettin' Merry Like Christmas* (1976).

The articles in the women's magazines did nothing to 1
help explain the deterioration of my marriage. We had no infidelity; my husband was a good provider and I was a good cook. He encouraged me to resume my dance classes and I listened to him practice the saxophone without interruption. He came directly home from work each afternoon and in the evening after my son was asleep I found as much enjoyment in our marital bed as he.

The form was there, but the spirit had disappeared. 2

A bizarre sensation pervades a relationship of pretense. No 3
truth seems true. A simple morning's greeting and response appear loaded with innuendo and fraught with implications.

"How are you?" Does he/she really care? 4

"Fine," I'm not really. I'm miserable, but I'll never tell you. 5

Each nicety becomes more sterile and each withdrawal more 6
permanent.

Bacon and coffee odors mingled with the aseptic aroma of 7
Lifebuoy soap. Wisps of escaping gas, which were as real a part of a fifty-year-old San Francisco house as the fourteen-foot high ceilings and the cantankerous plumbing, solidified my reality. Those were natural morning mists. The sense that order was departing my life was refuted by the daily routine. My family would awaken. I would shower and head for the kitchen to begin making breakfast. Clyde would then take over the shower as Tosh read the newspaper. Tosh would shower while Clyde dressed, collected his crayons and lunch pail for school. We would all sit at breakfast together. I would force unwanted pleasantries into my face. (My mother had taught me: "If you have only one smile in you, give it to the people you love. Don't be surly at home, then go out in the street and start grinning 'Good morning' at total strangers.")

Tosh was usually quiet and amiable. Clyde gabbled about his 8

dreams, which had to do with Roy Rogers as Jesus and Br'er Rabbit as God. We would finish breakfast in a glow of family life and they would both leave me with kisses, off to their separate excitements.

One new morning Tosh screamed from the bathroom, "Where in the hell are the goddamn dry towels?" The outburst caught me as unexpectedly as an upper cut. He knew that I kept the linen closet filled with towels folded as I had seen them photographed in the *Ladies' Home Journal*. More shocking than his forgetfulness, however, was his shouting. Anger generally rendered my husband morose and silent as a stone. 9

I went to the bathroom and handed him the thickest towel we owned. 10

"What's wrong, Tosh?" 11

"All the towels in here are wet. You know I hate fucking wet towels." 12

I didn't know because he had never told me. I went back to the kitchen, not really knowing him, either. 13

At breakfast, Clyde began a recounting of Roy Rogers on his horse and Red Ryder, riding on clouds up to talk to God about some rustlers in the lower forty. 14

Tosh turned, looking directly at him, and said, "Shut up, will you. I'd like a little fucking peace and quiet while I eat." 15

The statement slapped Clyde quiet; he had never been spoken to with such cold anger. 16

Tosh looked at me. "The eggs are like rocks. Can't you fry a decent goddamn egg? If not, I'll show you." 17

I was too confounded to speak. I sat, not understanding the contempt. Clyde asked to be excused from the table. I excused him and followed him to the door. 18

He whispered, "Is Dad mad at me?" 19

I picked up his belongings, saw him jacketed and told him, "No, not at you. You know grownups have a lot on their minds. Sometimes they're so busy thinking they forget their manners. It's not nice, but it happens." 20

He said, "I'll go back and tell him 'bye." 21

"No, I think you should just go on to school. He'll be in a better mood this evening." 22

I held the front door open. 23

He shouted, "'Bye, Dad." 24

There was no answer as I kissed him and closed the door. Fury quickened my footsteps. How could he scream at my son like that? Who the hell was he? A white-sheeted Grand Dragon of the Ku Klux Klan? I wouldn't have a white man talk to me in that tone of voice and I'd slap him with a coffeepot before he could yell at my child again. The midnight murmuring of soft words was forgotten. His 25

gentle hands and familiar body had become in those seconds the shelter of an enemy.

He was still sitting over coffee, brooding. I went directly to the table. 26

"What do you mean, screaming at us that way?" 27

He said nothing. 28

"You started, first with the towels, then it was Clyde's dream. Then my cooking. Are you going crazy?" 29

He said, "I don't want to talk about it," still looking down into a half-filled cup of near-cold coffee. 30

"You sure as hell will talk about it. What have I done to you? What's the matter with you?" 31

He left the table and headed for the door without looking at me. I followed, raising my protest, hoping to puncture his cloak of withdrawal. 32

"I deserve and demand an explanation." 33

He held the door open and turned at last to face me. His voice was soft again and tender. "I think I'm just tired of being married." He pulled the door closed. 34

There is a shock that comes so quickly and strikes so deep that the blow is internalized even before the skin feels it. The strike must first reach bone marrow, then ascend slowly to the brain where the slowpoke intellect records the deed. 35

I went about cleaning my kitchen. Wash the dishes, sweep the floor, swipe the sputtered grease from the stove, make fresh coffee, put a fresh starched cloth on the table. Then I sat down. A sense of loss suffused me until I was suffocating within the vapors. 36

What had I done? I had placed my life within the confines of my marriage. I was everything the magazines said a wife should be. Constant, faithful and clean. I was economical. I was compliant, never offering headaches as excuses for not sharing the marital bed. 37

I had generously allowed Tosh to share my son, encouraging Clyde to think of him as a permanent life fixture. And now Tosh was "tired of being married." 38

Experience had made me accustomed to make quick analyses and quick if often bad decisions. So I expected Tosh, having come to the conclusion that marriage was exhausting, to ask me for a divorce when he returned from work. My tears were for myself and my son. We would be thrown again into a maelstrom of rootlessness. I wept for our loss of security and railed at the brutality of fate. Forgotten were my own complaints of the marriage. Unadmitted was the sense of strangulation I had begun to feel, or the insidious quality of guilt for having a white husband, which surrounded me like an evil aura when we were in public. 39

At my table, immersed in self-pity, I saw my now dying 40
marriage as a union made in heaven, officiated over by St. Peter and sanctioned by God. It wasn't just that my husband was leaving me, I was losing a state of perfection, of grace.

My people would nod knowingly. Again a white man had 41
taken a Black woman's body and left her hopeless, helpless and alone. But I couldn't expect their sympathy. I hadn't been ambushed on a dark country lane or raped by a group of randy white toughs. I had sworn to obey the man and had accepted his name. Anger, first at injustice, then at Tosh, stopped my tears. The same words I had used to voice my anguish I now used to fan the fires of rage. I had been a good wife, kind and compliant. And that wasn't enough for him? It was better than he deserved. More than he could reasonably have expected had he married within his own race. Anyway, had he planned to leave me from the first? Had he intended in the beginning to lure me into trust, then break up our marriage and break my heart? Maybe he was a sadist, scheming to inflict pain on poor, unsuspecting me. Well, he didn't know me. I would show him. I was no helpless biddy to be beckoned, then belittled. He was tired of marriage; all right, then I would leave him.

I got up from the table and cooked dinner, placed the food in 42
the refrigerator and dressed in my best clothes. I left the dinner pots dirty and my bed unmade and hit the streets.

The noontime bar in the popular hotel on Eddy Street was 43
filled with just-awakened petty gamblers and drowsy whores. Pimps not yet clad in their evening air of exquisite brutality spent the whores' earnings on their fellow parasites. I was recognized by a few drinkers, because I was Clydell and Vivian's daughter, because I had worked at the popular record shop or because I was that girl who had married the white man. I knew nothing about strong liquor except the names of some cocktails. I sat down and ordered a Zombie.

I clung to the long, cold drink and examined my predica- 44
ment. My marriage was over, since I believed the legal bonds were only as good as the emotional desire to make them good. If a person didn't want you, he didn't want you. I could have thrown myself and my son on Tosh's mercy; he was a kind man, and he might have tolerated us in his home and on the edges of his life. But begging had always stuck, resisting, in my throat. I thought women who accepted their husbands' inattention and sacrificed all their sovereignty for a humiliating marriage more unsavory than the prostitutes who were drinking themselves awake in the noisy bar.

A short, thickset man sat down beside me and asked if he 45
could pay for my second Zombie. He was old enough to be my father and reminded me of a kindly old country doctor from sepia-colored B

movies. He asked my name and where I lived. I told his soft, near-feminine face that my name was Clara. When I said "No, I'm not married," he grinned and said, "I don't know what these young men are waiting for. If I was a few years younger, I'd give them a run for they money. Yes siree bob." He made me feel comfortable. His Southern accent was as familiar to me as the smell of baking cornbread and the taste of wild persimmons. He asked if I was "a, uh, a ah a fancy lady?"

I said, "No." Desperate, maybe. Fanciful, maybe. Fancy? No. 46

He told me he was a merchant marine and was staying in the 47
hotel and asked would I like to come upstairs and have a drink with him.

I would. 48

I sat on the bed in the close room, sipping the bourbon 49
diluted with tap water. He talked about Newport News and his family as I thought about mine. He had a son and daughter near my age and they were "some kinda good children" and the girl was "some kinda pretty."

He noticed that I was responding to the whiskey, and came 50
near the bed. "Why don't you just stretch out and rest a little while? You'll feel better. I'll rest myself. Just take off your shoes and your clothes. To keep them from wrinkling up on you."

My troubles and memories swam around, then floated out 51
the window when I laid my head on the single pillow.

When I awakened, the dark room didn't smell familiar and 52
my head throbbed. Confusion panicked me. I could have been picked up by an extraterrestrial being and teleported into some funky rocket ship. I jumped out of bed and fumbled along the walls, bumping until I found the light switch. My clothes were folded neatly and my shoes peeked their tidy toes from under the chair. I remembered the room and the merchant marine. I had no idea what had happened since I passed out. I examined myself and found no evidence that the old man had misused my drunkenness.

Dressing slowly, I wondered over the next move. Night had 53
fallen on my affairs, but the sharp edges of rejection were not softened. There was a note on the dresser. I picked it up to read under the naked bulb that dangled from the ceiling; it said in effect:

> Dear Clara, 54
>
> I tell you like I tell my own daughter. Be careful of strangers. Everybody smile at you don't have to mean you no good. I'll be back in two months from now. You be a good girl, hear? You'll make some boy a good wife.
>
> Abner Green

I walked through the dark streets to Ivonne's house. After I 55
explained what had happened, she suggested I telephone home.

"Hello, Tosh?" 56

"Marguerite, where are you?" The strain in his voice made 57
me smile.

He asked, "When are you coming home? Clyde hasn't 58
eaten."

I knew that was a lie. 59

"Nor have I. I can't eat," he said. I wasn't concerned about 60
his appetite.

I said, "You're tired of being married. Yes? Well, I'll be home 61
when I get there." I hung up before he could say more.

Ivonne said, "Maya, you're cold. Aren't you worried about 62
Clyde?"

"No. Tosh loves Clyde. He'll look after him. He loves me too, 63
but I gave up too much and gave in too much. Now we'll see."

The thought of his loneliness in the large apartment made my 64
own less acute. I slept badly on Ivonne's sofa.

I went home the next day and we resumed a sort of marriage, 65
but the center of power had shifted. I was no longer the dutiful wife ready with floors waxed and rugs beaten, with my finger between the pages of a cookbook and my body poised over the stove or spread-eagled on the bed.

One day my back began to hurt with a sullen ache, the kind 66
usually visited only on the arthritic aged. My head pulsed and my side was punished by short, hot stabs of pain. The doctor advised immediate hospitalization. A simple appendectomy developed complications and it was weeks before I was released. The house was weary with failure—I told my husband that I wanted to go to Arkansas. I would stay with my grandmother until I had fully recovered. I meant in mind, as well as body.

He came close and in a hoarse whisper said, "Marguerite. 67
Your grandmother died the day after your operation. You were too sick. I couldn't tell you."

Ah, Momma. I had never looked at death before, peered into 68
its yawning chasm for the face of a beloved. For days my mind staggered out of balance. I reeled on a precipice of knowledge that even if I were rich enough to travel all over the world, I would never find Momma. If I were as good as God's angels and as pure as the Mother of Christ, I could never have Momma's rough slow hands pat my cheek or braid my hair.

Death to the young is more than that undiscovered country; 69
despite its inevitability, it is a place having reality only in song or in other people's grief.

QUESTIONS

1. What does the author absorb from the women's magazines she mentions in the essay? Why does her behavior change? Trace this change through the main episodes in the narrative.

2. Explain the meaning of these sentences:
a. "A bizarre sensation pervades a relationship of pretense" (paragraph 3).
b. "There is a shock that comes so quickly and strikes so deep that the blow is internalized even before the skin feels it" (paragraph 35).
c. "Unadmitted was the sense of strangulation I had begun to feel, or the insidious quality of guilt for having a white husband, which surrounded me like an evil aura when we were in public" (paragraph 40).

3. Define these words: *innuendo* (paragraph 3); *refuted* (paragraph 7); *morose* (paragraph 9); *suffused* (paragraph 6); *compliant* (paragraph 7). Use them in sentences.

4. Analyze the author's handling of language in paragraph 7.

5. What is the function of exposition in this narrative essay? Point to sections in which you think exposition is used effectively and explain why.

6. What is the special quality associated with point of view in the essay?

7. What is the importance of the author's use of dialogue?

8. What is the relationship of the concluding paragraphs to the rest of the essay?

9. Speaking of her marriage, the author states, "The form was there, but the spirit had disappeared" (paragraph 2). Is this a common characteristic of relationships? What causes people to maintain such relationships? Are there solutions to relationships that have reached this point?

10. Write a narrative essay about the deterioration of a relationship in your life or that of a friend or family member.

GEORGE ORWELL

Shooting an Elephant

George Orwell (1903–1950) was the pseudonym of Eric Blair, an English novelist, essayist, and journalist. Orwell served with the Indian Imperial Police from 1922 to 1927 in Burma, fought in the Spanish Civil War, and acquired from his experiences a disdain of totalitarian and imperialistic systems. This attitude is reflected in the satiric fable *Animal Farm* (1945) and in his bleak, futuristic novel, *1984* (1949). In this essay, Orwell invokes personal experience to expose the contradictions inherent in British imperialism.

1 In Moulmein, in Lower Burma, I was hated by large numbers of people—the only time in my life that I have been important enough for this to happen to me. I was sub-divisional police officer of the town, and in an aimless, petty kind of way anti-European feeling was very bitter. No one had the guts to raise a riot, but if a European woman went through the bazaars alone somebody would probably spit betel juice over her dress. As a police officer I was an obvious target and was baited whenever it seemed safe to do so. When a nimble Burman tripped me up on the football field and the referee (another Burman) looked the other way, the crowd yelled with hideous laughter. This happened more than once. In the end the sneering yellow faces of young men that met me everywhere, the insults hooted after me when I was at a safe distance, got badly on my nerves. The young Buddhist priests were the worst of all. There were several thousands of them in the town and none of them seemed to have anything to do except stand on street corners and jeer at Europeans.

2 All this was perplexing and upsetting. For at that time I had already made up my mind that imperialism was an evil thing and the sooner I chucked up my job and got out of it the better. Theoretically—and secretly, of course—I was all for the Burmese and all against their oppressors, the British. As for the job I was doing, I hated it more bitterly than I can perhaps make clear. In a job like that you see the dirty work of Empire at close quarters. The wretched prisoners huddling in the stinking cages of the lock-ups, the grey, cowed faces of the long-term convicts, the scarred buttocks of the men who had been flogged with bamboos—all these oppressed me with an intolerable sense of guilt. But I could get nothing into perspective. I was young and ill-educated and I had had to think out my problems in the utter silence that is imposed on every Englishman in the East. I did not even know that the British Empire is dying, still less did I know that it is a great deal better than the younger empires that are going to supplant it. All I knew was that I was stuck between my hatred of the empire I served and my rage against the evil-spirited little beasts who tried to make my job impossible. With one part of my mind I thought of the British Raj as an unbreakable tyranny, as something clamped down, *in saecula saeculorum,* upon the will of prostrate peoples; with another part I thought that the greatest joy in

the world would be to drive a bayonet into a Buddhist priest's guts. Feelings like these are the normal by-products of imperialism; ask any Anglo-Indian official, if you can catch him off duty.

One day something happened which in a roundabout way 3 was enlightening. It was a tiny incident in itself, but it gave me a better glimpse than I had had before of the real nature of imperialism—the real motives for which despotic governments act. Early one morning the sub-inspector at a police station the other end of the town rang me up on the phone and said that an elephant was ravaging the bazaar. Would I please come and do something about it? I did not know what I could do, but I wanted to see what was happening and I got on to a pony and started out. I took my rifle, an old .44 Winchester and much too small to kill an elephant, but I thought the noise might be useful *in terrorem*. Various Burmans stopped me on the way and told me about the elephant's doings. It was not, of course, a wild elephant, but a tame one which had gone "must." It had been chained up as tame elephants always are when their attack of "must" is due, but on the previous night it had broken its chain and escaped. Its mahout, the only person who could manage it when it was in that state, had set out in pursuit, but he had taken the wrong direction and was now twelve hours' journey away, and in the morning the elephant had suddenly reappeared in the town. The Burmese population had no weapons and were quite helpless against it. It had already destroyed somebody's bamboo hut, killed a cow and raided some fruit-stalls and devoured the stock; also it had met the municipal rubbish van, and, when the driver jumped out and took to his heels, had turned the van over and inflicted violence upon it.

The Burmese sub-inspector and some Indian constables were 4 waiting for me in the quarter where the elephant had been seen. It was a very poor quarter, a labyrinth of squalid bamboo huts, thatched with palm-leaf, winding all over a steep hillside. I remember that it was a cloudy stuffy morning at the beginning of the rains. We began questioning the people as to where the elephant had gone, and, as usual, failed to get any definite information. That is invariably the case in the East; a story always sounds clear enough at a distance, but the nearer you get to the scene of events the vaguer it becomes. Some of the people said that the elephant had gone in one direction, some said that he had gone in another, some professed not even to have heard of any elephant. I had almost made up my mind that the whole story was a pack of lies, when we heard yells a little distance away. There was a loud, scandalised cry of "Go away, child! Go away this instant!" and an old woman with a switch in her hand came round the corner of a hut, violently shooing away a crowd of naked children. Some more women followed, clicking their tongues and exclaiming; evidently there was something there that the children ought not to have seen. I rounded the hut and saw a man's dead body sprawling in the mud. He was an Indian, a black Dravidian coolie, almost naked, and he could not have been dead many minutes. The people said that the elephant had come suddenly upon him round the corner of the hut, caught him with its trunk, put its foot on his back and ground him into the earth. This was the rainy season and the ground was soft, and his face had scored a trench a foot deep and a couple of yards long. He was lying on his belly with arms crucified and head sharply twisted to one side. His face was coated with mud, the eyes wide open, the teeth bared and grinning with an expression of unendurable agony. (Never tell me, by the way, that the dead look peaceful. Most of the corpses I have seen looked devilish.) The friction of the great beast's foot had stripped the skin from his back as neatly as one skins a rabbit. As soon as I saw the dead man I sent an orderly to a friend's house nearby to borrow an elephant rifle. I had already sent back the pony, not wanting it to go mad with fright and throw me if it smelled the elephant.

5 The orderly came back in a few minutes with a rifle and five cartridges, and meanwhile some Burmans had arrived and told us that the elephant was in the paddy fields below, only a few hundred yards away. As I started forward practically the whole population of the quarter flocked out of their houses and followed me. They had seen the rifle and were all shouting excitedly that I was going to shoot the elephant. They had not shown much interest in the elephant when he was merely ravaging their homes, but it was different now that he was going to be shot. It was a bit of fun to them, as it would be to an English crowd; besides, they wanted the meat. It made me vaguely uneasy. I had no intention of shooting the elephant—I had merely sent for the rifle to defend myself if necessary—and it is always unnerving to have a crowd following you. I marched down the hill, looking, and feeling a fool, with the rifle over my shoulder and an ever-growing army of people jostling at my heels. At the bottom, when you got away from the huts, there was a metalled road and beyond that a miry waste of paddy fields a thousand yards across, not yet ploughed but soggy from the first rains and dotted with coarse grass. The elephant was standing eighty yards from the road, his left side towards us. He took not the slightest notice of the crowd's approach. He was tearing up bunches of grass, beating them against his knees to clean them and stuffing them into his mouth.

6 I had halted on the road. As soon as I saw the elephant I knew with perfect certainty that I ought not to shoot him. It is a serious matter to shoot a working elephant—it is comparable to destroying a huge and costly piece of machinery—and obviously one ought not to do it if it can possibly be avoided. And at a distance, peacefully eating, the elephant looked no more dangerous than a

cow. I thought then and I think now that his attack of "must" was already passing off; in which case he would merely wander harmlessly about until the mahout came back and caught him. Moreover, I did not in the least want to shoot him. I decided that I would watch him for a little while to make sure that he did not turn savage again, and then go home.

But at that moment I glanced round at the crowd that had followed me. It was an immense crowd, two thousand at the least and growing every minute. It blocked the road for a long distance on either side. I looked at the sea of yellow faces above the garish clothes—faces all happy and excited over this bit of fun, all certain that the elephant was going to be shot. They were watching me as they would watch a conjuror about to perform a trick. They did not like me, but with the magical rifle in my hands I was momentarily worth watching. And suddenly I realised that I should have to shoot the elephant after all. The people expected it of me and I had got to do it; I could feel their two thousand wills pressing me forward, irresistibly. And it was at this moment, as I stood there with the rifle in my hands, that I first grasped the hollowness, the futility of the white man's dominion in the East. Here was I, the white man with his gun, standing in front of the unarmed native crowd—seemingly the leading actor of the piece; but in reality I was only an absurd puppet pushed to and fro by the will of those yellow faces behind. I perceived in this moment that when the white man turns tyrant it is his own freedom that he destroys. He becomes a sort of hollow, posing dummy, the conventionalised figure of a sahib. For it is the condition of his rule that he shall spend his life in trying to impress the "natives" and so in every crisis he has got to do what the "natives" expect of him. He wears a mask, and his face grows to fit it. I had got to shoot the elephant. I had committed myself to doing it when I sent for the rifle. A sahib has got to act like a sahib; he has got to appear resolute, to know his own mind and do definite things. To come all that way, rifle in hand, with two thousand people marching at my heels, and then to trail feebly away, having done nothing—no, that was impossible. The crowd would laugh at me. And my whole life, every white man's life in the East, was one long struggle not to be laughed at. 7

But I did not want to shoot the elephant. I watched him beating his bunch of grass against his knees, with that preoccupied grandmotherly air that elephants have. It seemed to me that it would be murder to shoot him. At that age I was not squeamish about killing animals, but I had never shot an elephant and never wanted to. (Somehow it always seems worse to kill a *large* animal.) Besides, there was the beast's owner to be considered. Alive, the elephant was worth at least a hundred pounds; dead, he would only be worth the 8 value of his tusks—five pounds, possibly. But I had got to act quickly. I turned to some experienced-looking Burmans who had been there when we arrived, and asked them how the elephant had been behaving. They all said the same thing: he took no notice of you if you left him alone, but he might charge if you went to close to him.

It was perfectly clear to me what I ought to do. I ought to walk up to within, say, twenty-five yards of the elephant and test his behaviour. If he charged I could shoot, if he took no notice of me it would be safe to leave him until the mahout came back. But also I knew that I was going to do no such thing. I was a poor shot with a rifle and the ground was soft mud into which one would sink at every step. If the elephant charged and I missed him, I should have about as much chance as a toad under a steam-roller. But even then I was not thinking particularly of my own skin, only the watchful yellow faces behind. For at that moment, with the crowd watching me, I was not afraid in the ordinary sense, as I would have been if I had been alone. A white man mustn't be frightened in front of "natives"; and so, in general, he isn't frightened. The sole thought in my mind was that if anything went wrong those two thousand Burmans would see me pursued, caught, trampled on and reduced to a grinning corpse like that Indian up the hill. And if that happened it was quite probable that some of them would laugh. That would never do. There was only one alternative. I shoved the cartridges into the magazine and lay down on the road to get a better aim. 9

The crowd grew very still, and a deep, low, happy sigh, as of people who see the theatre curtain go up at last, breathed from innumerable throats. They were going to have their bit of fun after all. The rifle was a beautiful German thing with cross-hair sights. I did not then know that in shooting an elephant one should shoot to cut an imaginary bar running from ear-hole to ear-hole. I ought therefore, as the elephant was sideways on, to have aimed straight at his ear-hole; actually I aimed several inches in front of this, thinking the brain would be further forward. 10

When I pulled the trigger I did not hear the bang or feel the kick—one never does when a shot goes home—but I heard the devilish roar of glee that went up from the crowd. In that instant, in too short a time, one would have thought, even for the bullet to get there, a mysterious, terrible change had come over the elephant. He neither stirred nor fell, but every line of his body had altered. He looked suddenly stricken, shrunken, immensely old, as though the frightful impact of the bullet had paralysed him without knocking him down. At last, after what seemed a long time—it might have been five seconds, I dare say—he sagged flabbily to his knees. His mouth slobbered. An enormous senility seemed to have settled upon him. One could have imagined him thousands of years old. I fired 11 again into the same spot. At the second shot he did not collapse but climbed with desperate slowness to his feet and stood weakly upright, with legs sagging and head drooping. I fired a third time. That was the shot that did for him. You could see the agony of it jolt his whole body and knock the last remnant of strength from his legs. But in falling he seemed for a moment to rise, for as his hind legs collapsed beneath him he seemed to tower upwards like a huge rock toppling, his trunk reaching skyward like a tree. He trumpeted, for the first and only time. And then down he came, his belly towards me, with a crash that seemed to shake the ground even where I lay.

I got up. The Burmans were already racing past me across the 12
mud. It was obvious that the elephant would never rise again, but he was not dead. He was breathing very rhythmically with long rattling gasps, his great mound of a side painfully rising and falling. His mouth was wide open—I could see far down into caverns of pale pink throat. I waited a long time for him to die, but his breathing did not weaken. Finally I fired my two remaining shots into the spot where I thought his heart must be. The thick blood welled out of him like red velvet, but still he did not die. His body did not even jerk when the shots hit him, the tortured breathing continued without a pause. He was dying, very slowly and in great agony, but in some world remote from me where not even a bullet could damage him further. I felt that I had got to put an end to that dreadful noise. It seemed dreadful to see the great beast lying there, powerless to move and yet powerless to die, and not even to be able to finish him. I sent back for my small rifle and poured shot after shot into his heart and down his throat. They seemed to make no impression. The tortured gasps continued as steadily as the ticking of a clock.

In the end I could not stand it any longer and went away. I 13
heard later that it took him half an hour to die. Burmans were arriving with dahs and baskets even before I left, and I was told they had stripped his body almost to the bones by the afternoon.

Afterwards, of course, there were endless discussions about 14
the shooting of the elephant. The owner was furious, but he was only an Indian and could do nothing. Besides, legally I had done the right thing, for a mad elephant has to be killed, like a mad dog, if its owner fails to control it. Among the Europeans opinion was divided. The older men said I was right, the younger men said it was a damn shame to shoot an elephant for killing a coolie, because an elephant was worth more than any damn Coringhee coolie. And afterwards I was very glad that the coolie had been killed; it put me legally in the right and it gave me a sufficient pretext for shooting the elephant. I often wondered whether any of the others grasped that I had done it solely to avoid looking a fool.

QUESTIONS

1. How does the shooting of the elephant give Orwell a better understanding of "the real nature of imperialism—the real motives for which despotic governments act" (paragraph 3)? Why does Orwell kill the elephant? What is his attitude toward the Burmese people?

2. Why does Orwell concentrate on the prolonged death of the elephant? What effect does it have?

3. How would you describe the level of language in the essay? Point to specific words, sentences, and phrases to support your answer.

4. Define *supplant* (paragraph 2); *labyrinth* (paragraph 4); *jostling* (paragraph 5); *conjuror* (paragraph 7); *senility* (paragraph 11).

5. What is the function of the first two paragraphs? Where is the thesis stated in the essay?

6. Analyze Orwell's use of dramatic techniques to develop the narrative. Examine consecutive paragraphs in the essay to determine the author's presentation of action from different perspectives.

7. Select and analyze some of the details in the essay that are designed to impress the reader's senses and emotions. Why does Orwell rely so heavily on the presentation and accumulation of detail in the essay?

8. How is the entire essay structured by irony of situation and paradox? How do these devices relate to the ethical issues raised by Orwell?

9. In this essay, written in 1936, Orwell declares: "I did not even know that the British Empire is dying, still less did I know that it is a great deal better than the younger empires that are going to supplant it" (paragraph 2). In what ways is Orwell's statement prophetic?

10. Write a narrative essay about an episode in your life when you came into conflict with social or political forces.

2 The Sense of Place

HARRY CREWS

Why I Live Where I Live

Harry Crews (1935–) is a Southern writer who is a master of the art of the grotesque. His novels include *Karate is a Thing of the Spirit* (1971), *The Gypsy's Curse* (1974), and *A Feast of Snakes* (1976). He contributes regularly to *Playboy, The Sewanee Review, Esquire,* and other publications. In this personal essay, Crews examines the relationship between the writer's surroundings and the creative process.

1 I can leave the place where I live a couple of hours before daylight and be on a deserted little strip of sand called Crescent Beach in time to throw a piece of meat on a fire and then, in a few minutes, lie back sucking on a vodka bottle and chewing on a hunk of bloody beef while the sun lifts out of the Atlantic Ocean (somewhat unnerving but also mystically beautiful to a man who never saw a body of water bigger than a pond until he was grown) and while the sun rises lie on a blanket, brain singing from vodka and a bellyful of beef, while the beautiful bikinied children from the University of Florida drift down the beach, their smooth bodies sweating baby oil and the purest kind of innocent lust (which of course is the rankest sort) into the bright air. If all that starts to pall—and what *doesn't* start to pall?—I can leave the beach and be

out on the end of a dock, sitting in the Captain's Table eating hearts-of-palm salad and hot boiled shrimp and sipping on a tall, icy glass of beer while the sun I saw lift out of the Atlantic that morning sinks into the warm, waveless Gulf of Mexico. It makes for a hell of a day. But that isn't really why I live in the north-central Florida town of Gainesville.

Nor do I live in Gainesville because seven blocks from my house there are two enormous libraries filled with the most courteous, helpful people you can imagine, people who, after explaining some of the more intricate mysteries of how the place works, including the purposes of numerous indices, will go ahead and cheerfully find what I cannot: for example, the car capacity of drive-in theaters in Bakersfield, California, in 1950. A man never knows when he may need a bit of information like that, but it isn't enough to keep him living in a little town in Florida as opposed to, say, Ann Arbor, Michigan. 2

I love the size of Gainesville. I can walk anywhere I want to go, and consequently I have very little to do with that abomination before the Lord, the car. It's a twenty-minute stroll to my two favorite bars, Lillian's Music Store and the Winnjammer; ten minutes to a lovely square of grass and trees called the Plaza of the Americas; less than ten minutes to the house of a young lady who has been hypnotizing me for six years. Some people get analyzed; I get hypnotized. It leaves me with the most astonishing and pleasurable memories. But there must be ten thousand towns like Gainesville in this country, and surely several hundred of them would have good places to drink and talk and at least one house where a young lady lived who would consent to hypnotize me into astonishing and pleasurable memories. So I cannot lean too heavily on walking and memories to justify being where I am. 3

The reason I live where I do is more complicated than the sorts of things I've been talking about thus far—more complicated and, I expect, ultimately inexplicable. Or, said another way: anyone other than I may find that the explanation does not satisfy. To start, I live right in the middle of town on three acres of land, land thick with pines a hundred feet tall, oak, wild plum trees, and all manner of tangled, unidentifiable underbrush. The only cleared space is the very narrow road leading down to the house. No lawn. (There are many things I absolutely refuse to do in this world, but the three things leading the list are: wash my car, shine my shoes, and mow a lawn.) The back wall of the room I work in at the rear of the house is glass, and when I raise my eyes from the typewriter I look past an enormous bull bay tree through a thin stand of reeds into a tiny creek, the banks of which are thick with the greenest fern God ever made. In my imagination I can follow that little creek upstream to the place 4 where, after a long, circuitous passage, it joins the Suwannee River, and then follow the dark waters of the Suwannee upriver to the place where it rises in the nearly impenetrable fastness of the Okefenokee Swamp. Okefenokee: Creek Indian word for Land of the Trembling Earth, because most of the islands in the swamp—some of them holding hundreds of huge trees growing so thick that their roots are matted and woven as closely as a blanket—actually float on the water, and when a black bear crashes across one of them, the whole thing trembles.

I saw the Okefenokee Swamp long before I saw the Suwannee River, and the Suwannee River long before I saw the little creek I'm looking at as I write this. When I was a boy, I was in the swamp a lot, on the edges of it practically all the time that I was not in the fields working. I went deep into the Okefenokee with T. J., the husband of one of my first cousins. His left leg was cut off at the knee and he wore a peg, but he got along fine with it because we were usually in a flat skiff casting nets for crawfish, which he sold for fish bait at a penny apiece. I did not know enough then and do not know enough now to go into the deep middle swamp, but T. J. did; he knew the twisting maze of sloughs like his back yard, could read every sign of every living thing in the swamp, and made a good living with the crawfish nets and his string of traps and his gun. He sold alligator, wore alligator, and ate alligator. This was long before the federal government made the place a national wildlife refuge. 5

T. J. made his living out of the swamp, and I make mine now out of how the swamp shaped me, how the rhythms and patterns of speech in that time and place are still alive in my mouth today and, more important, alive in my ear. I feed off now and hope always to feed off the stories I heard told in the early dark around fires where coffee boiled while our clothes, still wet from stringing traps all day, slowly dried to our bodies. Even when I write stories not set in Georgia and not at all about anything in the South, that writing is of necessity still informed by my notions of the world and of what it is to be caught in it. Those notions obviously come out of South Georgia and out of everything that happened to me there, or so I believe. 6

Living here in North Florida, I am a little more than a hundred miles from where I was born and raised to manhood. I am just far enough away from the only place that was ever mine to still see it, close enough to the only people to whom I was ever kin in ways deeper than blood to still hear them. I know that what I have just written will sound precious and pretentious to many people. So be it. Let them do their work as they will, and I'll do mine. 7

I've tried to work—that is, to write—in Georgia, but I could not. Even under the best of circumstances, at my mama's farm, for instance, it was all too much for me. I was too deep in it, too close to it 8 to use it, to make anything out of it. My memory doesn't even seem to work when I'm writing in Georgia. I can't seem to hold a story in my head. I write a page, and five pages later what I wrote earlier has begun to slide out of focus. If this is all symptomatic of some more profound malaise, I don't want to know about it and I certainly don't want to understand it.

Living here in Gainesville seems to give me a kind of geographic and emotional distance I need to write. I can't write if I get too far away. I tried to work on a novel in Tennessee once and after a ruined two months gave it up in despair. I once spent four months near Lake Placid in a beautiful house lent to me by a friend—perfect place to write—and I didn't do a damn thing but eat my guts and look out the window at the mountains. 9

And that, all of it, precious, pretentious, or whatever, is why I live where I live. And unless something happens that I cannot control, I plan to die here. 10

QUESTIONS

1. The author gives uncomplicated reasons to explain why he lives where he does. What are these reasons? Why does he raise them?

2. How does Crews's sense of place relate to his conception of himself as a writer?

3. What are the key words in the first, long sentence of the essay that create a persona for the author? To what extent is the language in this sentence sustained or modified throughout the essay?

4. Locate words and phrases in paragraphs 4 and 5 that convey connotations of mystery and the unknown. What do these words indicate about the theme of the essay?

5. Study Crews's introductory paragraph. What is the effect of the first sentence? Of the parenthetical asides? Of the last two sentences? How does the introduction function in relation to the next two paragraphs?

6. How does description function in relation to the causal patterns that Crews develops?

7. Notice the shift in tone between the first half of the essay (paragraphs 1 to 5) and the second half (paragraphs 6 to 10). Why does the author do this? What does he achieve by "breaking" tonal consistency?

8. Describe the method of development in the concluding paragraph. What new element is introduced? Justify its placement and effectiveness.

9. Crews speaks of "a kind of geographic and emotional distance" that

he needs to work or to create. Why can being too close to a place or neighborhood be harmful? Conversely, how can such closeness be a strength?

10. a. Write an essay on why you live where you live.
b. Write a paper about the ideal place for you to live if you had the opportunity.

HENRY DAVID THOREAU

Economy

Henry David Thoreau (1817–1862), author of the masterpiece *Walden* (1854), is one of the most important figures in American thought and literature. A social and political activist, he opposed the Mexican War, protested slavery, and refused to pay his poll taxes. As a naturalist, he believed in the preeminence of individualism and nature over technology, materialism, and nationalism. In 1845, Thoreau went to live at Walden Pond, "living deep and sucking the marrow out of life." *Walden,* describing his life at the pond, is one of the most challenging, exuberant, and innovative works of American literature. This account from Thoreau's masterpiece, tracing the construction of his dwelling, reflects his preoccupation with economy, natural process, and self-reliance.

Near the end of March, 1845, I borrowed an axe and went down to the woods by Walden Pond, nearest to where I intended to build my house, and began to cut down some tall arrowy white pines, still in their youth, for timber. It is difficult to begin without borrowing, but perhaps it is the most generous course thus to permit your fellow-men to have an interest in your enterprise. The owner of the axe, as he released his hold on it, said that it was the apple of his eye; but I returned it sharper than I received it. It was a pleasant hillside where I worked, covered with pine woods, through which I looked out on the pond, and a small open field in the woods where pines and hickories were springing up. The ice in the pond was not yet dissolved, though there were some open spaces, and it was all dark colored and saturated with water. There were some slight flurries of snow during the days that I worked there; but for the most part when I came out onto the 1 railroad, on my way home, its yellow sand heap stretched away gleaming in the hazy atmosphere, and the rails shone in the spring sun, and I heard the lark and pewee and other birds already come to commence another year with us. They were pleasant spring days, in which the winter of man's discontent was thawing as well as the earth, and the life that had lain torpid began to stretch itself. One day, when my axe had come off and I had cut a green hickory for a wedge, driving it with a stone, and had placed the whole to soak in a pond hole in order to swell the wood, I saw a striped snake run into the water, and he lay on the bottom, apparently without inconvenience, as long as I stayed there, or more than a quarter of an hour; perhaps because he had not yet fairly come out of the torpid state. It appeared to me that for a like reason men remain in their present low and primitive condition; but if they should feel the influence of the spring of springs arousing them, they would of necessity rise to a higher and more ethereal life. I had previously seen the snakes in frosty mornings in my path with portions of their bodies still numb and inflexible, waiting for the sun to thaw them. On the 1st of April it rained and melted the ice, and in the early part of the day, which was very foggy, I heard a stray goose groping about over the pond and cackling as if lost, or like the spirit of the fog.

So I went on for some days cutting and hewing timber, and 2
also studs and rafters, all with my narrow axe, not having many communicable or scholar-like thoughts, singing to myself.

> Men say they know many things;
> But lo! they have taken wings—
> The arts and sciences,
> And a thousand appliances;
> The wind that blows
> Is all that anybody knows.

I hewed the main timber six inches square, most of the studs on two sides only, and the rafters and floor timbers on one side, leaving the rest of the bark on, so that they were just as straight and much stronger than sawed ones. Each stick was carefully mortised or tenoned by its stump, for I had borrowed other tools by this time. My days in the woods were not very long ones; yet I usually carried my dinner of bread and butter, and read the newspaper in which it was wrapped, at noon, sitting amid the green pine boughs which I had cut off, and to my bread was imparted some of their fragrance, for my hands were covered with a thick coat of pitch. Before I had done I was more the friend than the foe of the pine tree, though I had cut down some of them, having become better acquainted with it. Sometimes a rambler in the wood was attracted by the sound of my axe, and we chatted pleasantly over the chips which I had made.

By the middle of April, for I made no haste in my work, but 3
rather made the most of it, my house was framed and ready for the raising. I had already bought the shanty of James Collins, an Irishman who worked on the Fitchburg Railroad, for boards. James Collins' shanty was considered an uncommonly fine one. When I called to see it he was not at home. I walked about the outside, at first unobserved from within, the window was so deep and high. It was of small dimensions, with a peaked cottage roof, and not much else to be seen, the dirt being raised five feet all around as if it were a compost heap. The roof was the soundest part, though a good deal warped and made brittle by the sun. Doorsill there was none, but a perennial passage for the hens under the door board. Mrs. C. came to the door and asked me to view it from the inside. The hens were driven in by my approach. It was dark, and had a dirt floor for the most part, dank, clammy, and aguish, only here a board and there a board which would not bear removal. She lighted a lamp to show me the inside of the roof and the walls, and also that the board floor extended under the bed, warning me not to step into the cellar, a sort of dust hole two feet deep. In her own words, they were "good boards overhead, good boards all around, and a good window"—of two whole squares originally, only the cat had passed out that way lately. There was a stove, a bed, and a place to sit, an infant in the house where it was born, a silk parasol, gilt-framed looking-glass, and a patent new coffee-mill nailed to an oak sapling, all told. The bargain was soon concluded, for James had in the meanwhile returned. I to pay four dollars and twenty-five cents tonight, he to vacate at five tomorrow morning, selling to nobody else meanwhile: I to take possession at six. It were well, he said, to be there early, and anticipate certain indistinct but wholly unjust claims on the score of ground rent and fuel. This he assured me was the only encumbrance. At six I passed him and his family on the road. One large bundle held their all—bed, coffee-mill, looking-glass, hens—all but the cat; she took to the woods and became a wild cat and, as I learned afterward, trod in a trap set for woodchucks, and so became a dead cat at last.

I took down this dwelling the same morning, drawing the 4
nails, and removed it to the pond side by small cartloads, spreading the boards on the grass there to bleach and warp back again in the sun. One early thrush gave me a note or two as I drove along the woodland path. I was informed treacherously by a young Patrick that neighbor Seeley, an Irishman, in the intervals of the carting, transferred the still tolerable, straight, and drivable nails, staples, and spikes to his pocket, and then stood when I came back to pass the time of day, and look freshly up, unconcerned, with spring thoughts, at the devastation; there being a dearth of work, as he said. He was

there to represent spectatordom, and help make this seemingly insignificant event one with the removal of the gods of Troy.

I dug my cellar in the side of a hill sloping to the south, where 5
a woodchuck had formerly dug his burrow, down through sumach and blackberry roots, and the lowest stain of vegetation, six feet square by seven deep, to a fine sand where potatoes would not freeze in any winter. The sides were left shelving, and not stoned; but the sun having never shone on them, the sand still keeps its place. It was but two hours' work. I took particular pleasure in this breaking of ground, for in almost all latitudes men dig into the earth for an equable temperature. Under the most splendid house in the city is still to be found the cellar where they store their roots as of old, and long after the superstructure had disappeared posterity remark its dent in the earth. The house is still but a sort of porch at the entrance of a burrow.

At length, in the beginning of May, with the help of some of 6
my acquaintances, rather to improve so good an occasion for neighborliness than from any necessity, I set up the frame of my house. No man was ever more honored in the character of his raisers than I. They are destined, I trust, to assist at the raising of loftier structures one day. I began to occupy my house on the 4th of July, as soon as it was boarded and roofed, for the boards were carefully feather-edged and lapped, so that it was perfectly impervious to rain, but before boarding I laid the foundation of a chimney at one end, bringing two cartloads of stones up the hill from the pond in my arms. I built the chimney after my hoeing in the fall, before a fire became necessary for warmth, doing my cooking in the meanwhile out of doors on the ground, early in the morning: which mode I still think is in some respects more convenient and agreeable than the usual one. When it stormed before my bread was baked, I fixed a few boards over the fire, and sat under them to watch my loaf, and passed some pleasant hours in that way. In those days, when my hands were much employed, I read but little, but the least scraps of paper which lay on the ground, my holder, or tablecloth, afforded me as much entertainment, in fact answered the same purpose as the Iliad.

QUESTIONS

1. Describe the process by which Thoreau builds his house.

2. What is Thoreau's attitude toward economy in this selection? Which of the details Thoreau has included most successfully reveal this attitude?

3. In paragraph 1, what connotation does the author develop for the

word "borrowing"? How do words related to economics serve as a motif in the essay?

4. What is the analogy in paragraph 1?

5. How does Thoreau use process analysis? Why is this rhetorical technique reinforced by the natural processes depicted in the essay?

6. How does Thoreau particularize the generalizations he makes in the essay?

7. What is the tone of the essay? Does an implied thesis for the essay emerge? Justify your answer.

8. What is the relationship of the last two sentences in paragraph 6 to the rest of the selection?

9. Analyze Thoreau's poem in paragraph 2. What is your response to the theme of the poem?

10. Using Thoreau's method, write an essay in which you trace the process of building or creating something that was important to you.

PABLO NERUDA

The Odors of Homecoming

Pablo Neruda (1904–1973), one of the greatest modern poets writing in Spanish, was born in Parral, Chile, the son of a railwayworker. He studied in Santiago from 1923 to 1926, publishing five volumes of poetry. Later he served as Chilean counsel in Burma, Ceylon, Java, Spain and Mexico. Neruda, a communist, was elected to the Chilean senate in 1945 but was driven into hiding and eventual exile in 1948. He returned to Chile in 1952 and remained active as a poet-politician up to his untimely death, twelve days after the coup that overthrew Allende. Neruda's major volumes of poetry include *Residence on Earth* (1925–1945), *Elementary Odes* (1954–1957), *Estravagaria* (1958), and *A Hundred Love Sonnets* (1960). The following essay, in a translation by Margaret Sayers Peden, comes from *Passions and Impressions* (1983). It reflects the broad range of images, figurative language, and heightened meanings that also endow Neruda's poetry with such power.

My house nestles among many trees. After a long 1
absence, I like to lose myself in hidden nooks to savor my homecoming. Mysterious, fragrant thickets have appeared that are new to me. The poplar I planted in the back of the garden, so slim it could barely be seen, is now an adult tree. Its bark is patterned with wrinkles of wisdom that rise toward the sky to express themselves in a constant tremor of new leaves in the treetop.

The chestnut trees were the last to recognize me. When I 2
arrived, their naked, dry branches, towering and unseeing, seemed imperious and hostile, though the pervading spring of Chile was germinating amid their trunks. Every day I went to call on them, for I understood that they demanded my homage, and in the cold of morning stood motionless beneath the leafless branches, until one day a timid green bud, high overhead, came out to look at me, and others followed. So my reappearance was communicated to the wary, hidden leaves of the tallest chestnut tree, which now greets me with condescension, tolerating my return.

In the trees the birds renew their age-old trills, as if nothing 3
ever happened beneath the leaves.

A pervasive odor of winter and years lingers in the library. 4
Of all places, this was the most suffused with absence.

There is something of mortality about the smell of musty 5
books; it assaults the nostrils and strikes the rugged terrain of the soul, because it is the odor of oblivion, of buried memory.

Standing beside the weathered window, staring at the blue 6
and white Andean sky, I sense that behind my back the aroma of spring is pitting its strength against the books. They resist being rooted out of their long neglect, and still exude signs of oblivion. Spring enters every room, clad in a new dress and the odor of honeysuckle.

The books have been unruly in my absence. None is missing, 7
but none is in its place. Beside an austere volume of Bacon, a rare seventeenth-century edition, I find Salgari's *The Captain of Yucatan*, and in spite of everything, they've got along rather well together. On the other hand, as I pick up a solitary Byron, its cover drops off like the dark wing of an albatross. Laboriously, I stitch spine and cover, but not before a puff of cold Romanticism clouds my eyes.

The shells are the most silent occupants of my house. They 8
endured the years of the ocean, solidifying their silence. Now, to those years have been added time and dust. Their cold, glinting mother-of-pearl, their concentric Gothic ellipses, their open valves, remind me of distant coasts, long-ago events. This incomparable lance of rosy light is the *Rostellaria*, which the Cuban malacologist Carlos de la Torre, a magus of the deep, once conferred upon me like

an underseas decoration. And here, slightly more faded and dusty, is the black "olive" of the California seas, and, of the same provenance, the oyster of red spines and the oyster of black pearls. We almost drowned in that treasure-laden sea.

There are new occupants, books and objects liberated from 9
boxes long sealed. The pine boxes come from France. The boards smell of sunny noon in the Midi, and as I pry them open, they creak and sing, and the golden light falls on the red bindings of Victor Hugo. *Les Misérables*, in an early edition, arrives to crowd the walls of my house with its multitude of heartrending lives.

Then, from a large box resembling a coffin, comes the sweet 10
face of a woman, firm wooden breasts that once cleaved the wind, hands saturated with music and brine. It is the figure of a woman, a figurehead. I baptize her María Celeste, because she has all the mystery of a lost ship. I discovered her radiant beauty in a Paris *bric-á-brac*, buried beneath used hardware, disfigured by neglect, hidden beneath the sepulchral rags and tatters of the slums. Now, aloft, she sails again, alive and new. Every morning her cheeks will be covered by mysterious dew or saltwater tears.

All at once the roses are in bloom. Once I was an enemy of 11
the rose, of its interminable literary associations, of its arrogance. But as I watched them grow, having endured the winter with nothing to wear and nothing to cover their heads, and then as snowy breasts or glowing fires peered from among hard and thorny stems, little by little I was filled with tenderness, with admiration for their ox-like health, for the daring, secret wave of perfume and light they implacably extract from the black earth at just the right moment, as if duty were a miracle, as if they thrived on precise maneuvers in harsh weather. And now roses grow everywhere, with a moving solemnity I share—remote, both they and I, from pomp and frivolity, each absorbed in creating its individual flash of lightning.

Now every wave of air bears a soft, trembling movement, a 12
flowery palpitation that pierces the heart. Forgotten names, forgotten springs, hands that touched briefly, haughty eyes of yellow stone, tresses lost in time: youth, insistently throbbing with memories and ecstatic aromas.

It is the perfume of the honeysuckle, the first kisses of spring. 13

QUESTIONS

1. What is the season? What are some of the "odors of homecoming" that Neruda detects? What do the odors and sights remind him of?

2. List the various objects that Neruda describes. What is his attitude toward them?

3. Analyze the sensory language in this essay. What senses does Neruda evoke? Cite examples. Describe the mood or atmosphere that the imagery creates.

4. Locate similes and metaphors in the essay. What do they contribute to the dominant impression?

5. What sentence in the introductory paragraph establishes the purpose of Neruda's description of his home? Is this the thesis statement? Why or why not?

6. How does Neruda arrange descriptive details in paragraphs 1 to 3, 4 to 6, 7 to 10, and 11 to 13 ?

7. Neruda employs a considerable amount of personification in this essay. Cite and explain examples of this method. What cumulative impression is created?

8. What effect is achieved by the relatively short paragraphs 3, 4, and 5, and by the one-sentence conclusion?

9. Is Neruda excessively impressionistic, romantic, or sentimental in this essay? Justify your response.

10. a. Describe a particularly vivid homecoming of your own. Incorporate sensory details and other poetic devices.
b. Write a descriptive essay that captures the dominant impression of a specific month or season.

MARGARET MEAD

A Day in Samoa

Margaret Mead (1901–1979), famed American anthropologist, was curator of ethnology at the American Museum of Natural History and a professor at Columbia University. Her field expeditions to Samoa, New Guinea, and Bali in the 1920s and 1930s produced several major studies, notably *Coming of Age in Samoa* (1928), *Growing Up in New Guinea* (1930), and *Sex and Temperament in Three Primitive Societies* (1935). Her interest in the development of personality in primitive culture is evident in this selection from *Coming of Age in Samoa.*

The life of the day begins at dawn, or if the moon has 1
shown until daylight, the shouts of the young men may be heard before dawn from the hillside. Uneasy in the night, populous with ghosts, they shout lustily to one another as they hasten with their work. As the dawn begins to fall among the soft brown roofs and the slender palm trees stand out against a colourless, gleaming sea, lovers slip home from trysts beneath the palm trees or in the shadow of beached canoes, that the light may find each sleeper in his appointed place. Cocks crow, negligently, and a shrill-voiced bird cries from the breadfruit trees. The insistent roar of the reef seems muted to an undertone for the sounds of a waking village. Babies cry, a few short wails before sleepy mothers give them the breast. Restless little children roll out of their sheets and wander drowsily down to the beach to freshen their faces in the sea. Boys, bent upon an early fishing, start collecting their tackle and go to rouse their more laggard companions. Fires are lit, here and there, the white smoke hardly visible against the paleness of the dawn. The whole village, sheeted and frowsy, stirs, rubs its eyes, and stumbles towards the beach. "Talofa!" "Talofa!" "Will the journey start to-day?" "Is it bonito fishing your lordship is going?" Girls stop to giggle over some young ne'er-do-well who escaped during the night from an angry father's pursuit and to venture a shrewd guess that the daughter knew more about his presence than she told. The boy who is taunted by another, who has succeeded him in his sweetheart's favour, grapples with his rival, his foot slipping in the wet sand. From the other end of the village comes a long drawn-out, piercing wail. A messenger has just brought word of the death of some relative in another village. Half-clad, unhurried women, with babies at their breasts, or astride their hips, pause in their tale of Losa's outraged departure from her father's house to the greater kindness in the home of her uncle, to wonder who is dead. Poor relatives whisper their requests to rich relatives, men make plans to set a fish trap together, a woman begs a bit of yellow dye from a kinswoman, and through the village sounds the rhythmic tattoo which calls the young men together. They gather from all parts of the village, digging sticks in hand, ready to start inland to the plantation. The older men set off upon their more lonely occupations, and each household, reassembled under its peaked roof, settles down to the routine of the morning. Little children, too hungry to wait for the late breakfast, beg lumps of cold taro which they munch greedily. Women carry piles of washing to the sea or to the spring at the far end of the village, or set off inland after weaving materials. The older girls go fishing on the reef, or perhaps set themselves to weaving a new set of Venetian blinds.

In the houses, where the pebbly floors have been swept bare with a stiff long-handled broom, the women great with child and the nursing mothers sit and gossip with one another. Old men sit apart, unceasingly twisting palm husk on their bare thighs and muttering old tales under their breath. The carpenters begin work on the new house, while the owner bustles about trying to keep them in good humour. Families who will cook to-day are hard at work; the taro, yams and bananas have already been brought from inland; the children are scuttling back and forth, fetching sea water, or leaves to stuff the pig. As the sun rises higher in the sky, the shadows deepen under the thatched roofs, the sand is burning to the touch, the hibiscus flowers wilt on the hedges, and little children bid the smaller ones, "Come out of the sun." Those whose excursions have been short return to the village, the women with strings of crimson jelly fish, or baskets of shell fish, the men with cocoanuts, carried in baskets slung on a shoulder pole. The women and children eat their breakfasts, just hot from the oven, if this is cook day, and the young men work swiftly in the mid-day heat, preparing the noon feast for their elders. 2

It is high noon. The sand burns the feet of the little children, who leave their palm leaf balls and their pin-wheels of frangipani blossoms to wither in the sun, as they creep into the shade of the houses. The women who must go abroad carry great banana leaves as sun-shades or wind wet cloths about their heads. Lowering a few blinds against the slanting sun, all who are left in the village wrap their heads in sheets and go to sleep. Only a few adventurous children may slip away for a swim in the shadow of a high rock, some industrious woman continues with her weaving, or a close little group of women bend anxiously over a woman in labour. The village is dazzling and dead; any sound seems oddly loud and out of place. Words have to cut through the solid heat slowly. And then the sun gradually sinks over the sea. 3

A second time, the sleeping people stir, roused perhaps by the cry of "a boat," resounding through the village. The fishermen beach their canoes, weary and spent from the heat, in spite of the slaked lime on their heads, with which they have sought to cool their brains and redden their hair. The brightly coloured fishes are spread out on the floor, or piled in front of the houses until the women pour water over them to free them from taboo. Regretfully, the young fishermen separate out the "Taboo fish," which must be sent to the chief, or proudly they pack the little palm leaf baskets with offerings of fish to take to their sweethearts. Men come home from the bush, grimy and heavy laden, shouting as they come, greeted in a sonorous rising cadence by those who have remained at home. They gather in 4 the guest house for their evening kava drinking. The soft clapping of hands, the high-pitched intoning of the talking chief who serves the kava echoes through the village. Girls gather flowers to weave into necklaces; children, lusty from their naps and bound to no particular task, play circular games in the half shade of the late afternoon. Finally the sun sets, in a flame which stretches from the mountain behind to the horizon on the sea, the last bather comes up from the beach, children straggle home, dark little figures etched against the sky; lights shine in the houses, and each household gathers for its evening meal. The suitor humbly presents his offering, the children have been summoned from their noisy play, perhaps there is an honoured guest who must be served first, after the soft, barbaric singing of Christian hymns and the brief and graceful evening prayer. In front of a house at the end of the village, a father cries out the birth of a son. In some family circles a face is missing, in others little runaways have found a haven! Again quiet settles upon the village, as first the head of the household, then the women and children, and last of all the patient boys, eat their supper.

After supper the old people and the little children are 5
bundled off to bed. If the young people have guests the front of the house is yielded to them. For day is the time for the councils of old men and the labours of youth, and night is the time for lighter things. Two kinsmen, or a chief and his councillor, sit and gossip over the day's events or make plans for the morrow. Outside a crier goes through the village announcing that the communal breadfruit pit will be opened in the morning, or that the village will make a great fish trap. If it is moonlight, groups of young men, women by twos and threes, wander through the village, and crowds of children hunt for land crabs or chase each other among the breadfruit trees. Half the village may go fishing by torchlight and the curving reef will gleam with wavering lights and echo with shouts of triumph or disappointment, teasing words or smothered cries of outraged modesty. Or a group of youths may dance for the pleasure of some visiting maiden. Many of those who have retired to sleep, drawn by the merry music, will wrap their sheets about them and set out to find the dancing. A white-clad, ghostly throng will gather in a circle about the gaily lit house, a circle from which every now and then a few will detach themselves and wander away among the trees. Sometimes sleep will not descend upon the village until long past midnight; then at last there is only the mellow thunder of the reef and the whisper of lovers, as the village rests until dawn.

QUESTIONS

1. Trace the daily cycle of Samoan life that Mead presents.

2. At first glance this essay seems to be a superbly crafted description of daily life in Samoa. However, it is more than a mere description. What anthropological inferences does Mead make about Samoan culture?

3. Certain words in the essay are indigenous to Samoan culture and geography. Locate these words and define them. Can these words be used in American culture?

4. Explain the images and figurative language in paragraph 1.

5. Discuss the effect of the author's lengthy introductory and concluding paragraphs.

6. What is the relationship of description to mood and tone in the essay?

7. How does narrative influence essay structure and theme?

8. Discuss the transitions from paragraph to paragraph in the essay.

9. To what extent do you think that Mead is seduced by primitive or exotic life in her treatment of Samoan culture? Justify your answer.

10. Write your own description of a vivid or memorable place that you have visited and observed.

N. SCOTT MOMADAY

The Way to Rainy Mountain

Navarre Scott Momaday (1934–   ), Pulitzer Prize–winning poet, critic, and academician, is the author of *House Made of Dawn* (1968), *The Way to Rainy Mountain* (1969), *The Names* (1976), and other works. "I am an American Indian (Kiowa), and am vitally interested in American Indian art, history and culture," Momaday has written. In this essay, he elevates personal experience to the realm of poety and tribal myth.

A single knoll rises out of the plain in Oklahoma, north and west of the Wichita Range. For my people, the Kiowas, it is an old landmark, and they gave it the name Rainy Mountain. The hardest weather in the world is there. Winter brings blizzards, hot tornadic winds arise in the spring, and in summer the prairie is an anvil's edge. The grass turns brittle 1 and brown, and it cracks beneath your feet. There are green belts along the rivers and creeks, linear groves of hickory and pecan, willow and witch hazel. At a distance in July or August the steaming foliage seems almost to writhe in fire. Great green and yellow grasshoppers are everywhere in the tall grass, popping up like corn to sting the flesh, and tortoises crawl about on the red earth, going nowhere in the plenty of time. Loneliness is an aspect of the land. All things in the plain are isolate; there is no confusion of objects in the eye, but *one* hill or *one* tree or *one* man. To look upon that landscape in the early morning, with the sun at your back, is to lose the sense of proportion. Your imagination comes to life, and this, you think, is where Creation was begun.

I returned to Rainy Mountain in July. My grandmother had 2
died in the spring, and I wanted to be at her grave. She had lived to be very old and at last infirm. Her only living daughter was with her when she died, and I was told that in death her face was that of a child.

I like to think of her as a child. When she was born, the 3
Kiowas were living the last great moment of their history. For more than a hundred years they had controlled the open range from the Smoky Hill River to the Red, from the headwaters of the Canadian to the fork of the Arkansas and Cimarron. In alliance with the Comanches, they had ruled the whole of the southern Plains. War was their sacred business, and they were among the finest horsemen the world has ever known. But warfare for the Kiowas was preeminently a matter of disposition rather than of survival, and they never understood the grim, unrelenting advance of the U.S. Cavalry. When at last, divided and ill-provisioned, they were driven onto the Staked Plains in the cold rains of autumn, they fell into panic. In Palo Duro Canyon they abandoned their crucial stores to pillage and had nothing then but their lives. In order to save themselves, they surrendered to the soldiers at Fort Sill and were imprisoned in the old stone corral that now stands as a military museum. My grandmother was spared the humiliation of those high gray walls by eight or ten years, but she must have known from birth the affliction of defeat, the dark brooding of old warriors.

Her name was Aho, and she belonged to the last culture to 4
evolve in North America. Her forebears came down from the high country in western Montana nearly three centuries ago. They were a mountain people, a mysterious tribe of hunters whose language has never been positively classified in any major group. In the late seventeenth century they began a long migration to the south and east. It was a journey toward the dawn, and it led to a golden age. Along the way the Kiowas were befriended by the Crows, who gave

them the culture and religion of the Plains. They acquired horses, and their ancient nomadic spirit was suddenly free of the ground. They acquired Tai-me, the sacred Sun Dance doll, from that moment the object and symbol of their worship, and so shared in the divinity of the sun. Not least, they acquired the sense of destiny, therefore courage and pride. When they entered upon the southern Plains they had been transformed. No longer were they slaves to the simple necessity of survival; they were a lordly and dangerous society of fighters and thieves, hunters and priests of the sun. According to their origin myth, they entered the world through a hollow log. From one point of view, their migration was the fruit of an old prophecy, for indeed they emerged from a sunless world.

Although my grandmother lived out her long life in the 5
shadow of Rainy Mountain, the immense landscape of the continental interior lay like memory in her blood. She could tell of the Crows, whom she had never seen, and of the Black Hills, where she had never been. I wanted to see in reality what she had seen more perfectly in the mind's eye, and traveled fifteen hundred miles to begin my pilgrimage.

Yellowstone, it seemed to me, was the top of the world, a 6
region of deep lakes and dark timber, canyons and waterfalls. But, beautiful as it is, one might have the sense of confinement there. The skyline in all directions is close at hand, the high wall of the woods and deep cleavages of shade. There is a perfect freedom in the mountains, but it belongs to the eagle and the elk, the badger and the bear. The Kiowas reckoned their stature by the distance they could see, and they were bent and blind in the wilderness.

Descending eastward, the highland meadows are a stairway 7
to the plain. In July the inland slope of the Rockies is luxuriant with flax and buckwheat, stonecrop and larkspur. The earth unfolds and the limit of the land recedes. Clusters of trees, and animals grazing far in the distance, cause the vision to reach away and wonder to build upon the mind. The sun follows a longer course in the day, and the sky is immense beyond all comparison. The great billowing clouds that sail upon it are shadows that move upon the grain like water, dividing light. Farther down, in the land of the Crows and Blackfeet, the plain is yellow. Sweet clover takes hold of the hills and bends upon itself to cover and seal the soil. There the Kiowas paused on their way; they had come to the place where they must change their lives. The sun is at home on the plains. Precisely there does it have the certain character of a god. When the Kiowas came to the land of the Crows, they could see the dark lees of the hills at dawn across the Bighorn River, the profusion of light on the grain shelves, the oldest deity ranging after the solstices. Not yet would they veer southward

to the caldron of the land that lay below; they must wean their blood from the northern winter and hold the mountains a while longer in their view. They bore Tai-me in procession to the east.

A dark mist lay over the Black Hills, and the land was like iron. At the top of a ridge I caught sight of Devil's Tower upthrust against the gray sky as if in the birth of time the core of the earth had broken through its crust and the motion of the world was begun. There are things in nature that engender an awful quiet in the heart of man; Devil's Tower is one of them. Two centuries ago, because they could not do otherwise, the Kiowas made a legend at the base of the rock. My grandmother said: 8

> Eight children were there at play, seven sisters and their brother. Suddenly the boy was struck dumb; he trembled and began to run upon his hands and feet. His fingers became claws, and his body was covered with fur. Directly there was a bear where the boy had been. The sisters were terrified; they ran, and the bear after them. They came to the stump of a great tree, and the tree spoke to them. It bade them climb upon it, and as they did so it began to rise into the air. The bear came to kill them, but they were just beyond its reach. It reared against the tree and scored the bark all around with its claws. The seven sisters were borne into the sky, and they became the stars of the Big Dipper.

From that moment, and so long as the legend lives, the Kiowas have kinsmen in the night sky. Whatever they were in the mountains, they could be no more. However tenuous their well-being, however much they had suffered and would suffer again, they had found a way out of the wilderness.

My grandmother had a reverence for the sun, a holy regard that now is all but gone out of mankind. There was a wariness in her, and an ancient awe. She was a Christian in her later years, but she had come a long way about, and she never forgot her birthright. As a child she had been to the Sun Dances; she had taken part in those annual rites, and by them she had learned the restoration of her people in the presence of Tai-me. She was about seven when the last Kiowa Sun Dance was held in 1887 on the Washita River above Rainy Mountain Creek. The buffalo were gone. In order to consummate the ancient sacrifice—to impale the head of a buffalo bull upon the medicine tree—a delegation of old men journeyed into Texas, there to beg and barter for an animal from the Goodnight herd. She was ten when the Kiowas came together for the last time as a living Sun Dance culture. They could find no buffalo; they had to hang an old hide from 9 the sacred tree. Before the dance could begin, a company of soldiers rode out from Fort Sill under orders to disperse the tribe. Forbidden without cause the essential act of their faith, having seen the wild herds slaughtered and left to rot upon the ground, the Kiowas backed away forever from the medicine tree. That was July 20, 1890, at the great bend of the Washita. My grandmother was there. Without bitterness, and for as long as she lived, she bore a vision of deicide.

Now that I can have her only in memory, I see my grand- 10
mother in the several postures that were peculiar to her: standing at the wood stove on a winter morning and turning meat in a great iron skillet; sitting at the south window, bent above her beadwork, and afterwards, when her vision failed, looking down for a long time into the fold of her hands; going out upon a cane, very slowly as she did when the weight of age came upon her; praying. I remember her most often at prayer. She made long, rambling prayers out of suffering and hope, having seen many things. I was never sure that I had the right to hear, so exclusive were they of all mere custom and company. The last time I saw her she prayed standing by the side of her bed at night, naked to the waist, the light of a kerosene lamp moving upon her dark skin. Her long, black hair, always drawn and braided in the day, lay upon her shoulders and against her breasts like a shawl. I do not speak Kiowa, and I never understood her prayers, but there was something inherently sad in the sound, some merest hesitation upon the syllables of sorrow. She began in a high and descending pitch, exhausting her breath to silence; then again and again—and always the same intensity of effort, of something that is, and is not, like urgency in the human voice. Transported so in the dancing light among the shadows of her room, she seemed beyond the reach of time. But that was illusion; I think I knew then that I should not see her again.

Houses are like sentinels in the plain, old keepers of the 11
weather watch. There, in a very little while, wood takes on the appearance of great age. All colors wear soon away in the wind and rain, and then the wood is burned gray and the grain appears and the nails turn red with rust. The windowpanes are black and opaque; you imagine there is nothing within, and indeed there are many ghosts, bones given up to the land. They stand here and there against the sky, and you approach them for a longer time than you expect. They belong in the distance; it is their domain.

Once there was a lot of sound in my grandmother's house, a 12
lot of coming and going, feasting and talk. The summers there were full of excitement and reunion. The Kiowas are a summer people; they abide the cold and keep to themselves, but when the season turns and the land becomes warm and vital they cannot hold still; an

old love of going returns upon them. The aged visitors who came to my grandmother's house when I was a child were made of lean and leather, and they bore themselves upright. They wore great black hats and bright ample shirts that shook in the wind. They rubbed fat upon their hair and wound their braids with strips of colored cloth. Some of them painted their faces and carried the scars of old and cherished enmities. They were an old council of warlords, come to remind and be reminded of who they were. Their wives and daughters served them well. The women might indulge themselves; gossip was at once the mark and compensation of their servitude. They made loud and elaborate talk among themselves, full of jest and gesture, fright and false alarm. They went abroad in fringed and flowered shawls, bright beadwork and German silver. They were at home in the kitchen, and they prepared meals that were banquets.

There were frequent prayer meetings, and great nocturnal 13
feasts. When I was a child I played with my cousins outside, where the lamplight fell upon the ground and the singing of the old people rose up around us and carried away into the darkness. There were a lot of good things to eat, a lot of laughter and surprise. And afterwards, when the quiet returned, I lay down with my grandmother and could hear the frogs away by the river and feel the motion of the air.

Now there is funeral silence in the rooms, the endless wake 14
of some final word. The walls have closed in upon my grandmother's house. When I returned to it in mourning, I saw for the first time in my life how small it was. It was late at night, and there was a white moon, nearly full. I sat for a long time on the stone steps by the kitchen door. From there I could see out across the land; I could see the long row of trees by the creek, the low light upon the rolling plains, and the stars of the Big Dipper. Once I looked at the moon and caught sight of a strange thing. A cricket had perched upon the handrail, only a few inches away from me. My line of vision was such that the creature filled the moon like a fossil. It had gone there, I thought, to live and die, for there, of all places, was its small definition made whole and eternal. A warm wind rose up and purled like the longing within me.

The next morning I awoke at dawn and went out on the dirt 15
road to Rainy Mountain. It was already hot, and the grasshoppers began to fill the air. Still, it was early in the morning, and the birds sang out of the shadows. The long yellow grass on the mountain shone in the bright light, and a scissortail hied above the land. There, where it ought to be, at the end of a long and legendary way, was my grandmother's grave. Here and there on the dark stones were ancestral names. Looking back once, I saw the mountain and came away.

QUESTIONS

1. Why does Momaday return to his grandmother's house and journey to her grave?

2. List the various myths and legends the author mentions in the essay. What subjects do they treat? How are these subjects interrelated?

3. Locate and explain instances of sensory, metaphorical, and symbolic language in the essay. Why are these modes of language consistent with the subject and theme elaborated by Momaday?

4. How does Momaday's use of abstract language affect the concrete vocabulary in the essay?

5. What is the method of development in the first paragraph? How does the introduction serve as a vehicle for the central meanings in the essay?

6. Consider the relationship of narration to description in the organization of the essay. What forms of narrative serve to unify the selection? Are the narrative patterns strictly linear, or do they shift for other purposes? Explain. In what sense is Momaday's descriptive technique cinematic?

7. How do the land, the Kiowas, and Momaday's grandmother serve as reinforcing frames of the essay?

8. Describe in detail the creation of mood in this essay. Explain specifically the mood at the conclusion.

9. Momaday implies that myth is central to his life and the life of the Kiowas. What *is* myth? Do you think that myth is as strong in general American culture as it is in Kiowa culture? In what ways does it operate? How can myth sustain the individual, community, and nation?

10. Write about a person and place that, taken together, hold a special reverence for you.

RENÉ DUBOS

A Family of Landscapes

René Dubos (1901–   ) was born in France but left Europe for the United States in 1924. A famous microbiologist and experimental pathologist, Dubos is professor emeritus at the Rockefeller University in New York. He is also a well-known author, whose books include *So Human an Animal* (1969

Pulitzer Prize winner), *A God Within* (1972), and *Louis Pasteur* (1976). In this selection from *The Wooing of Earth* (1980), Dubos offers a unique perspective on humanity's relationship to the natural world.

Some of the landscapes that we most admire are the products of environmental degradation. The denuded islands of the Aegean Sea, the rocky shores of the Mediterranean basin, the semidesertic areas of the American Southwest are regions that appeal to countless people from all social and ethnic groups, as well as professional ecologists. Yet these landscapes derive much of their color and sculptural beauty from deforestation and erosion, the two cardinal sins of ecology. The immense majority of people, furthermore, elect to live in places from which the wilderness has been eradicated and which have been profoundly transformed by human habitation. Orthodox ecological criteria are therefore not adequate to evaluate the quality of a particular environment for human life. 1

Since the humanization of Earth inevitably results in destruction of the wilderness and of many living species that depend on it, there is a fundamental conflict between ecological doctrine and human cultures, a conflict whose manifestations are most glaring in Greece. 2

On two occasions during the past few years, I visited the eleventh-century Byzantine monastery of Moni Kaisarianis, located some five miles southeast of Athens. The monastery is nestled on the slopes of Mount Hymettus at 1,100 feet elevation. A trail meanders from it toward the Hymettus mountain through an almost treeless landscape amidst thyme, lavender, sage, mint, and other aromatic plants. The rock formations of the area are denuded, but the luminous sky gives them an architectural quality particularly bewitching under the violet light of sunset. 3

A short distance from the monastery, the trail reaches an outcrop of rocks that affords a sudden view of the Acropolis, Mount Lycabettus, and the entire city of Athens. As is so often the case in Greece, the buildings—whether pagan or Christian—derive a dramatic quality independent of their architectural merit from their natural setting. But the landscape surrounding the monastery is not natural; it has been transformed by several thousand years of human occupation. 4

The grounds associated with the Moni Kaisarianis monastery are planted with almond and olive trees, two species that have long been part of the Greek flora but originated in south central or southeastern Asia. The road that leads from Athens to the monastery is shaded with eucalyptus trees introduced from Australia. Beyond 5 the monastery, the Hymettus is stark and luminous but its rock formations were originally masked by earth and trees. Its bold architecture became clearly visible only during historical times as a result of deforestation and erosion.

Ecologists and historians agree that most of the Mediterranean world was wooded before human occupation. What we now regard as the typical Greek landscape, often stark and treeless, is the result of human activities. The rock structures were revealed only after the felling of the trees, which resulted in extensive erosion. The slopes have been kept denuded by rabbits, sheep, and goats that continuously destroy any new growth either of trees or grass. Erosion and overgrazing are the forces, inadvertently set in motion by human activites, that enable light to play its bewitching game on the white framework of Attica. 6

The humanization of the Greek wilderness has been achieved at great ecological loss. Writers of the classical, Hellenistic, and Roman periods were aware of the transformations brought about by deforestation in the Mediterranean world. In *Critias,* Plato compared the land of Attica to the "bones of a wasted body . . . the richer and softer parts of the soil having fallen away, and the mere skeleton being left." In ancient times, still according to Plato, the buildings had "roofs of timber cut from trees which were of a size sufficient to cover the largest houses." After deforestation, however, "the mountains only afforded substenance to bees." The famous Hymettus honey is thus linked to deforestation, which permitted the growth of sun-loving aromatic plants. 7

As long as the mountain slopes were wooded, the land of Greece, as well as of other Mediterranean coutries, was enriched by rainfall, but by Plato's time erosion caused the water to "flow off the bare earth into the sea . . ." The sacred groves and other sanctuaries were originally established near springs and streams, but these progressively dried up as a consequence of deforestation. 8

The Ilissus River, which has its source on Mount Hymettus and runs through Athens, was still a lively stream in Plato's time. On a hot day in midsummer, Socrates and Phaedrus walked toward a tall plane tree on the banks of the Ilissus a short distance from the Agora. There, as reported in the famous dialogue, they discussed rhetoric, philosophy, and love while cooling their feet in the stream that they found "delightfully clear and bright." Today, the Ilissus is dry much of the year and, covered by a noisy roadway, serves as a sewer. There could not be a more dramatic symbol of the damage done by deforestation, erosion, and urban mismanagement. 9

The reforestation of Greece would certainly result in climatic and agricultural improvements. As Henry Miller writes in *The Colossus of Maroussi,* "The tree brings water, fodder, cattle, produce . . . 10

shade, leisure, song. Greece does not need archeologists—she needs arboriculturists." But a cover of trees would make the landscape very different from the image that we, and the Greeks themselves, have had of Greece since classical times. In his poem "The Satyr or the Naked Song," the Greek poet Kostes Palamas (1859–1943) sees in the stark eroded structures of the present landscape a symbol of the austerity and purity of the Greek genius; the landscape triumphantly proclaims the "divine nudity" of Greece. Henry Miller himself, a few pages before and after the passage quoted above in which he advocates reforestation, marvels at the quality given to the landscape by the rocks that "have been lying for centuries exposed to this divine illumination . . . nestling amid dancing colored shrubs in a blood-stained soil." In Miller's words, these rocks "are symbols of life eternal." He does not mention that they are visible only because of deforestation and erosion.

While visiting the Moni Kaisarianis monastery, I noticed a 11
dark opaque zone on the slopes of Mount Hymettus; this area had been reforested with pines. To me, it looked like an ink blot on the luminous landscape, especially at sunset, when the subtle violet atmosphere suffuses the bare rocks throughout the mountain range. The "divine illumination" lost much of its magic where it was absorbed by the pine trees.

The mountains of Attica were probably difficult to penetrate 12
and frightening when completely wooded, but they have now acquired some of the qualities of a park. The traveler can move on their open surfaces, and vision can extend into a distance of golden light. I have wondered whether the dark and ferocious divinities of the preclassical Greek period did not become more serene and more playful precisely because they had emerged from the dark forests into the open landscape. Would logic have flourished if Greece had remained covered with an opaque tangle of trees?

There is no doubt that people spoiled the water economy and 13
impoverished the land when they destroyed the forests of the Mediterranean world. But it is true also that deforestation allowed the landscape to express certain of its potentialities that had remained hidden under the dense vegetation. Not only did removal of the trees permit the growth of sun-loving aromatic plants and favor the spread of honeybees, as Plato had recognized; more importantly, it revealed the underlying architecture of the area and perhaps helped the soaring of the human mind.

The full expression of the Mediterranean genius may require 14
both the cool mysterious fountains in the sacred groves and the bright light shining on the sun-loving plants amid the denuded rocks. Ecology becomes a more complex but far more interesting science

when human aspirations are regarded as an integral part of the landscape.

QUESTIONS

1. What paradox does the author establish in the first paragraph? What is his attitude toward ecology?

2. Summarize the ecological conflicts that Dubos finds in Greece. What is the outcome?

3. Is Dubos' diction primarily abstract or concrete? Explain.

4. What "images" of Greece does the author evoke? Is there a dominant impression or series of impressions? Explain.

5. How does Dubos establish his thesis in the first paragraph? In what way does he augment the thesis in the concluding paragraph?

6. Analyze the types and patterns of illustration that the author uses to support his thesis and related ideas.

7. How does Dubos employ causal analysis in this essay?

8. How does description in this essay blend into a pattern of definition?

9. Discuss the preoccupation of Americans with ecology. Are conventional definitions of the term still useful or do we need stipulative definitions like the one that Dubos provides? Do you agree or disagree with Dubos' stance on ecology, and why?

10. Write an essay on a specific place that you know well and that permits you to assess or reassess your attitude toward ecological conflicts.

E. B. WHITE

Once More to the Lake

Elwyn Brooks White (1899–), perhaps the finest contemporary American essayist, is at his most distinctive in his treatments of people and nature. A recipient of the National Medal for Literature, and associated for years with *The New Yorker,* White is the author of *One Man's Meat* (1942), *Here Is*

New York (1949), and *The Second Tree from the Corner* (1954), among numerous works. He is also one of the most talented writers of literature for children, the author of *Stuart Little* (1945), *Charlotte's Web* (1952), and *The Trumpet of the Swan* (1970). In this essay, White combines narration and description to render a poignant and vivid statement about past and present, youth and age, life and death.

One summer, along about 1904, my father rented a camp on a lake in Maine and took us all there for the month of August. We all got ringworm from some kittens and had to rub Pond's Extract on our arms and legs night and morning, and my father rolled over in a canoe with all his clothes on; but outside of that the vacation was a success and from then on none of us ever thought there was any place in the world like that lake in Maine. We returned summer after summer—always on August 1st for one month. I have since become a salt-water man, but sometimes in summer there are days when the restlessness of the tides and the fearful cold of the sea water and the incessant wind which blows across the afternoon and into the evening make me wish for the placidity of a lake in the woods. A few weeks ago this feeling got so strong I bought myself a couple of bass hooks and a spinner and returned to the lake where we used to go, for a week's fishing and to revisit old haunts. 1

I took along my son, who had never had any fresh water up his nose and who had seen lily pads only from train windows. On the journey over to the lake I began to wonder what it would be like. I wondered how time would have marred this unique, this holy spot—the coves and streams, the hills that the sun set behind, the camps and the paths behind the camps. I was sure the tarred road would have found it out and I wondered in what other ways it would be desolated. It is strange how much you can remember about places like that once you allow your mind to return into the grooves which lead back. You remember one thing, and that suddenly reminds you of another thing. I guess I remembered clearest of all the early mornings, when the lake was cool and motionless, remembered how the bedroom smelled of the lumber it was made of and of the wet woods whose scent entered through the screen. The partitions in the camp were thin and did not extend clear to the top of the rooms, and as I was always the first up I would dress softly so as not to wake the others, and sneak out into the sweet outdoors and start out in the canoe, keeping close along the shore in the long shadows of the pines. I remembered being very careful never to rub my paddle against the gunwale for fear of disturbing the stillness of the cathedral. 2

The lake had never been what you would call a wild lake. There were cottages sprinkled around the shores, and it was in farming country although the shores of the lake were quite heavily wooded. Some of the cottages were owned by nearby farmers, and you would live at the shore and eat your meals at the farmhouse. That's what our family did. But although it wasn't wild, it was a fairly large and undisturbed lake and there were places in it which, to a child at least, seemed infinitely remote and primeval. 3

I was right about the tar: it led to within half a mile of the shore. But when I got back there, with my boy, and we settled into a camp near a farmhouse and into the kind of summertime I had known, I could tell that it was going to be pretty much the same as it had been before—I knew it, lying in bed the first morning, smelling the bedroom, and hearing the boy sneak quietly out and go off along the shore in a boat. I began to sustain the illusion that he was I, and therefore, by simple transposition, that I was my father. This sensation persisted, kept cropping up all the time we were there. It was not an entirely new feeling, but in this setting it grew much stronger. I seemed to be living a dual existence. I would be in the middle of some simple act, I would be picking up a bait box or laying down a table fork, or I would be saying something, and suddenly it would be not I but my father who was saying the words or making the gesture. It gave me a creepy sensation. 4

We went fishing the first morning. I felt the same damp moss covering the worms in the bait can, and saw the dragonfly alight on the tip of my rod as it hovered a few inches from the surface of the water. It was the arrival of this fly that convinced me beyond any doubt that everything was as it always had been, that the years were a mirage and there had been no years. The small waves were the same, chucking the rowboat under the chin as we fished at anchor, and the boat was the same boat, the same color green and the ribs broken in the same place, and under the floor-boards the same fresh-water leavings and débris—the dead hellgrammite, the wisps of moss, the rusty discarded fishhook, the dried blood from yesterday's catch. We stared silently at the tips of our rods, at the dragonflies that came and went. I lowered the tip of mine into the water, tentatively, pensively dislodging the fly, which darted two feet away, poised, darted two feet back, and came to rest again a little farther up the rod. There had been no years between the ducking of this dragonfly and the other one—the one that was part of memory. I looked at the boy, who was silently watching his fly, and it was my hands that held his rod, my eyes watching. I felt dizzy and didn't know which rod I was at the end of. 5

We caught two bass, hauling them in briskly as though they were mackerel, pulling them over the side of the boat in a business- 6 like manner without any landing net, and stunning them with a blow on the back of the head. When we got back for a swim before lunch, the lake was exactly where we had left it, the same number of inches from the dock, and there was only the merest suggestion of a breeze. This seemed an utterly enchanted sea, this lake you could leave to its own devices for a few hours and come back to, and find that it had not stirred, this constant and trustworthy body of water. In the shallows, the dark, water-soaked sticks and twigs, smooth and old, were undulating in clusters on the bottom against the clean ribbed sand, and the track of the mussel was plain. A school of minnows swam by, each minnow with its small individual shadow, doubling the attendance, so clear and sharp in the sunlight. Some of the other campers were in swimming, along the shore, one of them with a cake of soap, and the water felt thin and clear and unsubstantial. Over the years there had been this person with the cake of soap, this cultist, and here he was. There had been no years.

Up to the farmhouse to dinner through the teeming, dusty 7
field, the road under our sneakers was only a two-track road. The middle track was missing, the one with the marks of the hooves and the splotches of dried, flaky manure. There had always been three tracks to choose from in choosing which track to walk in; now the choice was narrowed down to two. For a moment I missed terribly the middle alternative. But the way led past the tennis court, and something about the way it lay there in the sun reassured me; the tape had loosened along the backline, the alleys were green with plaintains and other weeds, and the net (installed in June and removed in September) sagged in the dry noon, and the whole place steamed with midday heat and hunger and emptiness. There was a choice of pie for dessert, and one was blueberry and one was apple, and the waitresses were the same country girls, there having been no passage of time, only the illusion of it as in a dropped curtain—the waitresses were still fifteen; their hair had been washed, that was the only difference—they had been to the movies and seen the pretty girls with the clean hair.

Summertime, oh summertime, pattern of life indelible, the 8
fade-proof lake, the woods unshatterable, the pasture with the sweetfern and the juniper forever and ever, summer without end; this was the background, and the life along the shore was the design, the cottagers with their innocent and tranquil design, their tiny docks with the flagpole and the American flag floating against the white clouds in the blue sky, the little paths over the roots of the trees leading from camp to camp and the paths leading back to the outhouses and the can of lime for sprinkling, and at the souvenir counters at the store the miniature birch-bark canoes and the post cards that showed things looking a little better than they looked. This

was the American family at play, escaping the city heat, wondering whether the newcomers in the camp at the head of the cove were "common" or "nice," wondering whether it was true that the people who drove up for Sunday dinner at the farmhouse were turned away because there wasn't enough chicken.

It seemed to me, as I kept remembering all this, that those 9
times and those summers had been infinitely precious and worth saving. There had been jollity and peace and goodness. The arriving (at the beginning of August) had been so big a business in itself, at the railway station the farm wagon drawn up, the first smell of the pine-laden air, the first glimpse of the smiling farmer, and the great importance of the trunks and your father's enormous authority in such matters, and the feel of the wagon under you for the long ten-mile haul, and at the top of the last long hill catching the first view of the lake after eleven months of not seeing this cherished body of water. The shouts and cries of the other campers when they saw you, and the trunks to be unpacked, to give up their rich burden. (Arriving was less exciting nowadays, when you sneaked up in your car and parked it under a tree near the camp and took out the bags and in five minutes it was all over, no fuss, no loud wonderful fuss about trunks.)

Peace and goodness and jollity. The only thing that was 10
wrong now, really, was the sound of the place, an unfamiliar nervous sound of the outboard motors. This was the note that jarred, the one thing that would sometimes break the illusion and set the years moving. In those other summertimes all motors were inboard; and when they were at a little distance, the noise they made was a sedative, an ingredient of summer sleep. They were one-cylinder and two-cylinder engines, and some were make-and-break and some were jump-spark, but they all made a sleepy sound across the lake. The one-lungers throbbed and fluttered, and the twin-cylinder ones purred and purred, and that was a quiet sound too. But now the campers all had outboards. In the daytime, in the hot mornings, these motors made a petulant, irritable sound; at night, in the still evening when the afterglow lit the water, they whined about one's ears like mosquitoes. My boy loved our rented outboard, and his great desire was to achieve singlehanded mastery over it, and authority, and he soon learned the trick of choking it a little (but not too much), and the adjustment of the needle valve. Watching him I would remember the things you could do with the old one-cylinder engine with the heavy flywheel, how you could have it eating out of your hand if you got really close to it spiritually. Motor boats in those days didn't have clutches, and you would make a landing by shutting off the motor at the proper time and coasting in with a dead rudder. But there was a way of reversing them, if you learned the trick, by cutting the switch

and putting it on again exactly on the final dying revolution of the flywheel, so that it would kick back against compression and begin reversing. Approaching a dock in a strong following breeze, it was difficult to slow up sufficiently by the ordinary coasting method, and if a boy felt he had complete mastery over his motor, he was tempted to keep it running beyond its time and then reverse it a few feet from the dock. It took a cool nerve, because if you threw the switch a twentieth of a second too soon you would catch the flywheel when it still had speed enough to go up past center, and the boat would leap ahead, charging bull-fashion at the dock.

We had a good week at the camp. The bass were biting well 11
and the sun shone endlessly, day after day. We would be tired at night and lie down in the accumulated heat of the little bedrooms after the long hot day and the breeze would stir almost imperceptibly outside and the smell of the swamp drift in through the rusty screens. Sleep would come easily and in the morning the red squirrel would be on the roof, tapping out his gay routine. I kept remembering everything, lying in bed in the mornings—the small steamboat that had a long rounded stern like the lip of a Ubangi, and how quietly she ran on the moonlight sails, when the older boys played their mandolins and the girls sang and we ate doughnuts dipped in sugar, and how sweet the music was on the water in the shining night, and what it had felt like to think about girls then. After breakfast we would go up to the store and the things were in the same place—the minnows in a bottle, the plugs and spinners disarranged and pawed over by the youngsters from the boys' camp, the fig newtons and the Beeman's gum. Outside, the road was tarred and cars stood in front of the store. Inside, all was just as it had always been, except there was more Coca-Cola and not so much Moxie and root beer and birch beer and sarsaparilla. We would walk out with a bottle of pop apiece and sometimes the pop would backfire up our noses and hurt. We explored the streams, quietly, where the turtles slid off the sunny logs and dug their way into the soft bottom; and we lay on the town wharf and fed worms to the tame bass. Everywhere we went I had trouble making out which was I, the one walking at my side, the one walking in my pants.

One afternoon while we were there at that lake a thunder- 12
storm came up. It was like the revival of an old melodrama that I had seen long ago with childish awe. The second-act climax of the drama of the electrical disturbance over a lake in America had not changed in any important respect. This was the big scene, still the big scene. The whole thing was so familiar, the first feeling of oppression and heat and a general air around camp of not wanting to go very far away. In midafternoon (it was all the same) a curious darkening of the sky, and a lull in everything that had made life tick; and then the way

the boats suddenly swung the other way at their moorings with the coming of a breeze out of the new quarter, and the premonitory rumble. Then the kettle drum, then the snare, then the bass drum and cymbals, then crackling light against the dark, and the gods grinning and licking their chops in the hills. Afterward the calm, the rain steadily rustling in the calm lake, the return of light and hope and spirits, and the campers running out in joy and relief to go swimming in the rain, their bright cries perpetuating the deathless joke about how they were getting simply drenched, and the children screaming with delight at the new sensation of bathing in the rain, and the joke about getting drenched linking the generations in a strong industructible chain. And the comedian who waded in carrying an umbrella.

When the others went swimming my son said he was going 13
in too. He pulled his dripping trunks from the line where they had hung all through the shower, and wrung them out. Languidly, and with no thought of going in, I watched him, his hard little body, skinny and bare, saw him wince slightly as he pulled up around his vitals the small, soggy, icy garment. As he buckled the swollen belt suddenly my groin felt the chill of death.

QUESTIONS

1. What motivates White to return to the lake in Maine? Explain the "simple transposition" that he mentions in paragraph 4. List the illustrations that he gives of this phenomenon. What change does he detect in the lake?

2. Explain the significance of White's last sentence. Where are there foreshadowings of this statement?

3. Describe the author's use of figurative language in paragraphs 2, 10, and 12.

4. Identify those words and phrases that White invokes to establish the sense of mystery about the lake. Why are these words and their connotations important to the nature of the illusion that he describes?

5. Explain the organization of the essay in terms of the following paragraph units: 1 to 4; 5 to 7; 8 to 10; 11 to 13. Explain the function of paragraphs 8 and 12.

6. There are many vivid and unusual descriptive details in this essay—for example, the dragonfly in paragraph 2 and the two-track road in paragraph 7. How does White create symbolic overtones for these descriptive details and others? Why is the lake itself a complex symbol? Explain with reference to paragraph 6.

7. Describe the persona that White creates for himself in the essay. How does this persona function?

8. What is the relation between the introductory and concluding paragraphs, specifically in terms of irony of statement?

9. Discuss the type of nostalgia that White describes in "Once More to the Lake." What are the beauties and the dangers of nostalgia? Can the past ever be recaptured or relived? Justify your answer.

10. Write a descriptive account of a return to a favorite location and of your reaction to the experience. Explore the interrelationship of past and present.

GEORGE ORWELL

Marrakech

George Orwell (1903–1950) was the pseudonym of Eric Blair, an English novelist, essayist, and journalist. Orwell served with the Indian Imperial Police from 1922 to 1927 in Burma, fought in the Spanish Civil War, and acquired from his experiences a disdain of totalitarian and imperialistic systems. This attitude is reflected in the satiric fable *Animal Farm* (1945) and in his bleak, futuristic novel, *1984* (1949). In the following essay, Orwell depicts vividly third world poverty, and criticizes colonial responses to it.

As the corpse went past the flies left the restaurant table in a cloud and rushed after it, but they came back a few minutes later. 1

The little crowd of mourners—all men and boys, no women—threaded their way across the market-place between the piles of pomegranates and the taxis and the camels, wailing a short chant over and over again. What really appeals to the flies is that the corpses here are never put into coffins, they are merely wrapped in a piece of rag and carried on a rough wooden bier on the shoulders of four friends. When the friends get to the burying-ground they hack an oblong hole a foot or two deep, dump the body in it and fling over it a little of the dried-up, lumpy earth, which is like broken brick. No gravestone, no name, no identifying mark of any kind. The burying-ground is merely a huge waste of hummocky earth, like a derelict building-lot. After a month or two no one can even be certain where his own relatives are buried. 2

When you walk through a town like this—two hundred thousand inhabitants, of whom at least twenty thousand own literally nothing except the rags they stand up in—when you see how people live, and still more how easily they die, it is always difficult to believe that you are walking among human beings. All colonial empires are in reality founded upon that fact. The people have brown faces—besides, there are so many of them! Are they really the same flesh as yourself? Do they even have names? Or are they merely a kind of undifferentiated brown stuff, about as individual as bees or coral insects? They rise out of the earth, they sweat and starve for a few years, and then they sink back into the nameless mounds of the graveyard and nobody notices that they are gone. And even the graves themselves soon fade back into the soil. Sometimes, out for a walk, as you break your way through the prickly pear, you notice that it is rather bumpy underfoot, and only a certain regularity in the bumps tells you that you are walking over skeletons. 3

I was feeding one of the gazelles in the public gardens. 4

Gazelles are almost the only animals that look good to eat when they are still alive, in fact, one can hardly look at their hindquarters without thinking of mint sauce. The gazelle I was feeding seemed to know that this thought was in my mind, for though it took the piece of bread I was holding out it obviously did not like me. It nibbled rapidly at the bread, then lowered its head and tried to butt me, then took another nibble and then butted again. Probably its idea was that if it could drive me away the bread would somehow remain hanging in mid-air. 5

An Arab navvy working on the path nearby lowered his heavy hoe and sidled towards us. He looked from the gazelle to the bread and from the bread to the gazelle, with a sort of quiet amazement, as though he had never seen anything quite like this before. Finally he said shyly in French: 6

"*I* could eat some of that bread." 7

I tore off a piece and he stowed it gratefully in some secret place under his rags. This man is an employee of the Municipality. 8

When you go through the Jewish quarters you gather some idea of what the medieval ghettoes were probably like. Under their Moorish rulers the Jews were only allowed to own land in certain restricted areas, and after centuries of this kind of treatment they have ceased to bother about overcrowding. Many of the streets are a good deal less than six feet wide, the houses are completely windowless, and sore-eyed children cluster everywhere in unbelievable numbers, like clouds of flies. Down the centre of the street there is generally running a little river of urine. 9

In the bazaar huge families of Jews, all dressed in the long black robe and little black skull cap, are working in dark fly-infested 10 booths that look like caves. A carpenter sits cross-legged at a prehistoric lathe, turning chair-legs at lightning speed. He works the lathe with a bow in his right hand and guides the chisel with his left foot, and thanks to a lifetime of sitting in this position his left leg is warped out of shape. At his side his grandson, aged six, is already starting on the simpler parts of the job.

I was just passing the coppersmiths' booths when somebody noticed that I was lighting a cigarette. Instantly, from the dark holes all round, there was a frenzied rush of Jews, many of them old grandfathers with flowing grey beards, all clamouring for a cigarette. Even a blind man somewhere at the back of one of the booths heard a rumour of cigarettes and came crawling out, groping in the air with his hand. In about a minute I had used up the whole packet. None of these people, I suppose, works less than twelve hours a day, and every one of them looks on a cigarette as a more or less impossible luxury. 11

As the Jews live in self-contained communities they follow the same trades as the Arabs, except for agriculture. Fruit-sellers, potters, silversmiths, blacksmiths, butchers, leather-workers, tailors, water-carriers, beggars, porters—whichever way you look you see nothing but Jews. As a matter of fact there are thirteen thousand of them, all living in the space of a few acres. A good job Hitler isn't here. Perhaps he is on his way, however. You hear the usual dark rumours about the Jews, not only from the Arabs but from the poorer Europeans. 12

"Yes, *mon vieux,* they took my job away from me and gave it to a Jew. The Jews! They're the real rulers of this country, you know. They've got all the money. They control the banks, finance—everything." 13

"But," I said, "isn't it a fact that the average Jew is a labourer working for about a penny an hour?" 14

"Ah, that's only for show! They're all moneylenders really. They're cunning, the Jews." 15

In just the same way, a couple of hundred years ago, poor old women used to be burned for witchcraft when they could not even work enough magic to get themselves a square meal. 16

All people who work with their hands are partly invisible, and the more important the work they do, the less visible they are. Still, a white skin is always fairly conspicuous. In northern Europe, when you see a labourer ploughing a field, you probably give him a second glance. In a hot country, anywhere south of Gibraltar or east of Suez, the chances are that you don't even see him. I have noticed this again and again. In a tropical landscape one's eye takes in everything except the human beings. It takes in the dried-up soil, the prickly pear, the palm-tree and the distant mountain, but it always 17 misses the peasant hoeing at his patch. He is the same colour as the earth, and a great deal less interesting to look at.

It is only because of this that the starved countries of Asia and Africa are accepted as tourist resorts. No one would think of running cheap trips to the Distressed Areas. But where the human beings have brown skins their poverty is simply not noticed. What does Morocco mean to a Frenchman? An orange-grove or a job in government service. Or to an Englishman? Camels, castles, palm-trees, Foreign Legionnaires, brass trays and bandits. One could probably live here for years without noticing that for nine-tenths of the people the reality of life is an endless, back-breaking struggle to wring a little food out of an eroded soil. 18

Most of Morocco is so desolate that no wild animal bigger than a hare can live on it. Huge areas which were once covered with forest have turned into a treeless waste where the soil is exactly like broken-up brick. Nevertheless a good deal of it is cultivated, with frightful labour. Everything is done by hand. Long lines of women, bent double like inverted capital Ls, work their way slowly across the fields, tearing up the prickly weeds with their hands, and the peasant gathering lucerne for fodder pulls it up stalk by stalk instead of reaping it, thus saving an inch or two on each stalk. The plough is a wretched wooden thing, so frail that one can easily carry it on one's shoulder, and fitted underneath with a rough iron spike which stirs the soil to a depth of about four inches. This is as much as the strength of the animals is equal to. It is usual to plough with a cow and a donkey yoked together. Two donkeys would not be quite strong enough, but on the other hand two cows would cost a little more to feed. The peasants possess no harrows, they merely plough the soil several times over in different directions, finally leaving it in rough furrows, after which the whole field has to be shaped with hoes into small oblong patches, to conserve water. Except for a day or two after the rare rainstorms there is never enough water. Along the edges of the fields channels are hacked out to a depth of thirty or forty feet to get at the tiny trickles which run through the subsoil. 19

Every afternoon a file of very old women passes down the road outside my house, each carrying a load of firewood. All of them are mummified with age and the sun, and all of them are tiny. It seems to be generally the case in primitive communities that the women, when they get beyond a certain age, shrink to the size of children. One day a poor old creature who could not have been more than four feet tall crept past me under a vast load of wood. I stopped her and put a five-sou piece (a little more than a farthing) into her hand. She answered with a shrill wail, almost a scream, which was partly gratitude but mainly surprise. I suppose that from her point of view, by taking any notice of her, I seemed almost to be violating a 20 law of nature. She accepted her status as an old woman, that is to say as a beast of burden. When a family is travelling it is quite usual to see a father and a grown-up son riding ahead on donkeys, and an old woman following on foot, carrying the baggage.

But what is strange about these people is their invisibility. For several weeks, always at about the same time of day, the file of old women had hobbled past the house with their firewood, and though they had registered themselves on my eyeballs I cannot truly say that I had seen them. Firewood was passing—that was how I saw it. It was only that one day I happened to be walking behind them, and the curious up-and-down motion of a load of wood drew my attention to the human being underneath it. Then for the first time I noticed the poor old earth-coloured bodies, bodies reduced to bones and leathery skin, bent double under the crushing weight. Yet I suppose I had not been five minutes on Moroccan soil before I noticed the overloading of the donkeys and was infuriated by it. There is no question that the donkeys are damnably treated. The Moroccan donkey is hardly bigger than a St. Bernard dog, it carries a load which in the British army would be considered too much for a fifteen-hands mule, and very often its pack-saddle is not taken off its back for weeks together. But what is peculiarly pitiful is that it is the most willing creature on earth, it follows its master like a dog and does not need either bridle or halter. After a dozen years of devoted work it suddenly drops dead, whereupon its master tips it into the ditch and the village dogs have torn its guts out before it is cold. 21

This kind of thing makes one's blood boil, whereas—on the whole—the plight of the human beings does not. I am not commenting, merely pointing to a fact. People with brown skins are next door to invisible. Anyone can be sorry for the donkey with its galled back, but it is generally owing to some kind of accident if one even notices the old woman under her load of sticks. 22

As the storks flew northward the Negroes were marching southward—a long, dusty column, infantry, screw-gun batteries and then more infantry, four or five thousand men in all, winding up the road with a clumping of boots and a clatter of iron wheels. 23

They were Senegalese, the blackest Negroes in Africa, so black that sometimes it is difficult to see whereabouts on their necks the hair begins. Their splendid bodies were hidden in reach-me-down khaki uniforms, their feet squashed into boots that looked like blocks of wood, and every tin hat seemed to be a couple of sizes too small. It was very hot and the men had marched a long way. They slumped under the weight of their packs and the curiously sensitive black faces were glistening with sweat. 24

As they went past a tall, very young Negro turned and caught my eye. But the look he gave me was not in the least the kind of look 25 you might expect. Not hostile, not contemptuous, not sullen, not even inquisitive. It was the shy, wide-eyed Negro look, which actually is a look of profound respect. I saw how it was. This wretched boy, who is a French citizen and has therefore been dragged from the forest to scrub floors and catch syphilis in garrison towns, actually has feelings of reverence before a white skin. He has been taught that the white race are his masters, and he still believes it.

But there is one thought which every white man (and in this 26
connection it doesn't matter twopence if he calls himself a Socialist) thinks when he sees a black army marching past. "How much longer can we go on kidding these people? How long before they turn their guns in the other direction?"

It was curious, really. Every white man there has this thought 27
stowed somewhere or other in his mind. I had it, so had the other onlookers, so had the officers on their sweating chargers and the white NCOs marching in the ranks. It was a kind of secret which we all knew and were too clever to tell; only the Negroes didn't know it. And really it was almost like watching a flock of cattle to see the long column, a mile or two miles of armed men, flowing peacefully up the road, while the great white birds drifted over them in the opposite direction, glittering like scraps of paper.

QUESTIONS

1. Describe the major scenes that Orwell develops to render his impression of Marrakech. What relationships do you perceive among the scenes? What dominant impression emerges from the presentation of scenes?

2. What is Orwell's attitude toward the misery he describes? What does he say about certain foreign responses to misery and poverty?

3. Orwell uses both subjective and objective language in this essay. Cite examples of both. Why does he combine these two modes? What effect is created?

4. Locate and evaluate Orwell's use of similes, juxtaposed imagery, personification, and onomatopoeia in the essay.

5. How does Orwell's short initial paragraph set the stage for the entire essay?

6. Analyze Orwell's technique of juxtaposition in the presentation of major paragraph units in the essay. What is the effect of his decision not to provide normal transitions between major segments? How are the segments related in terms of theme, tone, and mood? Is there final essay coherence? Why or why not?

7. How does Orwell's persistent use of contrasting elements relate to his treatment of characterization? How does characterization relate to animal life?

8. Account for paragraphs 3, 8, 16, 22, and 27 in terms of their antecedents.

9. Orwell states that it is easy to ignore glaring poverty and to pretend that the poor and exploited do not exist. What explains this behavior? Offer your own examples to confirm or refute it.

10. Write a descriptive essay illuminating your personal encounter with poverty, as you have either observed or experienced it.

JEAN-PAUL SARTRE

American Cities

Jean-Paul Sartre (1905–1980), French philosopher, novelist, and playwright, was the leading exponent of secular existentialism in the years after World War II. His leftist convictions and commitment to political action, expressed in *Les Temps Modernes,* a journal he and Simone de Beauvoir founded, had enormous impact in France. Similarly, his literary works influenced the antinovel and new wave cinema. His major writing includes *Nausea* (1938), *The Flies* (1943), *Being and Nothingness* (1943), *No Exit* (1945), and *The Condemned of Altona* (1960). The following selection, which Sartre wrote during a trip to the United States in 1945, elevates the travel essay into a critique of American culture.

For the first few days I was lost. My eyes were not accustomed to the skyscrapers and they did not surprise me; they did not seem like man-made, man-inhabited constructions, but rather like rocks and hills, dead parts of the urban landscape one finds in cities built on a turbulent soil and which you pass without even noticing. At the same time, I was continually and vainly looking for something to catch my attention for a moment—a detail, a square, perhaps, or a public building. I did not yet know that these houses and streets should be seen in the mass. 1

In order to learn to live in these cities and to like them as 2
Americans do, I had to fly over the immense deserts of the west and south. Our European cities, submerged in human countrysides that have been worked over mile by mile, are continuous. And then we are vaguely aware that far away, across the sea, there is the desert, a myth. For the American, this myth is an everyday reality. We flew for hours between New Orleans and San Francisco, over an earth that was dry and red, clotted with verdigris bushes. Suddenly, a city, a little checkerboard flush with the ground, arose and then, again, the red earth, the Savannah, the twisted rocks of the Grand Canyon, and the snows of the Rocky Mountains.

After a few days of this diet, I came to understand that the 3
American city was, originally, a camp in the desert. People from far away, attracted by a mine, a petroleum field or fertile land, arrived one fine day and settled as quickly as possible in a clearing, near a river. They built the vital parts of the town, the bank, the town hall, the church, and then hundreds of one-storey frame houses. The road, if there was one, served as a kind of spinal column to the town, and then streets were marked out like vertebrae, perpendicular to the road. It would be hard to count the American cities that have that kind of parting in the middle.

Nothing has changed since the time of the covered wagons; 4
every year towns are founded in the United States, and they are founded according to the same methods.

Take Fontana, Tennessee, which is situated near one of the 5
great T.V.A. dams. Twelve years ago there were pine-trees growing in the mountain's red soil. As soon as the construction of the dam began, the pines were felled and three towns—two whites ones of 3000 and 5000 inhabitants each, and one Negro town—sprang from the soil. The workers live there with their families; four or five years ago, when work was in full swing, one birth was recorded each day. Half of the village looks like a pile-dwellers' community: the houses are of wood, with green roofs, and have been built on piles to avoid dampness. The other half is made of collapsible dwellings, "prefabricated houses." They too are of wood; they are constructed about 500 miles away and loaded onto trucks: a single team of men can set one up within four hours after its arrival. The smallest costs the employer two thousand dollars, and he rents them to his workers for nineteen dollars a month (thirty-one dollars if they are furnished). The interiors, with their mass-produced furniture, central heating, electric lamps, and refrigerators, remind one of ship cabins. Every square inch of these antiseptic little rooms has been utilized; the walls have clothes-presses and under the beds there are chests of drawers.

One leaves with a slightly depressed feeling, with the feeling 6 of having seen the careful, small-scale reconstitution of a 1944 flat in the year 3000. The moment one steps outside one sees hundreds of houses, all alike, piled up, squashed against the earth, but retaining in their very form some sort of nomadic look. It looks like a caravan graveyard. The pile-dweller community and the caravan cemetery face one another. Between them a wide road climbs toward the pines. There you have a city, or rather the nucleus of an American city, with all its essential parts. Below is the Woolworth's, higher up the hospital, and at the top, a "mixed" church in which what might be called a minimum service—that is, one valid for all creeds—is conducted.

The striking thing is the lightness, the fragility of these buildings. The village has no weight, it seems barely to rest on the soil; it has not managed to leave a human imprint on the reddish earth and the dark forest; it is a temporary thing. And besides, it will soon take to the road; in two years the dam will be finished, the workers will leave, and the prefabricated houses will be taken down and sent to a Texas oil well or a Georgia cotton plantation, to reconstitute another Fontana, under other skies, with new inhabitants. 7

This roving village is no exception; in the United States, communities are born as they die—in a day. The Americans have no complaint to make; the main thing is to be able to carry their homes with them. These homes are the collections of objects, furnishings, photographs, and souvenirs belonging to them, that reflect their own image and constitute the inner, living landscape of their dwellings. These are their penates. Like Aeneas, they haul them about everywhere. 8

The "house" is the shell; it is abandoned on the slightest pretext. 9

We have workers' communities in France. But they are sedentary, and then they never become real cities; on the contrary, they are the artificial product of neighbouring cities. In America, just as any citizen can theoretically become President, so each Fontana can become Detroit or Minneapolis; all that is needed is a bit of luck. And conversely, Detroit and Minneapolis are Fontanas which have had luck. To take only one example: in 1905 Detroit had a population of 300,000. Its population is now 1,000,000. 10

The inhabitants of this city are perfectly aware of this luck; they like to recall in their books and films the time when their community was only an outpost. And that is why they pass so easily from city to outpost; they make no distinction between the two. Detroit and Minneapolis, Knoxville and Memphis were *born temporary* and have stayed that way. They will never, of course, take to the road 11 again on the back of a truck. But they remain at the meeting point; they have never reached an internal temperature of solidification.

Things that would not constitute a change of situation for us are, for the American, occasions for real breaks with his past. There are many who, on going off to war, have sold their apartments and everything else, including their suits. What is the point of keeping something that will be outmoded upon their return? Soldiers' wives often reduce their scale of living and go to live more modestly in other neighbourhoods. Thus, sadness and faithfulness to the absent are marked by a removal. 12

The removals also indicate fluctuations in American fortunes. 13

It is customary, in the United States, for the fashionable neighbourhoods to slide from the centre to the outskirts of the city; after five years the centre of town is "polluted." If you walk about there, you come upon tumble-down houses that retain a pretentious look beneath their filth; you find a complicated kind of architecture, one-storey frame houses with entrances formed by peristyles supported by columns, gothic chalets, "colonial houses," etc. These were formerly aristocratic homes, now inhabited by the poor. Chicago's lurid Negro section contains some of these Greco-Roman temples; from the outside they still look well. But inside, twelve rat- and louse-plagued Negro families are crowded together in five or six rooms. 14

At the same time, changes are continually made within the same place. An apartment house is bought to be demolished, and a larger apartment house is built on the same plot. After five years, the new house is sold to a contractor who tears it down to build a third one. The result is that in the States a city is a moving landscape for its inhabitants, whereas our cities are our shells. 15

In France, one hears only from very old people what a forty-year-old American said to me in Chicago. "When I was young, this whole neighbourhood was taken up by a lake. But this part of the lake was filled in and built over." And a thirty-five-year-old lawyer who was showing me the Negro section said: "I was born here. Then it was a white section and, apart from servants, you would not have seen a Negro in the streets. Now the white people have left and 250,000 Negroes are crowded into their houses." 16

M. Verdier, the owner of the "City of Paris" department store in San Francisco, witnessed the earthquake and fire that destroyed three quarters of the city. At that time he was a young man; he remembers the disaster perfectly. He watched the reconstruction of the city which still had an Asiatic look around 1913, and then its rapid Americanization. Thus, he has superimposed memories of three San Franciscos. 17

We Europeans change within changeless cities, and our houses and neighbourhoods outlive us; American cities change faster than their inhabitants do, and it is the inhabitants who outlive the cities. 18

I am really visiting the United States in wartime; the vast life of the American city has suddenly become petrified; people hardly change their residences any more. But this stagnation is entirely temporary; the cities have been immobilized like the dancer on the film-screen who stays with his foot suspended in air when the film is stopped; one feels all about one the rising of the sap which will burst open the cities as soon as the war is ended. 19

First, there are immediate problems; Chicago's Negro section will have to be rebuilt, for instance. The government had begun this before Pearl Harbour. But the government-built apartment houses barely manage to shelter 7000 people. Now, there are 250,000 to be housed. Then the industrialists want to enlarge and transform their factories; the famous abattoirs of Chicago are going to be completely modernized. 20

Finally, the average American is obsessed by the image of the "modern house" which is considerably publicized and which will be, so we are told, a hundred times more comfortable than the present dwellings and whose construction in huge quantities certainly has its place in the plans for "industrial conversion" which are now springing up almost everywhere. 21

When the war is over, America will certainly be seized with a real construction fever. Today the American sees his city objectively; he does not dream of finding it ugly, but thinks it really old. If it were even older, like ours, he could find a social past, a tradition in it. We generally live in our grandfathers' houses. Our streets reflect the customs and ways of past centuries; they tend to filter the present; none of what goes on in the Rue Montorgueil or the Rue Pot-de-Fer is completely of the present. But the thirty-year-old American lives in a house that was built when he was twenty. 22

These houses that are too young to seem *old* seem merely outdated to them; they lag behind the other tools, the car that can be traded in every two years, the refrigerator or the wireless set. That is why they see their cities without vain sentimentality. They have grown slightly attached to them, as one becomes attached to one's car, but they consider them as instruments, rather than anything else, instruments to be exchanged for more convenient ones. 23

For us a city is, above all, a past; for them it is mainly a future; what they like in the city is everything it has not yet become and everything it can be. 24

What are the impressions of a European who arrives in an 25

American city? First, he thinks he has been taken in. He has heard only about skyscrapers; New York and Chicago have been described to him as "upright cities." Now his first feeling is, on the contrary, that the average height of an American city is noticeably smaller than that of a French one. The immense majority of houses have only two storeys. Even in the very large cities, the five-storey apartment house is an exception.

Then he is struck by the lightness of the materials used. In the 26
United States stone is less frequently used than in Europe. The skyscraper consists of a coating of concrete applied to a metal framework, and the other buildings are made of brick or wood. Even in the richest cities and the smartest sections, one often finds frame houses. New Orleans' lovely colonial houses are of wood; many of the pretty chalets belonging to the Hollywood stars and film-directors are made of wood; so are the "California style" cottages in San Francisco. Everywhere you find groups of frame houses crushed between two twenty-storeyed buildings.

The brick houses are the colour of dried blood, or, on the 27
contrary, daubed and smeared with bright yellow, green or raw white. In most of the cities, they are roofless cubes or rectangular parallelpipeds, with severely flat façades. All these houses, hastily constructed and made expressly to be hastily demolished, obviously bear a strange resemblance to Fontana's "prefabricated houses."

The lightness of these jerry-built houses, their loud colours 28
alternating with the sombre red of the bricks, the extraordinary variety of their decorations which does not manage to conceal the uniformity of their patterns, all give one the feeling, when in the middle of the city, of walking through the suburbs of a watering town, like Trouville or Cabourg or La Baule. Only those ephemeral seaside chalets with their pretentious architectural style and their fragility can convey to those of my French readers who have never seen the States an idea of the American apartment house.

To complete the impression, I should also like to add that 29
sometimes one also thinks of an exposition-city, but an obsolescent, dirty one, like those that ten years later, in some park, survive the celebration that occasioned them. For these shanties quickly grow dirty, particularly in industrial sections.

Chicago, blackened by its smoke, clouded by the Lake 30
Michigan fog, is a dark and gloomy red. Pittsburgh is more gloomy still. And there is nothing more immediately striking than the contrast between the formidable power, the inexhaustible abundance of what is called the "American Colossus" and the puny insignificance of those little houses that line the widest roads in the world. But

on second thought, there is no clearer indication that America is not finished, that her ideas and plans, her social structure and her cities have only a strictly temporary reality.

These perfectly straight cities bear no trace of organization. 31
Many of them have the rudimentary structure of a polypary. Los Angeles, in particular, is rather like a big earthworm that might be chopped into twenty pieces without being killed. If you go through this enormous urban cluster, probably the largest in the world, you come upon twenty juxtaposed cities, strictly identical, each with its poor section, its business streets, night-clubs and smart suburb, and you get the impression that a medium-sized urban centre has schizogenetically reproduced itself twenty times.

In America, where the neighbourhoods are added on to each 32
other as the region's prosperity attracts new immigrants, this juxtaposition is the rule. You pass without any transition from a poor street into an aristocratic avenue; a promenade lined with skyscrapers, museums and public monuments and adorned with lawns and trees, suddenly stops short above a smoky station; one frequently discovers at the feet of the largest buildings, along an aristocratic avenue, a "zone" of miserable little kitchen-gardens.

This is due to the fact that these cities that move at a rapid rate 33
are not constructed in order to grow old, but move forward like modern armies, encircling the islands of resistance they are unable to destroy; the past does not manifest itself in them as it does in Europe, through public monuments, but through survivals. The wooden bridge in Chicago which spans a canal two steps away from the world's highest skyscrapers is a survival. The elevated railways, rolling noisily through the central streets of New York and Chicago, supported by great iron pillars and cross-girders, nearly touching the façades of houses on either side, are survivals. They are there simply because no one has taken the time to tear them down, and as a kind of indication of work to be done.

You find this disorder in each individual vista. Nowhere have 34
I seen so many empty lots. Of course they do have a definite function; they are used as car parks. But they break the alignment of the street nonetheless sharply for all that. Suddenly it seems as if a bomb had fallen on three or four houses, reducing them to powder, and as if they had just been swept out: this is a "parking space," two hundred square metres of bare earth with its sole ornament, perhaps, a poster on a big hoarding. Suddenly the city seems unfinished, badly assembled; suddenly you rediscover the desert and the big empty site: noticeable at Fontana. I remember this Los Angeles landscape in the middle of the city, two modern apartment houses, two white cubes framing an empty lot with the ground torn up—a parking

space. A few abandoned-looking cars were parked there. A palm tree grew like a weed between the cars. Down at the bottom there was a steep grassy hill, rather like the fortification mounds we use for garbage disposal. On top of the mound was a frame house, and a little below this a string stretched between two little trees, with multi-coloured washing hanging out to dry. When one turned around the block of houses, the hill disappeared; its other side had been built up, covered with asphalt, streaked with tar roads, and pierced with a magnificent tunnel.

The most striking aspect of the American city is the vertical 35
disorder. These brick shanties are of varying heights; I noted at random during a walk in Detroit the following successive proportions: one storey, two storeys, one storey, one storey, three storeys. You find the same proportions in Albuquerque or San Antonio, at the other end of the country. In depth, above this irregular crenellation, you see apartment houses of all shapes and dimensions, long cases, thick thirty-storeyed boxes with forty windows to a storey. As soon as there is a bit of fog the colours fade away, and only volumes remain—every variety of polyhedron. Between them, you have enormous empty spaces, empty lots cut out in the sky.

In New York, and even in Chicago, the skyscraper is on home 36
ground, and imposes a new order upon the city. But everywhere else it is out of place, the eye is unable to establish any unity between these tall, gawky things and the little houses that run close to the ground; in spite of itself it looks for that line so familiar in European cities, the sky-line, and cannot find it. That is why the European feels at first as though he were travelling through a rocky chaos that resembles a city—something like Montpellier-le-Vieux—rather than a city.

But the European makes a mistake in visiting American cities 37
as one does Paris or Venice; they are not meant to be seen that way. The streets here do not have the same meaning as our streets. In Europe, a street is half-way between the path of communication and the sheltered "public place." It is on a footing with the cafés, as proved by the use of the "terrasses" that spring up on the sidewalks of the cafés in fine weather. Thus it changes its aspect more than a hundred times a day, for the crowd that throngs the European street changes, and men are its primary element. The American street is a piece of highway. It sometimes stretches over many miles. It does not stimulate one to walk. Ours are oblique and twisting, full of bends and secrets. The American street is a straight line that gives itself away immediately. It contains no mystery. You see the street straight through, from one end to the other no matter what your location in it. And the distances in American cities are too great to permit moving

about on foot; in most of them one gets about almost exclusively in cars, on buses and by underground. Sometimes, while going from one appointment to another, I have been carried like a parcel from underground to escalator, from escalator to elevator, from elevator to taxi, from taxi to bus and, again, by metro and elevator, without walking a step.

In certain cities I noticed a real atrophy of the sidewalk. In Los Angeles, for example, on La Cienega, which is lined with bars, theatres, restaurants, antique dealers and private residences, the sidewalks are scarcely more than side-streets that lead customers and guests from the roadway into the house. Lawns have been planted from the façades to the roadway of this luxurious avenue. I followed a narrow path between the lawns for a long time without meeting a living soul, while to my right, cars streaked by on the road; all animation in the street had taken refuge on the high road. 38

New York and Chicago do not have neighbourhoods, but they do have a neighbourhood life; the American is not familiar with his city; once he is ten "blocks" away from his home, he is lost. This does not mean that there are no crowds in the business streets, but they are crowds that do not linger; people shop or emerge from the Underground to go to their offices. 39

I rarely saw an occasional Negro day-dreaming before a shop. 40

Yet one quickly begins to like American cities. Of course they all look alike. And when you arrive at Wichita, Saint Louis or Albuquerque, it is disappointing to realize that, hidden behind these magnificent and promising names, is the same standard checker-board city with the same red and green traffic lights and the same provincial look. But one gradually learns to tell them apart. Chicago, the noble, lurid city, red as the blood that trickles through its abattoirs, with its canals, the grey water of Lake Michigan and its streets crushed between clumsy and powerful buildings, in no way resembles San Francisco, city of air, salt and sea, built in the shape of an amphitheatre. 41

And then one finally comes to like their common element, that temporary look. Our beautiful closed cities, full as eggs, are a bit stifling. Our slanting, winding streets run head on against walls and houses; once you are inside the city, you can no longer see beyond it. In America, these long, straight unobstructed streets carry one's glance, like canals, outside the city. You always see mountains or fields or the sea at the end of them, no matter where you may be. 42

Frail and temporary, formless and unfinished, they are haunted by the presence of the immense geographical space surrounding them. And precisely because their boulevards are high- 43 ways, they always seem to be stopping places on the roads. They are not oppressive, they do not close you in; nothing in them is definitive, nothing is arrested. You feel, from your first glance, that your contact with these places is a temporary one; either you will leave them or they will change around you.

Let us beware of exaggerating; I have spent Sundays in the American provinces that were more depressing than Sundays anywhere else; I have seen those suburban "colonial style" inns where, at two dollars a head, middle-class families go to eat shrimp cocktails and turkey with cranberry sauce in silence while listening to the electric organ. One must not forget the heavy boredom that weighs over America. 44

But these slight cities, still so similar to Fontana and the outposts of the Far West, reveal the other side of the United States: their freedom. Here everyone is free—not to criticize or to reform their customs—but to flee them, to leave for the desert or another city. The cities are open, open to the world, and to the future. This is what gives them their adventurous look and, even in their ugliness and disorder, a touching beauty. 45

QUESTIONS

1. Explain in the context of the whole essay Sartre's remark that the American city "is a moving landscape for its inhabitants" (paragraph 15).

2. What comparative points does Sartre draw between European and American cities?

3. Locate and explain the various analogies, metaphors, and similes Sartre employs to illuminate the qualities of American cities.

4. What terms from art, architecture, and mathematics does Sartre use to describe American cities?

5. On what details does the author focus to develop his analysis of the American city?

6. How does Sartre particularize his generalizations about American cities? What is the general thesis that he develops?

7. How does the author combine personal, aesthetic, and social judgments to create the tone of the essay?

8. What is Sartre's method of identification in the essay? How does he use identification to arrive at an informal definition of the American city?

9. Sartre's essay was written in 1945 for *Le Figaro*. Which of his observa-

tions still apply? How did he anticipate postwar developments in urban American life? How biased was Sartre in his analysis?

10. a. Write an analysis of American cities, attempting, as Sartre does, to capture their essence.
b. Write about one or more foreign cities from the perspective of a visitor.

ANAÏS NIN

Morocco

Anaïs Nin (1903–1977), diarist, novelist, essayist, and feminist, was an American born in Paris. A student of psychology under Otto Rank, Nin always retained her interest in the inner self and specifically in the consciousness of women. In her words, she wished "to unmask the deeper self that lies hidden behind the self that we present to the world." Her diaries, started as letters to her father in 1931, were published in seven volumes between 1966 and 1980. These diaries, an imposing collection termed by Gunther Stuhlmann "one of the unique literary documents of our century," have been compared in method to the work of Marcel Proust. In the following entry from *The Diaries of Anaïs Nin, 1934–39* (1967), the author reveals her debt to her literary friends Henry Miller and Lawrence Durrell in this remarkable evocation of exotic landscape.

A trip to Morocco. A short but vivid one. I fell in love with Fez. Peace, Dignity. Humility. I have just left the balcony where I stood listening to the evening prayer rising over the white city. A religious emotion roused by the Arabs' lives, by the simplicity of it, the fundamental beauty. Stepping into the labyrinth of their streets, streets like intestines, two yards wide, into the abyss of their dark eyes, into peace. The rhythm affects one first of all. The slowness. Many people on the streets. You touch elbows. They breathe into your face, but with a silence, a gravity, a dreaminess. Only the children cry and laugh and run. The Arabs are silent. The little square room open on the street in which they sit on the ground, on the mud, with their merchandise around them. They are weaving, they are sewing, baking bread, chiseling jewels, repairing knives, making guns for the Berbers in the mountains. They are 1 dying wool in vast cauldrons, big cauldrons full of dye emerald green, violet, Orient blue. They are making sienna earth pottery, weaving rugs, shaving, shampooing and writing legal documents right there, under your eyes. One Arab is asleep over his bag of saffron. Another is praying with his beads while selling herbs. Further, a big tintamarre, the street of copperwork. Little boys are beating copper trays with small hammers, beating a design into them, beating copper lamps, Aladdin's lamps. Little boys and old men do the work. They hold the tray between their legs. The younger men walk down the street in their burnouses, going I know not where, some so beautiful one thinks they are women. The women are veiled. They are going to the mosque, probably. At a certain hour all selling, all work ceases and they all go to the mosque. But first of all they wash their faces, their feet, their sore eyes, their leprous noses, their pock-marked skins at the fountain. They shed their sandals. Some of the old men and old women never leave the mosque. They squat there forever until death overtakes them. Women have their own entrance. They kiss the wall of the mosque as they pass. To make way for a donkey loaded with kindling wood, I step into a dark doorway. A choking stench overwhelms me. This stench is everywhere. It takes a day to get used to it. It makes you feel nauseated at first. It is the smell of excrement, saffron, leather being cured, sandalwood, olive oil being used for frying, nut oil on the bodies, incense, muskrat, so strong that at first you cannot swallow food. There is mud on the white burnous, on the Arab legs. Children's heads shaved, with one tuft of hair left. The women with faces uncovered and tattooed are the primitive Berbers from the mountains, wives of warriors, not civilized. I saw the wives of one Arab, five of them sitting on a divan, like mountains of flesh, enormous, with several chins and several stomachs, and diamonds set in their foreheads.

The streets and houses are inextricably woven, intricately 2
interwoven, by bridges from one house to another, passageways covered with lattice, creating shadows on the ground. They seem to be crossing within a house, you never know when you are out in a street or in a patio, or a passageway, as half of the houses are open on the street, you get lost immediately. Mosques run into a merchant's home, shops into mosques, now you are under a trellised roof covered with rose vines, now walking in utter darkness through a tunnel, behind a donkey raw and bleeding from being beaten, and now you are on a bridge built by the Portuguese. Now admire lacy trelliswork done by the Andalusians, and now look at the square next to the mosque where the poor are allowed to sleep on mats.

Everywhere the Arab squats and waits. Anywhere. An old 3
Arab is teaching a young one a religious chant. Another is defecating carefully, conscientiously. Another is begging, showing all his open

sores, standing near the baker baking bread in ovens built in the
earth.

The atmosphere is so clear, so white and blue, you feel you 4
can see the whole world as clearly as you see Fez. The birds do not
chatter as they do in Paris, they chant, trill with operatic and tropical
fervor. The poor are dressed in sackcloths, the semi-poor in sheets
and bathtowels, the well-to-do women in silks and muslins. The Jews
wear a black burnous. In the streets and in the houses of the poor the
floor is of stamped earth. Houses are built of sienna-red earth,
sometimes whitewashed. The olive oil is pressed out in the street too,
under large wooden wheels.

I had letters of introduction. First I visited Si Boubekertazi. 5
He sat in his patio, on pillows. A beautiful Negro woman, a con-
cubine, brought a copper tray full of delicacies. And tea served in
tiny cups without handles.

At the house of Driss Mokri Montasseb I was allowed to visit 6
the harem. Seven wives of various ages, but all of them fat, sat
around a low table eating candy and dates. We discussed nail polish.
They wanted some of mine, which was pearly. They told me how
they made up their eyes. They bought kohl dust at the market, filled
their eyes with it. The eyes smart and cry, and so the black kohl
marks the edges and gives that heavily accented effect.

Pasha El Glaoui de Marrakesh offered me a military escort to 7
visit the city. He said it was absolutely necessary. He signaled to a
soldier standing at his door, who never left me from then on except
when I went to my hotel room to sleep.

De Sidi Hassan Benanai received me under the fine spun- 8
gold colonnades. But he had just begun a forty-day fast and prayer,
so he sat in silence, counting his beads, and tea was served in silence,
and he continued to pray, occasionally smiling at me, and bowing his
head, until I left.

From outside, the houses are uniformly plain, with high 9
walls covered with flowers. One cannot tell when one is entering a
luxurious abode. The door may be of beautiful ironwork. There may
be two, or four, or six guards at the door. But inside, the walls are all
mosaics, or painted, and the stucco worked like lace, the ceilings
painted in gold. The pillows are of silk. The Negro women are simply
dressed but always beautiful. One does not see the children or the
wives.

The white burnous is called a *jelabba*. 10

Mystery and labyrinth. Complex streets. Anonymous walls. 11
Secret luxury. Secrecy of these houses without windows on the
streets. The windows and door open on the patio. The patio has a
fountain and lovely plants. There is a labyrinth design in the
arrangement of the gardens. Bushes are placed to form a puzzle so

you might get lost. They love the feeling of being lost. It has been interpreted as a desire to reproduce the infinite.

Fez. One always, sooner or later, comes upon a city which is an image of one's inner cities. Fez is an image of my inner self. This may explain my fascination for it. Wearing a veil, full and inexhaustible, labyrinthian, so rich and variable I myself get lost. Passion for mystery, the unknown, and for the infinite, the uncharted. 12

With my guide I visited the Quartier Réservé. It lay within medieval walls, guarded at each gate by a French soldier. The houses were full of prostitutes. Only the poor Arabs go there because the others have enough wives to satisfy their need of variety. Dark, dramatic, tortuous streets. Bare cellars which have become cafés. Arabs slinking in and out. Negroes. Beggars. Arab music heard now and then. The walls, ceilings covered with shabby rugs and potteries. *Thé à menthe* served, or beer. No wine drinking but much drug traffic. Bare, cellarlike rooms. Doors covered by muslin curtains, or beaded curtains. Front room is the bar or café where the men sit and the musicians play. Back room is for the prostitutes. The muslin curtain was parted and I found myself before Fatima, the queen of the prostitutes. 13

Fatima had a beautiful face, straight patrician nose, enormous black velvet eyes, tawny smooth skin, full but firm, and the usual Arabian attributes of several folds of stomach, several chins. She could only move with difficulty on her enormous legs. She was both queenly and magnificent, opulent, and voluptuous. She was dressed in a wedding costume, a pink chiffon dress embroidered with gold sequins laid over several layers of other chiffon petticoats. Heavy gold belt, bracelets, rings, a gold band across her forehead, enormous dangling gold earrings. Over her glistening black hair she wore a colored silk turban placed on the back of her head exposing the black curls. She had four gold teeth, considered beautiful by Arab women. The coal-black rim around her eyes exaggerated their size, as in Egyptian paintings. 14

She sat among pillows in a room shaped like many bedrooms in Fez, long and narrow. At each end of the room she had a brass bed, a sign of luxury and success. They are not used as beds, they are only a symbol of wealth. In between the two brass beds lay all the pillows, rugs, and low divans. (In rich homes the floors are tiled but the brass beds are displayed there too.) Fatima not only collected brass beds but also cuckoo clocks from Switzerland. One wall was covered with them, each one telling a different time. The other walls were covered with flowered cretonne. The atmosphere was heavy with perfume, enclosed and voluptuous, the womb itself. A young girl came in with an atomizer and lifting up my skirt gently atomized my underclothes with rose water. She came once more to throw rose petals around my 15 feet. Then she came carrying a tray with glass tea containers, sheathed in copper holders with handles. We sat cross-legged on vast pillows, Fatima in the center. She never made a vulgar gesture. Two blind, crippled musicians were invited in and played monotonously, but with such a beat that my excitement grew as if I had taken wine. Fatima began to prepare tea on the tray. Then she passed around a bottle of rose water and we perfumed our hands. Then she lit a sandalwood brazier and placed it at my feet. I was duly and thoroughly perfumed and the air grew heavier and richer. The Arab soldier lay back on the pillows. The handsome bodyguard in his white burnous, white turban and blue military costume conversed with Fatima, who could not speak French. He translated my compliments on her beauty. She asked him to translate a question about my nail polish. I promised to send her some. While we sat there dreaming between each phrase, there was a fight outside. A young Arab burst in, his face bleeding. "Aii, Aii, Aiii," he cried. Fatima sent her maid to see what could be done for the young Arab. She never lost her composure. The musicians played louder and faster so I would not notice the commotion and my pleasure would not be spoiled. I spent two hours with Fatima, as it is impolite to hurry here. It is a mortal insult to leave too soon or to seem hurried. It offends them deeply. Relationship does not depend so much on conversation or exchange as in the creation of a propitious, dreamy, meditative, contemplative atmosphere, a mood. Finally, when I was ready to leave, my escort made a parting speech.

It was after midnight. The city, so crowded during the day that I could hardly move in it, was silent and empty. The night watchman sleeps on the doorsteps. There are gates between different quarters. Six gates had to be opened for us with enormous keys. You are not allowed to circulate at night except by special permission and with a pass which the soldier showed to each watchman. 16

The frogs were croaking in the garden pools behind the walls, the crickets were announcing tomorrow's heat. The smell of roses won the battle of smells. A window was suddenly opened above me, an old woman stuck her head out and threw out a big rat she had just caught, with many curses. It fell at my feet. 17

Fez is a drug. It enmeshes you. The life of the senses, of poetry (even the poor Arabs who visit a prostitute will find a woman dressed in a wedding dress like a virgin), of illusion and dream. It made me passionate, just to sit there on pillows, with music, the birds, the fountains, the infinite beauty of the mosaic designs, the teakettle singing, the many copper trays shining, the twelve bottles of rose perfume and the sandalwood smoking in the brazier, and the cuckoo clocks chiming in disunion, as they pleased. 18

The layers of the city of Fez are like the layers and secrecies of 19
the inner life. One needs a guide.

I loved the racial nobility of the Arabs, the pride, the love of 20
sweets instead of alcohol, the gentleness, the peace, the hospitality, the reserve, pride, love of turquoise and coral colors, dignity of bearing, their silences. I love the way the men embrace in the street, proudly and nobly. I love the expression in their eyes, brooding, or fiery, but deep.

The river under the bridge was foul. Men held hands while 21
talking on the street. A dead Arab was carried on a stretcher, covered with narrow white bandages like an Egyptian mummy. Over his feet they had thrown a red rug. Silence and quietism. Contemplation and chanting. Music. Tea served on copper trays with a samovar kettle. Glasses have colored tops. On another tray a big silver box with big rough pieces of rock sugar. Trays with perfume bottles. Trays with almond cakes covered by a silk handkerchief or copper painted lids.

I met the Arab women walking to their baths. They went 22
there always in groups, and carrying a change of clothes in a basket over their heads. They walked veiled and laughing, showing only their eyes and the hennaed tips of their hands holding their veils. Their full white skirts and heavily embroidered belts made them heavy and full-looking, like the pillows they liked to sit on. It was heavy flesh moving in white robes, nourished on sweets and inertia, on passive watches behind grilled windows. This was one of their few moments of liberty, one of the few times they appeared in the street. They walked in groups with their servants, children, and bundles of fresh clothes, laughing and talking, and dragging their feet in embroidered mules.

I followed them. When they entered at the mosaic-covered 23
building near the mosque, I entered with them. The first room was very large and square, all of stone, with stone benches, and rugs on the floor. Here the women laid down their bundles and began undressing. This was a long ceremony, for they wore so many skirts, and several blouses, and belts which looked like bandages, so much white muslin, linen, cotton to unroll, unfold, and fold again on the bench. Then there were bracelets to take off, earrings, anklets, and then the long black hair to unwind from the ribbons tressed into the hair. So much white cotton fallen on the floor, a field of white petals, leaves, lace, shed by the full-fleshed women, and as I looked at them I felt they could never be really naked, that all this they wore must cling to them forever, grow with their bodies. I was already undressed and waiting, standing, as I would not sit naked on the stone bench. They were waiting for the children to be undressed by the African maids, waiting for the maids to get undressed.

An old woman was waiting for us, a completely shriveled old woman with only one eye. Her breasts were two long empty gourds hanging almost to the middle of her stomach. She wore a sackcloth around her waist. She gave me a little approving tap on the shoulder and smiled. She pointed to my finger nails and talked but I could not understand, and I smiled. 24

She opened the door to the steam room, another very large square room all of grey stone. But here there were no benches. All the women were sitting on the floor. The old woman filled pails of water from one of the fountains and occasionally poured one over their heads, after they had finished soaping themselves. The steam filled the room. The women sat on the floor, took their children between their knees and scrubbed them. Then the old woman threw a pail of water over them. This water flowed all around us, and it was dirty. We sat in rivulets of soapy, dirty water. The women did not hurry. They used the soap, then a piece of pumice stone, and then they began to use depilatories with great care and concentration. All of them were enormous. The flesh billowed, curved, folded in tremendous heavy waves. They seemed to be sitting on pillows of flesh of all colors, from the pale Northern Arab skin to the African. I was amazed that they could lift such heavy arms to comb their long hair. I had come to look at them, because the beauty of their faces was legendary, and proved not at all exaggerated. They had absolutely beautiful faces, enormous, jeweled eyes, straight noble noses with wide spaces between the eyes, full and voluptuous mouths, flawless skins, and always a royal bearing. The faces had a quality of statuary rather than painting, because the lines were so pure and clear. I sat in admiration of their faces, and then I noticed that they looked at me. They sat in groups, looking at me and smiling. They mimicked that I should wash my hair and face. I could not explain that I was hurrying through the ritual because I did not like sitting in the darkening waters. They offered me the pumice stone after using it thoroughly all over their ponderous bodies. I tried it but it scratched my face. The Arab women's skin was tougher. The women chatted in circles while washing themselves and their children. I could not bring myself to wash my face with the soap they all used for their feet and armpits. They laughed at what they must have thought was a European woman who did not know the rules of cleanliness. 25

They wanted me also to pull out superfluous eyebrows, hair under the arms, and to shave my pubic hair. I finally slipped away to the next room where pails of cooler water were thrown over me. 26

I wanted to see the Arab women clothed again, concealed in yards of white cotton. Such beautiful heads had risen out of these mountains of flesh, heads of incredible perfection, dazzling eyes 27 heavily fringed, sensual features. Sometimes moss-green eyes in dark sienna skins, sometimes coal-black eyes in pale moonlit skins, and always the long heavy black hair, the undulating tresses. But these heads rose from formless masses of flesh, heaving like plants in the sea, swelling, swaying, falling, the breasts like sea anemones, floating, the stomachs of perpetually pregnant women, the legs like pillows, the backs like cushions, the hips with furrows like a mattress.

They were all watching me, with friendly nodding of their 28
heads, commenting on my figure. By counting on their fingers they asked was I adolescent? I had no fat on me. I must be a girl. They came around me and we compared skin colors. They seemed amazed by my waist. They could enclose it in their two hands. They wanted to wash my hair. They soaped my face with tenderness. They touched me and talked with volubility. The old woman came with two pails and threw them over me. I was ready to leave, but the Arab women transmitted messages of all kinds with their eyes, smiles, talk. The old woman led me to the third room, which was cooler, and threw cold water over me, and then led me back to the dressing room.

QUESTIONS

1. Explain what the author means when she states in paragraph 12, "One always, sooner or later, comes upon a city which is an image of one's inner cities."

2. The Moroccan women dominate the author's description of life in Fez. What is Nin's attitude toward them? In what ways does she romanticize them? How do they contrast with the men?

3. How does the author's use of short sentence fragments, introduced in the first paragraph and woven into the essay, contribute to the mood and tone of the essay?

4. Where does the author use figurative and metaphorical language in paragraph 27? How are the prose rhythms in this paragraph typical of the essay as a whole?

5. What techniques of development does the author employ in the introductory paragraph? How does this paragraph establish motifs for the entire essay?

6. Which paragraph establishes the thesis for the essay? How is the paragraph prepared for in terms of the structure of the essay?

7. Examine paragraphs 13 to 15, 16 to 21, and 22 to 28. What dominant impression emerges from these paragraphs?

8. What methods does the author use to make point of view so distinctive in this essay?

9. Compare and contrast this essay with Orwell's "Marrakech."

10. Write about a place that has had an overwhelming, almost intoxicating, effect on you.

3 Manners and Morals

MARYA MANNES

Wasteland

Marya Mannes (1904–) has written several novels and some light verse, but she is best known for her essays, which have appeared in *Vogue, McCall's, Harper's,* and *The New Republic.* She has collected her essays in *More In Anger* (1958) and in *The New York I Know* (1961). Mannes has also written on such subjects as suicide and euthanasia in *Last Rights* (1974) and television in *Who Owns the Air?* (1960). Throughout her career, she has always been concerned with and critical of the quality of American life. In "Wasteland," Mannes describes the modern American landscape.

Cans. Beer cans. Glinting on the verges of a million miles of roadways, lying in scrub, grass, dirt, leaves, sand, mud, but never hidden. Piels, Rheingold, Ballantine, Schaefer, Schlitz, shining in the sun or picked by moon or the beams of headlights at night; washed by rain or flattened by wheels, but never dulled, never buried, never destroyed. Here is the mark of savages, the testament of wasters, the stain of prosperity. 1

Who are these men who defile the grassy borders of our roads and lanes, who pollute our ponds, who spoil the purity of our 2 ocean beaches with the empty vessels of their thirst? Who are the men who make these vessels in millions and then say, "Drink—and discard"? What society is this that can afford to cast away a million tons of metal and to make of wild and fruitful land a garbage heap?

What manner of men and women need thirty feet of steel and two hundred horsepower to take them, singly, to their small destinations? Who demand that what they eat is wrapped so that forests are cut down to make the paper that is thrown away, and what they smoke and chew is sealed so that the sealers can be tossed in gutters and caught in twigs and grass? 3

What kind of men can afford to make the streets of their towns and cities hideous with neon at night, and their roadways hideous with signs by day, wasting beauty; who leave the carcasses of cars to rot in heaps; who spill their trash into ravines and make smoking mountains of refuse for the town's rats? What manner of men choke off the life in rivers, streams and lakes with the waste of their produce, making poison of water? 4

Who is as rich as that? Slowly the wasters and despoilers are impoverishing our land, our nature, and our beauty, so that there will not be one beach, one hill, one lane, one meadow, one forest free from the debris of man and the stigma of his improvidence. 5

Who is so rich that he can squander forever the wealth of earth and water for the trivial needs of vanity or the compulsive demands of greed; or so prosperous in land that he can sacrifice nature for unnatural desires? The earth we abuse and the living things we kill will, in the end, take their revenge; for in exploiting their presence we are diminishing our future. 6

And what will we leave behind us when we are long dead? Temples? Amphora? Sunken treasure? 7

Or mountains of twisted, rusted steel, canyons of plastic containers, and a million miles of shores garlanded, not with the lovely wrack of the sea, but with the cans and bottles and light-bulbs and boxes of a people who conserved their convenience at the expense of their heritage, and whose ephemeral prosperity was built on waste. 8

QUESTIONS

1. What evidence of wastefulness does Mannes give in the essay?
2. How does Mannes relate prosperity to waste?
3. What are the multiple meanings of the title "Wasteland"? How are they represented in the essay?

4. Why does Mannes use fragments in the first paragraph and in paragraphs 7 and 8? What is the significance of the term "ephemeral prosperity" in the last paragraph?

5. What is the effect of the author's use of rhetorical questions to structure her essay? Explain the use of irony in Mannes's answers to her questions.

6. Identify the concrete objects listed in the essay. How does Mannes's selection of objects support her thesis?

7. How does Mannes describe such things as cars, cigarette wrappers, streetlights, and road signs? Why is her technique, called periphrasis, successful?

8. Paragraph 6 is made up of a question and a declarative sentence. Although the declarative sentence does not directly answer the question, the two are related. How?

9. How do you think Americans can become less wasteful?

10. Describe several objects that, taken as a whole, make a positive or negative statement about pollution, elections, education, or sports.

IMAMU AMIRI BARAKA

Soul Food

Imamu Amiri Baraka (1934–   ) is a playwright, novelist, editor, poet, essayist, and community leader. Baraka's most famous work, the play *Dutchman* (1964), is about the often destructive relations between black and white Americans. During his career, Baraka has, through the powerful use of the black idiom, introduced the public to the richness of black culture.

Recently, a young Negro novelist writing in *Esquire* about the beauties of America mentioned that one of the things wrong with Negroes was that, unlike the Chinese, boots have neither a language of their own nor a characteristic cuisine. And this to me is the deepest stroke, the unkindest cut, of oppression, especially as it has distorted Black Americans. America, where the suppliant, far from rebelling or even 1 disagreeing with the forces that have caused him to suffer, readily backs them up and finally tries to become an honorary oppressor himself.

No language? No characteristic food? Oh, man, come on. 2

Maws are things ofays seldom get to peck, nor are you likely 3 ever to hear about Charlie eating a chitterling. Sweet potato pies, a good friend of mine asked recently, "Do they taste anything like pumpkin?" Negative. They taste more like memory, if you're not uptown.

All those different kinds of greens (now quick frozen for 4 anyone) once were all Sam got to eat. (Plus the potlikker, into which one slipped some throwed away meat.) Collards and turnips and kale and mustards were not fit for anybody but the woogies. So they found a way to make them taste like something somebody would want to freeze and sell to a Negro going to Harvard as exotic European spinach.

The watermelon, friend, was imported from Africa (by 5 whom?) where it had been growing many centuries before it was necessary for some people to deny that they had ever tasted one.

Did you ever hear of a black-eyed pea? (Whitey used it for 6 forage, but some folks couldn't.) And all those weird parts of the hog? (After the pig was stripped of its choicest parts, the feet, snout, tail, intestines, stomach, etc., were all left for the "members," who treated them mercilessly.) Is it mere myth that shades are death on chickens? (Deep fat frying, the Dutch found out in 17th century New Amsterdam, was an African speciality: and if you can get hold of a fried chicken leg, or a fried porgie, you can find out what happened to that tradition.)

I had to go to Rutgers before I found people who thought 7 grits were meant to be eaten with milk and sugar, instead of gravy and pork sausage . . . and that's one of the reasons I left.

Away from home, you must make the trip uptown to get 8 really straight as far as a good grease is concerned. People kill chickens all over the world, but chasing them through the dark on somebody else's property would probably insure, once they went in the big bag, that you'd find some really beautiful way to eat them. I mean, after all the risk involved. The fruit of that tradition unfolds everywhere above 100th Street. There are probably more restaurants in Harlem whose staple is fried chicken, or chicken in the basket, than any other place in the world. Ditto, barbecued ribs—also straight out of the South with the West Indians, *i.e.*, Africans from farther south in the West, having developed the best sauce for roasting whole oxen and hogs, spicy and extremely hot.

Hoppin' John (black-eyed peas and rice), hushpuppies 9 (crusty cornmeal bread cooked in fish grease and best with fried fish, especially fried salt fish, which ought to soak overnight unless you're over fifty and can take all that salt), hoecake (pan bread), buttermilk biscuits and pancakes, fatback, *i.e.*, streak'alean-streak'afat, dumplings, neck bones, knuckles (both good for seasoning limas or string beans), okra (another African importation, other name gumbo), pork chops—some more staples of the Harlem cuisine. Most of the food came North when the people did.

There are hundreds of tiny restaurants, food shops, rib joints, 10
shrimp shacks, chicken shacks, "rotisseries" throughout Harlem that serve "soul food"—say, a breakfast of grits, eggs and sausage, pancakes and Alaga syrup—and even tiny booths where it's at least possible to get a good piece of barbecue, hot enough to make you whistle, or a chicken wing on a piece of greasy bread. You can *always* find a fish sandwich: a fish sandwich is something you walk with, or "Two of those small sweet potato pies to go." The Muslim temple serves bean pies which are really separate. It is never necessary to go to some big expensive place to get a good filling grease. You *can* go to the Red Rooster, or Wells, or Joch's, and get a good meal, but Jennylin's, a little place on 135th near Lenox, is more filling, or some place like the A&A food shop in a basement up in the 140's, and you can really get away. I guess a square is somebody who's in Harlem and eats at Nedicks.

QUESTIONS

1. According to Baraka, what foods and cooking styles originated in African or Afro-American culture?

2. The theme of white oppression and the black response to it recurs frequently in the essay. Identify some of the different ways in which the theme is put forth. Why does the author state and restate the theme?

3. List the various words that come from the black language and define them. There are also several references to "uptown" in the essay, which can be considered examples of metonymy. Explain.

4. Why is slang so effective in this essay?

5. What are the two opinions Baraka sets out to disprove? He uses two different methods of refuting these opinions. What are they?

6. How does the essay use inductive reasoning?

7. Why does Baraka present historical information in parentheses?

8. Analyze the development of Baraka's concluding paragraph.

9. Can you give examples of other systems of ethnic slang? What is the

purpose of slang? Why do composition teachers often discourage the use of slang?

10. a. Write an essay that develops your own definition of soul food.
b. Write an argumentative essay on the value of "separate" languages used by some ethnic, social, or professional group.

RUSSELL BAKER

Small Kicks in Superland

Russell Baker (1925–), Pulitzer Prize-winning humorist and journalist, has written a syndicated column called "The Observer" since 1962. His humor runs from allegorical satires on American politics and taste to witty criticisms of current jargon and slang. Baker's columns have been collected in such books as *An American in Washington* (1961), *No Cause for Panic* (1964), and *Poor Russell's Almanac* (1972). He has also written a fine autobiography, *Growing Up* (1982). In this essay, the author comically scrutinizes the mannerisms of some recognizable supermarket types.

I often go to the supermarket for the pure fun of it, and I 1
suspect a lot of other people do too. The supermarket fills some of the same needs the neighborhood saloon used to satisfy. There you can mix with neighbors when you are lonely, or feeling claustrophobic with family, or when you simply feel the urge to get out and be part of the busy, interesting world.

As in the old neighborhood saloon, something is being sold, 2
and this helps clothe the visit in wholesome material purpose. The national character tends to fear acts performed solely for pleasure; even our sexual hedonists usually justify themselves with the thought that they are doing a higher duty to social reform or mental hygiene.

It is hard to define the precise pleasure of the supermarket. 3
Unlike the saloon, it does not hold out promise of drugged senses commonly considered basic to pleasure.

There is, to be sure, the brilliant color of the fruit-and- 4
vegetable department to lift the spirit out of gray January's wearies, provided you do not look at the prices.

There are fantastic riches of pointless variety to make the mind delight in the excess that is America. In my neighborhood supermarket, for example, there are twenty or thirty yards of nothing but paper towels of varying colors, patterns and thicknesses. 5

What an amazing country that can make it so hard for a man to choose among things designed for the purpose of being thrown away! 6

The people, however, are the real lure. As in the traditional saloon, there are many who seem determined to leave nothing for anybody else. These sources prowl the aisles with carts overflowing with excesses of consumption. Twenty pounds of red meat, back-breaking cartons of powdered soap, onions wrapped lovingly in molded plastic, peanut butter by the hundredweight, cake mixes, sugar, oils, whole pineapples, wheels of cheese, candied watermelon rind, preserved camel humps from Persia . . . 7

Groaning and sweating, they heave their tonnage up to the checker, see it packaged in a forest's worth of paper bags and, the whole now reassembled as a tower of bags pyramided on another cart, they stagger off to their cars, drained of their wealth but filled with pride in their awesome capacity for consumption. 8

At times, seeing such a customer trying to buy up the whole supermarket, one is tempted to say, "Come now, my good woman, you've had enough for the day." Unfortunately, the ambience of supermarkets does not encourage verbal exchanges. In this it is inferior to the saloon. 9

Urban people, of course, are terribly scared nowadays. They may yearn for society, but it is risky to go around talking to strangers, for a lot of reasons, one being that people are so accustomed not to have many human contacts that they are afraid they may find out they really prefer life that way. 10

Whatever the reason, they go to the supermarket to be with people, but not to talk with people. The rule seems to be, you can look but you can't speak. Ah, well, most days there is a good bit to see. The other day in my own supermarket, for example, there was a woman who was sneakily lifting the cardboard lids on Sara Lee frozen coffee cakes and peeking under, eyeball to coffee cake, to see if—what? 11

Could she have misplaced something? Did she suspect that the contents were not as advertised? Whatever her purpose, she didn't buy. 12

Another woman was kneading a long package of white bread with her fingertips, rather like a doctor going over an abdomen for a yelp of pain that might confirm appendicitis. I had seen those silly women in the television commercial squeeze toilet paper, and so was 13 prepared for almost anything, but this medical examination of the bread was startling.

The woman, incidentally, did not buy. She left the store without a single purchase. This may have been because she looked at the "express checkout" line, saw that it would take forty-five minutes to pay for her bread and decided bread was not worth the wait. 14

(I am making a study of how supermarkets invariably manage to make the "express checkout" line the slowest in the store, and will report when interviews are completed.) 15

I suspect that woman who left empty-handed never intended to buy. I think she had simply become lonely sitting alone in her flat, or had begun to feel claustrophobic perhaps with her family, and had decided to go out to the supermarket and knead a loaf of white bread for the pure fun of feeling herself part of the great busy world. 16

QUESTIONS

1. For what purpose does Baker go to the supermarket? How does the title of the essay provide a clue? What does supermarket life tell him about human nature?

2. What similarities and differences does Baker draw between the supermarket and the saloon?

3. How does the author use action verbs in paragraphs 7 and 8 to capture character? What is the effect?

4. What descriptive details tend to stand out in this essay? How effective is Baker's use of concrete, sensory language? Are there any examples of figurative language? Explain.

5. How does Baker establish his thesis in this essay?

6. Explain how Baker uses comparison and contrast to develop his thesis.

7. What comic devices or techniques does Baker employ? Does he achieve a completely comic effect? Why, or why not?

8. Analyze the connections between the introductory and concluding paragraphs.

9. Baker tends to describe women in this essay. Is he fair and sensitive in his comic depiction of them, or do you think that his purpose is somewhat different?

10. Select any place where people tend to gather, and write an essay that captures the needs and eccentricities of human behavior there.

ANN GRACE MOJTABAI

Polygamy

Ann Grace Mojtabai (1938–   ) spent several years living in Iran. She has written three novels: *Mundome* (1974), *A Stopping Place* (1979), and *The Four Hundred Eels of Sigmund Freud* (1976). In the following essay, Mojtabai tries to look clearly at a particularly disturbing—from our perspective—aspect of Iranian culture.

Teheran, 1960. A warm evening. The courtyard in which 1
we were sitting was not very beautiful. There was a narrow strip of ground that ran along the edge of the wall, spotted with shrubbery and some insignificant roses; the rest was flagstone surrounding the customary small pool for ablutions, set like a turquoise in the center.

I had come to Iran expecting nightingales and roses, but had 2
not yet heard a nightingale above the sounds of street hawkers and traffic, and the famed rose gardens of Persia were nowhere in evidence; they remained out of sight, if they ever existed, sealed off by high proprietary walls.

But my interest of the moment was not in the garden; my 3
eyes were fixed on my father-in-law. He was a large, imposing man in his mid-90's, with high color, still-black eyebrows and the scrub of a heavy beard. He might have passed for a much younger man and, in fact, claimed to be in his young, vigorous 70's.

"What do you think of this?" he asked, pointing to his wives, 4
one large, one small, on either side of him. His wives smiled in my direction, then at each other. My father-in-law continued to stare at me and to wait; he really wanted to know what I thought.

For the few separate moments it took to translate his question 5
and my reply (with what distortion I shall never know), we gazed coolly at each other, each an anthropologist confronting opacity—the mind of a stranger. I thought I could hear him taking notes. I, for my part, was certainly jotting things down—but only impressions. I would see; I wasn't going to judge prematurely. My judgment, when it came, wouldn't be narrow, biased or culture-bound. "Customs differ," I said.

Long before meeting my father-in-law, I had been prepared 6
for this—or, rather, I had been briefed, and imagined that I was prepared. It had been a briefing full of history (polygamy as a practical solution to the decimation of the male population in warfare and the resulting disproportionate preponderance of females over males); it had been a briefing on principle as well (the Koranic

requirement that the husband distribute his affection equally among the co-wives).

7 But, of course, I was not ready to confront the live instance—three individuals who would bear an intimate family relation to me. Mother, father and what—aunt? mother-surrogate? I decided that the other party would simply be my Other Mother-in-Law. At that moment, the language barrier turned out to be an opportune cover for, really, I did not know what I thought.

8 The happy threesome sat cross-legged on a takhte, a low wooden platform, covered with a rug. My particular mother-in-law, the tiny one, was the junior wife, chosen, I later learned, by the older woman as someone agreeable to herself, someone she thought the old man would like, too. The senior wife's passion was for talking, and her husband's silence had long been wearing her down. She wanted someone in the house willing to hear her out and, she hoped, to respond from time to time.

9 I was left to imagine the precise formalities, but it seemed to me to be a marriage welcome to all the parties concerned. It was an arrangement not without its share of bickerings and quarrels, for however well-disposed the women were to each other, their respective children were rivals, and the wives were partisan for their children.

10 Still, as marriages go, theirs seemed to be a reasonably happy one.

11 When it grew chilly, we moved indoors. The sitting room was also my father-in-law's bedroom. He sat on a fine, ancient rug, with bolsters at his back, a bay of windows on his left and, in front of him, an array of small vials: vitamins, elixirs, purges. He didn't believe in modern medicine, but was taking no chances.

12 Stiff, wooden chairs of mismatching shapes were lined against the walls of the room. I eyed them, but, noticing that they were mantled in dust, furred with a thin, unbroken velvet, decided they were not really for use, and sat on the floor instead. In fact, the chairs were chiefly ceremonial, a reluctant concession to the times, to the imposition of Westernization around the world. Not like the television set, which was an ecstatic testimony to the march of *universal* human progress, and which held, along with the samovar, pride of place among the old man's possessions.

13 The wives stepped out to bring refreshments. With a sinking sense, I noticed my husband getting up to speak to his mother in private. I was utterly adrift, alone with my father-in-law, a total stranger. The old man turned to me and said what I later learned was: "When hearts speak, no language is necessary." I recognized none of the words, but I guessed from his face and tone that whatever it was

he had said was meant to be comforting and, trusting in a language of gesture and sign, I ventured a smile by way of reply.

Even today, I do not know what I think about polygamy. Or, 14
perhaps, I know what I think—it's only that my feelings are mixed. Abstractly, I oppose the custom. These bonds ought to be reciprocal, one-to-one. Sexual favors *may* be distributed equally as required (a night with A, a night with B), but I doubt whether affection can be distributed so neatly. And, of course, the custom speaks of the poverty of opportunities for women.

On the other hand, the custom of mut'a, or temporary 15
marriage, practiced by Shiites, though not by Sunnites, seems to me to be possessed of some merits and, on the whole, somewhat more enlightened than prostitution, or the vaguely polygamous custom of balancing wife (with legal rights) with mistress (having no rights), which is so widely prevalent in the West.

In the mut'a marriage, a term is stipulated—a night, a year, a 16
decade, an hour, whatever. A set term, a mehr—a wedding endowment for the woman—mutual consent and a contract specifying all this are required. The children of such unions are legitimate and entitled to a share of the father's inheritance, although the sigheh, the temporary wife, has no claim to maintenance beyond the initial marriage endowment.

But polygamy is meant to be more than a mere alternative to 17
such clearly deficient institutions as prostitution. And my feelings for polygamy as a true and viable form of marriage remain contrary, held in suspension. My opposition in theory is muffled by my observation of one palpable contrary fact. I saw a polygamous marriage work, and work well. That my mothers-in-law were deeply attached to each other, I have no doubt. I tend to question rather more their devotion to the husband who brought them together.

As for two mothers-in-law in one household, an old proverb 18
would seem to apply: "Better two tigers in one cage than two mistresses in one household." But, in point of fact, the laws of addition don't always apply. After all, one shark and one codfish equal one shark; one raindrop and one raindrop equal one raindrop. The two women worked off their intensities on each other, with less energy left for me. So, actually, I had one mother-in-law, which, as all the proverbs of all nations attest, was quite sufficient.

QUESTIONS

1. What effects of Westernization appear in the essay? Of which ones do the Iranians approve? Of which ones do they disapprove?

2. What academic-sounding reasons for polygamy has Mojtabai been given? Do they help her to confront the reality of it? Why or why not? What is her final attitude toward polygamy?

3. Identify Iranian words in the essay and explain what they mean.

4. What does Mojtabai mean when she describes her first meeting with her father-in-law as "each an anthropologist confronting opacity" (paragraph 5)? What level of language does that suggest Mojtabai uses in the essay? Can these words be used by Westerners to describe aspects of Western culture?

5. What is the function of the opening narrative? Why is it effective?

6. In this essay, the narrator is both actor and observer. How does this affect the tone of the essay?

7. Why does Mojtabai spend considerable time describing *mut'a?* What elements of contrast does she utilize here? For what purpose?

8. One paragraph is considerably shorter than the others. How does this contribute to the structure and meaning of the essay?

9. Discuss a custom you have confronted that was alien to your own values. Compare your response to Mojtabai's response.

10. a. Write an essay describing your confrontation with an alien custom and your response to it.
b. Write your own evaluation of polygamy.

D. H. LAWRENCE

Do Women Change?

David Herbert Lawrence (1885–1930), novelist, essayist, and poet, wrote in the great tradition of English romanticism. He chafed under the conventions of his age and zealously extended the content and style of the English novel. His novels, such as *Sons and Lovers* (1913), *The Rainbow* (1915), *Women in Love* (1921), *The Plumed Serpent* (1926), and *Lady Chatterley's Lover* (1928), are famous for their often disquieting depictions of love and ambition in the modern world. Lawrence also wrote criticism; his *Studies in Classic American Literature* (1923) is still a revealing, if idiosyncratic, look at

American literature. His inventive, powerful use of language is apparent in "Do Women Change?"

They tell of all the things that are going to happen in the future—babies bred in bottle, all the love-nonsense cut out, women indistinguishable from men. But it seems to me bosh. We like to imagine we are something very new on the face of the earth. But it seems to me we flatter ourselves. Motor-cars and aeroplanes are something novel, if not something new—one could draw a distinction. But the people in them are merely people, and not many steps up, if any, it seems to me, from the people who went in litters or palanquins or chariots, or who walked on foot from Egypt to Jordan, in the days of Moses. Humanity seems to have an infinite capacity for remaining the same—that is, human. 1

Of course, there are all kinds of ways of being human; but I expect almost every possible kind is alive and kicking today. There are little Cleopatras and Zenobias and Semiramises and Judiths and Ruths, and even Mother Eves, today just the same as in all the endless yesterdays. Circumstances make them little Cleopatras and little Semiramises instead of big ones, because our age goes in for quantity regardless of quality. But sophisticated people are sophisticated people, no matter whether it is Egypt or Atlantis. And sophisticated people are pretty well all alike. All that varies is the proportion of "modern" people to all the other unmodern sorts, the sophisticated to the unsophisticated. And today there is a huge majority of sophisticated people. And they are probably very little different from all the other sophisticated people of all the other civilizations, since man was man. 2

And women are just part of the human show. They aren't something apart. They aren't something new on the face of the earth, like the loganberry or artificial silk. Women are as sophisticated as men, anyhow, and they were never anything but women, and they are nothing but women today, whatever they may think of themselves. They say the modern woman is a new type. But is she? I expect, in fact I am sure, there have been lots of women like ours in the past, and if you'd been married to one of them, you wouldn't have found her any different from your present wife. Women are women. They only have phases. In Rome, in Syracuse, in Athens, in Thebes, more than two or three thousand years ago, there was the bob-haired, painted, perfumed Miss and Mrs. of today, and she inspired almost exactly the feelings that our painted and perfumed Misses and Mrses. inspire in the men. 3

I saw a joke in a German paper—a modern young man and a modern young woman leaning on an hotel balcony at night, overlook- 4 ing the sea. *He:* "See the stars sinking down over the dark restless ocean!" *She:* "Cut it out! My room number is 32!"

5 That is supposed to be very modern: the very modern woman. But I believe women in Capri under Tiberias said *"Cut it out"* to their Roman and Campanian lovers in just the same way. And women in Alexandria in Cleopatra's time. Certain phases of history are "modern." As the wheel of history goes round women become "modern," then they become unmodern again. The Roman women of the late Empire were most decidedly "modern"—so were the women of Ptolemaic Egypt. True modern cut-it-out women. Only the hotels were run differently.

6 Modernity or modernism isn't something we've just invented. It's something that comes at the end of civilizations. Just as leaves in autumn are yellow, so the women at the end of every known civilization—Roman, Greek, Egyptian, etc.—have been modern. They were smart, they were *chic,* they said cut-it-out, and they did as they jolly well pleased.

7 And then, after all, how deep does modernness go? Even in a woman? You give her a run for her money; and if you don't give it her, she takes it. The sign of modernness in a woman is that she says: Oh, cut it out, boy!—So the boy cuts it out—all the stars and ocean stuff.—My room number's thirty-two!—Come to the point!

8 But the point, when you come to it, is a very bare little place, a very meagre little affair. It's extraordinary how meagre the point is once you've come to it. It's not much better than a full-stop. So the modern girl comes to the point brutally and repeatedly, to find that her life is a series of full-stops, then a mere string of dots. Cut it out, boy! . . . When she comes to dot number one thousand, she's getting about tired of dots, and of the plain point she's come to. The point is all too plain and too obvious. It is so pointed that it is pointless. Following the series of dots comes a blank—a dead blank. There's nothing left to cut out. Blank-eye!

9 Then the thoroughly modern girl begins to moan: Oh, boy, do put something in again!—And the thoroughly modern boy, having cut it out so thoroughly that it will never grow again, tunes up with: I can't give you anything but love, Baby!—And the thoroughly modern girl accepts it with unction. She knows it's nothing but a most crestfallen echo from a sentimental past. But when you've cut everything out so that it will never grow again, you are thankful even for echoes from a sentimental past. And so the game begins again. Having cut it out, and brought it down to brass tacks, you find brass tacks are the last thing you want to lie down on.—Oh, boy, aren't you going to do something about it?—And the boy, having cut it all out so that it won't grow again, has no other bright inspiration but to turn the brass tacks round, when lo, they become the brass-headed nails

that go around Victorian plush furniture. And there they are, the hyper-modern two.

No, women don't change. They only go through a rather 10
regular series of phases. They are first the slave; then the obedient helpmeet; then the respected spouse; then the noble matron; then the splendid woman and citizen; then the independent female; then the modern girl, oh, cut-it-out, boy! and when the boy has cut it all out, the mills of God grind on, and having nothing else to grind, they grind the cut-it-out girl down, down, down—back to—we don't know where—but probably to the slave once more, and the whole cycle starts afresh, on and on, till in the course of a thousand years or two we come once more to the really "modern" girl. Oh, cut it out, boy!

A lead-pencil has a point, an argument may have a point, 11
remarks may be pointed, and a man who wants to borrow five pounds from you only comes to the point when he asks you for the fiver. Lots of things have points: especially weapons. But where is the point to life? Where is the point to love? Where, if it comes to the point, is the point to a bunch of violets? There is no point. Life and love are life and love, a bunch of violets is a bunch of violets, and to drag in the idea of a point is to ruin everything. Live and let live, love and let love, flower and fade, and follow the natural curve, which flows on, pointless.

Now women used to understand this better than men. Men, 12
who were keen on weapons, which all have points, used to insist on putting points to life and love. But women used to know better. They used to know that life is a flow, a soft curving flow, a flowing together and a flowing apart and a flowing together again, in a long subtle motion that has no full-stops and no points, even if there are rough places. Women used to see themselves as a softly flowing stream of attraction and desire and beauty, soft quiet rivers of energy and peace. Then suddenly the idea changes. They see themselves as isolated things, independent females, instruments, instruments for love, instruments for work, instruments for politics, instruments for pleasure, this, that and the other. And as instruments they become pointed and they want everything, even a small child, even love itself, to have a point. When women start coming to the point, they don't hesitate. They pick a daisy, and they say: There must be a point to this daisy, and I'm going to get at it.—So they start pulling off the white petals, till there are none left. Then they pull away the yellow bits of the centre, and come to a mere green part, still without having come to the point. Then in disgust they tear the green base of the flower across, and say: I call that a fool flower. It had no point to it!

Life is not a question of points, but a question of flow. It's the 13
flow that matters. If you come to think of it, a daisy even is like a little river flowing, that never for an instant stops. From the time when the

tiny knob of a bud appears down among the leaves, during the slow rising up a stem, the slow swelling and pushing out the white petal-tips from the green, to the full round daisy, white and gold and gay, that opens and shuts through a few dawns, a few nights, poised on the summit of her stem, then silently shrivels and mysteriously disappears—there is no stop, no halt, it is a perpetual little streaming of a gay little life out into full radiance and delicate shrivelling, like a perfect little fountain that flows and flows, and shoots away at last into the invisible, even then without any stop.

So it is with life, and especially with love. There is no point. 14
There is nothing you can cut out, except falsity, which isn't love or life. But the love itself is a flow, two little streams of feeling, one from the woman, one from the man, that flow and flow and never stop, and sometimes they twinkle with stars, sometimes they chafe, but still they flow on, intermingling; and if they rise to a floweriness like a daisy, that is part of the flow; and they will inevitably die down again, which is also part of a flow. And one relationship may produce many flowerinesses, as a daisy plant produces many daisies; but they will all die down again as the summer passes, though the green plant itself need not die. If flowers didn't fade they wouldn't be flowers, they'd be artificial things. But there are roots to faded flowers and in the root the flow continues and continues. And only the flow matters; live and let live, love and let love. There is no point to love.

QUESTIONS

1. Describe Lawrence's "cycle of womanhood."

2. According to Lawrence, what is the difference between new and novel? What novel things does he mention? Does he believe that the modern woman fits into either of these categories? Why or why not?

3. The level of language fluctuates radically in this essay. Why? Give some examples of high and low language.

4. Lawrence presents the clichés "cut it out," "down to brass tacks," and "what's the point" as symbols of the modern age. Explain the many different meanings for these terms.

5. There are references to several notable historical women. Who are they? Why does Lawrence choose to cite examples of classical women rather than modern ones? Where does he use general examples? Are they effective?

6. How does Lawrence use the symbols of the river and the flower to explain his view of love? What is the connection between the metaphors

point and *flow*? What other figurative and implied contrasts serve to structure the essay?

7. What is the significance of the anecdote in paragraph 4 for the structure of the essay?

8. Where does Lawrence state his thesis? How do earlier paragraphs prepare for it? Compare these paragraphs with those that follow the thesis statement.

9. Do you agree with Lawrence that we are at the end of civilization? Why or why not?

10. a. Write one of two essays: "Do Women Change?" or "Do Men Change?"
b. Write an essay in which you examine the levels of meaning of an old cliché. Then show how it symbolizes an aspect of our culture.

GLORIA STEINEM

Erotica and Pornography

Gloria Steinem (1934–   ) was born and raised in Toledo, Ohio; she attended Smith College, receiving a B.A. in government in 1956. A noted feminist and political activist, Steinem in 1968 helped to found *New York* magazine; in 1971 she cofounded *Ms.* magazine and has served as its editor since then. Whether campaigning for Robert Kennedy and George McGovern or helping to defend and raise money for Angela Davis and the United Farmworkers, Steinem has been on the cutting edge of American politics for more than two decades. Her most recent book, a collection of essays, is *Outrageous Acts and Everyday Rebellions* (1983). The essay that follows reflects Steinem's keen ability to relate ideas and issues to the lives of women today.

Human beings are the only animals that experience the same sex drive at times when we can—and cannot—conceive. 1

Just as we developed uniquely human capacities for language, planning, memory, and invention along our evolutionary path, we also developed sexuality as a form of expression; a way 2 of communicating that is separable from our need for sex as a way of perpetuating ourselves. For humans alone, sexuality can be and often is primarily a way of bonding, of giving and receiving pleasure, bridging differentness, discovering sameness, and communicating emotion.

We developed this and other human gifts through our ability 3 to change our environment, adapt physically, and in the long run, to affect our own evolution. But as an emotional result of this spiraling path away from other animals, we seem to alternate between periods of exploring our unique abilities to change new boundaries, and feelings of loneliness in the unknown that we ourselves have created; a fear that sometimes sends us back to the comfort of the animal world by encouraging us to exaggerate our sameness.

The separation of "play" from "work," for instance, is a 4 problem only in the human world. So is the difference between art and nature, or an intellectual accomplishment and a physical one. As a result, we celebrate play, art, and invention as leaps into the unknown; but any imbalance can send us back to nostalgia for our primate past and the conviction that the basics of work, nature, and physical labor are somehow more worthwhile or even moral.

In the same way, we have explored our sexuality as separable 5 from conception: a pleasurable, empathetic bridge to strangers of the same species. We have even invented contraception—a skill that has probably existed in some form since our ancestors figured out the process of birth—in order to extend this uniquely human difference. Yet we also have times of atavistic suspicion that sex is not complete—or even legal or intended-by-god—if it cannot end in conception.

No wonder the concepts of "erotica" and "pornography" can 6 be so crucially different, and yet so confused. Both assume that sexuality can be separated from conception, and therefore can be used to carry a personal message. That's a major reason why, even in our current culture, both may be called equally "shocking" or legally "obscene," a word whose Latin derivative means "dirty, containing filth." This gross condemnation of all sexuality that isn't harnessed to childbirth and marriage has been increased by the current backlash against women's progress. Out of fear that the whole patriarchal structure might be upset if women really had the autonomous power to decide our reproductive futures (that is, if we controlled the most basic means of production), right-wing groups are not only denouncing prochoice abortion literature as "pornographic," but are trying to stop the sending of all contraceptive information through the mails by invoking obscenity laws. In fact, Phyllis Schlafly recently denounced the entire Women's Movement as "obscene."

Not surprisingly, this religious, visceral backlash has a secu- 7 lar, intellectual counterpart that relies heavily on applying the "natural" behavior of the animal world to humans. That is questionable in itself, but these Lionel Tiger-ish studies make their political purpose even more clear in the particular animals they select and the habits they choose to emphasize. The message is that females should accept their "destiny" of being sexually dependent and devote themselves to bearing and rearing their young.

Defending against such reaction in turn leads to another temptation: to merely reverse the terms, and declare that *all* nonprocreative sex is good. In fact, however, this human activity can be as constructive as destructive, moral or immoral, as any other. Sex as communication can send messages as different as life and death; even the origins of "erotica" and "pornography" reflect that fact. After all, "erotica" is rooted in *eros* or passionate love, and thus in the idea of positive choice, free will, the yearning for a particular person. (Interestingly, the definition of erotica leaves open the question of gender.) "Pornography" begins with a root meaning "prostitution" or "female captives," thus letting us know that the subject is not mutual love, or love at all, but domination and violence against women. (Though, of course, homosexual pornography may imitate this violence by putting a man in the "feminine" role of victim.) It ends with a root meaning "writing about" or "description of" which puts still more distance between subject and object, and replaces a spontaneous yearning for closeness with objectification and a voyeur. 8

The difference is clear in the words. It becomes even more so by example. 9

Look at any photo or film of people making love; really making love. The images may be diverse, but there is usually a sensuality and touch and warmth, an acceptance of bodies and nerve endings. There is always a spontaneous sense of people who are there because they *want* to be, out of shared pleasure. 10

Now look at any depiction of sex in which there is clear force, or an unequal power that spells coercion. It may be very blatant, with weapons or torture or bondage, wounds and bruises, some clear humiliation, or an adult's sexual power being used over a child. It may be much more subtle: a physical attitude of conqueror and victim, the use of race or class difference to imply the same thing, perhaps a very unequal nudity, with one person exposed and vulnerable while the other is clothed. In either case, there is no sense of equal choice or equal power. 11

The first is erotic: a mutually pleasurable, sexual expression between people who have enough power to be there by positive choice. It may or may not strike a sense-memory in the viewer, or be creative enough to make the unknown seem real; but it doesn't require us to identify with a conqueror or a victim. It is truly sensuous, and may give us a contagion of pleasure. 12

The second is pornographic: its message is violence, dominance, and conquest. It is sex being used to reinforce some inequality, or to create one, or to tell us the lie that pain and humiliation (ours or someone else's) are really the same as pleasure. If we are to feel anything, we must identify with conqueror or victim. That means we can only experience pleasure through the adoption of some degree of sadism or masochism. It also means that we may feel diminished by the role of conqueror, or enraged, humiliated, and vengeful by sharing identity with the victim. 13

Perhaps one could simply say that erotica is about sexuality, but pornography is about power and sex-as-weapon—in the same way we have come to understand that rape is about violence, and not really about sexuality at all. 14

Yes, it's true that there are women who have been forced by violent families and dominating men to confuse love with pain; so much so that they have become masochists. (A fact that in no way excuses those who administer such pain.) But the truth is that, for most women—and for men with enough humanity to imagine themselves into the predicament of women—true pornography could serve as aversion therapy for sex. 15

Of course, there will always be personal differences about what is and is not erotic, and there may be cultural differences for a long time to come. Many women feel that sex makes them vulnerable and therefore may continue to need more sense of personal connection and safety before allowing any erotic feelings. We now find competence and expertise erotic in men, but that may pass as we develop those qualities in ourselves. Men, on the other hand, may continue to feel less vulnerable, and therefore more open to such potential danger as sex with strangers. As some men replace the need for submission from childlike women with the pleasure of cooperation from equals, they may find a partner's competence to be erotic, too. 16

Such group changes plus individual differences will continue to be reflected in sexual love between people of the same gender, as well as between women and men. The point is not to dictate sameness, but to discover ourselves and each other through sexuality that is an exploring, pleasurable, empathetic part of our lives; a human sexuality that is unchained both from unwanted pregnancies and from violence. 17

But that is a hope, not a reality. At the moment, fear of change is increasing both the indiscriminate repression of all nonprocreative sex in the religious and "conservative" male world, and the pornographic vengeance against women's sexuality in the secular world of "liberal" and "radical" men. It's almost futuristic to debate what is and is not truly erotic, when many women are again being 18 forced into compulsory motherhood, and the number of pornographic murders, tortures, and woman-hating images are on the increase in both popular culture and real life.

It's a familiar division: wife or whore, "good" woman who is constantly vulnerable to pregnancy or "bad" woman who is unprotected from violence. *Both* roles would be upset if we were to control our own sexuality. And that's exactly what we must do. 19

In spite of all our atavistic suspicions and training for the "natural" role of motherhood, we took up the complicated battle for reproductive freedom. Our bodies had borne the health burden of endless births and poor abortions, and we had a greater motive for separating sexuality and conception. 20

Now we have to take up the equally complex burden of explaining that all nonprocreative sex is *not* alike. We have a motive: our right to a uniquely human sexuality, and sometimes even to survival. As it is, our bodies have too rarely been enough our own to develop erotica in our own lives, much less in art and literature. And our bodies have too often been the objects of pornography and the woman-hating, violent practice that it preaches. Consider also our spirits that break a little each time we see ourselves in chains or full labial display for the conquering male viewer, bruised or on our knees, screaming a real or pretended pain to delight the sadist, pretending to enjoy what we don't enjoy, to be blind to the images of our sisters that really haunt us—humiliated often enough ourselves by the truly obscene idea that sex and the domination of women must be combined. 21

Sexuality *is* human, free, separate—and so are we. 22

But until we untangle the lethal confusion of sex with violence, there will be more pornography and less erotica. There will be little murders in our beds—and very little love. 23

QUESTIONS

1. How does Steinem define the terms *erotica* and *pornography*? What is the essential distinction that the author draws between these two words?

2. In what ways do the concepts of erotica and pornography affect women's lives?

3. Look up the words *erotica* and *pornography* in the *Oxford English Dictionary (OED)* or any large dictionary. Trace the etymology of these two words and any shifts in meaning.

4. Use the dictionary as necessary to understand the following biological, psychological, and sociological terms: *evolutionary* (paragraph 2), *environment* (paragraph 3), *primate* (paragraph 5), *atavistic* (paragraph 5),

patriarchal (paragraph 6), *voyeur* (paragraph 8), *sadism* and *masochism* (paragraph 12), and *aversion therapy* (paragraph 14).

5. Why does the author delay the introduction of her key topic until paragraph 6? What is the relevance of the first five paragraphs? How are these paragraphs developed?

6. What is the relevance of the definition to the essay's development?

7. Explain Steinem's use of comparison and contrast to structure parts of this essay.

8. Examine the author's use of illustration in three representative paragraphs.

9. Do you accept the author's distinction between erotica and pornography? Why or why not?

10. a. Using Steinem's essay as a guide, write your own definitions of erotica and pornography, relating the terms to contemporary manners and morals. b. Describe and evaluate an erotic scene that you have viewed in a film or read in a book.

CHARLES LAMB

A Bachelor's Complaint

Charles Lamb (1775–1834) was a famous essayist in England in the early nineteenth century. His writings ranged from children's tales to plays, but his forte was the personal essay. In *The Essays of Elia* (*London Magazine,* 1820–1825), Lamb described his friends, himself, and his society in a light, satiric style. In *Specimens of English Dramatic Poets* (1808), he inspired renewed interest in Elizabethan drama. Lamb describes the failures of matrimony under the persona of Elia, an eccentric bachelor, in the following selection, "A Bachelor's Complaint of the Behavior of Married People."

1 s a single man, I have spent a good deal of my time in noting down the infirmities of Married People, to console myself for those superior pleasures, which they tell me I have lost by remaining as I am.

2 I cannot say that the quarrels of men and their wives ever made any great impression upon me, or had much tendency to

strengthen me in those anti-social resolutions, which I took up long ago upon more substantial considerations. What oftenest offends me at the houses of married persons where I visit, is an error of quite a different description; it is that they are too loving.

Not too loving neither: that does not explain my meaning. 3
Besides, why should that offend me? The very act of separating themselves from the rest of the world, to have the fuller enjoyment of each other's society, implies that they prefer one another to all the world.

But what I complain of is, that they carry this preference so 4
undisguisedly, they perk it up in the faces of us single people so shamelessly, you cannot be in their company a moment without being made to feel, by some indirect hint or open avowal, that *you* are not the object of this preference. Now there are some things which give no offence, while implied or taken for granted merely; but expressed, there is much offence in them. If a man were to accost the first homely-featured or plain-dressed young woman of his acquaintance, and tell her bluntly, that she was not handsome or rich enough for him, and he could not marry her, he would deserve to be kicked for his ill manners; yet no less is implied in the fact, that having access and opportunity of putting the question to her, he has never yet thought fit to do it. The young woman understands this as clearly as if it were put into words; but no reasonable young woman would think of making this the ground of a quarrel. Just as little right have a married couple to tell me by speeches, and looks that are scarce less plain than speeches, that I am not the happy man—the lady's choice. It is enough that I know that I am not: I do not want this perpetual reminding.

The display of superior knowledge or riches may be made 5
sufficiently mortifying; but these admit of a palliative. The knowledge which is brought out to insult me, may accidentally improve me; and in the rich man's houses and pictures, his parks and gardens, I have a temporary usufruct at least. But the display of married happiness has none of these palliatives; it is throughout pure, unrecompensed, unqualified insult.

Marriage by its best title is a monopoly, and not of the least 6
invidious sort. It is the cunning of most possessors of any exclusive privilege to keep their advantage as much out of sight as possible, that their less favored neighbors, seeing little of the benefit, may be less disposed to question the right. But these married monopolists thrust the most obnoxious part of their patent into our faces.

Nothing is to me more distasteful than that entire complacen- 7
cy and satisfaction which beam in the countenances of a new-married couple—in that of the lady particularly; it tells you, that her lot is disposed of in this world: that *you* can have no hopes of her. It is true,

I have none; nor wishes either, perhaps; but this is one of those truths which ought, as I said before, to be taken for granted, not expressed.

The excessive airs which those people give themselves, founded on the ignorance of us unmarried people, would be more offensive if they were less irrational. We will allow them to understand the mysteries belonging to their own craft better than we, who have not had the happiness to be made free of the company: but their arrogance is not content within these limits. If a single person presume to offer his opinion in their presence, though upon the most indifferent subject, he is immediately silenced as an incompetent person. Nay, a young married lady of my acquaintance, who, the best of the jest was, had not changed her condition above a fortnight before, in a question on which I had the misfortune to differ from her, respecting the properest mode of breeding oysters for the London market, had the assurance to ask with a sneer, how such an old Bachelor as I could pretend to know anything about such matters! 8

But what I have spoken of hitherto is nothing to the airs which these creatures give themselves when they come, as they generally do, to have children. When I consider how little of a rarity children are—that every street and blind alley swarms with them—that the poorest people commonly have them in most abundance—that there are few marriages that are not blest with at least one of these bargains—how often they turn out ill, and defeat the fond hope of their parents, taking to vicious courses, which end in poverty, disgrace, the gallows, &c., I cannot for my life tell what cause for pride there can possibly be in having them. If they were young phoenixes, indeed, that were born but one in a year, there might be a pretext. But when they are so common— 9

I do not advert to the insolent merit which they assume with their husbands on these occasions. Let *them* look to that. But why *we*, who are not their natural-born subjects, should be expected to bring our spices, myrrh, and incense—our tribute and homage of admiration—I do not see. 10

"Like as the arrows in the hand of the giant, even so are the young children": so says the excellent office in our Prayer-book appointed for the churching of women. "Happy is the man that hath his quiver full of them": So say I; but then don't let him discharge his quiver upon us that are weaponless; let them be arrows, but not to gall and stick us. I have generally observed that these arrows are double-headed: they have two forks, to be sure to hit with one or the other. As for instance, where you come into a house which is full of children, if you happen to take no notice of them (you are thinking of something else, perhaps, and turn a deaf ear to their innocent caresses), you are set down as untractable, morose, a hater of children. On the other hand, if you find them more than usually 11 engaging—if you are taken with their pretty manners, and set about in earnest to romp and play with them, some pretext or other is sure to be found for sending them out of the room; they are too noisy or boisterous, or Mr.—— does not like children. With one or other of these forks the arrow is sure to hit you.

I could forgive their jealousy, and dispense with toying with their brats, if it gives them any pain; but I think it unreasonable to be called upon to *love* them, where I see no occasion—to love a whole family, perhaps eight, nine, or ten indiscriminately—to love all the pretty dears, because children are so engaging! 12

I know there is a proverb, "Love me, love my dog": that is not always so very practicable, particularly if the dog be set upon you to tease you or snap at you in sport. But a dog, or a lesser thing—any inanimate substance, as a keepsake, a watch or a ring, a tree, or the place where we last parted when my friend went away upon a long absence, I can make shift to love, because I love him, and anything that reminds me of him, provided it be in its nature indifferent, and apt to receive whatever hue fancy can give it. But children have a real character, and an essential being of themselves: they are amiable or unamiable *per se;* I must love or hate them, as I see cause for either in their qualities. A child's nature is too serious a thing to admit of its being regarded as a mere appendage to another being, and to be loved or hated accordingly: they stand with me upon their own stock, as much as men and women do. Oh! but you will say, sure it is an attractive age—there is something in the tender years of infancy that of itself charms us? That is the very reason why I am more nice about them. I know that a sweet child is the sweetest thing in nature, not even excepting the delicate creatures which bear them; but the prettier the kind of a thing is, the more desirable it is that it should be pretty of its kind. One daisy differs not much from another in glory; but a violet should look and smell the daintiest. I was always rather squeamish in my women and children. 13

But this is not the worst: one must be admitted into their familiarity at least, before they can complain of inattention. It implies visits, and some kind of intercourse. But if the husband be a man with whom you have lived on a friendly footing before marriage—if you did not come in on the wife's side—if you did not sneak into the house in her train, but were an old friend in fast habits of intimacy before their courtship was so much as thought on,—look about you—your tenure is precarious—before a twelve-month shall roll over your head, you shall find your old friend gradually grow cool and altered towards you, and at last seek opportunities of breaking with you. I have scarce a married friend of my acquaintance, upon whose firm faith I can rely, whose friendship did not commence *after the period of his marriage.* With some limitations, they can endure that; but 14 that the good man should have dared to enter into a solemn league of friendship in which they were not consulted, though it happened before they knew him,—before they that are now man and wife ever met,—this is intolerable to them. Every long friendship, every old authentic intimacy, must be brought into their office to be new stamped with their currency, as a sovereign prince calls in the good old money that was coined in some reign before he was born or thought of, to be new marked and minted with the stamp of his authority, before he will let it pass current in the world. You may guess what luck generally befalls such a rusty piece of metal as I am in these *new mintings.*

Innumerable are the ways which they take to insult and 15
worm you out of their husbands' confidence. Laughing at all you say with a kind of wonder, as if you were a queer kind of fellow that said good things, *but an oddity,* is one of the ways;—they have a particular kind of stare for the purpose;—till at last the husband, who used to defer to your judgment, and would pass over some excrescenses of understanding and manner for the sake of a general vein of observation (not quite vulgar) which he perceived in you, begins to suspect whether you are not altogether a humorist—a fellow well enough to have consorted with in his bachelor days, but not quite so proper to be introduced to ladies. This may be called the staring way; and is that which has oftenest been put in practice against me.

Then there is the exaggerating way, or the way of irony; that 16
is, where they find you an object of especial regard with their husband, who is not so easily to be shaken from the lasting attachment founded on esteem which he has conceived towards you, by never qualified exaggerations to cry up all that you say or do, till the good man, who understands well enough that it is all done in compliment to him, grows weary of the debt of gratitude which is due to so much candor, and by relaxing a little on his part, and taking down a peg or two in his enthusiasm, sinks at length to the kindly level of moderate esteem—that "decent affection and complacent kindness" towards you, where she herself can join in sympathy with him without much stress and violence to her sincerity.

Another way (for the ways they have to accomplish so 17
desirable a purpose are infinite) is, with a kind of innocent simplicity, continually to mistake what it was which first made their husband fond of you. If an esteem for something excellent in your moral character was that which riveted the chain which she is to break, upon any imaginary discovery of a want of poignancy in your conversation, she will cry, "I thought, my dear, you described your friend, Mr.——, as a great wit?" If, on the other hand, it was for some supposed charm in your conversation that he first grew to like you, and was content for this to overlook some trifling irregularities in

your moral deportment, upon the first notice of any of these she as readily exclaims, "This, my dear, is your good Mr.——!" One good lady whom I took the liberty of expostulating with for not showing me quite so much respect as I thought due to her husband's old friend, had the candor to confess to me that she had often heard Mr.—— speak of me before marriage, and that she had conceived a great desire to be acquainted with me, but that the sight of me had very much disappointed her expectations; for from her husband's representations of me, she had formed a notion that she was to see a fine, tall officer-like-looking man (I use her very words), the very reverse of which proved to be the truth. This was candid; and I had the civility not to ask her in return, how she came to pitch upon a standard of personal accomplishments for her husband's friends which differed so much from his own; for my friend's dimensions as near as possible approximate to mine; he standing five feet five in his shoes, in which I have the advantage of him by about half an inch; and he no more than myself exhibiting any indications of a martial character in his air or countenance.

These are some of the mortifications which I have encoun- 18
tered in the absurd attempt to visit at their houses. To enumerate them all would be a vain endeavor; I shall therefore just glance at the very common impropriety of which married ladies are guilty,—of treating us as if we were their husbands, and *vice versa*. I mean, when they use us with familiarity, and their husbands with ceremony. *Testacea*, for instance, kept me the other night two or three hours beyond my usual time of supping, while she was fretting because Mr.—— did not come home, till the oysters were all spoiled, rather than she would be guilty of the impoliteness of touching one in his absence. This was reversing the point of good manners; for ceremony is an invention to take off the uneasy feeling which we derive from knowing ourselves to be less the object of love and esteem with a fellow-creature than some other person is. It endeavors to make up, by superior attentions in little points, for that invidious preference which it is forced to deny in the greater. Had *Testacea* kept the oysters back for me, and withstood her husband's importunities to go to supper, she would have acted according to the strict rules of propriety. I know no ceremony that ladies are bound to observe to their husbands, beyond the point of a modest behavior and decorum: therefore I must protest against the vicarious gluttony of *Cerasia*, who at her own table sent away a dish of Morellas, which I was applying to with great good-will, to her husband at the other end of the table, and recommended a plate of less extraordinary gooseberries to my unwedded palate in their stead. Neither can I excuse the wanton affront of——

But I am weary of stringing up all my married acquaintance 19 by Roman denominations. Let them amend and change their manners, or I promise to record the full-length English of their names, to the terror of all such desperate offenders in future.

QUESTIONS

1. Lamb labels several ways that women alienate their husbands from their friends. What are the labels and what are the ways?

2. What are the author's complaints about children?

3. What is the effect of using such words as *usufruct, monopoly,* and *patent*? From what field are they derived?

4. Give examples of connotative words used to describe women and children. How do these words reveal the author's attitudes?

5. What is the thesis of the essay? Why is it so surprising?

6. Show where Lamb uses conventional essay techniques such as classification, definition, and exemplification.

7. This essay is part of the series *Essays of Elia;* thus, Lamb does not speak in his own voice. What effect does this have upon your sense of the tone of the essay?

8. What techniques does Lamb use to criticize conventional attitudes toward marriage?

9. Do you think that marriage is overrated? Justify your answer.

10. Write a satiric essay on the supposed "evils" of friendship, motherhood, patriotism, or another, similar convention.

VLADIMIR NABOKOV

Philistines and Philistinism

Vladimir Nabokov (1899–1977) was born into an aristocratic family in czarist Russia. Following the Russian Revolution, he went into exile in England in 1919. In 1922, he graduated with honors from Cambridge University. Subsequently he lived in Germany and France, writing in Russian, giving tennis lessons, and collecting butterflies—all recounted in his poignant autobiography, *Speak Memory* (1966). He came to the United States in 1940. Nabokov taught at Wellesley College from 1944 to 1948, and at Cornell University from 1948 to 1958.

Nabokov, who once termed himself the greatest Russian novelist writing in English, gained enormous success with *Lolita* (1956). His later novels include *Pale Fire* (1962) and *Ada* (1969). He died in Montreux, Switzerland. With stylistic grace and satiric precision, Nabokov in the following essay defines both a state of mind and a social condition of our times.

A philistine is a full-grown person whose interests are of a material and commonplace nature, and whose mentality is formed of the stock ideas and conventional ideals of his or her group and time. I have said "full-grown person" because the child or the adolescent who may look like a small philistine is only a small parrot mimicking the ways of confirmed vulgarians, and it is easier to be a parrot than to be a white heron. "Vulgarian" is more or less synonymous with "philistine": the stress in a vulgarian is not so much on the conventionalism of a philistine as on the vulgarity of some of his conventional notions. I may also use the terms *genteel* and *bourgeois*. *Genteel* implies the lace-curtain refined vulgarity which is worse than simple coarseness. To burp in company may be rude, but to say "excuse me" after a burp is genteel and thus worse than vulgar. The term *bourgeois* I use following Flaubert, not Marx. *Bourgeois* in Flaubert's sense is a state of mind, not a state of pocket. A bourgeois is a smug philistine, a dignified vulgarian. 1

A philistine is not likely to exist in a very primitive society although no doubt rudiments of philistinism may be found even there. We may imagine, for instance, a cannibal who would prefer the human head he eats to be artistically colored, just as the American philistine prefers his oranges to be painted orange, his salmon pink, and his whisky yellow. But generally speaking philistinism presupposes a certain advanced state of civilization where throughout the ages certain traditions have accumulated in a heap and have started to stink. 2

Philistinism is international. It is found in all nations and in all classes. An English duke can be as much of a philistine as an American Shriner or a French bureaucrat or a Soviet citizen. The mentality of a Lenin or a Stalin or a Hitler in regard to the arts and the sciences was utterly bourgeois. A laborer or a coal miner can be just as bourgeois as a banker or a housewife or a Hollywood star. 3

Philistinism implies not only a collection of stock ideas but also the use of set phrases, clichés, banalities expressed in faded words. A true philistine has nothing but these trivial ideas of which he entirely consists. But it should be admitted that all of us have our cliché side; all of us in everyday life often use words not as words but as signs, as coins, as formulas. This does not mean that we are all philistines, but it does mean that we should be careful not to indulge 4 too much in the automatic process of exchanging platitudes. On a hot day every other person will ask you, "Is it warm enough for you?" but that does not necessarily mean that the speaker is a philistine. He may be merely a parrot or a bright foreigner. When a person asks you "Hullo, how *are* you?" it is perhaps a sorry cliché to reply, "Fine"; but if you made to him a detailed report of your condition you might pass for a pedant and a bore. It also happens that platitudes are used by people as a kind of disguise or as the shortest cut for avoiding conversation with fools. I have known great scholars and poets and scientists who in the cafeteria sank to the level of the most commonplace give and take.

5 The character I have in view when I say "smug vulgarian" is, thus, not the part-time philistine, but the total type, the genteel bourgeois, the complete universal product of triteness and mediocrity. He is the conformist, the man who conforms to his group, and he also is typified by something else: he is a pseudo-idealist, he is pseudo-compassionate, he is pseudo-wise. The fraud is the closest ally of the true philistine. All such great words as "Beauty," "Love," "Nature," "Truth," and so on become masks and dupes when the smug vulgarian employs them. In *Dead Souls* you have heard Chichikov. In *Bleak House* you have heard Skimpole. You have heard Homais in *Madame Bovary*. The philistine likes to impress and he likes to be impressed, in consequence of which a world of deception, of mutual cheating, is formed by him and around him.

6 The philistine in his passionate urge to conform, to belong, to join, is torn between two longings: to act as everybody does, to admire, to use this or that thing because millions of people do; or else he craves to belong to an exclusive set, to an organization, to a club, to a hotel patronage or an ocean liner community (with the captain in white and wonderful food), and to delight in the knowledge that there is the head of a corporation or a European count sitting next to him. The philistine is often a snob. He is thrilled by riches and rank—"Darling, I've actually talked to a duchess!"

7 A philistine neither knows nor cares anything about art, including literature—his essential nature is anti-artistic—but he wants information and he is trained to read magazines. He is a faithful reader of the *Saturday Evening Post*, and when he reads he identifies himself with the characters. If he is a male philistine he will identify himself with the fascinating executive or any other big shot—aloof, single, but a boy and a golfer at heart; or if the reader is a female philistine—a philistinette—she will identify herself with the fascinating strawberry-blonde secretary, a slip of a girl but a mother at heart, who eventually marries the boyish boss. The philistine does not distinguish one writer from another; indeed, he reads little and only what may be useful to him, but he may belong to a book club

and choose beautiful, *beautiful* books, a jumble of Simone de Beauvoir, Dostoevski, Marquand, Somerset Maugham, *Dr. Zhivago*, and Masters of the Renaissance. He does not much care for pictures, but for the sake of prestige he may hang in his parlor reproductions of Van Gogh's or Whistler's respective mothers, although secretly preferring Norman Rockwell.

In his love for the useful, for the material goods of life, he becomes an easy victim of the advertisement business. Ads may be very good ads—some of them are very artistic—that is not the point. The point is that they tend to appeal to the philistine's pride in possessing things whether silverware or underwear. I mean the following kind of ad: just come to the family is a radio set or a television set (or a car, or a refrigerator, or table silver—anything will do). It has just come to the family: mother clasps her hands in dazed delight, the children crowd around all agog: junior and the dog strain up to the edge of the table where the Idol is enthroned; even Grandma of the beaming wrinkles peeps out somewhere in the background; and somewhat apart, his thumbs gleefully inserted in the armpits of his waistcoat, stands triumphant Dad or Pop, the Proud Donor. Small boys and girls in ads are invariably freckled, and the smaller fry have front teeth missing. I have nothing against freckles (in fact I find them very becoming in live creatures) and quite possibly a special survey might reveal that the majority of small American-born Americans *are* freckled, or else perhaps another survey might reveal that all successful executives and handsome housewives had been freckled in their childhood. I repeat, I have really nothing against freckles as such. But I do think there is considerable philistinism involved in the use made of them by advertisers and other agencies. I am told that when an unfreckled, or only slightly freckled, little boy actor has to appear on the screen in television, an artificial set of freckles is applied to the middle of his face. Twenty-two freckles is the minimum: eight over each cheekbone and six on the saddle of the pert nose. In the comics, freckles look like a case of bad rash. In one series of comics they appear as tiny circles. But although the good cute little boys of the ads are blond or redhaired, with freckles, the handsome young men of the ads are generally dark haired and always have thick dark eyebrows. The evolution is from Scotch to Celtic. 8

The rich philistinism emanating from advertisements is due not to their exaggerating (or inventing) the glory of this or that serviceable article but to suggesting that the acme of human happiness is purchasable and that its purchase somehow ennobles the purchaser. Of course, the world they create is pretty harmless in itself because everybody knows that it is made up by the seller with the understanding that the buyer will join in the make-believe. The 9 amusing part is not that it is a world where nothing spiritual remains except the ecstatic smiles of people serving or eating celestial cereals, or a world where the game of the senses is played according to bourgeois rules, but that it is a kind of satellite shadow world in the actual existence of which neither sellers nor buyers really believe in their heart of hearts—especially in this wise quiet country.

10 Russians have, or had, a special name for smug philistinism —*poshlust. Poshlism* is not only the obviously trashy but mainly the falsely important, the falsely beautiful, the falsely clever, the falsely attractive. To apply the deadly label of *poshlism* to something is not only an esthetic judgment but also a moral indictment. The genuine, the guileless, the good is never *poshlust*. It is possible to maintain that a simple, uncivilized man is seldom if ever a *poshlust* since *poshlism* presupposes the veneer of civilization. A peasant has to become a townsman in order to become vulgar. A painted necktie has to hide the honest Adam's apple in order to produce *poshlism*.

11 It is possible that the term itself has been so nicely devised by Russians because of the cult of simplicity and good taste in old Russia. The Russia of today, a country of moral imbeciles, of smiling slaves and poker-faced bullies, has stopped noticing *poshlism* because Soviet Russia is so full of its special brand, a blend of despotism and pseudo-culture; but in the old days a Gogol, a Tolstoy, a Chekhov in quest of the simplicity of truth easily distinguished the vulgar side of things as well as the trashy systems of pseudo-thought. But *poshlists* are found everywhere, in every country, in this country as well as in Europe—in fact *poshlism* is more common in Europe than here, despite our American ads.

QUESTIONS

1. What, according to the author, is a philistine? Explain the representative characteristics of a philistine.

2. What does philistinism tell us about the state of society? Why is philistinism international? What does Nabokov say about the degree of philistinism in Europe and America?

3. Nabokov employs several synonyms for *philistine* and *philistinism*. List them and explain their shades of meaning.

4. Identify and explain the effectiveness of the various literary allusions in the essay.

5. Identify the topic sentence in each paragraph. Why are they so consistently placed? Relate their placement to the movement from general or abstract to specific and concrete in three representative paragraphs.

6. Does the author use actual examples or hypothetical examples in the essay? Explain.

7. How does Nabokov use definition? For what purpose does he employ it? What instances of comparison and contrast and causal analysis do you find?

8. What is the tone of the essay? What effect does that tone have on the way that Nabokov describes the philistine?

9. What is your opinion of Nabokov's assertion that philistinism is rampant in the modern world?

10. a. Write an extended definition of philistinism, using examples drawn from personal experience, reading, and the media.
b. Write an essay that uses definition to make a comic or satiric point about manners or social behavior.

JOSEPH ADDISON

A Superstitious Household

Joseph Addison (1672–1719) was an essayist, poet, dramatist, statesman, and journalist. As a playwright, he wrote one of the most successful tragedies of the eighteenth century (*Cato,* in 1713). As a statesman, he served as secretary of state under George I. As an essayist, he wrote with reason and wit in *The Tatler* (1709–1711) and *The Spectator* (1711–1712, and 1714). Just as he excelled as a statesman and tragedian, he excelled as an essayist; he is often considered one of the best English essayists. Here, Addison examines one of the great foibles of his age—and ours.

Somnia, terrores magicos, miracula, sagas,
*Nocturnos, lemures, portentaque Thessala rides?**
Horace

oing yesterday to dine with an old acquaintance, I had 1
the misfortune to find his whole family very much
dejected. Upon asking him the occasion of it, he told me
that his wife had dreamt a very strange dream the night

*"Can you make sport of portents, gipsy crones, Hobgoblins, dreams, raw head and bloody bones?"

John Conington (translator)

before, which they were afraid portended some misfortune to themselves or to their children. At her coming into the room, I observed a settled melancholy in her countenance, which I should have been troubled for, had I not heard from whence it proceeded. We were no sooner sat down, but, after having looked upon me a little while, "My dear," says she, turning to her husband, "you may now see the stranger that was in the candle last night." Soon after this, as they began to talk of family affairs, a little boy at the lower end of the table told her that he was to go into join-hand on Thursday. "Thursday?" says she, "no, child, if it please God, you shall not begin upon Childermas Day, tell your writing master that Friday will be soon enough." I was reflecting with myself on the oddness of her fancy, and wondering that anybody would establish it as a rule to lose a day in every week. In the midst of these my musings, she desired me to reach her a little salt upon the point of my knife, which I did in such a trepidation and hurry of obedience, that I let it drop by the way; at which she immediately startled, and said it fell towards her. Upon this I looked very blank; and, observing the concern of the whole table, began to consider myself, with some confusion, as a person that had brought a disaster upon the family. The lady however recovering herself, after a little space, said to her husband with a sigh, "My dear, misfortunes never come single." My friend, I found, acted but an under part at his table, and being a man of more good nature than understanding, thinks himself obliged to fall in with all the passions and humors of his yoke-fellow. "Do not you remember, child," says she, "that the pigeon-house fell the very afternoon that our careless wench spilt the salt upon the table?" "Yes," says he, "my dear, and the next post brought us an account of the battle of Almanza." The reader may guess at the figure I made, after having done all this mischief. I despatched my dinner as soon as I could, with my usual taciturnity; when, to my utter confusion, the lady seeing me cleaning my knife and fork, and laying them across one another upon my plate, desired me that I would humor her so far as to take them out of that figure, and place them side by side. What the absurdity was which I had committed I did not know, but I suppose there was some traditionary superstition in it; and therefore, in obedience to the lady of the house, I disposed of my knife and fork in two parallel lines, which is the figure I shall always lay them in for the future, though I do not know any reason for it.

It is not difficult for a man to see that a person has conceived 2
an aversion to him. For my own part, I quickly found, by the lady's looks, that she regarded me as a very odd kind of fellow, with an unfortunate aspect: for which reason I took my leave immediately after dinner, and withdrew to my own lodgings. Upon my return home, I fell into a profound contemplation on the evils that attend

these superstitious follies of mankind; how they subject us to imaginary afflictions, and additional sorrows, that do not properly come within our lot. As if the natural calamities of life were not sufficient for it, we turn the most indifferent circumstances into misfortunes, and suffer as much from trifling accidents as from real evils. I have known the shooting of a star spoil a night's rest; and have seen a man in love grow pale and lose his appetite upon the plucking of a merry-thought. A screech owl at midnight has alarmed a family more than a band of robbers; nay, the voice of a cricket hath struck more terror than the roaring of a lion. There is nothing so inconsiderable, which may not appear dreadful to an imagination that is filled with omens and prognostics. A rusty nail, or a crooked pin, shoot up into prodigies.

I remember I was once in a mixed assembly, that was full of 3
noise and mirth, when on a sudden an old woman unluckily observed there were thirteen of us in company. This remark struck a panic terror into several who were present, insomuch that one or two of the ladies were going to leave the room; but a friend of mine taking notice that one of our female companions was big with child, affirmed there were fourteen in the room, and that, instead of portending one of the company should die, it plainly foretold one of them should be born. Had not my friend found this expedient to break the omen, I question not but half the women in the company would have fallen sick that very night.

An old maid, that is troubled with the vapors, produces 4
infinite disturbances of this kind among her friends and neighbors. I know a maiden aunt of a great family, who is one of these antiquated Sibyls, that forebodes and prophesies from one end of the year to the other. She is always seeing apparitions, and hearing death-watches, and was the other day almost frightened out of her wits by the great house-dog, that howled in the stable at a time when she lay ill of the tooth-ache. Such an extravagant cast of mind engages multitudes of people not only in impertinent terrors, but in supernumerary duties of life; and arises from that fear and ignorance which are natural to the soul of man. The horror with which we entertain the thoughts of death (or indeed of any future evil) and the uncertainty of its approach, fill a melancholy mind with innumerable apprehensions and suspicions, and consequently dispose it to the observation of such groundless prodigies and predictions. For as it is the chief concern of wise men to retrench the evils of life by the reasonings of philosophy; it is the employment of fools to multiply them by the sentiments of superstition.

For my own part, I should be very much troubled were I 5
endowed with this divining quality, though it should inform me truly of every thing that can befall me. I would not anticipate the relish of

any happiness, nor feel the weight of any misery, before it actually arrives.

I know but one way of fortifying my soul against these gloomy presages and terrors of mind, and that is, by securing to myself the friendship and protection of that Being who disposes of events, and governs futurity. He sees, at one view, the whole thread of my existence, not only that part of it which I have already passed through, but that which runs forward into all the depths of eternity. When I lay me down to sleep, I recommend myself to his care; when I awake, I give myself up to his direction. Amidst all the evils that threaten me, I will look up to him for help, and question not but he will either avert them, or turn them to my advantage. Though I know neither the time nor the manner of the death I am to die, I am not at all solicitous about it; because I am sure that he knows them both, and that he will not fail to comfort and support me under them. 6

QUESTIONS

1. Compare the attitude of Addison toward superstition with the attitude of his acquaintance's wife. What is the difference between wise men and fools?

2. Even if he could foretell the future, Addison would choose not to. Why?

3. Who was the Sibyl? Why is the allusion to her in paragraph 4 appropriate? Why does Addison compare elderly, superstitious women to the Sybil?

4. Define these words: *join-hard* (paragraph 1); *Childermas* (paragraph 1); *merry-thought* (paragraph 2); *death-watches* (paragraph 4).

5. How are superstitions examples of the logical fallacy *post hoc ergo propter hoc* in this essay?

6. Detail shifts of tone in the essay. What function does the difference serve?

7. Contrast Addison's ignorance or knowledge of superstitions in paragraphs 1 and 2 with that in the rest of the essay.

8. What assumptions about reason and superstition underly this essay?

9. What superstitions described in the essay are still prevalent today? Why do you think superstitions remain popular?

10. Write an argumentative essay on the value of superstition. Write it from the first-person point of view and cite examples.

A Treatise on Good Manners and Good Breeding

Jonathan Swift (1667–1745) is best known as the author of three satires: *A Tale of a Tub* (1704), *Gulliver's Travels* (1726), and *A Modest Proposal* (1729). In these satires, he pricks the balloons of many of his contemporaries and our own most cherished prejudices, pomposities, and delusions. Swift was also a famous churchman, an eloquent spokesman for Irish rights, and a political journalist. In this essay, he examines the uses and abuses of "good manners."

ood manners is the art of making those people easy with whom we converse. 1

Whoever makes the fewest persons uneasy is the best bred in the company. 2

As the best law is founded upon reason, so are the best manners. And as some lawyers have introduced unreasonable things into common law, so likewise many teachers have introduced absurd things into common good manners. 3

One principal point of this art is to suit our behaviour to the three several degrees of men; our superiors, our equals, and those below us. 4

For instance, to press either of the two former to eat or drink is a breach of manners; but a farmer or a tradesman must be thus treated, or else it will be difficult to persuade them that they are welcome. 5

Pride, ill nature, and want of sense, are the three great sources of ill manners; without some one of these defects, no man will behave himself ill for want of experience; or of what, in the language of fools, is called knowing the world. 6

I defy any one to assign an incident wherein reason will not direct us what we are to say or do in company, if we are not misled by pride or ill nature. 7

Therefore I insist that good sense is the principal foundation of good manners; but because the former is a gift which very few among mankind are possessed of, therefore all the civilized nations of the world have agreed upon fixing some rules for common behaviour, best suited to their general customs, or fancies, as a kind of artificial good sense, to supply the defects of reason. Without which the gentlemanly part of dunces would be perpetually at cuffs, as they seldom fail when they happen to be drunk, or engaged in squabbles about women or play. And, God be thanked, there hardly happens a duel in a year, which may not be imputed to one of those three 8 motives. Upon which account, I should be exceedingly sorry to find the legislature make any new laws against the practice of duelling; because the methods are easy and many for a wise man to avoid a quarrel with honour, or engage in it with innocence. And I can discover no political evil in suffering bullies, sharpers, and rakes, to rid the world of each other by a method of their own; where the law hath not been able to find an expedient.

As the common forms of good manners were intended for regulating the conduct of those who have weak understandings; so they have been corrupted by the persons for whose use they were contrived. For these people have fallen into a needless and endless way of multiplying ceremonies, which have been extremely troublesome to those who practise them, and insupportable to everybody else: insomuch that wise men are often more uneasy at the over civility of these refiners, than they could possibly be in the conversations of peasants or mechanics. 9

The impertinencies of this ceremonial behaviour are nowhere better seen than at those tables where ladies preside, who value themselves upon account of their good breeding; where a man must reckon upon passing an hour without doing any one thing he has a mind to; unless he will be so hardy to break through all the settled decorum of the family. She determines what he loves best, and how much he shall eat; and if the master of the house happens to be of the same disposition, he proceeds in the same tyrannical manner to prescribe in the drinking part: at the same time, you are under the necessity of answering a thousand apologies for your entertainment. And although a good deal of this humour is pretty well worn off among many people of the best fashion, yet too much of it still remains, especially in the country; where an honest gentleman assured me, that having been kept four days, against his will, at a friend's house, with all the circumstances of hiding his boots, locking up the stable, and other contrivances of the like nature, he could not remember, from the moment he came into the house to the moment he left it, any one thing, wherein his inclination was not directly contradicted; as if the whole family had entered into a combination to torment him. 10

But, besides all this, it would be endless to recount the many foolish and ridiculous accidents I have observed among these unfortunate proselytes to ceremony. I have seen a duchess fairly knocked down, by the precipitancy of an officious coxcomb running to save her the trouble of opening a door. I remember, upon a birthday at court, a great lady was utterly desperate by a dish of sauce let fall by a page directly upon her head-dress and brocade, while she gave a sudden turn to her elbow upon some point of ceremony with the person who sat next her. Monsieur Buys, the Dutch envoy, whose 11 politics and manners were much of a size, brought a son with him, about thirteen years old, to a great table at court. The boy and his father, whatever they put on their plates, they first offered round in order, to every person in the company; so that we could not get a minute's quiet during the whole dinner. At last their two plates happened to encounter, and with so much violence, that, being china, they broke in twenty pieces, and stained half the company with wet sweetmeats and cream.

There is a pedantry in manners, as in all arts and sciences; 12
and sometimes in trades. Pedantry is properly the overrating any kind of knowledge we pretend to. And if that kind of knowledge be a trifle in itself, the pedantry is the greater. For which reason I look upon fiddlers, dancing-masters, heralds, masters of the ceremony, &c. to be greater pedants than Lipsius, or the elder Scaliger. With these kind of pedants, the court, while I knew it, was always plentifully stocked; I mean from the gentleman usher (at least) inclusive, downward to the gentleman porter; who are, generally speaking, the most insignificant race of people that this island can afford, and with the smallest tincture of good manners, which is the only trade they profess. For being wholly illiterate, and conversing chiefly with each other, they reduce the whole system of breeding within the forms and circles of their several offices; and as they are below the notice of ministers, they live and die in court under all revolutions with great obsequiousness to those who are in any degree of favour or credit, and with rudeness or insolence to everybody else. Whence I have long concluded, that good manners are not a plant of the court growth: for if they were, those people who have understandings directly of a level for such acquirements, and who have served such long apprenticeships to nothing else, would certainly have picked them up. For as to the great officers, who attend the prince's person or councils, or preside in his family, they are a transient body, who have no better a title to good manners than their neighbours, nor will probably have recourse to gentlemen ushers for instruction. So that I know little to be learnt at court upon this head, except in the material circumstance of dress; wherein the authority of the maids of honour must indeed be allowed to be almost equal to that of a favourite actress.

I remember a passage my Lord Bolingbroke told me, that 13
going to receive Prince Eugene of Savoy at his landing, in order to conduct him immediately to the Queen, the prince said, he was much concerned that he could not see her Majesty that night; for Monsieur Hoffman (who was then by) had assured his Highness that he could not be admitted into her presence with a tied-up periwig; that his equipage was not arrived; and that he had endeavoured in vain to borrow a long one among all his valets and pages. My lord turned the

matter into a jest, and brought the Prince to her Majesty; for which he was highly censured by the whole tribe of gentlemen ushers; among whom Monsieur Hoffman, an old dull resident of the Emperor's, had picked up this material point of ceremony; and which, I believe, was the best lesson he had learned in five-and-twenty years' residence.

I make a difference between good manners and good breeding; although, in order to vary my expression, I am sometimes forced to confound them. By the first, I only understand the art of remembering and applying certain settled forms of general behaviour. But good breeding is of a much larger extent; for besides an uncommon degree of literature sufficient to qualify a gentleman for reading a play, or a political pamphlet, it takes in a great compass of knowledge; no less than that of dancing, fighting, gaming, making the circle of Italy, riding the great horse, and speaking French; not to mention some other secondary, or subaltern accomplishments, which are more easily acquired. So that the difference between good breeding and good manners lies in this, that the former cannot be attained to by the best understandings, without study and labour; whereas a tolerable degree of reason will instruct us in every part of good manners, without other assistance. 14

I can think of nothing more useful upon this subject, than to point out some particulars, wherein the very essentials of good manners are concerned, the neglect or perverting of which doth very much disturb the good commerce of the world, by introducing a traffic of mutual uneasiness in most companies. 15

First, a necessary part of good manners, is a punctual observance of time at our own dwellings, or those of others, or at third places; whether upon matter of civility, business, or diversion; which rule, though it be a plain dictate of common reason, yet the greatest minister I ever knew was the greatest trespasser against it; by which all his business doubled upon him, and placed him in a continual arrear. Upon which I often used to rally him, as deficient in point of good manners. I have known more than one ambassador, and secretary of state with a very moderate portion of intellectuals, execute their offices with good success and applause, by the mere force of exactness and regularity. If you duly observe time for the service of another, it doubles the obligation; if upon your own account, it would be manifest folly, as well as ingratitude, to neglect it. If both are concerned, to make your equal or inferior attend on you, to his own disadvantage, is pride and injustice. 16

Ignorance of forms cannot properly be styled ill manners; because forms are subject to frequent changes; and consequently, being not founded upon reason, are beneath a wise man's regard. Besides, they vary in every country; and after a short period of time, very frequently in the same; so that a man who travels, must needs be 17 at first a stranger to them in every court through which he passes; and perhaps at his return, as much a stranger in his own; and after all, they are easier to be remembered or forgotten than faces or names.

Indeed, among the many impertinencies that superficial young men bring with them from abroad, this bigotry of forms is one of the principal, and more prominent than the rest; who look upon them not only as if they were matters capable of admitting of choice, but even as points of importance; and are therefore zealous on all occasions to introduce and propagate the new forms and fashions they have brought back with them. So that, usually speaking, the worst bred person in the company is a young traveller just returned from abroad. 18

QUESTIONS

1. What does Swift say are the differences between good manners and ceremony?

2. According to Swift, what are artificial manners? Why have they developed? What examples of ceremonious manners does Swift offer?

3. Why are the allusions to Lipsius and Scaliger appropriate in paragraph 12?

4. In paragraph 12, Swift defines pedantry. Give examples of his use of hyperbole and connotative language in this paragraph.

5. How does Swift define a gentleman? Give examples from the essay.

6. Analyze Swift's use of comparison to support his thesis.

7. Explain how the anecdote concerning Lord Bolingbroke in paragraph 13 illustrates the general statements in paragraph 12. What other examples of anecdotes supporting assertions are there in the essay?

8. How does the digression in paragraph 8 reveal Swift's attitude toward aristocracy? Is there any contrary evidence in the essay? If so, where?

9. Would we be better off without manners? Have you ever been made uncomfortable by manners? Explain.

10. Write an essay exploring the absurdities of modern manners.

4 Education

ELLEN GOODMAN

Bamama Goes to College

Ellen Holtz Goodman (1941–) is an award-winning journalist who writes a syndicated column for *The Boston Globe.* She is the author of *Close to Home* (1979) and has been a commentator on television and radio. Goodman is an adept practitioner of the personal essay. In "Bamama Goes to College," she takes a jaundiced look at higher education.

Boston—My friend received another degree this month. She became a B.A., M.A., M.A., or as we fondly call her, a Bamama. 1

This latest degree raised her academic temperature and the quality of her resume. In fact, my friend Bamama officially became qualified to be unemployed in yet a better class of jobs. 2

Let me explain. When she got a B.A. in philosophy four years ago at the cost of $12,000 (them was the bargain basement days), Bamama had the choice between becoming an overeducated waitress 3 or an overeducated office worker. So she became an overeducated day-camp counselor and went back to school.

The next year, for $4,000, she got a degree in library science. Now, qualified as a librarian, she won a job as an overeducated part-time library assistant. In her off-hours, she became an overqualified clerk at a cheese counter. Rumors that she arranged the cheddar according to the Dewey Decimal system were greatly exaggerated. 4

In any case, her course was clear. Before she entirely coated her brain as well as her arteries with brie, she went back to school. Now, $5,000 later, she is qualified not only as a librarian, but as a school librarian, teacher, administrator, etc., for a school system in need of an efficient, caring, well-educated Bamama. No such luck or, rather, no such system. 5

So, Bamama has done the only logical thing: applied for and been accepted for a Ph.D. program. With that degree, Bamamaphd, three years older and deeper in debt, would be qualified as a college professor and might therefore be able to find a job as an overqualified school librarian. 6

She had, you see, followed the life pattern of Woody Allen, who says that success has meant that he is now turned down for dates by a better class of women. Bamama may be particularly adroit at choosing a career track on which 90 percent of the stations have been closed. But the problem is not uniquely hers. 7

There are more than one million Americans getting bachelor's degrees this year, more than 300,000 getting master's degrees and more than 32,000 getting doctorates. 8

They and/or their parents are up to their ears in debt. The economy is up to its ears in the overeducated underemployed. 9

Eighty percent of the recent college graduates, we are told, are doing work which was once done quite capably by people without college degrees. The point is that you don't need the degree to do the job. But nowadays you do need the degree to get the job. 10

College graduates may be getting the jobs once filled by nongraduates, but they are not automatically filling the spots once guaranteed by a degree. There is more educational competition at every level. In fact, by 1985, 2.5 college graduates will be competing for every "college" job. 11

This is the name of the 1980s war game called Defensive Education. As economist Lester Thurow put it: "As the supply of more highly educated labor increases, individuals find that they must improve their own education qualification simply to defend their current income position. If they do not go to college, others will and they will not find their current job open to them." 12

This is described as the "tiptoe syndrome" in Michael Harrington's Book, "Decade of Decision." At any parade, the people 13 in the second row stand on tiptoe to see over the heads of those in the front row. Then everyone else behind them stands on tiptoe, just to stay in the same position.

As more and more people go to college, a degree no longer guarantees who will get ahead. But the lack of a degree still can determine who will fall behind. We keep raising the education threshold to the job market. 14

This is the sort of new truth that makes us feel trapped and cynical and furious. Trapped into paying a fortune, not for advance but for defense. Cynical about the real motivation for "Higher Education." 15

Meanwhile, even as we play the game, the gap between our educational level and job level grows and is filled with the discontent of the "underemployed." 16

Remember the movie "Goodbye Columbus"? There was a moment when the father who owns a trucking business shakes his head watching his son work. Finally he sighs, "Four years of college, and he can't load a truck." 17

Just a few years ago, that was funny. But at the current rate of the education escalation war, the kid won't even be able to get a tryout without a Ph.D. 18

QUESTIONS

1. According to Goodman, how much does it cost to become a Bamama?

2. What does Goodman mean by "Defensive Education"?

3. What is the effect of using the acronym Bamama in the title and in identifying Goodman's friend?

4. Goodman uses two terms to describe modern higher education. Define "tiptoe syndrome" and "education escalation war."

5. What is the effect of repetition in the essay?

6. What different rhetorical strategies are used in paragraph groups 1 to 7, 8 to 11, 12 to 16, and 17 to 18?

7. How does Goodman use humor to forward her argument?

8. In this argumentative essay, what kinds of evidence are given? Why?

9. A second kind of education is alluded to in the essay: practical education. How valuable do you believe education through experience is to your career goals?

10. Statistics are crucial to this essay. Write an argumentative essay that combines anecdote and statistical information, and that addresses the proposition, "College is a waste of time and money."

E. B. WHITE

Education

Elwyn Brooks White (1899–), perhaps the finest contemporary American essayist, is at his most distinctive in his treatments of people, nature, and social conventions. A recipient of the National Medal for literature, and associated for years with *The New Yorker*, White is the author of *One Man's Meat* (1942), *Here Is New York* (1949), and *The Second Tree from the Corner* (1954), among numerous works. He is also one of the most talented writers of literature for children, the author of *Stuart Little* (1945), *Charlotte's Web* (1952), and *The Trumpet of the Swan* (1970). Most writers and lovers of language have read and reread his witty, cogent explanation of English grammar in *The Elements of Style* (1959). In the following essay, White reveals his abiding love for the country experience as he muses on the comparative values of urban and rural, private and public education.

1 I have an increasing admiration for the teacher in the country school where we have a third-grade scholar in attendance. She not only undertakes to instruct her charges in all the subjects of the first three grades, but she manages to function quietly and effectively as a guardian of their health, their clothes, their habits, their mothers, and their snowball engagements. She has been doing this sort of Augean task for twenty years, and is both kind and wise. She cooks for the children on the stove that heats the room, and she can cool their passions or warm their soup with equal competence. She conceives their costumes, cleans up their messes, and shares their confidences. My boy already regards his teacher as his great friend, and I think tells her a great deal more than he tells us.

2 The shift from city school to country school was something we worried about quietly all last summer. I have always rather favored public school over private school, if only because in public

school you meet a greater variety of children. This bias of mine, I suspect, is partly an attempt to justify my own past (I never knew anything but public schools) and partly an involuntary defense against getting kicked in the shins by a young ceramist on his way to the kiln. My wife was unacquainted with public schools, never having been exposed (in her early life) to anything more public than the washroom of Miss Winsor's. Regardless of our backgrounds, we both knew that change in schools was something that concerned not us but the scholar himself. We hoped it would work out all right. In New York our son went to a medium-priced private institution with semi-progressive ideas of education, and modern plumbing. He learned fast, kept well, and we were satisfied. It was an electric, colorful, regimented existence with moments of pleasurable pause and giddy incident. The day the Christmas angel fainted and had to be carried out by one of the Wise Men was educational in the highest sense of the term. Our scholar gave imitations of it around the house for weeks afterward, and I doubt if it ever goes completely out of his mind.

His days were rich in formal experience. Wearing overalls and 3
an old sweater (the accepted uniform of the private seminary), he sallied forth at morn accompanied by a nurse or a parent and walked (or was pulled) two blocks to a corner where the school bus made a flag stop. This flashy vehicle was as punctual as death: seeing us waiting at the cold curb, it would sweep to a halt, open its mouth, suck the boy in, and spring away with an angry growl. It was a good deal like a train picking up a bag of mail. At school the scholar was worked on for six or seven hours by half a dozen teachers and a nurse, and was revived on orange juice in mid-morning. In a cinder court he played games supervised by an athletic instructor, and in a cafeteria he ate lunch worked out by a dietitian. He soon learned to read with gratifying facility and discernment and to make Indian weapons of a semi-deadly nature. Whenever one of his classmates fell low of a fever the news was put on the wires and there were breathless phone calls to physicians, discussing periods of incubation and allied magic.

In the country all one can say is that the situation is different, 4
and somehow more casual. Dressed in corduroys, sweatshirt, and short rubber boots, and carrying a tin dinner-pail, our scholar departs at crack of dawn for the village school, two and a half miles down the road, next to the cemetery. When the road is open and the car will start, he makes the journey by motor, courtesy of his old man. When the snow is deep or the motor is dead or both, he makes it on the hoof. In the afternoons he walks or hitches all or part of the way home in fair weather, gets transported in foul. The schoolhouse is a two-room frame building, bungalow type, shingles stained a burnt

brown with weather-resistant stain. It has a chemical toilet in the basement and two teachers above stairs. One takes the first three grades, the other the fourth, fifth, and sixth. They have little or no time for individual instruction, and no time at all for the esoteric. They teach what they know themselves, just as fast and as hard as they can manage. The pupils sit still at their desks in class, and do their milling around outdoors during recess.

5 There is no supervised play. They play cops and robbers (only they call it "Jail") and throw things at one another—snowballs in winter, rose hips in fall. It seems to satisfy them. They also construct darts, pinwheels, and "pick-up sticks" (jackstraws), and the school itself does a brisk trade in penny candy, which is for sale right in the classroom and which contains "surprises." The most highly prized surprise is a fake cigarette, made of cardboard, fiendishly lifelike.

6 The memory of how apprehensive we were at the beginning is still strong. The boy was nervous about the change too. The tension, on that first fair morning in September when we drove him to school, almost blew the windows out of the sedan. And when later we picked him up on the road, wandering along with his little blue lunch-pail, and got his laconic report "All right" in answer to our inquiry about how the day had gone, our relief was vast. Now, after almost a year of it, the only difference we can discover in the two school experiences is that in the country he sleeps better at night—and *that* probably is more the air than the education. When grilled on the subject of school-in-country vs. school-in-city, he replied that the chief difference is that the day seems to go so much quicker in the country. "Just like lightning," he reported.

QUESTIONS

1. Why were the Whites "quietly" worried about the shift from private to public school? What were the two schools like? Which school does the author prefer? How do you know?

2. Explain the connections between the city and private schools and the country and public schools.

3. White refers to his son as the "scholar" several times in this essay. What are the purpose and effect of this strategy?

4. What is the significance of the word "Education" as used in the title? Is this significance a matter of connotation or denotation? Explain.

5. What is White's thesis? Is it ever explicitly stated? Why, or why not?

6. What standard means of exposition does the author employ in the introduction? Why is the introductory paragraph especially effective?

7. How does the author develop his pattern of comparison and contrast in this essay? What major and minor points in the contrast does he develop?

8. How are the rhetorical strategies of narration, description, and argumentation reflected in this essay?

9. Debate this proposition: Rural schools cannot provide the educational advantages of urban private schools.

10. a. Write a comparative essay on the type of school that you prefer—public or private.
b. Compare and contrast the relative advantages and disadvantages of urban and rural (or if you wish, suburban) education.

MAYA ANGELOU

Graduation

Maya Angelou (1928–) is an American poet, playwright, television screen writer, actress, and singer. Her autobiographical books, notably *I Know Why the Caged Bird Sings* (1970), from which the following selection is taken, provide one of the fullest accounts of the black female experience in contemporary literature. Fluent in six languages and active in artistic, educational, and political affairs, Angelou often presents autobiographical material against the backdrop of larger cultural concerns. In this vivid reminiscence of her 1940 graduation from grade school in Stamps, Arkansas, she provides insights into a community of young scholars who gain inspiration and wisdom from that "ancient tragedy" they are subjected to during commencement ceremonies.

1 The children in Stamps trembled visibly with anticipation. Some adults were excited too, but to be certain the whole young population had come down with graduation epidemic. Large classes were graduating from both the grammar school and the high school. Even those who were years removed from their own day of glorious release were anxious to help

with preparations as a kind of dry run. The junior students who were moving into the vacating classes' chairs were tradition-bound to show their talents for leadership and management. They strutted through the school and around the campus exerting pressure on the lower grades. Their authority was so new that occasionally if they pressed a little too hard it had to be overlooked. After all, next term was coming, and it never hurt a sixth grader to have a play sister in the eighth grade, or a tenth-year student to be able to call a twelfth grader Bubba. So all was endured in a spirit of shared understanding. But the graduating classes themselves were the nobility. Like travelers with exotic destinations on their minds, the graduates were remarkably forgetful. They came to school without their books, or tablets or even pencils. Volunteers fell over themselves to secure replacements for the missing equipment. When accepted, the willing workers might or might not be thanked, and it was of no importance to the pre-graduation rites. Even teachers were respectful of the now quiet and aging seniors, and tended to speak to them, if not as equals, as beings only slightly lower than themselves. After tests were returned and grades given, the student body, which acted like an extended family, knew who did well, who excelled, and what piteous ones had failed.

Unlike the white high school, Lafayette County Training 2
School distinguished itself by having neither lawn, nor hedges, nor tennis court, nor climbing ivy. Its two buildings (main classrooms, the grade school and home economics) were set on a dirt hill with no fence to limit either its boundaries or those of bordering farms. There was a large expanse to the left of the school which was used alternately as a baseball diamond or a basketball court. Rusty hoops on the swaying poles represented the permanent recreational equipment, although bats and balls could be borrowed from the P.E. teacher if the borrower was qualified and if the diamond wasn't occupied.

Over this rocky area relieved by a few shady tall persimmon 3
trees the graduating class walked. The girls often held hands and no longer bothered to speak to the lower students. There was a sadness about them, as if this old world was not their home and they were bound for higher ground. The boys, on the other hand, had become more friendly, more outgoing. A decided change from the closed attitude they projected while studying for finals. Now they seemed not ready to give up the old school, the familiar paths and classrooms. Only a small percentage would be continuing on to college—one of the South's A & M (agricultural and mechanical) schools, which trained Negro youths to be carpenters, farmers, handymen, masons, maids, cooks and baby nurses. Their future rode heavily on

their shoulders, and blinded them to the collective joy that had pervaded the lives of the boys and girls in the grammar school graduating class.

Parents who could afford it had ordered new shoes and ready-made clothes for themselves from Sears and Roebuck or Montgomery Ward. They also engaged the best seamstresses to make the floating graduating dresses and to cut down secondhand pants which would be pressed to a military slickness for the important event. 4

Oh, it was important, all right. Whitefolks would attend the ceremony, and two or three would speak of God and home, and the Southern way of life, and Mrs. Parsons, the principal's wife, would play the graduation march while the lower-grade graduates paraded down the aisles and took their seats below the platform. The high school seniors would wait in empty classrooms to make their dramatic entrance. 5

In the Store I was the person of the moment. The birthday girl. The center. Bailey had graduated the year before, although to do so he had had to forfeit all pleasures to make up for his time lost in Baton Rouge. 6

My class was wearing butter-yellow piqué dresses, and Momma launched out on mine. She smocked the yoke into tiny crisscrossing puckers, then shirred the rest of the bodice. Her dark fingers ducked in and out of the lemony cloth as she embroidered raised daisies around the hem. Before she considered herself finished she had added a crocheted cuff on the puff sleeves, and a pointy crocheted collar. 7

I was going to be lovely. A walking model of all the various styles of fine hand sewing and it didn't worry me that I was only twelve years old and merely graduating from the eighth grade. Besides, many teachers in Arkansas Negro schools had only that diploma and were licensed to impart wisdom. 8

The days had become longer and more noticeable. The faded beige of former times had been replaced with strong and sure colors. I began to see my classmate's clothes, their skin tones, and the dust that waved off pussy willows. Clouds that lazed across the sky were objects of great concern to me. Their shiftier shapes might have held a message that in my new happiness and with a little bit of time I'd soon decipher. During that period I looked at the arch of heaven so religiously my neck kept a steady ache. I had taken to smiling more often, and my jaws hurt from the unaccustomed activity. Between the two physical sore spots, I suppose I could have been uncomfortable, but that was not the case. As a member of the winning team (the graduating class of 1940) I had outdistanced unpleasant sensations by miles. I was headed for the freedom of open fields. 9

10 Youth and social approval allied themselves with me and we trammeled memories of slights and insults. The wind of our swift passage remodeled my features. Lost tears were pounded to mud and then to dust. Years of withdrawal were brushed aside and left behind, as hanging ropes of parasitic moss.

11 My work alone had awarded me a top place and I was going to be one of the first called in the graduating ceremonies. On the classroom blackboard, as well as on the bulletin board in the auditorium, there were blue stars and white stars and red stars. No absences, no tardiness, and my academic work was among the best of the year. I could say the preamble to the Constitution even faster than Baily. We timed ourselves often: "WethepeopleoftheUnitedStatesinordertoformamoreperfectunion . . ." I had memorized the Presidents of the United States from Washington to Roosevelt in chronological as well as alphabetical order.

12 My hair pleased me too. Gradually the black mass had lengthened and thickened, so that it kept at last to its braided pattern, and I didn't have to yank my scalp off when I tried to comb it.

13 Louise and I had rehearsed the exercises until we tired out ourselves. Henry Reed was class valedictorian. He was a small, very black boy with hooded eyes, a long, broad nose and an oddly shaped head. I had admired him for years because each term he and I vied for the best grades in our class. Most often he bested me, but instead of being disappointed, I was pleased that we shared top places between us. Like many Southern black children, he lived with his grandmother, who was as strict as Momma and as kind as she knew how to be. He was courteous, respectful and softspoken to elders, but on the playground he chose to play the roughest games. I admired him. Anyone, I reckoned, sufficiently afraid or sufficiently dull could be polite. But to be able to operate at a top level with both adults and children was admirable.

14 His valedictory speech was entitled "To Be or Not to Be." The rigid tenth-grade teacher had helped him write it. He'd been working on the dramatic stresses for months.

15 The weeks until graduation were filled with heady activities. A group of small children were to be presented in a play about buttercups and daisies and bunny rabbits. They could be heard throughout the building practicing their hops and their little songs that sounded like silver bells. The older girls (non-graduates, of course) were assigned the task of making refreshments for the night's festivities. A tangy scent of ginger, cinnamon, nutmeg and chocolate wafted around the home economics building as the budding cooks made samples for themselves and their teachers.

16 In every corner of the workshop, axes and saws split fresh timber as the woodshop boys made sets and stage scenery. Only the

graduates were left out of the general bustle. We were free to sit in the library at the back of the building or look in quite detachedly, naturally, on the measures being taken for our event.

Even the minister preached on graduation the Sunday before. His subject was, "Let your light so shine that men will see your good works and praise your Father, Who is in Heaven." Although the sermon was purported to be addressed to us, he used the occasion to speak to backsliders, gamblers and general ne'er-do-wells. But since he had called our names at the beginning of the service we were mollified. 17

Among Negroes the tradition was to give presents to children going only from one grade to another. How much more important this was when the person was graduating at the top of the class. Uncle Willie and Momma had sent away for a Mickey Mouse watch like Bailey's. Louise gave me four embroidered handkerchiefs. (I gave her three crocheted doilies.) Mrs. Sneed, the minister's wife, made me an underskirt to wear for graduation, and nearly every customer gave me a nickel or maybe even a dime with the instruction "Keep on moving to higher ground," or some such encouragement. 18

Amazingly the great day finally dawned and I was out of bed before I knew it. I threw open the back door to see it more clearly, but Momma said, "Sister, come away from that door and put your robe on." 19

I hoped the memory of that morning would never leave me. Sunlight was itself still young, and the day had none of the insistence maturity would bring it in a few hours. In my robe and barefoot in the backyard, under cover of going to see about my new beans, I gave myself up to the gentle warmth and thanked God that no matter what evil I had done in my life He had allowed me to live to see this day. Somewhere in my fatalism I had expected to die, accidentally, and never have the chance to walk up the stairs in the auditorium and gracefully receive my hard-earned diploma. Out of God's merciful bosom I had won reprieve. 20

Bailey came out in his robe and gave me a box wrapped in Christmas paper. He said he had saved his money for months to pay for it. It felt like a box of chocolates, but I knew Bailey wouldn't save money to buy candy when we had all we could want under our noses. 21

He was as proud of the gift as I. It was a soft-leather-bound copy of a collection of poems by Edgar Allan Poe, or, as Bailey and I called him, "Eap." I turned to "Annabel Lee" and we walked up and down the garden rows, the cool dirt between our toes, reciting the beautifully sad lines. 22

Momma made a Sunday breakfast although it was only Friday. After we finished the blessing, I opened my eyes to find the watch on my plate. It was a dream of a day. Everything went 23 smoothly and to my credit. I didn't have to be reminded or scolded for anything. Near evening I was too jittery to attend to chores, so Bailey volunteered to do all before his bath.

24 Days before, we had made a sign for the Store, and as we turned out the lights Momma hung the cardboard over the doorknob. It read clearly: CLOSED. GRADUATION.

25 My dress fitted perfectly and everyone said that I looked like a sunbeam in it. On the hill, going toward the school, Bailey walked behind with Uncle Willie, who muttered, "Go on, Ju." He wanted him to walk ahead with us because it embarrassed him to have to walk so slowly. Bailey said he'd let the ladies walk together, and the men would bring up the rear. We all laughed, nicely.

26 Little children dashed by out of the dark like fireflies. Their crepe-paper dresses and butterfly wings were not made for running and we heard more than one rip, dryly, and the regretful "uh uh" that followed.

27 The school blazed without gaiety. The windows seemed cold and unfriendly from the lower hill. A sense of ill-fated timing crept over me, and if Momma hadn't reached for my hand I would have drifted back to Bailey and Uncle Willie, and possibly beyond. She made a few slow jokes about my feet getting cold, and tugged me along to the now-strange building.

28 Around the front steps, assurance came back. There were my fellow "greats," the graduating class. Hair brushed back, legs oiled, new dresses and pressed pleats, fresh pocket handkerchiefs and little handbags, all homesewn. Oh, we were up to snuff, all right. I joined my comrades and didn't even see my family go in to find seats in the crowded auditorium.

29 The school band struck up a march and all classes filed in as had been rehearsed. We stood in front of our seats, as assigned, and on a signal from the choir director, we sat. No sooner had this been accomplished than the band started to play the national anthem. We rose again and sang the song, after which we recited the pledge of allegiance. We remained standing for a brief minute before the choir director and the principal signaled to us, rather desperately I thought, to take our seats. The command was so unusual that our carefully rehearsed and smooth-running machine was thrown off. For a full minute we fumbled for our chairs and bumped into each other awkwardly. Habits change or solidify under pressure, so in our state of nervous tension we had been ready to follow our usual assembly pattern: the American national anthem, then the pledge of allegiance, then the song every Black person I knew called the Negro National Anthem. All done in the same key, with the same passion and most often standing on the same foot.

30 Finding my seat at last, I was overcome with a presentiment

of worse things to come. Something unrehearsed, unplanned, was going to happen, an we were going to be made to look bad. I distinctly remember being explicit in the choice of pronoun. It was "we," the graduating class, the unit, that concerned me then.

The principal welcomed "parents and friends" and asked the Baptist minister to lead us in prayer. His invocation was brief and punchy, and for a second I thought we were getting back on the high road to right action. When the principal came back to the dais, however, his voice had changed. Sounds always affected me profoundly and the principal's voice was one of my favorites. During assembly it melted and lowed weakly into the audience. It has not been in my plan to listen to him, but my curiosity was piqued and I straightened up to give him my attention. 31

He was talking about Booker T. Washington, our "late great leader," who said we can be as close as the fingers on the hand, etc. . . . Then he said a few vague things about friendship and the friendship of kindly people to those less fortunate than themselves. With that his voice nearly faded, thin, away. Like a river diminishing to a stream and then to a trickle. But he cleared his throat and said, "Our speaker tonight, who is also our friend, came from Texarkana to deliver the commencement address, but due to the irregularity of the train scheule, he's going to, as they say, 'speak and run.' " He said that we understood and wanted the man to know that we were most grateful for the time he was able to give us and then something about how we were willing always to adjust to another's program, and without more ado—"I give you Mr. Edward Donleavy." 32

Not one but two white men came through the door offstage. The shorter one walked to the speaker's platform, and the tall one moved over to the center seat and sat down. But that was our principal's seat, and already occupied. The dislodged gentleman bounced around for a long breath or two before the Baptist minister gave him his chair, then with more dignity than the situation deserved, the minister walked off the stage. 33

Donleavy looked at the audience once (on reflection, I'm sure that he wanted only to reassure himself that we were really there), adjusted his glasses and began to read from a sheaf of papers. 34

He was glad "to be here and to see the work going on just as it was in the other schools." 35

At the first "Amen" from the audience I willed the offender to immediate death by choking on the word. But Amens and Yes, sir's began to fall around the room like rain through a ragged umbrella. 36

He told us of the wonderful changes we children in Stamps had in store. The Central School (naturally, the white school was Central) had already been granted improvements that would be in 37

use in the fall. A well-known artist was coming from Little Rock to teach art to them. They were going to have the newest microscopes and chemistry equipment for their labortory. Mr. Donleavy didn't leave us long in the dark over who made these improvements available to Central High. Nor were we to be ignored in the general betterment scheme he had in mind.

He said that he had pointed out to people at a very high level that one of the first-line football tacklers at Arkansas Agricultural and Mechanical College had graduated from good old Lafayette County Training School. Here fewer Amen's were heard. Those few that did break through lay dully in the air with the heaviness of habit. 38

He went on to praise us. He went on to say how he had bragged that "one of the best basketball players at Fisk sank his first ball right here at Lafayette County Training School." 39

The white kids were going to have a chance to become Galileos and Madame Curies and Edisons and Gauguins, and our boys (the girls weren't even in on it) would try to be Jesse Owenses and Joe Louises. 40

Owens and the Brown Bomber were great heroes in our world, but what school official in the white-goddom of Little Rock had the right to decide that those two men must be our only heroes? Who decided that for Henry Reed to become a scientist he had to work like George Washington Carver, as a bootblack, to buy a lousy microscope? Bailey was obviously always going to be too small to be an athlete, so which concrete angel glued to what country seat had decided that if my brother wanted to become a lawyer he had to first pay penance for his skin by picking cotton and hoeing corn and studying correspondence books at night for twenty years? 41

The man's dead words fell like bricks around the auditorium and too many settled in my belly. Constrained by hard-learned manners I couldn't look behind me, but to my left and right the proud graduating class of 1940 had dropped their heads. Every girl in my row had found something new to do with her handkerchief. Some folded the tiny squares into love knots, some into triangles, but most were wadding them, then pressing them flat on their yellow laps. 42

On the dais, the ancient tragedy was being replayed. Professor Parsons sat, a sculptor's reject, rigid. His large, heavy body seemed devoid of will or willingness, and his eyes said he was no longer with us. The other teachers examined the flag (which was draped stage right) or their notes, or the windows which opened on our now-famous playing diamond. 43

Graduation, the hush-hush magic time of frills and gifts and congratulations and diplomas, was finished for me before my name was called. The accomplishment was nothing. The meticulous maps, 44 drawn in three colors of ink, learning, and spelling decasyllabic words, memorizing the whole of *The Rape of Lucrece*—it was for nothing. Donleavy had exposed us.

We were maids and farmers, handymen and washerwomen, and anything higher that we aspired to was farcical and presumptuous. 45

Then I wished that Gabriel Prosser and Nat Turner had killed all whitefolks in their beds and that Abraham Lincoln had been assassinated before the signing of the Emancipation Proclamation, and that Harriet Tubman had been killed by that blow on her head and Christopher Columbus had drowned in the *Santa Maria*. 46

It was awful to be Negro and have no control over my life. It was brutal to be young and already trained to sit quietly and listen to charges brought against my color with no chance of defense. We should all be dead. I thought I should like to see us all dead, one on top of the other. A pyramid of flesh with the whitefolks on the bottom, as the broad base, then the Indians with their silly tomahawks and tepees and wigwams and treaties, the Negroes with their mops and recipes and cotton sacks and spirituals sticking out of their mouths. The Dutch children should all stumble in their wooden shoes and break their necks. The French should choke to death on the Louisiana Purchase (1803) while silkworms ate all the Chinese with their stupid pigtails. As a species, we were an abomination. All of us. 47

Donleavy was running for election, and assured our parents that if he won we could count on having the only colored paved playing field in that part of Arkansas. Also—he never looked up to acknowledge the grunts of acceptance—also, we were bound to get some new equipment for the home economics building and the workshop. 48

He finished, and since there was no need to give any more than the most perfunctory thank-you's, he nodded to the men on the stage, and the tall white man who was never introduced joined him at the door. They left with the attitude that now they were off to something really important. (The graduation ceremonies at Lafayette County Training School had been a mere preliminary.) 49

The ugliness they left was palpable. An uninvited guest who wouldn't leave. The choir was summoned and sang a modern arrangement of "Onward, Christian Soldiers," with new words pertaining to graduates seeking their place in the world. But it didn't work. Elouise, the daughter of the Baptist minister, recited "Invictus," and I could have cried at the impertinence of "I am the master of my fate, I am the captain of my soul." 50

My name had lost its ring of familiarity and I had to be nudged to go and receive my diploma. All my preparations had fled. I 51 neither marched up to the stage like a conquering Amazon, nor did I look in the audience for Bailey's nod of approval. Marguerite Johnson, I heard the name again, my honors were read, there were noises in the audience of appreciation, and I took my place on the stage as rehearsed.

I thought about colors I hated: ecru, puce, lavender, beige and black. 52

There was shuffling and rustling around me, then Henry Reed was giving his valedictory address, "To Be or Not to Be." Hadn't he heard the whitefolks? We couldn't *be* so the question was a waste of time. Henry's voice came clear and strong. I feared to look at him. Hadn't he got the message? There was no "nobler in the mind" for Negroes because the world didn't think we had minds, and they let us know it. "Outrageous fortune"? Now, that was a joke. When the ceremony was over I had to tell Henry Reed some things. That is, if I still cared. Not "rub," Henry, "erase." "Ah, there's the erase." Us. 53

Henry had been a good student in elocution. His voice rose on tides of promise and fell on waves of warnings. The English teacher had helped him to create a sermon winging through Hamlet's soliloquy. To be a man, a doer, a builder, a leader, or to be a tool, an unfunny joke, a crusher of funky toadstools, I marveled that Henry could go through the speech as if we had a choice. 54

I had been listening and silently rebutting each sentence with my eyes closed; then there was a hush, which in an audience warns that something unplanned is happening. I looked up and saw Henry Reed, the conservative, the proper, the A student, turn his back to the audience and turn to us (the proud graduating class of 1940) and sing, nearly speaking, 55

"Lift ev'ry voice and sing
Till earth and heaven ring
Ring with the harmonies of Liberty . . ."

It was the poem written by James Weldon Johnson. It was the music composed by J. Rosamond Johnson. It was the Negro national anthem. Out of habit we were singing it.

Our mothers and fathers stood in the dark hall and joined the hymn of encouragement. A kindergarten teacher led the small children onto the stage and the buttercups and daisies and bunny rabbits marked time and tried to follow: 56

"Stony the road we trod
Bitter the chastening rod

Felt in the days when hope, unborn, had died.
Yet with a steady beat
Have not our weary feet
Come to the place for which our father sighed?"

57 Every child I knew had learned that song with his ABC's and along with "Jesus Loves Me This I Know." But I personally had never heard it before. Never heard the words, despite the thousands of times I had sung them. Never thought they had anything to do with me.

58 On the other hand, the words of Patrick Henry had made such an impression on me that I had been able to stretch myself tall and trembling and say, "I know not what course others may take, but as for me, give me liberty or give me death."

59 And now I heard, really for the first time:

"We have come over a way that with tears has been watered,
We have come, treading our path through the blood of the slaughtered."

60 While echoes of the song shivered in the air, Henry Reed bowed his head, said "Thank you," and returned to his place in the line. The tears that slipped down many faces were not wiped away in shame.

61 We were on top again. As always, again. We survived. The depths had been icy and dark, but now a bright sun spoke to our souls. I was no longer simply a member of the proud graduating class of 1940; I was a proud member of the wonderful beautiful Negro race.

QUESTIONS

1. How is the author's "presentiment of worse things to come" actually borne out? What is the "ancient tragedy" alluded to? How, specifically, does education relate to that tragedy?

2. What do you learn about Marguerite—the young Maya Angelou—from this essay? What are her moods, emotions, thoughts, and attitudes? In what way is she "bound for higher ground"?

3. Angelou is a highly impressionistic stylist in this essay. Provide examples of details that create vivid descriptive impressions. How do these details control the shifting moods of the selection?

4. Explain Angelou's allusions to *The Rape of Lucrece*, Gabriel Prosser and Nat Turner, Harriet Tubman, and "Invictus." How are these allusions and others related to the thesis? State that thesis in your own words.

5. What is the purpose of the relatively long five-paragraph introduction? What contrasts and latent ironies do you detect?

6. Cite examples of the author's ability to blend description, narration, and exposition. At what points is the expository mode the strongest? What is Angelou's purpose?

7. Why are the descriptions of Henry Reed and Donleavy juxtaposed?

8. Which paragraphs constitute the conclusion? How does Angelou achieve the transition from the body to the end?

9. To what extent does American education still try to "track" students? What are the implications of such tracking?

10. a. Reconstruct your own graduation from grade school or high school. b. Analyze and evaluate the many strategies that Angelou employs to honor and celebrate black culture and black wisdom in this essay.

T. H. HUXLEY

A Liberal Education

Thomas Henry Huxley (1825–1895) was one of the nineteenth century's most brilliant adventurers, educators, polemicists, and scientists. He defended Charles Darwin's theory of evolution to an often hostile English scientific community. He reformed the organization of the English elementary school. He labored incessantly to explain science to Britain's middle and working classes. Most of Huxley's works were republished in his *Collected Essays* (nine volumes, 1894–1908). In this essay, Huxley employs striking allusions, metaphors, and analogies to explain the essence of a liberal education.

Suppose it were perfectly certain that the life and fortune of every one of us would, one day or other, depend upon his winning or losing a game of chess. Don't you think that we should all consider it to be a primary duty to learn at least the names and the moves of the pieces; to have a notion of a gambit, and a keen eye for all the means of giving and getting out of check? Do you not think that we should look with a disapprobation amounting to scorn, upon the father who allowed his son, or the state which allowed its members, to grow up without knowing a pawn from a knight? 1

Yet it is a very plain and elementary truth, that the life, the fortune, and the happiness of every one of us, and, more or less, of those who are connected with us, do depend upon our knowing something of the rules of a game infinitely more difficult and complicated than chess. It is a game which has been played for untold ages, every man and woman of us being one of the two players in a game of his or her own. The chessboard is the world, the pieces are the phenomena of the universe, the rules of the game are what we call the laws of Nature. The player on the other side is hidden from us. We know that his play is always fair, just, and patient. But also we know, to our cost, that he never overlooks a mistake, or makes the smallest allowance for ignorance. To the man who plays well, the highest stakes are paid, with that sort of overflowing generosity with which the strong shows delight in strength. And one who plays ill is checkmated—without haste, but without remorse. 2

My metaphor will remind some of you of the famous picture in which Retzsch has depicted Satan playing at chess with man for his soul. Substitute for the mocking fiend in that picture, a calm, strong angel who is playing for love, as we say, and would rather lose than win—and I should accept it as an image of human life. 3

Well, what I mean by Education is learning the rules of this mighty game. In other words, education is the instruction of the intellect in the laws of Nature, under which name I include not merely things and their forces, but men and their ways; and the fashioning of the affections and of the will into an earnest and loving desire to move in harmony with those laws. For me education means neither more nor less than this. Anything which professes to call itself education must be tried by this standard, and if it fails to stand the test, I will not call it education, whatever may be the force of authority, or of numbers, upon the other side. 4

It is important to remember that, in strictness, there is no such thing as an uneducated man. Take an extreme case. Suppose that an adult man, in the full vigor of his faculties, could be suddenly placed in the world, as Adam is said to have been, and then left to do as he best might. How long would he be left uneducated? Not five minutes. Nature would begin to teach him, through the eye, the ear, the touch, the properties of objects. Pain and pleasure would be at his elbow telling him to do this and avoid that; and by slow degrees the man would receive an education, which, if narrow, would be thorough, real, and adequate to his circumstances, though there would be no extras and very few accomplishments. 5

And if to this solitary man entered a second Adam, or better still, an Eve, a new and greater world, that of social and moral phenomena, would be revealed. Joys and woes, compared with which all others might seem but faint shadows, would spring from 6 the new relations. Happiness and sorrow would take the place of the coarser monitors, pleasure and pain; but conduct would still be shaped by the observation of the natural consequences of actions; or, in other words, by the laws of the nature of man.

To every one of us the world was once as fresh and new as to Adam. And then, long before we were susceptible of any other mode of instruction, Nature took us in hand, and every minute of waking life brought its educational influence, shaping our actions into rough accordance with Nature's laws, so that we might not be ended untimely by too gross disobedience. Nor should I speak of this process of education as past for any one, be he as old as he may. For every man the world is as fresh as it was at the first day, and as full of untold novelties for him who has the eyes to see them. And Nature is still continuing her patient education of us in that great university, the universe, of which we are all members—Nature having no Test Acts. 7

Those who take honors in Nature's university, who learn the laws which govern men and things and obey them, are the really great and successful men in this world. The great mass of mankind are the "Poll," who pick up just enough to get through without much discredit. Those who won't learn at all are plucked; and then you can't come up again. Nature's pluck means extermination. 8

Thus the question of compulsory education is settled so far as Nature is concerned. Her bill on that question was framed and passed long ago. But, like all compulsory legislation, that of Nature is harsh and wasteful in its operation. Ignorance is visited as sharply as willful disobedience—incapacity meets with the same punishment as crime. Nature's discipline is not even a word and a blow, and the blow first; but the blow without the word. It is left to you to find out why your ears are boxed. 9

The object of what we commonly call education—that education in which man intervenes and which I shall distinguish as artificial education—is to make good these defects in Nature's methods; to prepare the child to receive Nature's education, neither incapably nor ignorantly, nor with willful disobedience; and to understand the preliminary symptoms of her displeasure, without waiting for the box on the ear. In short, all artificial education ought to be an anticipation of natural education. And a liberal education is an artificial education, which has not only prepared a man to escape the great evils of disobedience to natural laws, but has trained him to appreciate and to seize upon the rewards, which Nature scatters with as free a hand as her penalties. 10

That man, I think, has had a liberal education, who has been so trained in youth that his body is the ready servant of his will, and does with ease and pleasure all the work that, as a mechanism, it is 11

capable of; whose intellect is a clear, cold, logic engine, with all its parts of equal strength, and in smooth working order; ready, like a steam engine, to be turned to any kind of work, and spin the gossamers as well as forge the anchors of the mind; whose mind is stored with a knowledge of the great and fundamental truths of Nature and of the laws of her operations; one who, no stunted ascetic, is full of life and fire, but whose passions are trained to come to heel by a vigorous will, the servant of a tender conscience; who has learned to love all beauty, whether of Nature or of art, to hate all vileness, and to respect others as himself.

Such a one and no other, I conceive, has had a liberal education; for he is, as completely as a man can be, in harmony with Nature. He will make the best of her, and she of him. They will get on together rarely; she as his ever beneficent mother; he as her mouthpiece, her conscious self, her minister and interpreter. 12

QUESTIONS

1. What is the main analogy in this essay? What concept does it explain? Define that concept in your own words.

2. According to the author, what is the relationship of mature people to Adam and Eve?

3. Does the author's use of analogy make his language more concrete or abstract? Explain.

4. In addition to analogy, what figurative language does Huxley employ, and for what purpose?

5. Exactly how does the author use analogy to structure this essay? Does he use a single analogy or multiple ones? Explain.

6. In what way is the author's essay a definition of "liberal education"?

7. How does the author use examples in the essay?

8. Of what value is Huxley's use of the pronouns "I," "we," and "us" in this essay?

9. Huxley speaks of taking "honors in Nature's university." What does Nature have to do with a liberal education? Why, do you think, would Huxley have based his definitions of a liberal education on the laws of nature?

10. a. Write your own definition of a liberal education.
b. Use an analogy to explain what Nature can teach us. Try to avoid sentimentality in handling this topic.

SANTHA RAMA RAU

By Any Other Name

Santha Rama Rau (1923–   ) is an Indian novelist and essayist who throughout her career has interpreted the Eastern experience for Western audiences. She is a gifted travel writer and memorist. Her principal works include *Home to India* (1944), *Remember the House* (1955), and *Gifts of Passage* (1961). This narrative essay sensitively portrays the conflict in cultures perceived by the author in her early childhood.

At the Anglo-Indian day school in Zorinabad to which my sister and I were sent when she was eight and I was five and a half, they changed our names. On the first day of school, a hot, windless morning of a north Indian September, we stood in the headmistress's study and she said, "Now you're the *new* girls. What are your names?" 1

My sister answered for us. "I am Premila, and she" nodding in my direction—"is Santha." 2

The headmistress had been in India, I suppose, fifteen years or so, but she still smiled her helpless inability to cope with Indian names. Her rimless half-glasses glittered, and the precarious bun on top of her head trembled as she shook her head. "Oh, my dears, those are much too hard for me. Suppose we give you pretty English names. Wouldn't that be more jolly? Let's see, now—Pamela for you, I think." She shrugged in a baffled way at my sister. "That's as close as I can get. And for *you*," she said to me, "how about Cynthia? Isn't that nice?" 3

My sister was always less easily intimidated than I was, and while she kept a stubborn silence, I said, "Thank you," in a very tiny voice. 4

We had been sent to that school because my father, among his responsibilities as an officer of the civil service, had a tour of duty to perform in the villages around that steamy little provincial town, where he had his headquarters at that time. He used to make his shorter inspection tours on horseback, and a week before, in the stale heat of a typically postmonsoon day, we had waved good-by to him and a little procession—an assistant, a secretary, two bearers, and the man to look after the bedding rolls and luggage. They rode away through our large garden, still bright green from the rains, and we turned back into the twilight of the house and the sound of fans whispering in every room. 5

Up to then, my mother had refused to send Premila to school 6

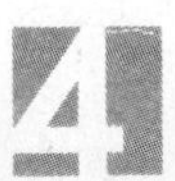

in the British-run establishments of that time, because, she used to say, "you can bury a dog's tail for seven years and it still comes out curly, and you can take a Britisher away from his home for a lifetime, and he still remains insular." The examinations and degrees from entirely Indian schools were not, in those days, considered valid. In my case, the question had never come up, and probably never would have come up if Mother's extraordinary good health had not broken down. For the first time in my life, she was not able to continue the lessons she had been giving us every morning. So our Hindi books were put away, the stories of the Lord Krishna as a little boy were left in mid-air, and we were sent to the Anglo-Indian school.

That first day at school is still, when I think of it, a remarkable 7
one. At that age, if one's name is changed, one develops a curious form of dual personality. I remember having a certain detached and disbelieving concern in the actions of "Cynthia," but certainly no responsibility. Accordingly, I followed the thin, erect back of the headmistress down the veranda to my classroom feeling, at most, a passing interest in what was going to happen to me in this strange, new atmosphere of School.

The building was Indian in design, with wide verandas 8
opening onto a central courtyard, but Indian verandas are usually whitewashed, with stone floors. These, in the tradition of British schools, were painted dark brown and had matting on the floors. It gave a feeling of extra intensity to the heat.

I suppose there were about a dozen Indian children in the 9
school—which contained perhaps forty children in all—and four of them were in my class. They were all sitting at the back of the room, and I went to join them. I sat next to a small, solemn girl who didn't smile at me. She had long, glossy-black braids and wore a cotton dress, but she still kept on her Indian jewelry—a gold chain around her neck, thin gold bracelets, and tiny ruby studs in her ears. Like most Indian children, she had a rim of black kohl around her eyes. The cotton dress should have looked strange, but all I could think of was that I should ask my mother if I couldn't wear a dress to school, too, instead of my Indian clothes.

I can't remember too much about the proceedings in class 10
that day, except for the beginning. The teacher pointed to me and asked me to stand up. "Now, dear, tell the class your name."

I said nothing. 11

"Come along," she said frowning slightly. "What's your 12
name, dear?"

"I don't know," I said, finally. 13

The English children in the front of the class—there were 14
about eight or ten of them—giggled and twisted around in their

chairs to look at me. I sat down quickly and opened my eyes very wide, hoping in that way to dry them off. The little girl with the braids put out her hand and very lightly touched my arm. She still didn't smile.

Most of that morning I was rather bored. I looked briefly at 15
the children's drawings pinned to the wall, and then concentrated on a lizard clinging to the ledge of the high, barred window behind the teacher's head. Occasionally it would shoot out its long yellow tongue for a fly, and then it would rest, with its eyes closed and its belly palpitating, as though it were swallowing several times quickly. The lessons were mostly concerned with reading and writing and simple numbers—things that my mother had already taught me—and I paid very little attention. The teacher wrote on the easel blackboard words like "bat" and "cat," which seemed babyish to me; only "apple" was new and incomprehensible.

When it was time for the lunch recess, I followed the girl with 16
braids out onto the veranda. There the children from the other classes were assembled. I saw Premila at once and ran over to her, as she had charge of our lunchbox. The children were all opening packages and sitting down to eat sandwiches. Premila and I were the only ones who had Indian food—thin wheat chapatties, some vegetable curry, and a bottle of buttermilk. Premila thrust half of it into my hand and whispered fiercely that I should go and sit with my class, because that was what the others seemed to be doing.

The enormous black eyes of the little Indian girl from my class 17
looked at my food longingly, so I offered her some. But she only shook her head and plowed her way solemnly through her sandwiches.

I was very sleepy after lunch, because at home we always 18
took a siesta. It was usually a pleasant time of day, with the bedroom darkened against the harsh afternoon sun, the drifting off into sleep with the sound of Mother's voice reading a story in one's mind, and, finally, the shrill, fussy voice of the ayah waking one for tea.

At school, we rested for a short time on low, folding cots on 19
the veranda, and then we were expected to play games. During the hot part of the afternoon we played indoors, and after the shadows had begun to lengthen and the slight breeze of the evening had come up we moved outside to the wide courtyard.

I had never really grasped the system of competitive games. 20
At home, whenever we played tag or guessing games, I was always allowed to "win"—"because," Mother used to tell Premila, "she is the youngest, and we have to allow for that." I had often heard her say it, and it seemed quite reasonable to me, but the result was that I had no clear idea of what "winning" meant.

When we played twos-and-threes that afternoon at school, in 21 accordance with my training, I let one of the small English boys catch me, but was naturally rather puzzled when the other children did not return the courtesy. I ran about for what seemed like hours without ever catching anyone, until it was time for school to close. Much later I learned that my attitude was called "not being a good sport," and I stopped allowing myself to be caught, but it was not for years that I really learned the spirit of the thing.

When I saw our car come up to the school gate, I broke away from my classmates and rushed toward it yelling, "Ayah! Ayah!" It seemed like an eternity since I had seen her that morning—a wizened, affectionate figure in her white cotton sari, giving me dozens of urgent and useless instructions on how to be a good girl at school. Premila followed more sedately, and she told me on the way home never to do that again in front of the other children. 22

When we got home we went straight to Mother's high, white room to have tea with her, and I immediately climbed onto the bed and bounced gently up and down on the springs. Mother asked how we had liked our first day in school. I was so pleased to be home and to have left that peculiar Cynthia behind that I had nothing whatever to say about school, except to ask what "apple" meant. But Premila told Mother about the classes, and added that in her class they had weekly tests to see if they learned their lessons well. 23

I asked, "What's a test?" 24

Premila said, "You're too small to have them. You won't have them in your class for donkey's years." She had learned the expression that day and was using it for the first time. We all laughed enormously at her wit. She also told Mother, in an aside, that we should take sandwiches to school the next day. Not, she said, that *she* minded. But they would be simpler for me to handle. 25

That whole lovely evening I didn't think about school at all. I sprinted barefoot across the lawns with my favorite playmate, the cook's son, to the stream at the end of the garden. We quarreled in our usual way, waded in the tepid water under the lime trees, and waited for the night to bring out the smell of the jasmine. I listened with fascination to his stories of ghosts and demons, until I was too frightened to cross the garden alone in the semidarkness. The ayah found me, shouted at the cook's son, scolded me, hurried me into supper—it was an entirely usual, wonderful evening. 26

It was a week later, the day of Premila's first test, that our lives changed rather abruptly. I was sitting at the back of my class, in my usual inattentive way, only half listening to the teacher. I had started a rather guarded friendship with the girl with the braids, whose name turned out to be Nalini (Nancy, in school). The three other Indian children were already fast friends. Even at that age it was apparent to all of us that friendship with the English or Anglo-Indian 27 children was out of the question. Occasionally, during the class, my new friend and I would draw pictures and show them to each other secretly.

The door opened sharply and Premila marched in. At first, the teacher smiled at her in a kindly and encouraging way and said, "Now, you're little Cynthia's sister?" 28

Premila didn't even look at her. She stood with her feet planted firmly apart and her shoulders rigid, and addressed herself directly to me. "Get up," she said. "We're going home." 29

I didn't know what had happened, but I was aware that it was a crisis of some sort. I rose obediently and started to walk toward my sister. 30

"Bring your pencils and your notebook," she said. 31

I went back for them, and together we left the room. The teacher started to say something just as Premila closed the door, but we didn't wait to hear what it was. 32

In complete silence we left the school grounds and started to walk home. Then I asked Premila what the matter was. All she would say was "We're going home for good." 33

It was a very tiring walk for a child of five and a half, and I dragged along behind Premila with my pencils growing sticky in my hand. I can still remember looking at the dusty hedges, and the tangles of thorns in the ditches by the side of the road, smelling the faint fragrance from the eucalyptus trees and wondering whether we would ever reach home. Occasionally a horse-drawn tonga passed us, and the women, in their pink or green silks, stared at Premila and me trudging along on the side of the road. A few coolies and a line of women carrying baskets of vegetables on their heads smiled at us. But it was nearing the hottest time of day, and the road was almost deserted. I walked more and more slowly, and shouted to Premila, from time to time, "Wait for me!" with increasing peevishness. She spoke to me only once, and that was to tell me to carry my notebook on my head, because of the sun. 34

When we got to our house the ayah was just taking a tray of lunch into Mother's room. She immediately started a long, worried questioning about what are you children doing back here at this hour of the day. 35

Mother looked very startled and very concerned, and asked Premila what had happened. 36

Premila said, "We had our test today, and she made me and the other Indians sit at the back of the room, with a desk between each one." 37

Mother said, "Why was that, darling?" 38

"She said it was because Indians cheat," Premila added. "So I don't think we should go back to that school." 39

40 Mother looked very distant, and was silent a long time. At last she said, "Of course not, darling." She sounded displeased.

41 We all shared the curry she was having for lunch, and afterward I was sent off to the beautifully familiar bedroom for my siesta. I could hear Mother and Premila talking through the open door.

42 Mother said, "Do you suppose she understood all that?"

43 Premila said, "I shouldn't think so. She's a baby."

44 Mother said, "Well, I hope it won't bother her."

45 Of course, they were both wrong. I understood it perfectly, and I remember it all very clearly. But I put it happily away, because it had all happened to a girl called Cynthia, and I never was really particularly interested in her.

QUESTIONS

1. Cite five examples the author gives to demonstrate that her attendance at the Anglo-Indian day school was an alien experience for her.

2. According to the author's inferences, what was the effect of British rule on Indian society? How does the headmistress embody this impact?

3. Define these Indian words, preferably from the contexts in which they are used: *kohl* (paragraph 9); *chapatties* (paragraph 17); *ayah* (paragraph 18); *sari* (paragraph 22); *tonga* (paragraph 34).

4. Explain the author's use of sensory language in paragraphs 1, 3, 5, 8, 9, 15, 26, and 34.

5. What is the theme of this narrative essay? How does the author state it?

6. Describe the tone and mood of the essay.

7. What is the utility and value of the author's use of dialogue in the essay?

8. How do various causal patterns inform the narrative?

9. Although dealing specifically with a colonial situation, the author also illuminates the universal experience of being made to feel different, strange, or alien. Why is this ironic for the author? Why does it remain so vivid in her memory? Do we become more or less conscious of this phenomenon at a later age?

10. a. Write a narrative essay centering on a time when you were made to feel strange or foreign in an educational situation.
b. Tell of a time when you felt that someone or some group was trying to change your identity or sense of self.

FRANCES FITZGERALD

America Revised:
HISTORY SCHOOLBOOKS IN THE TWENTIETH CENTURY

Frances Fitzgerald (1940–), winner of the Pulitzer Prize for *Fire in the Lake: The Vietnamese and Americans in Vietnam* (1972), is an American journalist who has contributed to the *Atlantic*, the *New Yorker*, the *New York Times Book Review*, and other magazines. Fitzgerald's interest in contemporary affairs and in the history of modern education resulted in the controversial study *America Revised: History Schoolbooks in the Twentieth Century* (1979), from which this selection is taken.

1 It is a commonplace to say that the texts of the fifties were superpatriotic—dominated, almost to the exclusion of all else, by the concerns of the Cold War. But it is now hard to remember exactly what this meant, or how it happened. It is interesting, therefore, to watch the ideological drift as it crossed over the subsequent junior-high-school texts of the mid-century. First published in 1931, Casner and Gabriel's *Exploring American History* has had a life span of almost fifty years and was for much of the time a best-selling American history for seventh and eighth graders. Initially, at least, it was the product of a collaboration between a Yale history professor, Ralph Henry Gabriel, and a West Haven, Connecticut, schoolteacher, Mabel B. Casner. According to its first editor, at Harcourt Brace, it did well in the market because of its thematic approach to American history and its "ingenious" teaching strategies.

2 The first edition is clearly the work of liberals, and it has more than a touch of John Dewey about it. The foreword states that history should be "socially helpful" and should lead to "an understanding of how the life about us has evolved out of the life of the past." The text begins by drawing a parallel between a child's exploration of his own world and the wanderings of an imaginary knight over medieval Europe—the point of which is to explain "why did Europeans wait 500 years to discover America again?" It goes on to draw a picture of pre-Colonial North American Indian life in a manner so stylized that it might have been taken from the backdrop of a case in the American Museum of Natural History. The forest is deep, birds are flitting, squirrels are chattering, and so forth. The Indians, so the book says, were "deeply religious," the proof being that they worshipped so many different spirits; their tragedy was that they had no domestic animals, and therefore "could not progress toward a higher way of

life." There are a certain number of poor people in the book—Jacob Riis is mentioned and there is a drawing of the immigrant boats—and very little chauvinism. The War of 1812 is said to have been won by no one, and the Mexican War to have occurred because President James Polk wanted to buy some empty land from the Mexicans and the Mexicans, though poor, were too proud to sell it. Such attempts at balance run through the narrative. The book reports that the United States was "drawn into" world affairs before the First World War, and in the title of the last foreign-policy chapter it asks, "What Steps Has the United States Taken Recently to Promote International Peace?" (a question that provides a perfect logical parallel to "When did you stop beating your wife?").

The 1938 edition of Casner and Gabriel has a new title, *The* 3
Rise of American Democracy, and is said to be a complete reworking of the original volume. It has a new rationale. In their foreword, the authors say that democracy is now being challenged by other forms of government, including "swift-striking dictatorships," and that we therefore have to ask, "What does the word, *democracy*, mean?" The book never quite gets around to answering this question, but its focus is more political than that of the first edition, and its tone more urgent. The story of the knight in the first chapter has been condensed, and the American scenery of birds, squirrels, and leafy boughs has largely disappeared. The Indians are now said to have practiced democracy, not religion; they are no longer "deeply religious." Jacob Riis is still around, but the United States government has become a much more positive actor in social reform. Whereas a mid-thirties edition seems to judge some of President Franklin Roosevelt's legislation to have been unconstitutional, this one simply credits him with having helped the country out of the Depression. In foreign policy, too, the government has taken a positive role: it "helps" the Allies in the First World War and "promotes" world peace thereafter, within the limits of its isolationist position. In the last part of the book, "American Democracy Faces a Confused World," the text maintains that Americans now have new ideals, including a balanced economy, Social Security, and well-being for all citizens. But it ends, rather ominously, "The struggle still goes on. It was never more intense than in our day. The outcome will depend upon the intelligence and alertness of this generation and of future generations."

The 1942 edition, now called *The Story of American Democracy*, 4
has an update on the Second World War and a new preface that refers to the "perilous times" we are living in. Apparently because of this emergency, the Indian sections have been condensed. (They drop out completely in subsequent editions.) In the central part of the book, the titles have changed, and these give a rather different tone to the

book. Where once there were "problems" to "challenge democracy," there is now only progress: "American Life Becomes Better for the Common Man," and so on. The Constitutional period is headed "Free Americans Organize a Strong Democratic Nation," and the words "freedom" and "strength" crop up a lot elsewhere. In the last chapter—a completely new one, entitled "The United States Fights for Its Life and for a Free, Democratic World"—there is a photograph caption that reads, "This picture shows citizens enjoying the democratic privilege of free discussion. . . . The leader is helping them to carry on their business in an orderly way." The photograph shows several men on a dais facing a seated audience; it is clearly a meeting of some sort. In contrast to the final worryings of the 1938 edition, this book ends on a note of optimism concerning air travel.

Over the next eight years, the authors—or whoever did the 5
revising of the text—must have felt justified in their optimism, for the 1950 text is a victorious book. The United States now "leads the struggle for democracy"; it has "faced problems," "met challenges"; it has risen "to a position of world leadership" and become "a bastion of the free nations." All of this is, of course, in the twentieth century, but retrospectively the nation has made other gains as well—notably in its nineteenth-century wars. It has not exactly won the War of 1812, but the war is now said to have helped "build the nation." (In earlier editions, the war, less grandly, "develops national feeling.") The Mexican War, which in the first two editions brought the country only empty land, now has brought it vast territories rich in oil and precious metals. In addition, the country has become more prosperous: there are no more poor people or bad social conditions. Pages have been added explaining the superiority of the American democratic system to the Russian police state.

In accordance with the authors' new belief that "perhaps the 6
most important event of the first half of the twentieth century was the rise of the United States to a position of world leadership," the last quarter of the book deals mainly with foreign affairs. These sections portray the United States as playing an essentially benevolent and pacific role in the world. The nation is always attempting to improve communications with the Soviet Union and to "gain peace by mutual understanding"—this in spite of continual rebuffs. In an echo of the liberal internationalism of the first edition, the book talks about the need for international control of atomic energy and the effort to remove the causes of war through the United Nations. The last section, "Democracy Enriches the Lives of Americans," confidently describes recent "advances" in art, education, and science, and points up the American belief in the importance of the individual, of whatever race or creed.

Five years later, this confidence has evaporated; the book is a 7

bundle of anxieties. In the first place, the authors no longer appear to believe that the United States exerts "world leadership." In their foreword, they say that the United States leads "those people in the world who believe in freedom" (a worrying kind of group), and that it is "locked in a struggle" with "another powerful world leader . . . the Soviet Union." Faced with the need to prepare "young people" for the "struggle" in a "complicated and often dangerous world," the authors propose to compare the Russian and American ways of life—American history apparently being of no use anymore. Later on in the book, the authors fulfill their promise by giving an account of Soviet institutions. In this section, one is told that "Russia" is a police state, where "the leader of the Communist party has absolute power over . . . every person." (The book cautiously does not name this leader; Stalin had died two years before publication.) Russia, one learns, is a "fake democracy" and a "fake republic"; worse yet, its industry is geared not to the production of television sets but to war production. In addition, one learns that Russia is tremendously powerful—perhaps even more powerful than the United States, because, in spite of all the American aid to free nations, Russia has managed to block progress and block the growth of prosperity. It is now threatening the free world. (In this section, there is a map of the world color-coded to show which nations are "Communist," which are "free," and which are "neutral." This map classifies all of Indo-China and all of sub-Sahara Africa as "free" and classifies Saudi Arabia, Iran, and most of Latin America, including Mexico, as "neutral." This assessment is mysterious, since the book appeared a year after Dien Bien Phu, several years before the decolonization of most of Africa, and some time after the C.I.A. had brought the Shah of Iran to power and had overturned the Arbenz government in Guatemala.) Internationally, nothing is safe from the Communists, and the home front is not very secure, either. The United States may be a free country, with "wonderful machines" and a free-enterprise system (over which the government now presides in the much reduced capacity of referee), but the Russians are in the process of undermining it. They have already stolen American state secrets through Alger Hiss and the Rosenbergs. They lie a lot, and the Communist Party in the United States espouses violent, undemocratic means. The book therefore approves of the Internal Security Act, the Loyalty Board, and the firm hand of J. Edgar Hoover in the F.B.I.

The most surprising thing about this 1955 edition is the 8
attitude that its authors take toward children. In the thirties editions, they had tried to engage their young readers with adventure stories and romance; here they do nothing but lecture—as if the children

might turn out to be small subversives. The last page, subheaded "A Citizen's Rights and Duties," is terribly stern. A citizen's duties, they warn, include military service, jury duty, and paying taxes without cheating. The last few pages—usually given over to science and technology—now include a warning against "false news" and "dangerous propaganda." What the authors are referring to here can only be conjectured, since they are no more explicit than they were when they warned in an earlier section against the questionable practices of "some investigating committees of Congress"—surely the House Un-American Activities Committee and Senator Joseph R. McCarthy's subcommittee. But these two things are probably connected, because the authors offer this explicit piece of advice:

> The FBI urges Americans to report directly to its offices any suspicions they may have about Communist activity on the part of their fellow Americans. The FBI is expertly trained to sift out the truth of such reports under the laws of our free nation. When Americans handle their suspicions in this way, rather than by gossip and publicity, they are acting in line with American traditions.

What this paragraph literally says is that an American tradition is that of the police informer. The authors, however, appear to have thought of the F.B.I. as the liberal alternative to the McCarthy subcommittee.

This edition of Casner and Gabriel was not untypical of the 9
texts of the period—certainly in its emphasis on the Communist threat. Virtually all the texts of the mid-fifties made the same estimates of Soviet power and Soviet aggressiveness in foreign policy. Virtually all of them expressed similar doubts about the survival of democracy in this country. The texts of the early forties had not portrayed the Nazis as half so aggressive, or the Second World War as half such a threat to the country. Now the danger was everywhere, invisible. According to Bragdon and McCutchen, one of the most respectable of the high-school texts of the period:

> Unquestioning party members are found everywhere. Everywhere they are willing to engage in spying, sabotage, and the promotion of unrest on orders from Moscow.

And

> Agents of the worldwide Communist conspiracy have been active inside the United States. Some of them have

> been trusted officials of the State Department, regularly furnishing information to Russia. Others have passed on atomic secrets; still others have even represented the United States in the UN.

Bragdon and McCutchen were quoting Senator McCarthy and representing his charges as true.

The subversion anxieties of the texts peaked in the mid- 10
fifties, subsiding gradually after that. The early-sixties texts did not repudiate McCarthy except by saying, "Some Americans said there was too much fuss being made about the Communists since there were so relatively few in the United States," or "The struggle divided us when we should have been united." Only now do some texts actually denounce McCarthy's "scare tactics" and take issue with the general assessment of the Soviet Union in the fifties. The aspect of fifties texts that persisted most strongly into the sixties was a certain tone of grimness toward children, and particularly toward young children. It was the junior-high-school books, rather than the high-school ones, that gave such warnings as "Some forces in the world today want to abolish freedom. [But] your heritage as an American provides you with the ideals and faith to give you strength to preserve the rights that are yours as a free American. It is your duty to preserve these rights." And so on. Since these books never defined what they meant by "freedom," the burden they laid on children was truly awesome.

QUESTIONS

1. Trace the changes in the "ideological drift" of the Casner and Gabriel textbook from 1931 to the mid-1950s.

2. What assumptions and inferences does Fitzgerald make about the teaching of American history in the junior high school classroom?

3. Although this is an analytical essay, the diction tends to be informal. Point to examples of this informal style. What is the effect of the diction on the analysis itself?

4. Explain the allusions to John Dewey and Jacob Riis in paragraph 2. Identify the allusion in paragraph 8.

5. How does the term *ideological drift* serve to structure the entire essay? What type of process analysis is involved in the development? Identify the steps in the process.

6. Comment on the effectiveness of the author's topic sentences. How do they reinforce the implied thesis in the essay?

7. Explain how Fitzgerald uses causal analysis. Analyze one paragraph in detail to illuminate this procedure.

8. What is the author's tone in her analysis of the Casner and Gabriel text? Cite examples to support your position.

9. Discuss the presentation of American history (or any other subject) in a textbook with which you are familiar. What connections can you make among the text, the author, and the era in which it was written?

10. Write an analysis of a textbook, dealing with its assumptions, its content, its intended audience, and its purpose. What view of American history, politics, or society does it project?

FRANCIS BACON

Of Studies

Francis Bacon (1561–1626), a contemporary of William Shakespeare, Queen Elizabeth, and James I, was a noted author, scientist, and statesman. In *The Advancement of Learning* (1605) and *The Novum Organum* (1620), Bacon argued the superiority of inductive over deductive reasoning. His literary reputation rests on his *Essays* (1597–1625), in which he examines human nature and society. "Of Studies," part of this collection, is considered one of Bacon's finest stylistic ventures into the art of the essay.

Studies serve for delight, for ornament, and for ability. 1
Their chief use for delight is in privateness and retiring; for ornament, is in discourse; and for ability, is in the judgment and disposition of business. For expert men can execute, and perhaps judge of particulars, one by one; but the general counsels, and the plots and marshalling of affairs come best from those that are learned. To spend too much time in studies is sloth; to use them too much for ornament is affectation; to make judgment wholly by their rules is the humour of a scholar. They perfect nature, and are perfected by experience: for natural abilities are like natural plants, that need pruning by study; and studies themselves do give forth directions too much at large, except they be bounded in by experience. Crafty men contemn studies, simple men admire them, and wise men use them; for they teach not their own use; but that is a wisdom without them and above them, won by

observation. Read not to contradict and confute, nor to believe and take for granted, nor to find talk and discourse, but to weigh and consider. Some books are to be tasted, others to be swallowed, and some few to be chewed and digested; that is, some books are to be read only in parts; others to be read, but not curiously; and some few to be read wholly, and with diligence and attention. Some books also may be read by deputy, and extracts made of them by others; but that would be only in the less important arguments and the meaner sort of books; else distilled books are, like common distilled waters, flashy things. Reading maketh a full man; conference a ready man; and writing an exact man. And, therefore, if a man write little, he had need have a great memory; if he confer little, he had need have a present wit; and if he read little, he had need have much cunning, to seem to know that he doth not. Histories make men wise; poets, witty; the mathematics, subtile; natural philosophy, deep; moral, grave; logic and rhetoric, able to contend. *Abeunt studia in mores*. Nay, there is no stond or impediment in the wit but may be wrought out by fit studies, like as diseases of the body may have appropriate exercises. Bowling is good for the stone and reins, shooting for the lungs and breast, gentle walking for the stomach, riding for the head and the like. So if a man's wit be wandering, let him study the mathematics; for in demonstrations, if his wit be called away never so little, he must begin again. If his wit be not apt to distinguish or find difference, let him study the school men; for they are *Cymini sectores*. If he be not apt to beat over matters, and to call up one thing to prove and illustrate another, let him study the lawyers' cases. So every defect of the mind may have a special receipt.

QUESTIONS

1. According to Bacon, what are the purposes of studies? How can study "perfect nature"? What is the best form of study, and why?

2. How can various branches of study improve human nature?

3. Bacon is a master of balance and parallelism in sentence structure. List five examples and explain their effect. How do these stylistic strategies affect the presentation of Bacon's ideas?

4. Identify and explain figures of speech in "Of Studies."

5. Bacon, an early experimenter with the essay as a genre, offers a single-paragraph essay to his audience. How does he develop this single-paragraph essay?

6. Bacon's essays are well known for their aphorisms. Identify several in this essay. How do they contribute to the unity of the essay?

7. Bacon uses classification and listing in this essay. Give examples of both.

8. Is this an argumentative or expository essay? Give reasons for your choice.

9. Bacon wrote this essay more than 350 years ago. Why is his advice still relevant? For example, how might you apply his statement: "Studies serve for delight, for ornament, and for ability"?

10. a. Write your own essay on the purpose of studies.
b. Argue for or against Bacon's proposition that "fit studies" can improve virtually any defect of the mind.

BERTRAND RUSSELL

Knowledge and Wisdom

Bertrand Arthur William Russell (1872–1970), who was born in Monmouthshire, England, was one of the great philosophers, mathematicians, liberal political theorists, and authors of the twentieth century. His works, comprising more than sixty volumes, range from abstract explanations of mathematical theory to fascinating memoirs that record British culture in the early years of the twentieth century. From the early *Principles of Mathematics* (1903) through *An Inquiry into Meaning and Truth* (1940), to his three-volume *Autobiography* (1967–1969), Russell demonstrated his multivarious talents as a writer, socialist thinker, and activist. He was awarded the Nobel Prize in Literature in 1950. In 1955 he received the Silver Pears Trophy for work on behalf of world peace. In this essay from *Portraits from Memory* (1956), Russell argues that as we advance in knowledge, wisdom becomes an increasingly necessary quality in peoples and cultures.

1 Most people would agree that, although our age far surpasses all previous ages in knowledge, there has been no correlative increase in wisdom. But agreement ceases as soon as we attempt to define "wisdom" and consider means of promoting it. I want to ask first what wisdom is, and then what can be done to teach it.

2 There are several factors that contribute to wisdom. Of these I should put first *a sense of proportion*: the capacity to take account of all the important factors in a problem and to attach to each its due

weight. This has become more difficult than it used to be owing to the extent and complexity of the specialised knowledge required of various kinds of technicians. Suppose, for example, that you are engaged in research in scientific medicine. The work is difficult and is likely to absorb the whole of your intellectual energy. You have not time to consider the effect which your discoveries or inventions may have outside the field of medicine. You succeed (let us say), as modern medicine has succeeded, in enormously lowering the infant death-rate, not only in Europe and America, but also in Asia and Africa. This has the entirely unintended result of making the food supply inadequate and lowering the standard of life in the most populous parts of the world. To take an even more spectacular example, which is in everybody's mind at the present time: you study the composition of the atom from a disinterested desire for knowledge, and incidentally place in the hands of powerful lunatics the means of destroying the human race. In such ways the pursuit of knowledge may become harmful unless it is combined with wisdom; and wisdom in the sense of comprehensive vision is not necessarily present in specialists in the pursuit of knowledge.

Comprehensiveness alone, however, is not enough to constitute wisdom. There must be, also, a certain awareness of the ends of human life. This may be illustrated by the study of history. Many eminent historians have done more harm than good because they viewed facts through the distorting medium of their own passions: Hegel had a philosophy of history which did not suffer from any lack of comprehensiveness, since it started from the earliest times and continued into an indefinite future. But the chief lesson of history which he sought to inculcate was that from the year A.D. 400 down to his own time, Germany had been the most important nation and the standard-bearer of progress in the world. Perhaps one could stretch the comprehensiveness that constitutes wisdom to include not only intellect but also feeling. It is by no means uncommon to find men whose knowledge is wide but whose feelings are narrow. Such men lack what I am calling wisdom. 3

It is not only in public ways, but in private life equally, that wisdom is needed. It is needed in the choice of ends to be pursued and in emancipation from personal prejudice. Even an end which it would be noble to pursue if it were attainable may be pursued unwisely if it is inherently impossible of achievement. Many men in past ages devoted their lives to a search for the Philosopher's Stone and the Elixir of Life. No doubt, if they could have found them, they would have conferred great benefits upon mankind, but as it was their lives were wasted. To descend to less heroic matters, consider the case of two men, Mr. A and Mr. B, who hate each other and, 4 through mutual hatred, bring each other to destruction. Suppose you go to Mr. A and say, "Why do you hate Mr. B?" He will no doubt give you an appalling list of Mr. B's vices, partly true, partly false. And now suppose you go to Mr. B. He will give you an exactly similar list of Mr. A's vices with an equal admixture of truth and falsehood. Suppose you now come back to Mr. A and say, "You will be surprised to learn that Mr. B says the same things about you as you say about him," and you go to Mr. B and make a similar speech. The first effect, no doubt, will be to increase their mutual hatred, since each will be so horrified by the other's injustice. But, perhaps, if you have sufficient patience and sufficient persuasiveness, you may succeed in convincing each that the other has only the normal share of human wickedness, and their enmity is harmful to both. If you do this, you will have instilled some fragment of wisdom.

The essence of wisdom is emancipation, as far as possible, 5
from the tyranny of the here and the now. We cannot help the egoism of our senses. Sight and sound and touch are bound up with our own bodies and cannot be made impersonal. Our emotions start similarly from ourselves. An infant feels hunger and discomfort, and is unaffected except by his own physical condition. Gradually, with the years, his horizon widens, and, in proportion as his thoughts and feelings become less personal and less concerned with his own physical states, he achieves growing wisdom. This is, of course, a matter of degree. No one can view the world with complete impartiality; and if anyone could, he would hardly be able to remain alive. But it is possible to make a continual approach towards impartiality: on the one hand, by knowing things somewhat remote in time or space; and, on the other hand, by giving to such things their due weight in our feelings. It is this approach towards impartiality that constitutes growth in wisdom.

Can wisdom in this sense be taught? And, if it can, should 6
the teaching of it be one of the aims of education? I should answer both these questions in the affirmative. We are told on Sundays that we should love our neighbour as ourselves. On the other six days of the week, we are exhorted to hate him. You may say that this is nonsense, since it is not our neighbour whom we are exhorted to hate. But you will remember that the precept was exemplified by saying that the Samaritan was our neighbour. We no longer have any wish to hate Samaritans and so we are apt to miss the point of the parable. If you want to get its point, you should substitute "communist" or "anticommunist," as the case may be, for "Samaritan." It might be objected that it is right to hate those who do harm. I do not think so. If you hate them, it is only too likely that you will become equally harmful; and it is very unlikely you will induce them to

abandon their evil ways. Hatred of evil is itself a kind of bondage to evil. The way out is through understanding, not through hate. I am not advocating non-resistance. But I am saying that resistance, if it is to be effective in preventing the spread of evil, should be combined with the greatest degree of understanding and the smallest degree of force that is compatible with the survival of the good things that we wish to preserve.

It is commonly urged that a point of view such as I have been 7
advocating is incompatible with vigour in action. I do not think history bears out this view. Queen Elizabeth I in England and Henry IV in France lived in a world where almost everybody was fanatical, either on the Protestant or on the Catholic side. Both remained free from the errors of their time and both, by remaining free, were beneficent and certainly not ineffective. Abraham Lincoln conducted a great war without ever departing from what I have been calling wisdom.

I have said that in some degree wisdom can be taught. I think 8
that this teaching should have a larger intellectual element than has been customary in what has been thought of as moral instruction. The disastrous results of hatred and narrow-mindedness to those who feel them can be pointed out incidentally in the course of giving knowledge. I do not think that knowledge and morals ought to be too much separated. It is true that the kind of specialised knowledge which is required for various kinds of skill has little to do with wisdom. But it should be supplemented in education by wider surveys calculated to put it in its place in the total of human activities. Even the best technicians should also be good citizens; and when I say "citizens," I mean citizens of the world and not of this or that sect or nation. With every increase of knowledge and skill, wisdom becomes more necessary, for every such increase augments our capacity for realising our purposes, and therefore augments our capacity for evil, if our purposes are unwise. The world needs wisdom as it has never needed it before; and if knowledge continues to increase, the world will need wisdom in the future even more than it does now.

QUESTIONS

1. According to Russell, what is the difference between knowledge and wisdom? What constitutes true wisdom? What is the essence of wisdom?
2. How does Russell answer this question, "can wisdom . . . be taught"?
3. Explain how the author shades his connotations of the words *knowl-*

edge and *wisdom* so that the audience understands that Russell thinks the latter more important.

4. Define these words: *correlative* (paragraph 1), *eminent* (paragraph 3), *enmity* (paragraph 4), *exhorted* (paragraph 6), and *advocating* (paragraph 7).

5. What sort of introductory paragraph does the author develop?

6. How does Russell employ a pattern of comparison and contrast to structure his essay?

7. Explain the way that Russell integrates a pattern of exemplification into his comparative essay. How does this strategy help him achieve the definition of wisdom?

8. What elements of argumentation and persuasion do you encounter in this essay?

9. How successful have your teachers been in imparting wisdom to you? Do you think that a teacher *should* impart wisdom, or is knowledge sufficient?

10. a. Write your own essay on knowledge and wisdom, using personal examples to highlight differences in the two concepts.
b. Argue for or against the proposition that wisdom can be taught.

JOHN HENRY CARDINAL NEWMAN

What Is a University?

John Henry Newman (1801–1890), English theologian, cardinal, and writer, was a leading thinker of the nineteenth century. His *Apologia pro Vita Sua* (1864) and *The Idea of a University* (1852) are considered literary classics. A convert from Anglicanism, Newman entered the Roman Catholic Church in 1845; in 1879, at the height of his fame, Pope Leo XIII created him a cardinal. In his *Collected Works* (1874–1921), Newman persistently tries to deal with the cultural problems of the modern world from a Christian perspective. In the following essay, from *The Office and Work of Universities* (1856), we sense the concern for moral values and Christian ideals as well as a mastery of prose style that made Newman one of the great figures of the Victorian period.

If I were asked to describe as briefly and popularly as I could, what a University was, I should draw my answer from its ancient designation of a *Studium Generale*, or "School of Universal Learning." This description implies the assemblage of strangers from all parts in one spot;—*from all parts;* else, how will you find professors and students for every department of knowledge? and *in one spot;* else, how can there be any school at all? Accordingly, in its simple and rudimental form, it is a school of knowledge of every kind, consisting of teachers and learners from every quarter. Many things are requisite to complete and satisfy the idea embodied in this description; but such as this a University seems to be in its essence, a place for the communication and circulation of thought, by means of personal intercourse, through a wide extent of country. 1

There is nothing farfetched or unreasonable in the idea thus presented to us; and if this be a University, then a University does but contemplate a necessity of our nature, and is but one specimen in a particular medium, out of many which might be adduced in others, of a provision for that necessity. Mutual education, in a large sense of the word, is one of the great and incessant occupations of human society, carried on partly with set purpose, and partly not. One generation forms another; and the existing generation is ever acting and reacting upon itself in the persons of its individual members. Now, in this process, books, I need scarcely say, that is, the *litera scripta*, are one special instrument. It is true; and emphatically so in this age. Considering the prodigious powers of the press, and how they are developed at this time in the never-intermitting issue of periodicals, tracts, pamphlets, works in series, and light literature, we must allow there never was a time which promised fairer for dispensing with every other means of information and instruction. What can we want more, you will say, for the intellectual education of the whole man, and for every man, than so exuberant and diversified and persistent a promulgation of all kinds of knowledge? Why, you will ask, need we go up to knowledge, when knowledge comes down to us? The Sibyl wrote her prophecies upon the leaves of the forest, and wasted them; but here such careless profusion might be prudently indulged, for it can be afforded without loss, in consequence of the almost fabulous fecundity of the instrument which these latter ages have invented. We have sermons in stones, and books in the running brooks; works larger and more comprehensive than those which have gained for ancients an immortality, issue forth every morning, and are projected onwards to the ends of the earth at the rate of hundreds of miles a day. Our seats are strewed, our pavements are powdered, with swarms of little tracts; and the very bricks of our city walls 2 preach wisdom, by informing us by their placards where we can at once cheaply purchase it.

I allow all this, and much more; such certainly is our popular education, and its effects are remarkable. Nevertheless, after all, even in this age, whenever men are really serious about getting what, in the language of trade, is called "a good article," when they aim at something precise, something refined, something really luminous, something really large, something choice, they go to another market; they avail themselves, in some shape or other, of the rival method, the ancient method, of oral instruction, of present communication between man and man, of teachers instead of learning, of the personal influence of a master, and the humble initiation of a disciple, and, in consequence, of great centers of pilgrimage and throng, which such a method of education necessarily involves. This, I think, will be found to hold good in all those departments or aspects of society, which possess an interest sufficient to bind men together, or to constitute what is called "a world." It holds in the political world, and in the high world, and in the religious world; and it holds also in the literary and scientific world. 3

If the actions of men may be taken as any test of their convictions, then we have reason for saying this, viz.: that the province and the inestimable benefit of the *litera scripta* is that of being a record of truth, and an authority of appeal, and an instrument of teaching in the hands of a teacher; but that, if we wish to become exact and fully furnished in any branch of knowledge which is diversified and complicated, we must consult the living man and listen to his living voice. I am not bound to investigate the cause of this, and anything I may say will, I am conscious, be short of its full analysis—perhaps we may suggest, that no books can get through the number of minute questions which it is possible to ask on any extended subject, or can hit upon the very difficulties which are severally felt by each reader in succession. Or again, that no book can convey the special spirit and delicate peculiarities of its subject with that rapidity and certainty which attend on the sympathy of mind with mind, through the eyes, the look, the accent, and the manner, in casual expressions thrown off at the moment, and the unstudied turns of familiar conversation. But I am already dwelling too long on what is but an incidental portion of my main subject. Whatever be the cause the fact is undeniable. The general principles of any study you may learn by books at home; but the detail, the color, the tone, the air, the life which makes it live in us, you must catch all these from those in whom it lives already. You must imitate the student in French or German, who is not content with his grammar, but goes to Paris or Dresden: you must take example from the young artist, who 4 aspires to visit the great Masters in Florence and in Rome. Till we have discovered some intellectual daguerreotype, which takes off the course of thought, and the form, lineaments, and features of truth, as completely and minutely, as the optical instrument reproduces the sensible object, we must come to the teachers of wisdom to learn wisdom, we must repair to the fountain, and drink there. Portions of it may go from thence to the ends of the earth by means of books; but the fullness is in one place alone. It is in such assemblages and congregations of intellect that books themselves, the masterpieces of human genius, are written, or at least originated.

The principle on which I have been insisting is so obvious, 5
and instances in point are so ready,that I should think it tiresome to proceed with the subject, except that one or two illustrations may serve to explain my own language about it, which may not have done justice to the doctrine which it has been intended to enforce.

For instance, the polished manners and highbred bearing 6
which are so difficult of attainment, and so strictly personal when attained—which are so much admired in society, from society are acquired. All that goes to constitute a gentlemen—the carriage, gait, address, gestures, voice; the ease, the self-possession, the courtesy, the power of conversing, the talent of not offending; the lofty principle, the delicacy of thought, the happiness of expression, the taste and propriety, the generosity and forbearance, the candor and consideration, the openness of hand;—these qualities, some of them come by nature, some of them may be found in any rank, some of them are a direct precept of Christianity; but the full assemblage of them, bound up in the unity of an individual character, do we expect they can be learned from books? Are they not necessarily acquired, where they are to be found, in high society? The very nature of the case leads us to say so; you cannot fence without an antagonist, nor challenge all comers in disputation before you have supported a thesis; and in like manner, it stands to reason, you cannot learn to converse till you have the world to converse with; you cannot unlearn your natural bashfulness, or awkwardness, or stiffness, or other besetting deformity, till you serve your time in some school of manners. Well, and is it not so in matter of fact? The metropolis, the court, the great houses of the land, are the centers to which at stated times the country comes up, as to shrines of refinement and good taste; and then in due time the country goes back again home, enriched with a portion of the social accomplishments, which those very visits serve to call out and heighten in the gracious dispensers of them. We are unable to conceive how the "gentlemanlike" can otherwise be maintained; and maintained in this way it is.

And now a second instance: and here, too, I am going to 7
speak without personal experience of the subject I am introducing. I

admit I have not been in Parliament, any more than I have figured in the *beau monde*; yet I cannot but think that statesmanship, as well as high breeding, is learned, not by books, but in certain centers of education. If it be not presumption to say so, Parliament puts a clever man *au courant* with politics and affairs of state in a way surprising to himself. A member of the Legislature, if tolerably observant, begins to see things with new eyes, even though his views undergo no change. Words have a meaning now, and ideas a reality, such as they had not before. He hears a vast deal in public speeches and private conversation, which is never put into print. The bearings of measures and events, the action of parties, and the persons of friends and enemies, are brought out to the man who is in the midst of them with a distinctness, which the most diligent perusal of newspapers will fail to impart to them. It is access to the fountainheads of political wisdom and experience, it is daily intercourse, of one kind or another, with the multitude who go up to them, it is familiarity with business, it is access to the contributions of fact and opinion thrown together by many witnesses from many quarters, which does this for him. However, I need not account for a fact, to which it is sufficient to appeal; that the Houses of Parliament and the atmosphere around them are a sort of University of politics.

8 As regards the world of science, we find a remarkable instance of the principle which I am illustrating, in the periodical meetings for its advance, which have arisen in the course of the last twenty years, such as the British Association. Such gatherings would to many persons appear at first sight simply preposterous. Above all subjects of study, Science is conveyed, is propagated, by books, or by private teaching; experiments and investigations are conducted in silence; discoveries are made in solitude. What have philosophers to do with festive celebrities, and panegyrical solemnities with mathematical and physical truth? Yet on a closer attention to the subject, it is found that not even scientific thought can dispense with the suggestions, the instruction, the stimulus, the sympathy, the intercourse with mankind on a large scale, which such meetings secure. A fine time of year is chosen, when days are long, skies are bright, the earth smiles, and all nature rejoices; a city or town is taken by turns, of ancient name or modern opulence, where buildings are spacious and hospitality hearty. The novelty of place and circumstance, the excitement of strange, or the refreshment of well-known faces, the majesty of rank or of genius, the amiable charities of men pleased both with themselves and with each other; the elevated spirits, the circulation of thought, the curiosity; the morning sections, the outdoor exercise, the well-furnished, well-earned board, the not ungraceful hilarity, the evening circle; the brilliant lecture, the discussions or collisions or guesses of great men one with another, the narratives of scientific

processes, of hopes, disappointments, conflicts, and successes, the splendid eulogistic orations; these and the like constituents of the annual celebration are considered to do something real and substantial for the advance of knowledge which can be done in no other way. Of course they can but be occasional; they answer to the Annual Act, or Commencement, or Commemoration, of a University, not to its ordinary condition; but they are of a University nature; and I can well believe in their utility. They issue in the promotion of a certain living and, as it were, bodily communication of knowledge from one to another, of a general interchange of ideas, and a comparison and adjustment of science with science, of an enlargement of mind, intellectual and social, of an ardent love of the particular study which may be chosen by each individual, and a noble devotion to its interests.

Such meetings, I repeat, are but periodical, and only partially 9
represent the idea of a University. The bustle and whirl, which are their usual concomitants, are in ill keeping with the order and gravity of earnest intellectual education. We desiderate means of instruction which involve no interruption of our ordinary habits; nor need we seek it long, for the natural course of things brings it about, while we debate over it. In every great country, the metropolis itself becomes a sort of necessary University, whether we will or no. As the chief city is the seat of the court, of high society, of politics, and of law, so as a matter of course is it the seat of letters also; and at this time, for a long term of years, London and Paris are in fact and in operation Universities, though in Paris its famous University is no more, and in London a University scarcely exists except as a board of administration. The newspapers, magazines, reviews, journals, and periodicals of all kinds, the publishing trade, the libraries, museums, and academies there found, the learned and scientific societies, necessarily invest it with the functions of a University; and that atmosphere of intellect, which in a former age hung over Oxford or Bologna or Salamanca, has, with the change of times, moved away to the center of civil government. Thither come up youths from all parts of the country, the students of law, medicine, and the fine arts, and the *employés* and *attachés* of literature. There they live, as chance determines; and they are satisfied with their temporary home, for they find in it all that was promised to them there. They have not come in vain, as far as their own object in coming is concerned. They have not learned any particular religion, but they have learned their own particular profession well. They have, moreover, become acquainted with the habits, manners, and opinions of their place of sojourn, and done their part in maintaining the tradition of them. We cannot then be without virtual Universities; a metropolis is such: the simple question is, whether the education sought and given should be based

on principle, formed upon rule, directed to the highest ends, or left to the random succession of masters and schools, one after another, with a melancholy waste of thought and an extreme hazard of truth.

Religious teaching itself affords us an illustration of our subject to a certain point. It does not, indeed, seat itself merely in centers of the world; this is impossible from the nature of the case. It is intended for the many, not the few; its subject matter is truth necessary for us, not truth recondite and rare; but it concurs in the principle of a University so far as this, that its great instrument, or rather organ, has ever been that which nature prescribes in all education, the personal presence of a teacher, or, in theological language, Oral Tradition. It is the living voice, the breathing form, the expressive countenance, which preaches, which catechizes. Truth, a subtle, invisible, manifold spirit, is poured into the mind of the scholar by his eyes and ears, through his affections, imagination, and reason; it is poured into his mind and is sealed up there in perpetuity, by propounding and repeating it, by questioning and requestioning, by correcting and explaining, by progressing and then recurring to first principles, by all those ways which are implied in the word "catechizing." In the first ages, it was a work of long time; months, sometimes years, were devoted to the arduous task of disabusing the mind of the incipient Christian of its pagan errors, and of molding it upon the Christian faith. The Scriptures, indeed, were at hand for the study of those who could avail themselves of them; but St. Irenaeus does not hesitate to speak of whole races who had been converted to Christianity without being able to read them. To be unable to read or write was in those times no evidence of want of learning: the hermits of the deserts were, in this sense of the word, illiterate; yet the great St. Anthony, though he knew not letters, was a match in disputation for the learned philosophers who came to try him. Didymus again, the great Alexandrian theologian, was blind. The ancient discipline, called the *Disciplina Arcani,* involved the same principle. The more sacred doctrines of Revelation were not committed to books but passed on by successive tradition. The teaching on the Blessed Trinity and the Eucharist appears to have been so handed down for some hundred years; and when at length reduced to writing, it has filled many folios, yet has not been exhausted. 10

But I have said more than enough in illustration; I end as I began;—a University is a place of concourse, whither students come from every quarter for every kind of knowledge. You cannot have the best of every kind everywhere; you must go to some great city or emporium for it. There you have all the choicest productions of nature and art all together, which you find each in its own separate place elsewhere. All the riches of the land, and of the earth, are carried up thither; there are the best markets, and there the best 11 workmen. It is the center of trade, the supreme court of fashion, the umpire of rival talents, and the standard of things rare and precious. It is the place for seeing galleries of first-rate pictures, and for hearing wonderful voices and performers of transcendent skill. It is the place for great preachers, great orators, great nobles, great statesmen. In the nature of things, greatness and unity go together; excellence implies a center. And such, for the third or fourth time, is a University; I hope I do not weary out the reader by repeating it. It is the place to which a thousand schools make contributions; in which the intellect may safely range and speculate, sure to find its equal in some antagonist activity, and its judge in the tribunal of truth. It is a place where inquiry is pushed forward, and discoveries verified and perfected, and rashness rendered innocuous, and error exposed, by the collision of mind with mind, and knowledge with knowledge. It is the place where the professor becomes eloquent, and is a missionary and a preacher, displaying his science in its most complete and most winning form, pouring it forth with the zeal of enthusiasm, and lighting up his own love of it in the breasts of his hearers. It is the place where the catechist makes good his ground as he goes, treading in the truth day by day into the ready memory, and wedging and tightening it into the expanding reason. It is a place which wins the admiration of the young by its celebrity, kindles the affections of the middle-aged by its beauty, and rivets the fidelity of the old by its associations. It is a seat of wisdom, a light of the world, a minister of the faith, an Alma Mater of the rising generation. It is this and a great deal more, and demands a somewhat better head and hand than mine to describe it well.

Such is a University in its idea and in its purpose; such in 12
good measure has it before now been in fact. Shall it ever be again? We are going forward in the strength of the Cross, under the patronage of the Blessed Virgin, in the name of St. Patrick, to attempt it.

QUESTIONS

1. How does Newman define a university? What specific purposes does it serve?

2. What distinctions does the author draw between popular education and university education? Why is the city a type of university?

3. Newman's style in this essay is distinguished by, among other elements, a consistent pattern of balance and parallelism in sentence structure. Locate examples and explain their effect.

4. Carefully analyze the diction in this essay, and evaluate the preconceptions Newman must have had of his reading audience.

5. What is the function of Newman's introductory paragraph?

6. Cite several representative examples of Newman's use of topic sentences to control the unity and coherence of his relatively long and dense paragraphs.

7. Explain the way in which a pattern of example serves to reinforce Newman's main rhetorical goal of offering a definition of a univeristy.

8. How do the author's comparisons help him support his thesis?

9. Evaluate the effectiveness of Newman's concluding paragraph. Can it be justified? Why, or why not?

10. a. Write your own definition of a university.
b. Compare and contrast university knowledge and "street" knowledge.

JOHN DEWEY

Education and Social Change

John Dewey (1859–1952), one of the most influential thinkers of his time, profoundly affected the course of education, politics, psychology, and law in America. First at the University of Chicago and then at Columbia University, Dewey between 1894 and 1930 was an internationally acclaimed educational experimenter, activist, and humanitarian. A proponent of "instrumentalism" or learning by doing, Dewey believed that active and free inquiry was the essence of both educational and democratic process. In *Democracy and Education* (1916), he wrote that people "have to *do* something to the things when they wish to find out something; they have to alter conditions." This belief is also at the basis of Dewey's progressive argument in the following essay.

Attention has been continually called of late to the fact that society is in process of change, and that the schools tend to lag behind. We are all familiar with the pleas that are urged to bring education in the schools into closer relation with the forces that are producing social change and with the needs that arise from these changes. Probably no question has 1 received so much attention in educational discussion during the past few years as the problem of integration of the schools with social life. Upon these general matters, I could hardly do more than reiterate what has often been said.

Nevertheless, there is as yet little consensus of opinion as to 2
what the schools can do in relation to the forces of social change and how they should do it. There are those who assert in effect that the schools must simply reflect social changes that have already occurred, as best they may. Some would go so far as to make the work of schools virtually parasitic. Others hold that the schools should take an active part in *directing* social change, and share in the construction of a new social order. Even among the latter there is, however, marked difference of attitude. Some think the schools should assume this directive role by means of indoctrination; others oppose this method. Even if there were more unity of thought than exists there would still be the practical problem of overcoming institutional inertia so as to realize in fact an agreed-upon program.

There is, accordingly, no need to justify further discussion of 3
the problem of the relation of education to social change. I shall do what I can, then, to indicate the factors that seem to me to enter into the problem, together with some of the reasons that prove that the schools do have a role—and an important one—in *production* of social change.

One factor inherent in the situation is that schools *do* follow 4
and reflect the social "order" that exists. I do not make this statement as a grudging admission, nor yet in order to argue that they should *not* do so. I make it rather as a statement of a *conditioning* factor which supports the conclusion that the schools thereby do take part in the determination of a future social order; and that, accordingly, the problem is not whether the schools *should* participate in the production of a future society (since they do so anyway) but whether they should do it blindly and irresponsibly or with the maximum possible of courageous intelligence and responsibility.

The grounds that lead me to make this statement are as 5
follows: The existing state of society, which the schools reflect, is not something fixed and uniform. The idea that such is the case is a self-imposed hallucination. Social conditions are not only in process of change, but the changes going on are in different directions, so different as to produce social confusion and conflict. There is no single and clear-cut pattern that pervades and holds together in a unified way the social conditions and forces that operate. It requires a good deal of either ignorance or intellectual naivete to suppose that these changes have all been tending to one coherent social outcome. The plaint of the conservative about the imperiling of old and

time-tried values and truths, and the efforts of reactionaries to stem the tide of changes that occur, are sufficient evidence, if evidence be needed to the contrary.

Of course the schools have mirrored the social changes that take place. The notion that the educational system has been static is too absurd for notice; it has been and still is in a state of flux. 6

The fact that it is possible to argue about the desirability of many of the changes that have occurred, and to give valid reasons for deploring aspects of the flux, is not relevant to the main point. For the stonger the arguments brought forth on these points, and the greater the amount of evidence produced to show that the educational system is in a state of disorder and confusion, the greater is the proof that the schools have responded to, and have reflected, social conditions which are themselves in a state of confusion and conflict. 7

Do those who hold the idea that the schools should not attempt to give direction to social change accept complacently the confusion that exists, because the schools *have* followed in the track of one social change after another? They certainly do not, although the logic of their position demands it. For the most part they are severe critics of the existing state of education. They are as a rule opposed to the studies called modern and the method called progressive. They tend to favor return to older types of studies and to strenuous "disciplinary" methods. What does this attitude mean? Does it not show that its advocates in reality adopt the position that the schools can do something to affect positively and constructively social conditions? For they hold in effect that the school should discriminate with respect to the social forces that play upon it; that instead of accepting the latter *in toto*, education should select and organize in a given direction. The adherents of this view can hardly believe that the effect of selection and organization will stop at the doors of school rooms. They must expect some ordering and healing influence to be exerted sooner or later upon the structure and movement of life outside. What they are really doing when they deny directive social effect to education is to express their opposition to some of the directions social change is actually taking, and their choice of other social forces as those with which education should throw in its lot so as to promote as far as may be their victory in the strife of forces. They are conservatives in education because they are socially conservative and vice-versa. 8

This is as it should be in the interest of clearness and consistency of thought and action. If these conservatives in education were more aware of what is involved in their position, and franker in stating its implications, they would help bring out the real issue. It is not whether the schools shall or shall not influence the course of 9 future social life, but in what direction they shall do so and how. In some fashion or other, the schools will influence social life anyway. But they can exercise such influence in different ways and to different ends, and the important thing is to become conscious of these different ways and ends, so that an intelligent choice may be made, and so that if opposed choices are made, the further conflict may at least be carried on with understanding of what is at stake, and not in the dark.

There are three possible directions of choice. Educators may 10
act so as to perpetuate the present confusion and possibly increase it. That will be the result of drift, and under present conditions to drift is in the end to make a choice. Or they may select the newer scientific, technological, and cultural forces that are producing change in the old order; may estimate the direction in which they are moving and their outcome if they are given freer play, and see what can be done to make the schools their ally. Or, educators may become intelligently conservative and strive to make the schools a force in maintaining the old order intact against the impact of new forces.

If the second course is chosen—as of course I believe it should 11
be—the problem will be other than merely that of accelerating the rate of the change that is going on. The problem will be to develop the insight and understanding that will enable the youth who go forth from the schools to take part in the great work of construction and organization that will have to be done,and to equip them with the attitudes and habits of action that will make their understanding and insight practically effective.

There is much that can be said for an intelligent conservatism. 12
I do not know anything that can be said for perpetuation of a wavering, uncertain, confused condition of social life and education. Nevertheless, the easiest thing is to refrain from fundamental thinking and let things go on drifting. Upon the basis of any other policy than drift—which after all is a policy, though a blind one—every special issue and problem, whether that of selection and organization of subject-matter of study, of methods of teaching, of school buildings and equipment, of school administration, is a special phase of the inclusive and fundamental problem: What movement of social forces, economic, political, religious, cultural, shall the school take to be controlling in its aims and methods, and with which forces shall the school align itself?

Failure to discuss educational problems from this point of 13
view but intensifies the existing confusion. Apart from this background, and outside of this perspective, educational questions have to be settled *ad hoc* and are speedily unsettled. What is suggested does not mean that the schools shall throw themselves into the political

and economic arena and take sides with some party there. I am not talking about parties; I am talking about social forces and their movement. In spite of absolute claims that are made for this party or that, it is altogether probable that existing parties and sects themselves suffer from existing confusions and conflicts, so that the understanding, the ideas, and attitudes that control their policies, need re-education and re-orientation. I know that there are some who think that the implications of what I have said point to abstinence and futility; that they negate the stand first taken. But I am surprised when educators adopt this position, for it shows a profound lack of faith in their own calling. It assumes that education as education has nothing or next to nothing to contribute; that formation of understanding and disposition counts for nothing; that only immediate overt action counts and that it can count equally whether or not it has been modified by education.

Before leaving this aspect of the subject, I wish to recur to the 14
utopian nature of the idea that the schools can be completely neutral. This idea sets up an end incapable of accomplishment. So far as it is acted upon, it has a definite social effect, but that effect is, as I have said, perpetuation of disorder and increase of blind because unintelligent conflict. Practically, moreover, the weight of such action falls upon the reactionary side. Perhaps the most effective way of reinforcing reaction under the name of neutrality, consists in keeping the oncoming generation ignorant of the conditions in which they live and the issues they have to face. This effect is the more pronounced because it is subtle and indirect; because neither teachers nor those taught are aware of what they are doing and what is being done to them. Clarity can develop only in the extent to which there is frank acknowledgment of the basic issue: Where shall the social emphasis of school life and work fall, and what are the educational policies which correspond to this emphasis?

QUESTIONS

1. Explain briefly Dewey's position on the debate over education and social change.

2. What is Dewey's attitude toward conservatives and conservatism in general? What can you infer about his own political, philosophical, and educational biases from this essay?

3. How important are the connotations of the following words to the reading of Dewey's essay: *social change, parasitic, indoctrination, self-imposed hallucination, reactionaries,* and *intelligent conservatism*?

4. How does the author's overall use of language reflect his purpose?

5. Which paragraphs constitute the introductory selection of this essay? How does the author establish an argumentative context for his discussion?

6. In what manner does the author use a pattern of cause and effect?

7. How does the author employ classification to logically develop his argument?

8. Explain the method and purpose of the last paragraph.

9. Dewey wrote this essay in 1937. What were the forces of social change, confusion, and conflict that he was alluding to? How do his observations apply to the social and educational situations today?

10. a. Argue for or against the proposition that schools should be agents of social change.
b. Analyze the factors and forces behind the current crisis in public school education.

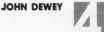

5 Human Development and Behavior

VIRGINIA WOOLF

The Death of the Moth

Virginia Woolf (1882–1941), English novelist and essayist, was the daughter of Leslie Stephen, a famous critic and writer on economics. An experimental novelist, Woolf attempted to portray consciousness through a poetic, symbolic, and concrete style. Her novels include *Jacob's Room* (1922), *Mrs. Dalloway* (1925), *To the Lighthouse* (1927), and *The Waves* (1931). She was also a perceptive reader and critic, and her criticism appears in *The Common Reader* (1925) and *The Second Common Reader* (1933). The following essay, which demonstrates Woolf's capacity to convey profound meaning even in commonplace events, appeared in *The Death of a Moth and Other Essays* (1948).

1 Moths that fly by day are not properly to be called moths; they do not excite that pleasant sense of dark autumn nights and ivy-blossom which the commonest yellow-underwing asleep in the shadow of the curtain never fails to rouse in us. They are hybrid creatures, neither gay like butterflies nor sombre like their own species. Nevertheless the present specimen, with his narrow hay-coloured wings, fringed with

a tassel of the same colour, seemed to be content with life. It was a pleasant morning, mid-September, mild, benignant, yet with a keener breath than that of the summer months. The plough was already scoring the field opposite the window, and where the share had been, the earth was pressed flat and gleamed with moisture. Such vigour came rolling in from the fields and the down beyond that it was difficult to keep the eyes strictly turned upon the book. The rooks too were keeping one of their annual festivities; soaring round the tree tops until it looked as if a vast net with thousands of black knots in it had been cast up into the air; which, after a few moments sank slowly down upon the trees until every twig seemed to have a knot at the end of it. Then, suddenly, the net would be thrown into the air again in a wider circle this time, with the utmost clamour and vociferation, as though to be thrown into the air and settle slowly down upon the tree tops were a tremendously exciting experience.

The same energy which inspired the rooks, the ploughmen, 2
the horses, and even, it seemed, the lean bare-backed downs, sent the moth fluttering from side to side of his square of the window-pane. One could not help watching him. One, was, indeed, conscious of a queer feeling of pity for him. The possibilities of pleasure seemed that morning so enormous and so various that to have only a moth's part in life, and a day moth's at that, appeared a hard fate, and his zest in enjoying his meagre opportunities to the full, pathetic. He flew vigorously to one corner of his compartment, and, after waiting there a second, flew across to the other. What remained for him but to fly to a third corner and then to a fourth? That was all he could do, in spite of the size of the downs, the width of the sky, the far-off smoke of houses, and the romantic voice, now and then, of a steamer out at sea. What he could do he did. Watching him, it seemed as if a fibre, very thin but pure, of the enormous energy of the world had been thrust into his frail and diminutive body. As often as he crossed the pane, I could fancy that a thread of vital light became visible. He was little or nothing but life.

Yet, because he was so small, and so simple a form of the 3
energy that was rolling in at the open window and driving its way through so many narrow and intricate corridors in my own brain and in those of other human beings, there was something marvellous as well as pathetic about him. It was as if someone had taken a tiny bead of pure life and decking it as lightly as possible with down and feathers, had set it dancing and zigzagging to show us the true nature of life. Thus displayed one could not get over the strangeness of it. One is apt to forget all about life, seeing it humped and bossed and garnished and cumbered so that it has to move with the greatest circumspection and dignity. Again, the thought of all that life might

have been had he been born in any other shape caused one to view his simple activities with a kind of pity.

After a time, tired by his dancing apparently, he settled on 4
the window ledge in the sun, and, the queer spectacle being at an end, I forgot about him. Then, looking up, my eye was caught by him. He was trying to resume his dancing, but seemed either so stiff or so awkward that he could only flutter to the bottom of the window-pane; and when he tried to fly across it he failed. Being intent on other matters I watched these futile attempts for a time without thinking, unconsciously waiting for him to resume his flight, as one waits for a machine, that has stopped momentarily, to start again without considering the reason of its failure. After perhaps a seventh attempt he slipped from the wooden ledge and fell, fluttering his wings, on to his back on the window sill. The helplessness of his attitude roused me. It flashed upon me that he was in difficulties; he could no longer raise himself; his legs struggled vainly. But, as I stretched out a pencil, meaning to help him to right himself, it came over me that the failure and awkwardness were the approach of death. I laid the pencil down again.

The legs agitated themselves once more. I looked as if for the 5
enemy against which he struggled. I looked out of doors. What had happened there? Presumably it was midday, and work in the fields had stopped. Stillness and quiet had replaced the previous animation. The birds had taken themselves off to feed in the brooks. The horses stood still. Yet the power was there all the same, massed outside, indifferent, impersonal, not attending to anything in particular. Somehow it was opposed to the little hay-coloured moth. It was useless to try to do anything. One could only watch the extraordinary efforts made by those tiny legs against an oncoming doom which could, had it chosen, have submerged an entire city, not merely a city, but masses of human beings; nothing, I knew had any chance against death. Nevertheless after a pause of exhaustion the legs fluttered again. It was superb this last protest, and so frantic that he succeeded at last in righting himself. One's sympathies, of course, were all on the side of life. Also, when there was nobody to care or to know, this gigantic effort on the part of an insignificant little moth, against a power of such magnitude, to retain what no one else valued or desired to keep, moved one strangely. Again, somehow, one saw life, a pure bead. I lifted the pencil again, useless though I knew it to be. But even as I did so, the unmistakable tokens of death showed themselves. The body relaxed, and instantly grew stiff. The struggle was over. The insignificant little creature now knew death. As I looked at the dead moth, this minute wayside triumph of so great a force over so mean an antagonist filled me with wonder. Just as life

had been strange a few minutes before, so death was now as strange. The moth having righted himself now lay most decently and uncomplainingly composed. O yes, he seemed to say, death is stronger than I am.

QUESTIONS

1. Why is Woolf so moved by the moth's death? Why does she call the moth's protest (paragraph 5) "superb"?

2. What, according to Woolf, is the "true nature of life"?

3. Examine Woolf's use of similes in paragraph 1. Where else does she use similes? Are any of them similar to the similes used in paragraph 1?

4. Why does the author personify the moth?

5. What sentences constitute the introduction of this essay? What rhetorical device do they use?

6. Divide the essay into two parts. Why did you divide the essay where you did? How are the two parts different? How are they similar?

7. Explain the importance of description in this essay. Where, particularly, does Woolf describe the setting of her scene? How does that description contribute to the development of her essay? How does she describe the moth, and how does this description affect tone?

8. How is narration used to structure the essay?

9. Woolf implicitly connects insect and human life. What else can we learn about human development by looking at other forms of life?

10. a. Write a detailed description of a small animal. Try to invest it with the importance that Woolf gives this moth.
b. Write a description of a scene, using details and metaphors.

ROLLO MAY

Powerlessness Corrupts

Rollo May (1909–) is a writer and psychologist. He was a student of Karen Horney and has written about the growth of the self. His works include *Man's Search for Himself* (1952), *Love and Will* (1969), *Power and Innocence* (1972), and *The*

Meaning of Anxiety (1977). In *Power and Innocence,* from which the following essay is excerpted, May details how violence arises from the individual's perception of his or her powerlessness.

1 The relationship of powerlessness and psychosis was impressed upon me a number of years ago when I started work as a psychotherapist. In the mentally troubled person psychotherapists are able to see the extremes of the behavior and the experience of us all. It bears out the words of Edgar Z. Friedenberg: "All weakness tends to corrupt, and impotence corrupts absolutely."

2 A young musician, Priscilla, was one of my first patients. According to the person who administered her Rorschach, she had "one foot in schizophrenia and the other on a banana peel." In her sessions with me she would give long, involved comparisons of the colors of the musical notes made by the train from Newark in contrast to those made by the train from New Brunswick. I had not the slightest idea about what she was talking much of the time—and she knew it. But she seemed to need me as a person who listened, wanting and trying to understand her whether I succeeded or not. She was also a woman with considerable dignity and a sense of humor, which helped us immeasurably.

3 But she could never get angry. Not at me or her parents or anyone else. Her self-esteem was so shaky and vague as to be almost nonexistent. Once a young man in a chorus to which she belonged asked her to go to a concert with him. She accepted. But the next day, in a surge of self-doubts, she phoned him to say: "You don't have to take me if you don't want to." She could not affirm or assert herself enough to conceive that someone might *like* to go to a concert with her. When, at the age of eight or nine, she would play football with a boy slightly older than she, he would run into her hard enough to hurt her. Another child might have yelled at the boy, or started a fight, or cried, or abandoned the game; these are all, good or bad, ways of coping. But Priscilla could utilize none of these methods; she could only sit there on the ground, looking at him and silently thinking that he shouldn't hit her so hard.

4 When she was exploited, as she often was, sexually and financially, she had no defenses, no way of drawing a line beyond which she could firmly say "no," no anger to support her. (One gets a feeling that such persons almost invite exploitation—it at least gives them some relationship and significance.) Along with her inability to get angry, there went, as a necessary corollary, a deep experience of powerlessness and an almost complete lack of capacity to influence or affect other people in interpersonal relations.

But such a person has another side which, as I have 5
confirmed in working with many borderline patients since, is completely different. Priscilla's dreams were of cut-up bodies put in bags, of blood and battles—in short, as *violent* as her conscious life was docile.

Since that time and partly due to this young woman, I have 6
frequently reflected on the relationship between powerlessness and madness. I am purposely stressing both meanings of the word *mad*: its personal sense of enragedness to the point of violence; and its historical psychiatric sense of psychosis. There is a relationship between the two, and this double use of the term may lead us to the center of the problem.

We know that a common characteristic of all mental patients 7
is their powerlessness, and with it goes a constant anxiety which is both cause and effect of the impotence. The patients' insignificance is so firmly assumed by them that they accept it as a given, often going through life making sad and pitiful gestures to get whatever bit of significance they can. An adolescent girl came to consult me in the middle of the day wearing a crinoline evening dress, possibly one of the prettiest things she had, as a gesture of how much she needed my attention and concern, unaware that it was likely to be regarded as out of place.

When a person like Priscilla can no longer support this way of 8
life, something "cracks" within her and she may then move into a state in which she is nothing but mad. The person then seems to be the exact opposite of what she had been. The violence of dreams like Priscilla's then becomes the content of her waking life. The person seems *all* madness, which is surely why psychosis through the centuries was called madness. Mad now at everybody, including herself, the person threatens or attempts suicide, cuts her wrists, smears blood over the doors in hospitals to dramatize her need of the attendants and interns. She does overt violence to herself and whoever gets in the range of her projections.

We see the same movement in other patients. In the autobio- 9
graphical novel on her own schizophrenia *I Never Promised You a Rose Garden,* Hannah Green was admitted to Chestnut Lodge at sixteen. She was the epitome of docility and placidity, never showing any anger at all. Whenever she needed to, she withdrew into the mythology of her private spirit world and talked with mythical figures. Dr. Frieda Fromm-Reichman, the psychiatrist at Chestnut Lodge who treated her, dealt with this mythology with respect, assuring Hannah that she would not take it away as long as the girl needed it. But when Dr. Fromm-Reichman went to Europe one summer, another, younger doctor was assigned to the girl. He charged in, blithely courageous, to break up her mythological world.

The results were disastrous. In her explosion of violence, the patient set fire to herself and to her belongings at the Lodge, scarring herself for life. The error of the young doctor was that he did not appreciate that the mythology was what gave significance to Hannah's existence. The question was not whether it was theoretically right or wrong, but its function for her. This placid patient, who seemed incapable of any aggressive act, swung from docility into outright violence.

This may seem and feel like power to the hospital attendants, 10
but it is a *pseudopower*, an expression of impotence. The patient may now be spoken of as "mad," which means that she does not fit the accepted criteria in our society which, like all societies, prefers a docile, placid "face." It is important to see that the violence is the end result of repressed anger and rage, combined with constant fear based on the patient's powerlessness. Behind the pseudopower of the madness we can often find a person struggling for some sense of significance, some way of making a difference and establishing some self-esteem.

When Priscilla was in treatment with me, she received a 11
newspaper from her home town in which it was reported that a certain man in her village had committed suicide. She said to me: "If only one other person in that town had known him, he would not have committed suicide." Note that she did not say, "If *he* had known someone," but "if someone had known *him*." She was telling me, I believed, that she would not put a violent end to her life so long as I was related to her. But she was also describing something critically important for a human being—*the necessity of having somebody listen, recognize, know him*. It gives a person the conviction that he counts, that he exists as part of the human race. It also gives him some orientation, a point where he can find meaning in an otherwise meaningless world.

It would be a red-letter day when Priscilla could get angry 12
with me, for I knew that she could then begin to protect herself in her contacts with other people in the wide world. And what is more, she could dare to live out her considerable capacities as an original and lovable as well as loving human being.

QUESTIONS

1. According to May, what is the relationship between madness and powerlessness?

2. According to May, how does violence manifest itself in a psychotic person? Who represses anger?

3. Explain the meanings of the following psychological terms: *psychosis* (paragraph 1); *anxiety* and *schizophrenia* (paragraph 2), *pseudopower* (paragraph 10), and *impotence* (paragraph 10).

4. Explain the allusion in the title and in Friedenberg's quote.

5. Explain how and where May uses cause and effect to develop his thesis.

6. Identify the extended examples in this essay. To what general ideas are they related? How do they contribute to the goals of the essay?

7. Show where and how May describes the process of psychoanalysis and how process analysis contributes to the structuring of the essay.

8. Look at the transition words in this essay. How do they mark the development of the essay?

9. How do most people respond to anger? Does our society encourage us to suppress anger? How do you feel about anger?

10. Using May's insights, describe a moment in your life when you either expressed or repressed anger and explain how it made you feel.

BENJAMIN FRANKLIN

Remarks Concerning the Savages of North America

Benjamin Franklin (1706–1790), statesman, inventor, philanthropist, printer, scientist, diplomat, and author, was a founding father of the United States and a seminal figure in the development of a native American humor, language, and culture. *Poor Richard's Almanack* (1732–1757) and his *Autobiography* (written between 1771 and 1789) have both had a tremendous influence upon American readers and authors. In the essay below, Franklin observes the American Indian with the scientific objectivity he often practiced.

Savages we call them, because their Manners differ from ours, which we think the Perfection of Civility; they think the same of theirs. 1

Perhaps, if we could examine the Manners of 2
different Nations with Impartiality, we should find no People so rude,

as to be without any Rules of Politeness; nor any so polite, as not to have some Remains of Rudeness.

The Indian Men, when young, are Hunters and Warriors; 3
when old, Counsellors; for all their Government is by Counsel of the Sages; there is no Force, there are no Prisons, no Officers to compel Obedience, or inflict Punishment. Hence they generally study Oratory, the best Speaker having the most Influence. The Indian Women till the Ground, dress the Food, nurse and bring up the Children, and preserve and hand down to Posterity the Memory of public Transactions. These Employments of Men and Women are accounted natural and honourable. Having few artificial Wants, they have abundance of Leisure for Improvement by Conversation. Our laborious Manner of Life, compared with theirs, they esteem slavish and base; and the Learning, on which we value ourselves, they regard as frivolous and useless. An Instance of this occurred at the Treaty of Lancaster, in Pennsylvania, *anno* 1744, between the Government of Virginia and the Six Nations. After the principal Business was settled, the Commissioners from Virginia acquainted the Indians by a Speech, that there was at Williamsburg a College, with a Fund for Educating Indian youth; and that, if the Six Nations would send down half a dozen of their young Lads to that College, the Government would take care that they should be well provided for, and instructed in all the Learning of the White People. It is one of the Indian Rules of Politeness not to answer a public Proposition the same day that it is made; they think it would be treating it as a light matter, and that they show it Respect by taking time to consider it, as of a Matter important. They therefore deferr'd their Answer till the Day following; when their Speaker began, by expressing their deep Sense of the kindness of the Virginia Government, in making them that Offer; "for we know," says he, "that you highly esteem the kind of Learning taught in those Colleges, and that the Maintenance of our young Men, while with you, would be very expensive to you. We are convinc'd, therefore, that you mean to do us Good by your Proposal; and we thank you heartily. But you, who are wise, must know that different Nations have different Conceptions of things; and you will therefore not take it amiss, if our Ideas of this kind of Education happen not to be the same with yours. We have had some Experience of it; Several of our young People were formerly brought up at the Colleges of the Northern Provinces; they were instructed in all your Sciences; but, when they came back to us, they were bad Runners, ignorant of every means of living in the Woods, unable to bear either Cold or Hunger, knew neither how to build a Cabin, take a Deer, or kill an Enemy, spoke our Language imperfectly, were therefore neither fit for Hunters, Warriors, nor Counsellors; they were totally good for nothing. We are however not the less oblig'd by your kind Offer, tho' we decline

accepting it; and, to show our grateful Sense of it, if the Gentlemen of Virginia will send us a Dozen of their Sons, we will take great Care of their Education, instruct them in all we know, and make *Men* of them."

Having frequent Occasions to hold public Councils, they have acquired great Order and Decency in conducting them. The old Men sit in the foremost Ranks, the Warriors in the next, and the Women and Children in the hindmost. The Business of the Women is to take exact Notice of what passes, imprint it in their Memories (for they have no Writing), and communicate it to their Children. They are the Records of the Council, and they preserve Traditions of the Stipulations in Treaties 100 Years back; which, when we compare with our Writings, we always find exact. He that would speak, rises. The rest observe a profound Silence. When he has finish'd and sits down, they leave him 5 or 6 Minutes to recollect, that, if he has omitted any thing he intended to say, or has any thing to add, he may rise again and deliver it. To interrupt another, even in common Conversation, is reckon'd highly indecent. How different this is from the conduct of a polite British House of Commons, where scarce a day passes without some Confusion, that makes the Speaker hoarse in calling *to Order;* and how different from the Mode of Conversation in many polite Companies of Europe, where, if you do not deliver your Sentence with great Rapidity, you are cut off in the middle of it by the Impatient Loquacity of those you converse with, and never suffer'd to finish it! 4

The Politeness of these Savages in Conversation is indeed carried to Excess, since it does not permit them to contradict or deny the Truth of what is asserted in their Presence. By this means they indeed avoid Disputes; but then it becomes difficult to know their Minds, or what Impression you make upon them. The Missionaries who have attempted to convert them to Christianity, all complain of this as one of the great Difficulties of their Mission. The Indians hear with Patience the Truths of the Gospel explain'd to them, and give their usual Tokens of Assent and Approbation; you would think they were convinc'd. No such matter. It is mere Civility. 5

A Swedish Minister, having assembled the chiefs of the Susquehanah Indians, made a Sermon to them, acquainting them with the principal historical Facts on which our Religion is founded; such as the Fall of our first Parents by eating an Apple, the coming of Christ to repair the Mischief, his Miracles and Suffering, &c. When he had finished an Indian Orator stood up to thank him. "What you have told us," says he, "is all very good. It is indeed bad to eat Apples. It is better to make them all into Cyder. We are much oblig'd by your kindness in coming so far, to tell us these Things which you have heard from your Mothers. In return, I will tell you some of those we have heard from ours. In the Beginning, our Fathers had only the 6

Flesh of Animals to subsist on; and if their Hunting was unsuccessful, they were starving. Two of our young Hunters, having kill'd a Deer, made a Fire in the Woods to broil some Part of it. When they were about to satisfy their Hunger, they beheld a beautiful young Woman descend from the Clouds, and seat herself on that Hill, which you see yonder among the blue Mountains. They said to each other, it is a Spirit that has smelt our broiling Venison, and wishes to eat of it; let us offer some to her. They presented her with the Tongue; she was pleas'd with the Taste of it, and said, 'Your kindness shall be rewarded; come to this Place after thirteen Moons, and you shall find something that will be of great Benefit in nourishing you and your Children to the latest Generations.' They did so, and, to their Surprise, found Plants they had never seen before; but which, from that ancient time, have been constantly cultivated among us, to our great Advantage. Where her right Hand had touched the Ground, they found Maize; where her left hand had touch'd it, they found Kidney-Beans; and where her Backside had sat on it, they found Tobacco." The good Missionary, disgusted with this idle Tale, said, "What I delivered to you were sacred Truths; but what you tell me is mere Fable, Fiction, and Falsehood." The Indian, offended, reply'd, "My brother, it seems your Friends have not done you Justice in your Education; they have not well instructed you in the Rules of common Civility. You saw that we, who understand and practise those Rules, believ'd all your stories; why do you refuse to believe ours?"

When any of them come into our Towns, our People are apt to 7
crowd round them, gaze upon them, and incommode them, where they desire to be private; this they esteem great Rudeness, and the Effect of the Want of Instruction in the Rules of Civility and good Manners. "We have," say they, "as much Curiosity as you, and when you come into our Towns, we wish for Opportunities of looking at you; but for this purpose we hide ourselves behind Bushes, where you are to pass, and never intrude ourselves into your Company."

Their Manner of entering one another's village has likewise 8
its Rules. It is reckon'd uncivil in travelling Strangers to enter a Village abruptly, without giving Notice of their Approach. Therefore, as soon as they arrive within hearing, they stop and hollow, remaining there till invited to enter. Two old Men usually come out to them, and lead them in. There is in every Village a vacant Dwelling, called *the Strangers' House.* Here they are plac'd, while the old Men go round from Hut to Hut, acquainting the Inhabitants, that Strangers are arriv'd, who are probably hungry and weary; and every one sends them what he can spare of Victuals, and Skins to repose on. When the Strangers are refresh'd, Pipes and Tobacco are brought; and then, but not before, Conversation begins, with Enquiries who they are, whither bound, what News, &c.; and it usually ends with offers of

Service, if the Strangers have occasion of Guides, or any Necessaries for continuing their Journey; and nothing is exacted for the Entertainment.

The same Hospitality, esteem'd among them as a principal 9
Virtue, is practis'd by private Persons; of which Conrad Weiser, our Interpreter, gave me the following Instance. He had been naturaliz'd among the Six Nations, and spoke well the Mohock Language. In going thro' the Indian Country, to carry a Message from our Governor to the Council at Onondaga, he call'd at the Habitation of Canassatego, an old Acquaintance, who embrac'd him, spread Furs for him to sit on, plac'd before him some boil'd Beans and Venison, and mix'd some Rum and Water for his Drink. When he was well refresh'd, and had lit his Pipe, Canassatego began to converse with him; ask'd how he had far'd the many Years since they had seen each other; whence he then came; what occasion'd the Journey, &c. Conrad answered all his Questions; and when the Discourse began to flag, the Indian, to continue it, said, "Conrad, you have lived long among the white People, and know something of their Customs; I have been sometimes at Albany, and have observed, that once in Seven Days they shut up their Shops, and assemble all in the great House; tell me what it is for? What do they do there?" "They meet there," says Conrad, "to hear and learn *good Things*." "I do not doubt," says the Indian, "that they tell you so; they have told me the same; but I doubt the Truth of what they say, and I will tell you my Reasons. I went lately to Albany to sell my Skins and buy Blankets, Knives, Powder, Rum, &c. You know I us'd generally to deal with Hans Hanson; but I was a little inclin'd this time to try some other Merchant. However, I call'd first upon Hans, and asked him what he would give for Beaver. He said he could not give any more than four Shillings a Pound; 'but,' says he, 'I cannot talk on Business now; this is the Day when we meet together to learn *Good Things*, and I am going to the Meeting.' So I thought to myself, 'Since we cannot do any Business to-day, I may as well go to the meeting too,' and I went with him. There stood up a Man in Black, and began to talk to the People very angrily. I did not understand what he said; but, perceiving that he look'd much at me and at Hanson, I imagin'd he was angry at seeing me there; so I went out, sat down near the House, struck Fire, and lit my Pipe, waiting till the Meeting should break up. I thought too, that the Man had mention'd something of Beaver, and I suspected it might be the Subject of their Meeting. So, when they came out, I accosted my Merchant. 'Well, Hans,' says I, 'I hope you have agreed to give more than four Shillings a Pound.' 'No,' says he, 'I cannot give so much; I cannot give more than three shillings and sixpence.' I then spoke to several other Dealers, but they all sung the

same song,—Three and sixpence,—Three and sixpence. This made it clear to me, that my Suspicion was right; and, that whatever they pretended of meeting to learn *good Things,* the real purpose was to consult how to cheat Indians in the Price of Beaver. Consider but a little, Conrad, and you must be of my Opinion. If they met so often to learn *good Things,* they would certainly have learnt some before this time. But they are still ignorant. You know our Practice. If a white Man, in travelling thro' our Country, enters one of our Cabins, we all treat him as I treat you; we dry him if he is wet, we warm him if he is cold, we give him Meat and Drink, that he may allay his Thirst and Hunger; and we spread soft Furs for him to rest and sleep on; we demand nothing in return. But, if I go into a white Man's House at Albany, and ask for Victuals and Drink, they say, 'Where is your Money?' and if I have none, they say, 'Get out, you Indian Dog.' You see they have not yet learned those little *Good Things,* that we need no Meetings to be instructed in, because our Mothers taught them to us when we were Children; and therefore it is impossible their Meetings should be, as they say, for any such purpose, or have any such Effect; they are only to contrive *the Cheating of Indians in the Price of Beaver.*"

NOTE.—It is remarkable that in all Ages and Countries Hospitality has been allow'd as the Virtue of those whom the civiliz'd were pleas'd to call Barbarians. The Greeks celebrated the Scythians for it. The Saracens possess'd it eminently, and it is to this day the reigning Virtue of the wild Arabs. St. Paul, too, in the Relation of his Voyage and Shipwreck on the Island of Melita says the Barbarous People shewed us no little kindness; for they kindled a fire, and received us every one, because of the present Rain, and because of the Cold.—F.

QUESTIONS

1. In the course of this letter, Franklin describes some of the customs and values of North American Indians. Describe them. Does he approve or disapprove of them? Why?

2. According to Franklin, what are some of the failings of Indian culture? What are the failings, if any, of white culture?

3. Is this essay written primarily in an objective or subjective style? Give evidence to support your opinion.

4. Locate and analyze examples of Franklin's irony in this essay.

5. Explain the importance of the first two sentences of the essay. What effect does Franklin achieve by making them separate paragraphs?

6. Explain how Franklin uses narrative in the essay. What paragraphs contain narrative examples? What words does he use to establish his chronology?

7. Where does Franklin use comparison and contrast in the essay? How do they support his thesis?

8. How is dialogue used in the essay? What is its function?

9. To a great extent, this essay is about prejudice, which of course is still a problem in America. How do you think Franklin would identify modern race problems? How would he respond to them?

10. Many of us are guilty of or have suffered from prejudice. Write a narrative essay in which you explain how you have suffered from or been guilty of prejudice.

FRANZ BOAS

The Diffusion of Cultural Traits

Franz Boas (1858–1942) was a highly influential anthropologist who was known for his rigorous use of scientific method. His most famous works are *The Mind of Primitive Man* (1911), *Primitive Art* (1927), *Anthropology and Modern Life* (1928), and two volumes of collected essays, *Race, Language, and Culture* (1940) and *Race and Democratic Society* (1945). "The Diffusion of Cultural Traits" shows Boas's wide-ranging cultural expertise and, perhaps more importantly, his humanism.

1 The study of the types of cultures found the world over gives the impression of an enormous diversity of forms. The differences are so great that we may be inclined to think that every one of these cultures developed quite independently and that the peculiar genius of the people has found expression in the forms under which they live. This impression is strengthened by the fact that the people themselves differ in appearance. The African Negro, the Australian, the Siberian native, the people of the Pacific Islands, each have their own peculiar bodily build and their own peculiar culture.

2 Added to this is the observation that the people constituting every one of these societies consider themselves as independent units, specifically distinct from all their neighbors. This finds its strongest expression in the fact that many primitive people designate themselves as human beings, while all their neighbors are designated by specific names in the same way as animals are designated by names. Thus the Eskimos call themselves human beings, the Indians

whom they know in some regions only by hearsay are considered as doglike animals, and the white people with whom they came into contact in later times are considered as descended from dogs. The specific differences are keenly felt, while the similarities are neglected.

The objective study of cultures and of types of man shows 3
that notwithstanding all these apparently fundamental differences cultural strains have passed from one people to the other, that no culture can be assumed to be self-developed and no type to be pure, unmixed with foreign strains.

This can be most easily shown by a study of the distribution 4
of languages. The migrations of primitive people in early times covered whole continents. A few examples will suffice. A certain American language is spoken in the vast area extending from the Yukon to Hudson Bay; south of this area live people speaking entirely different languages, but dialects of the same language which is spoken in the north reappear locally in Oregon and California and in the vast territory north and south of the Rio Grande. This can be understood only on the assumption that at one time these people migrated over this immense area. In southern Brazil the Carib language is spoken. It reappears locally north of the Amazon River and on the West Indian Islands. The Bantu languages spoken in Africa cover the whole district from south of the Sahara, southward almost to the extreme southern end of Africa. The language of the Malay, which is spoken in southeastern Asia, found its way eastward to all the islands of the Pacific Ocean and is also spoken by the inhabitants of part of Madagascar.

These inferences based on similarities of languages can also 5
be proved by historical migrations. The great Arab migration, which started in Arabia and at the time of its greatest extent covered the whole of north Africa and part of Spain, and which also influenced all the languages of the Near East, occurred after Mohammed's time. We know that the so-called Aryans invaded India at a very early time. The Greeks migrated from the north into what later became Greece. The Celts of western Europe migrated eastward as far as Asia Minor. The Teutonic migrations destroyed the Roman Empire, and later on the great Turkish migrations swept over a large part of eastern Europe as well as over a large part of Siberia. Thus we actually see mankind on the move since the very earliest times. The whole settlement of America occurred within a comparatively short period. Evidently the American aborigines lived on the continent not earlier than the beginning of the last warm period before the last ice age, coming presumably over the land bridge which is now Bering Sea, and spreading from there as far as the extreme southern part of South America.

It is not only language that was carried by migrations all over 6
the world; it is also easy to show that inventions and ideas were carried from one area to another, partly by migration, partly by cultural contact. One of the most striking examples is found in the distribution of folk tales. The European folk tale of the couple that escaped a pursuing monster by throwing backwards a number of objects which were transformed into obstacles is well known all over Europe. A comb thrown down becomes an impenetrable thicket, a whetstone an insurmountable mountain, a small amount of oil becomes an extensive lake, all of which detain the pursuer. This complicated story containing all the elements mentioned is found not only all over Europe but all over the Asiatic continent and also in northwestern America reaching as far as California, and eastward even in Greenland and Nova Scotia. In more recent times we find that the most isolated tribes of South America tell tales which were carried by Negro slaves to the coast of Brazil.

Equally striking are certain similarities in political organiza- 7
tion characteristic of the Old World but entirely absent in America and other outlying regions. The whole political organization of Africa shows a high development of administration through kings and their ministers in charge of war, judicial procedure and so on—analogous to the ancient organization of European states. Judicial procedure by means of courts taking evidence, administering the oath and finally ascertaining the truth by ordeal is found in a vast part of the Old World, while it is entirely foreign to people that had never been in contact with the Old World.

Perhaps still more convincing is the distribution of agricul- 8
ture. Wheat and barley are two characteristic plants on which early agriculture is based all over the temperate zone of the Old World, while rice is characteristic of another extended area. The home of the wild plants from which wheat and barley are derived must be looked for somewhere in western Asia, from where they spread from tribe to tribe. In the same way early American agriculture is based on the use of Indian corn which was developed from a native plant of the western highlands of Mexico, from where it spread southward as far as the Argentine republic and northward to the Great Lakes.

Thus a detailed study of cultural traits proves beyond cavil 9
that there is not a single people in the primitive world that has developed its culture independently.

Much of the diffusion must have been accompanied by actual 10
intermingling of tribes. The people speaking the language of the Yukon River, to whom we referred before and who live now on the Rio Grande, differ in type from the people of the north but are similar in appearance to their neighbors who speak an unrelated language. This would not have happened if they had not intermingled with

them at the same time that they adopted many important traits of their culture. In South Africa the intermingling of types is perhaps not equally clear but another striking feature of mutual influence may be seen in a linguistic change. The Bushmen of southern Africa have a peculiarity of speech which does not occur in any other part of the world. They produce sounds not by breathing out but by sucking in. This habit, which is considered an ancient African trait, is found in weak traits on the Gold Coast in equatorial West Africa, but only one of the Bantu tribes, who are neighbors of the Bushmen, have adopted the habit of producing strong sounds by sucking in, as the Bushmen do.

If we want to understand the way in which these fundamen- 11
tal modifications of cultures occur we have to remember that the conditions of contact among primitive tribes are very different from what has occurred in more modern times. Most primitive tribes are small; sometimes the whole number of individuals may not be more than a few hundred. Wars between neighboring groups are common and almost everywhere it is customary for the men to be killed, while the women are taken along as captives. These become the mothers of the following generation, so that it may happen that a large number of children grow up bilinguals, with the cultural habits of the mother having a far-reaching influence upon the behavior of the children.

The study of distribution of cultural traits brings out one very 12
characteristic feature: the details of the culture may be similar among different tribes but the general structure will retain fundamental differences. To give an example, one of the most important ceremonials of our North American Indians is the Sun Dance, an elaborate ceremonial the details of which are widespread over our western plains. The meaning of the ceremonial is quite different in the different areas and it is fitted into the fundamental religious ideas of each tribe. We can perhaps best understand these differences when we consider our own culture. All over Europe, and wherever the white race has gone, the fundamental traits are the same; inventions, religion, fundamental traits of state organization are alike. And nevertheless there are decided national patterns which allow us to differentiate between the cultural life of different areas as well as of different times.

It is interesting to follow the processes of acculturation. 13
Evidently in many cases it is due to war. We have already mentioned the importance of the introduction of foreign women. In many cases conquest leads to the establishment of stratified societies of a class of masters to whom the native population becomes subject. This has been the case in the history of Europe as well as in the history of Africa. In Africa we see that pastoral people conquered agricultural communities and became the nobility to whom the natives became

subjects. Such conquests led to economic adjustments, and in many traits the conquerors adopted the customs of the old population while these in turn adopted the traits of the invaders. It must not be assumed that every stratified society originated in this manner, because sometimes internal conditions, family privileges and so on have led to similar results. In other cases economic and social advantages favored the adoption of foreign customs. This was obviously the case in the spread of agriculture both in the Old World and in America. In a similar way new religious ideas which strengthen the emotional energy of the people and awaken them from indifferent attitudes have had a powerful influence in modifying cultural life.

One of the many remarkable changes of culture due to an 14
introduction of foreign invention is the change all over North America which occurred with the introduction of the horse. After the introduction of the horse the pursuit of the buffalo became easier and some of the tribes which had been hunting the buffalo on foot were now able to roam over a wider area and gave up agriculture almost entirely, becoming more or less nomadic hunters. Notwithstanding the readiness with which foreign cultural traits are adopted we may also observe in many cases a strong resistance to changes of life. This occurs particularly when new ideas cannot be fitted into the general cultural habits of the people. As an instance may be mentioned the difficulty of adjusting native tribes to the fundamental idea of capitalism. Very rarely do we find among primitive people that wealth can be used to produce more wealth by utilizing the power it may give over other members of the community. Wealth is of value only in so far as it enables the owner to improve his social standing by liberality, or by making a show with his property. In this lies one of the reasons which make it so difficult to assimilate the American Indians, to whom the idea of capital as producing wealth is entirely foreign.

In modern society the conditions favorable to cultural contact 15
are ever so much greater than those existing in primitive society. First of all, the numbers of individuals constituting each unit are infinitely larger than those occurring in primitive society, and within each group diffusion occurs with the greatest rapidity. Our schools, the commercial exploitation of inventions, are of such a character that new ideas and new objects are distributed with incredible rapidity. Most of these extend beyond national boundaries because international trade and international communication make it impossible for any idea to be confined to a single nation. On the other hand general, structural attitudes find much greater resistance than in the small tribes because the inertia of the enormous masses of the population is much greater than that of a small tribal group. It is less difficult to

introduce a new idea into the well established structure of a small group than to break down the habits of thought of millions.

We are too much inclined to consider the development of 16
civilization in Europe as an achievement of Europe alone, and to assume that Europe has always been the giver, not the recipient of new ideas. We are likely to forget that in antiquity the exchange of inventions and ideas extended from China all over the continent to Europe, and that the indirect contact between the Far East and Europe contributed much to the development of European civilization. We are likely to forget the immense service that Arab scientists did to Europe in re-establishing contact with Greek thought. Later on, when contact with the Far East was interrupted by the Turkish invasion of eastern Europe and the development of the Mongolian empire, the need for contact with the East led to maritime discoveries, and the discovery of America brought inventions to Europe which modified life in many parts of the Old World. I need only mention the introduction of Indian corn, which in an incredibly short time found its way to all parts of the Old World that were adapted to its cultivation, or the use of tobacco, which has reached all parts of the inhabitable world.

Peculiar types of cultural assimilation developed with coloni- 17
zation. Greek colonies sprang up on all the shores of the Mediterranean and hand in hand with them went a strong influence of Greek culture upon the surrounding people. Still more effective was Roman colonization, which not only carried the habits of Roman life into outlying provinces but led to Latin becoming the language of these countries, so that the languages of what is now Spain, of France, of what is now Romania disappeared and provincial Latin took their place. During the Middle Ages a similar process occurred in central Europe when German colonists reoccupied the former habitat of German tribes which had been filled by Slavic groups. The process that occurred there may still be observed in Mexico, where Spaniards are still colonizing in Indian territory and where we see the Indian languages gradually giving way to Spanish. There is little doubt that the process of assimilation which occurred in Greek and Roman colonization and later on in Germany was of the same type. In Mexico we see the Spaniards settling in small towns. A hybrid population develops with fair rapidity and the town as a trade center attracts the Indians. Intercourse is first by means of poorly developed Spanish, which is gradually adopted by a large part of the native population. Gradually the influence of the town increases in importance, with the final result that the native language disappears and the natives and the Spaniards form a single community. According to the character of the migrating population there would of course be differences in the

resultant social structure. When the colonists are poor and uneducated the native population and colonists may merge into a single community. When the colonists are supported by a central power they may become the masters of the territory and a stratified society results.

It is interesting to compare with this the conditions of immigration into countries which are already more or less settled. We may observe this in our own country as well as in South America, Australia, or South Africa. The immigrants who arrive are drawn from many different countries and form always a minority in a larger and economically stronger group, so that their only hope of success in the new country is based on a gradual assimilation. It is not only economic stress, however, which brings about the assimilation of the new colonists to the new environment but also the strong social influence of the majority among whom they live. An interesting example of this kind was observed about thirty years ago in a New York school in a part of the city which had been inhabited by an Irish population then being replaced by Italians. The school had been for some time Irish, with a sprinkling of Italian children. The Italian children had learned an Irish pronunciation of English, and even when they increased to about ninety per cent of all the children they all spoke English with an Irish accent. By the pressure of the majority all immigrants become assimilated, no matter what nationality they belong to, and their own influence is comparatively slight. 18

It is of considerable practical interest for us to understand what happens in the process of assimilation, how far old habits are stable and how far they are influenced by their new environment. A number of studies made on American immigrants throw light on this question. It has repeatedly been shown that the physical development of children of immigrants differs from that of their parents. During the last century the stature of Americans and also of Europeans has increased noticeably, but the immigrants who came here during the last seventy years have always belonged to the same economic level and their stature has remained quite stable. Their children, however, follow the general increase which is found in the American population. Furthermore, the form of the body of immigrants' children undergoes certain changes, and though the cause is still obscure the result is that in bodily form they differ from their parents. This does not mean that they tend to approach a general American type, but merely that the new environment and new mode of life influence the bodily build. 19

The changes in their behavior are much more noticeable. It is not only that they adopt American tastes and language, a process which results from contact between children of many nationalities in 20

school, but their motor habits also change from foreign types to what we might call an American type. The Italians and the Jews accompany speech with characteristic gestures. The Italian describes what he has to say with a wide sweep of motions, while the Jew follows his line of thought with short, rather jerky movements. The assimilated Italians and Jews substitute for these movements the descriptive and emphatic motions which are characteristic of American habits, or when they belong to more sophisticated classes tend to suppress all gestures. Statistics also show that the immigrant becomes adjusted very quickly to American social habits. This becomes particularly striking in criminal statistics. On the whole, crimes against property among the immigrants from Europe are comparatively rare, while they are exceedingly common in our American city population. But the distribution of crime in the second generation, that is, among the descendants of immigrants, is quite similar to that found in the American population of native parentage. All this is merely an expression of the fact that when an individual is exposed to a new environment his descent is almost irrelevant when compared to the stress to which he is exposed in his new mode of life.

A review of all the data which have been summarized here 21
altogether too briefly shows that the assumption that any culture is autonomous, uninfluenced from outside sources, or that each type of man produces a culture which is an expression of the biological make-up of the race to which he belongs, is quite untenable. We see everywhere types of culture which develop historically under the impact of multifarious influences that come from neighboring people or those living far away.

QUESTIONS

1. Does Boas believe that there is such a thing as a purely autonomous culture? What evidence does he give to prove or disprove this thesis?

2. What ways of acculturation does Boas present? What kinds of things are exchanged by cultures?

3. As an early anthropologist, Boas might be expected to write in a scientific style. Is there any reflection in word choice or point of view of a scientific method?

4. Explain Boas's use of the word *invention.* How does it differ from the way we use it? How does the difference reflect his anthropological viewpoint?

5. If you were to divide this essay into three parts, where would you divide it? Why did you divide it where you did?

6. How does Boas use process and analysis to support his thesis?

7. What kinds of evidence does he offer to support his thesis?

8. How does Boas use contrast and comparison? Are they his primary rhetorical methods? If so, why do you think he chose them? If not, why not?

9. All Americans either are immigrants or have forebearers who were. How thoroughly have you been assimilated into the mainstream of American life? Do you believe that assimilation is valuable? Explain.

10. Many of us have had to acclimate ourselves to new cultural settings. When we do that, we are in a small way repeating the acts of nations that Boas describes. Remaining scientifically objective, describe the process of assimilation you underwent when you did one of the following things: (a) went out for your first sports team; (b) moved to a new school, for instance, college; (c) moved into a new neighborhood.

JOAN DIDION

In Bed

Joan Didion (1934–) is a novelist and essayist. Her most recent novel is *A Book of Common Prayer* (1977). She has also written two collections of essays, *Slouching Towards Bethlehem* (1968) and *The White Album* (1979). Didion is an intensely introspective writer, and her writing in its very particularity takes on general significance. Here she examines one of the most subjective of experiences—pain.

Three, four, sometimes five times a month, I spend the 1
day in bed with a migraine headache, insensible to the world around me. Almost every day of every month, between these attacks, I feel the sudden irrational irritation and the flush of blood into the cerebral arteries which tell me that migraine is on its way, and I take certain drugs to avert its arrival. If I did not take the drugs, I would be able to function perhaps one day in four. The physiological error called migraine is, in brief, central to the given of my life. When I was 15, 16, even 25, I used to think that I could rid myself of this error by simply denying it, character over chemistry. "Do you have headaches *sometimes? frequently? never?*" the application forms would demand. "Check one." Wary of the trap,

wanting whatever it was that the successful circumnavigation of that particular form could bring (a job, a scholarship, the respect of mankind and the grace of God), I would check one. *"Sometimes,"* I would lie. That in fact I spent one or two days a week almost unconscious with pain seemed a shameful secret, evidence not merely of some chemical inferiority but of all my bad attitudes, unpleasant tempers, wrongthink.

For I had no brain tumor, no eyestrain, no high blood pressure, nothing wrong with me at all: I simply had migraine headaches, and migraine headaches were, as everyone who did not have them knew, imaginary. I fought migraine then, ignored the warnings it sent, went to school and later to work in spite of it, sat through lectures in Middle English and presentations to advertisers with involuntary tears running down the right side of my face, threw up in washrooms, stumbled home by instinct, emptied ice trays onto my bed and tried to freeze the pain in my right temple, wished only for a neurosurgeon who would do a lobotomy on house call, and cursed my imagination. 2

It was a long time before I began thinking mechanistically enough to accept migraine for what it was: something with which I would be living, the way some people lived with diabetes. Migraine is something more than the fancy of a neurotic imagination. It is an essentially hereditary complex of symptoms, the most frequently noted but by no means the most unpleasant of which is a vascular headache of blinding severity, suffered by a surprising number of women, a fair number of men (Thomas Jefferson had migraine, and so did Ulysses S. Grant, the day he accepted Lee's surrender), and by some unfortunate children as young as two years old. (I had my first when I was eight. It came on during a fire drill at the Columbia School in Colorado Springs, Colorado. I was taken first home and then to the infirmary at Peterson Field, where my father was stationed. The Air Corps doctor prescribed an enema.) Almost anything can trigger a specific attack of migraine: stress, allergy, fatigue, an abrupt change in barometric pressure, a contretemps over a parking ticket. A flashing light. A fire drill. One inherits, of course, only the predisposition. In other words I spent yesterday in bed with a headache not merely because of my bad attitudes, unpleasant tempers and wrongthink but because both my grandmothers had migraine, my father has migraine and my mother has migraine. 3

No one knows precisely what it is that is inherited. The chemistry of migraine, however, seems to have some connection with the nerve hormone named serotonin, which is naturally present in the brain. The amount of serotonin in the blood falls sharply at the onset of migraine, and one migraine drug, methysergide, or Sansert, 4 seems to have some effect on serotonin. Methysergide is a derivative of lysergic acid (in fact Sandoz Pharmaceuticals first synthesized LSD-25 while looking for a migraine cure), and its use is hemmed about with so many contraindications and side effects that most doctors prescribe it only in the most incapacitating cases. Methysergide, when it is prescribed, is taken daily, as a preventive; another preventive which works for some people is old-fashioned ergotamine tartrate, which helps to constrict the swelling blood vessels during the "aura," the period which in most cases precedes the actual headache.

Once an attack is under way, however, no drug touches it. 5
Migraine gives some people mild hallucinations, temporarily blinds others, shows up not only as a headache but as a gastrointestinal disturbance, a painful sensitivity to all sensory stimuli, an abrupt overpowering fatigue, a strokelike aphasia, and a crippling inability to make even the most routine connections. When I am in a migraine aura (for some people the aura lasts fifteen minutes, for others several hours), I will drive through red lights, lose the house keys, spill whatever I am holding, lose the ability to focus my eyes or frame coherent sentences, and generally give the appearance of being on drugs, or drunk. The actual headache, when it comes, brings with it chills, sweating, nausea, a debility that seems to stretch the very limits of endurance. That no one dies of migraine seems, to someone deep into an attack, an ambiguous blessing.

My husband also has migraine, which is unfortunate for him 6
but fortunate for me: perhaps nothing so tends to prolong an attack as the accusing eye of someone who has never had a headache. "Why not take a couple of aspirin," the unafflicted will say from the doorway, or "I'd have a headache, too, spending a beautiful day like this inside with all the shades drawn." All of us who have migraine suffer not only from the attacks themselves but from this common conviction that we are perversely refusing to cure ourselves by taking a couple of aspirins, that we are making ourselves sick, that we "bring it on ourselves." And in the most immediate sense, the sense of why we have a headache this Tuesday and not last Thursday, of course we often do. There certainly is what doctors call a "migraine personality," and that personality tends to be ambitious, inward, intolerant of error, rather rigidly organized, perfectionist. "You don't look like a migraine personality," a doctor once said to me. "Your hair's messy. But I suppose you're a compulsive housekeeper." Actually my house is kept even more negligently than my hair, but the doctor was right nonetheless: perfectionism can also take the form of spending most of a week writing and rewriting and not writing a single paragraph.

But not all perfectionists have migraine, and not all migrainous people have migraine personalities. We do not escape heredity. I have tried in most of the available ways to escape my own migrainous heredity (at one point I learned to give myself two daily injections of histamine with a hypodermic needle, even though the needle so frightened me that I had to close my eyes when I did it), but I still have migraine. And I have learned how to live with it, learned when to expect it, and how to outwit it, even how to regard it, when it does come, as more friend than lodger. We have reached a certain understanding, my migraine and I. It never comes when I am in real trouble. Tell me that my house is burned down, my husband has left me, that there is gunfighting in the streets and panic in the banks, and I will not respond by getting a headache. It comes instead when I am fighting not an open but a guerrilla war with my own life, during weeks of small household confusions, lost laundry, unhappy help, canceled appointments, on days when the telephone rings too much and I get no work done and the wind is coming up. On days like that my friend comes uninvited. 7

And once it comes, now that I am wise in its ways, I no longer fight it. I lie down and let it happen. At first every small apprehension is magnified, every anxiety a pounding terror. Then the pain comes, and I concentrate only on that. Right there is the usefulness of migraine, there in that imposed yoga, the concentration on the pain. For when the pain recedes, ten or twelve hours later, everything goes with it, all the hidden resentments, all the vain anxieties. The migraine has acted as a circuit breaker, and the fuses have emerged intact. There is a pleasant convalescent euphoria. I open the windows and feel the air, eat gratefully, sleep well. I notice the particular nature of a flower in a glass on the stair landing. I count my blessings. 8

QUESTIONS

1. What are the physical symptoms of migraine? Identify possible genetic and psychological causes of migraine.

2. What kinds of treatments are available to those who suffer from migraine? How does Didion treat her migraines?

3. Identify the analogies and metaphors Didion uses to describe migraines. How do they help you understand how she feels about migraines?

4. What is the tone of this essay? How does Didion maintain this tone even when she is giving medical information?

5. Didion says that migraine is a "physiological error" (paragraph 1). What rhetorical methods does she use to develop this idea?

6. What paragraphs relate personal experience? How does she use personal experience to structure her essay?

7. What other rhetorical techniques does Didion use to define migraine? Where does she use them?

8. Where and how does Didion use contrast in the essay?

9. Do you think Didion's response to migraine is an admirable one? Have you ever been bedridden or seriously ill? How did you respond?

10. Many people suffer from a disability. Write an essay about a disability you or a friend may have. Use personal experience and medical information to describe and define the disease.

ANAÏS NIN

Notes on Feminism

Anaïs Nin (1903–1977), diarist, novelist, essayist, and feminist, was an American born in Paris. A student of psychology under Otto Rank, Nin always retained her interest in the inner self and specifically in the consciousness of women. In her words, she wished "to unmask the deeper self that lies hidden behind the self that we present to the world." Her diaries, started as letters to her father in 1931, were published in seven volumes between 1966 and 1980. These diaries, an imposing collection termed by Gunther Stuhlmann "one of the unique literary documents of our century," have been compared in method to the work of Marcel Proust. In this essay, Nin writes about the need for women to develop their inner selves.

The nature of my contribution to the Women's Liberation Movement is not political but psychological. I get thousands of letters from women who have been liberated by the reading of my diaries, which are a long study of the psychological obstacles that have prevented woman from her fullest evolution and flowering. I studied the negative influence of religion, of racial and cultural patterns, which action alone and no political slogans can dissolve. I describe in the diaries the many restrictions 1 confining woman. The diary itself was an escape from judgment, a place in which to analyze the truth of woman's situation. I believe that is where the sense of freedom has to begin. I say begin, not remain. A reformation of woman's emotional attitudes and beliefs will enable her to act more effectively. I am not speaking of the practical, economic, sociological problems, as I believe many of them are solvable with clear thinking and intelligence. I am merely placing the emphasis on a confrontation of ourselves because it is a source of strength. Do not confuse my shifting of responsibility with blame. I am not blaming woman. I say that if we take the responsibility for our situation, we can feel less helpless than when we put the blame on society or man. We waste precious energy in negative rebellions. Awareness can give us a sense of captainship over our fate, and to take destiny into our own hands is more inspiring than to expect others to direct our destiny for us. No matter what ideas, psychology, history, or art I learned from man, I learned to convert it into the affirmation of my own identity and my own beliefs, to serve my own growth. At the same time, I loved woman and was fully aware of her problems, and I watched her struggles for development. I believe the lasting revolution comes from deep changes in ourselves which influence our collective life.

Many of the chores women accepted were ritualistic; they 2
were means of expressing love and care and protection. We have to find other ways of expressing these devotions. We cannot solve the problem of freeing ourselves of all chores without first understanding why we accomplished them and felt guilty when we did not. We have to persuade those we love that there are other ways of enriching their lives. Part of these occupations were compensatory. The home was our only kingdom, and it returned many pleasures. We were repaid with love and beauty and a sense of accomplishment. If we want our energy and strength to go into other channels, we have to work at a transitional solution which may deprive us of a personal world altogether. But I also think we have to cope with our deep-seated, deeply instilled sense of responsibility. That means finding a more creative way of love and collaboration, of educating our children, or caring for a house, and we have to convince those we love that there are other ways of accomplishing these things. The restrictions of women's lives, confined to the personal, also created in us qualities men lost to a degree in a competitive world. I think woman retains a more human relationship to human beings and is not corrupted by the impersonality of powerful interests. I have watched woman in law, in politics, and in education. Because of her gift for personal relationships she deals more effectively with injustice, war, prejudice. I have a dream about woman pouring into all professions a new quality. I want a different world, not the same world born of man's

need of power which is the origin of war and injustice. We have to create a new woman.

What of ghettos and poverty? A new kind of human being 3
would not allow them to be born in the first place. It is the quality of human beings I want to see improved, because we already know that drugs, crime, war, and injustice are not curable by a change of system. It is humanism which is lacking in our leaders. I do not want to see women follow in the same pattern. To assert individual qualities and thought was tabooed by puritanism and is now being equally tabooed by militant fanatics. But practical problems are often solved by psychological liberation. The imagination, the skills, the intelligence, are freed to discover solutions. I see so many women in the movement thinking in obsessional circles about problems which are solvable when one is emotionally free to think and act clearly. Undirected, blind anger and hostility are not effective weapons. They have to be converted into lucid action. Each woman has to consider her own problems before she can act effectively within her radius; otherwise she is merely adding the burden of her problems to the collective overburdened majority. Her individual solution, courage, become in turn like cellular growth, organic growth. It is added to the general synthesis. Slogans do not give strength because generalizations are untrue. Many intelligent women, many potentially collaborative men, are alienated by generalizations. To recruit all women for a work for which some are unfit is not effective. The group does not always give strength, because it moves only according to the lowest denominator of understanding. The group weakens the individual will and annihilates the individual contribution. To object to individual growth of awareness in women is to work against the benefit of the collective whose quality is raised by individual research and learning. Each woman has to know herself, her problems, her obstacles. I ask woman to realize she can be master of her own destiny. This is an inspiring thought. To blame others means one feels helpless. What I liked best about psychology is the concept that destiny is interior, in our own hands. While we wait for others to free us, we will not develop the strength to do it ourselves. When a woman has not solved her personal, intimate defeats, her private hostilities, her failures, she brings the dregs of this to the group and only increases its negative reactions. This is placing liberation on too narrow a basis. Liberation means the power to transcend obstacles. The obstacles are educational, religious, racial, and cultural patterns. These have to be confronted, and there is no political solution which serves them all. The real tyrants are guilt, taboos, educational inheritance—these are our enemies. And we can grapple with them. The real enemy is what we were taught, not always by man, but often by our mothers and grandmothers.

The trouble with anger is that it makes us overstate our case and prevents us from reaching awareness. We often damage our case by anger. It is like resorting to war. 4

Poverty and injustice and prejudice are not solved by any man-made system. I want them to be solved by a higher quality of human being who, by his own law of valuation upon human life, will not permit such inequalities. In that sense whatever we do for the development of this higher quality will eventually permeate all society. The belief that all of us, untrained, unprepared and unskilled, can be conscripted for mass action is what has prevented woman from developing, because it is the same old-fashioned assertion that the only good we can do is outside of ourselves, salvaging others. When we do this we ignore the fact that the evil comes from individual flaws, undeveloped human beings. We need models. We need heroes and leaders. Out of the many lawyers who came from Harvard, we were given only one Nader. But one Nader has incalculable influence. If we continue in the name of politics to denigrate those who have developed their skills to the maximum pitch as elite, privileged, or exceptional people, we will never be able to help others achieve their potential. We need blueprints for the creation of human beings as well as for architecture. 5

The attack against individual development belongs to the dark ages of socialism. If I am able to inspire or help women today, it is because I persisted in my development. I was often derailed by other duties, but I never gave up this relentless disciplined creation of my awareness because I realized that at the bottom of every failed system to improve the lot of man lies an imperfect, corruptible human being. 6

It is inspiring to read of the women who defied the codes and taboos of their period: Ninon de Lenclos in the seventeenth century, Lou Andreas-Salomé in the time of Freud, Nietzsche, and Rilke, and in our time Han Suyin. Or the four heroines of Lesley Blanch's *Wilder Shores of Love*. 7

I see a great deal of negativity in the Women's Liberation Movement. It is less important to attack male writers than to discover and read women writers, to attack male-dominated films than to make films by women. If the passivity of woman is going to erupt like a volcano or an earthquake, it will not accomplish anything but disaster. This passivity can be converted to creative will. If it expresses itself in war, then it is an imitation of man's methods. It would be good to study the writings of women who were more concerned with personal relationships than with the power struggles of history. I have a dream of a more human lawyer, a more human educator, a more human politician. To become man, or like man, is no solution. There is far too much imitation of man in the women's 8 movement. That is merely a displacement of power. Woman's definition of power should be different. It should be based on relationships to others. The women who truly identify with their oppressors, as the cliché phrase goes, are the women who are acting like men, masculinizing themselves, not those who seek to convert or transform man. There is no liberation of one group at the expense of another. Liberation can only come totally and in unison.

Group thinking does not give strength. It weakens the will. 9
Majority thinking is oppressive because it inhibits individual growth and seeks a formula for all. Individual growth makes communal living of higher quality. A developed woman will know how to take care of all her social duties and how to act effectively.

QUESTIONS

1. What arguments does Nin give against group action? What arguments does she offer for individual growth?

2. According to Nin, what are the main differences between man and woman? Why does this difference make women so important to the development of social justice?

3. Give examples of Nin's hortatory style. Examine particularly her point of view and verb forms.

4. Give examples of Nin's use of psychological vocabulary in this essay. How does the vocabulary reflect the theme?

5. Where in this essay does Nin describe her personal experience? How is this placement important for the development of the essay?

6. Does Nin use such conventional forms of organization as comparison and contrast or classification? If not, what kinds of organizational devices does she use? If she does, detail how.

7. The most explicit criticism of the woman's liberation movement occurs in paragraph 8. Why does Nin defer this criticism until so late in her essay?

8. Nin's conclusion clearly recapitulates most of the points of her essay. Why does she write such a conventional conclusion?

9. Do you agree that personal growth must precede social growth? Explain.

10. Write an essay describing your idea of the new woman.

MARYA MANNES

The New Therapy

Marya Mannes (1904–) has written several novels and some light verse, but she is best known for her essays, which have appeared in *Vogue, McCall's, Harpers,* and *The New Republic.* She has collected her essays in *More in Anger* (1958) and in *The New York I Know* (1961). Mannes has also written on television in *Who Owns the Air* (1960). The following essay is taken from *Last Rights* (1974), in which Mannes considers the issues of suicide and euthanasia.

1 When Sigmund Freud at seventy-two accepted young Doctor Schur as his personal internist, he stipulated that Schur would never lie to him, and then said, "Promise me. When the time comes, you won't let me suffer unnecessarily." (About his own dying father, Freud had said years before: "The unconscious is immortal.")

2 In 1939, after eleven years of acute suffering and countless operations on his cancerous mouth (added to the horror of Hitler's rise and Freud's own unremitting work), the time came. Now in English exile, the great psychoanalyst was not only too pain-racked to read, let alone write, but necrosis of the tissue emanated an odor so foul that his own long-loved dog lay twenty feet away, and even those dearest to him could barely endure to come close.

3 Freud then gave the word to Schur, and Schur gave him two injections of morphine, one at night and one in the early morning. By contemporary standards they were light doses. But since Freud had refused all pain killers through his many cancerous bouts, the drug brought death.

4 Schur, as his own brilliant psychobiography of Freud made clear, was constant witness to the struggle in this creative genius between the life force and the death wish.

5 The same struggle now is widely manifest in those psychiatrists who have to deal with it not only in themselves, but in professional contact with the dying.

6 They are as yet a relatively small band. The reasons are clear. Their profession is oriented to the healing or strengthening of the psyche so that it can withstand not only the pressures of external life but the anxieties of the inner self. It is aimed toward the patient's fullest realization of self, of his powers as well as his limitations, and toward an acceptance of truth that will free the hitherto shackled or impeded spirit. It is therefore deeply concerned with ongoing life.

7 Yet with the great lengthening of the human life span, and

the growing numbers of the fatally ill suspended in limbo to await their end with little spiritual comfort or support, some psychiatrists now feel impelled to come to their aid, to ease the final transition.

They seem to agree on only three points. One is the need to 8
strengthen the vital force by supporting their patient's sense of identity as an individual. The second (essential to the first) is to listen to them. And the third consensus is that the psychiatrists themselves cannot psychically sustain in their practice more than a few patients near death. "It is a terrible strain," said one of them, "because in order to communicate with the dying, we must ourselves understand—and try to feel—the process of dying."

It is because of this, and because the attitudes of the family 9
toward this process can deeply affect the doomed patient, that psychiatrists find the counseling of relatives so important.

They know what it can do to a husband aware of his cancer to 10
have a wife who never mentions it. The physical pain can be tempered by drugs, but for the pain of isolation there is no anodyne.

They know that if close family members cannot bring them- 11
selves to share the truth gently with those they are about to lose, then they must share it with a neutral but compassionate ear.

This ear need not be the psychiatrist's alone. In fact, very few 12
of us can afford his counsel, either in time or money. The psychiatrists themselves lack the firm base of knowledge in the psychic aspects of death that the doctor possesses in biological terms. One of their most eloquent spokesmen, Dr. Avery D. Weisman, concedes that psychosocial data on dying are not only very elusive, but much more difficult to obtain than observations about organic disease. An aged person may live for years in a chronic hospital, but his interests, actions, and ordinary habits are neither observed nor recorded.

Weisman also observes, as I have myself found in chronic and 13
terminal wards, that the higher the professional rank of staff members, the less familiar they are with patients as people.

A fascinating sidelight was a study made recently (and 14
surreptitiously) by a young psychologist in the geriatric ward of a big city hospital. Having counseled a patient there, he had acquainted himself with the numbers of the rooms that housed those on the critical list. He spent several hours one night in view of the call-board signaling requests from patients by means of lights used for nursing attention. After comparing these calls with the room numbers on his chart and the time it took for them to be answered, he saw—unequivocally—that the nearer the patient was to death, the longer the wait for nursing response.

The floor knew the score. Old Mrs. Jones always called just 15
for company, or some trivial thing. Old Mr. Smith didn't know what he was doing anymore. Miss Schwartz was a chronic complainer.

This tardy response from the nurses wasn't deliberate callousness: more a feeling of uselessness at this stage of the game. Those with a chance for life deserved priority. 16

Like many of us, inside and outside of the health professions, psychiatrist Kurt Eissler has noticed that all modern medicine has achieved is to make it more difficult for man to die, "although his preoccupation with his body, his worry about disease have not decreased. It may even have been augmented." 17

It is this worry, this call for help in the night or the day, that the "lower echelons" in the treatment hierarchy of the critically ill are now trying to answer. 18

Again in the death of Ivan Ilych, it was his humble servant Gerasim—holding his aching body, sharing his agony—who gave any comfort or peace. And those who have seen Ingmar Bergman's *Cries and Whispers* know that in this elaborate family mansion, cold and dark with unspoken words and ungiven love, it was the maid who held her cancer-ridden mistress to her breast, rocking and soothing her until the convulsive end. 19

So now, social workers, young aides, and unorthodox ministers sit at the bedside of the near-to-death to listen, to comfort, to pray—if asked to—to touch, to answer. They are also open to bewildered or agonized relatives in need of counsel and direction. 20

The growing trend is for less specialization, more interdependence in this ultimate care. Doctors, interns, and nurses should share their knowledge and observations with their subordinates instead of proceeding in virtual ignorance of each other's decisions and actions. 21

So far, only one out of a hundred private hospitals immediately involved with catastrophic disease and terminal care have established training courses for this new form of "consciousness raising." For one thing, they go against the grain of the medical hierarchy. For another, they are rejected by the hospital unions, who do not want to join any training program with management. 22

Since union members die as well as doctors, the familiar and fruitless act of cutting off the nose to spite the face is with us again. Or is it perhaps the territorial imperative? The turf? 23

Whatever the resistance, courses for this new kind of group counseling are being held under the auspices of the Foundation of Thanatology, Cancer Care, and other institutions dedicated to the study and alleviation of critical or terminal diseases ravishing human beings. 24

Last year the Foundation of Thanatology, spearheaded by its founder Dr. Austin Kutscher, held a conference at Columbia University devoted largely to this counseling. One session included psychiatrists, priests, nurses, doctors, and social workers. 25

They appeared to agree on several salient points, among them that city hospitals were largely dumping grounds for training doctors and for dying patients on Medicare and Medicaid, and of necessity often brutalized by their own bureaucracy. To reverse this trend, it was suggested that doctors should regain their philosophic control of hospitals, making them more human and less mechanical. 26

The conferees could not know that scarcely two months after this discussion the American Hospital Association, based in Chicago, would establish a patient's "Bill of Rights" which would include, among the twelve major points, the right to "obtain from his physician complete, current information concerning his diagnosis, treatment, and prognosis in terms the patient can reasonably hope to understand . . . the right to refuse treatment to the extent permitted by law, and to be informed of the medical consequences of his action . . . and the right to receive from his physician information necessary to give informed consent prior to the start of any procedure and/or treatment." 27

All these rights, moreover, are to include the guarantee of total privacy between patient, doctor, and hospital staff. Most importantly, copies of these rights are to be given to every patient entering or in the hospital. 28

Following this patient's Bill of Rights in a matter of days was a statement from the New York State Medical Society which, though prohibiting doctors from authorizing mercy killings, supported a patient's "right" to die with dignity if he so chooses; adding that when "there is irrefutable evidence that biological death is inevitable," this right must be "the joint decision of the patient and/or the immediate family with the approval of the family physician." 29

The door was open at last. But only ajar. 30

QUESTIONS

1. According to Mannes, how do the following types traditionally respond to dying patients: doctors, psychiatrists, nurses, and relatives?

2. Describe the patient's Bill of Rights and explain its effect on the terminally ill.

3. Detail the shifting level of diction in this essay. What effect does Mannes achieve by changing diction?

4. Explain how the style in paragraphs 15 and 19 differs from the general style of the essay. Why does Mannes change style here?

5. What paragraphs constitute the introduction of this essay? How does it help Mannes to develop her theme?

6. This essay is about a developing therapy. Show what methods Mannes uses to demonstrate that she is writing a narrative.

7. Paragraphs 13 and 18 are critical to the development of the essay. Why?

8. What is the purpose of the author's quotation of several people?

9. The right to "die with dignity" is, of course deeply controversial. Do you think that people should have this right? Justify your answer.

10. Write an essay exploring a moral issue such as abortion, capital punishment, or euthanasia.

BRUNO BETTELHEIM

Freud and Man's Soul

Bruno Bettelheim (1903–) is a world-renowned child psychologist. He was born in Vienna and received his doctorate from the University of Vienna. Bettelheim came to the United States in 1939. He is Distinguished Professor of Education Emeritus and Professor Emeritus of both psychology and psychiatry at the University of Chicago. His books include *The Informed Heart* (1950), *The Uses of Enchantment* (1977), and *Freud and Man's Soul* (1983), from which this selection on the literary origins of some of Freud's theories is taken.

Among the Greek words that Freud used in very significant ways are "Eros" and "erotic"; from these words is derived the important concept of erotogenic zones, the term Freud created to name areas of the body particulary sensitive to erotic stimulation, such as the oral, anal, and genital zones. The concept first appeared in *Three Essays on the Theory of Sexuality* (1905). In a preface to the fourth edition, written in 1920, Freud stressed "how closely the enlarged concept of sexuality of psychoanalysis coincides with the Eros of divine Plato." For readers who, like Freud, were steeped in the classic tradition, words such as "Eros" and "erotic" called up Eros's charm and cunning and—perhaps more important—his deep love for Psyche, the soul, to whom Eros is wedded in everlasting love and devotion. For those familiar with this myth, it is impossible to think of Eros without being reminded at the same time of Psyche, and how she had at first been 1 tricked into believing that Eros was disgusting, with the most tragic consequences. To view Eros or anything connected with him as grossly sexual or monstrous is an error that, according to the myth, can lead to catastrophe. (It would be equally erroneous to confuse Eros with Cupid: Cupid is an irresponsible, mischievous little boy; Eros is fully grown, at the height of the beauty and strength of young manhood.) In order for sexual love to be an experience of true erotic pleasure, it must be imbued with beauty (symbolized by Eros) and express the longings of the soul (symbolized by Psyche). These were some of the connotations that Freud had in mind when he used words like "Eros" and "erotic." Devoid of such connotations, which are closely related to their classical origin, these words not only lose much of the meaning he wished them to evoke but may even be invested with meanings opposite to those he intended.

This is true of the word "psychoanalysis" itself, which Freud coined. Those who use this now-familiar term are usually vaguely aware that it combines two words of Greek origin, but few are conscious of the fact that the two words refer to strongly contrasting phenomena. "Psyche" is the soul—a term full of the richest meaning, endowed with emotion, comprehensively human and unscientific. "Analysis" implies a taking apart, a scientific examination. English readers of Freud are further thrown off by the fact that in English the accent in "psychoanalysis" is on "analysis," thus emphasizing the part of the word whose connotations are scientific. With the German word *Psychoanalyse*, on the other hand, the accent is on the first syllable—on "psyche," the soul. By coining the term "psychoanalysis" to describe his work, Freud wished to emphasize that by isolating and examining the neglected and hidden aspects of our souls we can acquaint ourselves with those aspects and understand the roles they play in our lives. It was Freud's emphasis on the soul that made his analysis different from all others. What we think and feel about man's soul—our own soul—is all-important in Freud's view. Unfortunately, when we now use the word "psyche" in the compound word "psychoanalysis" or in other compound words, such as "psychology," we no longer react to the words with the feelings that Freud intended to evoke. This was not true for his contemporaries in Vienna; for them, "psyche" used in any combination never lost its real meaning. 2

The story of Psyche may have been particulary attractive to Freud because she had to enter the underworld and retrieve something there before she could attain her apotheosis. Freud, similarly, had to dare to enter the underworld—in his case, the underworld of the soul—to gain his illumination. He alluded to the story of Amor (or Eros) and Psyche in his essay "The Theme of the Three Caskets" (1913), in which he analyzed the unconscious motives that may 3 explain the frequently evoked image of the always fateful choice among three: three caskets in *The Merchant of Venice,* three daughters in *King Lear,* three goddesses in the judgment of Paris, and three sisters of whom Psyche was the most beautiful. Freud tried to show that two related topics underlie this motif: the wish to believe that we have a choice where we have none, and a symbolic expression of the three fateful roles that the female plays in the life of the male—as mother, as beloved, and, finally, as the symbolic mother (Mother Earth) to whom man returns when he dies. The tale of Amor and Psyche describes the deep attachment of a mother to her son—the relationship that Freud considered the most unambivalent in a man's life. It also depicts the extreme jealousy that a mother feels for the girl her son loves. As Apuleius tells it, Psyche's beauty was so great that she was more venerated than Venus, and that outraged Venus. "With parted lips," Venus "kissed her son long and fervently" to persuade him to destroy Psyche. But, despite his mother's efforts to seduce him into doing her bidding, Amor falls deeply in love with Psyche. This only increases Venus's jealousy, and she sets out to destroy Psyche by demanding tasks of her that she thinks will kill her, including that of bringing a casket filled with "a day's worth of beauty" up from the underworld. And, to make sure of Amor, Venus locks him up. In desperation, Amor turns for help to his father, Jupiter, who, remembering his own amorous experiences, accepts Psyche as his son's bride.

In some respects, the story of Amor and Psyche is a counter- 4
part of that of Oedipus, but there are important differences. The Oedipus legend tells of a father's fear that his son will replace him; to avert this, the father tries to destroy his son. Psyche's story tells of a mother who is afraid that a young girl will replace her in the affections of mankind and of her son, and who therefore tries to destroy the girl. But, while the tale of Oedipus ends tragically, the tale of Amor and Psyche has a happy ending, and this fact is significant. A mother's love for her son and her jealous rage against the girl he prefers to her can be openly acknowledged. That the young girl surpasses the mature woman in beauty, that a son turns away from his mother to embrace his bride, that a bride has to suffer from the jealousy of her lover's mother—all this, although extremely troublesome, accords with normal human emotions, and is in line with the natural conflict of the generations. That is why in the end Jupiter and Venus accept the situation; Amor and Psyche celebrate their wedding in the presence of all the gods; Psyche is made immortal; and Venus makes peace with her. But Oedipus, in killing his father and marrying his mother, acts out in reality a common childhood fantasy that ought to have remained just that. In doing so, Oedipus acts

against nature, which requires that a son marry a woman of his own generation, and not his mother, and that he make his peace with his father. Thus, his story results in tragedy for all involved in the events.

5 Whether Freud was impressed by the parallels and differences of these two ancient myths we do not know, but we do know how fascinated he was by Greek mythology: he studied it assiduously, and he collected Greek, Roman, and Egyptian statuary. He knew that Psyche was depicted as young and beautiful, and as having the wings of a bird or a butterfly. Birds and butterflies are symbols of the soul in many cultures, and serve to emphasize its transcendental nature. These symbols invested the word "psyche" with connotations of beauty, fragility, and insubstantiality—ideas we still connect with the soul—and they suggest the great respect, care, and consideration with which Psyche had to be approached, because any other approach would violate, even destroy her. Respect, care, and consideration are attitudes that psychoanalysis, too, requires.

QUESTIONS

1. According to Bettelheim, what did Freud learn from classical literature and mythology? What stories and legends were most relevent to his psychological theories?

2. How does Bettelheim define the term *psychoanalysis*?

3. Define these words: *oral, anal,* and *genital zones* (paragraph 1), *apotheosis* (paragraph 3), *unambivalent* (paragraph 3), *venerated* (paragraph 3), *assiduously* (paragraph 5), and *transcendental* (paragraph 5).

4. What is the language level of this essay? Cite examples to support your answer.

5. Why is summary important to the development of this essay? How effective is the method, and why?

6. Identify the topic sentence in each paragraph. The paragraphs themselves are relatively long. Does all material in each paragraph relate directly to the topic sentence? What is the final effect?

7. What kinds of definitions does Bettelheim develop? How does he use comparison and contrast? What types of illustration are there?

8. Analyze the effectiveness of the last paragraph. Why does Bettelheim withhold a complete thesis until the end?

9. What can literature and mythology tell you about human development and behavior? Does psychoanalysis get at the "truth" of human behavior better than literature? Justify your answer.

10. a. Show how a reading of a particular piece of literature contributed to your understanding of human behavior.
b. Compare and contrast Bettelheim's explanation of "eros" with Gloria Steinem's definition of "erotica" (see pages 125–129).

SIGMUND FREUD

Libidinal Types

Sigmund Freud (1856–1939), founder of psychoanalysis, was an excellent writer. His theories concerning the pleasure principle, repression, and infantile sexuality are still controversial; nevertheless, they have had a profound impact upon culture, education, and art. Some of Freud's psychological works include *The Interpretation of Dreams* (1900), *The Psychopathology of Everyday Life* (1904), and *The Ego and the Id* (1923). He also analyzed the relation of culture and psychology in *Totem and Taboo* (1913) and *Moses and Monotheism* (1939). In the following essay, Freud discusses several character types derived from his theory of the libido.

Observation teaches us that in individual human beings the general features of humanity are embodied in almost infinite variety. If we follow the promptings of a legitimate desire to distinguish particular types in this multiplicity, we must begin by selecting the characteristics to look for and the points of view to bear in mind in making our differentiation. For this purpose physical qualities will be no less useful than mental; it will be most valuable of all if we can make our classification on the basis of a regularly occurring combination of physical and mental characteristics. 1

It is doubtful whether we are as yet able to discover types of this order, although we shall certainly be able to do so sometime on a basis of which we are still ignorant. If we confine our efforts to defining certain purely psychological types, the libidinal situation will have the first claim to serve as the basis of our classification. It may fairly be demanded that this classification should not merely be deduced from our knowledge or our conjectures about the libido, but that it should be easily verified in actual experience and should help to clarify the mass of our observations and enable us to grasp 2 their meaning. Let it be admitted at once that there is no need to suppose that, even in the psychical sphere, these libidinal types are the only possible ones; if we take other characteristics as our basis of classification we might be able to distinguish a whole series of other psychological types. But there is one rule which must apply to all such types: they must not coincide with specific clinical pictures. On the contrary, they should embrace all the variations which according to our practical standards fall within the category of the normal. In their extreme developments, however, they may well approximate to clinical pictures and so help to bridge the gulf which is assumed to exist between the normal and the pathological.

Now we can distinguish three main libidinal types, according as the subject's libido is mainly allocated to one or another region of the mental apparatus. To name these types is not very easy; following the lines of our depth-psychology, I should be inclined to call them the *erotic*, the *narcissistic* and the *obsessional* type. 3

The *erotic* type is easily characterized. Erotics are persons whose main interest—the relatively largest amount of their libido—is focused on love. Loving, but above all being loved, is for them the most important thing in life. They are governed by the dread of loss of love, and this makes them peculiarly dependent on those who may withhold their love from them. Even in its pure form this type is a very common one. Variations occur according as it is blended with another type and as the element of aggression in it is strong or weak. From the social and cultural standpoint this type represents the elementary instinctual claims of the id, to which the other psychical agencies have become docile. 4

The second type is that which I have termed the *obsessional*—a name which may at first seem rather strange; its distinctive characteristic is the supremacy exercised by the super-ego, which is segregated from the ego with great accompanying tension. Persons of this type are governed by anxiety of conscience instead of by the dread of losing love; they exhibit, we might say, an inner instead of an outer dependence; they develop a high degree of self-reliance, from the social standpoint they are the true upholders of civilization, for the most part in a conservative spirit. 5

The characteristics of the third type, justly called the *narcissistic*, are in the main negatively described. There is no tension between ego and super-ego—indeed, starting from this type one would hardly have arrived at the notion of a super-ego; there is no preponderance of erotic needs; the main interest is focused on self-preservation; the type is independent and not easily overawed. The ego has a considerable amount of aggression available, one manifestation of this being a proneness to activity; where love is in question, loving is pre- 6 ferred to being loved. People of this type impress others as being "personalities"; it is on them that their fellow-men are specially likely to lean; they readily assume the role of leader, give a fresh stimulus to cultural development or break down existing conditions.

7 These pure types will hardly escape the suspicion of being deduced from the theory of the libido. But we feel that we are on the firm ground of experience when we turn to the mixed types which are to be found so much more frequently than the unmixed. These new types: the *erotic-obsessional,* the *erotic-narcissistic* and the *narcissistic-obsessional* do really seem to provide a good grouping of the individual psychical structures revealed in analysis. If we study these mixed types we find in them pictures of characters with which we have long been familiar. In the *erotic-obsessional* type the preponderance of the instincts is restricted by the influence of the super-ego: dependence on persons who are *contemporary* objects and, at the same time, on the residues of *former* objects—parents, educators and ideal figures—is carried by this type to the furthest point. The *erotic-narcissistic* type is perhaps the most common of all. It combines contrasting characteristics which are thus able to moderate one another; studying this type in comparison with the other two erotic types, we can see how aggressiveness and activity go with a predominance of narcissism. Finally, the *narcissistic-obsessional* type represents the variation most valuable from the cultural standpoint, for it combines independence of external factors and regard for the requirements of conscience with the capacity for energetic action, and it reinforces the ego against the super-ego.

8 It might be asked in jest why no mention has been made of another mixed type which is theoretically possible: the *erotic-obsessional-narcissistic.* But the answer to this jest is serious: such a type would no longer be a type at all, but the absolute norm, the ideal harmony. We thereupon realize that the phenomenon of different types arises just in so far as one or two of the three main modes of expending the libido in the mental economy have been favoured at the cost of the others.

9 Another question that may be asked is what is the relation of these libidinal types to pathology, whether some of them have a special disposition to pass over into neurosis and, if so, which types lead to which forms of neurosis. The answer is that the hypothesis of these libidinal types throws no fresh light on the genesis of the neuroses. Experience testifies that persons of all these types can live free from neurosis. The pure types marked by the undisputed predominance of a single psychical agency seem to have a better prospect of manifesting themselves as pure character-formations, while we might expect that the mixed types would provide a more

fruitful soil for the conditioning factors of neurosis. But I do not think that we should make up our mind on these points until they have been carefully submitted to appropriate tests.

10 It seems easy to infer that when persons of the erotic type fall ill they will develop hysteria, just as those of the obsessional type will develop obsessional neurosis; but even this conclusion partakes of the uncertainty to which I have just alluded. People of the narcissistic type, who, being otherwise independent, are exposed to frustration from the external world, are peculiarly disposed to psychosis; and their mental composition also contains some of the essential conditioning factors which make for criminality.

11 We know that we have not as yet exact certainty about the aetiological conditions of neurosis. The precipitating occasions are frustrations and inner conflicts: conflicts between the three great psychical agencies, conflicts arising in the libidinal economy by reason of our bisexual disposition, conflicts between the erotic and the aggressive instinctual components. It is the endeavour of the psychology of the neurosis to discover what imparts a pathogenic character to these processes, which are a part of the normal course of mental life.

QUESTIONS

1. According to Freud, what types of individuals uphold society? What are their psychological characteristics?

2. What relationship does Freud see between mental illness and these character types?

3. Freud assumes that the reader is familiar with several psychological terms. Make sure you understand the following: *depth-psychology* (paragraph 3); *id* (paragraph 4); *ego* (paragraph 5); *neuroses* (paragraph 9); *psychosis* (paragraph 10); and *aetiological* (paragraph 11).

4. Is Freud general or specific in this essay? How does his choice here relate to the conclusions he draws in paragraphs 9 to 11?

5. Freud's primary rhetorical technique is classification. Identify his categories and explain the method he uses to classify people.

6. Explain the relations of paragraphs 1 and 2 to the body of the essay.

7. Freud uses definition frequently in this essay. What kinds of definitions does he use? How do they contribute to the structuring of the essay?

8. Explain the importance of paragraph 7 to the essay's structure. What effect does it have on the classification the author has established?

9. Using Freud's "pure" categories, how would you categorize politicians, actors, teachers, religious leaders, and students?

10. There are innumerable ways to classify people. In essay form, devise your own method for classifying a particular group of people.

RICHARD WRIGHT

The Psychological Reactions of Oppressed People

Richard Wright (1908–1960), American author, spoke eloquently about the black experience in America in his novels and essays. Wright was born on a Mississippi plantation. As a young man he moved to Chicago, where he joined a Federal Writers' Project in the 1930s. His experiences in Mississippi and Chicago appear in his early fiction: *Uncle Tom's Children* (1938) is about racial oppression in the South, and *Native Son* (1940) is about discrimination and exploitation in Chicago during the Depression. Wright became an expatriate after World War II. From Paris, he wrote an autobiography, *Black Boy* (1945), and two novels, *The Outsider* (1953) and *The Long Dream* (1958). Wright visited the African Gold Coast where, as the following essay demonstrates, he observed the oppression of blacks once more.

Buttressed by their belief that their God had entrusted the earth into their keeping, drunk with power and possibility, waxing rich through trade in commodities, human and non-human, with awesome naval and merchant marines at their disposal, their countries filled with human debris anxious for any adventures, psychologically armed with new facts, white Western Christian civilization during the fourteenth, fifteenth, sixteenth, and seventeenth centuries, with a long, slow, and bloody explosion, hurled itself upon the sprawling masses of colored humanity in Asia and Africa. 1

I say to you white men of the West: Don't be too proud of how easily you conquered and plundered those Asians and Africans. You had unwitting allies in your campaigns; you had Fifth Columns in the form of indigenous cultures to facilitate your military, missionary, 2 and mercenary efforts. Your collaborators in those regions consisted of the mental habits of the people, habits for which they were in no way responsible, no more than you were responsible for yours. Those habits constituted corps of saboteurs, of spies, if you will, that worked in the interests of European aggression. You must realize that it was not your courage or racial superiority that made you win, nor was it the racial inferiority or cowardice of the Asians and Africans that made them lose. This is an important point that you must grasp, or your concern with this problem will be forever wide of the facts. How, then, did the West, numerically the minority, achieve, during the last four centuries, so many dazzling victories over the body of colored mankind? Frankly, it took you centuries to do a job that could have been done in fifty years! You had the motive, the fire power, the will, the religious spur, the superior organization, but you dallied. Why? You were not aware exactly of what you were doing. You didn't suspect your impersonal strength, or the impersonal weakness on the other side. You were as unconscious, at bottom, as were your victims about what was really taking place.

Your world of culture clashed with the culture-worlds of 3
colored mankind, and the ensuing destruction of traditional beliefs among a billion and a half of black, brown, and yellow men has set off a tide of social, cultural, political, and economic revolution that grips the world today. That revolution is assuming many forms, absolutistic, communistic, fascistic, theocratistic etc.—all marked by unrest, violence, and an astounding emotional thrashing about as men seek new objects about which they can center their loyalties.

It is of the reactions, tortured and turbulent, of those Asians 4
and Africans, in the New and Old World, that I wish to speak to you. Naturally I cannot speak for those Asians and Africans who are still locked in their mystical or ancestor-worshiping traditions. They are the voiceless ones, the silent ones. Indeed, I think that they are the doomed ones, men in a tragic trap. Any attempt on their part to wage a battle to protect their outmoded traditions and religions is a battle that is lost before it starts. And I say frankly that I suspect any white man who loves to dote upon those "naked nobles," who wants to leave them as they are, who finds them "primitive and pure," for such mystical hankering is, in my opinion, the last refuge of reactionary racists and psychological cripples tired of their own civilization. My remarks will, of necessity, be confined to those Asians and Africans who, having been partly Westernized, have a quarrel with the West. They are the ones who feel that they are oppressed. In a sense, this is a fight of the West with *itself*, a fight that the West blunderingly began, and the West does not to this day realize that it is the sole responsible agent, the sole instigator. For the West to disclaim responsibility for what it so clearly did is to make

every white man alive on earth today a criminal. In history as in law, men must be held strictly responsible for the consequences of their historic actions, whether they intended those consequences or not. For the West to accept its responsibility is to create the means by which white men can liberate themselves from their fears, panic, and terror while they confront the world's colored majority of men who are also striving for liberation from the irrational ties which the West prompted them to disown—ties of which the West has partially robbed them.

Let's imagine a mammoth flying saucer from Mars landing, 5
say, in a peasant Swiss village and debouching swarms of fierce-looking men whose skins are blue and whose red eyes flash lightning bolts that deal instant death. The inhabitants are all the more terrified because the arrival of these men had been predicted. The religious myths of the Western world—the Second Coming of Christ, the Last Judgment, etc., have conditioned Europeans for just such an improbable event. Hence, those Swiss natives will feel that resistance is useless for a while. As long as the blue strangers are casually kind, they are obeyed and served. They become the Fathers of the people. Is this a fragment of paperback science fiction? No. It's more prosaic than that. The image I've sketched above is the manner, by and large, in which white Europe overran Asia and Africa. (Remember the Cortés-Montezuma drama!)

But why did Europe do this? Did it only want gold, power, 6
women, raw materials? It was more complicated than that.

The fifteenth-, sixteenth-, and seventeenth-century neurotic 7
European, sick of his thwarted instincts, restless, filled with self-disgust, was looking for not only spices and gold and slaves when he set out; he was looking for an Arcadia, a Land's End, a Shangri-la, a world peopled by shadow men, a world that would permit free play for his repressed instincts. Stripped of tradition, these misfits, adventurers, indentured servants, convicts and freebooters were the most advanced individualists of their time. Rendered socially superfluous by the stifling weight of the Church and nobility, buttressed by the influence of the ideas of Hume and Descartes, they had been brutally molded toward attitudes of emotional independence and could doff the cloying ties of custom, tradition, and family. The Asian-African native, anchored in family-dependence systems of life, could not imagine why or how these men had left their homelands, could not conceive of the cold, arid emotions sustaining them. . . . Emotional independence was a state of mind not only utterly inconceivable, but an attitude toward life downright evil to the Asian-African native—something to be avoided at all costs. Bound by a charged array of humble objects that made up an emotionally satisfying and exciting world, they, trapped by their limited mental horizon, could not help

thinking that the white men invading their lands had been driven forcibly from their homes!

Living in a waking dream, generations of emotionally impoverished colonial European whites wallowed in the quick gratification of greed, reveled in the cheap superiority of racial domination, slaked their sensual thirst in illicit sexuality, draining off the dammed-up libido that European morality had condemned, amassing through trade a vast reservoir of economic fat, thereby establishing vast accumulations of capital which spurred the industrialization of the West. Asia and Africa thus became a neurotic habit that Europeans could forgo only at the cost of a powerful psychic wound, for this emotionally crippled Europe had, through the centuries, grown used to leaning upon this black crutch. 8

But what of the impact of those white faces upon the personalities of the native? Steeped in dependence systems of family life and anchored in ancestor-worshiping religions, the native was prone to identify those powerful white faces falling athwart his existence with the potency of his dead father who had sustained him in the past. Temporarily accepting the invasion, he transferred his loyalties to those white faces, but, because of the psychological, racial, and economic luxury which those faces derived from their domination, the native was kept at bay. 9

Today, as the tide of white domination of the land mass of Asia and Africa recedes, there lies exposed to view a procession of shattered cultures, disintegrated societies, and a writhing sweep of more aggressive, irrational religion than the world has known for centuries. And, as scientific research, partially freed from the blight of colonial control, advances, we are witnessing the rise of a new genre of academic literature dealing with colonial and post-colonial facts from a wider angle of vision than ever possible before. The personality distortions of hundreds of millions of black, brown, and yellow people that are being revealed by this literature are confounding and will necessitate drastic alteration of our past evaluations of colonial rule. In this new literature one enters a universe of menacing shadows where disparate images coalesce—white turning into black, the dead coming to life, the top becoming the bottom—until you think you are seeing Biblical beasts with seven heads and ten horns rising out of the sea. Imperialism turns out to have been much more morally foul a piece of business than even Marx and Lenin imagined! 10

An agony was induced into the native heart, rotting and pulverizing it as it tried to live under a white domination with which it could not identify in any real sense, a white domination that mocked it. The more Westernized that native heart became, the more anti-Western it had to be, for that heart was now weighing itself in 11 terms of white Western values that made it feel degraded. Vainly attempting to embrace the world of white faces that rejected it, it recoiled and sought refuge in the ruins of moldering tradition. But it was too late; it was trapped; it found haven in neither. This is the psychological stance of the elite of the populations, free or still in a state of subjection, of present-day Asia and Africa; this is the profound revolution that the white man cast into the world; this is the revolution (a large part of which has been successfully captured by the Communists) that the white man confronts today with fear and paralysis.

QUESTIONS

1. Whom does Wright blame for the state of oppressed nations? What reasons does he give for blaming them?

2. According to Wright, what are the cultural traits of Western people in the fifteenth, sixteenth, seventeenth, and eighteenth centuries?

3. Explain what Wright means by "advanced individualists" (paragraph 7). What other words does he use to describe Westerners? What connotations do these words tend to have?

4. Give examples of Wright's hortatory style. What other styles of writing appear in this essay?

5. How does Wright develop his history? Is his chronological structure linear? Does he repeat events? How does his choice here reflect the goals of the essay?

6. Explain how contrast is used as a structural device in this essay.

7. What words introduce the hypothetical example in paragraph 5? How does this example contribute to the theme of the essay?

8. Identify an instance of syllogistic reasoning in Wright's argument.

9. In an age of diminishing resources and burgeoning populations, can Americans afford to be concerned with the plight of oppressed peoples? How do you think Wright would answer this question? How do you?

10. a. Write your own essay on the psychological reactions of oppressor nations.
b. Write an essay on the new psychology of third world nations, notably OPEC (Organization of Petroleum Exporting Countries).
c. People often engage in actions whose consequences are damaging. Show how this insight is true in your experience.

Social Processes and Institutions

E. M. FORSTER

My Wood

Edward Morgan Forster (1879–1970), English essayist, novelist, biographer, and literary critic, wrote several notable works of fiction dealing with the constricting effects of social and national conventions upon human relationships. These novels include *A Room with a View* (1908), *Howards End* (1910), and *A Passage to India* (1924). In addition, his lectures on fiction, collected as *Aspects of the Novel* (1927), remain graceful elucidations of the genre. In "My Wood," taken from his essay collection *Abinger Harvest* (1936), Forster writes with wit and wisdom about the effect of property upon human behavior—notably his own.

A few years ago I wrote a book which dealt in part with the difficulties of the English in India. Feeling that they would have had no difficulties in India themselves, the Americans read the book freely. The more they read it the better it made them feel, and a cheque to the author was the result. I bought a wood with the cheque. It is not a large wood—it contains scarcely any trees, and it is intersected, blast it, by a public footpath. Still, it is the first property that I have owned, so it is right that other people should participate in my shame, and should ask 1 themselves, in accents that will vary in horror, this very important question: What is the effect of property upon the character? Don't let's touch economics; the effect of private ownership upon the community as a whole is another question—a more important question, perhaps, but another one. Let's keep to psychology. If you own things, what's their effect on you? What's the effect on me of my wood?

In the first place, it makes me feel heavy. Property does have 2
this effect. Property produces men of weight, and it was a man of weight who failed to get into the Kingdom of Heaven. He was not wicked, that unfortunate millionaire in the parable, he was only stout; he stuck out in front, not to mention behind, and as he wedged himself this way and that in the crystalline entrance and bruised his well-fed flanks, he saw beneath him a comparatively slim camel passing through the eye of a needle and being woven into the robe of God. The Gospels all through couple stoutness and slowness. They point out what is perfectly obvious, yet seldom realized: that if you have a lot of things you cannot move about a lot, that furniture requires dusting, dusters require servants, servants require insurance stamps, and the whole tangle of them makes you think twice before you accept an invitation to dinner or go for a bathe in the Jordan. Sometimes the Gospels proceed further and say with Tolstoy that property is sinful; they approach the difficult ground of asceticism here, where I cannot follow them. But as to the immediate effects of property on people, they just show straightforward logic. It produces men of weight. Men of weight cannot, by definition, move like the lightning from the East unto the West, and the ascent of a fourteen-stone bishop into a pulpit is thus the exact antithesis of the coming of the Son of Man. My wood makes me feel heavy.

In the second place, it makes me feel it ought to be larger. 3

The other day I heard a twig snap in it. I was annoyed at first, 4
for I thought that someone was blackberrying, and depreciating the value of the undergrowth. On coming nearer, I saw it was not a man who had trodden on the twig and snapped it, but a bird, and I felt pleased. My bird. The bird was not equally pleased. Ignoring the relation between us, it took fright as soon as it saw the shape of my face, and flew straight over the boundary hedge into a field, the property of Mrs. Henessy, where it sat down with a loud squawk. It had become Mrs. Henessy's bird. Something seemed grossly amiss here, something that would not have occurred had the wood been larger. I could not afford to buy Mrs. Henessy out, I dared not murder her, and limitations of this sort beset me on every side. Ahab did not want that vineyard—he only needed it to round off his property, preparatory to plotting a new curve—and all the land around my wood has become necessary to me in order to round off the wood. A

boundary protects. But—poor little thing—the boundary ought in its turn to be protected. Noises on the edge of it. Children throw stones. A little more, and then a little more, until we reach the sea. Happy Canute! Happier Alexander! And after all, why should even the world be the limit of possession? A rocket containing a Union Jack, will, it is hoped, be shortly fired at the moon. Mars. Sirius. Beyond which . . . But these immensities ended by saddening me. I could not suppose that my wood was the destined nucleus of universal dominion—it is so very small and contains no mineral wealth beyond the blackberries. Nor was I comforted when Mrs. Henessy's bird took alarm for the second time and flew clean away from us all, under the belief that it belonged to itself.

In the third place, property makes its owner feel that he ought to do something to it. Yet he isn't sure what. A restlessness comes over him, a vague sense that he has a personality to express—the same sense which, without any vagueness, leads the artist to an act of creation. Sometimes I think I will cut down such trees as remain in the wood, at other times I want to fill up the gaps between them with new trees. Both impulses are pretentious and empty. They are not honest movements towards money-making or beauty. They spring from a foolish desire to express myself and from an inability to enjoy what I have got. Creation, property, enjoyment form a sinister trinity in the human mind. Creation and enjoyment are both very, very good, yet they are often unattainable without a material basis, and at such moments property pushes itself in as a substitute, saying, "Accept me instead—I'm good enough for all three." It is not enough. It is, as Shakespeare said of lust, "The expense of spirit in a waste of shame": it is "Before, a joy proposed; behind, a dream." Yet we don't know how to shun it. It is forced on us by our economic system as the alternative to starvation. It is also forced on us by an internal defect in the soul, by the feeling that in property may lie the germs of self-development and of exquisite or heroic deeds. Our life on earth is, and ought to be, material and carnal. But we have not yet learned to manage our materialism and carnality properly; they are still entangled with the desire for ownership, where (in the words of Dante) "Possession is one with loss." 5

And this brings us to our fourth and final point: the blackberries. 6

Blackberries are not plentiful in this meagre grove, but they are easily seen from the public footpath which traverses it, and all too easily gathered. Foxgloves, too—people will pull up the foxgloves, and ladies of an educational tendency even grub for toadstools to show them on the Monday in class. Other ladies, less educated, roll 7 down the bracken in the arms of their gentlemen friends. There is paper, there are tins. Pray, does my wood belong to me or doesn't it? And, if it does, should I not own it best by allowing no one else to walk there? There is a wood near Lyme Regis, also cursed by a public footpath, where the owner has not hesitated on this point. He had built high stone walls each side of the path, and has spanned it by bridges, so that the public circulate like termites while he gorges on the blackberries unseen. He really does own his wood, this able chap. Dives in Hell did pretty well, but the gulf dividing him from Lazarus could be traversed by vision, and nothing traverses it here. And perhaps I shall come to this in time. I shall wall in and fence out until I really taste the sweets of property. Enormously stout, endlessly avaricious, pseudo-creative, intensely selfish, I shall weave upon my forehead the quadruple crown of possession until those nasty Bolshies come and take it off again and thrust me aside into the outer darkness.

QUESTIONS

1. List the four effects that property ownership has upon the author.

2. Describe the persona that emerges from the essay. What is the relationship of the last sentence to this persona?

3. What words and phrases does the author use to create a conversational style in the essay?

4. Analyze biblical, historical, and literary allusions in the essay. What is their function?

5. What is the purpose of Forster's reference to Americans at the outset of the essay?

6. How is the thesis reinforced in the first paragraph? How are essay clarity and proper sequence achieved through placement of topic sentences?

7. Analyze the manner in which Forster integrates the analysis of effects with a personal definition of property.

8. Explain the shift in tone, and the movement from concrete to abstract, in paragraph 5.

9. Do you agree with Forster that property ownership is as difficult as he declares it to be? Give the basis of your response and elucidate.

10. Write an essay of definition in which you explain an abstract term in personal, concrete, and carefully organized terms.

Are Families Passé?

Ruth Benedict (1887–1948), an anthropologist and educator, began her career as a poet. Later, she studied anthropology under Franz Boas and succeeded him as chairman of the department of anthropology at Columbia University (1936–1939). In 1934, she wrote *Patterns of Culture;* in 1940 *Race: Science and Politics.* In her work, Benedict attempted to study anthropology through sociology, psychology, and philosophy. The following essay illustrates her ability to work in an interdisciplinary manner in order to illuminate a core American institution.

A great many people today speak as if the family were in some special sort of danger in our times. We hear a great deal about "saving the family" and about "preserving the home." Authors and lecturers describe how the family is threatened by divorce, or by mothers who work outside of the home, or by unemployment, or by lack of religious training of children. Each of them, depending on his experience in his own home and on his observations in the families he knows, selects something which he thinks should be changed—or should be preserved—and says that, if this or that were done, the family would be "saved." 1

To an anthropologist such phrasings are dangerously misleading. He has studied the family among naked savages and in contemporary civilizations and he knows that it has survived in all human societies known in the record of mankind. Just as surely he knows that the family takes all kinds of different forms. It is not merely that unlettered primitive nomads have family arrangements different from Western industrial nations; even in Western nations around the Atlantic shores the family differs profoundly. The ethics of marriage, the specific close emotional ties which the family fosters, the disciplines and freedoms for the child, the nature of the dependency of the children upon the parents, even the personnel which makes up the family—all these differ in Western civilized nations. The anthropologist knows that the changes taking place in the home in any decade in any country do not mean that the family is now about to disintegrate under our eyes unless we do something about it. The problem as he states it is quite different: how do legal and customary arrangements in the family tally with the arrangements and premises of the whole way of life which is valued in any tribe or nation? If, for instance, the father has a heavy, authoritarian hand upon his children, the anthropologist asks: Is this in keeping with authoritarianism in the state and in industry? Or is it at odds with a society 2 which values non-authoritarianism and the pursuit of happiness? He asks the same kind of question about a nation's laws of inheritance from father to son, about the divorce laws, about the architectural layout of the house, about the reasons that are given to children when they are told to be good.

Customs enshrined in the family in any tribe or nation are likely to be sensitively adjusted to the values and customs of each particular people. This is no mystic correspondence; the persons who make up the family are the same people who are the citizens of that nation—the business men, the farmers, the churchgoers or non-churchgoers, the readers of newspapers, and the listeners to the radio. In all their roles they are molded more or less surely into a people with certain habits, certain hopes, and a certain *espirit de corps.* Americans come to share certain slogans, behavior, and judgments which differ from those of Frenchmen or Czechs. This is inevitable. And in the process the role of the family also becomes different. By the same token, just as economic and political changes occur over a period of time in the United States or in France or in Czechoslovakia, the family also changes. 3

An anthropologist, therefore, when he reads about the failure of the family, finds in such criticism a somewhat special meaning. He remembers how often the family is made a convenient whipping boy among many peoples who disapprove of the way their world is going. He has seen it in Amazon jungles and on the islands of the Pacific. The author remembers an American Indian tribe which used to talk about the family in a most uncomplimentary fashion. They were a people who, not long before, had roamed over the great plains hunting buffalo and proving their courage by war exploits. Now they lived on a reservation, and tending crops was no adequate substitute for their old way of life. Their old economic arrangements of boastful gift giving, their political life, and their religious practices had either been destroyed by circumstances or had lost their old meaningfulness. Life had become pointless to them. These men talked with gusto about the failure of the family. They said that in the family the children no longer learned manners, or religion, or generosity, or whatever it was the individual Indian favored as a cure-all. The family, too, weighed a man down, they said; it was a burden to him. 4

To the anthropologist studying this tribe, however, the family was precisely the best arranged, most trustworthy institution in their whole culture. It was hard beset and it had not escaped the tragic effects of the general disintegration of tribal life, but it was what provided the warm, human ties and the dependable security which were left in that Indian tribe. The children were loved and cared for, the husbands and wives often had comfortable relations with each 5 other, and family hospitality had a graciousness that was absent in more public life. At birth and marriage and death the family still functioned as an effective institution. And there seemed to be no man or woman of childbearing age who was not married or would not have preferred to be.

The writer thinks of this Indian tribe when she hears Americans talk about the decay of the family. Instead of viewing the family with such alarm, suppose we look at it as it exists in this decade in this country and see how it is arranged to fulfill its functions in American schemes of life. Let us leave aside for the moment the questions of whether conditions are provided that would keep it from preventable overstrain and of whether as human beings we are able to get all the satisfaction we might out of this institution; let us consider only the arrangements of the family as we know it and how these fit in with our values and with the way we should like to plan our lives. 6

Suppose we take marriage first. Marriage sets up the new family, and it seems to make a great deal of difference whether a society dictates that the new home shall be begun in tears and heartache or with rejoicing. Many human societies would not recognize a marriage without a wailing bride and a sullen groom. Often the bride has to be surrounded by her mourning women, who lament her coming lifelong separation from her parents and her brothers and sisters, as well as her future misery as she goes to work for her mother-in-law. Often they cut her long hair and remove her jewelry as a sign that she is now a worker and no longer alluring. The groom's role, too, may be that of an unwilling victim. Often marriages are arranged by the parents without giving the two young people any chance to know each other. 7

All these circumstances are absent in marriage in the United States. The young people are hardly hampered in their choice of a mate; if occasionally parents deplore their choice, public opinion allows the young couple to outface them and expects the parents to accept the inevitable with as much decency as they can muster. We expect that the bride and groom will be in love or will have chosen each other for reasons known to themselves. Whether they marry for love or for money or to show they can win a sought-after mate from a rival, in any case they are making a personal choice and are not acting on command. Because in every field of life American culture puts such a high value on this kind of freedom and so bitterly resents its curtailment in peace time, the fact that young people do make their own choice of a mate is an important and auspicious arrangement. The arranged marriage which is traditional in France or the careful class restrictions which have been observed in Holland would be difficult to manage in the United States. The wide range of choice of a 8

mate and the fact that the young people make their own selection are conditions which could hardly be made more satisfactory for Americans with their particular habits and demands.

After marriage, too, the new family has a wide range of choices about where to live, how the wife shall occupy herself, when to start a family, and a host of other important matters. Such freedom is extremely unusual in the world. Sometimes the couple must live with the husband's family, sometimes with the wife's. Often in other countries, until one or two children are born, the young man continues to work for his father and has no say about the farm or the flock and no money which he can control. But in the United States a young couple plans the family budget before the wedding and what they earn is theirs to spend. 9

The way the new family in this country sets up its own separate home makes possible a rare and delightful circumstance: the two of them can have an incomparable privacy. No matter how hard it has been to arrange for privacy before marriage, as soon as the wedding is over everybody expects them to have their own latch key and their own possessions around them. If they cannot manage this, they feel cheated and other people think something is wrong. It is the same if they have to give a home to a parent. In most civilized countries this is a duty to which as a good son and good daughter they are bound, but if it is necessary in the United States their friends and neighbors will regard them as exceptionally burdened. Even the scarcity and high wages of domestic servants give the young family a greater privacy. Considering that they have chosen each other to their own liking, this privacy in the home is made to order to gratify them; the only problem is whether they can use it to their own happiness. 10

When they cannot, and when they find that their choice of a mate was not fool-proof just because they made it on their own, there is in the United States great freedom to get a divorce. Our growing divorce rate is the subject of much viewing-with-alarm; yet in a culture built as ours is on ever expanding personal choice, an important goal of which is the pursuit of happiness, the right to terminate an unhappy marriage is the other side of the coin of which the fair side is the right to choose one's spouse. Weak and stunted individuals will of course abuse both privileges, yet it is difficult to see how divorce could consistently be denied in a culture like ours. Certainly if we accepted it more honestly as a necessary phase of our way of life, however sorrowful, and put honest effort and sympathy into not penalizing the divorced, we should be acting more appropriately and in our own best interests. At any rate, the high divorce rate in the United States is no attack on marriage, for it is precisely the divorced—those who have failed in one or two attempts—who have the highest rate of marriage. Between the ages of twenty-five and 11 thirty-five not even the unmarried or the widowed marry at so great a rate as the divorced.

Besides free choice and privacy, the American family has unusual potential leisure because of the labor-saving devices, prepared foods, and ready-made clothes available under modern conditions. The basic labor-saver is running water in the sink, and Americans have little idea how many millions of homes in civilized countries do not have it. Thus we are saved an endless round of drudgery that ties down women—and men also—in countries where homes have no running water, no gas and electricity, no farm tools but those which are driven into the earth by human hands or are swung in human arms, and no use of ready-made soaps and foods and clothes. Americans put high value on lessened drudgery, but they deprecate having free spaces of truly leisure time; the more time they save the more they fill up their days and nights with a round of engagements and complications. They are unwilling to admit that they have leisure, but the schedules of their lives prove clearly how much they have. 12

Universal schooling in the United States also frees the family of many duties when children have come. It is hard for Americans to imagine the difference which regular school hours make in a mother's role. For a great part of the working day, American children are in the responsibility of the teacher and not of the mother. As nursery schools spread over the country, younger and younger children get trained care outside the home and the mother's labors are correspondingly relieved. As the children grow older the mother's leisure increases until finally she reaches that idle middle age with its round of card parties and clubs and window shopping and movies which engross and waste the energy of so many millions of American women. Her husband is earning more money now than when he was younger, and her children have flown; she has a plethora of privileges and freedom and leisure. In one sense she has everything. 13

It is obviously unfair to talk about the incomparable freedom from drudgery which the American home offers without emphasizing that interval of a few years when there is no leisure for the mother in the home—the years when the babies are little. In our great cities where each family is strange to all the others, a mother is likely to have to be baby tender every hour of the day, with no one to relieve her. Along with these duties she must do all her cooking and washing and cleaning. And, as all our magazines and women's pages reiterate, she must make efforts to keep her husband. She must keep herself looking attractive, must keep up social contacts, and be a companion to him. To European wives this program looks formidable. "I was always told that American women were so free," a Polish woman said 14 to me, "but when I came here and saw how they had to manage with the babies and the house without any older women of the family to help, and then how they had to play around with their husbands in the evening to keep them happy, I decided I wouldn't change places with them for anything. In Poland a woman doesn't have to 'keep' her husband; it's all settled when they're married."

The striking fact about the nursery years in the United States 15
is that in comparison with those in other countries they are so short and that nevertheless we do not really treat them as an interim. Mothers who are going through this period give remarkably little thought to the leisure that will come soon. They are often vocal enough about the turmoil of their present lives, and sometimes bitter, but the fact that the nursery years last so short a time in the United States and could be treated as an interim—like a professor's going into the government during war time—is all too seldom part of their thinking. No doubt this is due in part to a lag in our culture, since even with our grandparents conditions were different; but in part it is a result of the sentiment which selects this period, no matter how short, as the fulfillment of a woman's chief duty in life. A social engineer looking at the family, however, would certainly put his major effort into better arrangements for the overburdened mother during these years and into thinking about effecting some transition from this period into that next one during which, in the United States, millions of women become idle parasites upon society—and dull and unhappy into the bargain.

Another notable feature of the American family is its peculiar- 16
ly non-authoritarian character. The old rules that a child should be seen and not heard and the adage, "Spare the rod and spoil the child," are anachronistic in the United States; they are dispensed with even in immigrant groups which honored them in their native country. The rule of the father over the family is still a reality in some European nations, but in the United States the mother is the chief responsible agent in bringing up her children; here the father's opinions are something the children are more likely to play off against the mother's, to their own advantage, rather than a court of last authority from which there is no appeal. Children take the noisy center of the stage at the breakfast table and in the living room in a way that is quite impossible in European countries. The fact that they are expected to know right from wrong in their tenderest years and to act upon it on their own is often commented on by European mothers who have lived here. A Dutch mother once spoke to the author about how hard we are on our children because we expect this of them; she said "I don't expect it of my children before they are seven; until then, I am there to see that they act correctly." But an American mother

expects a child of three or four to be a responsible moral agent, and she gives him great latitude in which to prove that he can manage his little affairs by himself.

All this lack of strong authoritarianism in American families accords well with the values that are chiefly sought after in this country. No strong father image is compatible with our politics or our economics. We seek the opportunity to prove that we are as good as the next person, and we do not find comfort in following an authoritarian voice—in the state or in the home, from the landowner or the priest—which will issue a command from on high. We learn as children to measure ourselves against Johnny next door, or against Mildred whose mother our mother knows in church, and this prepares us for living in a society with strongly egalitarian ideals. We do not learn the necessity of submitting to unquestioned commands as the children of many countries do. The family in the United States has become democratic. 17

These free-choice and non-authoritarian aspects of the family, along with its privacy and potential leisure, evidence only a few of the many ways in which it has become consistent with major emphases in our national life. They seem, when one compares them with arrangements of other civilized nations, to be quite well fitted to the role the family must play in a culture like the United States. This does not mean, however, that Americans capitalize to their own advantage upon all these consistently contrived arrangements which are institutionalized in the family as we know it. At the beginning of this essay two subjects were left for later discussion—how well our society protects the family from dangerous overstrain, and how well as human beings with special insights and blind spots we are able to get all the satisfactions we might out of our version of the home. These two subjects cannot be omitted. 18

In spite of all our American sentiment about the home and the family, we do not show great concern about buttressing it against catastrophe. Any well-considered national program must have regard for the children; if they are housed and fed below a certain minimum, if their health is not attended to, the nation suffers in the next generation. The lack of a tolerable economic floor under the family is especially crucial in a society like that of the United States, where competition is so thoroughly relied upon as an incentive and where so few families have anything but the weekly pay envelope to use for food and doctors' bills. When factories close, when inflation comes, the family gets little consideration in the United States. Especially in economic crises it gets the little end of the horn. Today the necessity of providing tens of thousands of new homes is of the greatest importance for healthy family life in the United States, but adequate 19 housing programs are notoriously unsupported. Sickness insurance, too, which would provide preventive care as well as relieve the family budget of all expenses in a crisis, needs high priority in a national program. When one reads about families in trouble, it is clear that many of the reefs which are threatening shipwreck are avoidable by intelligent local, state, or national programs. Such programs have worked satisfactorily in non-communist countries—as, for instance, in the Scandinavian nations. But they cost money, and Americans have not been willing to be taxed for the sake of taking the excessive strain off the family and providing better circumstances for growing children. It could be done, and if it were done the incidental disadvantages of our highly competitive and unregulated economic system would be largely removed; it should be the surest way to ensure the successful continuance of what is known as the democratic way of life.

Besides this American political attitude toward the family, 20
there is also a very different difficulty which threatens it. We have seen how as an institution it is particularly tailored to American ways of living. But the very best suit of clothes may be badly worn by a careless and irresponsible person. So, too, people may abuse a home well designed to suit them. It is no less true of marriage and the family. These exist as institutions remarkably well adjusted to American life. But many Americans are miserably unable to achieve happiness within them.

It is of course easy to say that a culture like that of the United 21
States, which allows individuals so much free choice among alternatives, is asking a great deal of human beings. In social life, as in literature, some of the finest human achievements have been within restrictions as rigid as those of the sonnet form. Our American culture is more like a sprawling novel where every page may deal with a new encounter and with a special choice. We ask a great deal of individuals when we give them such wide latitude and so little respected authority. But the United States is built on the premise that this is possible, and if ever we as a people decide otherwise our nation will change beyond recognition. We shall have lost the very thing we have been trying to build in this country.

It must not be imagined that this craving for individual 22
freedom is what prevents Americans from enjoying the family as much as it might be enjoyed. In so far as the family is an overheavy economic burden on some wage earners, a more careful welfare program could take care of this complaint. Certainly women and children have a freedom in the American family which is hard to match elsewhere in the world, and from all portents this will probably increase rather than diminish.

The crucial difficulty in American happiness in marriage is, rather, a certain blind spot which is especially fostered in our privileged United States. An extreme instance of this was mentioned in connection with the millions of idle, middle-aged wives in this country. These are women who as a group are well set up and favored beyond any such great numbers of women in any other part of the world. But privilege to them is separate from responsibility. Comparatively few of them feel that it is compatible with their status to do responsible work in which they have had experience in their own households and which must now be done outside their homes, and few take the initiative in getting the training they would need in jobs which they can see need to be done—except in war time. In periods of peace they have a blind spot about what it takes to live happily. For that the motto is *Noblesse oblige,* or "Privilege obligates one to do something in return." 23

It is not only the middle-aged woman who accepts privilege without a sense of obligation. In marriage, the right of both men and women to choose their mates freely is a privilege which carries with it, if they are to live happily, an accompanying conviction that when things go wrong it is doubly their obligation—to themselves as well as to their spouse—to deal tolerantly. Perhaps a young man realizes that his wife is more petulant than he knew; exactly because he chose her, however, she is "a poor thing; but his own." Privileged as he was to choose her, he has a corresponding responsibility. 24

It is the same with children. In the United States the reason for having children is not, as it is in most of the world, the perpetuation of the family line down many generations. In most countries people have children because there must be someone to till the piece of land in the village where the family has lived for centuries, there must be an heir to inherit the *Hof,* or there must be a son to perform the ancestral rites. In our atomistic American families these motivations seldom arise. We have children, not because our parents are sitting in judgment, not because of the necessity of having an heir, but because we personally want them—whether as company in the home or to show our friends we can have them. It is a privileged phase of parenthood, and if it is to bring us happiness it implies an acceptance of responsibility. Nothing is all pleasure in this life, and bringing up two or three noisy children in our small urban apartments is no exception to the rule. But with us it is based on choice—far more than it is elsewhere in the world—and we can only make the most of a choice if we follow it through wholeheartedly in all its implications. 25

It is partly because of this blind spot in the American family, this walling off of privilege from responsibility and tolerance, that we so often ask of life an average happiness—as if it could be presented 26 to us on a platter. Full normal happiness only comes to men and women who give as well as take—who, in this instance, give themselves warmly to their family life, and do not merely arrogate to themselves the rights they are so freely allowed in our society. In the United States, if happiness proves impossible they can get a divorce, but, until they have made this decision, they can capitalize on their privileges only if they bind around their arms the motto "Privilege has its obligations."

The family in the United States is an institution remarkably adapted to our treasured way of life. The changes that are occurring in it do not mean that it is decaying and needs to be saved. It offers a long array of privileges. It needs more consideration in political tax-supported programs, by means of which many difficulties that beset it could be eradicated. Finally, Americans, in order to get the maximum happiness out of such a free institution as the family in the United States, need to parallel their privileges with an awakening responsibility. It is hard to live up to being so privileged as we are in the United States, but it is not impossible. 27

QUESTIONS

1. Why is the anthropological perspective established by Benedict at the outset of the essay important to our understanding of the selection?

2. List the "notable features" about the American family that the author analyzes.

3. How does the writer achieve an informal yet reflective style in presenting her materials?

4. Define the following foreign words used by the author: *esprit de corps* (paragraph 3); *noblesse oblige* (paragraph 23); *Hof* (paragraph 25). Do they conflict with the intent of a popular essay?

5. What rhetorical strategies does Benedict employ in the introductory section, paragraphs 1 to 5? What is the function of paragraph 6? What other paragraph in the essay has a similar function?

6. How does the author's use of comparison and contrast throughout paragraphs 7 to 18 advance her thesis? What are the main comparative topics?

7. Analyze Benedict's presentation of illustration to develop the thesis. What is the unifying principle behind these illustrations? How are they ordered?

8. Explain the techniques in the development of the concluding paragraph.

9. Benedict wrote this essay in 1948. Do any of her observations require reconsideration today? What assumptions does the author make about "our treasured way of life"? Do you agree or disagree with her assumptions? Why?

10. Write an analysis of the relative strength or weakness of the American family today.

OLIVER GOLDSMITH

An Election

FROM LIEN CHI ALTANGI TO FUM HOAM, FIRST PRESIDENT OF THE CEREMONIAL ACADEMY AT PEKIN, IN CHINA.

Oliver Goldsmith (1730–1774), the son of an Anglican curate, was an Anglo-Irish essayist, poet, novelist, dramatist, and journalist. His reputation as an enduring figure in English literature is based on his novel, *The Vicar of Wakefield* (1766); his play *She Stoops to Conquer* (1773); his major poem, *The Deserted Village* (1770); and the essays and satiric letters collected in *The Bee* (1759) and *The Citizen of the World* (1762). In this sample from *The Citizen of the World,* Goldsmith assumes the role of a Chinese visitor to England who is amazed by one of the nation's ritualistic political conventions.

The English are at present employed in celebrating a feast 1
which becomes general every seventh year; the parliament of the nation being then dissolved, and another appointed to be chosen. This solemnity falls infinitely short of our Feast of the Lanterns in magnificence and splendour; it is also surpassed by others of the East in unanimity and pure devotion; but no festival in the world can compare with it for eating. Their eating, indeed, amazes me; had I five hundred heads, and were each head furnished with brains, yet would they all be insufficient to compute the number of cows, pigs, geese, and turkeys which upon this occasion die for the good of their country.

To say the truth, eating seems to make a grand ingredient in 2
all English parties of zeal, business, or amusement. When a church is to be built or a hospital endowed, the directors assemble and, instead

of consulting upon it, they eat upon it, by which means the business goes forward with success. When the poor are to be relieved, the officers appointed to dole out public charity assemble and eat upon it. Nor has it ever been known that they filled the bellies of the poor till they had previously satisfied their own. But in the election of magistrates the people seem to exceed all bounds; the merits of a candidate are often measured by the number of his treats; his constituents assemble, eat upon him, and lend their applause, not to his integrity or sense, but to the quantities of his beef and brandy.

And yet I could forgive this people their plentiful meals on 3
this occasion, as it is extremely natural for every man to eat a great deal when he gets it for nothing; but what amazes me is that all this good living no way contributes to improve their good-humour. On the contrary, they seem to lose their temper as they lose their appetites; every morsel they swallow, and every glass they pour down, serves to increase their animosity. Many an honest man, before as harmless as a tame rabbit, when loaded with a single election dinner has become more dangerous than a charged culverin. Upon one of these occasions I have actually seen a bloody-minded man-milliner sally forth at the head of a mob, determined to face a desperate pastry-cook who was general of the opposite party.

But you must not suppose they are without a pretext for thus 4
beating each other. On the contrary, no man here is so uncivilized as to beat his neighbour without producing very sufficient reasons. One candidate, for instance, treats with gin, a spirit of their own manufacture; another always drinks brandy, imported from abroad. Brandy is a wholesome liquor; gin, a liquor wholly their own. This, then, furnishes an obvious cause of quarrel—whether it be most reasonable to get drunk with gin or get drunk with brandy? The mob meet upon the debate, fight themselves sober, and then draw off to get drunk again, and charge for another encounter. So that the English may now properly be said to be engaged in war; since, while they are subduing their enemies abroad, they are breaking each other's heads at home.

I lately made an excursion to a neighbouring village, in order 5
to be a spectator of the ceremonies practised upon this occasion. I left town in company with three fiddlers, nine dozen of hams, and a corporation poet, which were designed as reinforcements to the gin-drinking party. We entered the town with a very good face; the fiddlers, no way intimidated by the enemy, kept handling their arms up the principal street. By this prudent manoeuvre, they took peaceable possession of their headquarters, amidst the shouts of multitudes, who seemed perfectly rejoiced at hearing their music, but above all at seeing their bacon.

I must own, I could not avoid being pleased to see all ranks of 6

people, on this occasion, levelled into an equality, and the poor, in some measure, enjoying the primitive privileges of nature. If there was any distinction shown, the lowest of the people seemed to receive it from the rich. I could perceive a cobbler with a levee at his door, and a haberdasher giving audience from behind his counter.

But my reflections were soon interrupted by a mob, who 7 demanded whether I was for the distillery or the brewery? As these were terms with which I was totally unacquainted, I chose at first to be silent; however, I know not what might have been the consequence of my reserve, had not the attention of the mob been called off to a skirmish between a brandy-drinker's cow and a gin-drinker's mastiff, which turned out, greatly to the satisfaction of the mob, in favour of the mastiff.

This spectacle, which afforded high entertainment, was at 8 last ended by the appearance of one of the candidates, who came to harangue the mob: he made a very pathetic speech upon the late excessive importation of foreign drams, and the downfall of the distillery; I could see some of the audience shed tears. He was accompanied in his procession by Mrs. Deputy and Mrs. Mayoress. Mrs. Deputy was not in the least in liquor; and as for Mrs. Mayoress, one of the spectators assured me in my ear that—she was a very fine woman before she had the small-pox.

Mixing with the crowd, I was now conducted to the hall 9 where the magistrates are chosen: but what tongue can describe this scene of confusion! The whole crowd seemed equally inspired with anger, jealousy, politics, patriotism, and punch. I remarked one figure that was carried up by two men upon this occasion. I at first began to pity his infirmities as natural, but soon found the fellow so drunk that he could not stand; another made his appearance to give his vote, but though he could stand, he actually lost the use of his tongue, and remained silent; a third, who, though excessively drunk, could both stand and speak, being asked the candidate's name for whom he voted, could be prevailed upon to make no other answer but "Tobacco and brandy." In short, an election hall seems to be a theatre, where every passion is seen without disguise; a school where fools may readily become worse, and where philosophers may gather wisdom.—Adieu.

QUESTIONS

1. Summarize Goldsmith's attitude toward English elections.

2. Why does Goldsmith pose as a visiting Chinese? What advantages does the role afford him?

3. Identify and analyze examples of exaggeration and understatement in the essay.

4. Explain the effect of the alliteration in paragraph 9.

5. How does the introductory paragraph alert readers to the ironic and satiric nature of the essay? Cite other examples of irony and satire in the essay.

6. Trace the method whereby the act of eating becomes an extended metaphor in the essay.

7. Examine paragraphs 5 to 8 as a self-contained unit. What key principle of rhetoric does Goldsmith utilize to develop these paragraphs?

8. Where does the author state his thesis most clearly? Evaluate the placement of the thesis.

9. What foibles do you encounter in the American political process that lend themselves to ironic or satiric treatment?

10. Write an essay on some aspect of American political life, treating the subject in a lightly satiric or tongue in cheek manner.

J. B. PRIESTLEY

Wrong Ism

John Boynton Priestley (1894–1984), best-selling English novelist and popular dramatist, was also a prolific writer of essays, many of them involving social and political criticism. His work includes *The English Novel* (1927), *The Good Companions* (1929), *Time and the Conways* (1937), *An Inspector Calls* (1946), and *The English* (1973). This selection from *Essays of Five Decades* (1968) offers an astute analysis of contemporary political habits.

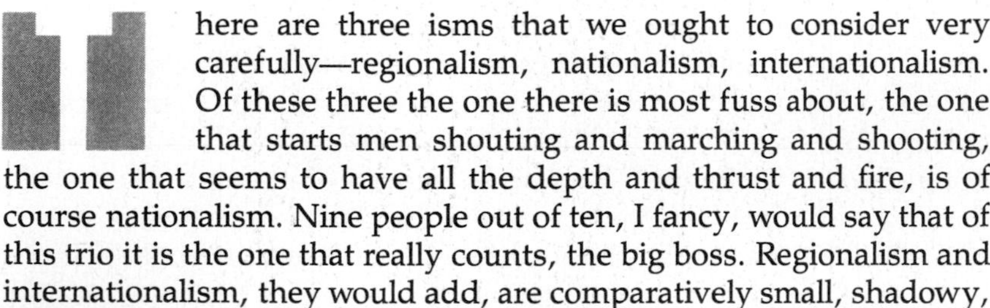

There are three isms that we ought to consider very carefully—regionalism, nationalism, internationalism. Of these three the one there is most fuss about, the one that starts men shouting and marching and shooting, the one that seems to have all the depth and thrust and fire, is of course nationalism. Nine people out of ten, I fancy, would say that of this trio it is the one that really counts, the big boss. Regionalism and internationalism, they would add, are comparatively small, shadowy, 1 rather cranky. And I believe all this to be quite wrong. Like many another big boss, nationalism is largely bogus. It is like a bunch of flowers made of plastics.

The real flowers belong to regionalism. The mass of people 2
everywhere may never have used the term. They are probably regionalists without knowing it. Because they have been brought up in a certain part of the world, they have formed perhaps quite unconsciously a deep attachment to its landscape and speech, its traditional customs, its food and drink, its songs and jokes. (There are of course always the rebels, often intellectuals and writers, but they are not the mass of people.) They are rooted in their region. Indeed, without this attachment a man can have no roots.

So much of people's lives, from earliest childhood onwards, 3
is deeply intertwined with the common life of the region, they cannot help feeling strongly about it. A threat to it is a knife pointing at the heart. How can life ever be the same if bullying strangers come to change everything? The form and colour, the very taste and smell of dear familiar things will be different, alien, life-destroying. It would be better to die fighting. And it is precisely this, the nourishing life of the region, for which common men have so often fought and died.

This attachment to the region exists on a level far deeper than 4
that of any political hocus-pocus. When a man says "my country" with real feeling, he is thinking about his region, all that has made up his life, and not about that political entity, the nation. There can be some confusion here simply because some countries are so small—and ours is one of them—and so old, again like ours, that much of what is national is also regional. Down the centuries, the nation, itself, so comparatively small, has been able to attach to itself the feeling really created by the region. (Even so there is something left over, as most people in Yorkshire or Devon, for example, would tell you.) This probably explains the fervent patriotism developed early in small countries. The English were announcing that they were English in the Middle Ages, before nationalism had arrived elsewhere.

If we deduct from nationalism all that it has borrowed or 5
stolen from regionalism, what remains is mostly rubbish. The nation, as distinct from the region, is largely the creation of power-men and political manipulators. Almost all nationalist movements are led by ambitious frustrated men determined to hold office. I am not blaming them. I would do the same if I were in their place and wanted power so badly. But nearly always they make use of the rich warm regional feeling, the emotional dynamo of the movement, while being almost untouched by it themselves. This is because they are not as a rule deeply loyal to any region themselves. Ambition and a love of power can eat like acid into the tissues of regional loyalty. It is hard, if not

impossible, to retain a natural piety and yet be for ever playing both ends against the middle.

Being itself a power structure, devised by men of power, the 6
nation tends to think and act in terms of power. What would benefit the real life of the region, where men, women and children actually live, is soon sacrificed for the power and prestige of the nation. (And the personal vanity of presidents and ministers themselves, which historians too often disregard.) Among the new nations of our time innumerable peasants and labourers must have found themselves being cut down from five square meals a week to three in order to provide unnecessary airlines, military forces that can only be used against them and nobody else, great conference halls and official yachts and the rest. The last traces of imperialism and colonialism may have to be removed from Asia and Africa, where men can no longer endure being condemned to a permanent inferiority by the colour of their skins; but even so, the modern world, the real world of our time, does not want and would be far better without more and more nations, busy creating for themselves the very paraphernalia that western Europe is now trying to abolish. You are compelled to answer more questions when trying to spend half a day in Cambodia than you are now travelling from the Hook of Holland to Syracuse.

This brings me to internationalism. I dislike this term, which I 7
used only to complete the isms. It suggests financiers and dubious promoters living nowhere but in luxury hotels; a shallow world of entrepreneurs and impresarios. (Was it Sacha Guitry who said that impresarios were men who spoke many languages but all with a foreign accent?) The internationalism I have in mind here is best described as world civilisation. It is life considered on a global scale. Most of our communications and transport already exist on this high wide level. So do many other things from medicine to meteorology. Our astronomers and physicists (except where they have allowed themselves to be hush-hushed) work here. The UN special agencies, about which we hear far too little, have contributed more and more to this world civilisation. All the arts, when they are arts and not chunks of nationalist propaganda, naturally take their place in it. And it grows, widens, deepens, in spite of the fact that for every dollar, ruble, pound or franc spent in explaining and praising it, a thousand are spent by the nations explaining and praising themselves.

This world civilisation and regionalism can get along togeth- 8
er, especially if we keep ourselves sharply aware of their quite different but equally important values and rewards. A man can make his contribution to world civilisation and yet remain strongly regional in feeling: I know several men of this sort. There is of course the danger—it is with us now—of the global style flattening out the

regional, taking local form, colour, flavour, away for ever, disinheriting future generations, threatening them with sensuous poverty and a huge boredom. But to understand and appreciate regionalism is to be on guard against this danger. And we must therefore make a clear distinction between regionalism and nationalism.

9 It is nationalism that tries to check the growth of world civilisation. And nationalism, when taken on a global scale, is more aggressive and demanding now than it has ever been before. This in the giant powers is largely disguised by the endless fuss in public about rival ideologies, now a largely unreal quarrel. What is intensely real is the glaring nationalism. Even the desire to police the world is nationalistic in origin. (Only the world can police the world.) Moreover, the nation-states of today are for the most part far narrower in their outlook, far more inclined to allow prejudice against the foreigner to impoverish their own style of living, than the old imperial states were. It should be part of world civilisation that men with particular skills, perhaps the product of the very regionalism they are rebelling against, should be able to move easily from country to country, to exercise those skills, in anything from teaching the violin to running a new type of factory to managing an old hotel. But nationalism, especially of the newer sort, would rather see everything done badly than allow a few non-nationals to get to work. And people face a barrage of passports, visas, immigration controls, labour permits; and in this respect are worse off than they were in 1900. But even so, in spite of all that nationalism can do—so long as it keeps its nuclear bombs to itself—the internationalism I have in mind, slowly creating a world civilisation, cannot be checked.

10 Nevertheless, we are still backing the wrong ism. Almost all our money goes on the middle one, nationalism, the rotten meat between the two healthy slices of bread. We need regionalism to give us roots and that very depth of feeling which nationalism unjustly and greedily claims for itself. We need internationalism to save the world and to broaden and heighten our civilisation. While regional man enriches the lives that international man is already working to keep secure and healthy, national man, drunk with power, demands our loyalty, money and applause, and poisons the very air with his dangerous nonsense.

QUESTIONS

1. Define regionalism, nationalism, and internationalism as Priestley presents these terms.

2. Explain Priestley's objections to nationalism. Where does he state these objections in the essay?

3. What striking metaphor does the author develop to capture the essence of nationalism? What is its sensory impact? Analyze another example of metaphorical language in the essay.

4. How does the suffix "-ism" function in the essay?

5. What is Priestley's principle of classification in this essay? How does he maintain proportion in the presentation of categories?

6. Analyze the relationship between definition and classification in the essay.

7. Examine Priestley's use of comparison and contrast.

8. Explain the connection between the introductory and concluding paragraphs.

9. Priestley makes many assumptions about regionalism, nationalism, and internationalism. Which assumptions do you accept? Which assumptions do you reject? Explain.

10. Write a classification essay on at least three related "-isms": capitalism, socialism, and communism; Protestantism, Catholicism, and Judaism; regionalism, nationalism, and internationalism.

W. E. B. DU BOIS

Of the Meaning of Progress

William Edward Burghardt Du Bois (1868–1963) was born in Massachusetts, the descendant of French Huguenots and slaves. He studied at Harvard and Berlin, and was a professor of economics and history at Atlanta University from 1896 to 1910. Emerging as a leader of the militant wing of the black movement in America, Du Bois wrote *The Souls of Black Folk* (1903) and other sociological studies. His increasing militancy moved him toward socialism and communism, culminating in renunciation of American citizenship and residence in Ghana, where he died. In this chapter from *The Souls of Black Folk,* Du Bois presents a highly personalized sociological account of black education in the South.

Once upon a time I taught school in the hills of Tennessee, where the broad dark vale of the Mississippi begins to roll and crumple to greet the Alleghenies. I was a Fisk student then, and all Fisk men thought that Tennessee—beyond the Veil—was theirs alone, and in vacation time they sallied forth in lusty bands to meet the county school-commissioners. Young and happy, I too went, and I shall not soon forget that summer, seventeen years ago. 1

First, there was a Teachers' Institute at the countyseat; and there distinguished guests of the superintendent taught the teachers fractions and spelling and other mysteries,—white teachers in the morning, Negroes at night. A picnic now and then, and a supper, and the rough world was softened by laughter and song. I remember how—But I wander. 2

There came a day when all the teachers left the Institute and began the hunt for schools. I learn from hearsay (for my mother was mortally afraid of firearms) that the hunting of ducks and bears and men is wonderfully interesting, but I am sure that the man who has never hunted a country school has something to learn of the pleasures of the chase. I see now the white, hot roads lazily rise and fall and wind before me under the burning July sun; I feel the deep weariness of heart and limb as ten, eight, six miles stretch relentlessly ahead; I feel my heart sink heavily as I hear again and again, "Got a teacher? Yes." So I walked on and on—horses were too expensive—until I had wandered beyond railways, beyond stage lines, to a land of "varmints" and rattlesnakes, where the coming of a stranger was an event, and men lived and died in the shadow of one blue hill. 3

Sprinkled over hill and dale lay cabins and farmhouses, shut out from the world by the forests and the rolling hills toward the east. There I found at last a little school. Josie told me of it; she was a thin, homely girl of twenty, with a dark-brown face and thick, hard hair. I had crossed the stream at Watertown, and rested under the great willows; then I had gone to the little cabin in the lot where Josie was resting on her way to town. The gaunt farmer made me welcome, and Josie, hearing my errand, told me anxiously that they wanted a school over the hill; that but once since the war had a teacher been there; that she herself longed to learn—and thus she ran on, talking fast and loud, with much earnestness and energy. 4

Next morning I crossed the tall round hill, lingered to look at the blue and yellow mountains stretching toward the Carolinas, then plunged into the wood, and came out at Josie's home. It was a dull frame cottage with four rooms, perched just below the brow of the hill, amid peach-trees. The father was a quiet, simple soul, calmly ignorant, with no touch of vulgarity. The mother was different,— 5 strong, bustling, and energetic, with a quick, restless tongue, and an ambition to live "like folks." There was a crowd of children. Two boys had gone away. There remained two growing girls; a shy midget of eight; John, tall awkward, and eighteen; Jim, younger, quicker, and better looking; and two babies of indefinite age. Then there was Josie herself. She seemed to be the centre of the family: always busy at service, or at home, or berrypicking, a little nervous and inclined to scold, like her mother, yet faithful, too, like her father. She had about her a certain fineness, the shadow of an unconscious moral heroism that would willingly give all of life to make life broader, deeper, and fuller for her and hers. I saw much of this family afterwards, and grew to love them for their honest efforts to be decent and comfortable, and for their knowledge of their own ignorance. There was with them no affectation. The mother would scold the father for being so "easy"; Josie would roundly berate the boys for carelessness; and all knew that it was a hard thing to dig a living out of a rocky side-hill.

I secured the school. I remember the day I rode horseback out 6
to the commissioner's house with a pleasant young white fellow who wanted the white school. The road ran down the bed of a stream; the sun laughed and the water jingled, and we rode on. "Come in," said the commissioner,—come in. Have a seat. Yes, that certificate will do. Stay to dinner. What do you want a month?" "Oh," thought I, "this is lucky"; but even then fell the awful shadow of the Veil, for they ate first, then I—alone.

The schoolhouse was a log hut, where Colonel Wheeler used 7
to shelter his corn. It sat in a lot behind a rail fence and thorn bushes, near the sweetest of springs. There was an entrance where a door once was, and within a massive rickety fireplace; great chinks between the logs served as windows. Furniture was scarce. A pale blackboard crouched in the corner. My desk was made of three boards, reinforced at critical points, and my chair, borrowed from the landlady, had to be returned every night. Seats for the children—these puzzled me much. I was haunted by a New England vision of neat little desks and chairs, but, alas! the reality was rough plank benches without backs, and at times without legs. They had the one virtue of making naps dangerous,—possibly fatal, for the floor was not to be trusted.

It was a hot morning late in July when the school opened. I 8
trembled when I heard the patter of little feet down the dusty road, and saw the growing row of dark solemn faces and bright eager eyes facing me. First came Josie and her brothers and sisters. The longing to know, to be a student in the great school at Nashville, hovered like a star above this child-woman amid her work and worry, and she studied doggedly. There were the Dowells from their farm over

toward Alexandria,—Fanny, with her smooth black face and wondering eyes; Martha, brown and dull; the pretty girl-wife of a brother, and the younger brood.

There were the Burkes,—two brown and yellow lads, and a 9
tiny haughty-eyed girl. Fat Reuben's little chubby girl came, with golden face and old-gold hair, faithful and solemn. Thenie was on hand early,—a jolly, ugly, goodhearted girl, who slyly dipped snuff and looked after her little bow-legged brother. When her mother could spare her, Tildy came,—a midnight beauty, with starry eyes and tapering limbs; and her brother, correspondingly homely. And then the big boys,—the hulking Lawrences; and lazy Neills, unfathered sons of mother and daughter; Hickman, with a stoop in his shoulders; and the rest.

There they sat, nearly thirty of them, on the rough benches, 10
their faces shading from a pale cream to a deep brown, the little feet bare and swinging, the eyes full of expectation, with here and there a twinkle of mischief, and the hands grasping Webster's blue-back spelling-book. I loved my school, and the fine faith the children had in the wisdom of their teacher was truly marvellous. We read and spelled together, wrote a little, picked flowers, sang, and listened to stories of the world beyond the hill. At times the school would dwindle away, and I would start out. I would visit Mun Eddings, who lived in two very dirty rooms, and ask why little Lugene, whose flaming face seemed ever ablaze with the dark-red hair uncombed, was absent all last week, or why I missed so often the inimitable rags of Mack and Ed. Then the father, who worked Colonel Wheeler's farm on shares, would tell me how the crops needed the boys; and the thin, slovenly mother, whose face was pretty when washed, assured me that Lugene must mind the baby. "But we'll start them again next week." When the Lawrences stopped, I knew that the doubts of the old folks about book-learning had conquered again, and so, toiling up the hill, and getting as far into the cabin as possible, I put Cicero "pro Archia Poeta" into the simplest English with local applications, and usually convinced them—for a week or so.

On Friday nights I often went home with some of the 11
children,—sometimes to Doc Burke's farm. He was a great, loud, thin Black, ever working, and trying to buy the seventy-five acres of hill and dale where he lived; but people said that he would surely fail, and the "white folks would get it all." His wife was a magnificent Amazon, with saffron face and shining hair, uncorseted and barefooted, and the children were strong and beautiful. They lived in a one-and-a-half room cabin in the hollow of the farm, near the spring. The front room was full of great fat white beds, scrupulously neat; and there were bad chromos on the walls, and a tired centre-table. In the tiny back kitchen I was often invited to "take out and help"

myself to fried chicken and wheat biscuit, "meat" and corn pone, string-beans and berries. At first I used to be a little alarmed at the approach of bedtime in the one lone bedroom, but embarrassment was very deftly avoided. First, all the children nodded and slept, and were stowed away in one great pile of goose feathers; next, the mother and the father discreetly slipped away to the kitchen while I went to bed; then, blowing out the dim light, they retired in the dark. In the morning all were up and away before I thought of awaking. Across the road, where fat Reuben lived, they all went outdoors while the teacher retired, because they did not boast the luxury of a kitchen.

I liked to stay with the Dowells, for they had four rooms and 12
plenty of good country fare. Uncle Bird had a small, rough farm, all woods and hills, miles from the big road; but he was full of tales,—he preached now and then,—and with his children, berries, horses, and wheat he was happy and prosperous. Often, to keep the peace, I must go where life was less lovely; for instance, Tildy's mother was incorrigibly dirty, Reuben's larder was limited seriously, and herds of untamed insects wandered over the Eddingses' beds. Best of all I loved to go to Josie's, and sit on the porch, eating peaches, while the mother bustled and talked: how Josie had bought the sewing-machine; how Josie worked at service in winter, but that four dollars a month was "mighty little" wages; how Josie longed to go away to school, but that it "looked like" they never could get far enough ahead to let her; how the crops failed and the well was yet unfinished; and, finally, how "mean" some of the white folks were.

For two summers I lived in this little world; it was dull and 13
humdrum. The girls looked at the hill in wistful longing, and the boys fretted and haunted Alexandria. Alexandria was "town,"—a straggling, lazy village of houses, churches, and shops, and an aristocracy of Toms, Dicks, and Captains. Cuddled on the hill to the north was the village of the colored folks who lived in three- or four-room unpainted cottages, some neat and homelike, and some dirty. The dwellings were scattered rather aimlessly, but they centered about the twin temples of the hamlet, the Methodist, and the Hard-Shell Baptist churches. These, in turn, leaned gingerly on a sad-colored schoolhouse. Hither my little world wended its crooked way on Sunday to meet other worlds, and gossip, and wonder, and make the weekly sacrifice with frenzied priest at the altar of the "old-time religion." Then the soft melody and mighty cadences of Negro song fluttered and thundered.

I have called my tiny community a world, and so its isolation 14
made it; and yet there was among us but a half-awakened common consciousness, sprung from common joy and grief, at burial, birth, or wedding; from a common hardship in poverty, poor land, and low wages; and, above all, from the sight of the Veil that hung between us

and Opportunity. All this caused us to think some thoughts together; but these, when ripe for speech, were spoken in various languages. Those whose eyes twenty-five and more years before had seen "the glory of the coming of the Lord," saw in every present hindrance or help a dark fatalism bound to bring all things right in His own good time. The mass of those to whom slavery was a dim recollection of childhood found the world a puzzling thing: it asked little of them, and they answered with little, and yet it ridiculed their offering. Such a paradox they could not understand, and therefore sank into listless indifference, or shiftlessness, or reckless bravado. There were, however, some—such as Josie, Jim, and Ben—to whom War, Hell, and Slavery were but childhood tales, whose young appetites had been whetted to an edge by school and story and half-awakened thought. Ill could they be content, born without and beyond the World. And their weak wings beat against their barriers,—barriers of caste, of youth, of life; at last, in dangerous moments, against everything that opposed even a whim.

The ten years that follow youth, the years when first the 15
realization comes that life is leading somewhere,—these were the years that passed after I left my little school. When they were past, I came by chance once more to the walls of Fisk University, to the halls of the chapel of melody. As I lingered there in the joy and pain of meeting old school-friends, there swept over me a sudden longing to pass again beyond the blue hill, and to see the homes and the school of other days, and to learn how life had gone with my school-children; and I went.

Josie was dead, and the gray-haired mother said simply, 16
"We've had a heap of trouble since you've been away." I had feared for Jim. With a cultured parentage and a social caste to uphold him, he might have made a venturesome merchant or a West Point cadet. But here he was, angry with life and reckless; and when Farmer Durham charged him with stealing wheat, the old man had to ride fast to escape the stones which the furious fool hurled after him. They told Jim to run away; but he would not run, and the constable came that afternoon. It grieved Josie, and great awkward John walked nine miles every day to see his little brother through the bars of Lebanon jail. At last the two came back together in the dark night. The mother cooked supper, and Josie emptied her purse, and the boys stole away. Josie grew thin and silent, yet worked the more. The hill became steep for the quiet old father, and with the boys away there was little to do in the valley. Josie helped them to sell the old farm, and they moved nearer town. Brother Dennis, the carpenter, built a new house with six rooms; Josie toiled a year in Nashville, and brought back ninety dollars to furnish the house and change it to a home.

When the spring came, and the birds twittered, and the stream ran proud and full, little sister Lizzie, bold and thoughtless, flushed with the passion of youth, bestowed herself on the tempter, and brought home a nameless child. Josie shivered and worked on, with the vision of schooldays all fled, with a face wan and tired,—worked until, on a summer's day, some one married another; then Josie crept to her mother like a hurt child, and slept—and sleeps. 17

I paused to scent the breeze as I entered the valley. The Lawrences have gone,—the father and son forever,—and the other son lazily digs in the earth to live. A new young widow rents out their cabin to fat Reuben. Reuben is a Baptist preacher now, but I fear as lazy as ever, though his cabin has three rooms; and little Ella has grown into a bouncing woman, and is ploughing corn on the hot hillside. There are babies a-plenty, and one half-witted girl. Across the valley is a house I did not know before, and there I found, rocking one baby and expecting another one of my schoolgirls, a daughter of Uncle Bird Dowell. She looked somewhat worried with her new duties, but soon bristled into pride over her neat cabin and the tale of her thrifty husband, and the horse and cow, and the farm they were planning to buy. 18

My log schoolhouse was gone. In its place stood Progress; and Progress, I understand, is necessarily ugly. The crazy foundation stones still marked the former site of my poor little cabin, and not far away, on six weary boulders, perched a jaunty board house, perhaps twenty by thirty feet, with three windows and a door that locked. Some of the window-glass was broken, and part of an old iron stove lay mournfully under the house. I peeped through the window half reverently, and found things that were more familiar. The blackboard had grown by about two feet, and the seats were still without backs. The county owns the lot now, I hear, and every year there is a session of school. As I sat by the spring and looked on the Old and the New I felt glad, very glad, and yet— 19

After two long drinks I started on. There was the great double log-house on the corner. I remembered the broken, blighted family that used to live there. The strong, hard face of the mother, with its wilderness of hair, rose before me. She had driven her husband away, and while I taught school a strange man lived there, big and jovial, and people talked. I felt sure that Ben and Tildy would come to naught from such a home. But this is an odd world; for Ben is a busy farmer in Smith County, "doing well, too," they say, and he had cared for little Tildy until last spring, when a lover married her. A hard life the lad had led, toiling for meat, and laughed at because he was homely and crooked. There was a Sam Carlon, an impudent old skinflint, who had definite notions about "niggers," and hired Ben a summer and would not pay him. Then the hungry boy gathered his 20 sacks together, and in broad daylight went to Carlon's corn; and when the hard-fisted farmer set upon him, the angry boy flew at him like a beast. Doc Burke saved a murder and a lynching that day.

The story reminded me again of the Burkes, and an impatience seized me to know who won in the battle, Doc or the seventy-five acres. For it is a hard thing to make a farm out of nothing, even in fifteen years. So I hurried on, thinking of the Burkes. They used to have a certain magnificent barbarism about them that I liked. They were never vulgar, never immoral, but rather rough and primitive, with an unconventionality that spent itself in loud guffaws, slaps on the back, and naps in the corner. I hurried by the cottage of the misborn Neill boys. It was empty, and they were grown into fat, lazy farm-hands. I saw the home of the Hickmans, but Albert, with his stooping shoulders, had passed from the world. Then I came to the Burkes' gate and peered through; the inclosure looked rough and untrimmed, and yet there were the same fences around the old farm save to the left, where lay twenty-five other acres. And Lo! the cabin in the hollow had climbed the hill and swollen to a half-finished six-room cottage. 21

The Burkes held a hundred acres, but they were still in debt. Indeed, the gaunt father who toiled night and day would scarcely be happy out of debt, being so used to it. Some day he must stop, for his massive frame is showing decline. The mother wore shoes, but the lion-like physique of other days was broken. The children had grown up. Rob, the image of his father, was loud and rough with laughter. Birdie, my school baby of six, had grown to a picture of maiden beauty, tall and tawny. "Edgar is gone," said the mother, with head half bowed,—"gone to work in Nashville; he and his father couldn't agree." 22

Little Doc, the boy born since the time of my school, took me horseback down the creek next morning toward Farmer Dowell's. The road and the stream were battling for mastery, and the stream had the better of it. We splashed and waded, and the merry boy, perched behind me, chattered and laughed. He showed me where Simon Thompson had bought a bit of ground and a home; but his daughter Lana, a plump, brown, slow girl, was not there. She had married a man and a farm twenty miles away. We wound on down the stream till we came to a gate that I did not recognize, but the boy insisted that it was "Uncle Bird's." The farm was fat with the growing crop. In that little valley was a strange stillness as I rode up; for death and marriage had stolen youth and left age and childhood there. We sat and talked that night after the chores were done. Uncle Bird was grayer, and his eyes did not see so well, but he was still jovial. We talked of the acres bought,—one hundred and twenty-five,—of the new guest-chamber added, of Martha's marrying. Then we talked of death: Fanny and 23

Fred were gone; a shadow hung over the other daughter and when it lifted she was to go to Nashville to school. At last we spoke of the neighbors, and as night fell, Uncle Bird told me how, on a night like that, 'Thenie came wandering back to her home over yonder, to escape the blows of her husband. And next morning she died in the home that her little bow-legged brother, working and saving, had bought for their widowed mother.

My journey was done, and behind me lay hill and dale, and 24
Life and Death. How shall man measure Progress there where the dark-faced Josie lies? How many heartfuls of sorrow shall balance a bushel of wheat? How hard a thing is life to the lowly, and yet how human and real! And all this life and love and strife and failure,—is it the twilight of nightfall or the flush of some faint-dawning day?

Thus sadly musing, I rode to Nashville in the Jim Crow car. 25

QUESTIONS

1. In general, what is the author's basic attitude toward progress? Where does he state this attitude most clearly?

2. Put into your own words the feelings Du Bois projects in his description of the people he taught in the hills of Tennessee.

3. Would you label the language in the essay subjective or objective? Justify your answer by citing passages from the text.

4. How does the symbolism of "the Veil," first introduced in paragraph 1, influence the tone of the essay? How does the author control mood through shifting patterns of imagery? Cite examples.

5. What are the primary rhetorical patterns employed by the author to develop his definition of progress?

6. The essay divides into two main narrative segments. What are they? Analyze the relationship between these segments. How does Du Bois maintain unity? How does the time element affect the mood and tone that are generated?

7. Analyze the spatial transitions that the author uses in the essay.

8. Assess the effectiveness of the short, concluding paragraph.

9. Discuss the value of personal experience and observation as a sociological method. Why do you think that Du Bois mistrusted scientific objectivity in sociological analysis? Compare and contrast the sociological methods of Du Bois and Mumford.

10. Write a definition of "progress" based on personal experience and observation.

THOMAS JEFFERSON

The Declaration of Independence

In CONGRESS, JULY 4, 1776

The Unanimous Declaration of the thirteen united States of America

Thomas Jefferson (1743–1826) was governor of Virginia during the American Revolution, America's first Secretary of State, and the third President of the United States. He had a varied and monumental career as politician, public servant, scientist, architect, educator (he founded the University of Virginia), and man of letters. Jefferson attended the Continental Congress in 1775, where he wrote the rough draft of the Declaration of Independence and revised it; other hands made contributions to the document that was signed on July 4, 1776, but the wording, style, structure, and spirit of the final version are distinctly Jefferson's. Like Thomas Paine, Benjamin Franklin, James Madison, and other major figures of the Revolutionary era, Jefferson was notable for his use of prose as an instrument for social and political change. In the Declaration of Independence, we see a direct, precise, logical, and persuasive statement of revolutionary principles that make the document one of the best known and best written texts in world history. Jefferson died in his home at Monticello on July 4, fifty years to the day of the signing of the Declaration of Independence.

When in the Course of human events it becomes necessary for one people to dissolve the political bands which have connected them with another, and to assume among the powers of the earth, the separate and equal station to which the Laws of Nature and of Nature's God entitle them, a decent respect to the opinions of mankind requires that they should declare the causes which impel them to the separation. 1

We hold these truths to be self-evident, that all men are created equal, that they are endowed by their Creator with certain unalienable Rights, that among these are Life, Liberty and the pursuit of Happiness. 2

That to secure these rights, Governments are instituted among Men, deriving their just powers from the consent of the governed. 3

That whenever any Form of Government becomes destructive of these ends, it is the Right of the People to alter or to abolish it, and to institute new Government, laying its foundation on such principles and organizing its powers in such form, as to them shall 4 seem most likely to effect their Safety and Happiness. Prudence, indeed, will dictate that Governments long established should not be changed for light and transient causes; and accordingly all experience hath shewn that mankind are more disposed to suffer, while evils are sufferable, than to right themselves by abolishing the forms to which they are accustomed. But when a long train of abuses and usurpations, pursuing invariably the same Object evinces a design to reduce them under absolute Despotism, it is their right, it is their duty, to throw off such Government, and to provide new Guards for their future security.

Such has been the patient sufferance of these Colonies; and 5
such is now the necessity which constrains them to alter their former Systems of Government. The history of the present King of Great Britain is a history of repeated injuries and usurpations, all having in direct object the establishment of an absolute Tyranny over these States. To prove this, let Facts be submitted to a candid world.

He has refused his Assent to Laws, the most wholesome and 6
necessary for the public good.

He has forbidden his Governors to pass Laws of immediate 7
and pressing importance, unless suspended in their operation till his Assent should be obtained; and when so suspended, he has utterly neglected to attend to them.

He has refused to pass other Laws for the accommodation of 8
large districts of people, unless those people would relinquish the right of Representation in the Legislature, a right inestimable to them and formidable to tyrants only.

He has called together legislative bodies at places unusual, 9
uncomfortable, and distant from the depository of their public Records, for the sole purpose of fatiguing them into compliance with his measures.

He has dissolved Representative Houses repeatedly, for 10
opposing with manly firmness his invasions on the rights of the people.

He has refused for a long time, after such dissolutions, to 11
cause others to be elected; whereby the Legislative powers, incapable of Annihilation, have returned to the People at large for their exercise; the State remaining in the mean time exposed to all the dangers of invasion from without, and convulsions within.

He has endeavoured to prevent the population of these 12
States; for that purpose obstructing the Laws for Naturalization of Foreigners; refusing to pass others to encourage their migrations hither, and raising the conditions of new Appropriations of Lands.

He has obstructed the Administration of Justice, by refusing 13
his Assent to Laws for establishing Judiciary powers.

He has made Judges dependent on his Will alone, for the 14

tenure of their offices, and the amount and payment of their salaries.

He has erected a multitude of New Offices, and sent hither swarms of Officers to harass our people, and eat out their substance. 15

He has kept among us, in times of peace, Standing Armies without the Consent of our legislatures. 16

He has affected to render the Military independent of and superior to the Civil power. 17

He has combined with others to subject us to a jurisdiction foreign to our constitution, and unacknowledged by our laws; giving his Assent to their Acts of pretended Legislation: 18

For quartering large bodies of armed troops among us:

For protecting them, by a mock Trial, from punishment of any Murders which they should commit on the Inhabitants of these States:

For cutting off our Trade with all parts of the world:

For imposing Taxes on us without our Consent:

For depriving us in many cases, of the benefits of Trial by Jury:

For transporting us beyond Seas to be tried for pretended offences:

For abolishing the free System of English Laws in a neighbouring Province, establishing therein an Arbitrary government, and enlarging its Boundaries so as to render it at once an example and fit instrument for introducing the same absolute rule into these Colonies:

For taking away our Charters, abolishing our most valuable Laws and altering fundamentally the Forms of our Governments:

For suspending our own Legislatures, and declaring themselves invested with power to legislate for us in all cases whatsoever.

He has abdicated Government here, by declaring us out of his Protection and waging War against us. 19

He has plundered our seas, ravaged our Coasts, burnt our towns, and destroyed the Lives of our people. 20

He is at this time transporting large Armies of foreign Mercenaries to compleat the works of death, desolation and tyranny, already begun with circumstances of Cruelty & perfidy scarcely paralleled in the most barbarous ages, and totally unworthy the Head of a civilized nation. 21

He has constrained our fellow Citizens taken Captive on the high Seas to bear Arms against their Country, to become the executioners of their friends and Brethren, or to fall themselves by their Hands. 22

He has excited domestic insurrections amongst us, and has endeavoured to bring on the inhabitants of our frontiers, the merci- 23 less Indian Savages, whose known rule of warfare, is an undistinguished destruction of all ages, sexes and conditions.

24 In every stage of these Oppressions We have Petitioned for Redress in the most humble terms: Our repeated Petitions have been answered only by repeated injury. A Prince, whose character is thus marked by every act which may define a Tyrant, is unfit to be the ruler of a free people. Nor have We been wanting in attentions to our British brethren. We have warned them from time to time of attempts by their legislature to extend an unwarrantable jurisdiction over us. We have reminded them of the circumstances of our emigration and settlement here. We have appealed to their native justice and magnanimity, and we have conjured them by the ties of our common kindred to disavow these usurpations, which would inevitably interrupt our connections and correspondence. They too have been deaf to the voice of justice and of consanguinity. We must, therefore, acquiesce in the necessity, which denounces our Separation, and hold them, as we hold the rest of mankind, Enemies in War, in Peace Friends.

25 We, therefore, the Representatives of the united States of America, in General Congress, Assembled, appealing to the Supreme Judge of the world for the rectitude of our intentions, do, in the Name, and by Authority of the good People of these Colonies, solemnly publish and declare, That these United Colonies are, and of Right ought to be, Free and Independent States; that they are Absolved from all Allegiance to the British Crown, and that all political connection between them and the State of Great Britian, is and ought to be totally dissolved; and that as Free and Independent States, they have full Power to levy War, conclude Peace, contract Alliances, establish Commerce, and to do all other Acts and Things which Independent States may of right do.

26 And for the support of this Declaration, with a firm reliance on the protection of divine Providence, we mutually pledge to each other our Lives, our Fortunes and our sacred Honor.

QUESTIONS

1. What is Jefferson's key assertion or argument? Mention several reasons that he gives to support his argument.

2. Summarize Jefferson's definition of human nature and of government.

3. There are many striking words and phrases in the Declaration of Independence, notably in the beginning. Locate three such examples, and explain their connotative power and effectiveness.

4. Jefferson and his colleagues had to draft a document designed for several audiences. What audiences did they have in mind? How do language and style reflect an awareness of multiple audiences?

5. The Declaration of Independence is a classic model of syllogistic reasoning and deductive argument (see the Glossary). What is the major premise, and where is it stated? The minor premise? The conclusion?

6. What sort of inductive evidence does Jefferson offer?

7. Why is the middle portion or body of the Declaration of Independence considerably longer than the introduction or conclusion? What holds the body together?

8. Explain the function and effect of parallel structure in this document.

9. Do you believe that "all men are created equal"? Justify your answer.

10. a. Discuss the relevance of the Declaration of Independence to politics today.
b. Explain why the Declaration of Independence is a model of effective prose.
c. Write your own declaration of independence—from family, employer, required courses, or the like.

ALEXIS DE TOCQUEVILLE

Some Reflections on American Manners

Alexis Charles Henri Clerél de Tocqueville (1805–1859), descended from an aristocratic Norman family, was a French lawyer, politician, statesman, and historian. Sent to the United States in 1831 to study the American penal system, he wrote instead one of the most penetrating inquiries into the nature of the American system, *Democracy in America* (1835). In this chapter from his study, Tocqueville compares and contrasts manners as manifested in the political and social contexts of democracy and aristocracy.

Nothing, at first sight, seems less important than the external formalities of human behavior, yet there is nothing to which men attach more importance. They can get used to anything except living in a society which does not share their manners. The influence of the social and political system on manners is therefore worth serious examination. 1

Manners, speaking generally, have their roots in mores; they are also sometimes the result of an arbitrary convention agreed between certain men. They are both natural and acquired. 2

When some see that, without dispute or effort of their own, they stand first in society; when they daily have great aims in view which keep them occupied, leaving details to others; and when they live surrounded by wealth they have not acquired and do not fear to lose, one can see that they will feel a proud disdain for all the petty interests and material cares of life and that there will be a natural grandeur in their thoughts that will show in their words and manners. 3

In democracies there is generally little dignity of manner, as private life is very petty. Manners are often vulgar, as thoughts have small occasion to rise above preoccupation with domestic interests. 4

True dignity in manners consists in always taking one's proper place, not too high and not too low; that is as much within the reach of a peasant as of a prince. In democracies everybody's status seems doubtful; as a result, there is often pride but seldom dignity of manners. Moreover, manners are never well regulated or well thought out. 5

There is too much mobility in the population of a democracy for any definite group to be able to establish a code of behavior and see that it is observed. So everyone behaves more or less after this own fashion, and a certain incoherence of manners always prevails, because they conform to the feelings and ideas of each individual rather than to an ideal example provided for everyone to imitate. 6

In any case, this is much more noticeable when an aristocracy has just fallen than when it has long been destroyed. 7

New political institutions and new mores then bring together in the same places men still vastly different in education and habits and compel them to a life in common; this constantly leads to the most ill-assorted juxtapositions. There is still some memory of the former strict code of politeness, but no one knows quite what it said or where to find it. Men have lost the common standard of manners but have not yet resolved to do without it, so each individual tries to shape, out of the ruins of former customs, some rule, however arbitrary and variable. Hence manners have neither the regularity and dignity frequent in aristocracies nor the qualities of simplicity and freedom which one sometimes finds in democracies; they are both constrained and casual. 8

But this is not a normal state of things. 9

When equality is complete and old-established, all men, having roughly the same ideas and doing roughly the same things, do not need to come to an understanding or to copy each other in order to behave and talk in the same way; one sees a lot of petty variations in their manners but no great differences. They are never exactly alike, since they do not copy one pattern; they are never very unlike, because they have the same social condition. At first sight one 10 might be inclined to say that the manners of all Americans are exactly alike, and it is only on close inspection that one sees all the variations among them.

The English make game of American manners, but it is odd that most of those responsible for those comic descriptions belong themselves to the English middle classes, and the cap fits them very well too. So these ruthless critics generally themselves illustrate just what they criticize in America; they do not notice that they are abusing themselves, to the great delight of their own aristocracy. 11

Nothing does democracy more harm than its outward forms of behavior; many who could tolerate its vices cannot put up with its manners. 12

But I will not admit that there is nothing to praise in democratic manners. 13

In aristocracies, all within reach of the ruling class are at pains to imitate it, and very absurd and insipid imitations result. Democracies, with no models of high breeding before them, at least escape the necessity of daily looking at bad copies thereof. 14

In democracies manners are never so refined as among aristocracies, but they are also never so coarse. One misses both the crude words of the mob and the elegant and choice phrases of the high nobility. There is much triviality of manner, but nothing brutal or degraded. 15

I have already said that a precise code of behavior cannot take shape in democracies. That has its inconveniences and its advantages. In aristocracies rules of propriety impose the same demeanor on all, making every member of the same class seem alike in spite of personal characteristics; they bedizen and conceal nature. Democratic manners are neither so well thought out nor so regular, but they often are more sincere. They form, as it were, a thin, transparent veil through which the real feelings and personal thoughts of each man can be easily seen. Hence there is frequently an intimate connection between the form and the substance of behavior; we see a less decorative picture, but one truer to life. One may put the point this way: democracy imposes no particular manners, but in a sense prevents them from having manners at all. 16

Sometimes the feelings, passions, virtues, and vices of an aristocracy may reappear in a democracy, but its manners never. They are lost and vanish past return when the democratic revolution is completed. It would seem that nothing is more lasting than the manners of an aristocratic class, for it preserves them for some time after losing property and power, nor more fragile, for as soon as they have gone, no trace of them is left, and it is even difficult to discover what they once were when they have ceased to exist. A change in the 17 state of society works this marvel, and a few generations are enough to bring it about.

The principal characteristics of the aristocracy remain engraved in history after its destruction, but the slight and delicate forms of its manners are lost to memory almost immediately after its fall. No one can imagine them when they are no longer seen. Their disappearance is unnoted and unfelt. For the heart needs an apprenticeship of custom and education to appreciate the refined pleasure derived from distinguished and fastidious manners; once the habit is lost, the taste for them easily goes too. 18

Thus, not only are democratic peoples unable to have aristocratic manners, but they cannot even conceive or desire them. As they cannot imagine them, from their point of view it is as if they had never existed. 19

One should not attach too much importance to this loss, but it is permissible to regret it. 20

I know it has happened that the same men have had very distinguished manners and very vulgar feelings; the inner life of courts has shown well enough what grand appearances may conceal the meanest hearts. But though the manners of an aristocracy by no means create virtue, they may add grace to virtue itself. It was no ordinary sight to see a numerous and powerful class whose every gesture seemed to show a constant and natural dignity of feeling and thought, an ordered refinement of taste and urbanity of manners. 21

The manners of the aristocracy created a fine illusion about human nature; though the picture was often deceptive, it was yet a noble satisfaction to look on it. 22

QUESTIONS

1. How does Tocqueville develop his introductory observation about the impact of the social and political system on manners?

2. What distinctions does the author draw between manners in aristocracies and manners in democracies?

3. Analyze the relationship between the parallelism of the first sentence in paragraph 3 and the author's purpose.

4. Show the importance of the connotations that develop around the author's application of the key words *aristocracy* and *democracy.*

5. What is Tocqueville's main thesis? Analyze the way he develops the thesis. Explain the tone that emerges from the essay.

6. Analyze the importance of definition in paragraphs 1 to 5.

7. Explain the significance of comparison and contrast and of causal analysis in the development of the essay. Cite instances of these rhetorical strategies.

8. Many of Tocqueville's paragraphs are relatively short. Analyze their length in relation to the topic treated.

9. How valid are Tocqueville's assumptions about manners today? Have

BARBARA TUCHMAN

An Inquiry into the Persistence of Unwisdom in Government

Barbara Tuchman (1912–), an eminent American historian, twice winner of the Pulitzer Prize, began her career as a research assistant for the Institute of Pacific Relations in 1933. She was a staff writer and correspondent for the *Nation,* covering the Spanish Civil War from 1935 to 1937. Tuchman gained her first significant literary recognition for *The Zimmerman Telegram* (1958); she followed this initial success with *The Guns of August* (1962), *The Proud Tower* (1966), and *Stilwell and the American Experience in China, 1911–45* (1971). This article offers a wide-ranging historical assessment of the causes of failure, mediocrity, and unwisdom in political life.

A problem that strikes one in the study of history, regardless of period, is why man makes a poorer performance of government than of almost any other human activity. In this sphere, wisdom—meaning judgment acting on experience, common sense, available knowledge, and a decent appreciation of probability—is less operative and more frustrated than it should be. Why do men in high office so often act contrary to the way that reason points and enlightened self-interest suggests? Why does intelligent mental process so often seem to be paralyzed? 1

Why, to begin at the beginning, did the Trojan authorities 2 drag that suspicious-looking wooden horse inside their gates? Why did successive ministries of George III—that "bundle of imbecility," as Dr. Johnson called them collectively—insist on coercing rather than conciliating the Colonies though strongly advised otherwise by many counselors? Why did Napoleon and Hitler invade Russia? Why did the kaiser's government resume unrestricted submarine warfare in 1917 although explicitly warned that this would bring in the United States and that American belligerency would mean Germany's defeat? Why did Chiang Kai-shek refuse to heed any voice of reform or alarm until he woke up to find that his country had slid from under him? Why did Lyndon Johnson, seconded by the best and the brightest, progressively involve this nation in a war both ruinous and halfhearted and from which nothing but bad for our side resulted? Why does the present Administration continue to avoid introducing effective measures to reduce the wasteful consumption of oil while members of OPEC follow a price policy that must bankrupt their customers? How is it possible that the Central Intelligence Agency, whose function it is to provide, at taxpayers' expense, the information necessary to conduct a realistic foreign policy, could remain unaware that discontent in a country crucial to our interests was boiling up to the point of insurrection and overthrow of the ruler upon whom our policy rested? It has been reported that the CIA was ordered *not* to investigate the opposition to the shah of Iran in order to spare him any indication that we took it seriously, but since this sounds more like the theater of the absurd than like responsible government, I cannot bring myself to believe it.

There was a king of Spain once, Philip III, who is said to have 3
died of a fever he contracted from sitting too long near a hot brazier, helplessly overheating himself because the functionary whose duty it was to remove the brazier when summoned could not be found. In the late twentieth century, it begins to appear as if mankind may be approaching a similar stage of suicidal incompetence. The Italians have been sitting in Philip III's hot seat for some time. The British trade unions, in a lunatic spectacle, seem periodically bent on dragging their country toward paralysis, apparently under the impression that they are separate from the whole. Taiwan was thrown into a state of shock by the United States' recognition of the People's Republic of China because, according to one report, in the seven years since the Shanghai Communiqué, the Kuomintang rulers of Taiwan had "refused to accept the new trend as a reality."

Wooden-headedness is a factor that plays a remarkably large 4
role in government. Wooden-headedness consists of assessing a situation in terms of preconceived, fixed notions while ignoring or rejecting any contrary signs. It is acting according to wish while not allowing oneself to be confused by the facts.

A classic case was the French war plan of 1914, which concentrated everything on a French offensive to the Rhine, leaving the French left flank from Belgium to the Channel virtually unguarded. This strategy was based on the belief that the Germans would not use reserves in the front line and, without them, could not deploy enough manpower to extend their invasion through the French left. Reports by intelligence agents in 1913 to the effect that the Germans were indeed preparing their reserves for the front line in case of war were resolutely ignored because the governing spirits in France, dreaming only of their own offensive, did not want to believe in any signals that would require them to strengthen their left at the expense of their march to the Rhine. In the event, the Germans could and did extend themselves around the French left with results that determined a long war and its fearful consequences for our century. 5

Wooden-headedness is also the refusal to learn from experience, a form in which fourteenth-century rulers were supreme. No matter how often and obviously devaluation of the currency disrupted the economy and angered the people, French monarchs continued to resort to it whenever they were desperate for cash until they provoked insurrection among the bourgeoisie. No matter how often a campaign that depended on living off a hostile country ran into want and even starvation, campaigns for which this fate was inevitable were regularly undertaken. 6

Still another form is identification of self with the state, as currently exhibited by the ayatollah Khomeini. No wooden-headedness is so impenetrable as that of a religious zealot. Because he is connected with a private wire to the Almighty, no idea coming in on a lesser channel can reach him, which leaves him ill equipped to guide his country in its own best interests. 7

Philosophers of government ever since Plato have devoted their thinking to the major issues of ethics, sovereignty, the social contract, the rights of man, the corruption of power, the balance between freedom and order. Few—except Machiavelli, who was concerned with government as it is, not as it should be—bothered with mere folly, although this has been a chronic and pervasive problem. "Know, my son," said a dying Swedish statesman in the seventeenth century, "with how little wisdom the world is governed." More recently, Woodrow Wilson warned, "In public affairs, stupidity is more dangerous than knavery." 8

Stupidity is not related to type of regime; monarchy, oligarchy, and democracy produce it equally. Nor is it peculiar to nation or class. The working class as represented by the Communist governments functions no more rationally or effectively in power than the aristocracy or the bourgeoisie, as has notably been demonstrated in recent history. Mao Tse-tung may be admired for many things, but 9 the Great Leap Forward, with a steel plant in every backyard, and the Cultural Revolution were exercises in unwisdom that greatly damaged China's progress and stability, not to mention the chairman's reputation. The record of the Russian proletariat in power can hardly be called enlightened, although after sixty years of control it must be accorded a kind of brutal success. If the majority of Russians are better off now than before, the cost in cruelty and tyranny has been no less and probably greater than under the czars.

After the French Revolution, the new order was rescued only by Bonaparte's military campaigns, which brought the spoils of foreign wars to fill the treasury, and subsequently by his competence as an executive. He chose officials not on the basis of origin or ideology but on the principle of "la carrière ouverte aux talents"—the said talents being intelligence, energy, industry, and obedience. That worked until the day of his own fatal mistake. 10

I do not wish to give the impression that men in office are incapable of governing wisely and well. Occasionally, the exception appears, rising in heroic size above the rest, a tower visible down the centuries. Greece had her Pericles, who ruled with authority, moderation, sound judgment, and a certain nobility that imposes natural dominion over others. Rome had Caesar, a man of remarkable governing talents, although it must be said that a ruler who arouses opponents to resort to assassination is probably not as smart as he ought to be. Later, under Marcus Aurelius and the other Antonines, Roman citizens enjoyed good government, prosperity, and respect for about a century. Charlemagne was able to impose order upon a mass of contending elements, to foster the arts of civilization no less than those of war, and to earn a prestige supreme in the Middle Ages—probably not equaled in the eyes of contemporaries until the appearance of George Washington. 11

Possessor of an inner strength and perseverance that enabled him to prevail over a sea of obstacles, Washington was one of those critical figures but for whom history might well have taken a different course. He made possible the physical victory of American independence, while around him, in extraordinary fertility, political talent bloomed as if touched by some tropical sun. For all their flaws and quarrels, the Founding Fathers, who established our form of government, were, in the words of Arthur Schlesinger Sr., "the most remarkable generation of public men in the history of the United States or perhaps of any other nation." It is worth noting the qualities Schlesinger ascribes to them: They were fearless, high-principled, deeply versed in ancient and modern political thought, astute and pragmatic, unafraid of experiment, and—this is significant—"convinced of man's power to improve his condition through the use of intelligence." That was the mark of the Age of Reason that formed 12 them, and though the eighteenth century had a tendency to regard men as more rational than they in fact were, it evoked the best in government from these men.

For our purposes, it would be invaluable if we could know what produced this burst of talent from a base of only two million inhabitants. Schlesinger suggests some contributing factors: wide diffusion of education, challenging economic opportunities, social mobility, training in self-government—all these encouraged citizens to cultivate their political aptitudes to the utmost. Also, he adds, with the Church declining in prestige and with business, science, and art not yet offering competing fields of endeavor, statecraft remained almost the only outlet for men of energy and purpose. Perhaps the need of the moment—the opportunity to create a new political system—is what brought out the best. 13

Not before or since, I believe, has so much careful and reasonable thinking been invested in the creation of a new political system. In the French, Russian, and Chinese revolutions, too much class hatred and bloodshed were involved to allow for fair results or permanent constitutions. The American experience was unique, and the system so far has always managed to right itself under pressure. In spite of accelerating incompetence, it still works better than most. We haven't had to discard the system and try another after every crisis, as have Italy and Germany, Spain and France. The founders of the United States are a phenomenon to keep in mind to encourage our estimate of human possibilities, but their example, as a political scientist has pointed out, is "too infrequent to be taken as a basis for normal expectations." 14

The English are considered to have enjoyed reasonably benign government during the eighteenth and nineteenth centuries, except for their Irish subjects, debtors, child laborers, and other unfortunates in various pockets of oppression. The folly that lost the American colonies reappeared now and then, notably in the treatment of the Irish and the Boers, but a social system can survive a good deal of folly when circumstances are historically favorable or when it is cushioned by large resources, as in the heyday of the British Empire, or absorbed by sheer size, as in this country during our period of expansion. Today there are no more cushions, which makes folly less affordable. 15

Elsewhere than in government, man has accomplished marvels: invented the means in our time to leave the world and voyage to the moon; in the past, harnessed wind and electricity, raised earthbound stone into soaring cathedrals, woven silk brocades out of the spinnings of a worm, composed the music of Mozart and the dramas of Shakespeare, classified the forms of nature, penetrated the mysteries of genetics. Why is he so much less accomplished in government? 16

What frustrates, in that sphere, the operation of the intellect? Isaac Bashevis Singer, discoursing as a Nobel laureate in mankind, offers the opinion that God had been frugal in bestowing intellect but lavish with passions and emotions. "He gave us," Singer says, "so many emotions and such strong ones that every human being, even if he is an idiot, is a millionaire in emotions."

I think Singer has made a point that applies to our inquiry. 17 What frustrates the workings of intellect is the passions and the emotions: ambition, greed, fear, facesaving, the instinct to dominate, the needs of the ego, the whole bundle of personal vanities and anxieties.

Reason is crushed by these forces. If the Athenians out of 18 pride and overconfidence had not set out to crush Sparta for good but had been content with moderate victory, their ultimate fall might have been averted. If fourteenth-century knights had not been obsessed by the idea of glory and personal prowess, they might have defeated the Turks at Nicopolis with incalculable consequence for all of Eastern Europe. If the English, 200 years ago, had heeded Chatham's knocking on the door of what he called "this sleeping and confounded Ministry" and his urgent advice to repeal the Coercive Acts and withdraw the troops before the "inexpiable drop of blood is shed in an impious war with a people contending in the great cause of publick liberty" or, given a last chance, if they had heeded Edmund Burke's celebrated plea for conciliation and his warning that it would prove impossible to coerce a "fierce people" of their own pedigree, we might still be a united people bridging the Atlantic, with incalculable consequence for the history of the West. It did not happen that way, because king and Parliament felt it imperative to affirm sovereignty over arrogant colonials. The alternative choice, as in Athens and medieval Europe, was close to psychologically impossible.

In the case we know best—the American engagement in 19 Vietnam—fixed notions, preconceptions, wooden-headed thinking, and emotions accumulated into a monumental mistake and classic humiliation. The original idea was that the lesson of the failure to halt fascist aggression during the appeasement era dictated the necessity of halting the so-called aggression by North Vietnam, conceived to be the spearhead of international communism. This was applying the wrong model to the wrong facts, which would have been obvious if our policy makers had taken into consideration the history of the people on the spot instead of charging forward wearing the blinkers of the cold war.

The reality of Vietnamese nationalism, of which Ho Chi Minh 20 had been the standard-bearer since long before the war, was certainly no secret. Indeed, Franklin Roosevelt had insisted that the French should not be allowed to return after the war, a policy that we instantly abandoned the moment the Japanese were out: Ignoring the Vietnamese demand for self-government, we first assisted the return of the French, and then, when incredibly, they had been put to rout by the native forces, we took their place, as if Dien Bien Phu had no significance whatever. Policy founded upon error multiplies, never retreats. The pretense that North versus South Vietnam represented foreign aggression was intensified. If Asian specialists with knowledge of the situation suggested a reassessment, they were not persuasive. As a Communist aggressor, Hanoi was presumed to be a threat to the United States, yet the vital national interest at stake, which alone may have justified belligerency, was never clear enough to sustain a declaration of war.

A further, more fundamental, error confounded our policy. 21
This was the nature of the client. In war, as any military treatise or any soldier who has seen active service will tell you, it is essential to know the nature—that is, the capabilities *and* intentions—of the enemy and no less so of an ally who is the primary belligerent. We fatally underestimated the one and foolishly overestimated the other. Placing reliance on, or hope in, South Vietnam was an advanced case of wooden-headedness. Improving on the Bourbons, who forgot nothing and learned nothing, our policy makers forgot everything and learned nothing. The oldest lesson in history is the futility and, often, fatality of foreign interference to maintain in power a government unwanted or hated at home. As far back as 500 B.C., Confucius stated, "Without the confidence of the people, no government can stand," and political philosophers have echoed him down through the ages. What else was the lesson of our vain support of Chiang Kai-shek, within such recent experience? A corrupt or oppressive government may be maintained by despotic means but not for long, as the English occupiers of France learned in the fifteenth century. The human spirit protests and generates a Joan of Arc, for people will not passively endure a government that is in fact unendurable.

The deeper we became involved in Vietnam during the 22
Johnson era, the greater grew the self-deception, the lies, the false body counts, the cheating on Tonkin Gulf, the military mess, domestic dissent, and all those defensive emotions in which, as a result, our leaders became fixed. Their concern for personal ego, public image, and government status determined policy. Johnson was not going to be the first President to preside over defeat; generals could not admit failure nor civilian advisers risk their jobs by giving unpalatable advice.

Males, who so far in history have managed government are 23
obsessed with potency, which is the reason, I suspect, why it is difficult for them to admit error. I have rarely known a man who, with a smile and a shrug, could easily acknowledge being wrong. Why

not? *I* can, without any damage to self-respect. I can only suppose the difference is that deep in their psyches, men somehow equate being wrong with being impotent. For a Chief of State, it is almost out of the question, and especially so for Johnson and Nixon, who both seem to me to have had shaky self-images. Johnson's showed in his deliberate coarseness and compulsion to humiliate others in crude physical ways. No self-confident man would have needed to do that. Nixon was a bundle of inferiorities and sense of persecution. I do not pretend to be a psychohistorian, but in pursuit of this inquiry, the psychological factors must be taken into account. Having no special knowledge of Johnson and Nixon, I will not pursue the question other than to say that it was our misfortune during the Vietnam period to have had two Presidents who lacked the self-confidence for a change of course, much less for a grand withdrawal. "Magnanimity in politics," said Edmund Burke, "is not seldom the truest wisdom, and a great Empire and little minds go ill together."

An essential component of that "truest wisdom" is the self-confidence to reassess. Congressman Morris Udall made this point in the first few days after the nuclear accident at Three Mile Island. Cautioning against a hasty decision on the future of nuclear power, he said, "We have to go back and reassess. There is nothing wrong about being optimistic or making a mistake. The thing that is wrong, as in Vietnam, is *persisting* in a mistake when you see you are going down the wrong road and are caught in a bad situation." 24

The test comes in recognizing when persistence has become a fatal error. A prince, says Machiavelli, ought always to be a great asker and a patient hearer of truth about those things of which he has inquired, and he should be angry if he finds that anyone has scruples about telling him the truth. Johnson and Nixon, as far as an outsider can tell, were not great askers; they did not want to hear the truth or to face it. Chiang Kai-shek knew virtually nothing of real conditions in his domain because he lived a headquarters life amid an entourage all of whom were afraid to be messengers of ill report. When, in World War I, a general of the headquarters staff visited for the first time the ghastly landscape of the Somme, he broke into tears, saying, "If I had known we sent men to fight in that, I could not have done it." Evidently he was no great asker either. 25

Neither, we now know, was the shah of Iran. Like Chiang Kai-shek, he was isolated from actual conditions. He was educated abroad, took his vacations abroad, and toured his country, if at all, by helicopter. 26

Why is it that the major clients of the United States, a country founded on the principle that government derives its just powers from the consent of the governed, tend to be unpopular autocrats? A certain schizophrenia between our philosophy and our practice 27 afflicts American policy, and this split will always make the policy based on it fall apart. On the day the shah left Iran, an article summarizing his reign said that "except for the generals, he has few friends or allies at home." How useful to us is a ruler without friends or allies at home? He is a kind of luftmensch, no matter how rich or how golden a customer for American business. To attach American foreign policy to a ruler who does not have the acceptance of his countrymen is hardly intelligent. By now, it seems to me, we might have learned that. We must understand conditions—and by conditions, I mean people and history—on the spot. Wise policy can only be made on the basis of *informed,* not automatic, judgments.

When it has become evident to those associated with it that a 28
course of policy is pointed toward disaster, why does no one resign in protest or at least for the peace of his own soul? They never do. In 1917, the German chancellor Bethmann Hollweg pleaded desperately against the proposed resumption of unrestricted submarine warfare, since, by bringing in the United States, it would revive the Allies' resources, their confidence in victory, and their will to endure. When he was overruled by the military, he told a friend who found him sunk in despair that the decision meant "finis Germaniae." When the friend said simply, "You should resign," Bethmann said he could not, for that would sow dissension at home and let the world know he believed Germany would fail.

This is always the refuge. The officeholder tells himself he 29
can do more from within and that he must not reveal division at the top to the public. In fact if there is to be any hope of change in a democratic society, that is exactly what he must do. No one of major influence in Johnson's circle resigned over our Vietnam policy, although several, hoping to play it both ways, hinted their disagreement. Humphrey, waiting for the nod, never challenged the President's policy, although he campaigned afterward as an opponent of the war. Since then, I've always thought the adulation given to him misplaced.

Basically, what keeps officeholders attached to a policy they 30
believe to be wrong is nothing more nor less, I believe, than the lure of office, or Potomac fever. It is the same whether the locus is the Thames or the Rhine or, no doubt, the Nile. When Herbert Lehman ran for a second term as senator from New York after previously serving four terms as governor, his brother asked him why on earth he wanted it. "Arthur," replied the senator, "after you have once ridden behind a motorcycle escort, you are never the same again."

Here is a clue to the question of why our performance in 31
government is worse than in other activities: because government offers power, excites that lust for power, which is subject to emotional drives—to narcissism, fantasies of omnipotence, and other sources of

folly. The lust for power, according to Tacitus, "is the most flagrant of all the passions" and cannot really be satisfied except by power over others. Business offers a kind of power but only to the very successful at the very top, and even they, in our day, have to play it down. Fords and Du Ponts, Hearsts and Pulitzers, nowadays are subdued, and the Rockefeller who most conspicuously wanted power sought it in government. Other activities—in sports, science, the professions, and the creative and performing arts—offer various satisfactions but not the opportunity for power. They may appeal to status seeking and, in the form of celebrity, offer crowd worship and limousines and recognition by headwaiters, but these are the trappings of power, not the essence. Of course, mistakes and stupidities occur in nongovernmental activities too, but since these affect fewer people, they are less noticeable than they are in public affairs. Government remains the paramount field of unwisdom because it is there that men seek power over others—and lose it over themselves.

There are, of course, other factors that lower competence in 32
public affairs, among them the pressure of overwork and overscheduling; bureaucracy, especially big bureaucracy; the contest for votes that gives exaggerated influence to special interests and an absurd tyranny to public opinion polls. Any hope of intelligent government would require that the persons entrusted with high office should formulate and execute policy according to their best judgment and the best knowledge available, not according to every breeze of public opinion. But reelection is on their minds, and that becomes the criterion. Moreover, given schedules broken down into fifteen-minute appointments and staffs numbering in the hundreds and briefing memos of never less than thirty pages, policy makers never have time to think. This leaves a rather important vacuum. Meanwhile, bureaucracy rolls on, impervious to any individual or cry for change, like some vast computer that when once penetrated by error goes on pumping it out forever.

Under the circumstances, what are the chances of improving 33
the conduct of government? The idea of a class of professionals trained for the task has been around ever since Plato's Republic. Something of the sort animates, I imagine, the new Kennedy School of Government at Harvard. According to Plato, the ruling class in a just society should be men apprenticed to the art of ruling, drawn from the rational and the wise. Since he acknowledged that in natural distribution these are few, he believed they would have to be eugenically bred and nurtured. Government, he said, was a special art in which competence, as in any other profession, could be acquired only by study of the discipline and could not be acquired otherwise.

Without reference to Plato, the Mandarins of China were 34

trained, if not bred, for the governing function. They had to pass through years of study and apprenticeship and weeding out by successive examinations, but they do not seem to have developed a form of government much superior to any other, and in the end, they petered out in decadence and incompetence.

In seventeenth-century Europe, after the devastation of the 35
Thirty Years' War, the electors of Brandenburg, soon to be combined with Prussia, determined to create a strong state by means of a disciplined army and a trained civil service. Applicants for the civil positions, drawn from commoners in order to offset the nobles' control of the military, had to complete a course of study covering political theory, law and legal philosophy, economics, history, penology, and statutes. Only after passing through various stages of examination and probationary terms of office did they receive definitive appointments and tenure and opportunity for advancement. The higher civil service was a separate branch, not open to promotion from the middle and lower levels.

The Prussian system proved so effective that the state was 36
able to survive both military defeat by Napoleon in 1807 and the revolutionary surge of 1848. By then it had begun to congeal, losing many of its most progressive citizens in emigration to America; nevertheless, Prussian energies succeeded in 1871 in uniting the German states in an empire under Prussian hegemony. Its very success contained the seed of ruin, for it nourished the arrogance and power hunger that from 1914 through 1918 was to bring it down.

In England, instead of responding in reactionary panic to the 37
thunders from the Continent in 1848, as might have been expected, the authorities, with commendable enterprise, ordered an investigation of their own government practices, which were then the virtually private preserve of the propertied class. The result was a report on the need for a permanent civil service to be based on training and specialized skills and designed to provide continuity and maintenance of the long view as against transient issues and political passions. Though heavily resisted, the system was adopted in 1870. It has produced distinguished civil servants but also Burgess, Maclean, Philby, and the fourth man. The history of British government in the last 100 years suggests that factors other than the quality of its civil service determine a country's fate.

In the United States, civil service was established chiefly as a 38
barrier to patronage and the pork barrel rather than in search of excellence. By 1937, a presidential commission, finding the system inadequate, urged the development of a "real career service . . . requiring personnel of the highest order, competent, highly trained, loyal, skilled in their duties by reason of long experience, and assured of continuity." After much effort and some progress, that goal is still

not reached, but even if it were, it would not take care of elected officials and high appointments—that is, of government at the top.

I do not know if the prognosis is hopeful or, given the underlying emotional drives, whether professionalism is the cure. In the Age of Enlightenment, John Locke thought the emotions should be controlled by intellectual judgment and that it was the distinction and glory of man to be able to control them. As witnesses of the twentieth century's record, comparable to the worst in history, we have less confidence in our species. Although professionalism can help, I tend to think that fitness of character is what government chiefly requires. How that can be discovered, encouraged, and brought into office is the problem that besets us. 39

No society has yet managed to implement Plato's design. Now, with money and image-making manipulating our elective process, the chances are reduced. We are asked to choose by the packaging, yet the candidate seen in a studio-filmed spot, sincerely voicing lines from the Tele-PrompTer, is not the person who will have to meet the unrelenting problems and crucial decisions of the Oval Office. It might be a good idea if, without violating the First Amendment, we could ban all paid political commercials and require candidates (who accept federal subsidy for their campaigns) to be televised live only. 40

That is only a start. More profound change must come if we are to bring into office the kind of person our form of government needs if it is to survive the challenges of this era. Perhaps rather than educating officials according to Plato's design, we should concentrate on educating the electorate—that is, ourselves—to look for, recognize, and reward character in our representatives and to reject the ersatz. 41

QUESTIONS

1. According to Tuchman, what are the causes of the persistence of unwisdom in government?

2. What is the author's attitude toward the French, Russian, Chinese, and Iranian revolutions respectively?

3. How do such phrases as the following contribute to the author's purpose and tone: "theatre of the absurd" (paragraph 2); "lunatic spectacle" (paragraph 3); "the whole bundle of personal vanities and anxieties" (paragraph 17); "charging forward wearing the blinkers of the Cold War" (paragraph 19); "schizophrenia between our philosophy and our practice" (paragraph 27)?

4. Analyze the connotations that develop around Tuchman's use of the word *unwisdom.*

5. How does the author's use of rhetorical questions, notably in the introduction, contribute to the thesis? To the causal analysis?

6. How selective are the author's illustrations? What types of illustration does she use in the essay?

7. Analyze the author's transitions for paragraphs 7 to 8, 14 to 15, 23 to 24, 30 to 31, and 39 to 40.

8. What particulars develop Tuchman's generalizations about the emotional and psychological drives of politicians?

9. A significant part of Tuchman's critique of unwisdom in government deals specifically with the problems of men as rulers. What is your response to her emotional and psychological profile of men as political leaders? Would women be less susceptible to these emotional and psychological problems?

10. a. Write your own inquiry into the persistence of unwisdom in government, using a series of relevant examples to support your generalizations. b. Write an essay on the failures of men as political leaders or, if you wish, on the desirability of having women as political leaders.

NICCOLO MACHIAVELLI

The Circle of Governments

Niccolo Machiavelli (1469–1527), Italian patriot, statesman, and writer, is one of the seminal figures in the history of Western political thought. His inquiries into the nature of the state, the amoral quality of political life, and the primacy of power are distinctly modernist in outlook. He began his studies of political and historical issues after being forced to retire from Florentine politics in 1512. Exiled outside the city, Machiavelli wrote *The Prince* (1513), *The Discourses* (1519), *The Art of War* (1519–1520), and *The Florentine History* (1525). The following selection from *The Discourses* (conceived as commentaries by the author on the first ten books of Livy's *History of Rome*) analyzes the varieties of government and their political implications in history.

Having proposed to myself to treat of the kind of government established at Rome, and of the events that led to its perfection, I must at the beginning observe that some of the writers on politics distinguished three kinds of government, vis. the monarchical, the aristocratic, and the democratic; and maintain that the legislators of a people must choose from these three the one that seems to them most suitable. Other authors, wiser according to the opinion of many, count six kinds of governments, three of which are very bad, and three good in themselves, but so liable to be corrupted that they become absolutely bad. The three good ones are those which we have just named; the three bad ones result from the degradation of the other three, and each of them resembles its corresponding original, so that the transition from the one to the other is very easy. Thus monarchy becomes tyranny; aristocracy degenerates into oligarchy; and the popular government lapses readily into licentiousness. So that a legislator who gives to a state which he founds either of these three forms of government, constitutes it but for a brief time; for no precautions can prevent either one of the three that are reputed good from degenerating into its opposite kind; so great are in these the attractions and resemblances between the good and the evil. 1

Chance has given birth to these different kinds of governments amongst men; for at the beginning of the world the inhabitants were few in number and lived for a time dispersed, like beasts. As the human race increased, the necessity for uniting themselves for defence made itself felt; the better to attain this object they chose the strongest and most courageous from amongst themselves and placed him at their head promising to obey him. Thence they began to know the good and the honest, and to distinguish them from the bad and vicious; for seeing a man injure his benefactor aroused at once two sentiments in every heart, hatred against the ingrate and love for the benefactor. They blamed the first, and on the contrary honoured those the more who showed themselves grateful, for each felt that he in turn might be subject to a like wrong; and to prevent similar evils, they set to work to make laws, and to institute punishments for those who contravened them. Such was the origin of justice. This caused them, when they had afterwards to choose a prince, neither to look to the strongest nor bravest, but to the wisest and most just. But when they began to make sovereignty hereditary and non-elective, the children quickly degenerated from their fathers; and, so far from trying to equal their virtues, they considered that a prince had nothing else to do than to excel all the rest in luxury, indulgence, and every other variety of pleasure. The prince consequently soon drew upon himself the general hatred. An object of hatred, he naturally felt fear; fear in turn dictated to him precautions and wrongs, and thus 2 tyranny quickly developed itself. Such were the beginning and causes of disorders, conspiracies, and plots against the sovereigns, set on foot, not by the feeble and timid, but by those citizens who, surpassing the others in grandeur of soul, in wealth, and in courage, could not submit to the outrages and excesses of their princes.

Under such powerful leaders the masses armed themselves 3
against the tyrant, and after having rid themselves of him, submitted to these chiefs as their liberators. These, abhorring the very name of prince, constituted themselves a new government; and at first bearing in mind the past tyranny, they governed in strict accordance with the laws which they had established themselves; preferring public interests to their own, and to administer and protect with greatest care both public and private affairs. The children succeeded their fathers, and ignorant of the changes of fortune, having never experienced its reverses, and indisposed to remain content with this civil equality, they in turn gave themselves up to cupidity, ambition, libertinage, and violence, and soon caused the aristocratic government to degenerate into an oligarchic tyranny, regardless of all civil rights. They soon, however, experienced the same fate as the first tyrant; the people, disgusted with their government, placed themselves at the command of whoever was willing to attack them, and this disposition soon produced an avenger, who was sufficiently well seconded to destroy them. The memory of the prince and the wrongs committed by him being still fresh in their minds, and having overthrown the oligarchy, the people were not willing to return to the government of a prince. A popular government was therefore resolved upon, and it was so organized that the authority would not again fall into the hands of a prince or a small number of nobles. And as all governments are at first looked up to with some degree of reverence, the popular state also maintained itself for a time, but which was never of long duration, and lasted generally only about as long as the generation that had established it; for it soon ran into that kind of licence which inflicts injury upon public as well as private interests. Each individual only consulted his own passions, and a thousand acts of injustice were daily committed, so that, constrained by necessity, or directed by the counsels of some good man, or for the purpose of escaping from this anarchy, they returned anew to the government of a prince, and from this they generally lapsed again into anarchy, step-by-step, in the same manner and from the same causes as we have indicated.

Such is the circle which all republics are destined to run 4
through. Seldom, however, do they come back to the original form of government, which results from the fact that their duration is not sufficiently long to be able to undergo these repeated changes and preserve their existence. But it may well happen that a republic

lacking strength and good counsel in its difficulties becomes subject after a while to some neighbouring state, that is better organized than itself; and if such is not the case, then they will be apt to revolve indefinitely in the circle of revolutions. I say, then, that all kinds of government are defective; those three which we have qualified as good because they are too short-lived, and the three bad ones because of their inherent viciousness. Thus sagacious legislators, knowing the vices of each of these systems of government by themselves, have chosen one that should partake of all of them, judging that to be the most stable and solid. In fact, when there is combined under the same constitution a prince, a nobility, and the power of the people, then these three powers will watch and keep each other reciprocally in check.

QUESTIONS

1. Explain the relation between the author's three forms of government and six forms of government.

2. Describe the "circle which all republics are destined to run through" (paragraph 4).

3. Analyze the definitions Machiavelli provides in context for the key political terms *monarchy, tyranny, aristocracy, oligarchy, democracy,* and *anarchy.*

4. What does the term *justice* mean to the author?

5. The author uses classification as a method of essay development. Analyze the way in which the key categories are introduced and developed.

6. Explain the relationship of the "circle" as a metaphor to the development of the essay. Is the application purely figurative or based on logic? Explain.

7. Explain the use of comparison and contrast as a strategy in the essay.

8. Where does the author present his thesis? How is it reinforced by other materials in the essay?

9. What is your opinion concerning Machiavelli's definition of good or viable government? Are Machiavelli's types of government obsolete, or are they universal? Explain.

10. Write a classification essay on the types of government in the modern world, or on the branches of government or levels of government in the United States.

JONATHAN SWIFT

A Modest Proposal

FOR PREVENTING THE CHILDREN OF POOR PEOPLE IN IRELAND FROM BEING A BURDEN TO THEIR PARENTS OR COUNTRY, AND FOR MAKING THEM BENEFICIAL TO THE PUBLIC

Jonathan Swift (1667–1745) is best known as the author of three satires: *A Tale of a Tub* (1704), *Gulliver's Travels* (1726), and *A Modest Proposal* (1729). In these satires, Swift pricks the balloon of many of his contemporaries' and our own most cherished prejudices, pomposities, and delusions. He was also a famous churchman, an eloquent spokesman for Irish rights, and a political journalist. The following selection, perhaps the most famous satiric essay in the English language, offers modest advice to a nation suffering from poverty, overpopulation, and political injustice.

1 It is a melancholy object to those who walk through this great town or travel in the country, when they see the streets, the roads, and cabin doors, crowded with beggars of the female-sex, followed by three, four, or six children, all in rags and importuning every passenger for an alms. These mothers, instead of being able to work for their honest livelihood, are forced to employ all their time in strolling to beg sustenance for their helpless infants, who, as they grow up, either turn thieves for want of work, or leave their dear native country to fight for the Pretender in Spain, or sell themselves to the Barbadoes.

2 I think it is agreed by all parties that this prodigious number of children in the arms, or on the backs, or at the heels of their mothers, and frequently of their fathers, is in the present deplorable state of the kingdom a very great additional grievance; and therefore whoever could find out a fair, cheap, and easy method of making these children sound, useful members of the commonwealth would deserve so well of the public as to have his statue set up for a preserver of the nation.

3 But my intention is very far from being confined to provide only for the children of professed beggars; it is of a much greater extent, and shall take in the whole number of infants at a certain age who are born of parents in effect as little able to support them as those who demand our charity in the streets.

4 As to my own part, having turned my thoughts for many years upon this important subject, and maturely weighed the several schemes of other projectors, I have always found them grossly

mistaken in their computation. It is true, a child just dropped from its dam may be supported by her milk for a solar year, with little other nourishment; at most not above the value of two shillings, which the mother may certainly get, or the value in scraps, by her lawful occupation of begging; and it is exactly at one year old that I propose to provide for them in such a manner as instead of being a charge upon their parents or the parish, or wanting food and raiment for the rest of their lives, they shall on the contrary contribute to the feeding, and partly to the clothing, of many thousands.

There is likewise another great advantage in my scheme, that 5
it will prevent those voluntary abortions, and that horrid practice of women murdering their bastard children, alas, too frequent among us, sacrificing the poor innocent babes, I doubt, more to avoid the expense than the shame, which would move tears and pity in the most savage and inhuman breast.

The number of souls in this kingdom being usually reckoned 6
one million and a half, of these I calculate there may be about two hundred thousand couple whose wives are breeders; from which number I subtract thirty thousand couples who are able to maintain their own children, although I apprehend there cannot be so many under the present distresses of the kingdom; but this being granted, there will remain an hundred and seventy thousand breeders. I again subtract fifty thousand for those women who miscarry, or whose children die by accident or disease within the year. There only remain an hundred and twenty thousand children of poor parents annually born. The question therefore is, how this number shall be reared and provided for, which, as I have already said, under the present situation of affairs, is utterly impossible by all the methods hitherto proposed. For we can neither employ them in handicraft or agriculture; we neither build houses (I mean in the country) nor cultivate land. They can very seldom pick up a livelihood by stealing till they arrive at six years old, except where they are of towardly parts; although I confess they learn the rudiments much earlier, during which time they can however be looked upon only as probationers, as I have been informed by a principal gentlemen in the county of Cavan, who protested to me that he never knew above one or two instances under the age of six, even in a part of the kingdom so renowned for the quickest proficiency in that art.

I am assured by our merchants that a boy or girl before twelve 7
years old is no salable commodity; and even when they come to this age they will not yield above three pounds, or three pounds and half a crown at most on the Exchange; which cannot turn to account either to the parents or the kingdom, the charge of nutriment and rags having been at least four times that value.

I shall now therefore humbly propose my own thoughts, which I hope will not be liable to the least objection. 8

I have been assured by a very knowing American of my acquaintance in London, that a young healthy child well nursed is at a year old a most delicious, nourishing, and wholesome food, whether stewed, roasted, baked or boiled; and I make no doubt that it will equally serve in a fricassee or a ragout. 9

I do therefore humbly offer it to public consideration that of the hundred and twenty thousand children, already computed, twenty thousand may be reserved for breed, whereof only one fourth part to be males, which is more than we allow to sheep, black cattle, or swine; and my reason is that these children are seldom the fruits of marriage, a circumstance not much regarded by our savages, therefore one male will be sufficient to serve four females. That the remaining hundred thousand may at a year old be offered in sale to the persons of quality and fortune through the kingdom, always advising the mother to let them suck plentifully in the last month, so as to render them plump and fat for a good table. A child will make two dishes at an entertainment for friends; and when the family dines alone, the fore or hind quarter will make a reasonable dish, and seasoned with a little pepper or salt will be very good boiled on the fourth day, especially in winter. 10

I have reckoned upon a medium that a child just born will weigh twelve pounds, and in a solar year if tolerably nursed increaseth to twenty-eight pounds. 11

I grant this food will be somewhat dear, and therefore very proper for landlords, who, as they have already devoured most of the parents, seem to have the best title to the children. 12

Infant's flesh will be in season throughout the year, but more plentiful in March, and a little before and after. For we are told by a grave author, an eminent French physician, that fish being a prolific diet, there are more children born in Roman Catholic countries about nine months after Lent than at any other season: therefore, reckoning a year after Lent, the markets will be more glutted than usual, because the number of popish infants is at least three to one in this kingdom; and therefore it will have one other collateral advantage, by lessening the number of Papists among us. 13

I have already computed the charge of nursing a beggar's child (in which list I reckon all cottagers, laborers, and four fifths of the farmers) to be about two shillings per annum, rags included: and I believe no gentleman would repine to give ten shillings for the carcass of a good fat child, which, as I have said, will make four dishes of excellent nutritive meat, when he hath only some particular friend or his own family to dine with him. Thus the squire will learn to be a 14 good landlord, and grow popular among the tenants; the mother will have eight shillings net profit, and be fit for work till she produces another child.

Those who are more thrifty (as I must confess the times 15
require) may flay the carcass; the skin of which artificially dressed will make admirable gloves for ladies, and summer boots for fine gentlemen.

As to our city of Dublin, shambles may be appointed for this 16
purpose in the most convenient parts of it, and butchers we may be assured will not be wanting; although I rather recommend buying the children alive, and dressing them hot from the knife as we do roasting pigs.

A very worthy person, a true lover of his country, and whose 17
virtues I highly esteem, was lately pleased in discoursing on this matter to offer a refinement upon my scheme. He said that many gentlemen of this kingdom, having of late destroyed their deer, he conceived that the want of venison might be well supplied by the bodies of young lads and maidens, not exceeding fourteen years of age nor under twelve, so great a number of both sexes in every county being now ready to starve for want of work and service; and these to be disposed of by their parents, if alive, or otherwise by their nearest relations. But with due deference to so excellent a friend and so deserving a patriot, I cannot be altogether in his sentiments; for as to the males, my American acquaintance assured me from frequent experience that their flesh was generally tough and lean, like that of our schoolboys, by continual exercise, and their taste disagreeable; and to fatten them would not answer the charge. Then as to the females, it would, I think with humble submission, be a loss to the public, because they soon would become breeders themselves: and besides, it is not improbable that some scrupulous people might be apt to censure such a practice (although indeed very unjustly) as a little bordering upon cruelty; which, I confess, hath always been with me the strongest objection against any project, how well soever intended.

But in order to justify my friend, he confessed that this 18
expedient was put into his head by the famous Psalmanazar, a native of the island Formosa, who came from thence to London above twenty years ago, and in conversation told my friend that in his country when any young person happened to be put to death, the executioner sold the carcass to persons of quality as a prime dainty; and that in his time the body of a plump girl of fifteen, who was crucified for an attempt to poison the emperor, was sold to his Imperial Majesty's prime minister of state, and other great mandarins of the court, in joints from the gibbet, at four hundred crowns.

Neither indeed can I deny that if the same use were made of several plump young girls in this town, who without one single groat to their fortunes cannot stir abroad without a chair, and appear at the playhouse and assemblies in foreign fineries which they never will pay for, the kingdom would not be the worse.

Some persons of a desponding spirit are in great concern 19
about that vast number of poor people who are aged, diseased, or maimed, and I have been desired to employ my thoughts what course may be taken to ease the nation of so grievous an encumbrance. But I am not in the least pain upon that matter, because it is very well known that they are every day dying and rotting by cold and famine, and filth and vermin, as fast as can be reasonably expected. And as to the younger laborers, they are now in almost as hopeful a condition. They cannot get work, and consequently pine away for want of nourishment to a degree that if at any time they are accidentally hired to common labor, they have not strength to perform it; and thus the country and themselves are happily delivered from the evils to come.

I have too long digressed, and therefore shall return to my 20
subject. I think the advantages by the proposal which I have made are obvious and many, as well as of the highest importance.

For first, as I have already observed, it would greatly lessen 21
the number of Papists, with whom we are yearly overrun, being the principal breeders of the nation as well as our most dangerous enemies; and who stay at home on purpose to deliver the kingdom to the Pretender, hoping to take their advantage by the absence of so many good Protestants, who have chosen rather to leave their country than to stay at home and pay tithes against their conscience to an Episcopal curate.

Secondly, the poorer tenants will have something valuable of 22
their own, which by law may be made liable to distress, and help to pay their landlord's rent, their corn and cattle being already seized and money a thing unknown.

Thirdly, whereas the maintenance of an hundred thousand 23
children, from two years old and upwards, cannot be computed at less than ten shillings a piece per annum, the nation's stock will be thereby increased fifty thousand pounds per annum, besides the profit of a new dish introduced to the tables of all gentlemen of fortune in the kingdom who have any refinement in taste. And the money will circulate among ourselves, the goods being entirely of our own growth and manufacture.

Fourthly, the constant breeders, besides the gain of eight 24
shillings sterling per annum by the sale of their children, will be rid of the charge of maintaining them after the first year.

Fifthly, this food would likewise bring great custom to 25
taverns, where the vinters will certainly be so prudent as to procure

the best receipts for dressing it to perfection, and consequently have their houses frequented by all the fine gentlemen, who justly value themselves upon their knowledge in good eating; and a skillful cook, who understands how to oblige his guests, will contrive to make it as expensive as they please.

Sixthly, this would be a great inducement to marriage, which all wise nations have either encouraged by rewards or enforced by laws and penalties. It would increase the care and tenderness of mothers toward their children, when they were sure of a settlement for life to the poor babes, provided in some sort by the public, to their annual profit instead of expense. We should see an honest emulation among the married women, which of them could bring the fattest child to the market. Men would become as fond of their wives during the time of their pregnancy as they are now of their mares in foal, their cows in calf, or sows when they are ready to farrow; nor offer to beat or kick them (as is too frequent a practice) for fear of a miscarriage. 26

Many other advantages might be enumerated. For instance, the addition of some thousand carcasses in our exportation of barreled beef, the propagation of swine's flesh, and improvement in the art of making good bacon, so much wanted among us by the great destruction of pigs, too frequent at our tables, which are no way comparable in taste or magnificence to a well-grown, fat yearling child, which roasted whole will make a considerable figure at a lord mayor's feast or any other public entertainment. But this and many others I omit, being studious of brevity. 27

Supposing that one thousand families in this city would be constant customers for infants' flesh, besides others who might have it at merry meetings, particularly weddings and christenings, I compute that Dublin would take off annually about twenty thousand carcasses, and the rest of the kingdom (where probably they will be sold somewhat cheaper) the remaining eighty thousand. 28

I can think of no one objection that will possibly be raised against this proposal, unless it should be urged that the number of people will be thereby much lessened in the kingdom. This I freely own, and it was indeed one principal design in offering it to the world. I desire the reader will observe, that I calculate my remedy for this one individual kingdom of Ireland and for no other that ever was, is, or I think ever can be upon earth. Therefore let no man talk to me of other expedients: of taxing our absentees at five shillings a pound: of using neither clothes nor household furniture except what is of our own growth and manufacture: of utterly rejecting the materials and instruments that promote foreign luxury: of curing the expensiveness of pride, vanity, idleness, and gaming in our women: of introducing a vein of parsimony, prudence, and temperance: of learning to love our 29 country, in the want of which we differ even from Laplanders and the inhabitants of Topinamboo: of quitting our animosities and factions, nor acting any longer like the Jews, who were murdering one another at the very moment their city was taken: of being a little cautious not to sell our country and conscience for nothing: of teaching landlords to have at least one degree of mercy toward their tenants: lastly, of putting a spirit of honesty, industry, and skill into our shopkeepers; who, if a resolution could be now taken to buy only our native goods, would immediately unite to cheat and exact upon us in the price, the measure and the goodness, nor could ever yet be brought to make one fair proposal of just dealing, though often and earnestly invited to it.

Therefore I repeat, let no man talk to me of these and the like 30
expedients, till he hath at least some glimpse of hope that there will ever be some hearty and sincere attempt to put them in practice.

But as to myself, having been wearied out for many years 31
with offering vain, idle, visionary thoughts, and at length utterly despairing of success, I fortunately fell upon this proposal, which, as it is wholly new, so it hath something solid and real, of no expense and little trouble, full in our own power, and whereby we can incur no danger in disobliging England. For this kind of commodity will not bear exportation, the flesh being of too tender a consistence to admit a long continuance in salt, although perhaps I could name a country which would be glad to eat up our whole nation without it.

After all, I am not so violently bent upon my own opinion as 32
to reject any offer proposed by wise men, which shall be found equally innocent, cheap, easy, and effectual. But before something of that kind shall be advanced in contradiction to my scheme, and offering a better, I desire the author or authors will be pleased maturely to consider two points. First, as things now stand, how they will be able to find food and raiment for an hundred thousand useless mouths and backs. And secondly, there being a round million of creatures in human figure throughout this kingdom, whose sole subsistence put into a common stock would leave them in debt two millions of pounds sterling, adding those who are beggars by profession to the bulk of farmers, cottagers, and laborers, with their wives and children who are beggars in effect; I desire those politicians who dislike my overture, and may perhaps be so bold to attempt an answer, that they will first ask the parents of these mortals whether they would not at this day think it a great happiness to have been sold for food at a year old in the manner I prescribe, and thereby have avoided such a perpetual scene of misfortunes as they have since gone through by the oppression of landlords, the impossibility of paying rent without money or trade, the want of common sustenance, with neither house nor clothes to cover them from the

inclemencies of the weather, and the most inevitable prospect of entailing the like or greater miseries upon their breed forever.

I profess, in the sincerity of my heart, that I have not the least personal interest in endeavoring to promote this necessary work, having no other motive than the public good of my country, by advancing our trade, providing for infants, relieving the poor, and giving some pleasure to the rich. I have no children by which I can propose to get a single penny; the youngest being nine years old, and my wife past childbearing. 33

QUESTIONS

1. Describe the persona in this essay. How is the unusual narrative personality (as distinguished from Swift's personality) revealed by the author in degrees? How can we tell that the speaker's opinions are not shared by Swift?

2. What are the major propositions behind Swift's modest proposal? What are the minor propositions?

3. Explain the importance of the word *modest* in the title.

4. What is the effect of Swift's persistent reference to people as "breeders," "dams," "carcass," and the like? Why does he define children in economic terms? Find other words that contribute to this motif.

5. Analyze the purpose of the relatively long introduction consisting of paragraphs 1 to 7. How does Swift establish his ironic-satiric tone in this initial section?

6. What contrasts and discrepancies are at the heart of Swift's ironic statement in paragraphs 9 and 10? Explain both the subtlety and savagery of the satire in paragraph 12.

7. Paragraphs 13 to 20 develop six advantages of Swift's proposal, while paragraphs 24 to 26 list them in enumerative manner. Analyze the progression of these propositions. What is the effect of the listing? Why is Swift parodying argumentative techniques?

8. How does the author both sustain and suspend the irony in paragraph 29? How is the strategy repeated in paragraph 32? How does the concluding paragraph cap his satiric commentary on human nature?

9. Discuss Swift's social, political, religious, and economic views as they are revealed in the essay.

10. a. Write a modest proposal, advancing an absurd proposition through various argumentative techniques.
b. Write an analysis of the ironic-satiric structure of Swift's essay.

7 Business and Economics

ADAM SMITH

"You Keep Bringing Up Exogenous Variables"

Adam Smith (1930–) is the pseudonym of George J. W. Goodman, who in 1966 started a witty and irreverant column on business and economics in *New York* magazine. Born in St. Louis and educated at Harvard and Oxford universities, he has successfully combined careers as a corporate director, financial analyst, editor, essayist, and novelist. His books include *The Money Game, Supermoney,* and *Paper Money.* In this selection from *Paper Money* (1981), the modern day "Adam Smith" talks about his eighteenth-century predecessor and other figures as he shrewdly pokes fun at certain types of economic inquiry.

have a friend called Arthur, who has a pleasant smile, a 1
wife, two children, two sets of skis, and who has, in economics, what is called an ideal quantitative background. Practically from second grade, Arthur loved

math. It was a mystery to him why some people had to chew their pencils in math exams; to him, math was as easy as watching television was to some of his contemporaries. And although excellent marks came showering upon him all through school, he was never a serious, innovative mathematician. Great mathematicians, like competitive swimmers, mature early. At sixteen they have solved Fermat's Last Theorem, and at twenty-six they had better be teaching somewhere, because they are burned out. Arthur knew, at eighteen, that he was not that kind of scholar-mathematician, so he looked around at college and found a congenial home in economics. Arthur's hardest course came in his freshman year; it was English, and he had to write a paper on two Joseph Conrad stories, *Heart of Darkness* and *The Secret Agent*. He had a ghastly time with it. When he finished the Conrad paper, he says, he was very glad that he would never again have to do anything like that.

The graduate students who taught sections of the economics courses were very strong in econometrics, which is a mathematical and statistical form of economics, and Arthur was marvelously adept at that. After he got his Ph.D., Arthur thought about teaching. But one of his professors was a consultant to a commercial firm I will call Economics, Inc., which had built a computer model of the whole economy and which sold this service to various businesses. Economics, Inc., offered Arthur such a high starting salary that he went right to work there and has been very happy ever since. 2

At various times I visited Arthur, and we would sit at his computer console. His cuffs would shoot out of his sport jacket, and his fingers would be poised over the computer keyboard like those of E. Power Biggs at the organ. The computer keyboard was like a typewriter keyboard, *q-w-e-r-t-y-u-i-o-p*, except that it had a lot of extra keys you had to press before you could ask it questions. Once, I had just come back from the Middle East and I was worried that the price of oil might go to $15 a barrel, or even $20 a barrel. 3

"Ask it what the inflation rate will be if oil goes to fifteen dollars a barrel," I would say, and Arthur would go tapety-tapety-tap on the keyboard. The answer—when the computer did not ask us for more information, or tell us to start over—would appear on the CRT screen. "Wow," said Arthur. "Inflation of nine percent, all other things being equal." 4

"Ask it what the mortgage rate will be with oil at fifteen dollars a barrel," I said. Tapety-tapety-tap. "Ten percent?" Arthur said. "That's awfully high. It can't be right. Maybe we have to have an assumption about housing starts, too." Tapety-tapety-tapety-tapety-*tap*. 5

I have called Arthur, periodically, over the years, but I have never had to act specifically on his information. In 1973, for example, 6

Economics, Inc., missed the inflation rate by a wide margin. "Well, we did better than the Council of Economic Advisers," Arthur said, referring to the group appointed by the President, which sits in Washington. "They predicted inflation would be down to two and a half percent." Indeed they had, and Economics, Inc., had done better.

In order to have something as neat and symmetrical as an 7
equation, you have to have assumptions, even if the assumption is very basic—let x equal the unknown, let Σ mean "the sum of." There is an old joke, used by economists at departmental dinners, in which three men are stranded on a desert island and all they have is one huge can of tuna, but the tuna is inside the can and they are starving. The first man, a physicist, suggests a way to make a fire hot enough to melt the can. The second is an engineer, who is thinking up a complicated slingshot that will hurl the can against a rock with enough force to puncture it. The third is an economist. He has the answer. He says, "Assume a can opener." Then he proceeds with a theory.

Economics, Inc., had all kinds of assumptions and all kinds of 8
assessments.

None of this, by the way, hurt Economics, Inc. Businessmen 9
and institutions quested for certainty, and the computer at Economics, Inc., was very certain, even if it was not always right. The CRT screen would say ERROR if the processing was inconsistent, but not if the conclusions didn't match the brawling world outside.

As I said, I was worried about the Middle East. If the price of 10
oil went high enough fast enough, we would have a depression because all that money for imports would get taken out of our economy, unless the oil countries reinvested the money productively, unless the Federal Reserve loosened the money to make up for the oil, unless the new price of oil brought up more oil . . . you see the process. So I was talking to Arthur about Saudi Arabia, and the health of King Khalid, and the Shiites of the eastern province who worked in the oil fields, and I could tell it all sounded to Arthur like Conrad's Congo in *Heart of Darkness*—unfathomable. Revolutionary Iran had thrown out the Shah, the price of oil was doubling, gold was going to new highs, and I had been saying how far off the great Economics, Inc., model was; it wasn't telling me what I so urgently needed to know. Arthur lost his temper.

"You keep bringing up exogenous variables!" he shouted. 11

Like *economist*, *exogenous* is another Greek-rooted word, from *exo*, "outside, coming from outside."

"Who the hell knew there was an ayatollah?" Arthur said. 12
"Who knew the Russian wheat crop was going to bomb? Who cares about whoever it is in the eastern province?"

"But *life* is exogenous variables," I said. All I wanted was the 13
answers. I was worried that if *one* ayatollah could, in a short time, cause oil to go up, the truckers then to go on strike, the airlines to flirt with bankruptcy, the defense budget to gather momentum, the Japanese to replace us as the buyers of Iranian oil—what if there was *another* fanatic Islamic cleric somewhere dictating into cassettes? What if there was a sorehead colonel in an oil country deciding that Allah wished the prime minister to meet with a nine-millimeter bullet?

But Arthur had hung up. And suddenly I knew one of the 14
problems with economics. Arthur was brilliant. He had never sold a can of shoe polish, or bought a carload of lumber, or hired anybody, or fired anybody, or even worried about his checking account; in fact, he had never done anything but economics. In his own shop he could make lemmas dance around stochastic equilibria, he could rip off multiple regressions, he could make equations whistle "Dixie." The trouble came from that joke, "Assume a can opener." For deep, deep in the Economics, Inc., computer was a very tiny person upon whom the assumptions were based. Would the tiny person spend? Would the tiny person save? If you tapped the tiny person on the knee, his leg would jerk; if you tickled him, he would laugh. But the tiny, tiny person, upon whom all the vast panoply of computer modeling had been done, *was an economist*. If you asked him something, he would take a tiny sheet of yellow paper and ask, "What are the costs, and what are the benefits?" With a column for each, very coolly and rationally. He never threw an ashtray at his tiny wife, breaking a window and raising the gross national product by the price of the new window. Fear and greed and panic and emotion and nationalism and religious fervor, ayatollahs and Shiites and sinister Middle Eastern colonels were not part of his world.

This is *not* meant to be a trivial complaint about the limits of 15
models. That is of interest to the people who use them, who naturally want to do the best possible job, and the subject has been well debated by such respected figures as Harvard's Hendrik Houthakker, an expert on econometric models and the varying relationships known as elasticities. I have another friend, Princeton's Geoffrey Watson, who, many years ago, with James Durbin, derived an equation that made them both famous in the field. The Durbin-Watson equation is one test for the mathematical work upon which the complex computer models are based. "Mathematics has so much prestige," Geoffrey says, "that people sometimes back away from their own intuitive judgments. What used to be called 'political economy' at Oxford and Cambridge has been overshadowed. I had a distinguished economics professor at Cambridge, Richard Stern, whose background was in classics."

There were once two kinds of economists, one might argue: 16

the Smiths and the Ricardos. The Smith is the 1723 Adam Smith, and the Ricardo is David Ricardo, his immediate successor. Both the Smiths and the Ricardos were concerned with human activity and with the institutions that produce, preserve, and distribute wealth. The Smiths observed; the Ricardos sought the universal and logical principles, using algebra and its succeeding languages. The Smiths looked for what is to be explained, the Ricardos for the principles that did the explaining. Until comparatively recently, economists could write in both languages; that is, they could describe human activity in some detail, using the detail in written analysis, and they could reason mathematically and abstractly about the governing principles.

Today the Ricardos are fashionable and the Smiths are not. 17
Economists who write well in English—there may be eight of them—run the risk of being labeled with the pejorative term "literary." The Ricardos admire the elegance of perfect equations; the highest terms of their praise are "rigorous" and "scientific."

When the problem was contained enough, when the num- 18
bers were discrete enough, the mathematical descriptions of the Ricardos worked. Government economists who favored deregulation of the airline industry found that scenario unfolding much as they had planned. But too often the real world did not match the movements of that tiny economist inside the computer. All through the 1970s, the economists missed the impact of OPEC because, when they described it mathematically, they treated it as if it were a rational, profit-maximizing convention of economists. They did not know about *asibaya*, the Arab sense of community, nor could they quantify Third World indignation at past histories, or Middle East rivalries, or Western myopia, all of which became more important than the more easily quantified data. Some years ago the sociologist and pollster Daniel Yankelovich described a process he called the McNamara fallacy, after the Secretary of Defense who had so carefully quantified the Vietnam War.

"The first step," he said, "is to measure what can easily be 19
measured. The second is to disregard what can't be measured, or give it an arbitrary quantitative value. This is artificial and misleading. The third step is to presume that what can't be measured easily isn't very important. This is blindness. The fourth step is to say that what can't be easily measured really doesn't exist." The philosopher A. N. Whitehead called this tendency, in another form, "the fallacy of misplaced concreteness."

The Hopi language, an American Indian language, contains 20
no words, grammatical forms, constructions, or expressions that refer to what we call "time," or to past, present, future. The whole structure we base on "time"—wages, rent, credit, interest, deprecia-

tion, insurance—cannot be expressed in Hopi and is not part of that world view. The main Eskimo language has twenty-seven different words for snow, each connoting another nuance of texture, utility, and consistency, so the Eskimo's ability to communicate about snow is far greater than ours. The picture of the universe, of "reality," shifts from language to language. The economists whose counsel we seek—as do presidents and prime ministers—speak from a world within the world, just as the Hopi spoke from a world without time, credit, wages, and rent. That cold, neat, elegant world of mathematics views a different reality than blunt, ambiguous English.

Poets know they must use the slippery sibilances and jagged edges of language, as well as the meanings of the words, to communicate. Poets know that life throws up exogenous variables. I made a note that at the next meeting of the Advisory Council of the university Department of Economics on which I serve I would propose that we recruit some poets. I am sure the council will treat the suggestion as merely amusing, and I'm not totally sure it's a great idea; but I know it's aimed in the right direction. I sent Arthur the classic *Language, Thought, and Reality* by Benjamin Whorf, from which I took the example of the Hopi, but I haven't heard back. Maybe it reminds him of *Heart of Darkness*, and maybe he's just too busy. 21

QUESTIONS

1. Who uses the phrase "exogenous variables"? What does it mean? How does it serve to characterize contemporary economists?

2. Explain the distinction between the Smiths and the Ricardos. According to the author, which group or school of economists is more powerful today, and why? What are the consequences?

3. Explain what the language of paragraph 1 gains from the author's use of hyperbolic style. Explain.

4. Analyze the various levels of diction in this essay. What impression emerges?

5. Cite and explain the author's use of anecdotes in this essay. What is the effect?

6. What use does the author make of the personal "I" in this essay? What dominant impression of the speaker emerges?

7. How important is proportion in this essay? In other words, how does the author arrange the major parts of his analysis?

8. What is the relationship of logical reasoning to the ironic pattern of development in this essay?

9. Discuss the value of humor in exposing the foibles and problems of economic operations.

10. a. Create an imaginary economics expert and write a comic account of this person.
b. Is economics a science or discipline that is as precise as mathematics?
c. Analyze the ways in which economists use specialized language to confuse lay readers, deceive the public, or cover up the obvious.

ELLEN GOODMAN

Being a Secretary Can Be Hazardous to Your Health

Ellen Holtz Goodman (1941–) is an award-winning journalist who writes a syndicated column for *The Boston Globe*. She is the author of *Close to Home* (1979) and *At Large* (1981) and has been a commentator on television and radio. Goodman is an adept practitioner of the personal essay. In the following selection, her celebrated penchant for irony and satire finds a perfect focus in the working lives of women.

They used to say it with flowers or celebrate it with a somewhat liquid lunch. National Secretaries Week was always good for at least a token of appreciation. But the way the figures add up now, the best thing a boss can do for a secretary this week is cough up for her cardiogram. 1

"Stress and the Secretary" has become the hottest new syndrome on the heart circuit. 2

It seems that it isn't those Daring Young Women in their Dress-for-Success Suits who are following men down the cardiovascular trail to ruin. Nor is it the female professionals who are winning their equal place in intensive care units. 3

It is powerlessness and not power that corrupts women's hearts. And clerical workers are the number one victims. 4

In the prestigious Framingham study, Dr. Suzanne Haynes, an epidemiologist with the National Heart, Lung and Blood Institute, found that working women as a whole have no higher rate of heart 5 disease than housewives. But women employed in clerical and sales occupations do. Their coronary disease rates are twice that of other women.

"This is not something to ignore," says Dr. Haynes, "since such a high percent of women work at clerical jobs." In fact, 35 percent of all working women, or 18 million of us, hold these jobs. 6

When Dr. Haynes looked into their private lives, she found the women at greatest risk — with a one in five chance of heart disease — were clerical workers with blue-collar husbands, and three or more children. When she then looked at their work lives, she discovered that the ones who actually developed heart disease were those with nonsupportive bosses who hadn't changed jobs very often and who had trouble letting their anger out. 7

In short, being frustrated, dead-ended, without a feeling of control over your life is bad for your health. 8

The irony in all the various and sundry heart statistics is that we now have a weird portrait of the Cardiovascular Fun Couple of the Office: The Type A Boss and his secretary. The male heart disease stereotype is, after all, the Type A aggressive man who always needs to be in control, who lives with a great sense of time urgency . . . and is likely to be a white-collar boss. 9

"The Type A man is trying to be in control. But given the way most businesses are organized there are, in fact, few ways for them to be in control of their jobs," says Dr. Haynes. The only thing the Type A boss can be in control of is his secretary who in turn feels . . . well you get the picture. He's not only getting heart disease, he's giving it. 10

As if all this weren't enough to send you out for the annual three martini lunch, clerical workers are increasingly working for a new Type A boss: the computer. 11

These days fewer women are sitting in front of bosses with notepads and more are sitting in front of Visual Display Terminals. Word processors, data processors, microprocessors . . . these are the demanding, time-conscious, new automatons of automation. 12

There is nothing intrinsically evil about computers. I am writing this on a VDT and if you try to take it away from me, I will break your arm. But as Working Women, the national association of office workers, puts it in their release this week, automation is increasingly producing clerical jobs that are de-skilled, down-graded, dead-ended and dissatisfying. 13

As Karen Nussbaum of the Cleveland office described it, the office of the future may well be the factory of the past. Work on computers is often reduced to simple, repetitive, monotonous tasks. Workers are often expected to produce more for no more pay, and there are also reports of a disturbing trend to processing speed-ups 14

and piece-rate pay, and a feeling among clerical workers that their jobs are computer controlled.

"It's not the machine, but the way it's used by employers," 15
says Working Women's research director, Judith Gregory. Too often, automation's most important product is stress.

Groups, like Working Women, are trying to get clerical 16
workers to organize in what they call "a race against time" so that computers will become their tools instead of their supervisors.

But in the meantime, if you are 1) a female clerical worker, 2) 17
with a blue-collar husband, 3) with three or more children, 4) in a dead-end job, 5) without any way to express anger, 6) with a Type A boss, 7) or a Type A computer controlling your work day . . . *You better start jogging.*

QUESTIONS

1. What major problem does Goodman discuss in this essay? What are the causes of the problem?

2. How does the author describe the Type A boss and the Type A female employee?

3. How does Goodman use colloquial language to help establish the tone of the essay?

4. List examples of comic language. What is Goodman's purpose?

5. What technique does Goodman use to establish the topic of her essay?

6. What types of examples does Goodman use to reinforce her generalizations? Do any of the examples qualify as expert testimony? Explain.

7. Where does Goodman state her thesis? How does her conclusion reinforce this thesis?

8. What patterns of comparison and contrast do you find? Why does the author employ it?

9. Does Goodman's range of humor work for or against the seriousness of her topic? Explain your response.

10. a. Analyze the varieties of stress that you have felt while employed.
b. Argue for or against the proposition that working women do not experience any more stress than working men.
c. Describe the Type A worker or professional, and propose solutions to his or her problem.

JOHN KENNETH GALBRAITH

The Higher Economic Purpose of Women

John Kenneth Galbraith (1908–), America's best known economist and commentator on our economic system, was born on a farm in Ontario, Canada. He received his doctorate from the University of California at Berkeley and has taught at Princeton and Harvard Universities. Galbraith also has held posts in government since 1940; from 1961 to 1963, he served as U.S. ambassador to India. Among Galbraith's numerous books are *American Capitalism, The Concept of Countervailing Power* (1952), *The Affluent Society* (1958), and *The New Industrial State* (1967). In this essay from *Annals of an Abiding Liberal* (1979) Galbraith relates economic theory to "convenient social virtue."

IN THE NINETEEN-FIFTIES, for reasons that were never revealed to me, for my relations with academic administrators have often been somewhat painful, I was made a trustee of Radcliffe College. It was not a highly demanding position. Then, as now, the college had no faculty of its own, no curriculum of its own and, apart from the dormitories, a gymnasium and a library, no academic plant of its own. We were a committee for raising money for scholarships and a new graduate center. The meetings or nonmeetings of the trustees did, however, encourage a certain amount of reflection on the higher education of women, there being no appreciable distraction. This reflection was encouraged by the mood of the time at Harvard. As conversation and numerous formal and informal surveys reliably revealed, all but a small minority of the women students felt that they were a failure unless they were firmly set for marriage by the time they got their degree. I soon learned that my fellow trustees of both sexes thought this highly meritorious. Often at our meetings there was impressively solemn mention of our responsibility, which was to help women prepare themselves for their life's work. Their life's work, it was held, was care of home, husband and children. In inspired moments one or another of my colleagues would ask, "Is there anything else so important?" 1

Once, and rather mildly, for it was more to relieve tedium than to express conviction, I asked if the education we provided wasn't rather expensive and possibly also ill-adapted for these tasks, even assuming that they were combined with ultimate service to the New Rochelle Library and the League of Women Voters. The re- 2 sponse was so chilly that I subsided. I've never minded being in a minority, but I dislike being thought eccentric.

It was, indeed, mentioned that a woman should be prepared for what was called a *second* career. After her children were raised and educated, she should be able to essay a re-entry into intellectual life — become a teacher, writer, researcher or some such. All agreed that this was a worthy, even imaginative design which did not conflict with *basic* responsibilities. I remember contemplating but censoring the suggestion that this fitted in well with the common desire of husbands at about this stage in life to take on new, younger and sexually more inspiring wives. 3

In those years I was working on the book that eventually became *The Affluent Society.* The task was a constant reminder that much information solemnly advanced as social wisdom is, in fact, in the service of economic convenience — the convenience of some influential economic interest. I concluded that this was so of the education of women and resolved that I would one day explore the matter more fully. This I have been doing in these last few years, and I've decided that while the rhetorical commitment of women to home and husband as a career has been weakened in the interim, the economic ideas by which they are kept persuaded to serve economic interests are still almost completely intact. Indeed, these ideas are so generally assumed that they are very little discussed. 4

Women are kept in the service of economic interests by ideas that they do not examine and that even women who are professionally involved as economists continue to propagate, often with some professional pride. The husband, home and family that were celebrated in those ghastly Radcliffe meetings are no longer part of the litany. But the effect of our economic education is still the same. 5

Understanding of this begins with a look at the decisive but little-perceived role of women in modern economic development and at the economic instruction by which this perception is further dulled. 6

The decisive economic contribution of women in the developed industrial society is rather simple — or at least it so becomes once the disguising myth is dissolved. It is, overwhelmingly, to make possible a continuing and more or less unlimited increase in the sale and use of consumer goods. 7

The test of success in modern economic society, as all know, is the annual rate of increase in Gross National Product. At least until recent times this test was unquestioned; a successful society was one with a large annual increase in output, and the most successful society was the one with the largest increase. Even when the social validity of this measure is challenged, as on occasion it now is, those 8 who do so are only thought to be raising an interesting question. They are not imagined to be practical.

Increasing production, in turn, strongly reflects the needs of the dominant economic interest, which in modern economic society, as few will doubt, is the large corporation. The large corporation seeks relentlessly to get larger. The power, prestige, pay, promotions and perquisites of those who command or who participate in the leadership of the great corporation are all strongly served by its expansion. That expansion, if it is to be general, requires an expanding or growing economy. As the corporation became a polar influence in modern economic life, economic growth became the accepted test of social performance. This was not an accident. It was the predictable acceptance of the dominant economic value system. 9

Economic growth requires manpower, capital and materials for increased production. It also, no less obviously, requires increased consumption, and if population is relatively stable, as in our case, this must be increased per-capita consumption. But there is a further and equally unimpeachable truth which, in economics at least, has been celebrated scarcely at all: just as the production of goods and services requires management or administration, so does their consumption. The one is no less essential than the other. Management is required for providing automobiles, houses, clothing, food, alcohol and recreation. And management is no less required for their possession and use. 10

The higher the standard of living, that is to say the greater the consumption, the more demanding is this management. The larger the house, the more numerous the automobiles, the more elaborate the attire, the more competitive and costly the social rites involving food and intoxicants, the more complex the resulting administration. 11

In earlier times this administration was the function of a menial servant class. To its great credit, industrialization everywhere liquidates this class. People never remain in appreciable numbers in personal service if they have alternative employment. Industry supplies this employment, so the servant class, the erstwhile managers of consumption, disappears. If consumption is to continue and expand, it is an absolute imperative that a substitute administrative force be found. This, in modern industrial societies, is the function that wives perform. The higher the family income and the greater the complexity of the consumption, the more nearly indispensable this role. Within broad limits the richer the family, the more indispensably menial must be the role of the wife. 12

It is, to repeat, a vital function for economic success as it is now measured. Were women not available for managing consumption, an upper limit would be set thereon by the administrative task involved. At some point it would become too time-consuming, too 13

burdensome. We accept, without thought, that a bachelor of either sex will lead a comparatively simple existence. (We refer to it as the bachelor life.) That is because the administrative burden of a higher level of consumption, since it must be assumed by the individual who consumes, is a limiting factor. When a husband's income passes a certain level, it is expected that his wife will be needed "to look after the house" or simply "to manage things." So, if she has been employed, she quits her job. The consumption of the couple has reached the point where it requires full-time attention.

Although without women appropriately conditioned to the task there would be an effective ceiling on consumption and thus on production and economic expansion, this would not apply uniformly. The ceiling would be especially serious for high-value products for the most affluent consumers. The latter, reflecting their larger share of total income — the upper 20 percent of income recipients received just under 42 percent of all income in 1977 — account for a disproportionate share of total purchases of goods. So women are particularly important for lifting the ceiling on this kind of consumption. And, by a curious quirk, their doing so opens the way for a whole new range of consumer products — washing machines, dryers, dishwashers, vacuum cleaners, automatic furnaces, sophisticated detergents, cleaning compounds, tranquilizers, pain-relievers — designed to ease the previously created task of managing a high level of consumption. 14

Popular sociology and much associated fiction depict the extent and complexity of the administrative tasks of the modern diversely responsible, high-bracket, suburban woman. But it seems likely that her managerial effectiveness, derived from her superior education, her accumulating experience as well as her expanding array of facilitating gadgetry and services, keeps her more or less abreast of her increasingly large and complex task. Thus the danger of a ceiling on consumption, and therefore on economic expansion, caused by the exhaustion of her administrative capacities does not seem imminent. One sees here, more than incidentally, the economic rationale, even if it was unsuspected for a long time by those involved, of the need for a superior education for the upper-bracket housewife. Radcliffe prepared wives for the higher-income family. The instinct that this required superior intelligence and training was economically sound. 15

The family of higher income, in turn, sets the consumption patterns to which others aspire. That such families be supplied with intelligent, well-educated women of exceptional managerial competence is thus of further importance. It allows not only for the continued high-level consumption of these families, but it is important for its demonstration effect for families of lesser income. 16

That many women are coming to sense that they are instruments of the economic system is not in doubt. But their feeling finds no support in economic writing and teaching. On the contrary, it is concealed, and on the whole with great success, by modern neoclassical economics — the everyday economics of the textbook and classroom. This concealment is neither conspiratorial nor deliberate. It reflects the natural and very strong instinct of economics for what is convenient to influential economic interest — for what I have called the convenient social virtue. It is sufficiently successful that it allows many hundreds of thousands of women to study economics each year without their developing any serious suspicion as to how they will be used. 17

The general design for concealment has four major elements: 18

First, there is the orthodox identification of an increasing consumption of goods and services with increasing happiness. The greater the consumption, the greater the happiness. This proposition is not defended; it is again assumed that only the philosophically minded will cavil. They are allowed their dissent, but, it is held, no one should take it seriously. 19

Second, the tasks associated with the consumption of goods are, for all practical purposes, ignored. Consumption being a source of happiness, one cannot get involved with the problems in managing happiness. The consumer must exercise choice; happiness is maximized when the enjoyment from an increment of expenditure for one object of consumption equals that from the same expenditure for any other object or service. As all who have ever been exposed, however inadequately, to economic instruction must remember, satisfactions are maximized when they are equalized at the margin. 20

Such calculation does require some knowledge of the quality and technical performance of goods as well as thought in general. From it comes the subdivision of economics called consumer economics; this is a moderately reputable field that, not surprisingly, is thought especially appropriate for women. But this decision-making is not a burdensome matter. And once the decision between objects of expenditure is made, the interest of economics is at an end. No attention whatever is given to the effort involved in the care and management of the resulting goods.[1] 21

[1]There is a branch of learning — home economics or home science — that does concern itself with such matters. This field is a nearly exclusive preserve of women. It has never been accorded any serious recognition by economists or scholars generally; like physical education or poultry science, it is part of an academic underworld. And home economists or home scientists, in their natural professional enthusiasm for their subject matter and their natural resentment of their poor academic status, have sought to elevate their subject, homemaking, into a thing of unique dignity, profound spiritual reward, infinite social value as well as great nutritional significance. Rarely have they asked whether it cons women into a role that is exceedingly important for economic interest and also highly convenient for the men and institutions they are trained to serve. Some of the best home economists were once students of mine. I thought them superbly competent in their commitment to furthering a housewifely role for women.

The third requisite for the concealment of women's economic role is the avoidance of any accounting for the value of household work. This greatly helps it to avoid notice. To include in the Gross National Product the labor of housewives in managing consumption, where it would be a very large item which would increase as consumption increases, would be to invite thought on the nature of the service so measured. And some women would wonder if the service was one they wished to render. To keep these matters out of the realm of statistics is also to help keep them innocuously within the sacred domain of the family and the soul. It helps sustain the pretense that, since they are associated with consumption, the toil involved is one of its joys. 22

The fourth and final element in the concealment is more complex and concerns the concept of the household. The intellectual obscurantism that is here involved is accepted by all economists, mostly without thought. It would, however, be defended by very few. 23

The avowed focus of economics is the individual. It is the individual who distributes her or his expenditures so as to maximize satisfactions. From this distribution comes the instruction to the market and ultimately to the producing firm that makes the individual the paramount power in economic society. (There are grave difficulties with this design, including the way in which it reduces General Motors to the role of a mere puppet of market forces, but these anomalies are not part of the present story.) 24

Were this preoccupation with the individual pursued to the limit, namely to the individual, there would be grave danger that the role of women would attract attention. There would have to be inquiry as to whether, within the family, it is the husband's enjoyments that are equalized and thus maximized at the margin. Or, in his gallant way, does he defer to the preference system of his wife? Or does marriage unite only men and women whose preference schedules are identical? Or does marriage make them identical? 25

Investigation would turn up a yet more troublesome thing. It would be seen that, in the usual case, the place and style of living accord with the preferences and needs of the member of the family who makes the money — in short, the husband. Thus, at least partly his titles: "head of the household," "head of the family." And he would be seen to have a substantial role in decisions on the individual objects of expenditure. But the management of the resulting house, automobile, yard, shopping and social life would be by the wife. It would be seen that this arrangement gives the major decisions concerning consumption extensively to one person and the toil associated with that consumption to another. There would be further 26 question as to whether consumption decisions reflect with any precision or fairness the preferences of the person who has the resulting toil. Would the style of life and consumption be the same if the administration involved were equally shared?

None of these questions gets asked, for at precisely the point they obtrude, the accepted economics abruptly sheds its preoccupation with the individual. The separate identities of men and women are merged into the concept of the household. The inner conflicts and compromises of the household are not explored; by nearly universal consent, they are not the province of economics. The household, by a distinctly heroic simplification, is assumed to be the same as an individual. It thinks, acts and arranges its expenditures as would an individual; it is so treated for all purposes of economic analysis. 27

That, within the household, the administration of consumption requires major and often tedious effort, that decisions on consumption are heavily influenced by the member of the household least committed to such tasks, that these arrangements are extremely important if consumption is to expand, are all things that are thus kept out of academic view. Those who study and those who teach are insulated from such adverse thoughts. The concept of the household is an outrageous assault on personality. People are not people; they are parts of a composite or collective that is deemed somehow to reflect the different or conflicting preferences of those who make it up. This is both analytically and ethically indefensible. But for concealing the economic function of women even from women it works. 28

One notices, at this point, an interesting convergence of economics with politics. It has long been recognized that women are kept on political leash primarily by urging their higher commitment to the family. Their economic role is also concealed and protected by submerging them in the family or household. There is much, no doubt, to be said for the institution of the family. And it is not surprising that conservatives say so much. 29

In modern society power rests extensively on persuasion. Such reverse incentives as flogging, though there are law-and-order circles that seek their revival, are in limbo. So, with increasing affluence, is the threat of starvation. And even affirmative pecuniary reward is impaired. For some, at least, enough is enough — the hope for more ceases to drive. In consequence, those who have need for a particular behavior in others resort to persuasion — to instilling the belief that the action they need is reputable, moral, virtuous, socially beneficent or otherwise good. It follows that what women are persuaded to believe about their social role and, more important, 30

what they are taught to overlook are of prime importance in winning the requisite behavior. They must believe that consumption is happiness and that, however onerous its associated toil, it all adds up to greater happiness for themselves and their families.

31 If women were to see and understand how they are used, the consequence might be a considerable change in the pattern of their lives, especially in those income brackets where the volume of consumption is large. Thus, suburban life sustains an especially large consumption of goods, and, in consequence, is especially demanding in the administration required. The claims of roofs, furniture, plumbing, crabgrass, vehicles, recreational equipment and juvenile management are all very great. This explains why unmarried people, regardless of income, favor urban living over the suburbs. If women understood that they are the facilitating instrument of this consumption and were led to reject its administration as a career, there would, one judges, be a general return to a less demanding urban life.

32 More certainly there would be a marked change in the character of social life. Since they are being used to administer consumption, women are naturally encouraged to do it well. In consequence, much social activity is, in primary substance, a competitive display of managerial excellence. The cocktail party or dinner party is, essentially, a fair, more refined and complex than those at which embroidery or livestock are entered in competition but for the same ultimate purpose of displaying and improving the craftsmanship or breed. The cleanliness of the house, the excellence of the garden, the taste, quality and condition of the furnishings and the taste, quality and imagination of the food and intoxicants and the deftness of their service are put on display before the critical eye of those invited to appraise them. Comparisons are made with other exhibitors. Ribbons are not awarded, but the competent administrator is duly proclaimed a good housekeeper, a gracious hostess, a clever manager or, more simply, a really good wife. These competitive social rites and the accompanying titles encourage and confirm women in their role as administrators and thus facilitators of the high levels of consumption on which the high-production economy rests. It would add measurably to economic understanding were they so recognized. But perhaps for some it would detract from their appeal.

33 However, the more immediate reward to women from an understanding of their economic role is in liberalizing the opportunity for choice. What is now seen as a moral compulsion — the diligent and informed administration of the family consumption — emerges as a service to economic interests. When so seen, the moral compulsion disappears. Once women see that they serve purposes which are *not* their own, they will see that they can serve purposes which *are* their own.

QUESTIONS

1. What does Galbraith mean by "convenient social virtue"? How do women enter into this socioeconomic equation?

2. In what ways are the economic lives of women concealed, and for what reasons?

3. Why does the author begin his essay with a personal style? What tone is established? What is the impact of this style and tone on the rest of the essay? How would you characterize this later style?

4. Cite the various economic terms that Galbraith uses. Does he employ them concretely or abstractly, and why?

5. Is there a thesis statement in this essay? If so, where is it positioned? If not, why has Galbraith chosen to develop an implied thesis?

6. Explain the cause-effect pattern in this essay. How does the causal chain of economic and social phenomena support Galbraith's thesis?

7. Where does the author use examples? Discuss their relative effectiveness.

8. Which paragraphs constitute the conclusion? How does this conclusion reinforce the argumentative edge of the entire essay?

9. Galbraith states, "the concept of household is an outrageous assault on personality." Defend or attack this assertion.

10. a. Using Galbraith's final paragraph as a focus, write an essay on the new economic status of women.
b. Develop your own analysis of consumption and the economic roles of women.

GLORIA STEINEM

Why Do Women Work?

Gloria Steinem (1934–) was born and raised in Toledo, Ohio; she attended Smith College, receiving a B.A. in government in 1963. A noted writer, editor, feminist, and political activist, Steinem helped to found *New York* magazine in 1968; in 1971 she cofounded *Ms.* magazine and has served as its editor since then. Whether campaigning for Robert Kennedy and George McGovern or helping to defend and raise money for Angela Davis and the United Farmworkers, Stein-

em has been on the cutting edge of American politics for more than two decades. Her most recent book, a collection of essays, is *Outrageous Acts and Everyday Rebellions* (1983). In this essay, Steinem analyzes both the false and legitimate arguments underpinning the basic questions reflected in her title.

Toward the end of the 1970s, *The Wall Street Journal* 1
devoted an eight-part, front-page series to "the working woman"—that is, the influx of women into the paid-labor force—as the greatest change in American life since the Industrial Revolution.

Many women readers greeted both the news and the defini- 2
tion with cynicism. After all, women have always worked. If all the productive work of human maintenance that women do in the home were valued at its replacement cost, the gross national product of the United States would go up by 26 percent. It's just that we are now more likely than ever before to leave our poorly rewarded, low-security, high-risk job of homemaking (though we're still trying to explain that it's a perfectly good one and that the problem is male society's refusal both to do it and to give it an economic value) for more secure, independent, and better-paid jobs outside the home.

Obviously, the real work revolution won't come until all 3
productive work is rewarded—including child rearing and other jobs done in the home—and men are integrated into so-called women's work as well as vice versa. But the radical change being touted by the *Journal* and other media is one part of that long integration process: the unprecedented flood of women into salaried jobs, that is, into the labor force as it has been male-defined and previously occupied by men. We are already more than 41 percent of it—the highest proportion in history. Given the fact that women also make up a whopping 69 percent of the "discouraged labor force" (that is, people who need jobs but don't get counted in the unemployment statistics because they've given up looking), plus an official female unemployment rate that is substantially higher than men's, it's clear that we could expand to become fully half of the national work force by 1990.

Faced with this determination of women to find a little 4
independance and to be paid and honored for our work, experts have rushed to ask: "Why?" It's a question rarely directed at male workers. Their basic motivations of survival and personal satisfaction are taken for granted. Indeed, men are regarded as "odd" and therefore subjects for sociological study and journalistic reports only when they *don't* have work, even if they are rich and don't need jobs or are poor and can't find them. Nonetheless, pollsters and sociologists have gone to great expense to prove that women work outside the home

because of dire financial need, or if we persist despite the presence of a wage-earning male, out of some desire to buy "little extras" for our families, or even out of good old-fashioned penis envy.

Job interviewers and even our own families may still ask 5
salaried women the big "Why?" If we have small children at home or are in some job regarded as "men's work," the incidence of such questions increases. Condescending or accusatory versions of "What's a nice girl like you doing in a place like this?" have not disappeared from the workplace.

How do we answer these assumptions that we are "working" 6
out of some pressing or peculiar need? Do we feel okay about arguing that it's as natural for us to have salaried jobs as for our husbands—whether or not we have young children at home? Can we enjoy strong career ambitions without worrying about being thought "unfeminine"? When we confront men's growing resentment of women competing in the work force (often in the form of such guilt-producing accusations as "You're taking men's jobs away" or "You're damaging your children"), do we simply state that a decent job is a basic human right for everybody?

I'm afraid the answer is often no. As individuals and as a 7
movement, we tend to retreat into some version of a tactically questionable defense: "Womenworkbecausewehaveto." The phrase has become one word, one key on the typewriter—an economic form of the socially "feminine" stance of passivity and self-sacrifice. Under attack, we still tend to present ourselves as creatures of economic necessity and familial devotion. "Womenworkbecausewehaveto" has become the easiest thing to say.

Like most truisms, this one is easy to prove with statistics. 8
Economic need *is* the most consistent work motive—for women as well as men. In 1976, for instance, 43 percent of all women in the paid-labor force were single, widowed, separated, or divorced, and working to support themselves and their dependents. An additional 21 percent were married to men who had earned less than ten thousand dollars in the previous year, the minimum then required to support a family of four. In fact, if you take men's pension, stocks, real estate, and various forms of accumulated wealth into account, a good statistical case can be made that there are more women who "have" to work (that is, who have neither the accumulated wealth, nor husbands whose work or wealth can support them for the rest of their lives) than there are men with the same need. If we were going to ask one group "Do you really need this job?", we should ask men.

But the first weakness of the whole "have to work" defense is 9
its deceptiveness. Anyone who has ever experienced dehumanized life on welfare or any other confidence-shaking dependency knows that a paid job may be preferable to the dole, even when the handout

is coming from a family member. Yet the will and self-confidence to work on one's own can diminish as dependency and fear increase. That may explain why—contrary to the "have to" rationale—wives of men who earn less than three thousand dollars a year are actually *less* likely to be employed than wives whose husbands make ten thousand dollars a year or more.

10 Furthermore, the greatest proportion of employed wives is found among families with a total household income of twenty-five to fifty thousand dollars a year. This is the statistical underpinning used by some sociologists to prove that women's work is mainly important for boosting families into the middle or upper middle class. Thus, women's incomes are largely used for buying "luxuries" and "little extras": a neat doublewhammy that renders us secondary within our families, and makes our jobs expendable in hard times. We may even go along with this interpretation (at least, up to the point of getting fired so a male can have our job). It preserves a husbandly ego-need to be seen as the primary breadwinner, and still allows us a safe "feminine" excuse for working.

11 But there are often rewards that we're not confessing. As noted in *The Two-Career Couple,* by Francine and Douglas Hall: "Women who hold jobs by choice, even blue-collar routine jobs, are more satisfied with their lives than are the full-time housewives."

12 In addition to personal satisfaction, there is also society's need for all its members' talents. Suppose that jobs were given out on only a "have to work" basis to both women and men—one job per household. It would be unthinkable to lose the unique abilities of, for instance, Eleanor Holmes Norton, the distinguished chair of the Equal Employment Opportunity Commission. But would we then be forced to question the important work of her husband, Edward Norton, who is also a distinguished lawyer? Since men earn more than twice as much as women on the average, the wife in most households would be more likely to give up her job. Does that mean the nation could do as well without millions of its nurses, teachers, and secretaries? Or that the rare man who earns less than his wife should give up his job?

13 It was this kind of waste of human talents on a society-wide scale that traumatized millions of unemployed or underemployed Americans during the Depression. Then, a one-job-per-household rule seemed somewhat justified, yet the concept was used to displace women workers only, create intolerable dependencies, and waste female talent that the country needed. That Depression experience, plus the energy and example of women who were finally allowed to work during the manpower shortage created by World War II, led Congress to reinterpret the meaning of the country's full-employment goal in its Economic Act of 1946. Full employment was

officially defined as "the employment of those who want to work, without regard to whether their employment is, by some definition, necessary. This goal applies equally to men and to women." Since bad economic times are again creating a resentment of employed women—as well as creating more need for women to be employed—we need such a goal more than ever. Women are again being caught in a tragic double bind: We are required to be strong and then punished for our strength.

Clearly, anything less than government and popular commit- 14
ment to this 1946 definition of full employment will leave the less powerful groups, whoever they may be, in danger. Almost as important as the financial penalty paid by the powerless is the suffering that comes from being shut out of paid and recognized work. Without it, we lose much of our self-respect and our ability to prove that we are alive by making some difference in the world. That's just as true for the suburban woman as it is for the unemployed steel worker.

But it won't be easy to give up the passive defense of "we- 15
workbecausewehaveto."

When a woman who is struggling to support her children and 16
grandchildren on welfare sees her neighbor working as a waitress, even though that neighbor's husband has a job, she may feel resentful, and the waitress (of course, not the waitress's husband) may feel guilty. Yet unless we establish the obligation to provide a job for everyone who is willing and able to work, that welfare woman may herself be penalized by policies that give out only one public-service job per household. She and her daughter will have to make a painful and divisive decision about which of them gets that precious job, and the whole household will have to survive on only one salary.

A job as a human right is a principle that applies to men as 19
well as women. But women have more cause to fight for it. The phenomenon of the "working woman" has been held responsible for everything from an increase in male impotence (which turned out, incidently, to be attributable to medication for high blood pressure) to the rising cost of steak (which was due to high energy costs and beef import restrictions, not women's refusal to prepare the cheaper, slower-cooking cuts). Unless we see a job as part of every citizen's right to autonomy and personal fulfillment, we will continue to be vulnerable to someone else's idea of what 'need' is, and whose 'need' counts the most.

In many ways, women who do not have to work for simple 18
survival, but who choose to do so nonetheless, are on the frontier of asserting this right for all women. Those with well-to-do husbands are dangerously easy for us to resent and put down. It's easier still to resent women from families of inherited wealth, even though men

generally control and benefit from that wealth. (There is no Rockefeller Sisters Fund, no J. P. Morgan & Daughters, and sons-in-law may be the ones who really sleep their way to power.) But to prevent a woman whose husband or father is wealthy from earning her own living, and from gaining the self-confidence that comes with that ability, is to keep her needful of that unearned power and less willing to disperse it. Moreover, it is to lose forever her unique talents.

Perhaps modern feminists have been guilty of a kind of reverse snobbism that keeps us from reaching out to the wives and daughters of wealthy men; yet it was exactly such women who refused the restrictions of class and financed the first wave of feminist revolution. 19

For most of us, however, "womenworkbecausewehaveto" is just true enough to be seductive as a personal defense. 20

If we use it without also staking out the larger human right to a job, however, we will never achieve that right. And we will always be subject to the false argument that independence for women is a luxury affordable only in good economic times. Alternatives to layoffs will not be explored, acceptable unemployment will always be used to frighten those with jobs into accepting low wages, and we will never remedy the real cost, both to families and to the country, of dependent women and a massive loss of talent. 21

Worst of all, we may never learn to find productive, honored work as a natural part of ourselves and as one of life's basic pleasures. 22

QUESTIONS

1. What is the false rationale for "the working woman"? Why do women really work?

2. Explain in your own words the essence of Steinem's argument.

3. Where does Steinem employ the pronouns "we" and "our"? Who is her audience? What is the effect on the tone of the essay?

4. In paragraphs 4 to 6, the author asks a series of rhetorical questions. What is her purpose?

5. How does the author employ analysis of immediate causes? In what parts of the essay does she analyze ultimate causes?

6. What varieties of evidence does Steinem present? How effective or persuasive is it in supporting her argument?

7. Analyze the nature or function of comparison and contrast in this essay.

8. Where does the concluding section of this essay begin? What is the author's strategy?

9. Steinem asserts that women must fight to assert their right to work. How does this reality manifest itself in today's business world?

10. a. Write your own definition of today's "working woman."
b. Compare and contrast the modern working man and woman.
c. Analyze the ways in which men can be integrated into "so-called woman's work."

VIRGINIA WOOLF

Professions for Women

Virginia Woolf (1882–1941), novelist and essayist, was the daughter of Leslie Stephen, a famous critic and writer on economics. An experimental novelist, Woolf attempted to portray consciousness through a poetic, symbolic, and concrete style. Her novels include *Jacob's Room* (1922), *Mrs. Dalloway* (1925), *To the Lighthouse* (1927), and *The Waves* (1931). She was also a perceptive reader and critic; her criticism appears in *The Common Reader* (1925) and *The Second Common Reader* (1933). In the following essay, which was delivered originally as a speech to The Women's Service League in 1931, Woolf argues that women must overcome several "angels" or phantoms in order to succeed in professional careers.

When your secretary invited me to come here, she told me that your Society is concerned with the employment of women and she suggested that I might tell you something about my own professional experiences. It is true I am a woman; it is true I am employed; but what professional experiences have I had? It is difficult to say. My profession is literature; and in that profession there are fewer experiences for women than in any other, with the exception of the stage—fewer, I mean, that are peculiar to women. For the road was cut many years ago—by Fanny Burney, by Aphra Behn, by Harriet Martineau, by Jane Austen, by George Eliot—many famous women, and many more unknown and forgotten, have been before me, making the path smooth, and regulating my steps. Thus, when I came to write, there were very few material obstacles in my way. Writing was a reputable and harmless occupation. The family peace was not broken by the scratching of a pen. No demand was made upon the family purse. For 1

ten and sixpence one can buy paper enough to write all the plays of Shakespeare—if one has a mind that way. Pianos and models, Paris, Vienna and Berlin, masters and mistresses, are not needed by a writer. The cheapness of writing paper is, of course, the reason why women have succeeded as writers before they have succeeded in the other professions.

But to tell you my story—it is a simple one. You have only got 2
to figure to yourselves a girl in a bedroom with a pen in her hand. She had only to move that pen from left to right—from ten o'clock to one. Then it occurred to her to do what is simple and cheap enough after all—to slip a few of those pages into an envelope, fix a penny stamp in the corner, and drop the envelope into the red box at the corner. It was thus that I became a journalist; and my effort was rewarded on the first day of the following month—a very glorious day it was for me—by a letter from an editor containing a cheque for one pound ten shillings and sixpence. But to show you how little I deserve to be called a professional woman, how little I know of the struggles and difficulties of such lives, I have to admit that instead of spending that sum upon bread and butter, rent, shoes and stockings, or butcher's bills, I went out and bought a cat—a beautiful cat, a Persian cat, which very soon involved me in bitter disputes with my neighbours.

What could be easier than to write articles and to buy Persian 3
cats with the profits? But wait a moment. Articles have to be about something. Mine, I seem to remember, was about a novel by a famous man. And while I was writing this review, I discovered that if I were going to review books I should need to do battle with a certain phantom. And the phantom was a woman, and when I came to know her better I called her after the heroine of a famous poem, The Angel in the House. It was she who used to come between me and my paper when I was writing reviews. It was she who bothered me and wasted my time and so tormented me that at last I killed her. You who come of a younger and happier generation may not have heard of her—you may not know what I mean by the Angel in the House. I will describe her as shortly as I can. She was intensely sympathetic. She was immensely charming. She was utterly unselfish. She excelled in the difficult arts of family life. She sacrificed herself daily. If there was chicken, she took the leg; if there was a draught she sat in it—in short she was so constituted that she never had a mind or a wish of her own, but preferred to sympathize always with the minds and wishes of others. Above all—I need not say it—she was pure. Her purity was supposed to be her chief beauty—her blushes, her great grace. In those days—the last of Queen Victoria—every house had its Angel. And when I came to write I encountered her with the very first words. The shadow of her wings fell on my page; I heard the rustling of her skirts in the room. Directly, that is to say, I took my pen in

hand to review that novel by a famous man, she slipped behind me and whispered: "My dear, you are a young woman. You are writing about a book that has been written by a man. Be sympathetic; be tender; flatter; deceive; use all the arts and wiles of our sex. Never let anybody guess that you have a mind of your own. Above all, be pure." And she made as if to guide my pen. I now record the one act for which I take some credit to myself, though the credit rightly belongs to some excellent ancestors of mine who left me a certain sum of money—shall we say five hundred pounds a year?—so that it was not necessary for me to depend solely on charm for my living. I turned upon her and caught her by the throat. I did my best to kill her. My excuse, if I were to be had up in a court of law, would be that I acted in self-defense. Had I not killed her she would have killed me. She would have plucked the heart out of my writing. For, as I found, directly I put pen to paper, you cannot review even a novel without having a mind of your own, without expressing what you think to be the truth about human relations, morality, sex. And all these questions, according to the Angel in the House, cannot be dealt with freely and openly by women; they must charm, they must conciliate, they must—to put it bluntly—tell lies if they are to succeed. Thus, whenever I felt the shadow of her wing or the radiance of her halo upon my page, I took up the inkpot and flung it at her. She died hard. Her fictitious nature was of great assistance to her. It is far harder to kill a phantom than a reality. She was always creeping back when I thought I had dispatched her. Though I flatter myself that I killed her in the end, the struggle was severe; it took much time that had better have been spent upon learning Greek grammar; or in roaming the world in search of adventures. But it was a real experience; it was an experience that was bound to befall all women writers at that time. Killing the Angel in the House was part of the occupation of a woman writer.

But to continue my story. The Angel was dead; what then 4
remained? You may say that what remained was a simple and common object—a young woman in a bedroom with an inkpot. In other words, now that she had rid herself of falsehood, that young woman had only to be herself. Ah, but what is "herself"? I mean, what is a woman? I assure you, I do not know. I do not believe that you know. I do not believe that anybody can know until she has expressed herself in all the arts and professions open to human skill. That indeed is one of the reasons why I have come here—out of respect for you, who are in process of showing us by your experiments what a woman is, who are in process of providing us, by your failures and successes, with that extremely important piece of information.

But to continue the story of my professional experiences. I 5 made one pound ten and six by my first review; and I bought a Persian cat with the proceeds. Then I grew ambitious. A Persian cat is all very well, I said; but a Persian cat is not enough. I must have a motor car. And it was thus that I became a novelist—for it is a very strange thing that people will give you a motor car if you will tell them a story. It is a still stranger thing that there is nothing so delightful in the world as telling stories. It is far pleasanter than writing reviews of famous novels. And yet, if I am to obey your secretary and tell you my professional experiences as a novelist, I must tell you about a very strange experience that befell me as a novelist. And to understand it you must try first to imagine a novelist's state of mind. I hope I am not giving away professional secrets if I say that a novelist's chief desire is to be as unconscious as possible. He has to induce in himself a state of perpetual lethargy. He wants life to proceed with the utmost quiet and regularity. He wants to see the same faces, to read the same books, to do the same things day after day, month after month, while he is writing, so that nothing may break the illusion in which he is living—so that nothing may disturb or disquiet the mysterious nosings about, feelings round, darts, dashes and sudden discoveries of that very shy and illusive spirit, the imagination. I suspect that this state is the same both for men and women. Be that as it may, I want you to imagine me writing a novel in a state of trance. I want you to figure to yourselves a girl sitting with a pen in her hand, which for minutes, and indeed for hours, she never dips into the inkpot. The image that comes to my mind when I think of this girl is the image of a fisherman lying sunk in dreams on the verge of a deep lake with a rod held out over the water. She was letting her imagination sweep unchecked round every rock and cranny of the world that lies submerged in the depths of our unconscious being. Now came the experience, the experience that I believe to be far commoner with women writers than with men. The line raced through the girl's fingers. Her imagination had rushed away. It had sought the pools, the depths, the dark places where the largest fish slumber. And then there was a smash. There was an explosion. There was foam and confusion. The imagination had dashed itself against something hard. The girl was roused from her dream. She was indeed in a state of the most acute and difficult distress. To speak without figure she had thought of something, something about the body, about the passions which it was unfitting for her as a woman to say. Men, her reason told her, would be shocked. The consciousness of what men will say of a woman who speaks the truth about her passions had roused her from her artist's state of unconsciousness. She could write no more. The trance was over. Her imagination could work no longer. This I believe to be a very common experience with women writers—they are impeded by the extreme conventionality of the other sex. For

though men sensibly allow themselves great freedom in these respects, I doubt that they realize or can control the extreme severity with which they condemn such freedom in women.

These then were two very genuine experiences of my own. These were two of the adventures of my professional life. The first—killing the Angel in the House—I think I solved. She died. But the second, telling the truth about my own experiences as a body, I do not think I solved. I doubt that any woman has solved it yet. The obstacles against her are still immensely powerful—and yet they are very difficult to define. Outwardly, what is simpler than to write books? Outwardly, what obstacles are there for a woman rather than for a man? Inwardly, I think, the case is very different; she has still many ghosts to fight, many prejudices to overcome. Indeed it will be a long time still, I think, before a woman can sit down to write a book without finding a phantom to be slain, a rock to be dashed against. And if this is so in literature, the freest of all professions for women, how is it in the new professions which you are now for the first time entering?

Those are the questions that I should like, had I time, to ask you. And indeed, if I have laid stress upon these professional experiences of mine, it is because I believe that they are, though in different forms, yours also. Even when the path is nominally open—when there is nothing to prevent a woman from being a doctor, a lawyer, a civil servant—there are many phantoms and obstacles, as I believe, looming in her way. To discuss and define them is I think of great value and importance; for thus only can the labour be shared, the difficulties be solved. But besides this, it is necessary also to discuss the ends and the aims for which we are fighting, for which we are doing battle with these formidable obstacles. Those aims cannot be taken for granted; they must be perpetually questioned and examined. The whole position, as I see it—here in this hall surrounded by women practising for the first time in history I know not how many different professions—is one of extraordinary interest and importance. You have won rooms of your own in the house hitherto exclusively owned by men. You are able, though not without great labour and effort, to pay the rent. You are earning your five hundred pounds a year. But this freedom is only a beginning; the room is your own, but it is still bare. It has to be furnished; it has to be decorated; it has to be shared. How are you going to furnish it, how are you going to decorate it? With whom are you going to share it, and upon what terms? These, I think are questions of the utmost importance and interest. For the first time in history you are able to ask for them; for the first time you are able to decide for yourselves what the answers should be. Willingly would I stay and discuss those questions and answers—but not tonight. My time is up; and I must cease.

QUESTIONS

1. Who or what is the "angel" that Woolf describes in this essay? Why must she kill it? What other obstacles does a professional woman encounter?

2. Paraphrase the last two paragraphs of this essay. What is the essence of Woolf's argument?

3. There is a significant amount of figurative language in the essay. Locate and explain examples. What does the figurative language contribute to the tone of the essay?

4. How do we know that Woolf is addressing an audience of women? Why does she pose so many questions, and what does this strategy contribute ot the rapport that she wants to establish? Explain the effect of the last two sentences.

5. How does Woolf use analogy to structure part of her argument?

6. Why does Woolf rely on personal narration? How does it affect the logic of her argument?

7. Evaluate Woolf's use of contrast to advance her argument.

8. Where does Woolf place her main proposition? How emphatic is it, and why?

9. How effectively does Woolf use her own example as a professional writer to advance a broader proposition concerning all women entering professional life?

10. a. Explain the value of Woolf's essay for women today.
b. Discuss the problems and obstacles that you anticipate when you enter your chosen career.
c. Compare and contrast the essays by Galbraith, Steinem, and Woolf.

ADAM SMITH

Of the Division of Labor

Adam Smith (1723–1790), whose *The Wealth of Nations* (1776) exerted a profound influence on economic thought, was born in Scotland and educated at the University of Glasgow and Oxford University. From 1743 to 1766 he was a professor of economics and moral philosophy at Edinburgh and Glasgow Universities. Smith moved easily among the intellectual celebrities of his age—Franklin, Voltaire, Burke, Johnson, and Gibbon. In *The Wealth of Nations* he developed his theory of the "laissez-faire" economy—a relatively unfettered free enterprise society based on an efficient division of labor. The following chapter contains Smith's famous example of pin-making as an instance where the division of labor promotes effective production.

he greatest improvement in the productive powers of 1
labour, and the greater part of the skill, dexterity, and judgment with which it is any where directed, or applied, seem to have been the effects of the division of labour.

The effects of the division of labour, in the general business of 2
society, will be more easily understood, by considering in what manner it operates in some particular manufactures. It is commonly supposed to be carried furthest in some very trifling ones; not perhaps that it really is carried further in them than in others of more importance: but in those trifling manufactures which are destined to supply the small wants of but a small number of people, the whole number of workmen must necessarily be small; and those employed in every different branch of the work can often be collected into the same workhouse, and placed at once under the view of the spectator. In those great manufactures, on the contrary, which are destined to supply the great wants of the great body of the people, every different branch of the work employs so great a number of workmen, that it is impossible to collect them all into the same workhouse. We can seldom see more, at one time, than those employed in one single branch. Though in such manufactures, therefore, the work may really be divided into a much greater number of parts, than in those of a more trifling nature, the division is not near so obvious, and has accordingly been much less observed.

To take an example, therefore, from a very trifling manufac- 3
ture; but one in which the division of labour has been very often taken notice of, the trade of the pin-maker; a workman not educated to this business (which the division of labour has rendered a distinct trade), nor acquainted with the use of the machinery employed in it (to the invention of which the same division of labour has probably given occasion), could scarce, perhaps, with his utmost industry, make one pin in a day, and certainly could not make twenty. But in the way in which this business is now carried on, not only the whole work is a peculiar trade, but it is divided into a number of branches, of which the greater part are likewise peculiar trades. One man draws out the wire, another straights it, a third cuts it, a fourth points it, a fifth grinds it at the top for receiving the head; to make the head

requires two or three distinct operations; to put it on, is a peculiar business, to whiten the pins is another; it is even a trade by itself to put them into the paper; and the important business of making a pin is, in this manner, divided into about eighteen distinct operations, which, in some manufactories, are all performed by distinct hands, though in others the same man will sometimes perform two or three of them. I have seen a small manufactory of this kind where ten men only were employed, and where some of them consequently performed two or three distinct operations. But though they were very poor, and therefore but indifferently accommodated with the necessary machinery, they could, when they exerted themselves, make among them about twelve pounds of pins a day. There are in a pound upwards of four thousand pins of a middling size. Those ten persons, therefore, could make among them upwards of forty-eight thousand pins in a day. Each person, therefore, making a tenth part of forty-eight thousand pins might be considered as making four thousand eight hundred pins in a day. But if they had all wrought separately and independently, and without any of them having been educated to this peculiar business, they certainly could not each of them have made twenty, perhaps not one pin in a day; that is, certainly, not the two hundred and fortieth, perhaps not the four thousand eight hundredth part of what they are at present capable of performing, in consequence of a proper division and combination of their different operations.

In every other art and manufacture, the effects of the division of labour are similar to what they are in this very trifling one; though, in many of them, the labour can neither be so much subdivided, nor reduced to so great a simplicity of operation. The division of labour, however, so far as it can be introduced, occasions, in every art, a proportionable increase of the productive powers of labour. The separation of different trades and employments from one another, seems to have taken place, in consequence of this advantage. This separation too is generally carried furthest in those countries which enjoy the highest degree of industry and improvement; what is the work of one man in a rude state of society, being generally that of several in an improved one. In every improved society, the farmer is generally nothing but a farmer; the manufacturer, nothing but a manufacturer. The labour too which is necessary to produce any one complete manufacture, is almost always divided among a great number of hands. How many different trades are employed in each branch of the linen and woollen manufactures, from the growers of the flax and the wool, to the bleachers and smoothers of the linen, or to the dyers and dressers of the cloth! The nature of agriculture, indeed, does not admit of so many subdivisions of labour, nor of so 4

complete a separation of one business from another, as manufactures. It is impossible to separate so entirely, the business of the grazier from that of the corn-farmer, as the trade of the carpenter is commonly separated from that of the smith. The spinner is almost always a distinct person from the weaver; but the ploughman, the harrower, the sower of the seed, and the reaper of the corn, are often the same. The occasions for those different sorts of labour returning with the different seasons of the year, it is impossible that one man should be constantly employed in any one of them. This impossibility of making so complete and entire a separation of all the different branches of labour employed in agriculture, is perhaps the reason why the improvement of the productive powers of labour in this art, does not always keep pace with their improvement in manufactures. The most opulent nations, indeed, generally excel all their neighbours in agriculture as well as in manufactures; but they are commonly more distinguished by their superiority in the latter than in the former. Their lands are in general better cultivated, and having more labour and expence bestowed upon them, produce more in proportion to the extent and natural fertility of the ground. But this superiority of produce is seldom much more than in proportion to the superiority of labour and expence. In agriculture, the labour of the rich country is not always much more productive than that of the poor; or, at least, it is never so much more productive, as it commonly is in manufactures. The corn of the rich country, therefore, will not always, in the same degree of goodness, come cheaper to market than that of the poor. The corn of Poland, in the same degree of goodness, is as cheap as that of France, notwithstanding the superior opulence and improvement of the latter country. The corn of France is, in the corn provinces, fully as good, and in most years nearly about the same price with the corn of England, though, in opulence and improvement, France is perhaps inferior to England. The corn-lands of England, however, are better cultivated than those of France, and the corn-lands of France are said to be much better cultivated than those of Poland. But though the poor country, notwithstanding the inferiority of its cultivation, can, in some measure, rival the rich in the cheapness and goodness of its corn, it can pretend to no such competition in its manufactures; at least if those manufacturers suit the soil, climate, and situation of the rich country. The silks of France are better and cheaper than those of England, because the silk manufacture, at least under the present high duties upon the importation of raw silk, does not so well suit the climate of England as that of France. But the hard-ware and the coarse woollens of England are beyond all comparison superior to those of France, and much cheaper too in the same degree of goodness. In Poland there are said to be

scarce any manufactures of any kind, a few of those coarser household manufactures excepted, without which no country can well subsist.

This great increase of the quantity of work, which, in conse- 5
quence of the division of labour, the same number of people are capable of performing, is owing to three different circumstances; first, to the increase of dexterity in every particular workman; secondly, to the saving of the time which is commonly lost in passing from one species of work to another; and lastly, to the invention of a great number of machines which facilitate and abridge labour, and enable one man to do the work of many.

First, the improvement of the dexterity of the workman 6
necessarily increases the quantity of the work he can perform; and the division of labour, by reducing every man's business to some one simple operation, and by making this operation the sole employment of his life, necessarily increases very much the dexterity of the workman. A common smith, who, though accustomed to handle the hammer, has never been used to make nails, if upon some particular occasion he is obliged to attempt it, will scarce, I am assured, be able to make above two or three hundred nails in a day, and those too very bad ones. A smith who has been accustomed to make nails, but whose sole or principal business has not been that of a nailer, can seldom with his utmost diligence make more than eight hundred or a thousand nails in a day. I have seen several boys under twenty years of age who had never exercised any other trade but that of making nails, and who, when they exerted themselves, could make, each of them, upwards of two thousand three hundred nails in a day. The making of a nail, however, is by no means one of the simplest operations. The same person blows the bellows, stirs or mends the fire as there is occasion, heats the iron, and forges every part of the nail: In forging the head too he is obliged to change his tools. The different operations into which the making of a pin, or of a metal button, is subdivided, are all of them much more simple, and the dexterity of the person, of whose life it has been the sole business to perform them, is usually much greater. The rapidity with which some of the operations of those manufactures are performed, exceeds what the human hand could, by those who had never seen them, be supposed capable of acquiring.

Secondly, the advantage which is gained by saving the time 7
commonly lost in passing from one sort of work to another, is much greater than we should at first view be apt to imagine it. It is impossible to pass very quickly from one kind of work to another, that is carried on in a different place, and with quite different tools. A country weaver, who cultivates a small farm, must lose a good deal of time in passing from his loom to the field, and from the field to his

loom. When the two trades can be carried on in the same workhouse, the loss of time is no doubt much less. It is even in this case, however, very considerable. A man commonly saunters a little in turning his hand from one sort of employment to another. When he first begins the new work he is seldom very keen and hearty; his mind, as they say, does not go to it, and for some time he rather trifles than applies to good purpose. The habit of sauntering and of indolent careless application, which is naturally, or rather necessarily acquired by every country workman who is obliged to change his work and his tools every half hour, and to apply his hand in twenty different ways almost every day of his life; renders him almost always slothful and lazy, and incapable of any vigorous application even on the most pressing occasions. Independent, therefore, of his deficiency in point of dexterity, this cause alone must always reduce considerably the quantity of work which he is capable of performing.

Thirdly, and lastly, every body must be sensible how much labour is facilitated and abridged by the application of proper machinery. It is unnecessary to give any example. I shall only observe, therefore, that the invention of all those machines by which labour is so much facilitated and abridged, seems to have been originally owing to the division of labour. Men are much more likely to discover easier and readier methods of attaining any object, when the whole attention of their minds is directed towards that single object, than when it is dissipated among a great variety of things. But in consequence of the division of labour, the whole of every man's attention comes naturally to be directed towards some one very simple object. It is naturally to be expected, therefore, that some one or other of those who are employed in each particular branch of labour should soon find out easier and readier methods of performing their own particular work, wherever the nature of it admits of such improvement. A great part of the machines made use of in those manufactures in which labour is most subdivided, were originally the inventions of common workmen, who, being each of them employed in some very simple operation, naturally turned their thoughts towards finding out easier and readier methods of performing it. Whoever has been much accustomed to visit such manufactures, must frequently have been shewn very pretty machines, which were the inventions of such workmen, in order to facilitate and quicken their own particular part of the work. In the first fire-engines, a boy was constantly employed to open and shut alternately the communication between the boiler and the cylinder, according as the piston either ascended or descended. One of those boys, who loved to play with his companions, observed that, by tying a string from the handle of the valve which opened this communication to another part of the machine, the valve would open and shut without his assist- 8 ance, and leave him at liberty to divert himself with his play-fellows. One of the greatest improvements that has been made upon this machine, since it was first invented, was in this manner the discovery of a boy who wanted to save his own labour.

All the improvements in machinery, however, have by no means been the inventions of those who had occasion to use the machines. Many improvements have been made by the ingenuity of the makers of the machines, when to make them became the business of a peculiar trade; and some by that of those who are called philosophers or men of speculation, whose trade it is not to do any thing, but to observe every thing; and who, upon that account, are often capable of combining together the powers of the most distant and dissimilar objects. In the progress of society, philosophy or speculation becomes, like every other employment, the principal or sole trade and occupation of a particular class of citizens. Like every other employment too, it is subdivided into a great number of different branches, each of which affords occupation to a peculiar tribe or class of philosophers; and this subdivision of employment in philosophy, as well as in every other business, improves dexterity, and saves time. Each individual becomes more expert in his own peculiar branch, more work is done upon the whole, and the quantity of science is considerably increased by it. 9

It is the great multiplication of the productions of all the different arts, in consequence of the division of labour, which occasions, in a well-governed society, that universal opulence which extends itself to the lowest ranks of the people. Every workman has a great quantity of his own work to dispose of beyond what he himself has occasion for; and every other workman being exactly in the same situation, he is enabled to exchange a great quantity of his own goods for a great quantity, or what comes to the same thing, for the price of a great quantity of theirs. He supplies them abundantly with what they have occasion for, and they accommodate him as amply with what he has occasion for, and a general plenty diffuses itself through all the different ranks of the society. 10

Observe the accommodation of the most common artificer or day-labourer in a civilized and thriving country, and you will perceive that the number of people of whose industry a part, though but a small part, has been employed in procuring him this accommodation, exceeds all computation. The woollen coat, for example, which covers the day-labourer, as coarse and rough as it may appear, is the produce of the joint labour of a great multitude of workmen. The shepherd, the sorter of the wool, the wool-comber or carder, the dyer, the scribbler, the spinner, the weaver, the fuller, the dresser, with many others, must all join their different arts in order to complete 11

even this homely production. How many merchants and carriers, besides, must have been employed in transporting the materials from some of those workmen to others who often live in a very distant part of the country! How much commerce and navigation in particular, how many ship-builders, sailors, sail-makers, rope-makers, must have been employed in order to bring together the different drugs made use of by the dyer, which often come from the remotest corner of the world! What a variety of labour too is necessary in order to produce the tools of the meanest of those workmen! To say nothing of such complicated machines as the ship of the sailor, the mill of the fuller, or even the loom of the weaver, let us consider only what a variety of labour is requisite in order to form that very simple machine, the shears with which the shepherd clips the wool. The miner, the builder of the furnace for smelting the ore, the feller of the timber, the burner of the charcoal to be made use of in the smelting-house, the brick-maker, the brick-layer, the workmen who attend the furnace, the mill-wright, the forger, the smith, must all of them join their different arts in order to produce them. Were we to examine, in the same manner, all the different parts of his dress and household furniture, the coarse linen shirt which he wears next his skin, the shoes which cover his feet, the bed which he lies on, and all the different parts which compose it, the kitchen-grate at which he prepares his victuals, the coals which he makes use of for that purpose, dug from the bowels of the earth, and brought to him perhaps by a long sea and a long land carriage, all the other utensils of his kitchen, all the furniture of his table, the knives and forks, the earthen or pewter plates upon which he serves up and divides his victuals, the different hands employed in preparing his bread and his beer, the glass window which lets in the heat and the light, and keeps out the wind and the rain, with all the knowledge and art requisite for preparing that beautiful and happy invention, without which these northern parts of the world could scarce have afforded a very comfortable habitation, together with the tools of all the different workmen employed in producing those different conveniencies; if we examine, I say, all these things, and consider what a variety of labour is employed about each of them, we shall be sensible that without the assistance and co-operation of many thousands, the very meanest person in a civilized country could not be provided, even according to, what we very falsely imagine, the easy and simple manner in which he is commonly accommodated. Compared, indeed, with the more extravagant luxury of the great, his accommodation must no doubt appear extremely simple and easy; and yet it may be true, perhaps, that the accommodation of a European prince does not always so much exceed that of an industrious and frugal peasant, as

the accommodation of the latter exceeds that of many an African king, the absolute master of the lives and liberties of ten thousand naked savages.

QUESTIONS

1. What is the division of labor? How does it operate in pin-making? In what other economic sectors does the concept operate? What three reasons does Smith give for the increase in the quantity of work as a result of the division of labor?

2. According to the author, how does the division of labor contribute to a well-governed society?

3. Explain the connotations for the word "labour" in the essay.

4. Would you label the diction of this essay as informal or technical? Explain.

5. Why is it necessary for the author to employ an extensive series of examples?

6. Where does process analysis enter into the development of the essay?

7. Name instances where the author employs the pattern of cause and effect.

8. Which stylistic and rhetorical devices does Smith use in the lengthy concluding paragraph?

9. Smith maintains the division of labor benefits everyone in a society, from the humblest worker to the privileged or affluent person. Do you agree or disagree with this assertion, and why?

10. a. Analyze the way in which the division of labor benefits a particular economic enterprise in the United States today.
b. Describe any division of labor that you have had personal experience with, such as in your home, dormitory, club, or company.

JOSEPH ADDISON

The Royal Exchange

Joseph Addison (1672–1719) was an essayist, poet, dramatist, statesman, and journalist. As a playwright, he wrote one of the most successful tragedies of the eighteenth century

(*Cato,* in 1713). As a statesman, he served as secretary of state under George I. As an essayist, he wrote with reason and wit in *The Tatler* (1709–1711) and *The Spectator* (1711–1712, and 1714). He not only excelled as a statesman and tragedian, but also is often considered one of the best English essayists. In this periodical essay, Addison pays tribute to one of Britain's sacred institutions.

There is no place in the town which I so much love to 1
frequent as the Royal Exchange. It gives me a secret satisfaction, and, in some measure, gratifies my vanity, as I am an Englishman, to see so rich an assembly of countrymen and foreigners consulting together upon the private business of mankind, and making this metropolis a kind of emporium for the whole earth. I must confess I look upon high-change to be a great council, in which all considerable nations have their representatives. Factors in the trading world are what ambassadors are in the politic world; they negotiate affairs, conclude treaties, and maintain a good correspondence between those wealthy societies of men that are divided from one another by seas and oceans, or live on the different extremities of a continent. I have often been pleased to hear disputes adjusted between an inhabitant of Japan and an alderman of London, or to see a subject of the Great Mogul entering into a league with one of the Czar of Muscovy. I am infinitely delighted in mixing with these several ministers of commerce, as they are distinguished by their different walks and different languages: sometimes I am justled among a body of Armenians: sometimes I am lost in a crowd of Jews; and sometimes make one in a group of Dutchmen. I am a Dane, Swede, or Frenchman at different times, or rather fancy myself like the old philosopher, who upon being asked what country-man he was, replied, that he was a citizen of the world.

Though I very frequently visit this busy multitude of people, I 2
am known to nobody there but my friend Sir Andrew, who often smiles upon me as he sees me bustling in the crowd, but at the same time connives at my presence without taking any further notice of me. There is indeed a merchant of Egypt, who just knows me by sight, having formerly remitted me some money to Grand Cairo; but as I am not versed in the modern Coptic, our conferences go no further than a bow and a grimace.

This grand scene of business gives me an infinite variety of 3
solid and substantial entertainments. As I am a great lover of mankind, my heart naturally overflows with pleasure at the sight of a prosperous and happy multitude, insomuch that at many public solemnities I cannot forbear expressing my joy with tears that have stolen down my cheeks. For this reason I am wonderfully delighted to

see such a body of men thriving in their own private fortunes, and at the same time promoting the public stock; or in other words, raising estates for their own families, by bringing into their country whatever is wanting, and carrying out of it whatever is superfluous.

Nature seems to have taken a particular care to disseminate 4
her blessings among the different regions of the world, with an eye to this mutual intercourse and traffic among mankind, that the natives of the several parts of the globe might have a kind of dependence upon one another, and be united together by their common interest. Almost every degree produces something peculiar to it. The food often grows in one country, and the sauce in another. The fruits of Portugal are corrected by the products of Barbadoes: the infusion of a China plant sweetened with the pith of an Indian cane. The Philippick Islands give a flavour to our European bowls. The single dress of a woman of quality is often the product of an hundred climates. The muff and the fan come together from the different ends of the earth. The scarf is sent from the torrid zone, and the tippet from beneath the Pole. The brocade petticoat rises out of the mines of Peru, and the diamond necklace out of the bowels of Indostan.

If we consider our own country in its natural prospect, 5
without any of the benefits and advantages of commerce, what a barren uncomfortable spot of earth falls to our share! Natural historians tell us that no fruit grows originally among us, besides hips and haws, acorns and pig-nuts, with other delicacies of the like nature; that our climate of itself, and without the assistances of art, can make no further advances towards a plum than to a sloe, and carries an apple to no greater a perfection than a crab: that our melons, our peaches, our figs, our apricots, and cherries, are strangers among us, imported in different ages, and naturalized in our English gardens; and that they would all degenerate and fall away into the trash of our own country, if they were wholly neglected by the planter, and left to the mercy of our sun and soil.

Nor has traffic more enriched our vegetable world than it has 6
improved the whole face of nature among us. Our ships are laden with the harvest of every climate: our tables are stored with spices, and oils, and wines: our rooms are filled with pyramids of China, and adorned with the workmanship of Japan: our morning's-draught comes to us from the remotest corners of the earth: we repair our bodies by the drugs of America, and repose ourselves under Indian canopies. My friend Sir Andrew calls the vineyards of France our gardens; the spice-islands our hot-beds; the Persians our silk-weavers, and the Chinese our potters. Nature indeed furnishes us with the bare necessaries of life, but traffic gives us a great variety of what is useful, and at the same time supplies us with every thing that

is convenient and ornamental. Nor is it the least part of this our happiness, that whilst we enjoy the remotest products of the north and south, we are free from those extremities of weather which give them birth; that our eyes are refreshed with the green fields of Britain, at the same time that our palates are feasted with fruits that rise between the tropics.

For these reasons there are not more useful members in a commonwealth than merchants. They knit mankind together in a mutual intercourse of good offices, distribute the gifts of nature, find work for the poor, add wealth to the rich, and magnificence to the great. Our English merchant converts the tin of his own country into gold, and exchanges his wool for rubies. The Mahometans are clothed in our British manufacture, and the inhabitants of the frozen zone warmed with the fleeces of our sheep. 7

When I have been upon the 'Change, I have often fancied one of our old kings standing in person, where he is represented in effigy, and looking down upon the wealthy concourse of people with which that place is every day filled. In this case, how would he be surprized to hear all the languages of Europe spoken in this little spot of his former dominions, and to see so many private men, who in his time would have been the vassals of some powerful baron, negotiating like princes for greater sums of money than were formerly to be met with in the royal treasury! Trade, without enlarging the British territories, has given us a kind of additional empire: it has multiplied the number of the rich, made our landed estates infinitely more valuable than they were formerly, and added to them an accession of other estates as valuable as the lands themselves. 8

QUESTIONS

1. How is Addison's description of himself as a "citizen of the world" and "lover of mankind" reflected in his attitude toward the Royal Exchange?

2. What is Addison's opinion about merchants? About capitalism? About colonialism? About internationalism?

3. Locate and define these words as they would have been used in Addison's time: *high-change* (paragraph 1); *grimace* (paragraph 2); *Philip-pick Islands* (paragraph 4); *tippet* (paragraph 4); *concourse* (paragraph 8). Even though these words are out of date, can they be used in contemporary contexts? Try using them in sentences.

4. What words and phrases in the first paragraph set the tone of the essay? How do sentence balance and parallel structure affect the tone? Find other examples of balance and parallel structure in the essay.

5. Show the structural function of Addison's extended metaphor of the Royal Exchange as a "grand scene of business." To what extent is the Royal Exchange itself a symbol? Explain.

6. What types of illustration does Addison use to advance his thesis?

7. Describe the strength or weakness of Addison's logic in paragraphs 4 to 7.

8. What techniques of development appear in Addison's concluding paragraph?

9. Why might Addison be termed a forerunner of today's business booster? What traits does he share with today's apostles of business?

10. Focus on a financial landmark—your local bank, the Stock Exchange, and so forth—and write a speculative essay about it in the manner of Addison.

THORSTEIN VEBLEN

Conspicuous Waste

Thorstein Veblen (1857–1929), best known for his theory of conspicuous consumption, taught economics at several major universities, including the University of Chicago, Stanford University, and the New School for Social Research. In *The Theory of the Leisure Class* (1899), Veblen analyzes consumption as a group process, a dynamics of style and imitation that embraces everyone from the lower class to the wealthiest leisure class. Veblen, a highly original thinker, was a biting critic of social and industrial waste and, in *The Theory of Business Enterprise* (1904), a critic of the capitalist system. In this section from *The Theory of the Leisure Class*, Veblen offers a test for evaluating conspicuous waste.

The use of the term "waste" is in one respect an unfortunate one. As used in the speech of everyday life the word carries an undertone of deprecation. It is here used for want of a better term that will adequately describe the same range of motives and of phenomena, and it is not to be taken in an odious sense, as implying an illegitimate expenditure of human products or of human life. In the view of economic theory 1 the expenditure in question is no more and no less legitimate than any other expenditure. It is here called "waste" because this expenditure does not serve human life or human well-being on the whole, not because it is waste or misdirection of effort or expenditure as viewed from the standpoint of the individual consumer who chooses it. If he chooses it, that disposes of the question of its relative utility to him, as compared with other forms of consumption that would not be deprecated on account of their wastefulness. Whatever form of expenditure the consumer chooses, or whatever end he seeks in making his choice, has utility to him by virtue of his preference. As seen from the point of view of the individual consumer, the question of wastefulness does not arise within the scope of economic theory proper. The use of the word "waste" as a technical term, therefore, implies no deprecation of the motives or of the ends sought by the consumer under this canon of conspicuous waste.

But it is, on other grounds, worth noting that the term 2 "waste" in the language of everyday life implies deprecation of what is characterised as wasteful. This common-sense implication is itself an outcropping of the instinct of workmanship. The popular reprobation of waste goes to say that in order to be at peace with himself the common man must be able to see in any and all human effort and human enjoyment an enhancement of life and well-being on the whole. In order to meet with unqualified approval, any economic fact must approve itself under the test of impersonal usefulness—usefulness as seen from the point of view of the generically human. Relative or competitive advantage of one individual in comparison with another does not satisfy the economic conscience, and therefore competitive expenditure has not the approval of this conscience.

In strict accuracy nothing should be included under the head 3 of conspicuous waste but such expenditure as is incurred on the ground of an invidious pecuniary comparison. But in order to bring any given item or element in under this head it is not necessary that it should be recognized as waste in this sense by the person incurring the expenditure. It frequently happens that an element of the standard of living which set out with being primarily wasteful, ends with becoming, in the apprehension of the consumer, a necessary of life; and it may in this way become as indispensable as any other item of the consumer's habitual expenditure. As items which sometimes fall under this head, and are therefore available as illustrations of the manner in which this principle applies, may be cited carpets and tapestries, silver table service, waiter's services, silk hats, starched linen, many articles of jewellery and of dress. The indispensability of these things after the habit and the convention have been formed, however, has little to say in the classification of expenditures as waste or not waste in the technical meaning of the word. The test to which all expenditure must be brought in an attempt to decide that point is the question whether it serves directly to enhance human life on the whole—whether it furthers the life process taken impersonally. For this is the basis of award of the instinct of workmanship, and that instinct is the court of final appeal in any question of economic truth or adequacy. It is a question as to the award rendered by a dispassionate common sense. The question is, therefore, not whether, under the existing circumstances of individual habit and social custom, a given expenditure conduces to the particular consumer's gratification or peace of mind; but whether, aside from acquired tastes and from the canons of usage and conventional decency, its result is a net gain in comfort or in the fulness of life. Customary expenditure must be classed under the head of waste in so far as the custom on which it rests is traceable to the habit of making an invidious pecuniary comparison—in so far as it is conceived that it could not have become customary and prescriptive without the backing of this principle of pecuniary reputability or relative economic success.

4 It is obviously not necessary that a given object of expenditure should be exclusively wasteful in order to come in under the category of conspicuous waste. An article may be useful and wasteful both, and its utility to the consumer may be made up of use and waste in the most varying proportions. Consumable goods, and even productive goods, generally show the two elements in combination, as constituents of their utility; although, in a general way, the element of waste tends to predominate in articles of consumption, while the contrary is true of articles designed for productive use. Even in articles which appear at first glance to serve for pure ostentation only, it is always possible to detect the presence of some, at least ostensible, useful purpose; and on the other hand, even in special machinery and tools contrived for some particular industrial process, as well as in the rudest appliances of human industry, the traces of conspicuous waste, or at least of the habit of ostentation, usually become evident on a close scrutiny. It would be hazardous to assert that a useful purpose is ever absent from the utility of any article or of any service, however obviously its prime purpose and chief element is conspicuous waste; and it would be only less hazardous to assert of any primarily useful product that the element of waste is in no way concerned in its value, immediately or remotely.

QUESTIONS

1. What is the relationship of "waste" to economics? How does the "common sense" definition relate to the economic definition?

2. How does Veblen explain some of the paradoxes of "conspicuous waste" as it relates to the enhancement of human life?

3. Explain the way in which the author uses the following terms: *expenditure, consumption, impersonal usefulness, invidious pecuniary comparison, conspicuous waste,* and *utility.*

4. How does Veblen's style in this selection reflect his purpose?

5. Would you label Veblen's definition as subjective or objective? Cite internal evidence to support your response. To what extent does Veblen offer a stipulative definition?

6. How does the essay's structure reflect a pattern of comparison and contrast?

7. What is the role of analysis in this essay? How does it relate to Veblen's pattern of definition?

8. Analyze the connections between the opening sentences of each of the author's four paragraphs. What do they contribute to the definition, and to essay unity and development?

9. Discuss the relevance of Veblen's theory of conspicuous waste to economic and social life in America today.

10. Write in your own words a definition of conspicuous waste, offering several examples and explaining the effects on economic and social well-being.

GUNNAR MYRDAL

The Direction of Aid

Gunnar Myrdal (1898–   ), cowinner of the 1974 Nobel Prize in Economic Science, is an internationally acclaimed economist, politician, and educator. He was born in Sweden and received a degree in law and a doctorate of jurisprudence in economics from the University of Stockholm. From 1933 to 1950 he was a professor of economics and a leading figure in the Swedish government and the United Nations. Myrdal's study, *An American Dilemma: The Negro Problem and Modern Democracy* (1941), is a landmark text. His books dealing with economic theory include *Monetary Equilibrium* (1939) and *Asian Drama: An Inquiry into the Poverty of Nations* (1968). The following section from *Beyond the Welfare State* (1960) reflects Myrdal's long-standing interest in the economic state of underdeveloped nations.

1 I have felt for a long time that aid to underdeveloped countries should be placed in a definite and more rational order of priorities. This type of international cooperation, where there is not a *quid pro quo* in the ordinary way of business relations, should in my opinion be concentrated on a few fields where such aid would be particularly natural, and felt to be so, both in the countries that are giving aid and in those that are receiving it.

2 Firstly, those underdeveloped nations who are short of food should be given what they need for attaining adequate nutritional standards. The rich countries should make up their mind that they do not want to make money out of selling food to starving peoples. In many countries, a major limitation of economic development is the valid fear that, when the unemployed and underemployed are set to work, they will consume more food than is available. It should be recognized that when, at the same time, other countries are laboring with the problems of food surpluses, this limitation of development is not only cruel but unnecessary and, indeed, absurd. This is, however, no reason why only those rich countries which have food surpluses should carry the burden of the costs of such aid. In any reasonable scheme of international cooperation, the costs for such a scheme should be shared by all the rich nations.

3 What is more, aid should never be looked upon as a permanent solution to the problems of poverty. Aid should always be a help to self-help. For that reason a definite time limit should be set to the provision of food without pay, and a condition should be made that the aid-receiving country do everything it can to raise yields in agriculture. Otherwise there is always the danger that the food aid would only buttress its complacency. Secondly, therefore, the rich countries should also decide to give, free of charge, everything that it would be practical and economic to import from abroad in terms of tools and equipment, technical assistance, and training in order to assist underdeveloped countries to raise their agricultural production of food for consumption. Insofar as surpluses of fertilizers were available, those could be part of the aid. Otherwise, aid should instead be given to set up fertilizer factories in underdeveloped countries where conditions for fertilizer production are favorable.

4 In a rational scheme of international cooperation, this prob-

lem of providing enough food for rapid economic development should be viewed not as a narrowly national problem, but as regional and, indeed, world-wide. Some underdeveloped countries are, and should increasingly become, food exporters, while others could concentrate more on non-food crops and manufactured industrial goods for export. The interests of the former countries should be guarded. They are not, of course, in a position to give away food as the rich countries are. They should in many cases even be aided economically to produce more food for commercial export. If their exports went to other underdeveloped countries as part of the food aid they received, the rich countries' contribution would consist in paying the former countries for their food export to the latter.

Thirdly, the rich countries should, in addition to meeting the 5
fundamental request for more food to eat, agree to give everything that can be provided from abroad in the way of equipment, advice, personnel training, etc., for the most rapid advance the underdeveloped countries can manage to engender in sanitation, health, education at all levels, and research, including surveys of their natural resources.

There should be one general condition for aid in these three 6
directions: that the recipient should use the aid in an economic and efficient manner. If, as I am proposing, the rich countries declared themselves willing to provide all the additional food that some underdeveloped countries need, and all financial help which they can effectively administer for raising productivity in their agriculture, and improving levels of sanitation, health, education, training, and research, the costs would not imply any substantial lowering of economic levels in the rich Western countries.

The great desirability of giving aid generously for these 7
specific purposes would be more readily understood by the general public in the rich Western countries. If aid was given to feed hungry people, to make it more possible for them to grow more food themselves, and to raise the poor nations' levels of health and education, fewer people in the rich countries would be inclined to raise political conditions or to discriminate in giving aid. It would be less tempting to conceal aid in the twilight of "soft loans." In the underdeveloped countries themselves, there would be less suspicion of ulterior motives. Aid would be understood and accepted as the purely humanitarian effort it is, or rather should be.

If there were more funds available for aid to underdeveloped 8
countries than are needed for these three forms, I would give the fourth priority to paying for equipment and other productive necessities from abroad, in order to speed up the formation of various types of overall capital such as irrigation and power facilities, ports, roads,

store houses, etc. Such large-scale investment is necessary in order to give the basis for development, both in industry and agriculture. It is of a particular strategic importance in economic development, as it is labor-intensive and can thus make use of the productive resources of which an underdeveloped country has surplus, labor. If food ceased to be the cruel bottleneck it is at present in many countries, and if undertaking these investments in overall capital would not compete for foreign exchange, underdeveloped countries would find it advantageous to give them a higher priority rating. A large part of the loans from the International Bank have this purpose, but it would be rational to use grant aid in order to make it possible for many underdeveloped countries to intensify their efforts in this direction.

If these forms of economic aid were made available in 9
considerably larger quantities, industrial development, which rightly is such a paramount objective in all underdeveloped countries, could then be left with more hope to their own efforts, upon which it will anyhow have to depend. I have already referred to the fact that, at present, the lack of food, and the fear of increasing the scarcity of food in an inflationary process are often limitations to all development, and in particular to rapid industrialization. That limitation would then have been removed. In all underdeveloped countries, raising the levels of health, education, training, and research would decrease the impact of other brakes on industrialization. The widening of the basis of available social capital would have the same effect. Moreover, other favorable conditions for industrial development in underdeveloped countries would have been created if the rich countries were prepared to undertake the changes in their ordinary commercial and financial policies and business relations which I have referred to above, and which would be so much in the interests of international integration. In the final instance, those reforms in regard to trade and capital movements are, of course, more important than any grant aid for development could ever be.

It is difficult to see how these changes could be brought 10
about, except under concerted and sustained pressure exerted by the poor countries, making the maximum possible use of the existing inter-governmental organizations. A rational organization of aid and technical assistance, and in particular the inauguration of a priority system of the type sketched above, is only possible, of course, if aid is being planned internationally by inter-governmental agencies, instead of being handed out unilaterally by individual governments. And only an internationalization of aid can provide the political and psychological basis for so raising its level that aid becomes a really important means of policy for the economic development of underdeveloped countries.

QUESTIONS

1. What specific steps must the affluent nations take to promote economic development in the poorer nations? What is the goal or purpose of such aid?

2. According to the author, what is the best way to funnel aid to underdeveloped nations?

3. What connotations does Myrdal establish for the term *underdeveloped countries*?

4. Make a list of those transitional phrases at the start of various paragraphs that contribute to the unity of the essay.

5. What is Myrdal's thesis? Where does he state it, and why?

6. How does the author use a pattern of examples to structure this essay?

7. Why doesn't the author employ specific examples or offer concrete evidence? Is this a defect or not? Explain.

8. What is the implied paradox in the concluding paragraph?

9. Explain why you think that Myrdal is practical or utopian in his thinking in this selection.

10. a. Argue for or against the proposition that affluent nations have a humanitarian duty to offer economic assistance to poor nations.
b. Present your own program for aid to developing nations.

KARL MARX

Bourgeois and Proletarians

Karl Marx (1818–1883), the chief founder of democratic socialism and revolutionary communism, was born in Germany and studied at the Universities of Bonn and Berlin. He met Friedrich Engels, his closest friend and collaborator, in 1843 while living in Paris; he resided in Belgium from 1845 to 1848 and on his return to Germany became spokesperson for radical reform. He (and Engels) wrote *The Communist Manifesto* in 1848 on the eve of the revolution in France. After the collapse of the German revolution that same year, Marx fled from Prussia to London, where he spent the rest of his life,

often sick and impoverished, in exile. In addition to *The Communist Manifesto*, Marx's major works include *The German Ideology* (1845–1846) and *Das Kapital* (three volumes, 1867, 1885, and 1894). Here is the first chapter of *The Communist Manifesto*.

The history of all hitherto existing society is the history of class struggles. 1

Freeman and slave, patrician and plebeian, lord and serf, guild-master and journeyman, in a word, oppressor and oppressed, stood in constant opposition to one another, carried on uninterrupted, now hidden, now open fight, a fight that each time ended, either in a revolutionary re-constitution of society at large, or in the common ruin of the contending classes. 2

In the earlier epochs of history we find almost everywhere a complicated arrangement of society into various orders, a manifold gradation of social rank. In ancient Rome we have patricians, knights, plebeians, slaves; in the middle ages, feudal lords, vassals, guild-masters, journeymen, apprentices, serfs; in almost all of these classes, again, subordinate gradations. 3

The modern bourgeois society that has sprouted from the ruins of feudal society, has not done away with class antagonisms. It has but established new classes, new conditions of oppression, new forms of struggle in place of the old ones. 4

Our epoch, the epoch of the bourgeoisie, possesses, however, this distinctive feature; it has simplified the class antagonisms. Society as a whole is more and more splitting up into two great hostile camps, into two great classes directly facing each other: Bourgeoisie and Proletariat. 5

From the serfs of the middle ages sprang the chartered burghers of the earliest towns. From these burgesses the first elements of the bourgeoisie were developed. 6

The discovery of America, the rounding of the Cape, opened up fresh ground for the rising bourgeoisie. The East Indian and Chinese markets, the colonization of America, trade with the colonies, the increase in the means of exchange and in commodities generally, gave to commerce, to navigation, to industry, an impulse never before known, and thereby, to the revolutionary element in the tottering feudal society, a rapid development. 7

The feudal system of industry, under which industrial production was monopolized by closed guilds, now no longer sufficed for the growing wants of the new market. The manufacturing system took its place. The guild-masters were pushed on one side by the manufacturing middle-class: division of labor between the different corporate guilds vanished in the face of division of labor in each single workshop. 8

9 Meantime the markets kept ever growing, the demand ever rising. Even manufacture no longer sufficed. Thereupon, steam and machinery revolutionized industrial production. The place of manufacture was taken by the giant, Modern Industry, the place of the industrial middle-class, by industrial millionaires, the leaders of whole industrial armies, the modern bourgeois.

10 Modern industry has established the world market, for which the discovery of America paved the way. This market has given an immense development to commerce, to navigation, to communication by land. This development has, in its turn, reacted on the extension of industry; and in proportion as industry, commerce, navigation, railways extended, in the same proportion the bourgeoisie developed, increased its capital, and pushed into the background every class handed down from the Middle Ages.

11 We see, therefore, how the modern bourgeoisie is itself the product of a long course of development, of a series of revolutions in the modes of production and of exchange.

12 Each step in the development of the bourgeoisie was accompanied by a corresponding political advance of that class. An oppressed class under the sway of the feudal nobility, an armed and self-governing association in the mediaeval commune, here independent urban republic (as in Italy and Germany), there taxable "third estate" of the monarchy (as in France), afterwards, in the period of manufacture proper, serving either the semi-feudal or the absolute monarchy as a counterpoise against nobility, and, in fact, corner stone of the great monarchies in general, the bourgeoisie has at last, since the establishment of Modern Industry and of the world-market, conquered for itself, in the modern representative State, exclusive political sway. The executive of the modern State is but a committee for managing the common affairs of the whole bourgeoisie.

13 The bourgeoisie, historically, has played a most revolutionary part.

14 The bourgeoisie, wherever it has got the upper hand, has put an end to all feudal, patriarchal, idyllic relations. It has pitilessly torn asunder the motley feudal ties that bound man to his "natural superiors," and has left no other nexus between man and man than naked self-interest, than callous "cash payment." It has drowned the most heavenly ecstasies of religious fervor, of chivalrous enthusiasm, of Philistine sentimentalism, in the icy water of egotistical calculation. It has resolved personal worth into exchange value, and in place of the numberless indefeasible chartered freedoms, has set up that single, unconscionable freedom—Free Trade. In one word, for exploitation, veiled by religious and political illusions, it has substituted naked, shameless, direct, brutal exploitation.

15 The bourgeoisie has stripped of its halo every occupation

hitherto honored and looked up to with reverent awe. It has converted the physician, the lawyer, the priest, the poet, the man of science, into its paid wage laborers.

The bourgeoisie has torn away from the family its sentimental veil, and has reduced the family relation to a mere money relation. 16

The bourgeoisie has disclosed how it came to pass that the brutal display of vigor in the Middle Ages, which reactionists so much admire, found its fitting complement in the most slothful indolence. It has been the first to show what man's activity can bring about. It has accomplished wonders far surpassing Egyptian pyramids, Roman aqueducts and Gothic cathedrals; it has conducted expeditions that put in the shade all former Exoduses of nations and crusades. 17

The bourgeoisie cannot exist without constantly revolutionizing the instruments of production, and thereby the relations of production, and with them the whole relations of society. Conservation of the old modes of production in unaltered form was, on the contrary, the first condition of existence for all earlier industrial classes. Constant revolutionizing of production, uninterrupted disturbance of all social conditions, everlasting uncertainty and agitation distinguish the bourgeois epoch from all earlier ones. All fixed, fast frozen relations, with their train of ancient and venerable prejudices and opinions, are swept away, all new formed ones become antiquated before they can ossify. All that is solid melts into the air, all that is holy is profaned, and man is at last compelled to face with sober senses, his real conditions of life, and his relations with his kind. 18

The need of a constantly expanding market for its products chases the bourgeoisie over the whole surface of the globe. It must nestle everywhere, settle everywhere, establish connections everywhere. 19

The bourgeoisie has through its exploitation of the world-market given a cosmopolitan character to production and consumption in every country. To the great chagrin of reactionists, it has drawn from under the feet of industry the national ground on which it stood. All old-established national industries have been destroyed or are daily being destroyed. They are dislodged by new industries, whose introduction becomes a life and death question for all civilized nations, by industries that no longer work up indigenous raw material, but raw material drawn from the remotest zones; industries whose products are consumed, not only at home, but in every quarter of the globe. In place of the old wants, satisfied by the productions of the country, we find new wants, requiring for their satisfaction the products of distant lands and climes. In place of the old local and national seclusion and self-sufficiency, we have intercourse in every direction, universal interdependence of nations. And 20 as in material, so also in intellectual production. The intellectual creations of individual nations become common property. National onesidedness and narrowmindedness become more and more impossible, and from the numerous national local literatures there arises a world-literature.

The bourgeoisie, by the rapid improvement of all instruments of production, by the immensely facilitated means of communication draws all, even the most barbarian nations into civilization. The cheap prices of its commodities are the heavy artillery with which it batters down all Chinese walls, with which it forces the barbarians' intensely obstinate hatred of foreigners to capitulate. It compels all nations on pain of extinction, to adopt the bourgeois mode of production; it compels them to introduce what it calls civilization into their midst, *i. e.*, to become bourgeois themselves. In a word, it creates a world after its own image. 21

The bourgeoisie has subjected the country to the rule of the towns. It has created enormous cities, has greatly increased the urban population as compared with the rural, and has thus rescued a considerable part of the population from the idiocy of rural life. Just as it has made the country dependent on the towns, so it has made barbarian and semi-barbarian countries dependent on civilized ones, nations of peasants on nations of bourgeois, the East on the West. 22

The bourgeoisie keeps more and more doing away with the scattered state of the population, of the means of production, and of property. It has agglomerated population, centralized means of production, and has concentrated property in a few hands. The necessary consequence of this was political centralization. Independent, or but loosely connected provinces, with separate interests, laws, governments, and systems of taxation, became lumped together in one nation, with one government, one code of laws, one national class interest, one frontier and one customs tariff. 23

The bourgeoisie, during its rule of scarce one hundred years, has created more massive and more colossal productive forces than have all preceding generations together. Subjection of Nature's forces to man, machinery, application of chemistry to industry and agriculture, steam-navigation, railways, electric telegraphs, clearing of whole continents for cultivation, canalization of rivers, whole populations conjured out of the ground—what earlier century had even a presentiment that such productive forces slumbered in the lap of social labor? 24

We see then: the means of production and of exchange on whose foundation the bourgeoisie built itself up, were generated in feudal society. At a certain stage in the development of these means of production and of exchange, the conditions under which feudal society produced and exchanged, the feudal organization of agricul- 25 ture and manufacturing industry, in one word, the feudal relations of property became no longer compatible with the already developed productive forces; they became so many fetters. They had to burst asunder; they were burst asunder.

Into their places stepped free competition, accompanied by social and political constitution adapted to it, and by economical and political sway of the bourgeois class. 26

A similar movement is going on before our own eyes. Modern bourgeois society with its relations of production, of exchange and of property, a society that has conjured up such gigantic means of production and of exchange, is like the sorcerer, who is no longer able to control the powers of the nether world whom he has called up by his spells. For many a decade past, the history of industry and commerce is but the history of the revolt of modern productive forces against modern conditions of production, against the property relations that are the conditions for the existence of the bourgeoisie and of its rule. It is enough to mention the commercial crises that by their periodical return put on its trial, each time more threateningly, the existence of the entire bourgeois society. In these crises a great part not only of the existing products, but also of the previously created productive forces, are periodically destroyed. In these crises there breaks out an epidemic that, in all earlier epochs, would have seemed an absurdity—the epidemic of overproduction. Society suddenly finds itself put back into a state of momentary barbarism; it appears as if a famine, a universal war of devastation, had cut off the supply of every means of subsistence; industry and commerce seem to be destroyed; and why? Because there is too much civilization, too much means of subsistence, too much industry, too much commerce. The productive forces at the disposal of society no longer tend to further the development of the conditions of the bourgeois property; on the contrary, they have become too powerful for these conditions by which they are fettered, and as soon as they overcome these fetters they bring disorder into the whole of bourgeois society, endanger the existence of bourgeois property. The conditions of bourgeois society are too narrow to comprise the wealth created by them. And how does the bourgeoisie get over these crises? On the one hand by enforced destruction of a mass of productive forces; on the other, by the conquest of new markets, and by the more thorough exploitation of the old ones. That is to say, by paving the way for more extensive and more destructive crises, and by diminishing the means whereby crises are prevented. 27

The weapons with which the bourgeoisie felled feudalism to the ground are now turned against the bourgeoisie itself. 28

But not only has the bourgeoisie forged the weapons that bring death to itself; it has also called into existence the men who are 29 to wield those weapons—the modern working-class—the proletarians.

In proportion as the bourgeoisie, *i. e.*, capital, is developed, 30
in the same proportion is the proletariat, the modern working-class, developed, a class of laborers who live only so long as they find work, and who find work only so long as their labor increases capital. These laborers, who must sell themselves piecemeal, are a commodity, like every other article of commerce, and are consequently exposed to all the vicissitudes of competition, to all the fluctuations of the market.

Owing to the extensive use of machinery and to division of 31
labor, the work of the proletarians has lost all individual character, and, consequently, all charm for the workman. He becomes an appendage of the machine, and it is only the most simple, most monotonous and most easily acquired knack that is required of him. Hence, the cost of production of a workman is restricted almost entirely to the means of subsistence that he requires for his maintenance, and for the propagation of his race. But the price of a commodity, and also of labor, is equal to its cost of production. In proportion, therefore, as the repulsiveness of the work increases the wage decreases. Nay more, in proportion as the use of machinery and division of labor increases, in the same proportion the burden of toil increases, whether by prolongation of the working hours, by increase of the work enacted in a given time, or by increased speed of the machinery, etc.

Modern industry has converted the little workshop of the 32
patriarchal master into the great factory of the industrial capitalist. Masses of laborers, crowded into factories, are organized like soldiers. As privates of the industrial army they are placed under the command of a perfect hierarchy of officers and sergeants. Not only are they the slaves of the bourgeois class and of the bourgeois state, they are daily and hourly enslaved by the machine, by the overlooker, and above all, by the individual bourgeois manufacturer himself. The more openly this despotism proclaims gain to be its end and aim, the more petty, the more hateful and the more embittering it is.

The less the skill and exertion or strength implied in manual 33
labor, in other words, the more modern industry becomes developed, the more is the labor of men superseded by that of women. Differences of age and sex have no longer any distinctive social validity for the working class. All are instruments of labor, more or less expensive to use, according to their age and sex.

No sooner is the exploitation of the laborer by the manufac- 34
turer, so far at an end, that he receives his wages in cash, than he is set upon by the other portions of the bourgeoisie, the landlord, the shopkeeper, the pawnbroker, etc.

The lower strata of the middle class—the small tradespeople, 35

shopkeepers and retired tradesmen generally, the handicraftsmen and peasants—all these sink gradually into the proletariat, partly because their diminutive capital does not suffice for the scale on which Modern Industry is carried on, and is swamped in the competition with the large capitalists, partly because their specialized skill is rendered worthless by new methods of production. Thus the proletariat is recruited from all classes of the population.

The proletariat goes through various stages of development. 36
With its birth begins its struggle with the bourgeoisie. At first the contest is carried on by individual laborers, then by the workpeople of a factory, then by the operatives of one trade, in one locality, against the individual bourgeois who directly exploits them. They direct their attacks not against the bourgeois conditions of production, but against the instruments of production themselves; they destroy imported wares that compete with their labor, they smash to pieces machinery, they set factories ablaze, they seek to restore by force the vanished status of the workman of the Middle Ages.

At this stage the laborers still form an incoherent mass 37
scattered over the whole country, and broken up by their mutual competition. If anywhere they unite to form more compact bodies, this is not yet the consequence of their own active union, but of the union of the bourgeoisie, which class, in order to attain its own political ends, is compelled to set the whole proletariat in motion, and is moreover yet, for a time, able to do so. At this stage, therefore, the proletarians do not fight their enemies, but the enemies of their enemies, the remnants of absolute monarchy, the landowners, the non-industrial bourgeois, the petty bourgeoisie. Thus the whole historical movement is concentrated in the hands of the bourgeoisie, every victory so obtained is a victory for the bourgeoisie.

But with the development of industry the proletariat not only 38
increases in number; it becomes concentrated in greater masses, its strength grows and it feels that strength more. The various interests and conditions of life within the ranks of the proletariat are more and more equalized, in proportion as machinery obliterates all distinctions of labor, and nearly everywhere reduces wages to the same low level. The growing competition among the bourgeois, and the resulting commercial crises, make the wages of the workers even more fluctuating. The unceasing improvement of machinery, ever more rapidly developing, makes their livelihood more and more precarious; the collisions between individual workmen and individual bourgeois take more and more the character of collisions between two classes. Thereupon the workers begin to form combinations (Trades' Unions) against the bourgeois; they club together in order to keep up the rate of wages; they found permanent associations in order to

make provision beforehand for these occasional revolts. Here and there the contest breaks out into riots.

Now and then the workers are victorious, but only for a time. 39
The real fruit of their battle lies not in the immediate result but in the ever-expanding union of workers. This union is helped on by the improved means of communication that are created by modern industry, and that places the workers of different localities in contact with one another. It was just this contact that was needed to centralize the numerous local struggles, all of the same character, into one national struggle between classes. But every class struggle is a political struggle. And that union, to attain which the burghers of the Middle Ages with their miserable highways, required centuries, the modern proletarians, thanks to railways, achieve in a few years.

This organization of the proletarians into a class, and conse- 40
quently into a political party, is continually being upset again by the competition between the workers themselves. But it ever rises up again, stronger, firmer, mightier. It compels legislative recognition of particular interests of the workers by taking advantage of the divisions among the bourgeoisie itself. Thus the ten hours' bill in England was carried.

Altogether collisions between the classes of the old society 41
further, in many ways, the course of development of the proletariat. The bourgeoisie finds itself involved in a constant battle. At first with the aristocracy; later on, with those portions of the bourgeoisie itself whose interests have become antagonistic to the progress of industry; at all times, with the bourgeoisie of foreign countries. In all these battles it sees itself compelled to appeal to the proletariat, to ask for its help, and thus, to drag it into the political arena. The bourgeoisie itself, therefore, supplies the proletariat with its own elements of political and general education; in other words, it furnishes the proletariat with weapons for fighting the bourgeoisie.

Further, as we have already seen, entire sections of the ruling 42
class are, by the advance of industry, precipitated into the proletariat, or are at least threatened in their conditions of existence. These also supply the proletariat with fresh elements of enlightenment and progress.

Finally, in times when the class-struggle nears the decisive 43
hour, the process of dissolution going on within the ruling class—in fact, within the whole range of an old society—assumes such a violent, glaring character that a small section of the ruling class cuts itself adrift and joins the revolutionary class, the class that holds the future in its hands. Just as, therefore, at an earlier period, a section of the nobility went over to the bourgeoisie, so now a portion of the bourgeoisie goes over the the proletariat, and in particular a portion

of the bourgeois ideologists, who have raised themselves to the level of comprehending theoretically the historical movements as a whole.

Of all the classes that stand face to face with the bourgeoisie 44
to-day the proletariat alone is a really revolutionary class. The other classes decay and finally disappear in the face of modern industry; the proletariat is its special and essential product.

The lower middle class, the small manufacturer, the shop- 45
keeper, the artisan, the peasant, all these fight against the bourgeoisie, to save from extinction their existence as fractions of the middle class. They are therefore not revolutionary, but conservative. Nay more; they are reactionary, for they try to roll back the wheel of history. If by chance they are revolutionary, they are so only in view of their impending transfer into the proletariat; they thus defend not their present, but their future interests; they desert their own standpoint to place themselves at that of the proletariat.

The "dangerous class," the social scum, that passively rotting 46
mass thrown off by the lowest layers of old society, may, here and there, by swept into the movement by a proletarian revolution; its conditions of life, however, prepare it far more for the part of a bribed tool of reactionary intrigue.

In the conditions of the proletariat, those of the old society at 47
large are already virtually swamped. The proletarian is without property; his relation to his wife and children has no longer anything in common with the bourgeois family relations; modern industrial labor, modern subjection to capital, the same in England as in France, in America as in Germany, has stripped him of every trace of national character. Law, morality, religion, are to him so many bourgeois prejudices, behind which lurk in ambush just as many bourgeois interests.

All the preceding classes that got the upper hand sought to 48
fortify their already acquired status by subjecting society at large to their conditions of appropriation. The proletarians cannot become masters of the productive forces of society, except by abolishing their own previous mode of appropriation, and thereby also every other previous mode of appropriation. They have nothing of their own to secure and to fortify; their mission is to destroy all previous securities for and insurances of individual property.

All previous historical movements were movements of minor- 49
ities, or in the interest of minorities. The proletarian movement is the self-conscious, independent movement of the immense majority. The proletariat, the lowest stratum of our present society, cannot stir, cannot raise itself up without the whole superincumbent strata of official society being sprung into the air.

Though not in substance, yet in form, the struggle of the 50
proletariat with the bourgeoisie is at first a national struggle. The

proletariat of each country must, of course, first of all settle matters with its own bourgeoisie.

In depicting the most general phases of the development of the proletariat, we traced the more or less veiled civil war, raging within existing society, up to the point where that war breaks out into open revolution and where the violent overthrow of the bourgeoisie, lays the foundations for the sway of the proletariat. 51

Hitherto every form of society has been based, as we have already seen, on the antagonism of oppressing and oppressed classes. But in order to oppress a class, certain conditions must be assured to it under which it can, at least, continue its slavish existence. The serf, in the period of serfdom, raised himself to membership in the commune, just as the petty bourgeois, under the yoke of feudal absolutism, managed to develop into a bourgeois. The modern laborer, on the contrary, instead of rising with the progress of industry, sinks deeper and deeper below the conditions of existence of his own class. He becomes a pauper, and pauperism develops more rapidly than population and wealth. And here it becomes evident that the bourgeoisie is unfit any longer to be the ruling class in society, and to impose its conditions of existence upon society as an over-riding law. It is unfit to rule, because it is incompetent to assure an existence to its slave within his slavery, because it cannot help letting him sink into such a state that it has to feed him, instead of being fed by him. Society can no longer live under this bourgeoisie; in other words, its existence is no longer compatible with society. 52

The essential condition for the existence, and for the sway of the bourgeois class is the formation and augmentation of capital; the condition for capital is wage labor. Wage labor rests exclusively on competition between the laborers. The advance of industry, whose involuntary promoter is the bourgeoisie, replaces the isolation of the laborers, due to competition, by their involuntary combination, due to association. The development of Modern Industry, therefore, cuts from under its feet the very foundation on which the bourgeoisie produces and appropriates products. What the bourgeoisie therefore produces, above all, are its own grave diggers. Its fall and the victory of the proletariat are equally inevitable. 53

QUESTIONS

1. On what concept is Marx's economic history predicated? How did bourgeois society come into existence? What are the sins of the bourgeoisie? Why did the modern proletariat arise? How does it develop in relation to the bourgeoisie?

2. Explain the relationship of capital to class struggle.

3. What extended metaphor does Marx develop to describe the proletariat? Why is it particularly insightful? Cite other instances of figurative language in the essay.

4. Cite examples of words or phrases that Marx uses for both their intellectual and emotive value. What do they contribute to the overall tone of the essay?

5. How does the author develop the main contrast in this essay? What is his central purpose?

6. Demonstrate by reference to various paragraphs the ways in which Marx supports generalizations through the use of specific examples.

7. What are the strengths and weaknesses of this selection as a form of argumentation?

8. Does the last paragraph seem fully justified by the preceding analysis? Explain.

9. Do you agree or disagree with Marx's thesis that history is predicated on economic class struggles? Justify your answer.

10. a. Compare and contrast various conflicting groups, as you perceive them, in contemporary economic history.
b. Argue for or against Marx's assertion that the revolution of the proletariat against the bourgeoisie (the capitalist system) is inevitable.

8 Language, Writing, and Communication

HENRY DAVID THOREAU

On Keeping a Private Journal

Henry David Thoreau (1817–1862), author of the masterpiece *Walden* (1854), is one of the most important figures in American thought and literature. A social and political activist, Thoreau opposed the Mexican War, protested slavery, and refused to pay his poll taxes. As a naturalist, he believed in the preeminence of individualism and nature over technology, materialism, and nationalism. In 1845, he went to live at Walden Pond, "living deep and sucking the marrow out of life." Thoreau began writing a journal in 1837, and he used his journals to write his two most famous books, *A Week on the Concord and Merrimack Rivers* (1849) and *Walden.* No wonder that Thoreau, as he explains below at the age of 18, valued journal keeping.

As those pieces which the painter sketches for his own amusement in his leisure hours, are often superior to his most elaborate productions, so it is that ideas often suggest themselves to us spontaneously, as it were, far surpassing in beauty those which arise in the mind upon applying ourselves to any particular subject. Hence, could a machine be 1 invented which would instantaneously arrange on paper each idea as it occurs to us, without any exertion on our part, how extremely useful would it be considered! The relation between this and the practice of keeping a journal is obvious. But yet, the preservation of our scattered thoughts is to be considered an object but of minor importance.

Every one can think, but comparatively few can write, can express their thoughts. Indeed, how often do we hear one complain of his inability to express what he feels! How many have occasion to make the following remark, "I am sensible that I understand this perfectly, but am not able to find words to convey my idea to others". 2

But if each one would employ a certain portion of each day in looking back upon the time which has passed, and in writing down his thoughts and feelings, in reckoning up his daily gains, that he may be able to detect whatever false coins have crept into his coffers, and, as it were, in settling accounts with his mind, not only would his daily experience be greatly increased, since his feelings and ideas would thus be more clearly defined, but he would be ready to turn over a new leaf, having carefully perused the preceding one, and would not continue to glance carelessly over the same page, without being able to distinguish it from a new one. 3

Most of us are apt to neglect the study of our own characters, thoughts, and feelings, and for the purpose of forming our own minds, look to others, who should merely be considered as different editions of the same great work. To be sure, it would be well for us to examine the various copies, that we might detect any errors, but yet, it would be foolish for one to borrow a work which he possessed himself, but had not perused. 4

In fine, if we endeavoured more to improve ourselves by reflection, by making a business of thinking, and giving our thoughts form and expression, we should be led to "read not to contradict and confute, nor to believe and take for granted, nor to find talk and discourse, but to weigh and consider". 5

QUESTIONS

1. What reasons does Thoreau give for writing a journal?

2. Why does Thoreau value reflection? How does a journal forward that goal?

3. There are several metaphors, excluding the extended metaphor in paragraphs 3 and 4. Identify them. What do they have in common?

4. Do you believe that this essay is written in the typical style of a journal? If not, how does it differ? If so, how is it similar?

5. What evidence can you offer that this is an argumentative or persuasive essay?

6. Explain the analogy that introduces the essay. How does this analogy help Thoreau introduce his subject?

7. An extended metaphor is crucial to the development of this essay. Identify the metaphor and explain how it contributes to the organization of the essay.

8. Divide this essay into two parts. Where did you divide it and why?

9. Do you feel you do your best thinking when you write? What other devices, such as tape recorders, help you think?

10. a. For the next week, write a daily description of your life.
b. Write an essay on the value of keeping a private journal.

JOAN DIDION

On Keeping a Notebook

Joan Didion (1934–) is a novelist and essayist. Her most recent novel is *A Book of Common Prayer* (1977). She has also written two collections of essays, *Slouching towards Bethlehem* (1968) and *The White Album* (1979). Didion is an intensely introspective writer, who in her writing attempts to draw general significance from the particulars of her own life. Here she describes one of the sources of her work: her own notebooks.

"'That woman Estelle,'" the note reads, "'is partly the 1
reason why George Sharp and I are separated today.' *Dirty crepe-de-Chine wrapper, hotel bar, Wilmington RR, 9:45 a.m. August Monday morning.*"

Since the note is in my notebook, it presumably has some 2
meaning to me. I study it for a long while. At first I have only the most general notion of what I was doing on an August Monday morning in the bar of the hotel across from the Pennsylvania Railroad station in Wilmington, Delaware (waiting for a train? missing one? 1960? 1961? why Wilmington?), but I do remember being there. The woman in the dirty crepe-de-Chine wrapper had come down from her room for a beer, and the bartender had heard before the reason why George Sharp and she were separated today. "Sure," he said, and

went on mopping the floor. "You told me." At the other end of the bar is a girl. She is talking, pointedly, not to the man beside her but to a cat lying in the triangle of sunlight cast through the open door. She is wearing a plaid silk dress from Peck & Peck, and the hem is coming down.

Here is what it is: the girl has been on the Eastern Shore, and now she is going back to the city, leaving the man beside her, and all she can see ahead are the viscous summer sidewalks and the 3 a.m. long-distance calls that will make her lie awake and then sleep drugged through all the steaming mornings left in August (1960? 1961?). Because she must go directly from the train to lunch in New York, she wishes that she had a safety pin for the hem of the plaid silk dress, and she also wishes that she could forget about the hem and the lunch and stay in the cool bar that smells of disinfectant and malt and make friends with the woman in the crepe-de-Chine wrapper. She is afflicted by a little self-pity, and she wants to compare Estelles. That is what that was all about. 3

Why did I write it down? In order to remember, of course, but exactly what was it I wanted to remember? How much of it actually happened? Did any of it? Why do I keep a notebook at all? It is easy to deceive oneself on all those scores. The impulse to write things down is a peculiarly compulsive one, inexplicable to those who do not share it, useful only accidentally, only secondarily, in the way that any compulsion tries to justify itself. I suppose that it begins or does not begin in the cradle. Although I have felt compelled to write things down since I was five years old, I doubt that my daughter ever will, for she is a singularly blessed and accepting child, delighted with life exactly as life presents itself to her, unafraid to go to sleep and unafraid to wake up. Keepers of private notebooks are a different breed altogether, lonely and resistant rearrangers of things, anxious malcontents, children afflicted apparently at birth with some presentiment of loss. 4

My first notebook was a Big Five tablet, given to me by my mother with the sensible suggestion that I stop whining and learn to amuse myself by writing down my thoughts. She returned the tablet to me a few years ago; the first entry is an account of a woman who believed herself to be freezing to death in the Arctic night, only to find, when day broke, that she had stumbled onto the Sahara Desert, where she would die of the heat before lunch. I have no idea what turn of a five-year-old's mind could have prompted so insistently "ironic" and exotic a story, but it does reveal a certain predilection for the extreme which has dogged me into adult life; perhaps if I were analytically inclined I would find it a truer story than any I might have told about Donald Johnson's birthday party or the day my cousin Brenda put Kitty Litter in the aquarium. 5

So the point of my keeping a notebook has never been, nor is it now, to have an accurate factual record of what I have been doing or thinking. That would be a different impulse entirely, an instinct for reality which I sometimes envy but do not possess. At no point have I ever been able successfully to keep a diary; my approach to daily life ranges from the grossly negligent to the merely absent, and on those few occasions when I have tried dutifully to record a day's events, boredom has so overcome me that the results are mysterious at best. What is this business about "shopping, typing piece, dinner with E, depressed"? Shopping for what? Typing what piece? Who is E? Was this "E" depressed, or was I depressed? Who cares? 6

In fact I have abandoned altogether that kind of pointless entry; instead I tell what some would call lies. "That's simply not true," the members of my family frequently tell me when they come up against my memory of a shared event. "The party was *not* for you, the spider was *not* a black widow, *it wasn't that way at all.*" Very likely they are right, for not only have I always had trouble distinguishing between what happened and what merely might have happened, but I remain unconvinced that the distinction, for my purposes, matters. The cracked crab that I recall having for lunch the day my father came home from Detroit in 1945 must certainly be embroidery, worked into the day's pattern to lend verisimilitude; I was ten years old and would not now remember the cracked crab. The day's events did not turn on cracked crab. And yet it is precisely that fictitious crab that makes me see the afternoon all over again, a home movie run all too often, the father bearing gifts, the child weeping, an exercise in family love and guilt. Or that is what it was to me. Similarly, perhaps it never did snow that August in Vermont; perhaps there never were flurries in the night wind, and maybe no one else felt the ground hardening and summer already dead even as we pretended to bask in it, but that was how it felt to me, and it might as well have snowed, could have snowed, did snow. 7

How it felt to me: that is getting closer to the truth about a notebook. I sometimes delude myself about why I keep a notebook, imagine that some thrifty virtue derives from preserving everything observed. See enough and write it down, I tell myself, and then some morning when the world seems drained of wonder, some day when I am only going through the motions of doing what I am supposed to do, which is write—on that bankrupt morning I will simply open my notebook and there it will all be, a forgotten account with accumulated interest, paid passage back to the world out there: dialogue overheard in hotels and elevators and at the hatcheck counter in Pavillon (one middle-aged man shows his hatcheck to another and says, "That's my old football number"); impressions of Bettina Aptheker and Benjamin Sonnenberg and Teddy ("Mr. Acapulco") 8

Stauffer; careful *apercus* about tennis bums and failed fashion models and Greek shipping heiresses, one of whom taught me a significant lesson (a lesson I could have learned from F. Scott Fitzgerald, but perhaps we all must meet the very rich for ourselves) by asking, when I arrived to interview her in her orchid-filled sitting room on the second day of a paralyzing New York blizzard, whether it was snowing outside.

I imagine, in other words, that the notebook is about other 9
people. But of course it is not. I have no real business with what one stranger said to another at the hat-check counter in Pavillon; in fact I suspect that the line "That's my old football number" touched not my own imagination at all, but merely some memory of something once read, probably "The Eighty-Yard Run." Nor is my concern with a woman in a dirty crepe-de-Chine wrapper in a Wilmington bar. My stake is always, of course, in the unmentioned girl in the plaid silk dress. *Remember what it was to be me:* that is always the point.

It is a difficult point to admit. We are brought up in the ethic 10
that others, any others, all others, are by definition more interesting than ourselves; taught to be diffident, just this side of self-effacing. ("You're the least important person in the room and don't forget it," Jessica Mitford's governess would hiss in her ear on the advent of any social occasion; I copied that into my notebook because it is only recently that I have been able to enter a room without hearing some such phrase in my inner ear.) Only the very young and the very old may recount their dreams at breakfast, dwell upon self, interrupt with memories of beach picnics and favorite Liberty lawn dresses and the rainbow trout in a creek near Colorado Springs. The rest of us are expected, rightly, to affect absorption in other people's favorite dresses, other people's trout.

And so we do. But our notebooks give us away, for however 11
dutifully we record what we see around us, the common denominator of all we see is always, transparently, shamelessly, the implacable "I." We are not talking here about the kind of notebook that is patently for public consumption, a structural conceit for binding together a series of graceful *pensées;* we are talking about something private, about bits of the mind's string too short to use, an indiscriminate and erratic assemblage with meaning only for its maker.

And sometimes even the maker has difficulty with the 12
meaning. There does not seem to be for example, any point in my knowing for the rest of my life that, during 1964, 720 tons of soot fell on every square mile of New York City, yet there it is in my notebook, labeled "FACT." Nor do I really need to remember that Ambrose Bierce liked to spell Leland Stanford's name "£eland $tanford" or that "smart women almost always wear black in Cuba," a fashion hint

without much potential for practical application. And does not the relevance of these notes seem marginal at best?:

> In the basement museum of the Inyo County Courthouse in Independence, California, sign pinned to a mandarin coat: "This MANDARIN COAT was often worn by Mrs. Minnie S. Brooks when giving lectures on her TEAPOT COLLECTION." Redhead getting out of car in front of Beverly Wilshire Hotel, chinchilla stole, Vuitton bags with tags reading:
>
> MRS. LOU FOX
> HOTEL SAHARA
> VEGAS

Well, perhaps not entirely marginal. As a matter of fact, Mrs. Minnie S. Brooks and her MANDARIN COAT pull me back into my own childhood, for although I never knew Mrs. Brooks and did not visit Inyo County until I was thirty, I grew up in just such a world, in houses cluttered with Indian relics and bits of gold ore and ambergris and the souvenirs my Aunt Mercy Farnsworth brought back from the Orient. It is a long way from that world to Mrs. Lou Fox's world, where we all live now, and is it not just as well to remember that? Might not Mrs. Minnie S. Brooks help me to remember what I am? Might not Mrs. Lou Fox help me to remember what I am not? 13

But sometimes the point is harder to discern. What exactly did I have in mind when I noted down that it cost the father of someone I know $650 a month to light the place on the Hudson in which he lived before the Crash? What use was I planning to make of this line by Jimmy Hoffa: "I may have my faults, but being wrong ain't one of them"? And although I think it interesting to know where the girls who travel with the Syndicate have their hair done when they find themselves on the West Coast, will I ever make suitable use of it? Might I not be better off just passing it on to John O'Hara? What is a recipe for sauerkraut doing in my notebook? What kind of magpie keeps this notebook? *"He was born the night the Titanic went down."* That seems a nice enough line, and I even recall who said it, but is it not really a better line in life than it could ever be in fiction? 14

But of course that is exactly it: not that I should ever use the line, but that I should remember the woman who said it and the afternoon I heard it. We were on her terrace by the sea, and we were finishing the wine left from lunch, trying to get what sun there was, a California winter sun. The woman whose husband was born the night the *Titanic* went down wanted to rent her house, wanted to go back to her children in Paris. I remember wishing that I could afford the house, which cost $1,000 a month. "Someday you will," she said 15 lazily. "Someday it all comes." There in the sun on her terrace it seemed easy to believe in someday, but later I had a low-grade afternoon hangover and ran over a black snake on the way to the supermarket and was flooded with inexplicable fear when I heard the checkout clerk explaining to the man ahead of me why she was finally divorcing her husband. "He left me no choice," she said over and over as she punched the register. "He has a little seven-month-old baby by her, he left me no choice." I would like to believe that my dread then was for the human condition, but of course it was for me, because I wanted a baby and did not then have one and because I wanted to own the house that cost $1,000 a month to rent and because I had a hangover.

It all comes back. Perhaps it is difficult to see the value in 16
having one's self back in that kind of mood, but I do see it; I think we are well advised to keep on nodding terms with the people we used to be whether we find them attractive company or not. Otherwise they turn up unannounced and surprise us, come hammering on the mind's door at 4 a.m. of a bad night and demand to know who deserted them, who betrayed them, who is going to make amends. We forget all too soon the things we thought we could never forget. We forget the loves and the betrayals alike, forget what we whispered and what we screamed, forget who we were. I have already lost touch with a couple of people I used to be; one of them, a seventeen-year-old, presents little threat, although it would be of some interest to me to know again what it feels like to sit on a river levee drinking vodka-and-orange-juice and listening to Les Paul and Mary Ford and their echoes sing "How High the Moon" on the car radio. (You see I still have the scenes, but I no longer perceive myself among those present, no longer could even improvise the dialogue.) The other one, a twenty-three-year-old, bothers me more. She was always a good deal of trouble, and I suspect she will reappear when I least want to see her, skirts too long, shy to the point of aggravation, always the injured party, full of recriminations and little hurts and stories I do not want to hear again, at once saddening me and angering me with her vulnerability and ignorance, an apparition all the more insistent for being so long banished.

It is a good idea, then, to keep in touch, and I suppose that 17
keeping in touch is what notebooks are all about. And we are all on our own when it comes to keeping those lines open to ourselves: your notebook will never help me, nor mine you. *"So what's new in the whiskey business?"* What could that possibly mean to you? To me it means a blonde in a Pucci bathing suit sitting with a couple of fat men by the pool at the Beverly Hills Hotel. Another man approaches, and they all regard one another in silence for a while. "So what's new in the whiskey business?" one of the fat men finally says by way of

welcome, and the blonde stands up, arches one foot and dips it in the pool, looking all the while at the cabana where Baby Pignatari is talking on the telephone. That is all there is to that, except that several years later I saw the blonde coming out of Saks Fifth Avenue in New York with her California complexion and a voluminous mink coat. In the harsh wind that day she looked old and irrevocably tired to me, and even the skins in the mink coat were not worked the way they were doing them that year, not the the way she would have wanted them done, and there is the point of the story. For a while after that I did not like to look in the mirror, and my eyes would skim the newspapers and pick out only the deaths, the cancer victims, the premature coronaries, the suicides, and I stopped riding the Lexington Avenue IRT because I noticed for the first time that all the strangers I had seen for years—the man with the seeing-eye dog, the spinster who read the classified pages every day, the fat girl who always got off with me at Grand Central—looked older than they once had.

It all comes back. Even that recipe for sauerkraut: even that 18
brings it back. I was on Fire Island when I first made that sauerkraut, and it was raining, and we drank a lot of bourbon and ate the sauerkraut and went to bed at ten, and I listened to the rain and the Atlantic and felt safe. I made the sauerkraut again last night and it did not make me feel any safer, but that is, as they say, another story.

QUESTIONS

1. Why does Didion mention "keeping" a notebook in her title? How is her essay about keeping rather than writing a notebook?

2. What sort of entries does Didion make in her notebooks? How and why does Didion alter the reality of the events she describes in her notebooks?

3. What is the function of the numerous rhetorical questions in the essay?

4. How does the style of Didion's notebooks differ from her regular writing style?

5. How do the introductory quote and other quotes from her notebook help Didion develop the theme of her essay?

6. Repetition is a key device used to unify the essay. Identify examples of important repetitions.

7. Identify topic sentences in the essay. How does Didion prepare us for the thesis through her topic sentences?

8. Analyze causal patterns of development that appear in the essay.

9. To a great degree, Didion is also describing the process of writing fiction in this essay. Do you think fiction is a lie? How is it also true?

10. a. Write an essay about some events that have occurred in your own past that you feel were significant to your growth.
b. Write an essay about trivial objects and events that nevertheless have been important to you.

BENJAMIN FRANKLIN

The Art of Writing

Benjamin Franklin (1706–1790), statesman, inventor, philanthropist, printer, scientist, diplomat, and author, was founding father not only of the American nation, but of American humor, language, and values. His *Poor Richard's Almanack* (1732–1757) and *Autobiography* (written between 1771 and 1789) have had a tremendous influence on American readers and authors. Addressing the printer of *The Philadelphia Gazette* in 1773, Franklin offers sound advice for "all lovers of Writing" who seek improvement.

1 There are few Men, of Capacity for making any considerable Figure in Life, who have not frequent Occasion to communicate their Thoughts to others in *Writing*; if not sometimes publickly as Authors, yet continually in the Management of their private Affairs, both of Business and Friendship: and since, when ill-express'd, the most proper Sentiments and justest Reasoning lose much of their native Force and Beauty, it seems to me that there is scarce any Accomplishment more necessary to a Man of Sense, than that of *Writing well* in his Mother Tongue: But as most other polite Acquirements, make a greater Appearance in a Man's Character, this however useful, is generally neglected or forgotten.

2 I believe there is no better Means of learning to write well, than this of attempting to entertain the Publick now and then in one of your Papers. When the Writer conceals himself, he has the Advantage of hearing the Censure both of Friends and Enemies, express'd with more Impartiality. And since, in some degree, it concerns the Credit of the Province, that such Things as are printed

be performed tolerably well, mutual Improvement seems to be the Duty of all Lovers of Writing: I shall therefore frankly request those of others in Return.

I have thought in general, that whoever would write so as not to displease good Judges, should have particular Regard to these three Things, viz. That his Performance be *smooth, clear,* and *short:* For the contrary Qualities are apt to offend, either the Ear, the Understanding, or the Patience. 3

'Tis an Observation of Dr. Swift, that modern Writers injure the Smoothness of our Tongue, by omitting Vowels wherever it is possible, and joining the harshest Consonants together with only an Apostrophe between; thus for *judged,* in it self not the smoothest of Words, they say *judg'd;* for *disturbed, disturb'd,* etc. It may be added to this, say another, that by changing *eth* into *s,* they have shortned one Syllable in a multitude of Words, and have thereby encreased, not only the *Hissing,* too offensive before, but also the great Number of Monosyllables, of which, without great Difficulty, a smooth Sentence cannot be composed. The Smoothness of a Period is also often Hurt by Parentheses, and therefore the best Writers endeavour to avoid them. 4

To write *clearly,* not only the most expressive, but the plainest Words should be chosen. In this, as well as in every other Particular requisite to Clearness, Dr. Tillotson is an excellent Example. The Fondness of some Writers for such Words as carry with them an Air of Learning, renders them unintelligible to more than half their Countrymen. If a Man would that his Writings have an Effect on the Generality of Readers, he had better imitate that Gentleman, who would use no Word in his Works that was not well understood by his Cook-maid. 5

A too frequent Use of Phrases ought likewise to be avoided by him that would write clearly. They trouble the Language, not only rendring it extreamly difficult to Foreigners, but make the Meaning obscure to a great number of English Readers. Phrases, like learned Words, are seldom used without Affectation; when, with all true Judges, the simplest Stile is the most beautiful. 6

But supposing the most proper Words and Expressions chosen, the Performance may yet be weak and obscure, if it has not *Method.* If a Writer would *persuade,* he should proceed gradually from Things already allow'd to those from which Assent is yet with-held, and make their Connection manifest. If he would *inform,* he must advance regularly from Things known to things unknown, distinctly without Confusion, and the lower he begins the better. It is a common Fault in Writers, to allow their Readers too much Knowledge: They begin with that which should be the Middle, and skipping 7 backwards and forwards, 'tis impossible for any one but he who is perfect in the Subject before, to understand their Work, and such an one has no Occasion to read it. Perhaps a Habit of using good Method, cannot be better acquired, than by learning a little Geometry or Algebra.

Amplification, or the Art of saying Little in Much, should only be allowed to Speakers. If they preach, a Discourse of considerable Length is expected from them, upon every Subject they undertake, and perhaps they are not stock'd with naked Thoughts sufficient to furnish it out. If they plead in the Courts, it is of Use to speak abundance, tho' they reason little; for the Ignorant in a Jury, can scarcely believe it possible that a Man can talk so much and so long without being in the Right. Let them have the Liberty then, of repeating the same Sentences in other Words; let them put an Adjective to every Substantive, and double every Substantive with a Synonima; for this is more agreeable than hauking, spitting, taking Snuff, or any other Means of concealing Hesitation. Let them multiply Definitions, Comparisons, Similitudes and Examples. Permit them to make a Detail of Causes and Effects, enumerate all the Consequences, and express one Half by Metaphor and Circumlocution: Nay, allow the Preacher to tell us whatever a Thing is negatively, before he begins to tell us what it is affirmatively; and suffer him to divide and subdivide as far as *Two and fiftiethly*. All this is not intolerable while it is not written. But when a Discourse is to be bound down upon Paper, and subjected to the calm leisurely Examination of nice Judgment, everything that is needless gives Offense; and therefore should be retrenched, that does not directly conduce to the End design'd. Had this been always done, many large and tiresome Folio's would have shrunk into Pamphlets, and many a Pamphlet into a single Period. However, tho' a multitude of Words obscure the Sense, and 'tis necessary to abridge a verbose Author in order to understand him; yet a Writer should take especial Care on the other Hand, that his Brevity doth not hurt his Perspicuity. 8

After all, if the Author does not intend his Piece for general Reading, he must exactly suit his Stile and Manner to the particular Taste of those he proposes for his Readers. Every one observes, the different Ways of Writing and Expression used by the different Sects of Religion; and can readily enough pronounce, that it is improper to use some of these Stiles in common, or to use the common Stile, when we address some of these Sects in particular. 9

To conclude, I shall venture to lay it down as a Maxim, *That no Piece can properly be called good, and well written, which is void of any Tendency to benefit the Reader, either by improving his Virtue or his Knowledge*. This Principle every Writer would do well to have in View, 10 whenever he undertakes to write. All Performances done for meer Ostentation of Parts, are really contemptible; and withal far more subject to the Severity of Criticism, than those more meanly written, wherein the Author appears to have aimed at the Good of others. For when 'tis visible to every one, that a Man writes to show his Wit only, all his Expressions are sifted, and his Sense examined, in the nicest and most ill-natur'd manner; and everyone is glad of an Opportunity to mortify him. But, what a vast Destruction would there be of Books, if they were to be saved or condemned on a Tryal by this Rule!

Besides, Pieces meerly humorous, are of all Sorts the hardest 11
to succeed in. If they are not natural, they are stark naught; and there can be no real Humour in an Affectation of Humour.

Perhaps it may be said, that an ill Man is able to write an ill 12
Thing well; that is, having an ill Design, and considering who are to be his Readers, he may use the properest Stile and Arguments to attain his Point. In this Sense, that is best wrote, which is best adapted to the Purpose of the Writer.

I am apprehensive, dear Readers, lest in this Piece, I should 13
be guilty of every Fault I condemn, and deficient in every Thing I recommend; so much easier it is to offer Rules than to practise them. I am sure, however, of this, that I am Your very sincere Friend and Servant.

QUESTIONS

1. Identify and explain the main qualities that Franklin recommends for sound writing.

2. What aspects of the style of his era does Franklin dislike? How, according to Franklin, do writers fail their audience?

3. What unique aspects of eighteenth-century language and style can you locate in this essay? Identify the allusions to Swift (paragraph 4) and Tillotson (paragraph 5).

4. Is this essay written primarily in an objective or subjective style? Give evidence to support your opinion.

5. What is the thesis of this essay? How does its placement in the essay reflect the orderliness of Franklin's reasoning?

6. Explain how Franklin uses illustration.

7. What methods of definition does Franklin use?

8. What paragraphs constitute the conclusion? How do you know? What is the special purpose of the conclusion?

9. Why is Franklin's advice on "writing well" as sound today as it was more than 250 years ago?

10. a. Using Franklin's essay as a guide, compose your own essay on writing well.
b. Compare and contrast the arts of speaking and writing.

S. I. HAYAKAWA

Words and Children

Samuel Ichize Hayakawa (1906–) began his career as a professor of linguistics and was the author of numerous books on language such as *Language in Thought and Action* (1941), *Our Language and Our World* (1959), and *Symbol, Status, and Personality* (1963). When Hayakawa became president of San Francisco State College, student unrest was at its height. By defending traditional values and, indeed, authority itself, Hayakawa became a national and controversial figure. His notoriety has propelled him into the United States Senate. The present essay reflects his original career as a semanticist.

Those who still believe, after all the writing that semanti- 1
cists have done, that semantics is a science of words, may be surprised to learn that semantics has the effect—at least, it has had on me and on many others—of reducing rather than increasing one's preoccupation with words. First of all, there is that vast area of nonverbal communication with children that we accomplish through holding, touching, rocking, caressing our children, putting food in their mouths, and all of the little attentions that we give them. These are all communication, and we communicate in this way for a long time before the children even start to talk.

Then, after they start to talk, there is always the problem of 2
interpretation. There is a sense in which small children are recent immigrants in our midst. They have trouble both in understanding and in using the language, and they often make errors. Many people (you can notice this in the supermarkets, especially with parents of two- and three-year-old children) get angry at their children when they don't seem to mind. Anyone standing within earshot of one of

these episodes can tell that the child just hasn't understood what the mother said. But the mother feels, "Well, I said it, didn't I? What's wrong with the child that he doesn't understand? It's English, isn't it?" But, as I say, the child is a recent immigrant in our midst and there are things that the child doesn't understand.

There are curious instances. Once, when our daughter was 3
three years old, she found the bath too hot and she said, "Make it warmer." It took me a moment to figure out that she meant, "Bring the water more nearly to the condition we call warm." It makes perfectly good sense looked at that way. Confronted with unusual formulations such as these which children constantly make, many of us react with incredible lack of imagination. Sometimes children are laughed at for making "silly statements," when it only requires understanding their way of abstracting and their way of formulating their abstractions to see that they are not silly at all.

Children are newcomers to the language. Learning a lan- 4
guage isn't just learning words; rules of the language are learned at the same time. Prove this? Very simple. Little children use a past tense like "I runned all the way to the park and I swimmed in the pool." "Runned" and "swimmed" are words they did not hear. They made them up by analogy from other past tenses they had heard. This means that they learned not only the vocabulary, they learned the rule for making the past tense—except that the English language doesn't follow its own rules. And when the child proves himself to be more logical than the English language, we take it out on the child—which is nonsense. Children's language should be listened to with great attentiveness and respect.

Again, when our daughter was three years old, I was 5
pounding away at my typewriter in my study and she was drawing pictures on the floor when she suddenly said, "I want to go see the popentole."

I kept typing. 6

Then I stopped and said, "What?!" 7

She said, "I want to see the popentole." 8

"Did you say *popentole?*" 9

I just stopped. It was a puzzle to figure out, but I did. In a few 10
seconds I said, "You mean like last Saturday, you want to go to Lincoln Park and see the totem pole?"

She said, "Yes." 11

And what was so warm about this, so wonderful about it, 12
was that having got her point across she played for another twenty minutes singing to herself, happy that she had communicated. I didn't say to her, "Okay, I'll take you next Sunday to see the popentole." The mere fact that she'd made her point and got it

registered was a source of satisfaction to her. And I felt very proud of myself at the time for having understood.

One of the things we tend to overlook in our culture is the tremendous value of the acknowledgment of message. Not, "I agree with you" or "I disagree with you" or "That's a wonderful idea" or "That's a silly idea," but just the acknowledgment, "I know exactly what you've said. It goes on the record. You said that." She said, "I want to go see the totem pole." I said, "Okay, you want to go see the totem pole." The acknowledgment of message says in effect, "I know you're around. I know what you're thinking. I acknowledge your presence." 13

There is also a sense in which a child understands far more than we suspect. Because a child doesn't understand words too well (and also because his nervous system is not yet deadened by years spent as a lawyer, accountant, advertising executive, or professor of philosophy), a child attends not only to what we say but to everything about us as we say it—tone of voice, gesture, facial expression, bodily tensions, and so on. A child attends to a conversation between grown-ups with the same amazing absorption. Indeed, a child listening is, I hope, like a good psychiatrist listening— or like a good semanticist listening—because she watches not only the words but also the nonverbal events to which words bear, in all too many cases, so uncertain a relationship. Therefore a child is in some matters quite difficult to fool, especially on the subject of one's true attitude toward her. For this reason many parents, without knowing it, are to a greater or lesser degree in the situation of the worried mother who said to the psychiatrist to whom she brought her child, "I tell her a dozen times a day that I love her, but the brat still hates me. Why, doctor?" 14

"Life in a big city is dangerous," a mother once said to me. "You hear so often of children running thoughtlessly out in the street and being struck by passing cars. They will never learn unless you keep telling them and telling them." This is the communication theory that makes otherwise pleasant men and women into nagging parents: You've got to keep telling them; then you've got to remind them; then tell 'em again. Are there no better ways to teach children not to run out into the street? Of course there are. I think it was done in our family without words. 15

Whenever my wife crossed the street with our boy Alan—he was then about three—she would come to a stop at the curb whether there was any traffic in sight or not, and look up and down the boulevard before crossing. It soon became a habit. One day I absentmindedly started crossing the street without looking up and down—the street was empty. Alan grabbed my coat and pulled me 16 back on the curb to look up and down before we started out again. Children love to know the right way to do things. They learn by imitation far more than by precept.

The uncritical confidence that many people place in words is a matter of constant amazement to me. When we were living in Chicago there was a concrete courtyard behind our apartment house. I heard a great deal of noise and shouting out there one day, and I looked out and saw a father teaching his boy to ride a bicycle. The father was shouting instructions: "Keep your head up. Now push down with your left foot. Now look out, you're running into the wall. Steer away from it. *Steer away from it!* Now push down with your right foot. Don't fall down!" and so on and so on. The poor boy was trying to keep his balance, manage the bicycle, obey his father's instructions all at the same time, and he looked about as totally confused as it is possible for a little boy to get. One thing we learn from general semantics, if we haven't learned it some other way already, is that there are limits to what can be accomplished in words. Learning to ride a bicycle is beyond those limits. Having sensed those limits, we become content to let many things take care of themselves without words. All this makes for a quieter household. 17

The anthropologist Ray Birdwhistell has undertaken a study that he calls "kinesics,"* which is the systematic examination of gesture and body motion in communication; this is a rich area of concern about which many students of human behavior have been much excited. But there is a danger in going too far in this direction—in going overboard to the extent of saying that words are of *no* importance. There are thousands of things children must know and enjoy that it is not possible for them to get *without* words. 18

The sense of what one misses through the lack of words has been brought home to us by the fact that our second boy, Mark, now twenty-nine, is seriously mentally retarded. At the age of six he was hardly able to talk at all. Now he talks quite a bit, but his speech is very difficult to understand; members of the family can understand it about half the time. He was always able to understand words with direct physical referents—watch, glass of water, orange juice, record-player, television, and so on. But there are certain things that exist only in words, like the concept of the future. I remember the following incident when he was six years old. He came across a candy bar at ten minutes to twelve when lunch was just about to be served. I tried to take it away from him and said, "Look, Mark, you can have it right after lunch. Don't eat it now. You can have it right after lunch." Well, when he was six all he could understand was that it was being 19

*Ray Birdwhistell, *Kinesics and Context*. Philadelphia: University of Pennsylvania Press, 1970.

taken away from him *now,* and the idea that there was a future in which he'd have it back was something he just couldn't get at the time. Of course, the concept of futurity developed later, but it took him much longer to develop it than it took the other children.

20 For human beings, the future, which exists *only in language,* is a wonderful dimension in which to live. That is, human beings can readily endure and even enjoy postponement; the anticipation of future pleasures is itself a pleasure. But futurity is something that has no physical referent like "a glass of water." It exists only in language. Mark's frequent frustrations and rage when he was younger were a constant reminder to us that all the warmth and richness of nonverbal communication, all that we could communicate by holding him and feeding him and patting his head and playing on the floor with him, were not enough for the purposes of human interaction. Organized games of any kind all have linguistically formulated rules. Take an organized game like baseball. Can there be a baseball without language? No, there can't. What's the difference between a ball and a strike? There are linguistically formulated rules by which we define the difference. All systematic games, even much simpler games that children play, have to have a language to formulate the rules. An enormous amount of human life is possible only with language, and without it one is very much impoverished.

QUESTIONS

1. Hayakawa says that as a semanticist he has learned that we don't only communicate through words. What other ways of communication does he mention?

2. Hayakawa also points out some of the advantages of language as a communicative skill. What are they?

3. Hayakawa uses two metaphors to explain a child's relation to language. What are they?

4. Cite examples of Hayakawa's use of scientific jargon. What does this suggest about the audience for which he is writing?

5. Explain how Hayakawa uses process to develop his essay.

6. Hayakawa makes several statements about communication. What are they? How does he use examples to illustrate these points?

7. Where does Hayakawa use personal examples? How do they contribute to the development of the essay?

8. Explain the importance of paragraphs 3, 14, and 18 to the development of the essay.

9. Hayakawa introduces the idea that we often communicate without words. What examples beyond the ones he mentions can you think of?

10. a. Write an essay describing how we use a nonverbal form of communication such as signals in sports, streetlights, or arts such as music, ballet, and painting.
b. Write an essay about the language of children based on your personal experience.

RUSSELL BAKER

Little Red Riding Hood Revisited

Russell Baker (1925–), humorist and journalist, has written a syndicated column called "The Observer" since 1962. His humor runs from allegorical satires of American politics and taste to witty criticisms of current jargon and slang. His column has been collected in such books as *An American in Washington* (1961), *No Cause for Panic (1964),* and *Poor Russell's Almanac* (1972). In this essay, Baker offers a brilliant parody of one of our best-known children's stories.

In an effort to make the classics accessible to contemporary readers, I am translating them into the modern American language. Here is the translation of "Little Red Riding Hood": 1

Once upon a point in time, a small person named Little Red Riding Hood initiated plans for the preparation, delivery and transportation of foodstuffs to her grandmother, a senior citizen residing at a place of residence in a forest of indeterminate dimension. 2

In the process of implementing this program, her incursion into the forest was in midtransportation process when it attained interface with an alleged perpetrator. This individual, a wolf, made inquiry as to the whereabouts of Little Red Riding Hood's goal as well as inferring that he was desirous of ascertaining the contents of Little Red Riding Hood's foodstuffs basket, and all that. 3

"It would be inappropriate to lie to me," the wolf said, displaying his huge jaw capability. Sensing that he was a mass of repressed hostility intertwined with acute alienation, she indicated. 4

"I see you indicating," the wolf said, "but what I don't see is whatever it is you're indicating at, you dig?" 5

Little Red Riding Hood indicated more fully, making one thing perfectly clear—to wit, that it was to her grandmother's residence and with a consignment of foodstuffs that her mission consisted of taking her to and with. 6

At this point in time the wolf moderated his rhetoric and proceeded to grandmother's residence. The elderly person was then subjected to the disadvantages of total consumption and transferred to residence in the perpetrator's stomach. 7

"That will raise the old woman's consciousness," the wolf said to himself. He was not a bad wolf, but only a victim of an oppressive society, a society that not only denied wolves' rights, but actually boasted of its capacity for keeping the wolf from the door. An interior malaise made itself manifest inside the wolf. 8

"Is that the national malaise I sense within my digestive tract?" wondered the wolf. "Or is it the old person seeking to retaliate for her consumption by telling wolf jokes to my duodenum?" It was time to make a judgment. The time was now, the hour had struck, the body lupine cried out for decision. The wolf was up to the challenge. He took two stomach powders right away and got into bed. 9

The wolf had adopted the abdominal-distress recovery posture when Little Red Riding Hood achieved his presence. 10

"Grandmother," she said, "your ocular implements are of an extraordinary order of magnitude." 11

"The purpose of this enlarged viewing capability," said the wolf, "is to enable your image to register a more precise impression upon my sight systems." 12

"In reference to your ears," said Little Red Riding Hood, "it is noted with the deepest respect that far from being underprivileged, their elongation and enlargement appear to qualify you for unparalleled distinction." 13

"I hear you loud and clear, kid," said the wolf, "but what about these new choppers?" 14

"If it is not inappropriate," said Little Red Riding Hood, "it might be observed that with your new miracle masticating products you may even be able to chew taffy again." 15

This observation was followed by the adoption of an aggressive posture on the part of the wolf and the assertion that it was also possible for him, due to the high efficiency ratio of his jaw, to consume little persons, plus, as he stated, his firm determination to do so at once without delay and with all due process and propriety, notwithstanding the fact that the ingestion of one entire grandmother had already provided twice his daily recommended cholesterol intake. 16

There ensued flight by Little Red Riding Hood accompanied 17 by pursuit in respect to the wolf and a subsequent intervention on the part of a third party, heretofore unnoted in the record.

Due to the firmness of the intervention, the wolf's stomach underwent ax-assisted aperture with the result that Red Riding Hood's grandmother was enabled to be removed with only minor discomfort. 18

The wolf's indigestion was immediately alleviated with such effectiveness that he signed a contract with the intervening third party to perform with grandmother in a television commercial demonstrating the swiftness of this dramatic relief for stomach discontent. 19

"I'm going to be on television," cried grandmother. 20

And they all joined her happily in crying, "What a phenomena!" 21

QUESTIONS

1. What difference is there between the conclusion of this tale and that of the traditional fairy tale? Why do you think Baker has changed the ending?

2. What political allusions are made in this essay?

3. Baker uses several flaws of modern language such as repetition, excessive Latinisms, and jargon. Find examples of these flaws.

4. Diction is also a crucial issue in this essay. How does word choice contribute to Baker's satire?

5. What is Baker's thesis? Is it ever explicitly stated? Why, or why not?

6. This essay is, of course, a narrative. Identify those transitional devices that keep the development of the story clear.

7. Although never explicitly stated, this essay compares modern American English with traditional English. Are there any suggestions of this in the essay?

8. Why does Baker introduce fads, political and social, into a satire on modern English? How do they modify the meaning of the essay?

9. Do you think Baker's critique of modern English is correct or snobbish? Explain. Can you give reasons we should write the way we do?

10. a. Write a modern version of another fairy tale, using Baker's satiric methods.
b. Locate a particularly egregious example of modern American English and write a critique of its faults.

Names

Mary McCarthy (1912–) was born in Seattle, Washington, and attended Vassar College; among her friends at Vassar were future poets Elizabeth Bishop and Muriel Rukeyser. Her second husband, Edmund Wilson, was first to encourage her to write fiction. A novelist, journalist, essayist, and literary critic, McCarthy is the author of *The Company She Keeps* (1942), *The Groves of Academe* (1952), *Memories of a Catholic Girlhood* (1957), *The Group* (1963), and *Vietnam* (1967), among numerous works. Known for her elegant style and sharp comic wit, McCarthy has been a foremost—and controversial—literary figure for more than three decades. In the following essay, she reflects with witty and penetrating vigor on the importance of names at Forest Ridge Convent in Seattle, which she attended as a child.

Anna Lyons, Mary Louise Lyons, Mary von Phul, Emilie von Phul, Eugenia McLellan, Majorie McPhail, Marie-Louise L'Abbé, Mary Danz, Julia Dodge, Mary Fordyce Blake, Janet Preston—these were the names (I can still tell them over like a rosary) of some of the older girls in the convent: the Virtues and Graces. The virtuous ones wore wide blue or green moire goodconduct ribbons, bandoleer-style, across their blue serge uniforms; the beautiful ones wore rouge and powder or at least were reputed to do so. Our class, the eighth grade, wore pink ribbons (I never got one myself) and had names like Patricia ("Pat") Sullivan, Eileen Donohoe, and Joan Kane. We were inelegant even in this respect; the best name we could show, among us, was Phyllis ("Phil") Chatham, who boasted that her father's name, Ralph, was pronounced "Rafe" as in England. 1

Names had a great importance for us in the convent, and foreign names, French, German, or plain English (which, to us, were foreign, because of their Protestant sound), bloomed like prize roses among a collection of spuds. Irish names were too common in the school to have any prestige either as surnames (Gallagher, Sheehan, Finn, Sullivan, McCarthy) or as Christian names (Kathleen, Eileen). Anything exotic had value: an "olive" complexion, for example. The pet girl of the convent was a fragile Jewish girl named Susie Lowenstein, who had pale red-gold hair and an exquisite retroussé nose, which, if we had had it, might have been called "pug." We liked her name too and the name of a child in the primary grades: Abbie Stuart Baillargeon. My favorite name, on the whole, though, was Emilie von Phul (pronounced "Pool"); her oldest sister, recently 2 graduated, was called Celeste. Another name that appealed to me was Genevieve Albers, Saint Genevieve being the patron saint of Paris who turned back Attila from the gates of the city.

All these names reflected the still-pioneer character of the 3
Pacific Northwest. I had never heard their like in the parochial school in Minneapolis, where "foreign" extraction, in any case, was something to be ashamed of, the whole drive being toward Americanization of first name and surname alike. The exceptions to this were the Irish, who could vaunt such names as Catherine O'Dea and the name of my second cousin, Mary Catherine Anne Rose Violet McCarthy, while an unfortunate German boy named Manfred was made to suffer for his. But that was Minneapolis. In Seattle, and especially in the convent of the Ladies of the Sacred Heart, foreign names suggested not immigration but emigration—distinguished exile. Minneapolis was a granary; Seattle was a port, which had attracted a veritable Foreign Legion of adventurers—soldiers of fortune, younger sons, gamblers, traders, drawn by the fortunes to be made in virgin timber and shipping and by the Alaska Gold Rush. Wars and revolutions had sent the defeated out to Puget Sound, to start a new life; the latest had been the Russian Revolution, which had shipped us, via Harbin, a Russian colony, complete with restaurant, on Queen Anne Hill. The English names in the convent, when they did not testify to direct English origin, as in the case of "Rafe" Chatham, had come to us from the South and represented a kind of internal exile; such girls as Mary Fordyce Blake and Mary McQueen Street (a class ahead of me; her sister was named Francesca) bore their double-barreled first names like titles of aristocracy from the ante-bellum South. Not all our girls, by any means, were Catholic; some of the very prettiest ones—Julia Dodge and Janet Preston, if I remember rightly—were Protestants. The nuns had taught us to behave with special courtesy to these strangers in our midst, and the whole effect was of some superior hostel for refugees of all the lost causes of the past hundred years. Money could not count for much in such an atmosphere; the fathers and grandfathers of many of our "best" girls were ruined men.

Names, often, were freakish in the Pacific Northwest, particu- 4
larly girls' names. In the Episcopal boarding school I went to later, in Tacoma, there was a girl called De Vere Utter, and there was a girl called Rocena and another called Hermonie. Was Rocena a mistake for Rowena and Hermonie for Hermoine? And was Vere, as we called her, Lady Clara Vere de Vere? Probably. You do not hear names like those often, in any case, east of the Cascade Mountains; they belong to the frontier, where books and libraries were few and memory seems to have been oral, as in the time of Homer.

Names have more significance for Catholics than they do for 5 other people; Christian names are chosen for the spiritual qualities of the saints they are taken from; Protestants used to name their children out of the Old Testament and now they name them out of novels and plays, whose heroes and heroines are perhaps the new patron saints of a secular age. But with Catholics it is different. The saint a child is named for is supposed to serve, literally, as a model or pattern to imitate; your name is your fortune and it tells you what you are or must be. Catholic children ponder their names for a mystic meaning, like birthstones; my own, I learned, besides belonging to the Virgin and Saint Mary of Egypt, originally meant "bitter" or "star of the sea." My second name, Thérése, could dedicate me either to Saint Theresa or to the saint called the Little Flower, Soeur Thérése of Lisieux, on whom God was supposed to have descended in the form of a shower of roses. At Confirmation, I had added a third name (for Catholics then rename themselves, as most nuns do, yet another time, when they take orders); on the advice of a nun, I had taken "Clementina," after Saint Clement, an early pope—a step I soon regretted on account of "My Darling Clementine" and her number nine shoes. By the time I was in the convent, I would no longer tell anyone what my Confirmation name was. The name I had nearly picked was "Agnes," after a little Roman virgin martyr, always shown with a lamb, because of her purity. But Agnes would have been just as bad, I recognized in Forest Ridge Convent—not only because of the possibility of "Aggie," but because it was subtly, indefinably *wrong* in itself. Agnes would have made me look like an ass.

The fear of appearing ridiculous first entered my life, as a 6
governing motive, during my second year in the convent. Up to then, a desire for prominence had decided many of my actions and, in fact, still persisted. But in the eighth grade, I became aware of mockery and perceived that I could not seek prominence without attracting laughter. Other people could, but I couldn't. This laughter was proceeding, not from my classmates, but from the girls of the class just above me, in particular from two boon companions. Elinor Heffernan and Mary Harty, a clownish pair—oddly assorted in size and shape, as teams of clowns generally are, one short, plump, and baby-faced, the other tall, lean, and owlish—who entertained the high-school department by calling attention to the oddities of the younger girls. Nearly every school has such a pair of satirists, whose marks are generally low and who are tolerated just because of their laziness and non-conformity; one of them (in this case, Mary Harty, the plump one) usually appears to be half asleep. Because of their low standing, their indifference to appearances, the sad state of their uniforms, their clowning is taken to be harmless, which, on the whole, it is, their object being not to wound but to divert; such girls

are bored in school. We in the eighth grade sat directly in front of the two wits in study hall, so that they had us under close observation; yet at first I was not afraid of them, wanting, if anything, to identify myself with their laughter, to be initiated into the joke. One of their specialties was giving people nicknames, and it was considered an honor to be the first in the eighth grade to be let in by Elinor and Mary on their latest invention. This often happened to me; they would tell me, on the playground, and I would tell the others. As their intermediary, I felt myself almost their friend and it did not occur to me that I might be next on their list.

I had achieved prominence not long before by publicly losing my faith and regaining it at the end of a retreat. I believe Elinor and Mary questioned me about this on the playground, during recess, and listened with serious, respectful faces while I told them about my conversations with the Jesuits. Those serious faces ought to have been an omen, but if the two girls used what I had revealed to make fun of me, it must have been behind my back. I never heard any more of it, and yet just at this time I began to feel something, like a cold breath on the nape of my neck, that made me wonder whether the new position I had won for myself in the convent was as secure as I imagined. I would turn around in study hall and find the two girls looking at me with speculation in their eyes. 7

It was just at this time, too, that I found myself in a perfectly absurd situation, a very private one, which made me live, from month to month, in horror of discovery. I had waked up one morning, in my convent room, to find a few small spots of blood on my sheet; I had somehow scratched a trifling cut on one of my legs and opened it during the night. I wondered what to do about this, for the nuns were fussy about bedmaking, as they were about our white collars and cuffs, and if we had an inspection these spots might count against me. It was best, I decided, to ask the nun on dormitory duty, tall, stout Mother Slattery, for a clean bottom sheet, even though she might scold me for having scratched my leg in my sleep and order me to cut my toenails. You never know what you might be blamed for. But Mother Slattery, when she bustled in to look at the sheet, did not scold me at all; indeed, she hardly seemed to be listening as I explained to her about the cut. She told me to sit down: she would be back in a minute. "You can be excused from athletics today," she added, closing the door. As I waited, I considered this remark, which seemed to me strangely munificent, in view of the unimportance of the cut. In a moment, she returned, but without the sheet. Instead, she produced out of her big pocket a sort of cloth girdle and a peculiar flannel object which I first took to be a bandage, and I began to protest that I did not need or want a bandage; all I needed was a bottom sheet. "The sheet can wait," said Mother Slattery, succinctly, 8 handing me two large safety pins. It was the pins that abruptly enlightened me; I saw Mother Slattery's mistake, even as she was instructing me as to how this flannel article, which I now understood to be a sanitary napkin, was to be put on.

"Oh no, Mother," I said, feeling somewhat embarrassed. "You don't understand. It's just a little cut, on my leg." But Mother, again, was not listening; she appeared to have grown deaf, as the nuns had a habit of doing when what you were saying did not fit in with their ideas. And now that I knew what was in her mind, I was conscious of a funny constraint; I did not feel it proper to name a natural process, in so many words, to a nun. It was like trying not to think of their going to the bathroom or trying not to see the straggling irongray hair coming out of their coifs (the common notion that they shaved their heads was false). On the whole, it seemed better just to show her my cut. But when I offered to do so and unfastened my black stocking, she only glanced at my leg, cursorily. "That's only a scratch dear," she said. "Now hurry up and put this on or you'll be late for chapel. Have you any pain?" "No, no, Mother!" I cried. "You don't understand!" "Yes, yes, I understand," she replied soothingly, "and you will too, a little later. Mother Superior will tell you about it some time during the morning. There's nothing to be afraid of. You have become a woman." 9

"I know all about that," I persisted. "Mother, please listen. I just cut my leg. On the athletic field. Yesterday afternoon." But the more excited I grew, the more soothing, and yet firm, Mother Slattery became. There seemed to be nothing for it but to give up and do as I was bid. I was in the grip of a higher authority, which almost had the power to persuade me that it was right and I was wrong. But of course I was not wrong; that would have been too good to be true. While Mother Slattery waited, just outside my door, I miserably donned the equipment she had given me, for there was no place to hide it, on account of drawer inspection. She led me down the hall to where there was a chute and explained how I was to dispose of the flannel thing, by dropping it down the chute into the laundry. (The convent arrangements were very old-fashioned, dating back, no doubt, to the days of Louis Philippe.) 10

The Mother Superior, Madame MacIllvra, was a sensible woman, and all through my early morning classes, I was on pins and needles, chafing for the promised interview with her which I trusted would clear things up. *"Ma Mére,"* I would begin, "Mother Slattery thinks . . ." Then I would tell her about the cut and the athletic field. But precisely the same impasse confronted me when I was summoned to her office at recess-time. *I* talked about my cut, and *she* talked about becoming a woman. It was rather like a round, in which 11 she was singing "Scotland's burning, Scotland's burning," and I was singing "Pour on water, pour on water." Neither of us could hear the other, or, rather, I could hear her, but she could not hear me. Owing to our different positions in the convent she was free to interrupt me, whereas I was expected to remain silent until she had finished speaking. When I kept breaking in, she hushed me, gently, and took me on her lap. Exactly like Mother Slattery, she attributed all my references to the cut to a blind fear of this new, unexpected reality that had supposedly entered my life. Many young girls, she reassured me, were frightened if they had not been prepared. "And you, Mary, have lost your dear mother, who could have made this easier for you." Rocked on Madame MacIllvra's lap, I felt paralysis overtake me and I lay, mutely listening, against her bosom, my face being tickled by her white, starched, fluted wimple, while she explained to me how babies were born, all of which I had heard before.

There was no use fighting the convent. I had to pretend to 12
have become a woman, just as, not long before, I had had to pretend to get my faith back—for the sake of peace. This pretense was decidedly awkward. For fear of being found out by the lay sisters downstairs in the laundry (no doubt an imaginary contingency, but the convent was so very thorough), I reopened the cut on my leg, so as to draw a little blood to stain the napkins, which were issued me regularly, not only on this occasion, but every twenty-eight days thereafter. Eventually, I abondoned this bloodletting, for fear of lockjaw, and trusted to fate. Yet I was in awful dread of detection; my only hope, as I saw it, was either to be released from the convent or to become a woman in reality, which might take a year at least, since I was only twelve. Getting out of athletics once a month was not sufficient compensation for the farce I was going through. It was not my fault; they had forced me into it; nevertheless, it was I who would look silly—worse than silly; half mad—if the truth ever came to light.

I was burdened with this guilt and shame when the nickname 13
finally found me out. "Found me out," in a general sense, for no one ever did learn the particular secret I bore about with me, pinned to the linen band. "We've got a name for you,," Elinor and Mary called out to me, one day on the playground. "What is it?" I asked half hoping, half fearing, since not all their sobriquets were unfavorable. "Cye," they answered, looking at each other and laughing. "Si?" I repeated, supposing that it was based on Simple Simon. Did they regard me as a hick? "C.Y.E.," they elucidated, spelling it out in chorus. "The letters stand for something. Can you guess?" I could not and I cannot now. The closest I could come to it in the convent was "Clean Your Ears." Perhaps that was it, though in later life I have wondered whether it did not stand, simply, for "Clever Young Egg"

or "Champion Young Eccentric." But in the convent I was certain that it stood for something horrible, something even worse than dirty ears (as far as I knew, my ears were clean), something I could never guess because it represented some aspect of myself that the world could see and I couldn't, like a sign pinned on my back. Everyone in the convent must have known what the letters stood for, but no one would tell me. Elinor and Mary had made them promise. It was like halitosis; not even my best friend, my deskmate, Louise, would tell me, no matter how much I pleaded. Yet everyone assured me that it was "very good," that is, very apt. And it made everyone laugh.

This name reduced all my pretensions and solidified my 14
sense of *wrongness*. Just as I felt I was beginning to belong to the convent, it turned me into an outsider, since I was the only pupil who was not in the know. I liked the convent, but it did not like me, as people say of certain foods that disagree with them. By this, I do not mean that I was actively unpopular, either with the pupils or with the nuns. The Mother Superior cried when I left and predicted that I would be a novelist, which surprised me. And I had finally made friends; even Emilie von Phul smiled upon me softly out of her bright blue eyes from the far end of the study hall. It was just that I did not fit into the convent pattern; the simplest thing I did, like asking for a clean sheet, entrapped me in consequences that I never could have predicted. I was not bad; I did not consciously break the rules; and yet I could never, not even for a week, get a pink ribbon, and this was something I could not understand, because I was trying as hard as I could. It was the same case as with the hated name; the nuns, evidently, saw something about me that was invisible to me.

The oddest part was all that pretending. There I was, a 15
walking mass of lies, pretending to be a Catholic and going to confession while really I had lost my faith, and pretending to have monthly periods by cutting myself with nail scissors; yet all this had come about without my volition and even contrary to it. But the basest pretense I was driven to was the acceptance of the nickname. Yet what else could I do? In the convent, I could not live it down. To all those girls, I had become "Cye McCarthy." That was who I was. That was how I had to identify myself when telephoning my friends during vacations to ask them to the movies: "Hello, this is Cye." I loathed myself when I said it, and yet I succumbed to the name totally, making myself over into a sort of hearty to go with it–the kind of girl I hated. "Cye" was my new patron saint. This false personality stuck to me, like the name, when I entered public high school, the next fall, as a freshman, having finally persuaded my grandparents to take me out of the convent, although they could never get to the bottom of my reasons, since, as I admitted, the nuns were kind, and I

had made many nice new friends. What I wanted was a fresh start, a chance to begin life over again, but the first thing I heard in the corridors of the public high school was that name called out to me, like the warmest of welcomes: "Hi, there, Si!" That was the way they thought it was spelled. But this time I was resolute. After the first weeks, I dropped the hearties who called me "Si" and I never heard it again. I got my own name back and sloughed off Clementina and even Therese—the names that did not seem to me any more to be mine but to have been imposed on me by others. And I preferred to think that Mary meant "bitter" rather than "star of the sea."

QUESTIONS

1. According to McCarthy, what was the significance of names in her Catholic convent? What is the relationship of names to culture?

2. Describe the author's life in the convent school. How does she respond to her nickname? Why does she leave the convent school?

3. Locate "names" in the essay that have unusually vivid connotations for the author. What is the cumulative effect of the listing of so many names on the tone of the essay?

4. Why does the author use the word "names" at the beginning of paragraphs 1, 2, 3, 4, and 5? How does this one word contribute to the unity of the essay?

5. Does McCarthy use examples objectively or subjectively in this essay? Explain. Select one paragraph and show how the examples contribute to an understanding of McCarthy's view of the importance of names and "naming" things properly.

6. How does the author use personal experience as an example? What other types of example does she use?

7. Where do the patterns of explanation and description blend in this essay?

8. In what sense is this a definition essay? What is the thesis? What does the last paragraph contribute to the thesis?

9. Why do personal names actually mean certain things? What does your name mean? What does it reveal of you?

10. a. Write about your nickname or the nicknames of a group of friends. b. Evaluate the importance of names and naming as symbolic acts that tell us about ourselves and our culture.

Expressive Language

Imamu Amiri Baraka (1934–) is a playwright, novelist, editor, essayist, and community leader. His most famous work, the play *Dutchman* (1964), is about the often destructive relations between blacks and whites in America. During his career, Baraka has, through the powerful use of the black idiom, introduced both whites and blacks to the richness of black culture. Here, he explores the causes behind the connotations of particular words in black and white English.

Speech is the effective form of a culture. Any shape or cluster of human history still apparent in the conscious and unconscious habit of groups of people is what I mean by culture. All culture is necessarily profound. The very fact of its longevity, of its being what it is, *culture,* the epic memory of practical tradition, means that it is profound. But the inherent profundity of culture does not necessarily mean that its *uses* (and they are as various as the human condition) will be profound. German culture is profound. Generically. Its uses, however, are specific, as are all uses . . . of ideas, inventions, products of nature. And specificity, as a right and passion of human life, breeds what it breeds as a result of its context. 1

Context, in this instance, is most dramatically social. And the social, though it must be rooted, as are all evidences of existence, in culture, depends for its impetus for the most part on a multiplicity of influences. Other cultures, for instance. Perhaps, and this is a common occurrence, the reaction or interreaction of one culture on another can produce a social context that will extend or influence any culture in many strange directions. 2

Social also means *economic,* as any reader of nineteenth-century European philosophy will understand. The economic is part of the social—and in our time much more so than what we have known as the spiritual or metaphysical, because the most valuable canons of power have either been reduced or traduced into stricter economic terms. That is, there has been a shift in the actual meaning of the world since Dante lived. As if Brooks Adams were right. Money does not mean the same thing to me it must mean to a rich man. I cannot, right now, think of one meaning to name. This is not so simple to understand. Even as a simple term of the English language, *money* does not possess the same meanings for the rich man as it does 3 for me, a lower-middle-class American, albeit of laughably "aristocratic" pretensions. What possibly can "money" mean to a poor man? And I am not talking now about those courageous products of our permissive society who walk knowledgeably into "poverty" as they would into a public toilet. I mean, The Poor.

I look in my pocket; I have seventy cents. Possibly I can buy a beer. A quart of ale, specifically. Then I will have twenty cents with which to annoy and seduce my fingers when they wearily search for gainful employment. I have no idea at this moment what that seventy cents will mean to my neighbor around the corner, a poor Puerto Rican man I have seen hopefully watching my plastic garbage can. But I am certain it cannot mean the same thing. Say to David Rockefeller, "I have money," and he will think you mean something entirely different. That is, if you also dress the part. He would not for a moment think, "Seventy cents." But then neither would many New York painters. 4

Speech, the way one describes the natural proposition of being alive, is much more crucial than even most artists realize. Semantic philosophers are certainly correct in their emphasis on the final dictation of words over their users. But they often neglect to point out that, after all, it is the actual importance, *power*, of the words that remains so finally crucial. Words have users, but as well, users have words. And it is the users that establish the world's realities. Realities being those fantasies that control your immediate span of life. Usually they are not your own fantasies, *i.e.*, they belong to governments, traditions, etc., which, it must be clear by now, can make for conflict with the singular human life all ways. The fantasy of America might hurt you, but it is what should be meant when one talks of "reality." Not only the things you can touch or see, but the things that make such touching or seeing "normal." Then words, like their users, have a hegemony. Socially—which is final, right now. If you are some kind of artist, you naturally might think this is not so. There is the future. But *immortality* is a kind of drug, I think—one that leads to happiness at the thought of death. Myself, I would rather live forever . . . just to make sure. 5

The social hegemony, one's position in society, enforces more specifically one's terms (even the vulgar have "pull"). Even to the mode of speech. But also it makes these terms an available explanation of any social hierachy, so that the words themselves become, even informally, laws. And of course they are usually very quickly stitched together to make formal statutes only fools or the faithfully intrepid would dare to question beyond immediate necessity. 6

The culture of the powerful is very infectious for the sophisti- 7 cated, and strongly addictive. To be any kind of "success" one must be fluent in this culture. Know the words of the users, the semantic rituals of power. This is a way into wherever it is you are not now, but wish, very desperately, to get into.

Even speech then signals a fluency in this culture. A knowledge at least. "He's an educated man," is the barest acknowledgment of such fluency . . . in any time. "He's hip," my friends might say. They connote a similar entrance. 8

And it is certainly the meanings of words that are most important, even if they are no longer consciously acknowledged, but merely, by their use, trip a familiar lever of social accord. To recreate instantly the understood hierarchy of social, and by doing that, cultural, importance. And cultures are thought by most people in the world to do their business merely by being hierarchies. Certainly this is true in the West, in as simple a manifestation as Xenophobia, the naïve bridegroom of antihuman feeling, or in economic terms, Colonialism. For instance, when the first Africans were brought into the New World, it was thought that it was all right for them to be slaves because "they were heathens." It is a perfectly logical assumption. 9

And it follows, of course, that slavery would have been an even stranger phenomenon had the Africans spoken English when they first got here. It would have complicated things. Very soon after the first generations of Afro-Americans mastered this language, they invented white people called Abolitionists. 10

Words' meanings, but also the rhythm and syntax that frame and propel their concatenation, seek their culture as the final reference for what they are describing of the world. An A flat played twice on the same saxophone by two different men does not have to sound the same. If these men have different ideas of what they want this note to do, the note will not sound the same. Culture is the form, the overall structure of organized thought (as well as emotion and spiritual pretension). There are many cultures. Many ways of organizing thought, or having thought organized. That is, the form of thought's passage through the world will take on as many diverse shapes as there are diverse groups of travelers. Environment is one organizer of *groups,* at any level of its meaning. People who live in Newark, New Jersey, are organized, for whatever purpose, as Newarkers. It begins that simply. Another manifestation, at a slightly more complex level, can be the fact that blues singers from the Midwest sing through their noses. There is an explanation past the geographical, but that's the idea in tabloid. And singing through the nose does propose that the definition of singing be altered . . . even if ever so slightly. (At this point where someone's definitions 11 must be changed, we are flitting around at the outskirts of the old city of Aesthetics. A solemn ghost town. Though some of the bones of reason can still be gathered there.)

But we still need definitions, even if there already are many. 12
The dullest men are always satisfied that a dictionary lists everything in the world. They don't care that you may find out something *extra,* which one day might even be valuable to them. Of course, by that time it might even be in the dictionary, or at least they'd hope so, if you asked them directly.

But for every item in the world, there are a multiplicity of 13
definitions that fit. And every word we use *could* mean something else. And at the same time. The culture fixes the use, and usage. And in "pluralistic" America, one should always listen very closely when he is being talked to. The speaker might mean something completely different from what we think we're hearing. "Where is your pot?"

I heard an old Negro street singer last week, Reverend Pearly 14
Brown, singing, "God don't never change!" This is a precise thing he is singing. He does not mean "God does not ever change!" He means "God don't never change!" The difference, and I said it was crucial, is in the final human reference . . . the form of passage through the world. A man who is rich and famous who sings, "God don't never change," is confirming his hegemony and good fortune . . . or merely calling the bank. A blind hopeless black American is saying something very different. He is telling you about the extraordinary order of the world. But he is not telling you about his "fate." Fate is a luxury available only to those fortunate citizens with alternatives. The view from the top of the hill is not the same as that from the bottom of the hill. Nor are most viewers at either end of the hill, even certain that, in fact, there is any other place from which to look. Looking down usually eliminates the possibility of understanding what it must be like to look up. Or try to imagine yourself as not existing. It is difficult, but poets and politicians try every other day.

Being told to "speak proper," meaning that you become 15
fluent with the jargon of power, is also a part of not "speaking proper." That is, the culture which desperately understands that it does not "speak proper," or is not fluent with the terms of social strength, also understands somewhere that its desire to gain such fluency is done at a terrifying risk. The bourgeois Negro accepts such risk as profit. But does *close-ter* (in the context of "jes a close-ter, walk withee") mean the same thing as *closer?* Close-ter, in the term of its user is, believe me, exact. It means a quality of existence, of actual physical disposition perhaps . . . in its manifestation as a *tone* and *rhythm* by which people live, most often in response to common modes of thought best enforced by some factor of environmental

emotion that is exact and specific. Even the picture it summons is different, and certainly the "Thee" that is used to connect the implied "Me" with, is different. The God of the damned cannot know the God of the damner, that is, cannot know he is God. As no Blues person can really believe emotionally in Pascal's God, or Wittgenstein's question, "Can the concept of God exist in a perfectly logical language?" Answer: "God don't never change."

Communication is only important because it is the broadest root of education. And all cultures communicate exactly what they have, a powerful motley of experience. 16

QUESTIONS

1. Why do words have power, according to Baraka? Explain the different ways Baraka says they have power.

2. Explain the different meanings of "money" and "God don't never change." Why, according to Baraka, do these words have different meanings?

3. How does Baraka account for different meanings of words? Give examples of low, slangy, vulgar diction and scholarly diction. What is the effect of both?

4. Identify any sentence fragments in the essay. How do they contribute to Baraka's style?

5. Detail how Baraka uses contrasts between the rich and the poor to explain his thesis.

6. Give three examples that Baraka offers to prove his point. Explain how examples help him to support his thesis.

7. What methods of definition does Baraka use?

8. Explain how Baraka uses allusion and metaphor to support his thesis.

9. Relate Baraka's description of the differences in words to the words that you or your parents use or words that you or your teachers use.

10. Write an expository essay in which you try to define the "social hegemony" of several words of your own choice.

MARSHALL McLUHAN

Sight, Sound, and the Fury

Marshall McLuhan (1911–1980) has been called the "oracle of the electronic age." He began his career as a literary scholar, but later shifted his studies from the message to the medium through which the message is transmitted. Beginning with *Understanding Media: The Extensions of Man* (1964) and *The Gutenberg Galaxy: The Making of Typographic Man* (1967), McLuhan attempted to show the influence of the technology of communication upon culture. His later books include *The Medium Is the Message: An Inventory to Effects* (1967) and *From Cliché to Archetype* (1972). The following essay exhibits in brief the interplay of technology, language, and culture that McLuhan investigated in his major work.

1 On his recent visit to America, Roy Campbell mentioned that when Dylan Thomas had discovered he could read poetry on the radio, this discovery transformed his later poetry for the better. Thomas discovered a new dimension in his language when he established a new relation with the public.

2 Until Gutenberg, poetic publication meant the reading or singing of one's poems to a small audience. When poetry began to exist primarily on the printed page, in the seventeenth century, there occurred that strange mixture of sight and sound later known as "metaphysical poetry" which has so much in common with modern poetry.

3 American colonization began when the only culture available to most men was that of the printed book. European culture was then, as now, as much an affair of music, painting, sculpture, and communication as it was of literature. So that to this day North Americans associate culture mainly with books. But, paradoxically, it is in North America that the new media of sight and sound have had the greatest popular sway. Is it precisely because we make the widest separation between culture and our new media that we are unable to see the new media as serious culture? Have four centuries of book-culture hypnotized us into such concentration on the content of books and the new media that we cannot see that the very form of any medium of communication is as important as anything that it conveys?

4 Ireland is perhaps the only part of the English-speaking

world where the oral tradition of culture has strongly persisted in spite of the printed page. And Ireland has given us Wilde, Shaw, Yeats, Synge, and Joyce in recent years—all of them masters of the magic of the spoken word. A Ballynooley farmer who returned to Ireland from America said to his neighbor: "In three years I didn't meet a man who could sing a ballad, let alone compose one on his feet."

The printed page was itself a highly specialized (and spatia- 5
lized) term of communication. In 1500 A.D. it was revolutionary. And Erasmus was perhaps the first to grasp the fact that the revolution was going to occur above all in the classroom. He devoted himself to the production of textbooks and to the setting up of grammar schools. The printed book soon liquidated two thousand years of manuscript culture. It created the solitary student. It set up the rule of private interpretation against public disputation. It established the divorce between "literature and life." It created a new and highly abstract culture because it was itself a mechanized form of culture. Today, when the textbook has yielded to the classroom project and the classroom as social workshop and discussion group, it is easier for us to notice what was going on in 1500. Today we know that the turn to the visual on one hand, that is, to photography, and to the auditory media of radio and public address systems on the other hand, has created a totally new environment for the educational process.

André Malraux has recently popularized the notion of the art 6
revolution of our time in his *Museum Without Walls.* His theme is that the picture book today can embrace a greater range of art than any museum. By bringing such a range of art within portable compass, however, it has changed even the painter's approach to painting. Again, it is not just a question of message, image, or content. The picture book as a museum without walls has for the artist a new technical meaning, just as for the spectator pictorial communication means a large but unconscious shift in his ways of thought and feeling.

We have long been accustomed to the notion that a person's 7
beliefs shape and color his existence. They provide the windows which frame, and through which he views, all events. We are less accustomed to the notion that the shapes of a technological environment are also idea-windows. Every shape (gimmick or metropolis), every situation planned and realized by man's factive intelligence, is a window which reveals or distorts reality. Today when power technology has taken over the entire global environment to be manipulated as the material of art, nature has disappeared with nature-poetry. And the effectiveness of the classroom has diminished

with the decline of the monopoly of book-culture. If Erasmus saw the classroom as the new stage for the drama of the printing-press, we can see today that the new situation for young and old alike is classrooms without walls. The entire urban environment has become aggressively pedagogic. Everybody and everything has a message to declare, a line to plug.

This is the time of transition from the commercial age, when it was the production and distribution of commodities which occupied the ingenuity of men. Today we have moved from the production of packaged goods to the packaging of information. Formerly we invaded foreign markets with goods. Today we invade whole cultures with packaged information, entertainment, and ideas. In view of the instantaneous global scope of the new media of sight and sound, even the newspaper is slow. But the press ousted the book in the nineteenth century because the book arrived too late. The newspaper page was not a mere enlargement of the book page. It was, like the movie, a new collective art form. 8

To retrace some of this ground, it will help to recall that in the *Phaedrus*, Plato argued that the new arrival of writing would revolutionize culture for the worse. He suggested that it would substitute reminiscence for thought and mechanical learning for the true dialect of the living quest for truth by discourse and conversation. It was as if he foresaw the library of Alexandria and the unending exegesis upon previous exegesis of the scholiasts and grammarians. 9

It would seem that the great virtue of writing is its power to arrest the swift process of thought for steady contemplation and analysis. Writing is the translation of the audible into the visual. In large measure it is the spatialization of thought. Yet writing on papyrus and parchment fostered a very different set of mental habits from those we associate with print and books. In the first place silent reading was unknown until the macadamized, streamlined surfaces of the printed page arrived to permit swift traverse of the eye alone. In the second place, difficulty of access to manuscripts impelled students to memorize so far as possible everything they read. This led to encyclopedism, but also to having on tap in oral discourse one's entire erudition. 10

The child at school in the Middle Ages had first to make his own copies of texts from dictation. He had next to compile his own grammar and lexicon and commonplace book. The arrival of plenty of cheap, uniform, printed texts changed all this. The mechanization of writing by means of the assembly line of movable type speedily expanded the range of available reading and just as quickly reduced the habit of oral discourse as a way of learning. During the sixteenth century, however, a degree of equilibrium persisted between oral and 11 written learning which we associate with the special excellence of Elizabethan drama, sermon, and poetry.

In the reverse direction, much of the vivid energy of American speech and writing in the twentieth century is the result of the movement away from book-culture towards oral communication. This non-literary direction of speech has been felt to a much smaller degree in England and in Europe during the same period. Radio in particular has encouraged the return to the panel discussion and the round-table. But the spontaneous move towards the seminar and class discussion as learning process has been helped by press and photography too, in so far as these have challenged the monopoly of the book. 12

Above all, the habits of the business community in demanding conference and discussion as the swift way of establishing insight into method and procedure in various specialized branches of business—these have prompted the new reliance on speech as a means of discovery. It is significant, for example, that the atomic physicists found that only by daily, face-to-face association could they get on with their tasks during the past war. 13

It has long been a truism that changes in material culture cause shifts in the patterns of the entire culture. The ancient road made possible armies and empires and destroyed the isolated city states of Greece. But the road depended in the first place on writing. Behind the imperial command of great land areas stood the written word in easily transportable form. In the nineteenth century the newspapers, especially after the telegraph, paid for new roads and faster transport by land and sea. The press altered the forms of government, and the telegraph brought secret diplomacy to an end. When events in Egypt or Russia, London, Paris, or New York were known everywhere at once, the time for secret negotiation was reduced to hours and minutes. And the great national populations of the world, altered and emotionalized by the press, could confront one another immediately for a show-down. 14

Printing had from the first fostered nationalism because the vernaculars with their large reading publics were more profitable to commercial publishers than Latin. The press has pushed this nationalism to its ultimate point. There it remains. But photography and movies, like music and painting, are international in their power of appeal. The power of pictures to leap over national frontiers and prejudices is well-known, for good and ill. 15

One aspect of the press deserves special comment in this same respect. The contents of newspapers, their messages and information, have steadily promoted nationalism. But the form of the newspaper page is powerfully inter-cultural and international. The 16 unformulated message of an assembly of news items from every quarter of the globe is that the world today is one city. All war is civil war. All suffering is our own. So that regardless of the political line, or the time or the place, the mere format of the press exerts a single pressure. Basic acceptance of this fact is recorded in the steady weakening of interest in political parties everywhere.

17 From the point of view of its format, the press as a daily cross-section of the globe is a mirror of the technological instruments of communication. It is the popular daily book, the great collective poem, the universal entertainment of our age. As such it has modified poetic techniques and in turn has already been modified by the newer media of movie, radio, and television. These represent revolutions in communication as radical as printing itself. In fact, they are "magic casements opening on the foam of perilous seas," on which few of us have yet ventured in thought, art or living. If Erasmus was the first to size up and exploit the printing-press as a new force in art and education, James Joyce was the first to seize upon newspaper, radio, movie, and television to set up his "verbivoco-visual" drama in *Finnegans Wake*. Pound and Eliot are, in comparison with Joyce, timid devotees of the book as art form. But most of the difficulties which the ordinary person encounters with the poetry of Pound and Eliot disappear if it is viewed as a historical newsreel of persons, myths, ideas, and events with thematic musical score built in. Joyce had a much greater trust of language and reality than Pound or Eliot. By contrast they give their language and reality the Holly-wood glamor treatment. Joyce is closer to a De Sica film with its awareness of the intimate riches of the most ordinary scenes and situations.

18 But the reader who approaches Pound, Eliot, and Joyce alike as exploiters of the cinematic aspects of language will arrive at appreciation more quickly than the one who unconsciously tries to make sense of them by reducing their use of the new media of communication to the abstract linear forms of the book page.

19 The basic fact to keep in mind about the movie camera and projector is their resemblance to the process of human cognition. That is the real source of their magical, transforming power. The camera rolls up the external world on a spool. It does this by rapid still shots. The projector unwinds this spool as a kind of magic carpet which conveys the enchanted spectator anywhere in the world in an instant. The camera records and analyzes the daylight world with more than human intensity because of the forty-five degree angle of the camera eye. The projector reveals this daylight world on a dark screen where it becomes a dream world.

20 The wonderful resemblance in all this to human cognition

extends at least this far: in cognition we have to interiorize the exterior world. We have to recreate in the medium of our senses and inner faculties the drama of existence. This is the work of the *logos poietikos*, the agent intellect. In speech we utter that drama which we have analogously recreated within us. In speech we make or *poet* the world even as we may say that the movie parrots the world. Languages themselves are thus the greatest of all works of art. They are the collective hymns to existence. For in cognition itself is the whole of the poetic process. But the artist differs from most men in his power to arrest and then reverse the stages of human apprehension. He learns how to embody the stages of cognition (Aristotle's "plot") in an exterior work which can be held up for contemplation.

Even in this respect the movie resembles the cognitive process since the daylight world which the camera rolls up on the spool is reversed and projected to become the magical dream world of the audience. But all media of communication share something of this cognitive character which only a Thomist vision of existence and cognition dare do justice to. 21

Television, for example, differs from the movie in the immediacy with which it picks up and renders back the visible. The TV camera is like the microphone in relation to the voice. The movie has no such immediacy of pick-up and feedback. As we begin to look into the inevitably cognitive character of the various media we soon get over the jitters that come from exclusive concern with any one form of communication. 22

In his *Theory of the Film*, Bela Balazs notes how "the discovery of printing gradually rendered illegible the faces of men. So much could be read from paper that the method of conveying meaning by facial expression fell into desuetude. Victor Hugo wrote once that the printed book took over the part played by the cathedral in the Middle Ages and became the carrier of the spirit of the people. But the thousands of books tore the one spirit. . . . into thousands of opinions . . . tore the church into a thousand books. The visible spirit was thus turned into a legible spirit and visual culture into a culture of concepts." 23

Before printing, a reader was one who discerned and probed riddles. After printing, it meant one who scanned, who skipped along the macadamized surfaces of print. Today at the end of that process we have come to equate reading skill with speed and distraction rather than wisdom. But print, the mechanization of writing, was succeeded in the nineteenth century by photography and then by the mechanization of human gesture in the movie. This was followed by the mechanization of speech in telephone, phonograph and radio. In the talkies, and finally with TV, came the 24 mechanization of the totality of human expression, of voice, gesture, and human figure in action.

Each of these steps in the mechanization of human expres- 25
sion was comparable in its scope to the revolution brought about by the mechanization of writing itself. The changes in the ways of human association, social and political, were telescoped in time and so hidden from casual observers.

If there is a truism in the history of human communication it 26
is that any innovation in the external means of communication brings in its train shock on shock of social change. One effect of writing was to make possible cities, roads, armies, and empires. The letters of the alphabet were indeed the dragon's teeth. The printed book not only fostered nationalism but made it possible to bring the world of the past into every study. The newspaper is a daily book which brings a slice of all the cultures of the world under our eyes every day. To this extent it reverses the tendency of the printing press to accentuate merely national culture. Pictorial journalism and reportage tend strongly in the same international direction. But is this true of radio? Radio has strengthened the oral habit of communication and extended it, via the panel and round-table, to serious learning. Yet radio seems to be a form which also strengthens the national culture. Merely oral societies, for example, are the ultimate in national exclusiveness.

A group of us recently performed an experiment with a large 27
group of students. We divided them into four sections and assigned each section to a separate communication channel. Each section got the identical lecture simultaneously, but one read it, one heard it as a regular lecture in a studio, one heard it on radio and one heard and saw it as a TV broadcast. Immediately afterwards we administered a quiz to determine apprehension and understanding of this new and difficult material. The TV section came out on top, then the radio section, then the studio, and reading sections at the bottom. This was a totally unexpected result and it is too soon to generalize; but it is quite certain that the so-called mass media are not necessarily ordained to be channels of popular entertainment only.

It is "desirable" in thinking about the new media that we 28
should recall that buildings are mass communications and that the first mechanical medium was print from movable type. In fact, the discovery of movable type was the ancestor of all assembly lines, and it would be foolish to overlook the impact of the technological form involved in print on the psychological life of readers. To overlook this would be as unrealistic as to ignore rhythm and tempo in music. Likewise it is only common sense to recognize that the general situation created by a communicative channel and its audience is a

large part of that in which and by which the individuals commune. The encoded message cannot be regarded as a mere capsule or pellet produced at one point and consumed at another. Communication is communication all along the line.

One might illustrate from sports. The best brand of football played before fifty people would lack something of the power to communicate. The large enthusiastic crowd is necessary to represent the community at large, just as the players enact a drama which externalizes certain motivations and tensions in the communal life which would not otherwise be visible or available for audience participation. In India huge crowds assemble to experience *"darshan,"* which they consider to occur when they are massed in the presence of a visible manifestation of their collective life. 29

The new media do something similar for us in the West. Movies, radio, and TV establish certain personalities on a new plane of existence. They exist not so much in themselves but as types of collective life felt and perceived through a mass medium. L'il Abner, Bob Hope, Donald Duck, and Marilyn Monroe become points of collective awareness and communication for an entire society. And as technology increasingly undertakes to submit the entire planet as well as the contents of consciousness to the purposes of man's factive intelligence, it behooves us to consider the whole process of magical transformation involved in the media acutely and extensively. 30

From this point of view it should be obvious, for example, that the framers of the Hollywood morality code were operating with a very inadequate set of perceptions and concepts about the nature of the movie medium. Modern discussions of censorship, in the same way, are helplessly tied to conceptions borrowed from book culture alone. And the defenders of book culture have seldom given any thought to any of the media as art forms, the book least of all. The result is that their "defense" might as well be staged on an abandoned movie lot for all the effect it has on the actual situation. 31

When I wrote *The Mechanical Bride* some years ago I did not realize that I was attempting a defense of book culture against the new media. I can now see that I was trying to bring some of the critical awareness fostered by literary training to bear on the new media of sight and sound. My strategy was wrong, because my obsession with literary values blinded me to much that was actually happening for good and ill. What we have to defend today is not the values developed in any particular culture or by any one mode of communication. Modern technology presumes to attempt a total transformation of man and his environment. This calls in turn for an inspection and defense of all human values. And so far as merely human aid goes, the citadel of this defense must be located in 32 analytical awareness of the nature of the creative process involved in human cognition. For it is in this citadel that science and technology have already established themselves in their manipulation of the new media.

QUESTIONS

1. McLuhan's definition of communication is far broader than most of our definitions of that word. Give some examples of his more unusual applications of the word "communication."

2. According to the author, what effects have writing, printed words, newspapers, radio, and finally television had upon Western culture?

3. There are numerous allusions in this essay. Identify the following: Gutenberg (paragraph 2); Wilde, Shaw, Yeats, Synge, and Joyce (paragraph 4); André Malraux (paragraph 6); Erasmus (paragraph 7); Plato (paragraph 9); the library of Alexandria (paragraph 9); Ezra Pound, Eliot, and De Sica (paragraph 17); Thomist (paragraph 21); and Victor Hugo (paragraph 23). What effect does the range of allusions have on the reader?

4. In his effort to explain his argument, McLuhan uses numerous metaphors. Identify five of them and explain their relevance to McLuhan's discussion.

5. To a great degree, this essay is a "history of human communications." Does McLuhan present this history in a simple linear way? If not, how does he keep order among his historical events? How does his presentation reflect his sense of modern culture?

6. How and where does McLuhan use cause-and-effect analysis?

7. McLuhan uses contrast to develop meaning. Give examples of contrast in the essay.

8. Explain the importance of paragraph 30 in the essay. What sentence here could serve as the essay's thesis? Why does McLuhan defer his thesis for so long?

9. What effect do you think new technologies such as video cassettes, holography, videophones, and computer terminals will have on our culture?

10. a. Write an essay on the new communications systems in our culture.
b. Use McLuhan's ideas to analyze differences between watching movies and reading.

GEORGE ORWELL

Politics and the English Language

George Orwell (1903–1950) was the pseudonym of Eric Blair, an English novelist, essayist, and journalist. Orwell served with the Indian Imperial Police from 1922 to 1927 in Burma, fought in the Spanish Civil War, and acquired from his experiences a disdain of totalitarian and imperialistic systems. This attitude is reflected in the satiric fable *Animal Farm* (1945) and in the bleak, futuristic novel *1984* (1949). This essay, one of the more famous of the twentieth century, relates sloppy thinking and writing with political oppression.

Most people who bother with the matter at all would admit that the English language is in a bad way, but it is generally assumed that we cannot by conscious action do anything about it. Our civilisation is decadent, and our language—so the argument runs—must inevitably share in the general collapse. It follows that any struggle against the abuse of language is a sentimental archaism, like preferring candles to electric light or hansom cabs to aeroplanes. Underneath this lies the half-conscious belief that language is a natural growth and not an instrument which we shape for our own purposes. 1

Now, it is clear that the decline of a language must ultimately have political and economic causes: it is not due simply to the bad influence of this or that individual writer. But an effect can become a cause, reinforcing the original cause and producing the same effect in an intensified form, and so on indefinitely. A man may take to drink because he feels himself to be a failure, and then fail all the more completely because he drinks. It is rather the same thing that is happening to the English language. It becomes ugly and inaccurate because our thoughts are foolish, but the slovenliness of our language makes it easier for us to have foolish thoughts. The point is that the process is reversible. Modern English, especially written English, is full of bad habits which spread by imitation and which can be avoided if one is willing to take the necessary trouble. If one gets rid of these habits one can think more clearly, and to think clearly is a necessary first step towards political regeneration: so that the fight against bad English is not frivolous and is not the exclusive concern of professional writers. I will come back to this presently, and I hope that by that time the meaning of what I have said here will have become clearer. Meanwhile, here are five specimens of the English language as it is now habitually written. 2

These five passages have not been picked out because they 3
are especially bad—I could have quoted far worse if I had chosen—but because they illustrate various of the mental vices from which we now suffer. They are a little below the average, but are fairly representative samples. I number them so that I can refer back to them when necessary:

> 1. I am not, indeed, sure whether it is not true to say that the Milton who once seemed not unlike a seventeenth-century Shelley had not become, out of an experience ever more bitter in each year, more alien (sic) to the founder of that Jesuit sect which nothing could induce him to tolerate.
>
> Professor Harold Laski (Essay in *Freedom of Expression*).
>
> 2. Above all, we cannot play ducks and drakes with a native battery of idioms which prescribes such egregious collocations of vocables as the Basic *put up with* for *tolerate* or *put at a loss* for *bewilder*.
>
> Professor Lancelot Hogben (*Interglossa*).
>
> 3. On the one side we have the free personality: by definition it is not neurotic, for it has neither conflict nor dream. Its desires, such as they are, are transparent, for they are just what institutional approval keeps in the forefront of consciousness; another institutional pattern would alter their number and intensity; there is little in them that is natural, irreducible, or culturally dangerous. But *on the other side*, the social bond itself is nothing but the mutual reflection of these self-secure integrities. Recall the definition of love. Is not this the very picture of a small academic? Where is there a place in this hall of mirrors for either personality or fraternity?
>
> Essay on psychology in *Politics* (New York).
>
> 4. All the "best people" from the gentlemen's clubs, and all the frantic Fascist captains, united in common hatred of Socialism and bestial horror of the rising tide of the mass revolutionary movement, have turned to acts of provocation, to foul incendiarism, to medieval legends of poisoned wells, to legalise their own destruction to proletarian organisations, and rouse the agitated petty-bourgeoisie to chauvinistic fervour on behalf of the fight against the revolutionary way out of the crisis.
>
> Communist pamphlet.
>
> 5. If a new spirit *is* to be infused into this old country, there is one thorny and contentious reform which must be tackled, and that is the humanisation and galvanisation of the BBC. Timidity here will bespeak canker and atrophy of the soul. The heart of Britain may be sound and of strong beat,

> for instance, but the British lion's roar at present is like that of Bottom in Shakespeare's *Midsummer Night's Dream*—as gentle as any sucking dove. A virile new Britain cannot continue indefinitely to be traduced in the eyes, or rather ears, of the world by the effete languors of Langham Place, brazenly masquerading as "standard English". When the Voice of Britain is heard at nine o'clock, better far and infinitely less ludicrous to hear aitches honestly dropped than the present priggish, inflated, inhibited, school-ma'amish arch braying of blameless bashful mewing maidens!
>
> Letter in *Tribune.*

Each of these passages has faults of its own, but, quite apart from avoidable ugliness, two qualities are common to all of them. The first is staleness of imagery: the other is lack of precision. The writer either has a meaning and cannot express it, or he inadvertently says something else, or he is almost indifferent as to whether his words mean anything or not. This mixture of vagueness and sheer incompetence is the most marked characteristic of modern English prose, and especially of any kind of political writing. As soon as certain topics are raised, the concrete melts into the abstract and no one seems able to think of turns of speech that are not hackneyed: prose consists less and less of *words* chosen for the sake of their meaning, and more of *phrases* tacked together like the sections of a prefabricated hen-house. I list below, with notes and examples, various of the tricks by means of which the work of prose construction is habitually dodged: 4

Dying metaphors. A newly invented metaphor assists thought by evoking a visual image, while on the other hand a metaphor which is technically "dead" (e.g. *iron resolution*) has in effect reverted to being an ordinary word and can generally be used without loss of vividness. But in between these two classes there is a huge dump of worn-out metaphors which have lost all evocative power and are merely used because they save people the trouble of inventing phrases for themselves. Examples are: *Ring the changes on, take up the cudgels for, toe the line, ride roughshod over, stand shoulder to shoulder with, play into the hands of, no axe to grind, grist to the mill, fishing in troubled waters, rift within the lute, on the order of the day, Achilles' heel, swan song, hotbed.* Many of these are used without knowledge of their meaning (what is a "rift", for instance?), and incompatible metaphors are frequently mixed, a sure sign that the writer is not interested in what he is saying. Some metaphors now current have been twisted out of their original meaning without those who use them even being aware of the fact. For example, *toe the line* is sometimes written *tow the line.* Another example is *the hammer and the anvil,* now always used 5 with the implication that the anvil gets the worst of it. In real life it is always the anvil that breaks the hammer, never the other way about: a writer who stopped to think what he was saying would be aware of this, and would avoid perverting the original phrase.

Operators, or verbal false limbs. These save the trouble of picking out appropriate verbs and nouns, and at the same time pad each sentence with extra syllables which give it an appearance of symmetry. Characteristic phrases are: *render inoperative, militate against, prove unacceptable, make contact with, be subjected to, give rise to, give grounds for, have the effect of, play a leading part (rôle) in, make itself felt, take effect, exhibit a tendency to, serve the purpose of,* etc. etc. The keynote is the elimination of simple verbs. Instead of being a single word, such as *break, stop, spoil, mend, kill,* a verb becomes a *phrase,* made up of a noun or adjective tacked on to some general-purposes verb such as *prove, serve, form, play, render.* In addition, the passive voice is wherever possible used in preference to the active, and noun constructions are used instead of gerunds (*by examination of* instead of *by examining*). The range of verbs is further cut down by means of the *-ise* and *de-* formations, and banal statements are given an appearance of profundity by means of the *not un-* formation. Simple conjunctions and prepositions are replaced by such phrases as *with respect to, having regard to, the fact that, by dint of, in view of, in the interests of, on the hypothesis that;* and the ends of sentences are saved from anticlimax by such resounding commonplaces as *greatly to be desired, cannot be left out of account, a development to be expected in the near future, deserving of serious consideration, brought to a satisfactory conclusion,* and so on and so forth. 6

Pretentious diction. Words like *phenomenon, element, individual* (as noun), *objective, categorical, effective, virtual, basic, primary, promote, constitute, exhibit, exploit, utilise, eliminate, liquidate,* are used to dress up simple statements and give an air of scientific impartiality to biassed judgements. Adjectives like *epoch-making, epic, historic, unforgettable, triumphant, age-old, inevitable, inexorable, veritable,* are used to dignify the sordid processes of international politics, while writing that aims at glorifying war usually takes on an archaic colour, its characteristic words being: *realm, throne, chariot, mailed fist, trident, sword, shield, buckler, banner, jackboot, clarion.* Foreign words and expressions such as *cul de sac, ancien régime, deus ex machina, mutatis mutandis, status quo, Gleichschaltung, Weltanschauung,* are used to give an air of culture and elegance. Except for the useful abbreviations *i.e., e.g.,* and *etc.,* there is no real need for any of the hundreds of foreign phrases now current in English. Bad writers, and especially scientific, political and sociological writers, are nearly always haunted by the 7 notion that Latin or Greek words are grander than Saxon ones, and unnecessary words like *expedite, ameliorate, predict, extraneous, deracinated, clandestine, sub-aqueous* and hundreds of others constantly gain ground from their Anglo-Saxon opposite numbers.[1] The jargon peculiar to Marxist writing (*hyena, hangman, cannibal, petty bourgeois, these gentry, lacquey, flunkey, mad dog, White Guard,* etc.) consists largely of words and phrases translated from Russian, German or French; but the normal way of coining a new word is to use a Latin or Greek root with the appropriate affix and, where necessary, the *-ise* formation. It is often easier to make up words of this kind (*deregionalise, impermissible, extramarital, non-fragmentatory* and so forth) than to think up the English words that will cover one's meaning. The result, in general, is an increase in slovenliness and vagueness.

Meaningless words. In certain kinds of writing, particularly in art 8
criticism and literary criticism, it is normal to come across long passages which are almost completely lacking in meaning.[2] Words like *romantic, plastic, values, human, dead, sentimental, natural, vitality,* as used in art criticism, are strictly meaningless, in the sense that they not only do not point to any discoverable object, but are hardly even expected to do so by the reader. When one critic writes, "The outstanding features of Mr X's work is its living quality", while another writes, "The immediately striking thing about Mr X's work is its peculiar deadness", the reader accepts this as a simple difference of opinion. If words like *black* and *white* were involved, instead of the jargon words *dead* and *living,* he would see at once that language was being used in an improper way. Many political words are similarly abused. The word *Fascism* has now no meaning except in so far as it signifies "something not desirable". The words *democracy, socialism, freedom, patriotic, realistic, justice,* have each of them several different meanings which cannot be reconciled with one another. In the case of a word like *democracy,* not only is there no agreed definition, but the attempt to make one is resisted from all sides. It is almost universally felt that when we call a country democratic we are praising it: consequently the defenders of every kind of régime claim that it is a democracy, and fear that they might have to stop using the word if it were tied down to any one meaning. Words of this kind are often

[1]An interesting illustration of this is the way in which the English flower names which were in use till very recently are being ousted by Greek ones, *snapdragon* becoming *antirrhinum, forget-me-not* becoming *myosotis,* etc. It is hard to see any practical reason for this change of fashion: it is probably due to an instinctive turning-away from the more homely word and a vague feeling that the Greek word is scientific.

[2]Example: "Comfort's catholicity of perception and image, strangely Whitmanesque in range, almost the exact opposite in aesthetic compulsion, continues to evoke that trembling atmospheric accumulative hinting at a cruel, an inexorably serene timelessness . . . Wrey Gardiner scores by aiming at simple bullseyes with precision. Only they are not so simple, and through this contented sadness runs more than the surface bitter-sweet of resignation." *(Poetry Quarterly).*

used in a consciously dishonest way. That is, the person who uses them has his own private definition, but allows his hearer to think he means something quite different. Statements like *Marshal Pétain was a true patriot, The Soviet press is the freest in the world, The Catholic Church is opposed to persecution,* are almost always made with intent to deceive. Other words used in variable meanings, in most cases more or less dishonestly, are: *class, totalitarian, science, progressive, reactionary, bourgeois, equality.*

Now that I have made this catalogue of swindles and perversions, let me give another example of the kind of writing that they lead to. This time it must of its nature be an imaginary one. I am going to translate a passage of good English into modern English of the worst sort. Here is a well-known verse from *Ecclesiastes:* 9

> I returned, and saw under the sun, that the race is not to the swift, nor the battle to the strong, neither yet bread to the wise, nor yet riches to men of understanding, nor yet favour to men of skill; but time and chance happeneth to them all.

Here it is in modern English: 10

> Objective consideration of contemporary phenomena compels the conclusion that success or failure in competitive activities exhibits no tendency to be commensurate with innate capacity, but that a considerable element of the unpredictable must invariably be taken into account.

This is a parody, but not a very gross one. Exhibit 3, above, for instance, contains several patches of the same kind of English. It will be seen that I have not made a full translation. The beginning and ending of the sentence follow the original meaning fairly closely, but in the middle the concrete illustrations—race, battle, bread—dissolve into the vague phrase "success or failure in competitive activities". This had to be so, because no modern writer of the kind I am discussing—no one capable of using phrases like "objective consideration of contemporary phenomena"—would ever tabulate his thoughts in that precise and detailed way. The whole tendency of modern prose is away from concreteness. Now analyse these two sentences a little more closely. The first contains 49 words but only 60 syllables, and all its words are those of everyday life. The second contains 38 words of 90 syllables: 18 of its words are from Latin roots, and one from Greek. The first sentence contains six vivid images, and only one phrase ("time and chance") that could be called vague. The second contains not a single fresh, arresting phrase, and in spite of its 90 syllables it gives only a shortened version of the meaning con- 11 tained in the first. Yet without a doubt it is the second kind of sentence that is gaining ground in modern English. I do not want to exaggerate. This kind of writing is not yet universal, and outcrops of simplicity will occur here and there in the worst-written page. Still, if you or I were told to write a few lines on the uncertainty of human fortunes, we should probably come much nearer to my imaginary sentence than to the one from *Ecclesiastes*.

As I have tried to show, modern writing at its worst does not 12
consist in picking out words for the sake of their meaning and inventing images in order to make the meaning clearer. It consists in gumming together long strips of words which have already been set in order by someone else, and making the results presentable by sheer humbug. The attraction of this way of writing is that it is easy. It is easier—even quicker, once you have the habit—to say *In my opinion it is a not unjustifiable assumption that* than to say *I think.* If you use ready-made phrases, you not only don't have to hunt about for words; you also don't have to bother with the rhythms of your sentences, since these phrases are generally so arranged as to be more or less euphonious. When you are composing in a hurry—when you are dictating to a stenographer, for instance, or making a public speech—it is natural to fall into a pretentious, latinised style. Tags like *a consideration which we should do well to bear in mind* or *a conclusion to which all of us would readily assent* will save many a sentence from coming down with a bump. By using stale metaphors, similes and idioms, you save much mental effort, at the cost of leaving your meaning vague, not only for your reader but for yourself. This is the significance of mixed metaphors. The sole aim of a metaphor is to call up a visual image. When these images clash—as in *The Fascist octopus has sung its swan song, the jackboot is thrown into the melting-pot*—it can be taken as certain that the writer is not seeing a mental image of the objects he is naming; in other words he is not really thinking. Look again at the examples I gave at the beginning of this essay. Professor Laski (1) uses five negatives in 53 words. One of these is superfluous, making nonsense of the whole passage, and in addition there is the slip *alien* for akin, making further nonsense, and several avoidable pieces of clumsiness which increase the general vagueness. Professor Hogben (2) plays ducks and drakes with a battery which is able to write prescriptions, and, while disapproving of the everyday phrase *put up with,* is unwilling to look *egregious* up in the dictionary and see what it means. (3), if one takes an uncharitable attitude towards it, is simply meaningless: probably one could work out its intended meaning by reading the whole of the article in which it occurs. In (4) the writer knows more or less what he wants to say, but an accumulation of stale phrases chokes him like tea-leaves blocking a sink. In (5) words and meaning have almost parted company. People

who write in this manner usually have a general emotional meaning—they dislike one thing and want to express solidarity with another—but they are not interested in the detail of what they are saying. A scrupulous writer, in every sentence that he writes, will ask himself at least four questions, thus: What am I trying to say? What words will express it? What image or idiom will make it clearer? Is this image fresh enough to have an effect? And he will probably ask himself two more: Could I put it more shortly? Have I said anything that is avoidably ugly? But you are not obliged to go to all this trouble. You can shirk it by simply throwing your mind open and letting the ready-made phrases come crowding in. They will construct your sentences for you—even think your thoughts for you, to a certain extent—and at need they will perform the important service of partially concealing your meaning even from yourself. It is at this point that the special connection between politics and the debasement of language becomes clear.

In our time it is broadly true that political writing is bad 13
writing. Where it is not true, it will generally be found that the writer is some kind of rebel, expressing his private opinions, and not a "party line". Orthodoxy, of whatever colour, seems to demand a lifeless, imitative style. The political dialects to be found in pamphlets, leading articles, manifestos, White Papers and the speeches of Under-Secretaries do, of course, vary from party to party, but they are all alike in that one almost never finds in them a fresh, vivid, home-made turn of speech. When one watches some tired hack on the platform mechanically repeating the familiar phrases—*bestial atrocities, iron heel, blood-stained tyranny, free peoples of the world, stand shoulder to shoulder*—one often has a curious feeling that one is not watching a live human being but some kind of dummy: a feeling which suddenly becomes stronger at moments when the light catches the speaker's spectacles and turns them into blank discs which seem to have no eyes behind them. And this is not altogether fanciful. A speaker who uses that kind of phraseology has gone some distance towards turning himself into a machine. The appropriate noises are coming out of his larynx, but his brain is not involved as it would be if he were choosing his words for himself. If the speech he is making is one that he is accustomed to make over and over again, he may be almost unconscious of what he is saying, as one is when one utters the responses in church. And this reduced state of consciousness, if not indispensable, is at any rate favourable to political conformity.

In our time, political speech and writing are largely the 14
defence of the indefensible. Things like the continuance of British rule in India, the Russian purges and deportations, the dropping of the atom bombs on Japan, can indeed be defended, but only by arguments which are too brutal for most people to face, and which do

not square with the professed aims of political parties. Thus political language has to consist largely of euphemism, question-begging and sheer cloudy vagueness. Defenceless villages are bombarded from the air, the inhabitants driven out into the countryside, the cattle machine-gunned, the huts set on fire with incendiary bullets: this is called *pacification*. Millions of peasants are robbed of their farms and sent trudging along the roads with no more than they can carry: this is called *transfer of population* or *rectification of frontiers*. People are imprisoned for years without trial, or shot in the back of the neck or sent to die of scurvy in Arctic lumber camps: this is called *elimination of unreliable elements*. Such phraseology is needed if one wants to name things without calling up mental pictures of them. Consider for instance some comfortable English professor defending Russian totalitarianism. He cannot say outright, "I believe in killing off your opponents when you can get good results by doing so". Probably, therefore, he will say something like this:

> While freely conceding that the Soviet régime exhibits certain features which the humanitarian may be inclined to deplore, we must, I think, agree that a certain curtailment of the right to political opposition is an unavoidable concomitant of transitional periods, and that the rigours which the Russian people have been called upon to undergo have been amply justified in the sphere of concrete achievement.

The inflated style is itself a kind of euphemism. A mass of 15
Latin words falls upon the facts like soft snow, blurring the outlines and covering up all the details. The great enemy of clear language is insincerity. When there is a gap between one's real and one's declared aims, one turns as it were instinctively to long words and exhausted idioms, like a cuttlefish squirting out ink. In our age there is no such thing as "keeping out of politics". All issues are political issues, and politics itself is a mass of lies, evasions, folly, hatred and schizophrenia. When the general atmosphere is bad, language must suffer. I should expect to find—this is a guess which I have not sufficient knowledge to verify—that the German, Russian and Italian languages have all deteriorated in the last ten or fifteen years, as a result of dictatorship.

But if thought corrupts language, language can also corrupt 16
thought. A bad usage can spread by tradition and imitation, even among people who should and do know better. The debased language that I have been discussing is in some ways very convenient. Phrases like *a not unjustifiable assumption, leaves much to be desired, would serve no good purpose, a consideration which we should do well to bear in mind,* are a continuous temptation, a packet of aspirins always at

one's elbow. Look back through this essay, and for certain you will find that I have again and again committed the very faults I am protesting against. By this morning's post I have received a pamphlet dealing with conditions in Germany. The author tells me that he "felt impelled" to write it. I open it at random, and here is almost the first sentence that I see: "(The Allies) have an opportunity not only of achieving a radical transformation of Germany's social and political structure in such a way as to avoid a nationalistic reaction in Germany itself, but at the same time of laying the foundations of a co-operative and unified Europe." You see, he "feels impelled" to write—feels, presumably, that he has something new to say—and yet his words, like cavalry horses answering the bugle, group themselves automatically into the familiar dreary pattern. This invasion of one's mind by ready-made phrases *(lay the foundations, achieve a radical transformation)* can only be prevented if one is constantly on guard against them, and every such phrase anaesthetises a portion of one's brain.

I said earlier that the decadence of our language is probably 17
curable. Those who deny this would argue, if they produced an argument at all, that language merely reflects existing social conditions, and that we cannot influence its development by any direct tinkering with words and constructions. So far as the general tone or spirit of a language goes, this may be true, but it is not true in detail. Silly words and expressions have often disappeared, not through any evolutionary process but owing to the conscious action of a minority. Two recent examples were *explore every avenue* and *leave no stone unturned,* which were killed by the jeers of a few journalists. There is a long list of fly-blown metaphors which could similarly be got rid of if enough people would interest themselves in the job; and it should also be possible to laugh the *not un-* formation out of existence,[3] to reduce the amount of Latin and Greek in the average sentence, to drive out foreign phrases and strayed scientific words, and, in general, to make pretentiousness unfashionable. But all these are minor points. The defence of the English language implies more than this, and perhaps it is best to start by saying what it does *not* imply.

To begin with, it has nothing to do with archaism, with the 18
salvaging of obsolete words and turns of speech, or with the setting-up of a "standard English" which must never be departed from. On the contrary, it is especially concerned with the scrapping of every word or idiom which has outworn its usefulness. It has nothing to do with correct grammar and syntax, which are of no importance so long as one makes one's meaning clear, or with the avoidance of Americanisms, or with having what is called a "good

[3]One can cure oneself of the *not un-* formation by memorising this sentence: *A not unblack dog was chasing a not unsmall rabbit across a not ungreen field.*

prose style". On the other hand it is not concerned with fake simplicity and the attempt to make written English colloquial. Nor does it even imply in every case preferring the Saxon word to the Latin one, though it does imply using the fewest and shortest words that will cover one's meaning. What is above all needed is to let the meaning choose the word, and not the other way about. In prose, the worst thing one can do with words is to surrender to them. When you think of a concrete object, you think wordlessly, and then, if you want to describe the thing you have been visualising, you probably hunt about till you find the exact words that seem to fit it. When you think of something abstract you are more inclined to use words from the start, and unless you make a conscious effort to prevent it, the existing dialect will come rushing in and do the job for you, at the expense of blurring or even changing your meaning. Probably it is better to put off using words as long as possible and get one's meaning as clear as one can through pictures or sensations. Afterwards one can choose—not simply *accept*—the phrases that will best cover the meaning, and then switch round and decide what impression one's words are likely to make on another person. This last effort of the mind cuts out all stale or mixed images, all prefabricated phrases, needless repetitions, and humbug and vagueness generally. But one can often be in doubt about the effect of a word or a phrase, and one needs rules that one can rely on when instinct fails. I think the following rules will cover most cases:

i. Never use a metaphor, simile or other figure of speech which you are used to seeing in print.

ii. Never use a long word where a short one will do.

iii. If it is possible to cut a word out, always cut it out.

iv. Never use the passive where you can use the active.

v. Never use a foreign phrase, a scientific word or a jargon word if you can think of an everyday English equivalent.

vi. Break any of these rules sooner than say anything outright barbarous.

These rules sound elementary, and so they are, but they demand a deep change of attitude in anyone who has grown used to writing in the style now fashionable. One could keep all of them and still write bad English, but one could not write the kind of stuff that I quoted in those five specimens at the beginning of this article.

I have not here been considering the literary use of language, 19
but merely language as an instrument for expressing and not for

concealing or preventing thought. Stuart Chase and others have come near to claiming that all abstract words are meaningless, and have used this as a pretext for advocating a kind of political quietism. Since you don't know what Fascism is, how can you struggle against Fascism? One need not swallow such absurdities as this, but one ought to recognise that the present political chaos is connected with the decay of language, and that one can probably bring about some improvement by starting at the verbal end. If you simplify your English, you are freed from the worst follies of orthodoxy. You cannot speak any of the necessary dialects, and when you make a stupid remark its stupidity will be obvious, even to yourself. Political language—and with variations this is true of all political parties, from Conservatives to Anarchists—is designed to make lies sound truthful and murder respectable, and to give an appearance of solidity to pure wind. One cannot change this all in a moment, but one can at least change one's own habits, and from time to time one can even, if one jeers loudly enough, send some worn-out and useless phrase—some *jackboot, Achilles' heel, hotbed, melting pot, acid test, veritable inferno* or other lump of verbal refuse—into the dustbin where it belongs.

QUESTIONS

1. According to Orwell, "thought corrupts language" and "language can also corrupt thought." Give examples of these assertions in the essay.

2. In what ways does Orwell believe that politics and language are related?

3. Orwell himself uses similes and metaphors. Locate five of them and explain their relationship to the author's analysis.

4. Orwell claims that concrete language is superior to abstract language. Give examples of Orwell's attempt to write concretely.

5. One of the most crucial rhetorical devices in this essay is definition. What important concepts does Orwell define? What methods of definition does he tend to use?

6. Identify an example of hypothetical reasoning in the essay. How does it contribute to the thesis of the essay?

7. After having given five examples of bad English, why does Orwell in paragraph 9 give another example? How does this example differ from the others? What does it add to the essay?

8. Explain the use of extended analogy in paragraph 13.

9. Do you think that language has deteriorated even further or has it improved? Explain.

10. a. Write an essay defending the value of simplified English.
b. In an analytical essay, assess the state of language in politics today.

JONATHAN SWIFT

The Art of Political Lying

Jonathan Swift (1667–1745) is best known as the author of three satires: *A Tale of a Tub* (1704), *Gulliver's Travels* (1726), and *A Modest Proposal* (1729). In these satires, he pricks the balloon of many of his contemporaries' and our own most cherished prejudices, pomposities, and delusions. Swift was also a famous churchman, an eloquent spokesman for Irish rights, and a political journalist. In this essay, he examines a characteristic of politicians that apparently has not changed over the years: lying.

We are told the devil is the father of lies, and was a liar from the beginning; so that, beyond contradiction, the invention is old: and, which is more, his first Essay of it was purely political, employed in undermining the authority of his prince, and seducing a third part of the subjects from their obedience: for which he was driven down from heaven, where (as Milton expresses it) he had been viceroy of a great western province; and forced to exercise his talent in inferior regions among other fallen spirits, poor or deluded men, whom he still daily tempts to his own sin, and will ever do so, till he be chained in the bottomless pit. 1

But although the devil be the father of lies, he seems, like other great inventors, to have lost much of his reputation by the continual improvements that have been made upon him. 2

Who first reduced lying into an art, and adapted it to politics, is not so clear from history, although I have made some diligent inquiries. I shall therefore consider it only according to the modern system, as it has been cultivated these twenty years past in the southern part of our own island. 3

The poets tell us that, after the giants were overthrown by the gods, the earth in revenge produced her last offspring, which was Fame. And the fable is thus interpreted: that when tumults and 4 seditions are quieted, rumours and false reports are plentifully spread through a nation. So that, by this account, lying is the last relief of a routed, earth-born, rebellious party in a state. But here the moderns have made great additions, applying this art to the gaining of power and preserving it, as well as revenging themselves after they have lost it; as the same instruments are made use of by animals to feed themselves when they are hungry, and to bite those that tread upon them.

But the same genealogy cannot always be admitted for 5
political lying; I shall therefore desire to refine upon it, by adding some circumstances of its birth and parents. A political lie is sometimes born out of a discarded statesman's head, and thence delivered to be nursed and dandled by the rabble. Sometimes it is produced a monster, and licked into shape: at other times it comes into the world completely formed, and is spoiled in the licking. It is often born an infant in the regular way, and requires time to mature it; and often it sees the light in its full growth, but dwindles away by degrees. Sometimes it is of noble birth, and sometimes the spawn of a stockjobber. Here it screams aloud at the opening of the womb, and there it is delivered with a whisper. I know a lie that now disturbs half the kingdom with its noise, [of] which, although too proud and great at present to own its parents, I can remember its whisperhood. To conclude the nativity of this monster; when it comes into the world without a sting it is still-born; and whenever it loses its sting it dies.

No wonder if an infant so miraculous in its birth should be 6
destined for great adventures; and accordingly we see it has been the guardian spirit of a prevailing party for almost twenty years. It can conquer kingdoms without fighting, and sometimes with the loss of a battle. It gives and resumes employments; can sink a mountain to a mole-hill, and raise a mole-hill to a mountain; has presided for many years at committees of elections; can wash a blackmoor white; make a saint of an atheist, and a patriot of a profligate; can furnish foreign ministers with intelligence, and raise or let fall the credit of the nation. This goddess flies with a huge looking-glass in her hands, to dazzle the crowd, and make them see, according as she turns it, their ruin in their interest, and their interest in their ruin. In this glass you will behold your best friends, clad in coats powdered with *fleurs de lis* and triple crowns; their girdles hung round with chains, and beads, and wooden shoes; and your worst enemies adorned with the ensigns of liberty, property, indulgence, moderation, and a cornucopia in their hands. Her large wings, like those of a flying-fish, are of no use but while they are moist; she therefore dips them in mud, and, soaring aloft, scatters it in the eyes of the multitude, flying with great swiftness; but at every turn is forced to stoop in dirty ways for new supplies.

I have been sometimes thinking, if a man had the art of the second sight for seeing lies, as they have in Scotland for seeing spirits, how admirably he might entertain himself in this town, by observing the different shapes, sizes, and colours of those swarms of lies which buzz about the heads of some people, like flies about a horse's ears in summer; or those legions hovering every afternoon in Exchange-alley, enough to darken the air; or over a club of discontented grandees, and thence sent down in cargoes to be scattered at elections. 7

There is one essential point wherein a political liar differs from others of the faculty, that he ought to have but a short memory, which is necessary according to the various occasions he meets with every hour of differing from himself and swearing to both sides of a contradiction, as he finds the persons disposed with whom he has to deal. In describing the virtues and vices of mankind, it is convenient, upon every article, to have some eminent person in our eye, from whom we copy our description. I have strictly observed this rule, and my imagination this minute represents before me a certain great man famous for this talent, to the constant practice of which he owes his twenty years' reputation of the most skilful head in England for the management of nice affairs. The superiority of his genius consists in nothing else but an inexhaustible fund of political lies, which he plentifully distributes every minute he speaks, and by an unparalleled generosity forgets, and consequently contradicts, the next half-hour. He never yet considered whether any proposition were true or false, but whether it were convenient for the present minute or company to affirm or deny it; so that, if you think fit to refine upon him by interpreting everything he says, as we do dreams, by the contrary, you are still to seek, and will find yourself equally deceived whether you believe or not: the only remedy is to suppose that you have heard some inarticulate sounds, without any meaning at all; and besides, that will take off the horror you might be apt to conceive at the oaths wherewith he perpetually tags both ends of every proposition; although, at the same time, I think he cannot with any justice be taxed with perjury when he invokes God and Christ, because he has often fairly given public notice to the world that he believes in neither. 8

Some people may think that such an accomplishment as this can be of no great use to the owner, or his party, after it has been often practised and is become notorious; but they are widely mistaken. Few lies carry the inventor's mark, and the most prostitute enemy to truth may spread a thousand without being known for the author: besides, as the vilest writer has his readers, so the greatest liar has his believers; and it often happens that, if a lie be believed only for an 9 hour, it has done its work, and there is no farther occasion for it. Falsehood flies, and truth comes limping after it, so that when men come to be undeceived it is too late; the jest is over, and the tale has had its effect: like a man who has thought of a good repartee when the discourse is changed or the company parted; or like a physician who has found out an infallible medicine after the patient is dead.

Considering that natural disposition in many men to lie, and in multitudes to believe, I have been perplexed what to do with that maxim so frequent in everybody's mouth, that truth will at last prevail. Here has this island of ours, for the greatest part of twenty years, lain under the influence of such counsels and persons, whose principle and interest it was to corrupt our manners, blind our understanding, drain our wealth, and in time destroy our constitution both in church and state, and we at last were brought to the very brink of ruin; yet, by the means of perpetual misrepresentations, have never been able to distinguish between our enemies and friends. We have seen a great part of the nation's money got into the hands of those who, by their birth, education, and merit, could pretend no higher than to wear our liveries; while others, who, by their credit, quality, and fortune, were only able to give reputation and success to the Revolution, were not only laid aside as dangerous and useless, but loaded with the scandal of Jacobites, men of arbitrary principles, and pensioners to France; while truth, who is said to lie in a well, seemed now to be buried there under a heap of stones. But I remember it was a usual complaint among the Whigs, that the bulk of the landed men was not in their interests, which some of the wisest looked on as an ill omen; and we saw it was with the utmost difficulty that they could reserve a majority, while the court and ministry were on their side, till they had learned those admirable expedients for deciding elections and influencing distant boroughs by powerful motives from the city. But all this was more force and constraint, however upheld by most dexterous artifice and management, until the people began to apprehend their properties, their religion, and the monarchy itself in danger; when we saw them greedily laying hold on the first occasion to interpose. But of this mighty change in the dispositions of the people I shall discourse more at large in some following paper: wherein I shall endeavour to undeceive or discover those deluded or deluding persons who hope or pretend it is only a short madness in the vulgar, from which they may soon recover; whereas, I believe it will appear to be very different in its causes, its symptoms, and its consequences; and prove a great example to illustrate the maxim I lately mentioned, that truth (however sometimes late) will at last prevail.

QUESTIONS

1. According to Swift, what effects can be traced to political lying?

2. According to Swift, why aren't liars discovered and known to be liars?

3. In paragraphs 8 to 10, Swift uses numerous metaphors and similes. Identify and interpret them, and also explain why Swift uses metaphors and allusive language.

4. How does Swift employ ironic language?

5. Swift employs several extended metaphors, almost fables, to describe liars and lying. Identify these metaphors and explain how they characterize the liar. What is the effect of using this method of definition?

6. Which paragraphs constitute the introductory part of Swift's essay? What methods of development does he employ here?

7. At what point does Swift divide his essay into two parts? How are these parts different? How are they similar?

8. Swift frequently uses deductive reasoning in this essay. Give examples and explain how, particularly in paragraphs 8 to 10, deductions further his argument.

9. One effect Swift says political liars hope to achieve is to confuse friends and enemies. Give examples of similar political behavior today.

10. Write an essay on the art of lying as it relates to particular institutions or subjects—college life, business, politics, marriage, or other relevant topics.

Literature, Media, and the Arts

JUDITH VIORST

How Books Helped Shape My Life

Judith Viorst (193? –), a contributing editor to *Redbook,* is an American poet, journalist, and writer of children's books. Her work includes *People and Other Aggravations* (1971) and *Yes, Married: A Saga of Love and Complaint* (1972). Measured, witty, and affirmative, Viorst in her typical writing tries to mediate between extremes, seeking wisdom from the ordinary and commonplace. In this essay, Viorst investigates the books and fictive heroines that have molded her personality.

In books I've read since I was young I've searched for heroines who could serve as ideals, as models, as possibilities—some reflecting the secret self that dwelled inside me, others pointing to whole new ways that a woman (if only she dared!) might try to be. The person that I am today was shaped by Nancy Drew; by Jo March, Jane Eyre and Heathcliff's soul mate Cathy; and by other fictional females whose attractiveness or character or audacity for a time were the standards by which I measured myself. 1

I return to some of these books to see if I still understand the powerful hold that these heroines once had on me. I still understand. 2

Consider teen-aged Nancy Drew—beautiful, blond-haired, blue-eyed girl detective—who had the most terrific life that I as a ten-year-old could ever imagine. Motherless (in other words, quite free of maternal controls), she lived with her handsome indulgent lawyer father in a large brick house set back from the street with a winding tree-lined driveway on the outside and a faithful, nonintrusive housekeeper Hannah cooking yummy meals on the inside. She also had a boy friend, a convertible, nice clothes and two close girl friends—not as perfect as she, but then it seemed to me that no one could possibly be as perfect as Nancy Drew, who in dozens and dozens of books (*The Hidden Staircase, The Whispering Statue, The Clue in the Diary, The Clue of the Tapping Heels*) was resourceful and brave and intelligent as she went around solving mysteries left and right, while remaining kind to the elderly and invariably polite and absolutely completely delightfully feminine. 3

I mean, what else *was* there? 4

I soon found out what else when I encountered the four March sisters of *Little Women*, a sentimental, old-fashioned book about girls growing up in Civil War time in New England. About spoiled, vain, pretty Amy. And sickly, saintly Beth. And womanly, decent Meg. And about—most important of all—gawky, bookworm Jo. Dear Jo, who wasn't as flawless as the golden Nancy Drew but who showed me that girls like her—like *us*—could be heroines. Even if we weren't much to look at. Even if we were clumsy and socially gauche. And even if the transition into young womanhood often appeared to our dubious eye to be difficult and scary and even unwelcome. 5

Jo got stains on her dress and laughed when she shouldn't and lost her temper and didn't display tact or patience or restraint. Jo brought a touch of irreverence to the cultural constraints of the world she lived in. And yet her instincts were good and her heart was pure and her headstrong ways led always to virtue. And furthermore Jo—as I yearned to be—was a writer! 6

In the book the years go by, Beth dies, Meg and Amy marry and Jo—her fierce heart somewhat tamed—is alone. "An old maid, that's what I'm to be. A literary spinster, with a pen for a spouse, a family of stories for children, and twenty years hence a morsel of fame, perhaps!' . . . Jo sighed, as if the prospect was not inviting." 7

This worried young reader concurred—not inviting at all! 8

And so I was happy to read of Jo's nice suitor, Mr. Bhaer, not handsome or rich or young or important or witty, but possessed of kindness and dignity and enough intelligence to understand that 9 even a girl who wasn't especially pretty, who had no dazzling charms and who wanted to write might make a wonderful wife. And a wonderful mother. And live happily ever after.

What a relief! 10

What Jo and Nancy shared was active participation in life— 11
they went out and *did*; they weren't simply done to—and they taught and promised me (at a time when mommies stayed home and there was no Women's Movement) that a girl could go out and do and still get a man. Jo added the notion that brusque, ungainly girls could go out and do and still get a man. And Jane of *Jane Eyre,* whose author once said, "I will show you a heroine as small and as plain as myself," added the further idea that such women were able to "feel just as men feel" and were capable of being just as passionate.

Orphaned Jane, a governess at stately Thornfield Hall, was a 12
no-nonsense lady, cool and self-contained, whose lonely, painful childhood had ingrained in her an impressive firmness of character, an unwillingness to charm or curry favor and a sense of herself as the equal of any man. Said Jane to Mr. Rochester, the brooding, haughty, haunted master of Thornfield: "Do you think I am an automaton?—a machine without feelings? Do you think, because I am poor, obscure, plain, and little, I am soulless and heartless? You think wrong!—I have as much soul as you, and full as much heart!"

I loved it that such hot fires burned inside so plain a Jane. I 13
loved her for her unabashed intensity. And I loved her for being so pure that when she learned of Mr. Rochester's lunatic wife, she sacrificed romance for honor and left him immediately.

For I think it's important to note that Nancy and Jo and Jane, 14
despite their independence, were basically as good as girls can be: honest, generous, kind, sincere, reliable, respectable, possessed of absolute integrity. They didn't defy convention. They didn't challenge the rules. They did what was right, although it might cause them pain. And their virtue was always rewarded—look at Jane, rich and married at last to her Mr. Rochester. Oh, how I identified with Jane!

But then I read *Wuthering Heights,* a novel of soul-consuming 15
love on the Yorkshire moors, and Catherine Earnshaw totally captured me. And she captured me, not in spite of her dangerous, dark and violent spirit, but *because* of it.

Cathy was as wild as the moors. She lied and connived and 16
deceived. She was insolent, selfish, manipulative and cruel. And by marrying meek, weak Edgar instead of Heathcliff, her destiny, she betrayed a love she described in throbbing, unforgettable prose as . . . elemental:

"My love for Heathcliff resembles the eternal rocks beneath— 17 a source of little visible delight, but necessary. Nelly, I *am* Heathcliff—he's always, always in my mind—not as a pleasure, any more than I am always a pleasure to myself—but as my own being. . . ."

Now who, at the age of 16, could resist such quivering intensity? Who would settle for less than elemental? Must we untamed creatures of passion—I'd muse as I lay awake in my red flannel nightie—submit ourselves to conventional morality? Or could I actually choose not to be a good girl? 18

Cathy Earnshaw told me that I could. And so did lost Lady Brett, of *The Sun Also Rises*. 19

Brett Ashley was to me, at 18, free, modern, woman incarnate, and she dangled alluring new concepts before my eyes: 20

The value of style: "She wore a slipover jersey sweater and a tweed skirt, and her hair was brushed back like a boy's. She started all that." 21

The glamour of having a dark and tortured past: "Finally, when he got really bad, he used to tell her he'd kill her. . . . She hasn't had an absolutely happy life." 22

The excitement of nonconformity: "I've always done just what I wanted." 23

The importance of (understated) grace under pressure: "Brett was rather good. She's always rather good." 24

And the thrill of unrepressed sexuality: "Brett's had affairs with men before. She tells me all about everything." 25

Brett married lovelessly and drank too much and drifted too much and had an irresponsible fling with a bullfighter. But she also had class—and her own morality. She set her bullfighter free—"I'd have lived with him if I hadn't seen it was bad for him." And even though she was broke, she lied and "told him I had scads of it. . . . I couldn't take his money, you know." 26

Brett's wasn't the kind of morality that my mother was teaching me in suburban New Jersey. But maybe I wasn't meant for suburban life. Maybe—I would muse as I carefully lined my eyes with blue liner—maybe I'm meant for something more . . . emancipated. 27

I carried Brett's image with me when, after college, I lived for a while in Greenwich Village, in New York. But I couldn't achieve her desperate gallantry. And it struck me that Brett was too lonely and sad, and that Cathy had died too young (and that Scarlett O'Hara got Tara but lost her Rhett), and that maybe I ought to forget about unconventionality if the price was going to be so painfully high. Although I enjoyed my Village fling, I had no wish to live anguishedly ever after. I needed a heroine who, like me, wanted just a small taste of the wild before settling down into happy domesticity. 28

I found her in *War and Peace*. Her name was Natasha. 29

Natasha, the leading lady of this epic of Russian society 30 during Napoleon's time, was "poetic . . . charming . . . overflowing with life," an enchanting girl whose sweet eagerness and passionate impulsivity were tempered by historic and private tragedies. Betrothed to the handsome and excellent Prince Andrew, she fell in love with a heel named Anatole, and when she was warned that this foolish and dangerous passion would lead to her ruin, "I'll go to my ruin . . .," she said, "as soon as possible."

It ended badly with Anatole. Natasha tried suicide. Prince Andrew died. Natasha turned pale, thin, subdued. But unlike Brett and Cathy, her breach with convention was mended and, at long last, she married Pierre—a decent, substantial, loving man, the kind of man all our mothers want us to marry. 31

In marriage Natasha grew stouter and "the old fire very rarely kindled in her face now." She became an exemplary mother, an ideal wife. "She felt that her unity with her husband was maintained not by the poetic feelings that had attracted him to her but by something else—indefinite but firm as the bond between her own body and soul." 32

It sounded—if not elemental and doomed—awfully nice. 33

I identified with Natasha when, the following year, I married and left Greenwich Village. I too was ready for domesticity. And yet . . . her husband and children became "the subject which wholly engrossed Natasha's attention." She had lost herself—and I didn't want to lose me. What I needed next was a heroine who could reconcile all the warring wants of my nature—for fire and quiet, independence and oneness, ambition and love, and marriage and family. 34

But such reconciling heroines, in novels and real life, may not yet exist. 35

Nevertheless Natasha and Jane and Jo, Cathy, Nancy and Brett—each spoke to my heart and stirred me powerfully. On my journey into young womanhood I was fortunate to have them as my companions. They were, they will always remain, a part of me. 36

QUESTIONS

1. Analyze the process of growth and maturation reflected in the heroines the author was attracted to between the age of 10 and her adult years. What principle of unity does Viorst find in her early heroines?

2. Explain the author's need for "reconciling heroines." What can we infer about her personality from this statement?

3. What do words like "yummy" (paragraph 3) and "nightie" (paragraph 18) contribute to the tone of the essay? How do the conjunctions "and" in paragraphs 5, 9, and elsewhere reinforce this aspect of tone?

4. Locate examples of one of Viorst's favorite techniques—the use of adjectives in series. Explain the purpose of this technique.

5. Analyze the introductory paragraph in terms of its delineation of thesis and its function in establishing the organizing frame for the essay.

6. Discuss the manner in which Viorst integrates rhetorical strategies of illustration, causal analysis, and process analysis in the essay.

7. Find and analyze those paragraphs that rely on comparative methods of development. Why do they contribute to the unity of the essay?

8. What is the relationship between Viorst's use of summary, characterization, and character analysis and her attitude toward the reading audience?

9. Do you accept Viorst's thesis that books shape our lives? Explain your answer.

10. a. Write an essay entitled "How Books Shaped My Life," "How Music Shaped My Life," or "How Television Shaped My Life."
b. Write an essay focusing on one character from literature, radio, or film who had an impact on your life.

SYLVIA PLATH

A Comparison

Sylvia Plath (1932–1963), American poet and novelist, graduated from Smith College and took a master's at Cambridge University. She married the English poet Ted Hughes in 1956. Plath committed suicide at the age of 30. Her best known work is *The Bell-Jar* (1963), a highly autobiographical novel about a young woman overwhelmed by crises and suicidal tendencies. Plath's poetry, often reflecting a fascination with suffering, pain, and death, is collected in *The Colossus* (1960), *Ariel* (1965), *Crossing the Water* (1971), and *Winter Trees* (1972). This essay, written in 1962, is an energetic and highly poetic celebration of the artist's craft.

ow I envy the novelist! 1

I imagine him—better say her, for it is the women I look 2
to for . . . a parallel—I imagine her, then, pruning a rosebush with a large pair of shears, adjusting her

spectacles, shuffling about among the teacups, humming, arranging ashtrays or babies, absorbing a slant of light, a fresh edge to the weather, and piercing, with a kind of modest, beautiful X-ray vision, the psychic interiors of her neighbors—her neighbors on trains, in the dentist's waiting room, in the corner teashop. To her, this fortunate one, what is there that *isn't* relevant! Old shoes can be used, doorknobs, air letters, flannel nightgowns, cathedrals, nail varnish, jet planes, rose arbors and budgerigars; little mannerisms—the sucking at a tooth, the tugging at a hemline—any weird or warty or fine or despicable thing. Not to mention emotions, motivations—those rumbling, thunderous shapes. Her business is Time, the way it shoots forward, shunts back, blooms, decays and double-exposes itself. Her business is people in Time. And she, it seems to me, has all the time in the world. She can take a century if she likes, a generation, a whole summer.

I can take about a minute. 3

I'm not talking about epic poems. We all know how long *they* 4
can take. I'm talking about the smallish, unofficial garden-variety poem. How shall I describe it?—a door opens, a door shuts. In between you have had a glimpse: a garden, a person, a rainstorm, a dragonfly, a heart, a city. I think of those round glass Victorian paperweights which I remember, yet can never find—a far cry from the plastic mass-productions which stud the toy counters in Woolworth's. This sort of paperweight is a clear globe, self-complete, very pure, with a forest or village or family group within it. You turn it upside down, then back. It snows. Everything is changed in a minute. It will never be the same in there—not the fir trees, nor the gables, nor the faces.

So a poem takes place. 5

And there is really so little room! So little time! The poet 6
becomes an expert packer of suitcases:

The apparition of these faces in the crowd;
Petals on a wet black bough.

There it is: the beginning and the end in one breath. How 7
would the novelist manage that? In a paragraph? In a page? Mixing it, perhaps, like paint, with a little water, thinning it, spreading it out.

Now I am being smug, I am finding advantages. 8

If a poem is concentrated, a closed fist, then a novel is relaxed 9
and expansive, an open hand: it has roads, detours, destinations; a heart line, a head line; morals and money come into it. Where the fist excludes and stuns, the open hand can touch and encompass a great deal in its travels.

I have never put a toothbrush in a poem.  10

I do not like to think of all the things, familiar, useful and worthy things, I have never put into a poem. I did, once, put a yew tree in. And that yew tree began, with astounding egotism, to manage and order the whole affair. It was not a yew tree by a church on a road past a house in a town where a certain woman lived . . . and so on, as it might have been in a novel. Oh, no. It stood squarely in the middle of my poem, manipulating its dark shades, the voices in the churchyard, the clouds, the birds, the tender melancholy with which I contemplated it—everything! I couldn't subdue it. And, in the end, my poem was a poem about a yew tree. That yew tree was just too proud to be a passing black mark in a novel. 11

Perhaps I shall anger some poets by implying that the *poem* is proud. The poem, too, can include everything, they will tell me. And with far more precision and power than those baggy, disheveled and undiscriminate creatures we call novels. Well, I concede these poets their steamshovels and old trousers. I really *don't* think poems should be all that chaste. I would, I think, even concede a toothbrush, if the poem was a real one. But these apparitions, these poetical toothbrushes, are rare. And when they do arrive, they are inclined, like my obstreperous yew tree, to think themselves singled out and rather special. 12

Not so in novels. 13

There the toothbrush returns to its rack with beautiful promptitude and is forgot. Time flows, eddies, meanders, and people have leisure to grow and alter before our eyes. The rich junk of life bobs all about us: bureaus, thimbles, cats, the whole much-loved, well-thumbed catalog of the miscellaneous which the novelist wishes us to share. I do not mean that there is no pattern, no discernment, no rigorous ordering here. 14

I am only suggesting that perhaps the pattern does not insist so much. 15

The door of the novel, like the door of the poem, also shuts. 16

But not so fast, nor with such manic, unanswerable finality. 17

QUESTIONS

1. What distinctions does the author draw between the poem and the novel? Why does she envy the novelist? What stated and implied preferences does she have for the poem rather than the novel?

2. Explain the relevance of rosebushes, toothbrushes, and yew trees to Plath's discussion.

3. The author employs a remarkable variety of poetic techniques in this

essay, including metaphors, symbols, allusions, imagery, personification, onomatopoeia, alliteration, consonance, and assonance. Locate and analyze examples of these techniques.

4. Analyze Plath's use of parallelism in paragraphs 2, 4, and 14.

5. Plath uses a series of figurative comparisons to structure the entire essay. Trace and examine the main figurative comparisons that serve to organize the selection.

6. Examine the spatial and rhetorical effects of the numerous one-sentence paragraphs in the essay.

7. What purpose does Plath's method serve in identification and definition of the novelist and poet?

8. Analyze the cumulative use of illustration to achieve emphasis in this essay.

9. Comment on Plath's view that the poem, unlike the novel, closes with "manic, unanswerable finality."

10. Write an essay that compares and contrasts—either figuratively or literally—two forms of literature, art, music, or film.

D. H. LAWRENCE

Why the Novel Matters

David Herbert Lawrence (1885–1930), novelist, essayist, and poet, wrote in the great tradition of English romanticism. He chafed under the conventions of his age and zealously extended the content and style of the English novel. His novels, such as *Sons and Lovers* (1913), *The Rainbow* (1915), *Women in Love* (1921), *The Plumed Serpent* (1926), and *Lady Chatterley's Lover* (1928), are famous for their often disquieting depictions of love and ambition in the modern world. Lawrence also wrote criticism: his *Studies in Classic American Literature* (1923) is still a revealing, if idiosyncratic, look at American literature. In the following essay, what matters for Lawrence is not simply the novel, which he treats with energy and enthusiasm, but life itself.

We have curious ideas of ourselves. We think of ourselves as a body with a spirit in it, or a body with a soul in it, or a body with a mind in it. *Mens sana in corpore sano*. The years drink up the wine, and at last throw the bottle away, the body, of course, being the bottle. 1

It is a funny sort of superstition. Why should I look at my hand, as it so cleverly writes these words, and decide that it is a mere nothing compared to the mind that directs it? Is there really any huge difference between my hand and my brain? Or my mind? My hand is alive, it flickers with a life of its own. It meets all the strange universe in touch, and learns a vast number of things, and knows a vast number of things. My hand, as it writes these words, slips gaily along, jumps like a grasshopper to dot an *i*, feels the table rather cold, gets a little bored if I write too long, has its own rudiments of thought, and is just as much *me* as is my brain, my mind, or my soul. Why should I imagine that there is a *me* which is more *me* than my hand is? Since my hand is absolutely alive, me alive. 2

Whereas, of course, as far as I am concerned, my pen isn't alive at all. My pen *isn't me* alive. Me alive ends at my finger-tips. 3

Whatever is me alive is me. Every tiny bit of my hands is alive, every little freckle and hair and fold of skin. And whatever is me alive is me. Only my finger-nails, those ten little weapons between me and an inanimate universe, they cross the mysterious Rubicon between me alive and things like my pen, which are not alive, in my own sense. 4

So, seeing my hand is all alive, and me alive, wherein is it just a bottle, or a jug, or a tin can, or a vessel of clay, or any of the rest of that nonsense? True, if I cut it it will bleed, like a can of cherries. But then the skin that is cut, and the veins that bleed, and the bones that should never be seen, they are all just as alive as the blood that flows. So the tin can business, or vessel of clay, is just bunk. 5

And that's what you learn, when you're a novelist. And that's what you are very liable *not* to know, if you're a parson, or a philosopher, or a scientist, or a stupid person. If you're a parson, you talk about souls in heaven. If you're a novelist, you know that paradise is in the palm of your hand, and on the end of your nose, because both are alive; and alive, and man alive, which is more than you can say, for certain, of paradise. Paradise is after life, and I for one am not keen on anything that is *after* life. If you are a philosopher, you talk about infinity, and the pure spirit which knows all things. But if you pick up a novel, you realize immediately that infinity is just a handle to this self-same jug of a body of mine; while as for knowing, if I find my finger in fire, I know that fire burns, with a knowledge so emphatic and vital, it leaves Nirvana merely a conjecture. Oh, yes, my body, me alive, *knows*, and knows intensely. And as for the sum 6 of all knowledge, it can't be anything more than an accumulation of all the things I know in the body, and you, dear reader, know in the body.

These damned philosophers, they talk as if they suddenly went off in steam, and were then much more important than they are when they're in their shirts. It is nonsense. Every man, philosopher included, ends in his own finger-tips. That's the end of his man alive. As for the words and thoughts and sighs and aspirations that fly from him, they are so many tremulations in the ether, and not alive at all. But if the tremulations reach another man alive, he may receive them into his life, and his life may take on a new colour, like a chameleon creeping from a brown rock on to a green leaf. All very well and good. It still doesn't alter the fact that the so-called spirit, the message or teaching of the philosopher or the saint, isn't alive at all, but just a tremulation upon the ether, like a radio message. All this spirit stuff is just tremulations upon the ether into new life, that is because you are man alive, and you take sustenance and stimulation into your alive man in a myriad ways. But to say that the message, or the spirit which is communicated to you, is more important than your living body, is nonsense. You might as well say that the potato at dinner was more important. 7

Nothing is important but life. And for myself, I can absolutely see life nowhere but in the living. Life with a capital L is only man alive. Even a cabbage in the rain is cabbage alive. All things that are alive are amazing. And all things that are dead are subsidiary to the living. Better a live dog than a dead lion. But better a live lion than a live dog. *C'est la vie!* 8

It seems impossible to get a saint, or a philosopher, or a scientist, to stick to this simple truth. They are all, in a sense, renegades. The saint wishes to offer himself up as spiritual food for the multitude. Even Francis of Assisi turns himself into a sort of angel-cake, of which anyone may take a slice. But an angel-cake is rather less than man alive. And poor St. Francis might well apologize to his body, when he is dying: "Oh, pardon me, my body, the wrong I did you through the years!" It was no wafer, for others to eat. 9

The philosopher, on the other hand, because he can think, decides that nothing but thoughts matter. It is as if a rabbit, because he can make little pills, should decide that nothing but little pills matter. As for the scientist, he has absolutely no use for me so long as I am man alive. To the scientist, I am dead. He puts under the microscope a bit of dead me, and calls it me. He takes me to pieces, and says first one piece, and then another piece, is me. My heart, my liver, my stomach have all been scientifically me, according to the scientist; and nowadays I am either a brain, or nerves, or glands, or something more up-to-date in the tissue line. 10

Now I absolutely flatly deny that I am a soul, or a body, or a mind, or an intelligence, or a brain, or a nervous system, or a bunch of glands, or any of the rest of these bits of me. The whole is greater than the part. And therefore, I, who am man alive, am greater than my soul, or spirit, or body, or mind, or consciousness, or anything else that is merely a part of me. I am a man, and alive. I am man alive, and as long as I can, I intend to go on being man alive. 11

For this reason I am a novelist. And being a novelist, I consider myself superior to the saint, the scientist, the philosopher, and the poet, who are all great masters of different bits of man alive, but never get the whole hog. 12

The novel is the one bright book of life. Books are not life. They are only tremulations on the ether. But the novel as a tremulation can make the whole man alive tremble. Which is more than poetry, philosophy, science, or any other book-tremulation can do. 13

The novel is the book of life. In this sense, the Bible is a great confused novel. You may say, it is about God. But it is really about man alive. Adam, Eve, Sarai, Abraham, Isaac, Jacob, Samuel, David, Bath-Sheba, Ruth, Esther, Solomon, Job, Isaiah, Jesus, Mark, Judas, Paul, Peter: what is it but man alive, from start to finish? Man alive, not mere bits. Even the Lord is another man alive, in a burning bush, throwing the tablets of stone at Moses's head. 14

I do hope you begin to get my idea, why the novel is supremely important, as a tremulation on the ether. Plato makes the perfect ideal being tremble in me. But that's only a bit of me. Perfection is only a bit, in the strange make-up of man alive. The Sermon on the Mount makes the selfless spirit of me quiver. But that, too, is only a bit of me. The Ten Commandments set the old Adam shivering in me, warning me that I am a thief and a murderer, unless I watch it. But even the old Adam is only a bit of me. 15

I very much like all these bits of me to be set trembling with life and the wisdom of life. But I do ask that the whole of me shall tremble in its wholeness, some time or other. 16

And this, of course, must happen in me, living. 17

But as far as it can happen from a communication, it can only happen when a whole novel communicates itself to me. The Bible—but *all* the Bible—and Homer, and Shakespeare: these are the supreme old novels. These are all things to all men. Which means that in their wholeness they affect the whole man alive, which is the man himself, beyond any part of him. They set the whole tree trembling with a new access of life, they do not just stimulate growth in one direction. 18

I don't want to grow in any one direction any more. And, if I can help it, I don't want to stimulate anybody else into some 19 particular direction. A particular direction ends in a *cul-de-sac*. We're in a *cul-de-sac* at present.

I don't believe in any dazzling revelation, or in any supreme 20
Word. "The grass withereth, the flower fadeth, but the Word of the Lord shall stand for ever." That's the kind of stuff we've drugged ourselves with. As a matter of fact, the grass withereth, but comes up all the greener for that reason, after the rains. The flower fadeth, and therefore the bud opens. But the Word of the Lord, being man-uttered and a mere vibration on the ether, becomes staler and staler, more and more boring, till at last we turn a deaf ear and it ceases to exist, far more finally than any withered grass. It is grass that renews its youth like the eagle, not any Word.

We should ask for no absolutes, or absolute. Once and for all 21
and for ever, let us have done with the ugly imperialism of any absolute. There is no absolute good, there is nothing absolutely right. All things flow and change, and even change is not absolute. The whole is a strange assembly of apparently incongruous parts, slipping past one another.

Me, man alive, I am a very curious assembly of incongruous 22
parts. My yea! of today is oddly different from my yea! of yesterday. My tears of tomorrow will have nothing to do with my tears of a year ago. If the one I love remains unchanged and unchanging, I shall cease to love her. It is only because she changes and startles me into change and defies my inertia, and is herself staggered in her inertia by my changing, that I can continue to love her. If she stayed put, I might as well love the pepper-pot.

In all this change, I maintain a certain integrity. But woe 23
betide me if I try to put my finger on it. If I say of myself, I am this, I am that!—then, if I stick to it, I turn into a stupid fixed thing like a lamp-post. I shall never know wherein lies my integrity, my individuality, my me. I *can* never know it. It is useless to talk about my ego. That only means that I have made up an *idea* of myself, and that I am trying to cut myself out to pattern. Which is no good. You can cut your cloth to fit your coat, but you can't clip bits off your living body, to trim it down to your idea. True, you can put yourself into ideal corsets. But even in ideal corsets, fashions change.

Let us learn from the novel. In the novel, the characters can 24
do nothing but *live*. If they keep on being good, according to pattern, or bad, according to pattern, or even volatile, according to pattern, they cease to live, and the novel falls dead. A character in a novel has got to live, or it is nothing.

We, likewise, in life have got to live, or we are nothing. 25

What we mean by living is, of course, just as indescribable as 26
what we mean by *being*. Men get ideas into their heads, of what they

mean by Life, and they proceed to cut life out to pattern. Sometimes they go into the desert to seek God, sometimes they go into the desert to seek cash, sometimes it is wine, woman, and song, and again it is water, political reform, and votes. You never know what it will be next: from killing your neighbour with hideous bombs and gas that tears the lungs, to supporting a Foundlings Home and preaching infinite Love, and being co-respondent in a divorce.

In all this wild welter, we need some sort of guide. It's no 27
good inventing Thou Shalt Nots!

What then? Turn truly, honourably to the novel, and see 28
wherein you are man alive, and wherein you are dead man in life. You may love a woman as man alive, and you may be making love to a woman as sheer dead man in life. You may eat your dinner as man alive, or as a mere masticating corpse. As man alive you may have a shot at your enemy. But as a ghastly simulacrum of life you may be firing bombs into men who are neither your enemies nor your friends, but just things you are dead to. Which is criminal, when the things happen to be alive.

To be alive, to be man alive, to be whole man alive: that is the 29
point. And at its best, the novel, and the novel supremely, can help you. It can help you not to be dead man in life. So much of man walks about dead and a carcass in the street and house, today: so much of women is merely dead. Like a pianoforte with half the notes mute.

But in the novel you can see, plainly, when the man goes 30
dead, the woman goes inert. You can develop an instinct for life, if you will, instead of a theory of right and wrong, good and bad.

In life, there is right and wrong, good and bad, all the time. 31
But what is right in one case is wrong in another. And in the novel you see one man becoming a corpse, because of his so-called goodness, another going dead because of his so-called wickedness. Right and wrong is an instinct: but an instinct of the whole consciousness in a man, bodily, mental, spiritual at once. And only in the novel are *all* things given full play, or at least, they may be given full play, when we realize that life itself, and not inert safety, is the reason for living. For out of the full play of all things emerges the only thing that is anything, the wholeness of a man, the wholeness of a woman, man alive, and live woman.

QUESTIONS

1. According to Lawrence, what is the relationship between life and the novel? Why does the novel matter?

2. What contrasts does Lawrence establish between the novelist and the parson, philosopher, and scientist?

3. Analyze the levels of diction, the very "sound" of Lawrence's prose. Examine the admixture of declarative, interrogative, and exclamatory sentence structures in the essay. Explain the author's use of fragments, his application of figurative language, his use of italics for typographical emphasis. Examine Lawrence's persistent devices of repetition and overstatement in the essay. Evaluate the effect of these numerous strategies on the tone of the essay.

4. What patterns of imagery do you detect in the essay? How do they relate to the thesis?

5. How do the terms "tremulation on the ether" and "bright book of life" serve as structuring principles in the essay?

6. Trace the association of ideas advancing Lawrence's thesis. In the absence of strictly logical development, how unified and coherent is the essay?

7. Analyze patterns of comparison and contrast in the essay.

8. Examine the relation of point of view to theme and tone in the essay.

9. Do you agree with Lawrence's assertion that the novelist is better equipped than the scientist, philosopher, or theologian to capture the wholeness of life? Explain.

10. Write a personalized essay on why music matters; why film matters; why drama matters; or a similar subject.

RALPH ELLISON

On Becoming a Writer

Ralph Ellison (1914–　　) was born in Oklahoma City and attended Tuskegee Institute. Subsequently he moved to New York, working with the Federal Writers Project and editing *Negro Quarterly*. He has taught at numerous colleges, including the University of Chicago and Yale University. *Invisible Man* (1956), Ellison's only novel and a contemporary classic, portrays in vivid and often grotesque detail the crises in the black experience in America. This subject is also the thematic center of Ellison's collection of essays *Shadow and Act* (1964), from which the following selection is taken. In "On Becoming a Writer," Ellison offers a highly personalized account of the causal connections between the writer, literature, and American life.

In the beginning writing was far from a serious matter; it was a reflex of reading, an extension of a source of pleasure, escape, and instruction. In fact, I had become curious about writing by way of seeking to understand the aesthetic nature of literary power, the devices through which literature could command my mind and emotions. It was not, then, the *process* of writing which initially claimed my attention, but the finished creations, the artifacts, poems, plays, novels. The act of learning writing technique was, therefore, an amusing investigation of what seemed at best a secondary talent, an exploration, like dabbling in sculpture, of one's potentialities as a "Renaissance Man." This, surely, would seem a most unlikely and even comic concept to introduce here; and yet, it is precisely because I come from where I do (the Oklahoma of the years between World War I and the Great Depression) that I must introduce it, and with a straight face. 1

Anything and everything was to be found in the chaos of Oklahoma; thus the concept of the Renaissance Man has lurked long within the shadow of my past, and I shared it with at least a half dozen of my Negro friends. How we actually acquired it I have never learned, and since there is no true sociology of the dispersion of ideas within the American democracy, I doubt if I ever shall. Perhaps we breathed it in with the air of the Negro community of Oklahoma City, the capital of that state whose Negroes were often charged by exasperated white Texans with not knowing their "place." Perhaps we took it defiantly from one of them. Or perhaps I myself picked it up from some transplanted New Englander whose shoes I had shined of a Saturday afternoon. After all, the most meaningful tips do not always come in the form of money, nor are they intentionally extended. Most likely, however, my friends and I acquired the idea from some book or from some idealistic Negro teacher, some dreamer seeking to function responsibly in an environment which at its most normal took on some of the mixed character of nightmare and of dream. 2

One thing is certain, ours was a chaotic community, still characterized by frontier attitudes and by that strange mixture of the naive and sophisticated, the benign and malignant, which makes the American past so puzzling and its present so confusing; that mixture which often affords the minds of the young who grow up in the far provinces such wide and unstructured latitude, and which encourages the individual's imagination—up to the moment "reality" closes in upon him—to range widely and, sometimes, even to soar. 3

We hear the effects of this in the Southwestern jazz of the thirties, that joint creation of artistically free and exhuberantly creative adventurers, of artists who had stumbled upon the freedom lying within the restrictions of their musical tradition as within the 4 limitations of their social background, and who in their own unconscious way have set an example for any Americans, Negro or white, who would find themselves in the arts. They accepted themselves and the complexity of life as they knew it, they loved their art and through it they celebrated American experience definitively in sound. Whatever others thought or felt, this was their own powerful statement, and only nonmusical assaults upon their artistic integrity—mainly economically inspired changes of fashion—were able to compromise their vision.

5 Much of so-called Kansas City jazz was actually brought to perfection in Oklahoma by Oklahomans. It is an important circumstance for me as a writer to remember, because while these musicians and their fellows were busy creating out of tradition, imagination, and the sounds and emotions around them, a freer, more complex, and driving form of jazz, my friends and I were exploring an idea of human versatility and possibility which went against the barbs or over the palings of almost every fence which those who controlled social and political power had erected to restrict our roles in the life of the country. Looking back, one might say that the jazzmen, some of whom we idolized, were in their own way better examples for youth to follow than were most judges and ministers, legislators and governors (we were stuck with the notorious Alfalfa Bill Murray). For as we viewed these pillars of society from the confines of our segregated community we almost always saw crooks, clowns, or hypocrites. Even the best were revealed by their attitudes toward us as lacking the respectable qualities to which they pretended and for which they were accepted outside by others, while despite the outlaw nature of their art, the jazzmen were less torn and damaged by the moral compromises and insincerities which have so sickened the life of our country.

6 Be that as it may, our youthful sense of life, like that of many Negro children (though no one bothers to note it—especially the specialists and "friends of the Negro" who view our Negro-American life as essentially nonhuman) was very much like that of Huckleberry Finn, who is universally so praised and enjoyed for the clarity and courage of his moral vision. Like Huck, we observed, we judged, we imitated and evaded as we could the dullness, corruption, and blindness of "civilization." We were undoubtedly comic because, as the saying goes, we weren't supposed to know what it was all about. But to ourselves we were "boys," members of a wild, free, outlaw tribe which transcended the category of race. Rather we were Americans born into the forty-sixth state, and thus, into the context of Negro-American post-Civil War history, "frontiersmen." And isn't one of the implicit functions of the American frontier to encourage

the individual to a kind of dreamy wakefulness, a state in which he makes—in all ignorance of the accepted limitations of the possible—rash efforts, quixotic gestures, hopeful testings of the complexity of the known and the given?

Spurring us on in our controlled and benign madness was the voracious reading of which most of us were guilty and the vicarious identification and empathetic adventuring which it encouraged. This was due, in part, perhaps to the fact that some of us were fatherless—my own father had died when I was three—but most likely it was because boys are natural romantics. We were seeking examples, patterns to live by, out of a freedom which for all its being ignored by the sociologists and subtle thinkers, was implicit in the Negro situation. Father and mother substitutes also have a role to play in aiding the child to help create himself. Thus we fabricated our own heroes and ideals catch-as-catch-can; and with an outrageous and irreverent sense of freedom. Yes, and in complete disregard of ideas of respectability or the surreal incongruity of some of our projections. Gamblers and scholars, jazz musicians and scientists, Negro cowboys and soldiers from the Spanish-American and First World Wars, movie stars and stunt men, figures from the Italian Renaissance and literature, both classical and popular, were combined with the special virtues of some local bootlegger, the eloquence of some Negro preacher, the strength and grace of some local athlete, the ruthlessness of some businessman-physician, the elegance in dress and manners of some headwaiter or hotel doorman. 7

Looking back through the shadows upon this absurd activity, I realize now that we were projecting archetypes, re-creating folk figures, legendary heroes, monsters even, most of which violated all ideas of social hierarchy and order and all accepted conceptions of the hero handed down by cultural, religious, and racist tradition. But we, remember, were under the intense spell of the early movies, the silents as well as the talkies; and in our community, life was not so tightly structured as it would have been in the traditional South—or even in deceptively "free" Harlem. And our imaginations processed reality and dream, natural man and traditional hero, literature and folklore, like maniacal editors turned loose in some frantic film-cutting room. Remember, too, that being boys, yet in the play-stage of our development, we were dream-serious in our efforts. But serious nevertheless, for *culturally* play is a preparation, and we felt that somehow the human ideal lay in the vague and constantly shifting figures—sometimes comic but always versatile, picaresque, and self-effacingly heroic—which evolved from our wildly improvisatory projections: figures neither white nor black, Christian nor 8

Jewish, but representative of certain desirable essences, of skills and powers, physical, aesthetic, and moral.

The proper response to these figures was, we felt, to develop ourselves for the performance of many and diverse roles, and the fact that certain definite limitations had been imposed upon our freedom did not lessen our sense of obligation. Not only were we to prepare but we were to perform—not with mere competence but with an almost reckless verve; with, may we say (without evoking the quaint and questionable notion of *négritude*) Negro-American style? Behind each artist there stands a traditional sense of style, a sense of the felt tension indicative of expressive completeness; a mode of humanizing reality and of evoking a feeling of being at home in the world. It is something which the artist shares with the group, and part of our boyish activity expressed a yearning to make any and everything of quality *Negro-American*; to appropriate it, possess it, re-create it in our own group and individual images. 9

And we recognized and were proud of our group's own style where-ever we discerned it, in jazzmen and prizefighters, ballplayers, and tap dancers; in gesture, inflection, intonation, timbre, and phrasing. Indeed, in all those nuances of expression and attitude which reveal a culture. We did not fully understand the cost of that style, but we recognized within it an affirmation of life beyond all question of our difficulties as Negroes. 10

Contrary to the notion currently projected by certain specialists in the "Negro problem" which characterizes the Negro-American as self-hating and defensive, we did not so regard ourselves. We felt, among ourselves at least, that we were supposed to be whoever we would and could be and do anything and everything which other boys did, and do it better. Not defensively, because we were ordered to do so; nor because it was held in the society at large that we were naturally, as Negroes, limited—but because we demanded it of ourselves. Because to measure up to our own standards was the only way of affirming our notion of manhood. 11

Hence it was no more incongruous, as seen from our own particular perspective in this land of incongruities, for young Negro Oklahomans to project themselves as Renaissance men than for white Mississippians to see themselves as ancient Greeks or noblemen out of Sir Walter Scott. Surely our fantasies have caused far less damage to the nation's sense of reality, if for no other reason than that ours were expressive of a more democratic ideal. Remember, too, as William Faulkner made us so vividly aware, that the slaves often took the essence of the aristocratic ideal (as they took Christianity) with far more seriousness than their masters, and that we, thanks to the tight telescoping of American history, were but two generations from that previous condition. Renaissance men, indeed! 12

I managed, by keeping quiet about it, to cling to our boyish ideal during three years in Alabama, and I brought it with me to New York, where it not only gave silent support to my explorations of what was then an unknown territory, but served to mock and caution me when I became interested in the communist ideal. And when it was suggested that I try my hand at writing it was still with me. 13

The act of writing requires a constant plunging back into the shadow of the past where time hovers ghostlike. When I began writing in earnest I was forced, thus, to relate myself consciously and imaginatively to my mixed background as American, as Negro-American, and as a Negro from what in its own belated way was a pioneer background. More important, and inseparable from this particular effort, was the necessity of determining my true relationship to that body of American literature to which I was most attracted and through which, aided by what I could learn from the literatures of Europe, I would find my own voice and to which I was challenged, by way of achieving myself, to make some small contribution, and to whose composite picture of reality I was obligated to offer some necessary modifications. 14

This was no matter of sudden insight but of slow and blundering discovery, of a struggle to stare down the deadly and hypnotic temptation to interpret the world and all its devices in terms of race. To avoid this was very important to me, and in light of my background far from simple. Indeed, it was quite complex, involving as it did, a ceaseless questioning of all those formulas which historians, politicians, sociologists, and an older generation of Negro leaders and writers—those of the so-called "Negro Renaissance"—had evolved to describe my group's identity, its predicament, its fate, and its relation to the larger society and the culture which we share. 15

Here the question of reality and personal identity merge. Yes, and the question of the nature of the reality which underlies American fiction and thus the human truth which gives fiction viability. In this quest, for such it soon became, I learned that nothing could go unchallenged; especially that feverish industry dedicated to telling Negroes who and what they are, and which can usually be counted upon to deprive both humanity and culture of their complexity. I had undergone, not too many months before taking the path which led to writing, the humiliation of being taught in a class in sociology at a Negro college (from Park and Burgess, the leading textbook in the field) that Negroes represented the "lady of the races." This contention the Negro instructor passed blandly along to us without even bothering to wash his hands, much less his teeth. 16

Well, I had no intention of being bound by any such humiliating definition of my relationship to American literature. Not even to those works which depicted Negroes negatively. Negro-Americans have a highly developed ability to abstract desirable qualities from those around them, even from their enemies, and my sense of reality could reject bias while appreciating the truth revealed by achieved art. The pleasure which I derived from reading had long been a necessity, and in the *act* of reading, that marvelous collaboration between the writer's artful vision and the reader's sense of life, I had become acquainted with other possible selves; freer, more courageous and ingenuous and, during the course of the narrative at least, even wise.

At the time I was under the influence of Ernest Hemingway, and his description, in *Death in the Afternoon*, of his thinking when he first went to Spain became very important as translated in my own naive fashion. He was trying to write, he tells us, 17

> and I found the greatest difficulty aside from knowing truly what you really felt, rather than what you were supposed to feel, and had been taught to feel, was to put down what really happened in action; what the actual things were which produced the emotion that you experienced . . .

His statement of moral and aesthetic purpose which followed focused my own search to relate myself to American life through literature. For I found the greatest difficulty for a Negro writer was the problem of revealing what he truly felt, rather than serving up what Negroes were supposed to feel, and were encouraged to feel. And linked to this was the difficulty, based upon our long habit of deception and evasion, of depicting what really happened within our areas of American life, and putting down with honesty and without bowing to ideological expediencies the attitudes and values which give Negro-American life its sense of wholeness and which render it bearable and human and, when measured by our own terms, desirable. 18

I was forced to this awareness through my struggles with the craft of fiction; yes, and by my attraction (soon rejected) to Marxist political theory, which was my response to the inferior status which society sought to impose upon me (I did not then, now, or ever *consider* myself inferior). 19

I did not know my true relationship to America—what citizen of the United States really does?—but I did know and accept how I felt inside. And I also knew, thanks to the old Renaissance Man, what I expected of myself in the matter of personal discipline and creative quality. Since by the grace of the past and the examples of manhood 20 picked willy-nilly from the continuing-present of my background, I rejected all negative definitions imposed upon me by others, there was nothing to do but search for those relationships which were fundamental.

In this sense fiction became the agency of my efforts to answer the questions, Who am I, what am I, how did I come to be? What shall I make of the life around me, what celebrate, what reject, how confront the snarl of good and evil which is inevitable? What does American society *mean* when regarded out of my *own* eyes, when informed by my *own* sense of the past and viewed by my *own* complex sense of the present? How, in other words, should I think of myself and my pluralistic sense of the world, how express my vision of the human predicament, without reducing it to a point which would render it sterile before that necessary and tragic—though enhancing—reduction which must occur before the fictive vision can come alive? It is quite possible that much potential fiction by Negro-Americans fails precisely at this point: through the writers' refusal (often through provincialism or lack of courage or through opportunism) to achieve a vision of life and a resourcefulness of craft commensurate with the complexity of their actual situation. Too often they fear to leave the uneasy sanctuary of race to take their chances in the world of art. 21

QUESTIONS

1. Why did Ellison become a writer? Trace the influences and events in this process.

2. Paraphrase Ellison's commentary on the relationship between the black artist and American society.

3. Explain in context the following terms and phrases: "the aesthetic nature of literary power" (paragraph 1); "the concept of the Renaissance Man" (paragraph 2); "that joint creation of artistically free and exuberantly creative adventurers" (paragraph 4); "we were projecting archetypes . . ." (paragraph 8); "a traditional sense of style, a sense of the felt tension indicative of expressive completeness" (paragraph 9); "moral and aesthetic purpose" (paragraph 18). What do these terms have in common?

4. How does the relative difficulty of the syntax in this essay influence the effectiveness of the selection?

5. What do Ellison's use of narrative and first-person point of view contribute to the essay?

6. Where does the author introduce causal analysis? Is he interested in causes, effects, or both? What is the chain of causality? How does he treat primary and secondary causes?

7. Explain the function and purpose of paragraphs 6, 14, and 17.

8. Why is Ellison's concluding paragraph especially significant and successful? What is the purpose of the rhetorical questions?

9. Develop more fully Ellison's observation that reading (and exposure to any form of art) often produces "vicarious identification and empathetic adventuring" (paragraph 7).

10. a. Write an essay that analyzes the ways in which literature, music, television, and film permit us to relate to some aspect of American life.
b. Ellison implies that appreciating the arts is an act of liberation. Comment on this thesis.

ALICE WALKER

Saving the Life That Is Your Own: The Importance of Models in the Artist's Life

Alice Walker (1944–) was born in Eatonton, Georgia, and now lives in San Francisco and Mendocino County, California. A celebrated poet, short story writer, and novelist, she is the author of *Revolutionary Petunias, In Love and Trouble,* and *Meredian*, among other works. Her 1983 novel *The Color Purple* won the American Book Award and the Pulitzer Prize. The following essay, from *In Search of Our Mothers' Gardens* (1983), offers a highly personalized and perceptive analysis of the importance of influence in both art and life.

There is a letter Vincent Van Gogh wrote to Emile Bernard 1
that is very meaningful to me. A year before he wrote the letter, Van Gogh had had a fight with his domineering friend Gauguin, left his company, and cut off, in desperation and anguish, his own ear. The letter was written in Saint-Remy, in the South of France, from a mental institution to which Van Gogh had voluntarily committed himself.

I imagine Van Gogh sitting at a rough desk too small for him, looking out at the lovely Southern light, and occasionally glancing critically next to him at his own paintings of the landscape he loved so much. The date of the letter is December 1889, Van Gogh wrote: 2

> However hateful painting may be, and however cumbersome in the times we are living in, if anyone who has chosen this handicraft pursues it zealously, he is a man of duty, sound and faithful.
>
> Society makes our existence wretchedly difficult at times, hence our impotence and the imperfection of our work.
>
> . . . I myself am suffering under an absolute lack of models.
>
> But on the other hand, there are beautiful spots here. I have just done five size 30 canvasses, olive trees. And the reason I am staying on here is that my health is improving a great deal.
>
> What I am doing is hard, dry, but that is because I am trying to gather new strength by doing some rough work, and I'm afraid abstractions would make me soft.

Six months later, Van Gogh—whose health was "improving a great deal"—committed suicide. He had sold one painting during his lifetime. Three times was his work noticed in the press. But these are just details. 3

The real Vincent Van Gogh is the man who has "just done five size 30 canvasses, olive trees." To me, in context, one of the most moving and revealing descriptions of how a real artist thinks. And the knowledge that when he spoke of "suffering under an absolute lack of models" he spoke of that lack in terms of both the intensity of his commitment and the quality and singularity of his work, which was frequently ridiculed in his day. 4

The absence of models, in literature as in life, to say nothing of painting, is an occupational hazard for the artist, simply because models in art, in behavior, in growth of spirit and intellect—even if rejected—enrich and enlarge one's view of existence. Deadlier still, to the artist who lacks models, is the curse of ridicule, the bringing to bear on an artist's best work, especially his or her most original, most strikingly deviant, only a fund of ignorance and the presumption that, as an artist's critic, one's judgment is free of the restrictions imposed by prejudice, and is well informed, indeed, about all the art in the world that really matters. 5

What is always needed in the appreciation of art, or life, is the larger perspective. Connections made, or at least attempted, where 6 none existed before, the straining to encompass in one's glance at the varied world the common thread, the unifying theme through immense diversity, a fearlessness of growth, of search, of looking, that enlarges the private and the public world. And yet, in our particular society, it is the narrowed and narrowing view of life that often wins.

Recently, I read at a college and was asked by one of the audience what I considered the major difference between the literature written by black and by white Americans. I had not spent a lot of time considering this question, since it is not the difference between them that interests me, but, rather, the way black writers and white writers seem to me to be writing one immense story—the same story, for the most part—with different parts of this immense story coming from a multitude of different perspectives. Until this is generally recognized, literature will always be broken into bits, black and white, and there will always be questions, wanting neat answers, such as this. 7

Still, I answered that I thought, for the most part, white American writers tended to end their books and their characters' lives as if there were no better existence for which to struggle. The gloom of defeat is thick. 8

By comparison, black writers seem always involved in a moral and/or physical struggle, the result of which is expected to be some kind of larger freedom. Perhaps this is because our literary tradition is based on the slave narratives, where escape for the body and freedom for the soul went together, or perhaps this is because black people have never felt themselves guilty of global, cosmic sins. 9

This comparison does not hold up in every case, of course, and perhaps does not really hold up at all. I am not a gatherer of statistics, only a curious reader, and this has been my impression from reading many books by black and white writers. 10

There are, however, two books by American women that illustrate what I am talking about: *The Awakening*, by Kate Chopin, and *Their Eyes Were Watching God*, by Zora Neale Hurston. 11

The plight of Mme Pontellier is quite similar to that of Janie Crawford. Each woman is married to a dull, society-conscious husband and living in a dull, propriety-conscious community. Each woman desires a life of her own and a man who loves her and makes her feel alive. Each woman finds such a man. 12

Mme Pontellier, overcome by the strictures of society and the existence of her children (along with the cowardice of her lover), kills herself rather than defy the one and abandon the other. Janie Crawford, on the other hand, refuses to allow society to dictate behavior to her, enjoys the love of a much younger, freedom-loving man, and lives to tell others of her experience. 13

When I mentioned these two books to my audience, I was not surprised to learn that only one person, a young black poet in the first row, had ever heard of *Their Eyes Were Watching God (The Awakening* they had fortunately read in their "Women in Literature" class), primarily because it was written by a black woman, whose experience —in love and life—was apparently assumed to be unimportant to the students (and the teachers) of a predominantly white school. 14

Certainly, as a student, I was not directed toward this book, which would have urged me more toward freedom and experience than toward comfort and security, but was directed instead toward a plethora of books by mainly white male writers who thought most women worthless if they didn't enjoy bullfighting or hadn't volunteered for the trenches in World War I. 15

Loving both these books, knowing each to be indispensable to my own growth, my own life, I choose the model, the example, of Janie Crawford. And yet this book, as necessary to me and to other women as air and water, is again out of print* But I have distilled as much as I could of its wisdom in this poem about its heroine, Janie Crawford: 16

I love the way Janie Crawford
left her husbands
the one who wanted to change her
into a mule
and the other who tried to interest her
in being a queen.
A woman, unless she submits,
is neither a mule
nor a queen
though like a mule she may suffer
and like a queen pace the floor.

It has been said that someone asked Toni Morrison why she writes the kind of books she writes, and that she replied: Because they are the kind of books I want to read. 17

This remains my favorite reply to that kind of question. As if anyone reading the magnificent, mysterious *Sula* or the grim, poetic *The Bluest Eye* would require more of a reason for their existence than for the brooding, haunting *Wuthering Heights*, for example, or the melancholy, triumphant *Jane Eyre*. (I am not speaking here of the 18

*Reissued by the University of Illinois Press, 1979.

most famous short line of that book, "Reader, I married him," as the triumph, but, rather, of the triumph of Jane Eyre's control over her own sense of morality and her own stout will, which are but reflections of her creator's, Charlotte Brontë, who no doubt wished to write the sort of book *she* wished to read.)

Flannery O'Connor has written that more and more the serious novelist will write, not what other people want, and certainly not what other people expect, but whatever interests her or him. And that the direction taken, therefore, will be away from sociology, away from the "writing of explanation," of statistics, and further into mystery, into poetry, and into prophecy. I believe this is true, *fortunately true*; especially for "Third World Writers"; Morrison, Marquez, Ahmadi, Camara Laye make good examples. And not only do I believe it is true for serious writers in general, but I believe, as firmly as did O'Connor, that this is our only hope—in a culture so in love with flash, with trendiness, with superficiality, as ours—of acquiring a sense of essence, of timelessness, and of vision. Therefore, to write the books one wants to read is both to point the direction of vision and, at the same time, to follow it. 19

When Toni Morrison said she writes the kind of books she wants to read, she was acknowledging the fact that in a society in which "accepted literature" is so often sexist and racist and otherwise irrelevant or offensive to so many lives, she must do the work of two. She must be her own model as well as the artist attending, creating, learning from, realizing the model, which is to say, herself. 20

(It should be remembered that, as a black person, one cannot completely identify with a Jane Eyre, or with her creator, no matter how much one admires them. And certainly, if one allows history to impinge on one's reading pleasure, one must cringe at the thought of how Heathcliff, in the New World far from Wuthering Heights, amassed his Cathy-dazzling fortune.) I have often been asked why, in my own life and work, I have felt such a desperate need to know and assimilate the experiences of earlier black women writers, most of them unheard of by you and by me, until quite recently, why I felt a need to study them and to teach them. 21

I don't recall the exact moment I set out to explore the works of black women, mainly those in the past, and certainly, in the beginning, I had no desire to teach them. Teaching being for me, at that time, less rewarding than star-gazing on a frigid night. My discovery of them—most of them out of print, abandoned, discredited, maligned, nearly lost—came about, as many things of value do, almost by accident. As it turned out—and this should not have surprised me—I found I was in need of something that only one of them could provide. 22

Mindful that throughout my four years at a prestigious black and then a prestigious white college I had heard not one word about early black women writers, one of my first tasks was simply to determine whether they had existed. After this, I could breathe easier, with more assurance about the profession I myself had chosen. 23

But the incident that started my search began several years ago: I sat down at my desk one day, in a room of my own, with key and lock, and began preparations for a story about voodoo, a subject that had always fascinated me. Many of the elements of this story I had gathered from a story my mother several times told me. She had gone, during the Depression, into town to apply for some government surplus food at the local commissary, and had been turned down, in a particularly humiliating way, by the white woman in charge. 24

My mother always told this story with a most curious expression on her face. She automatically raised her head higher than ever—it was always high—and there was a look of righteousness, a kind of holy *heat* coming from her eyes. She said she had lived to see this same white woman grow old and senile and so badly crippled she had to get about on *two* sticks. 25

To her, this was clearly the working of God, who, as in the old spiritual, ". . . may not come when you want him, but he's right on time!" To me, hearing the story for about the fiftieth time, something else was discernible: the possibilities of the story, for fiction. 26

What, I asked myself, would have happened if, after the crippled old lady died, it was discovered that someone, my mother perhaps (who would have been mortified at the thought, Christian that she is), had voodooed her? 27

Then, my thoughts sweeping me away into the world of hexes and conjurings of centuries past, I wondered how a larger story could be created out of my mother's story; one that would be true to the magnitude of her humiliation and grief, and to the white woman's lack of sensitivity and compassion. 28

My third quandary was: How could I find out all I needed to know in order to write a story that used *authentic* black witchcraft? 29

Which brings me back, almost, to the day I became really interested in black women writers. I say "almost" because one other thing, from my childhood, made the choice of black magic a logical and irresistible one for my story. Aside from my mother's several stories about root doctors she had heard of or known, there was the story I had often heard about my "crazy" Walker aunt. 30

Many years ago, when my aunt was a meek and obedient girl growing up in a strict, conventionally religious house in the rural South, she had suddenly thrown off her meekness and had run away 31 from home, escorted by a rogue of a man permanently attached elsewhere.

When she was returned home by her father, she was declared quite mad. In the backwoods South at the turn of the century, "madness" of this sort was cured not by psychiatry but by powders and by spells. (One can see Scott Joplin's *Treemonisha* to understand the role voodoo played among black people of that period.) My aunt's madness was treated by the community conjurer, who promised, and delivered, the desired results. His treatment was a bag of white powder, bought for fifty cents, and sprinkled on the ground around her house, with some of it sewed, I believe, into the bodice of her nightgown. 32

So when I sat down to write my story about voodoo, my crazy Walker aunt was definitely on my mind. 33

But she had experienced her temporary craziness so long ago that her story had all the excitement of a might-have-been. I needed, instead of family memories, some hard facts about the *craft* of voodoo, as practiced by Southern blacks in the nineteenth century. (It never once, fortunately, occurred to me that voodoo was not worthy of the interest I had in it, or was too ridiculous to study seriously.) 34

I began reading all I could find on the subject of "The Negro and His Folkways and Superstitions." There were Botkin and Puckett and others, all white, most racist. How was I to believe anything they wrote, since at least one of them, Puckett, was capable of wondering, in his book, if "The Negro" had a large enough brain? 35

Well, I thought, where are the *black* collectors of folklore? Where is the *black* anthropologist? Where is the *black* person who took the time to travel the back roads of the South and collect the information I need: how to cure heat trouble, treat dropsy, hex somebody to death, lock bowels, cause joints to swell, eyes to fall out, and so on. Where was this black person? 36

And that is when I first saw, in a *footnote* to the white voices of authority, the name Zora Neale Hurston. 37

Folklorist, novelist, anthropologist, serious student of voodoo, also all-around black woman, with guts enough to take a slide rule and measure random black heads in Harlem; not to prove their inferiority, but to prove that whatever their size, shape, or present condition of servitude, those heads contained all the intelligence anyone could use to get through this world. 38

Zora Hurston, who went to Barnard to learn how to study what she really wanted to learn: the ways of her own people, and what ancient rituals, customs, and beliefs had made them unique. 39

Zora, of the sandy-colored hair and the daredevil eyes, a girl who escaped poverty and parental neglect by hard work and a sharp eye for the main chance. 40

Zora, who left the South only to return to look at it again. 41
Who went to root doctors from Florida to Louisiana and said, "Here I am. I want to learn your trade."

Zora, who had collected all the black folklore I could ever use. 42

That Zora. 43

And having found *that Zora* (like a golden key to a storehouse 44
of varied treasure), I was hooked.

What I had discovered, of course, was a model. A model, 45
who, as it happened, provided more than voodoo for my story, more than one of the greatest novels America had produced—though, being America, it did not realize this. She had provided, as if she knew someday I would come along wandering in the wilderness, a nearly complete record of her life. And though her life sprouted an occasional wart, I am eternally grateful for that life, warts and all.

It is not irrelevant, nor is it bragging (except perhaps to gloat 46
a little on the happy relatedness of Zora, my mother and me), to mention here that the story I wrote, called "the Revenge of Hannah Kemhuff," based on my mother's experiences during the Depression, and on Zora Hurston's folklore collection of the 1920s, and on my own response to both out of a contemporary existence, was immediately published and was later selected, by a reputable collector of short stories, as one of the *Best Short Stories of 1974*.

I mention it because this story might never have been 47
written, because the very bases of its structure, authentic black folklore, viewed from a black perspective, might have been lost.

Had it been lost, my mother's story would have had no 48
historical underpinning, none I could trust, anyway. I would not have written the story, which I enjoyed writing as much as I've enjoyed writing anything in my life, had I not known that Zora had already done a thorough job of preparing the ground over which I was then moving.

In that story I gathered up the historical and psychological 49
threads of the life my ancestors lived, and in the writing of it I felt joy and strength and my own continuity. I had that wonderful feeling writers get sometimes, not very often, of being *with* a great many people, ancient spirits, all very happy to see me consulting and acknowledging them, and eager to let me know, through the joy of their presence, that, indeed, I am not alone.

To take Toni Morrison's statement further, if that is possible, 50
in my own work I write not only what I want to read—understanding fully and indelibly that if I don't do it no one else is so vitally interested, or capable of doing it to my satisfaction—I write all the things *I should have been able to read*. Consulting, as belatedly discovered models, those writers—most of whom, not surprisingly, are women—who understood that their experience as ordinary human

beings was also valuable, and in danger of being misrepresented, distorted, or lost:

Zora Hurston—novelist, essayist, anthropologist, autobiographer;

Jean Toomer—novelist, poet, philosopher, visionary, a man who cared what women felt;

Colette—whose crinkly hair enhances her French, part-black face; novelist, playwright, dancer, essayist, newspaperwoman, lover of women, men, small dogs; fortunate not to have been born in America;

Anaïs Nin—recorder of everything, no matter how minute;

Tillie Olson—a writer of such generosity and honesty, she literally saves lives;

Virginia Woolf—who has saved so many of us.

It is, in the end, the saving of lives that we writers are about. 51
Whether we are "minority" writers or "majority." It is simply in our power to do this.

We do it because we care. We care that Vincent Van Gogh 52
mutilated his ear. We care that behind a pile of manure in the yard he destroyed his life. We care that Scott Joplin's music *lives*! We care because we know this: *the life we save is our own.*

QUESTIONS

1. According to the author, what is the importance of models in art? What is the relationship of models to life? List the models in Walker's life. Which figures stand out?

2. Paraphrase Walker's commentary on the relationship between black American and white American writing.

3. Walker uses many allusions in this essay. Identify as many as you can. What is the allusion in the title? Comment on their general effectiveness.

4. Is the author's style and choice of diction suitable to her subject matter and to her audience? Why or Why not?

5. What is Walker's thesis? Where is it stated most eloquently?

6. Why does the author personalize her treatment of the topic? What does she gain? Is there anything lost?

7. Walker employs several unique structuring devices in this essay. Cite at least three and analyze their utility.

8. Explain Walker's use of examples to reinforce her generalizations and to organize the essay.

9. Discuss the meaning of Walker's remark, "What is always needed in the appreciation of art, or life, is the larger perspective."

10. a. If you were planning on a career as a writer, artist, actor, or musician, who would your models be, and why?
b. Analyze the various models—personal, cultural, and artistic—in your own life.
c. Explore the types of literature, art, film, and music that you like. How do these varieties of art influence your life?

E. M. FORSTER

Not Looking at Pictures

Edward Morgan Forster (1879–1970), English essayist, novelist, biographer, and literary critic, wrote several notable works of fiction dealing with the constrictive effects of social and national conventions on human relationships. These novels include *A Room with a View* (1908), *Howard's End* (1910), and *A Passage to India* (1924). In addition, his lectures on fiction, collected as *Aspects of the Novel* (1927), remain graceful elucidations of the genre. In "Not Looking at Pictures," an essay taken from *Two Cheers for Democracy* (1939), Forster offers a whimsical account of difficulties when trying to evaluate art.

Pictures are not easy to look at. They generate private fantasies, they furnish material for jokes, they recall scraps of historical knowledge, they show landscapes where one would like to wander and human beings whom one would like to resemble or adore, but looking at them is another matter, yet they must have been painted to be looked at. They were intended to appeal to the eye, but almost as if it were gazing at the sun itself the eye often reacts by closing as soon as it catches sight of them. The mind takes charge instead and goes off on some alien vision. The mind has such a congenial time that it forgets what set it going. Van Gogh and Corot and Michelangelo are three different painters, but if the mind is undisciplined and uncontrolled by the eye, they may all three induce the same mood; we may take just the same course through dreamland or funland from them, each time, and never experience anything new. 1

I am bad at looking at pictures myself, and the late Roger Fry 2 enjoyed going to a gallery with me now and then, for this very reason. He found it an amusing change to be with someone who scarcely ever saw what the painter had painted. "Tell me, why do you like this, why do you prefer it to that?" he would ask, and listen agape for the ridiculous answer. One day we looked at a fifteenth-century Italian predella, where a St. George was engaged in spearing a dragon of the plesiosaurus type. I laughed. "Now, *what* is there funny in this?" pounced Fry. I readily explained. The fun was to be found in the expression upon the dragons' face. The spear had gone through its hooped-up neck once, and now startled it by arriving at a second thickness. "Oh dear, here it comes again, I hoped that was all" it was thinking. Fry laughed too, but not at the misfortunes of the dragon. He was amazed that anyone could go so completely off the lines. There was no harm in it—but really, really! He was even more amazed when our enthusiasms coincided: "I fancy we are talking about different things," he would say, and we always were; I liked the mountain-back because it reminded me of a peacock, he because it had some structural significance, though not as much as the sack of potatoes in the foreground.

Long years of wandering down miles of galleries have convinced me that there must be something rare in those coloured slabs called "pictures," something which I am incapable of detecting for myself, though glimpses of it are to be had through the eyes of others. How much am I missing? And what? And are other modern sight-seers in the same fix? Ours is an aural rather than a visual age, we do not get so lost in the concert hall, we seem able to hear music for ourselves, and to hear it as music, but in galleries so many of us go off at once into a laugh or a sigh or an amorous day-dream. In vain does the picture recall us. "What have your obsessions got to do with me?" it complains. "I am neither a theatre of varieties nor a spring-mattress, but paint. Look at my paint." Back we go—the picture kindly standing still meanwhile, and being to that extent more obliging than music—and resume the looking-business. But something is sure to intervene—a tress of hair, the half-open door of a summer-house, a Crivelli dessert, a Bosch fish-and-fiend salad—and to draw us away. 3

One of the things that helps us to keep looking is composition. For many years now I have associated composition with a diagonal line, and when I find such a line I imagine I have gutted the picture's secret. Giorgione's Castelfranco Madonna has such a line in the lance of the warrior-saint, and Titian's Entombment at Venice has a very good one indeed. Five figures contribute to make up the diagonal; beginning high on the left with the statue of Moses, it passes through the heads of the Magdalene, Mary, and the dead Christ, and plunges through the body of Joseph of Arimathea into the 4

ground. Making a right angle to it, flits the winged Genius of Burial. And to the right, apart from it, and perpendicular, balancing the Moses, towers the statue of Faith. Titian's Entombment is one of my easiest pictures. I look at photographs of it intelligently, and encourage the diagonal and the pathos to reinforce one another. I see, with more than usual vividness, the grim alcove at the back and the sinister tusked pedestals upon which the two statues stand. Stone shuts in flesh; the whole picture is a tomb. I hear sounds of lamentation, though not to the extent of shattering the general scheme; that is held together by the emphatic diagonal, which no emotion breaks. Titian was a very old man when he achieved this masterpiece; that too I realise, but not immoderately. Composition here really has been a help, and it is a composition which no one can miss: the diagonal slopes as obviously as the band on a threshing-machine, and vibrates with power.

Unfortunately, having no natural esthetic aptitude, I look for 5
diagonals everywhere, and if I cannot find one think the composition must be at fault. It is a word which I have learnt—a solitary word in a foreign language. For instance, I was completely baffled by Velasquez's Las Meninas. Wherever was the diagonal? Then the friend I was with—Charles Mauron, the friend who, after Roger Fry, has helped me with pictures most—set to work on my behalf, and cautiously underlined the themes. There is a wave. There is a half-wave. The wave starts up on the left, with the head of the painter, and curves down and up through the heads of the three girls. The half-wave starts with the head of Isabel de Velasco, and sinks out of the canvas through the dwarfs. Responding to these great curves, or inverting them, are smaller ones on the women's dresses or elsewhere. All these waves are not merely pattern; they are doing other work too—e.g., helping to bring out the effect of depth in the room, and the effect of air. Important too is the pushing forward of objects in the extreme left and right foregrounds, the easel of the painter in the one case, the paws of a placid dog in the other. From these, the composition curves back to the central figure, the lovely child-princess. I put it more crudely than did Charles Mauron, nor do I suppose that his account would have been Velasquez's, or that Velasquez would have given any account at all. But it is an example of the way in which pictures should be tackled for the benefit of us outsiders: coolly and patiently, as if they were designs, so that we are helped at last to the appreciation of something non-mathematical. Here again, as in the case of the Entombment, the composition and the action reinforced one another. I viewed with increasing joy that adorable party, which had been surprised not only by myself but by the King and Queen of Spain. There they were in the looking-glass!

Las Meninas has a snap-shot quality. The party might have been taken by Philip IV, if Philip IV had had a Kodak. It is all so casual—and yet it is all so elaborate and sophisticated, and I suppose those curves and the rest of it help to bring this out, and to evoke a vanished civilisation.

Besides composition there is colour. I look for that, too, but 6
with even less success. Colour is visible when thrown in my face—like the two cherries in the great grey Michael Sweertz group in the National Gallery. But as a rule it is only material for dream.

On the whole, I am improving, and after all these years. I am 7
learning to get myself out of the way a little, and to be more receptive, and my appreciation of pictures does increase. If I can make any progress at all, the average outsider should do better still. A combination of courage and modesty is what he wants. It is so unenterprising to annihilate everything that's made to a green thought, even when the thought is an exquisite one. Not looking at art leads to one goal only. Looking at it leads to so many.

QUESTIONS

1. Why does the author declare, "Pictures are not easy to look at"? Why is Forster himself "bad at looking at pictures"?

2. What does the author seem to like about art? Why does he persist in viewing art works, despite his difficulties?

3. Identify these allusions in the essay: Van Gogh, Corot, Michelangelo (paragraph 1); Roger Frye (paragraph 2); Crivelli, Bosch (paragraph 3); Glorgione, Titian (paragraph 4), and Velasquez (paragraph 5). What do these allusions tell us about the degree of Forster's expertise?

4. Examine Forster's use of punctuation to establish tone in paragraphs 2 and 3.

5. Analyze the material presented in the Introduction and the strategies employed.

6. How does Forster employ illustration to help structure each paragraph in this essay?

7. Explain the author's use of comparison and contrast in this essay.

8. What elements contribute to the gently humorous tone of this essay?

9. Forster declares, "Ours is an aural rather than visual age" (paragraph 3). Do you agree or disagree with his assertion, and why?

10. a. Write an essay explaining your own difficulties in appreciating a particular art form.

b. Forster mentions "composition" and "color" as two aspects of art appreciation. Elaborate on these qualities and others in an essay explaining how you evaluate pictures.

c. Analyze a particular work of art based on a museum trip or an illustration.

KATHARINE KUH

Break-up:
THE CORE OF MODERN ART

Katharine W. Kuh (1904–), specialist in modern art, was from 1946 to 1957 associated as curator and editor with the Art Institute of Chicago. Subsequently she was art editor for *Saturday Review.* Kuh is the author of *Art Has Many Faces* (1951), *Leger* (1953), *The Artist's Voice* (1962), *Break-up: The Core of Modern Art* (1965), and *The Open Eye* (1971). In this essay from her fourth book, Kuh examines the stages in and causes of the altered vision and style of modern art.

The art of our century has been characterized by shat- 1
tered surfaces, broken color, segmented compositions, dissolving forms and shredded images. Curiously insistent is this consistent emphasis on break-up. However, dissolution today does not necessarily mean lack of discipline. It can also mean a new kind of discipline, for disintegration is often followed by reconstruction, the artist deliberately smashing his material only to reassemble it in new and unexpected relationships. Moreover, the process of breaking up is quite different from the process of breaking down. And during the last hundred years, every aspect of art has been broken up—color, light, pigment, form, line, content, space, surface and design.

In the nineteenth century, easels were moved out-of-doors 2
and color was broken into relatively minute areas in order to approximate the reality of sunlight and to preserve on canvas nature's own fleeting atmospheric effects. Known as Impressionism, this movement was the first step in a long sequence of experiments that finally banished the Renaissance emphasis on humanism, on three-

dimensional form and on a traditional center of interest. Here was the beginning of a gradual but steady tendency toward diffusion in art. A few years later, Vincent Van Gogh transformed broken color into broken pigment. Less interested in realistic light than in his own highly charged emotions, he allowed smashing rhythmic brushstrokes to mirror his personal turbulence. In doing so he foretold twentieth-century Expressionism, that aptly named movement which relied on pitted surfaces, broken outlines, unpredictable color and scarred textures to intensify emotional expression. As the Impressionists were bent on freeing nature from sham, so the Expressionists hoped to liberate their own feelings from all trace of artificiality.

Perhaps the most revolutionary break-up in modern art took place a little more than fifty years ago with the advent of Cubism. It was the Cubists, Picasso, Braque, Duchamp, Picabia, Léger, Delaunay and Juan Gris, who responded to the inordinate multiplicity of present-day life by breaking up and arbitrarily rearranging transparent planes and surfaces so that all sides of an object could be seen at once. As the Cubists broke through the boundaries of conventional form to show multiple aspects simultaneously, their Italian colleagues, the Futurists, hoped to encompass the uninterrupted motion of an object at one time. This they tried to do by a series of overlapping transparent forms illustrating the path of an object as it moved through space. 3

With Surrealism came still another kind of break-up, the break-up of chronology. Frankly influenced by Freudian discoveries, this movement splintered time sequence with an abandon borrowed from the world of fragmented dreams. Content was purposely unhinged in denial of all rational expression, allowing disconnected episodes to recreate the disturbing life of our unconscious. At the same time, perspective and distance often became severely dislocated. Denying the orderly naturalism of the Renaissance, painters today project space and distance from innumerable eye levels, intentionally segmenting their compositions into conflicting perspectives. We look from above, from below, from diverse angles, from near, from far—all at one and the same time (not an unfamiliar experience for eyes accustomed to air travel). Here again is the Cubist idea of simultaneity, the twentieth-century urge to approach a scene from many different directions in a single condensed encounter. 4

Finally we come to the total break-up of Abstract Expressionism, a technique that celebrates the specific act of painting (sometimes appropriately called Action Painting). Now everything is shattered—line, light, color, form, pigment, surface and design. These canvases defy all the old rules as they reveal the immediate spontaneous feelings of the artist in the process of painting. There is 5 no one central idea, no beginning, no end—only an incessant flow and flux where lightning brushstrokes report the artist's impulsive and compulsive reactions. The pigment actually develops a life of its own, almost strong enough to hypnotize the painter. Here break-up turns into both content and form, with the impetuous paint itself telling the full story. No naturalistic image is needed to describe these artists' volatile feelings.

As one looks back over the last hundred years, the history of 6
break-up becomes a key to the history of art. Why painters and sculptors of this period have been so involved with problems of dissolution is a question only partly answered by the obvious impact of modern scientific methods of destruction. One cannot deny that the last two devastating wars and the possibility of a still more devastating one to come do affect our daily thinking. Since the discovery of the atom bomb, science has become almost synonymous with destruction. The influence of contemporary warfare with its colossal explosions and upheavals has unquestionably had much to do with the tendency toward fragmentation in art, but there have been other and earlier causes.

From the beginning, it was science in one form or another 7
that affected modern painting and sculpture. In nineteenth-century Europe the interest in atmospheric phenomena was not an isolated expression limited to the Impressionists. At that time, numerous scientists were experimenting with all manner of optical color laws, writing widely on the subject as they investigated the relationship of color to the human eye. Artists like Monet and Seurat were familiar with these findings and not unnaturally applied them to their paintings. It would be a grave mistake to underestimate the influence of contemporary scientific research on the development of Impressionism. The wonders of natural light became a focus for nineteenth-century artists exactly as the magic of artificial light stimulated painters of the precentury. If the earlier men were more interested in rural landscapes seen out-of-doors in the sunlight, the later artists quite reasonably concentrated on city scenes, preferably at night when man-made luminosity tends to puncture both form and space.

Other scientific investigations also exerted considerable influ- 8
ence on present-day painters and sculptors. Inventions like the microscope and telescope, with their capacity to enlarge, isolate and probe, offer the artist provocative new worlds to explore. These instruments, which break up structures only to examine them more fully, demonstrate how details can be magnified and separated from the whole and operate as new experiences. Repeatedly artists in recent years have exploited this idea, allowing one isolated symbol to represent an entire complex organism. Miró often needs merely part

of a woman's body to describe all women, or Léger, one magnified letter of the alphabet to conjure up the numberless printed words that daily bombard us.

As scientists smash the atom, so likewise artists smash traditional forms. For how, indeed, can anyone remain immune to the new mushroom shape that haunts us day and night? The American painter, Morris Graves, put it well recently, "You simply can't keep the world out any longer. Like everyone else, I've been caught in our scientific culture." This is not to say that painters are interested in reproducing realistic scenes of atomic explosions, but rather that they are concerned with the reactions accompanying these disasters. It is just possible that, with their extra-sensitized intuition, artists may have unconsciously predicted the discovery of atomic energy long before "the bomb" became a familiar household world, for the history of break-up in art antedates the history of nuclear break-up. 9

Even the invention of the X-ray machine has brought us closer to penetrating form. We no longer think of outer coverings as solid or final; we know they can be visually pierced merely by rendering them transparent. We have also learned from science that space penetrates everything. 10

The sculptor Gabo claims, "Space is a reality in all of our experiences and it is present in every object. . . . That's what I've tried to show in certain of my stone carvings. When they turn, observe how their curved forms seem interpenetrated by space." For the artist today, nothing is static or permanent. The new popular dances are no more potently kinetic than the new staccato art forms that everywhere confront us. 11

With the dramatic development of speedier transportation and swifter communication comes a visual overlapping responsible for much of contemporary art. In modern life one is simultaneously subjected to countless experiences that become fragmented, superimposed, and finally rebuilt into new experiences. Speed is a cogent part of our daily life. 12

How natural, then, that artists reflect this pressure by showing all sides of an object, its entire motion, its total psychological content in one concerted impact. It is almost as if the pressures of time had necessitated a visual speed-up not unlike the industrial one associated with the assembly line and mass production. Speed with its multiple overlays transforms our surroundings into jagged, interrupted images. 13

Modern technology and science have produced a wealth of new materials and new ways of using old materials. For the artist this means wider opportunities. There is no doubt that the limitations of materials and nature of tools both restrict and shape a man's work. 14

Observe how the development of plastics and light metals along with new methods of welding and brazing have changed the direction of sculpture. Transparent plastic materials allow one to look through an object, to see its various sides superimposed on each other (as in Cubism or in an X ray). Today, welding is as prevalent as casting was in the past. This new method encourages open designs, often of great linear agility, where surrounding and intervening space becomes as important as form itself. In fact, it becomes a kind of negative form. While bronze casting and stone carving are techniques more readily adapted to solid volumes, welding permits perforated metal designs of extreme versatility that free sculpture from the static restrictions which for centuries have moored it to the floor.

More ambiguous than other scientific inventions familiar to 15
modern artists, but no less influential, are the psychoanalytic studies of Freud and his followers, discoveries that have infiltrated recent art, especially Surrealism. The Surrealists, in their struggle to escape the monotony and frustrations of everyday life, claimed that dreams were the only hope. Turning to the irrational world of their unconscious, they banished all time barriers and moral judgments to combine disconnected dream experiences from the past, present and intervening psychological states. The Surrealists were concerned with overlapping emotions more than with overlapping forms. Their paintings often become segmented capsules of associative experiences. For them, obsessive and often unrelated images replaced the direct emotional messages of Expressionism. They did not need to smash pigment and texture; they went beyond this to smash the whole continuity of logical thought.

There is little doubt that contemporary art has taken much 16
from contemporary life. In a period when science has made revolutionary strides, artists in their studios have not been unaware of scientists in their laboratories. But this has rarely been a one-way street. Painters and sculptors, though admittedly influenced by modern science, have also molded and changed our world. If break-up has been a vital part of their expression, it has not always been a symbol of destruction. Quite the contrary: it has been used to examine more fully, to penetrate more deeply, to analyze more thoroughly, to enlarge, isolate and make more familiar certain aspects of life that earlier we were apt to neglect. In addition, it sometimes provides rich multiple experiences so organized as not merely to reflect our world, but in fact to interpret it.

QUESTIONS

1. Trace Kuh's theory of breakup from the impressionists to the abstract expressionists.

2. What examples does the author provide to illustrate the effect of science, technology, and psychology on modern painting?

3. Examine the essay and locate synonyms that Kuh employs for breakup. What connotations does she seem to emphasize for her core term?

4. What stylistic characteristics of art criticism—and criticism in general—does the essay reflect?

5. Analyze the development and function of the introductory paragraph.

6. Examine the combined modes of illustration and process analysis in paragraphs 2 to 5. What modes of definition does Kuh employ to convey essential information about modern art movements?

7. Describe the pattern of causal analysis employed by Kuh throughout the essay. Examine the role of topic sentences in guiding causal relationships.

8. What strategies for essay conclusions are evident in paragraph 16?

9. Kuh suggests that breakup is not necessarily destruction. What social and political implications do you perceive in her statement?

10. a. Write an essay on the impact of contemporary life on a literary, artistic, or media form.
b. Select one of the artists or art movements mentioned by Kuh and write a paper on the subject.

PAULINE KAEL

Rocky

Pauline Kael (1919–   ) has been a film critic for *McCall's, The New Republic*, and *The New Yorker* and a frequent contributor to other national publications. Perhaps the best known and most controversial film critic in the United States today, Kael is the author of *I Lost It at the Movies* (1965), *Kiss Kiss Bang Bang* (1968), *Going Steady* (1970), *Deeper into the Movies* (1973), and *When the Lights Go Down* (1980). The following review of *Rocky* reflects the energy, brilliance, range, and provocative tone characteristic of Kael's best film interpretation.

Chunky, muscle-bound Sylvester Stallone looks repulsive one moment, noble the next, and sometimes both at once. In *Rocky*, which he wrote and stars in, he's a thirty-year-old club fighter who works as a strong-arm man, collecting money for a loan shark. Rocky never got anywhere, and he has nothing; he lives in a Philadelphia tenement, and even the name he fights under—the Italian Stallion—has become a joke. But the world heavyweight champion, Apollo Creed (Carl Weathers), who's a smart black jester, like Muhammad Ali, announces that for his Bicentennial New Year's fight he'll give an unknown a shot at the title, and he picks the Italian Stallion for the racial-sexual overtones of the contest. This small romantic fable is about a palooka gaining his manhood; it's Terry Malloy finally getting his chance to be somebody. *Rocky* is a threadbare patchwork of old-movie bits (*On the Waterfront, Marty, Somebody Up There Likes Me*, Capra's *Meet Joe Doe*, and maybe even a little of Preston Sturges' *Hail the Conquering Hero*), yet it's engaging, and the naïve elements are emotionally effective. John G. Avildsen's directing is his usual strictly-from-hunger approach; he slams through a picture like a poor man's Sidney Lumet. But a more painstaking director would have been too proud to shoot the mildewed ideas and would have tried to throw out as many as possible and to conceal the others—and would probably have wrecked the movie. *Rocky* is shameless, and that's why—on a certain level—it works. What holds it together is innocence. 1

In his offscreen bravado, Stallone (in Italian *stallone* means stallion) has claimed that he wrote the script in three and a half days, and some professional screenwriters, seeing what a ragtag of a script it is, may think that they could have done it in two and a half. But they wouldn't have been able to believe in what they did, and it wouldn't have got the audience cheering, the way *Rocky* does. The innocence that makes this picture so winning emanates from Sylvester Stallone. It's a street-wise, flowers-blooming-in-the-garbage innocence. Stallone plays a waif, a strong-arm man who doesn't want to hurt anybody, a loner with only his pet turtles to talk to. Yet the character doesn't come across as maudlin. Stallone looks like a big, battered Paul McCartney. There's bullnecked energy in him, smoldering; he has a field of force, like Brando's. And he knows how to use his overripe, cartoon sensuality—the eyelids at half-mast, the sad brown eyes and twisted, hurt mouth. Victor Mature also had this thick sensuality, but the movies used him as if it were simple plushy handsomeness, and so he became ridiculous, until he learned—too late—to act. Stallone is aware that we see him as a hulk, and he plays against this comically and tenderly. In his deep, caveman's voice, he gives the most surprising, sharp, fresh shadings to his lines. He's at 2 his funniest trying to explain to his boss why he didn't break somebody's thumbs, as he'd been told to; he's even funny talking to his turtles. He pulls the whiskers off the film's cliché situations, so that we're constantly charmed by him, waiting for what he'll say next. He's like a child who never ceases to amaze us.

Stallone has the gift of direct communication with the audi- 3
ence. Rocky's naïve observations come from so deep inside him that they have a Lewis Carroll enchantment. His unworldliness makes him seem dumb, but we know better; we understand what he feels at every moment. Rocky is the embodiment of the out-of-fashion pure-at-heart. His macho strut belongs with the ducktails of the fifties—he's a sagging peacock. I'm not sure how much of his archaism is thought out, how much is the accidental result of Stallone's overdeveloped, weight lifter's muscles combined with his simplistic beliefs, but Rocky represents the redemption of an earlier ideal—the man as rock for woman to cleave to. Talia Shire plays Adrian, a shy girl with glasses who works in a pet store; she's the Betsy Blair to Stallone's Marty. It's unspeakably musty, but they put it over, her delicacy (that of a button-faced Audrey Hepburn) is the right counterpoint to his primitivism. It's clear that he's drawn to her because she isn't fast or rough and doesn't make fun of him; she doesn't make hostile wisecracks, like the kids in the street. We don't groan at this, because he's such a *tortured* macho nice-guy—he has failed his own high ideals. And who doesn't have a soft spot for the teen-age aspirations congealed inside this thirty-year-old bum?

Stallone is the picture, but the performers who revolve 4
around him are talented. Carl Weathers, a former Oakland Raiders linebacker, is a real find. His Apollo Creed has the flash and ebullience to put the fairy-tale plot in motion; when the champ arrives at the ring dressed as Uncle Sam, no one could enjoy the racial joke as much as he does. Adrian's heavyset brother Paulie is played by Burt Young, who has been turning up in movies more and more frequently in the past three years and still gives the impression that his abilities haven't begun to be tapped. Young, who actually was a professional fighter, has the cracked, mottled voice of someone who's taken a lot of punishment in the sinuses; the resonance is gone. As Mickey, the ancient pug who runs a fighters' gym, Burgess Meredith uses the harsh, racking sound of a man who's been punched too often in the vocal cords. The director overemphasizes Meredith's performance (much as John Schlesinger did in *The Day of the Locust*); Meredith would look better if we were left to discover how good he is for ourselves. I found *Marty* dreary, because the people in it were sapped of energy. But Stallone and Talia Shire and the others here have a restrained force; you feel that they're being pressed down, that

they're under a lid. The only one who gets a chance to explode is Paulie, when, in a rage, he wields a baseball bat, and it's a poor scene, out of tune. Yet the actors themselves have so much more to them than they're using that what comes across in their performances is what's under the lid. The actors—and this includes Joe Spinell as Gazzo, Rocky's gangster boss—enable us to feel their reserves of intelligence; they provide tact and taste, which aren't in long supply in an Avildsen film.

Rocky is the kind of movie in which the shots are under- 5
lighted, because the characters are poor and it's wintertime. I was almost never convinced that the camera was in the right place. The shots don't match well, and they're put together jerkily, with cheap romantic music thrown in like cement blocks of lyricism, and sheer noise used to build up excitement at the climactic prizefight, where the camera is so close to the fighters that you can't feel the rhythm of the encounter. And the film doesn't follow through on what it prepares. Early on, we see Rocky with the street-corner kids in his skid-row neighborhood, but we never get to see how these kids react to his training or to the fight itself. Even the bull mastiff who keeps Rocky company on his early-morning runs is lost track of. I get the feeling that Avildsen is so impatient to finish a film on schedule (or before, as if it were a race) that he hardly bothers to think it out. I hate the way *Rocky* is made, yet better might be worse in this case. Unless a director could take this material and transform it into sentimental urban poetry—a modern equivalent of what Frank Borzage used to do in pictures such as *Man's Castle*, with Spencer Tracy and Loretta Young—we're probably better off with Avildsen's sloppiness than with careful planning; a craftsmanlike *Rocky* would be obsolete, like a TV play of the fifties.

Stallone can certainly write; that is, he can write scenes and 6
dialogue. But as a writer he stays inside the character; we never get a clear outside view of Rocky. For that, Stallone falls back on clichés, on an urban-primitive myth: at the end, Rocky has everything a man needs—his manhood, his woman, maybe even his dog. (If it were rural-primitive, he'd have some land, too.) In a sense, *Rocky* is a piece of innocent art, but its innocence doesn't sit too well. The bad side of *Rocky* is its resemblance to *Marty*—its folklorish, grubby littleness. Unpretentiousness shouldn't be used as a virtue. This warmed-over bum-into-man myth is unworthy of the freak macho force of its star; talking to turtles is too endearing. What separates Stallone from a Brando is that everything Stallone does has one purpose: to make you like him. He may not know how good he could be if he'd stop snuggling into your heart. If not—well, he may be to acting what Mario Lanza was to singing, and that's a form of bumminess.

QUESTIONS

1. What does the author like about *Rocky*? What does she dislike about the film?

2. Examine the value judgments that the author makes about older movies, notably *Marty*; about Stallone and Brando, and about sentimentality in film. Why does she seem to like *Rocky* despite herself?

3. Locate and discuss examples of figurative language in paragraphs 1 to 3.

4. List and identify five to ten allusions to film culture (films, actors, directors, etc.). What does Kael presuppose about her audience?

5. Why is the author's introductory paragraph a model of film criticism? What is her thesis, and where does she place it?

6. Analyze the overall structure of this essay. What are the focal points of each paragraph? How does Kael handle transitions? Which mode of paragraph development does Kael prefer?

7. How do Kael's descriptive powers reinforce central meanings in the essay?

8. Analyze the relationship of the concluding paragraph to the opening one. What value judgment does she make at the end? How does this affect the tone?

9. Kael implies at several points that we like fairy tales—"a Lewis Carroll enchantment"—in films. Do you agree or disagree? What films that you have seen project this fairy tale aura?

10. a. Write your own review of *Rocky I*, *Rocky II*, *Rocky III*, or the entire trilogy.
b. Explore the theme of innocence in American film.
c. Select a film that you like but have mixed feelings about and evaluate your response to it.

MARYA MANNES

How Do You Know It's Good?

Marya Mannes (1904–) has written several novels and some light verse, but she is best known for her essays, which have appeared in *Vogue*, *McCall's*, *Harper's*, and *The New*

Republic. She has collected her essays in *More in Anger* (1958) and in *The New York I Know* (1961). Mannes has also written on such subjects as suicide and euthanasia in *Last Rights* (1974) and television in *Who Owns the Air?* (1960). In this essay from *But Will It Sell?* (1964), she establishes standards for judging excellence in the arts.

Suppose there were no critics to tell us how to react to a picture, a play, or a new composition of music. Suppose we wandered innocent as the dawn into an art exhibition of unsigned paintings. By what standards, by what values would we decide whether they were good or bad, talented or untalented, successes or failures? How can we ever know that what we think is right? 1

For the last fifteen or twenty years the fashion in criticism or appreciation of the arts has been to deny the existence of any valid criteria and to make the words "good" or "bad" irrelevant, immaterial, and inapplicable. There is no such thing, we are told, as a set of standards, first acquired through experience and knowledge and later imposed on the subject under discussion. This has been a popular approach, for it relieves the critic of the responsibility of judgment and the public of the necessity of knowledge. It pleases those resentful of disciplines, it flatters the empty-minded by calling them open-minded, it comforts the confused. Under the banner of democracy and the kind of equality which our forefathers did *not* mean, it says, in effect, "Who are you to tell us what *is* good or bad?" This is the same cry used so long and so effectively by the producers of mass media who insist that it is the public, not they, who decides what it wants to hear and see, and that for a critic to say that *this* program is bad and *this* program is good is purely a reflection of personal taste. Nobody recently has expressed this philosophy more succinctly than Dr. Frank Stanton, the highly intelligent president of CBS television. At a hearing before the Federal Communications Commission, this phrase escaped him under questioning: "One man's mediocrity is another man's good program." 2

There is no better way of saying "No values are absolute." There is another important aspect to this philosophy of *laissez faire:* It is the fear, in all observers of all forms of art, of guessing wrong. This fear is well come by, for who has not heard of the contemporary outcries against artists who later were called great? Every age has its arbiters who do not grow with their times, who cannot tell evolution from revolution or the difference between frivolous faddism, amateurish experimentation, and profound and necessary change. Who wants to be caught *flagrante delicto* with an error of judgment as serious as this? It is far safer, and certainly easier, to look at a picture 3 or a play or a poem and to say "This is hard to understand, but it may be good," or simply to welcome it as a new form. The word "new"—in our country especially—has magical connotations. What is new must be good; what is old is probably bad. And if a critic can describe the new in language that nobody can understand, he's safer still. If he has mastered the art of saying nothing with exquisite complexity, nobody can quote him later as saying anything.

But all these, I maintain, are forms of abdication from the 4
responsibility of judgment. In creating, the artist commits himself; in appreciating, you have a commitment of your own. For after all, it is the audience which makes the arts. A climate of appreciation is essential to its flowering, and the higher the expectations of the public, the better the performance of the artist. Conversely, only a public ill-served by its critics could have accepted as art and as literature so much in these last years that has been neither. If anything goes, everything goes; and at the bottom of the junkpile lie the discarded standards too.

But what are these standards? How do you get them? How do 5
you know they're the right ones? How can you make a clear pattern out of so many intangibles, including that greatest one, the very private I?

Well for one thing, it's fairly obvious that the more you read 6
and see and hear, the more equipped you'll be to practice that art of association which is at the basis of all understanding and judgment. The more you live and the more you look, the more aware you are of a consistent pattern—as universal as the stars, as the tides, as breathing, as night and day—underlying everything. I would call this pattern and this rhythm an order. Not order—*an* order. Within it exists an incredible diversity of forms. Without it lies chaos—the wild cells of destruction—sickness. It is in the end up to you to distinguish between the diversity that is health and the chaos that is sickness, and you can't do this without a process of association that can link a bar of Mozart with the corner of a Vermeer painting, or a Stravinsky score with a Picasso abstraction; or that can relate an aggressive act with a Franz Kline painting and a fit of coughing with a John Cage composition.

There is no accident in the fact that certain expressions of art 7
live for all time and that others die with the moment, and although you may not always define the reasons, you can ask the questions. What does an artist say that is timeless; how does he say it? How much is fashion, how much is merely reflection? Why is Sir Walter Scott so hard to read now, and Jane Austen not? Why is baroque right for one age and too effulgent for another?

Can a standard of craftsmanship apply to art of all ages, or 8 does each have its own, and different, definitions? You may have been aware, inadvertently, that craftsmanship has become a dirty word these years because, again, it implies standards—something done well or done badly. The result of this convenient avoidance is a plentitude of actors who can't project their voices, singers who can't phrase their songs, poets who can't communicate emotion, and writers who have no vocabulary—not to speak of painters who can't draw. The dogma now is that craftsmanship gets in the way of expression. You can do better if you don't know *how* you do it, let alone *what* you're doing.

I think it is time you helped reverse this trend by trying to rediscover craft: the command of the chosen instrument, whether it is a brush, a word, or a voice. When you begin to detect the difference between freedom and sloppiness, between serious experimentation and egotherapy, between skill and slickness, between strength and violence, you are on your way to separating the sheep from the goats, a form of segregation denied us for quite a while. All you need to restore it is a small bundle of standards and a Geiger counter that detects fraud, and we might begin our tour of the arts in an area where both are urgently needed: contemporary painting. 9

I don't know what's worse: to have to look at acres of bad art to find the little good, or to read what the critics say about it all. In no other field of expression has so much double-talk flourished, so much confusion prevailed, and so much nonsense been circulated: further evidence of the close interdependence between the arts and the critical climate they inhabit. It will be my pleasure to share with you some of this double-talk so typical of our times. 10

Item one: preface for a catalogue of an abstract painter: 11

"Time-bound meditation experiencing a life; sincere with plastic piety at the threshold of hallowed arcana; a striving for pure ideation giving shape to inner drive; formalized patterns where neural balances reach a fiction." End of quote. Know what this artist paints like now? 12

Item two: a review in the *Art News:* 13

". . . a weird and disparate assortment of material, but the monstrosity which bloomed into his most recent cancer of aggregations is present in some form everywhere. . . ." Then, later, "A gluttony of things and processes terminated by a glorious constipation." 14

Item three, same magazine, review of an artist who welds automobile fragments into abstract shapes: 15

"Each fragment . . . is made an extreme of human exasperation, torn at and fought all the way, and has its rightness of form as if by accident. *Any technique that requires order or discipline would just be the human ego.* No, these must be egoless, uncontrolled, undesigned and 16 different enough to give you a bang—fifty miles an hour around a telephone pole. . . ."

"Any technique that requires order of discipline would just be the human ego." What does he mean—"just be"? What are they really talking about? Is this journalism? Is it criticism? Or is it that other convenient abdication from standards of performance and judgment practiced by so many artists and critics that they, like certain writers who deal only in sickness and depravity, "reflect the chaos about them"? Again, whose chaos? Whose depravity? 17

I had always thought that the prime function of art was to create order *out* of chaos—again, not the order of neatness or rigidity or convention or artifice, but the order of clarity by which one will and one vision could draw the essential truth out of apparent confusion. I still do. It is not enough to use parts of a car to convey the brutality of the machine. This is as slavishly representative, and just as easy, as arranging dried flowers under glass to convey nature. 18

Speaking of which, i.e., the use of real materials (burlap, old gloves, bottletops) in lieu of pigment, this is what one critic had to say about an exhibition of Assemblage at the Museum of Modern Art last year: 19

"Spotted throughout the show are indisputable works of art, accounting for a quarter or even a half of the total display. But the remainder are works of non-art, anti-art, and art substitutes that are the aesthetic counterparts of the social deficiencies that land people in the clink on charges of vagrancy. These aesthetic bankrupts . . . have no legitimate ideological roof over their heads and not the price of a square intellectual meal, much less a spiritual sandwich, in their pockets." 20

I quote these words of John Canaday of *The New York Times* as an example of the kind of criticism which puts responsibility to an intelligent public above popularity with an intellectual coterie. Canaday has the courage to say what he thinks and the capacity to say it clearly: two qualities notably absent from his profession. 21

Next to art, I would say that appreciation and evaluation in the field of music is the most difficult. For it is rarely possible to judge a new composition at one hearing only. What seems confusing or fragmented at first might well become clear and organic a third time. Or it might not. The only salvation here for the listener is, again, an instinct born of experience and association which allows him to separate intent from accident, design from experimentation, and pretense from conviction. Much of contemporary music is, like its sister art, merely a reflection of the composer's own fragmentation: an absorption in self and symbols at the expense of communication with others. The artist, in short, says to the public: If you don't understand this, it's because you're dumb. I maintain that you are not. You may 22 have to go part way or even halfway to meet the artist, but if you must go the whole way, it's his fault, not yours. Hold fast to that. And remember it too when you read new poetry, that estranged sister of music.

"A multitude of causes, unknown to former times, are now acting with a combined force to blunt the discriminating powers of the mind, and, unfitting it for all voluntary exertion, to reduce it to a state of almost savage torpor. The most effective of these causes are the great national events which are daily taking place and the increasing accumulation of men in cities, where the uniformity of their occupations produces a craving for extraordinary incident, which the rapid communication of intelligence hourly gratifies. To this tendency of life and manners, the literature and theatrical exhibitions of the country have conformed themselves." 23

This startlingly applicable comment was written in the year 1800 by William Wordsworth in the preface to his "Lyrical Ballads"; and it has been cited by Edwin Muir in his recently published book "The Estate of Poetry." Muir states that poetry's effective range and influence have diminished alarmingly in the modern world. He believes in the inherent and indestructible qualities of the human mind and the great and permanent objects that act upon it, and suggests that the audience will increase when "poetry loses what obscurity is left in it by attempting greater themes, for great themes have to be stated clearly." If you keep that firmly in mind and resist, in Muir's words, "the vast dissemination of secondary objects that isolate us from the natural world," you have gone a long way toward equipping yourself for the examination of any work of art. 24

When you come to theatre, in this extremely hasty tour of the arts, you can approach it on two different levels. You can bring to it anticipation and innocence, giving yourself up, as it were, to the life on the stage and reacting to it emotionally, if the play is good, or listlessly, if the play is boring; a part of the audience organism that expresses its favor by silence or laughter and its disfavor by coughing and rustling. Or you can bring to it certain critical faculties that may heighten, rather than diminish, your enjoyment. 25

You can ask yourselves whether the actors are truly in their parts or merely projecting themselves; whether the scenery helps or hurts the mood; whether the playwright is honest with himself, his characters, and you. Somewhere along the line you can learn to distinguish between the true creative act and the false arbitrary gesture; between fresh observation and stale cliché; between the avant-garde play that is pretentious drivel and the avant-garde play that finds new ways to say old truths. 26

Purpose and craftsmanship—end and means—these are the keys to your judgment in all the arts. What is this painter trying to say 27 when he slashes a broad band of black across a white canvas and lets the edges dribble down? Is it a statement of violence? Is it a self-portrait? If it is *one* of these, has he made you believe it? Or is this a gesture of the ego or a form of therapy? If it shocks you, what does it shock you into?

And what of this tight little painting of bright flowers in a vase? Is the painter saying anything new about flowers? Is it different from a million other canvases of flowers? Has it any life, any meaning, beyond its statement? Is there any pleasure in its forms or texture? The question is not whether a thing is abstract or representational, whether it is "modern" or conventional. The question, inexorably, is whether it is good. And this is a decision which only you, on the basis of instinct, experience, and association, can make for yourself. It takes independence and courage. It involves, moreover, the risk of wrong decision and the humility, after the passage of time, of recognizing it as such. As we grow and change and learn, our attitudes can change too, and what we once thought obscure or "difficult" can later emerge as coherent and illuminating. Entrenched prejudices, obdurate opinions are as sterile as no opinions at all. 28

Yet standards there are, timeless as the universe itself. And when you have committed yourself to them, you have acquired a passport to that elusive but immutable realm of truth. Keep it with you in the forests of bewilderment. And never be afraid to speak up. 29

QUESTIONS

1. What examples does Mannes provide of the "abdication from the responsibility of judgment" (paragraph 4)?

2. Explain Mannes's criteria or standards for judging excellence in the arts.

3. Account for the author's use of the pronoun "you" in addressing her audience. How does it affect tone, notably at the end of the essay?

4. Explain Mannes's strategy of formulating questions, starting with the title and moving consistently through the essay to the conclusion.

5. Where does the author's introduction end? Analyze the material presented in the introduction and the rhetorical strategies involved. What paragraphs constitute the conclusion of the essay? Describe the nature of the conclusion.

6. Explain the function of paragraphs 5 to 9.

7. How does Mannes employ illustration to structure paragraphs 10 to 26? Analyze the main stages in the organization of this section.

8. Explain the author's use of process and causal analysis in the essay.

9. Mannes maintains that standards are absolutely necessary in distinguishing good from bad work in the arts. Do you agree or disagree with her premise, and why? What standards do you employ in determining whether an artistic product is good or bad?

10. a. Write your own essay entitled "How Do You Know It's Good?"
b. Evaluate one literary, artistic, or media work, making clear the standards that you are applying.

VIRGIL THOMSON

Taste in Music

Virgil Garnett Thomson (1896–), the dean of American composers and music critics, graduated from Harvard University in 1923 and studied in Paris. From 1940 to 1954, Thomas was music critic for *The New York Herald Tribune.* His musical compositions include the operas *Four Saints in Three Acts* (1928) and *The Mother of Us All* (1947), for which Gertrude Stein wrote the librettos; and the scores for the documentary films *The River* (1937), *The Plough That Broke the Plains* (1936), and *Louisiana Story* (1948). In this essay, Thomson investigates the nature of taste in music and the manner in which it can be cultivated.

A taste *for* music, a taste for anything, is an ability to consume it with pleasure. Taste *in* music is preferential consumption, a greater liking for certain kinds of it than for others. A broad taste in music involves the ability to consume with pleasure many kinds of it. 1

(2) Vast numbers of persons, many of them highly intelligent, derive no pleasure at all from organized sound. An even larger number can take it or leave it alone. They find it agreeable for the most part, stimulating to the sentiments and occasionally interesting to the mind. But music is not for them a passional experience, a transport, an auditory universe. Everybody, however, has some kind of taste *in* music, even persons with little or no taste *for* it. No subject, save perhaps the theory of money, is disputed about so constantly in contemporary life as the diverse styles of musical expression, both popular and erudite, their nature and likability. 2

(3)There are often striking contradictions between what musi- 3 cal people admire and what they like. Admiration, being a judgment, is submissive to reason. But liking is an inspiration, a datum exigent, unreasonable, and impossible by any act of the will to alter. It will frequently alter itself, however, without warning. And loyalty to things we once loved dearly brings tension into everybody's taste. Persons whose musical experience is limited may, indeed, be more loyal to old likings than persons who deal with music all the time. The latter tend to reject and to accept with vehemence; they are choosy. And their choosiness is quite independent of their judgment; it is personal and profoundly capricious. They can switch from Beethoven to boogie-woogie, from Bach to barbershop, with a facility that is possible only to those who take all music for their clothes closet. For practical living, man needs to be free in his thought and responsible in his actions. But in dealing with art, responsibility of thought, which makes for flexibility of taste, constitute the mechanics of vigor.

(4) The development of taste is not a major objective in musical education. What the young need is understanding, that whole paraphernalia of analysis and synthesis whereby a piece is broken up into its component details, mastered, restored to integrity, and possessed. Musical understanding depends not so much on the number of works one has learned in this fashion, provided examples from several schools have been included, as on the completeness with which the procedure has been carried out. Any student can be convinced by study that Mozart is a more accomplished workman than Grieg or Rachmaninoff. If he still likes Grieg and Rachmaninoff better, that is his privilege. Maturity is certain to alter, whatever they may be, his youthful predilections. 4

(5) Persons unprepared by training to roam the world of music in freedom but who enjoy music and wish to increase that enjoyment are constantly searching for a key, a passport that will hasten their progress. There is none, really, except study. And how far it is profitable to spend time cultivating talent where there is no vocation every man must decide for himself. But if there is any door opener to taste it is knowledge. One cannot know whether one likes, can use, a work unless one has some method beyond mere instinct for tasting it. The only known ways to taste a piece of music are to read it in score or to follow it in performance. And it is quite impossible to follow unfamiliar kinds of music without an analytical method, a set of aids to memory that enables one to discern the pattern of what is taking place. 5

(6) But an ability to hear is not the whole of musical reception. A vote seems to be required, a yes or no as to whether one desires for the present, further acquaintance. Now, the enjoyment of old musical acquaintance is such a pleasant thing for all and so quite sufficiently absorbing for the unskilled that nearly everybody leans toward a 6

timid conservatism with regard to unfamiliar music. The too old, the too new, the in-any-way strange we resist simply because we do not know how to take them on. The lay public will try anything; but it will be disappointed, on first hearing, in anything it has no method for remembering. We like the idea of being musically progressive, because progress is one of our national ideals; but we do not always know how to conduct a progress.

(7) Well, the way of that is long. It is nothing less, if one 7
wishes to take part in America's musical growing-up, than learning to hear music correctly and learning to know one's mind. Persons who cannot follow music at all do well to admit the fact and let music alone. Persons who really hear it, whom *it* will not let alone, usually improve themselves by one means and another in their ability to hear patterns in sound; and with more and more music thus rendered available to them, they can choose at any moment their personal allegiances with a modicum of liberty. The tolerant but untrained, however, will always be a bit uncertain in their tastes. They will never know, for instance, whether they are entitled to vote publically or not. They will consequently assume the privilege more proudly, more dogmatically, and more irresponsibly than musicians themselves are likely to do. And they will rarely know the difference between their tastes and their opinions.

(8) It is the ignorantly formed and categorically expressed 8
opinions of the amateur, in fact, that make the music world companionable. Professional musicians express, for the most part, responsible opinions; and these show a surprising tendency to approach, within twenty-five years, unanimity. There is not much difference of opinion any more, for instance, about either the nature or the value of Debussy's music, or of Puccini's, or of what Stravinsky wrote before 1914. But musicians' personal likings are eclectic; they imply no agreement of any kind. It is laymen who like to like together. Musicians' opinions influence nothing; they simply recognize, with a certain delay but correctly, the history of music. Lay opinion influences everything—even, at times, creation. And at all times it is the pronouncements of persons who know something about music but not much, and a bit more about what they like but still not too much, that end by creating those modes or fashions in consumption that make up the history of taste.

(9) There is no doubt that lay opinion is in large part 9
organized and directed by knowledgeable persons—by critics, college instructors, conductors, publishers' employees, and leaders of fashion. It is nevertheless not wholly under their control. The leaders of taste can no more create deliberately a mode in music than advertising campaigns can make popular a product that the public doesn't want. They can only manipulate a trend. And trends follow folk

patterns. Nobody connected with a trend in music—whether composer, executant, manager, critic, consumer, or even resister—is a free agent with regard to it. That is why unsuccessful or unfashionable music, music that seems to ignore what the rest of world is listening to, is sometimes the best music, the freest, the most original—though there is no rule about that either.

10 (10) And so, thus caught up on the wheel of fatality, how can anybody really know anything about music, beyond its immediate practice or perception, least of all what he likes? Learning is a precious thing and knowing one's mind is even more so. But let none of us who think we belong to music fancy too highly our opinions about it, since in twenty-five years most of these will have either gone down the drain or become every man's private conviction. And please let none imagine, either, that his personal tastes are unique, indissoluble, and free. Those who think themselves most individual in their likings are most easily trapped by the appeal of chic, since chic is no more than the ability to accept trends in fashion with grace, to vary them ever so slightly, to follow a movement under the sincere illusion that one is being oneself. And those who imagine themselves most independent as judges make up the most predictable public in the world, that known to managements as the university trade, since intellectuals will always pay for the privilege of exercising their intellectual powers. Rarities of any kind, ancient or modern, are merely stones to whet their minds against. You can always sell to the world of learning acquaintance with that which it does not know.

11 (11) In the long run, such freedom as anybody has is the reward of labor, much study, and inveterate wariness. And the pleasures of taste, at best, are transitory, since nobody, professional or layman, can be sure that what he finds beautiful this year may not be just another piece of music to him next. The best any of us can do about any piece, short of memorizing its actual sounds and storing it away intact against lean musical moments, is to consult his appetite about its immediate consumption, his appetite and his digestive experience. And after consumption to argue about the thing interminably with all his friends. *De gustibus disputandum est.*

QUESTIONS

1. Explain the author's distinction between taste for music and taste in music. How is a sound appreciation of music best developed? Why does Thomson say that "The development of taste is not a major objective in musical education" (paragraph 4)?

2. What is the importance of "lay opinion"?

3. Is the author interested in the denotative or connotative meaning of the term "taste"? Explain.

4. Explain the significance of the author's last sentence and the wordplay involved.

5. What is the thesis of Thomson's essay?

6. How would you explain the tone achieved by the author in the introductory paragraph? In the essay as a whole?

7. In what sense does the essay involve process analysis? Definition of terms? Explanation of causes and effects?

8. Analyze Thomson's development of paragraphs from his topic sentences, and transitions from paragraph to paragraph.

9. Discuss this comment in paragraph 11: ". . . the pleasures of taste, at best, are transitory, since nobody, professional or layman, can be sure that what he finds beautiful this year may not be just another piece of music to him the next."

10. a. Write an essay on your taste in music.
b. Write an essay on how to acquire taste in music.

10 Philosophy, Ethics, and Religious Thought

ROBERT COLES

I Listen to My Parents and I Wonder What They Believe

Robert Coles (1929–   ), author and psychologist, won the Pulitzer Prize for his multivolume work, *Children of Crisis,* in which he examines with compassion and intelligence the effects of the controversy over integration on children in the South. Walker Percy has praised Coles because he "spends his time listening to people and trying to understand them." In its final form, *Children of Crisis* has five volumes, and Coles has widened its focus to include the children of the wealthy and poor, the exploited and the exploiters. In collaboration with Jane Coles, he recently completed *Women of Crisis II* (1980). Below, Coles demonstrates his capacity to listen to and to understand children.

ot so long ago children were looked upon in a sentimental fashion as "angels" or as "innocents." Today, thanks to Freud and his followers, boys and girls are understood to have complicated inner lives; to feel love, hate, 1 envy and rivalry in various and subtle mixtures; to be eager participants in the sexual and emotional politics of the home, neighborhood and school. Yet some of us parents still cling to the notion of childhood innocence in another way. We do not see that our children also make ethical decisions every day in their own lives, or realize how attuned they may be to moral currents and issues in the larger society.

In Appalachia I heard a girl of eight whose father owns coal fields (and gas stations, a department store and much timberland) wonder about "life" one day: "I'll be walking to the school bus, and I'll ask myself why there's some who are poor and their daddies can't find a job, and there's some who are lucky like me. Last month there was an explosion in a mine my daddy owns, and everyone became upset. Two miners got killed. My daddy said it was their own fault, because they'll be working and they get careless. When my mother asked if there was anything wrong with the safety down in the mine, he told her no and she shouldn't ask questions like that. Then the Government people came and they said it was the owner's fault—Daddy's. But he has a lawyer and the lawyer is fighting the Government and the union. In school, kids ask me what I think, and I sure do feel sorry for the two miners and so does my mother—I know that. She told me it's just not a fair world and you have to remember that. Of course, there's no one who can be sure there won't be trouble; like my daddy says, the rain falls on the just and the unjust. My brother is only six and he asked Daddy awhile back who are the 'just' and the 'unjust,' and Daddy said there are people who work hard and they live good lives, and there are lazy people and they're always trying to sponge off others. But I guess you have to feel sorry for anyone who has a lot of trouble, because it's poured-down, heavy rain." 2

Listening, one begins to realize that an elementary-school child is no stranger to moral reflection—and to ethical conflict. This girl was torn between her loyalty to her particular background, its values and assumptions, and to a larger affiliation—her membership in the nation, the world. As a human being whose parents were kind and decent to her, she was inclined to be thoughtful and sensitive with respect to others, no matter what their work or position in society. But her father was among other things a mineowner, and she had already learned to shape her concerns to suit that fact of life. The result: a moral oscillation of sorts, first toward nameless others all over the world and then toward her own family. As the girl put it later, when she was a year older: "You should try to have 'good thoughts' about everyone, the minister says, and our teacher says that too. But you should honor your father and mother most of all; that's why you should find out what they think and then sort of copy them. But sometimes you're not sure if you're on the right track." 3

Sort of copy them. There could be worse descriptions of how children acquire moral values. In fact, the girl understood how girls and boys all over the world "sort of" develop attitudes of what is right and wrong, ideas of who the just and the unjust are. And they also struggle hard and long, and not always with success, to find out where the "right track" starts and ends. Children need encouragement or assistance as they wage that struggle. 4

In home after home that I have visited, and in many classrooms, I have met children who not only are growing emotionally and intellectually but also are trying to make sense of the world morally. That is to say, they are asking themselves and others about issues of fair play, justice, liberty, equality. Those last words are abstractions, of course—the stuff of college term papers. And there are, one has to repeat, those in psychology and psychiatry who would deny elementary-school children access to that "higher level" of moral reflection. But any parent who has listened closely to his or her child knows that girls and boys are capable of wondering about matters of morality, and knows too that often it is their grown-up protectors (parents, relatives, teachers, neighbors) who are made uncomfortable by the so-called "innocent" nature of the questions children may ask or the statements they may make. Often enough the issue is not the moral capacity of children but the default of us parents who fail to respond to inquiries put to us by our daughters and sons—and fail to set moral standards for both ourselves and our children. 5

Do's and don't's are, of course, pressed upon many of our girls and boys. But a moral education is something more than a series of rules handed down, and in our time one cannot assume that every parent feels able—sure enough of her own or his own actual beliefs and values—to make even an initial explanatory and disciplinary effort toward a moral education. Furthermore, for many of us parents these days it is a child's emotional life that preoccupies us. 6

In 1963, when I was studying school desegregation in the South, I had extended conversations with Black and white elementary-school children caught up in a dramatic moment of historical change. For longer than I care to remember, I concentrated on possible psychiatric troubles, on how a given child was managing under circumstances of extreme stress, on how I could be of help—with "support," with reassurance, with a helpful psychological observation or interpretation. In many instances I was off the mark. These children weren't "patients"; they weren't even complaining. They were worried, all right, and often enough they had things to say that were substantive—that had to do not so much with troubled emotions as with questions of right and wrong in the real-life dramas taking place in their worlds. 7

Here is a nine-year-old white boy, the son of ardent segregationists, telling me about his sense of what desegregation meant to Louisiana in the 1960s: "They told us it wouldn't happen—never. My daddy said none of us white people would go into schools with the colored. But then it did happen, and when I went to school the first day I didn't know what would go on. Would the school stay open or would it close up? We didn't know what to do; the teacher kept telling us that we should be good and obey the law, but my daddy said the law was wrong. Then my mother said she wanted me in school even if there were some colored kids there. She said if we all stayed home she'd be a 'nervous wreck.' So I went. 8

"After a while I saw that the colored weren't so bad. I saw that there are different kinds of colored people, just like with us whites. There was one of the colored who was nice, a boy who smiled, and he played real good. There was another one, a boy, who wouldn't talk with anyone. I don't know if it's right that we all be in the same school. Maybe it isn't right. My sister is starting school next year, and she says she doesn't care if there's 'mixing of the races.' She says they told her in Sunday school that everyone is a child of God, and then a kid asked if that goes for the colored too and the teacher said yes, she thought so. My daddy said that it's true, God made everyone—but that doesn't mean we all have to be living together under the same roof in the home or the school. But my mother said we'll never know what God wants of us but we have to try to read His mind, and that's why we pray. So when I say my prayers I ask God to tell me what's the right thing to do. In school I try to say hello to the colored, because they're kids, and you can't be mean or you'll be 'doing wrong,' like my grandmother says." 9

Children aren't usually long-winded in the moral discussions they have with one another or with adults, and in quoting this boy I have pulled together comments he made to me in the course of several days. But everything he said was of interest to me. I was interested in the boy's changing racial attitudes. It was clear he was trying to find a coherent, sensible moral position too. It was also borne in on me that if one spends days, weeks in a given home, it is hard to escape a particular moral climate just as significant as the psychological one. 10

In many homes parents establish moral assumptions, mandates, priorities. They teach children what to believe in, what not to believe in. They teach children what is permissible or not permissible—and why. They may summon up the Bible, the flag, history, novels, aphorisms, philosophical or political sayings, personal memories—all in an effort to teach children how to behave, what and whom to respect and for which reasons. Or they may neglect to do so, and in so doing teach their children *that*—a moral abdication, of 11 sorts—and in this way fail their children. Children need and long for words of moral advice, instruction, warning, as much as they need words of affirmation or criticism from their parents about other matters. They must learn how to dress and what to wear, how to eat and what to eat; and they must also learn how to behave under X or Y or Z conditions, and why.

All the time, in 20 years of working with poor children and rich children, Black children and white children, children from rural areas and urban areas and in every region of this country, I have heard questions—thoroughly intelligent and discerning questions—about social and historical matters, about personal behavior, and so on. But most striking is the fact that almost all those questions, in one way or another, are moral in nature: Why did the Pilgrims leave England? Why didn't they just stay and agree to do what the king wanted them to do? . . . Should you try to share all you've got or should you save a lot for yourself? . . . What do you do when you see others fighting—do you try to break up the fight, do you stand by and watch or do you leave as fast as you can? . . . Is it right that some people haven't got enough to eat? . . . I see other kids cheating and I wish I could copy the answers too; but I won't cheat, though sometimes I feel I'd like to and I get all mixed up. I go home and talk with my parents, and I ask them what should you do if you see kids cheating—pay no attention, or report the kids or do the same thing they are doing? 12

Those are examples of children's concerns—and surely millions of American parents have heard versions of them. Have the various "experts" on childhood stressed strongly enough the importance of such questions—and the importance of the hunger we all have, no matter what our age or background, to examine what we believe in, are willing to stand up for, and what we are determined to ask, likewise, of our children? 13

Children not only need our understanding of their complicated emotional lives; they also need a constant regard for the moral issues that come their way as soon as they are old enough to play with others and take part in the politics of the nursery, the back yard and the schoolroom. They need to be told what they must do and what they must not do. They need control over themselves and a sense of what others are entitled to from them—co-operation, thoughtfulness, an attentive ear and eye. They need discipline not only to tame their excesses of emotion but discipline also connected to stated and clarified moral values. They need, in other words, something to believe in that is larger than their own appetites and urges and, yes, bigger than their "psychological drives." They need a larger view of the world, a moral context, as it were—a faith that addresses itself to the meaning of this life we all live and, soon enough, let go of. 14

Yes, it is time for us parents to begin to look more closely at what ideas our children have about the world; and it would be well to do so before they become teen-agers and young adults and begin to remind us, as often happens, of how little attention we did pay to their moral development. Perhaps a nine-year-old girl from a well-off suburban home in Texas put it better than anyone else I've met: 15

"I listen to my parents, and I wonder what they believe in more than anything else. I asked my mom and my daddy once: What's the thing that means most to you? They said they didn't know but I shouldn't worry my head too hard with questions like that. So I asked my best friend, and she said she wonders if there's a God and how do you know Him and what does He want you to do—I mean, when you're in school or out playing with your friends. They talk about God in church, but is it only in church that He's there and keeping an eye on you? I saw a kid steal in a store, and I know her father has a lot of money—because I hear my daddy talk. But stealing's wrong. My mother said she's a 'sick girl,' but it's still wrong what she did. Don't you think?" 16

There was more—much more—in the course of the months I came to know that child and her parents and their neighbors. But those observations and questions—a "mere child's"—reminded me unforgettably of the aching hunger for firm ethical principles that so many of us feel. Ought we not begin thinking about this need? Ought we not all be asking ourselves more intently what standards we live by—and how we can satisfy our children's hunger for moral values? 17

QUESTIONS

1. According to Coles, why do parents have difficulty explaining ethics to their children? On what aspects of their children's development to they tend to concentrate? Why?

2. There is an implied contrast between mothers' and fathers' attitudes toward morality in Coles's essay. Explain this contrast and cite examples for your explanation.

3. What point of view does Coles use here? How does that viewpoint affect the tone of the essay?

4. Compare Coles's sentence structure with the sentence structure of the children he quotes. How do they differ?

5. Does this essay present an inductive or deductive argument? Give evidence for your answer.

6. How does paragraph 13 differ from paragraphs 3, 10, and 17? How do all four paragraphs contribute to the development of the essay?

7. Explain the line of reasoning in the first paragraph. Why does Coles allude to Freud? How is that allusion related to the final sentence of the paragraph?

8. What paragraphs constitute the conclusion of the essay? Why? How do they summarize Coles's argument?

9. Coles asserts the need for clear ethical values. Do you feel your parents provided such values? What kind of values will you give your children?

10. a. Write an essay describing conflict between your parents' ethical views and your own.
b. Gather evidence, based upon conversations, from your friends and relatives about an ethical issue such as poverty, world starvation, abortion, or capital punishment. Incorporate their opinions through direct and indirect quotation into your essay.

EPICURUS

We Should Seek Our Own Pleasure

Epicurus (341–270 B.C.), Greek philosopher, was a contemporary of Aristotle and is best known for asserting that pleasure is the highest good toward which people can strive. Epicurus himself favored a reclusive, moderate life and urged people to practice prudence, justice, and honesty. Although he was a voluminous writer, only a few fragments of his works have survived. One of the more extensive fragments appears below.

Let no one when young delay to study philosophy, nor when he is old grow weary of his study. For no one can come too early or too late to secure the health of his soul. And the man who says that the age for philosophy has either not yet come or has gone by is like the man who says that the age for happiness is not yet come to him, or has passed away. Wherefore both when young and old a man must study philosophy, 1

that as he grows old he may be young in blessings through the grateful recollection of what has been, and that in youth he may be old as well, since he will know no fear of what is to come. We must then meditate on the things that make our happiness, seeing that when that is with us we have all, but when it is absent we do all to win it.

The things which I used unceasingly to commend to you, these do and practise, considering them to be the first principles of the good life. First of all believe that god is a being immortal and blessed, even as the common idea of a god is engraved on men's minds, and do not assign to him anything alien to his immortality or ill-suited to his blessedness: but believe about him everything that can uphold his blessedness and immortality. For gods there are, since the knowledge of them is by clear vision. But they are not such as the many believe them to be: for indeed they do not consistently represent them as they believe them to be. And the impious man is not he who denies the gods of the many, but he who attaches to the gods the beliefs of the many. For the statements of the many about the gods are not conceptions derived from sensation, but false suppositions, according to which the greatest misfortunes befall the wicked and the greatest blessings the good by the gift of the gods. For men being accustomed always to their own virtues welcome those like themselves, but regard all that is not of their nature as alien. 2

Become accustomed to the belief that death is nothing to us. For all good and evil consists in sensation, but death is deprivation of sensation. And therefore a right understanding that death is nothing to us makes the mortality of life enjoyable, not because it adds to it an infinite span of time, but because it takes away the craving for immortality. For there is nothing terrible in life for the man who has truly comprehended that there is nothing terrible in not living. So that the man speaks but idly who says that he fears death not because it will be painful when it comes, but because it is painful in anticipation. For that which gives no trouble when it comes, is but an empty pain in anticipation. So death, the most terrifying of ills, is nothing to us, since so long as we exist death is not with us; but when death comes, then we do not exist. It does not then concern either the living or the dead, since for the former it is not, and the latter are no more. 3

But the many at one moment shun death as the greatest of evils, at another yearn for it as a respite from the evils in life. But the wise man neither seeks to escape life nor fears the cessation of life, for neither does life offend him nor does the absence of life seem to be any evil. And just as with food he does not seek simply the larger 4

share and nothing else, but rather the most pleasant, so he seeks to enjoy not the longest period of time, but the most pleasant.

And he who counsels the young man to live well, but the old 5
man to make a good end, is foolish, not merely because of the desirability of life, but also because it is the same training which teaches to live well and to die well. Yet much worse still is the man who says it is good not to be born, but

> once born make haste to pass the gates of Death. (Theognis, 427)

For if he says this from conviction why does he not pass away out of life? For it is open to him to do so, if he had firmly made up his mind to this. But if he speaks in jest, his words are idle among men who cannot receive them.

We must then bear in mind that the future is neither ours, nor 6
yet wholly not ours, so that we may not altogether expect it as sure to come, nor abandon hope of it, as if it will certainly not come.

We must consider that of desires some are natural, others 7
vain, and of the natural some are necessary and others merely natural; and of the necessary some are necessary for happiness, others for the repose of the body, and others for very life. The right understanding of these facts enables us to refer all choice and avoidance to the health of the body and the soul's freedom from disturbance, since this is the aim of the life of blessedness. For it is to obtain this end that we always act, namely, to avoid pain and fear. And when this is once secured for us, all the tempest of the soul is dispersed, since the living creature has not to wander as though in search of something that is missing, and to look for some other thing by which he can fulfil the good of the soul and the good of the body. For it is then that we have need of pleasure, when we feel pain owing to the absence of pleasure; but when we do not feel pain, we no longer need pleasure. And for this cause we call pleasure the beginning and end of the blessed life. For we recognize pleasure as the first good innate in us, and from pleasure we begin every act of choice and avoidance, and to pleasure we return again, using the feeling as the standard by which we judge every good.

And since pleasure is the first good and natural to us, for this 8
very reason we do not choose every pleasure, but sometimes we pass over many pleasures, when greater discomfort accrues to us as the result of them: and similarly we think many pains better than pleasures, since a greater pleasure comes to us when we have endured pains for a long time. Every pleasure then because of its natural kinship to us is good, yet not every pleasure is to be chosen:

even as every pain also is an evil, yet not all are always of a nature to be avoided. Yet by a scale of comparison and by the consideration of advantages and disadvantages we must form our judgment on all these matters. For the good on certain occasions we treat as bad, and conversely the bad as good.

And again independence of desire we think a great good— 9
not that we may at all times enjoy but a few things, but that, if we do not possess many, we may enjoy the few in the genuine persuasion that those have the sweetest pleasure in luxury who least need it, and that all that is natural is easy to be obtained, but that which is superfluous is hard. And so plain savours bring us a pleasure equal to a luxurious diet, when all the pain due to want is removed; and bread and water produce the highest pleasure, when one who needs them puts them to his lips. To grow accustomed therefore to simple and not luxurious diet gives us health to the full, and makes a man alert for the needful employments of life, and when after long intervals we approach luxuries, disposes us better towards them, and fits us to be fearless of fortune.

When, therefore, we maintain that pleasure is the end, we do 10
not mean the pleasures of profligates and those that consist in sensuality, as is supposed by some who are either ignorant or disagree with us or do not understand, but freedom from pain in the body and from trouble in the mind. For it is not continuous drinkings and revellings, nor the satisfaction of lusts, nor the enjoyment of fish and other luxuries of the wealthy table, which produce a pleasant life, but sober reasoning, searching out the motives for all choice and avoidance, and banishing mere opinions, to which are due the greatest disturbance of the spirit.

Of all this the beginning and the greatest good is prudence. 11
Wherefore prudence is a more precious thing even than philosophy: for from prudence are sprung all the other virtues, and it teaches us that it is not possible to live pleasantly without living prudently and honourably and justly, nor again, to live a life of prudence, honour, and justice without living pleasantly. For the virtues are by nature bound up with the pleasant life, and the pleasant life is inseparable from them. For indeed who, think you, is a better man than he who holds reverent opinions concerning the gods, and is at all times free from fear of death, and has reasoned out the end ordained by nature? He understands that the limit of good things is easy to fulfil and easy to attain, whereas the course of ills is either short in time or slight in pain: he laughs at destiny, whom some have introduced as the mistress of all things. He thinks that with us lies the chief power in determining events, some of which happen by necessity and some by chance, and some are within our control; for while necessity cannot

be called to account, he sees that chance is inconstant, but that which is in our control is subject to no master, and to it are naturally attached praise and blame. For, indeed, it were better to follow the myths about the gods than to become a slave to the destiny of the natural philosophers: for the former suggests a hope of placating the gods by worship, whereas the latter involves a necessity which knows no placation. As to chance, he does not regard it as a god as most men do (for in god's acts there is no disorder), nor as an uncertain cause of all things: for he does not believe that good and evil are given by chance to man for the framing of a blessed life, but that opportunities for great good and great evil are afforded by it. He therefore thinks it better to be unfortunate in reasonable action than to prosper in unreason. For it is better in a man's actions that what is well chosen should fail, rather than that what is ill chosen should be successful owing to chance.

Meditate therefore on these things and things akin to them 12
night and day by yourself, and with a companion like to yourself, and never shall you be disturbed waking or asleep, but you shall live like a god among men. For a man who lives among immortal blessings is not like to a mortal being.

QUESTIONS

1. How does Epicurus define "pain," "death," and "pleasure"? Of what kinds of pleasure does Epicurus approve?

2. Why does he believe "independence of desire" is a "great good"?

3. Examine the tone of the essay. Particularly look for evidence of a hortatory style and explain its function.

4. What are the connotations of "the many" and "the wise man"? How many people do you think Epicurus believes will profit from his advice?

5. Explain how Epicurus uses classification to order paragraph 7. Are there other examples of classification in the essay? If so, where do they appear?

6. Does Epicurus tend to use deductive or inductive reasoning? Examine particularly paragraph 3 for evidence. Are there other examples elsewhere in the essay of the kind of reasoning that appears in paragraph 3? If so, where?

7. What is the topic sentence in paragraph 11? How important is this sentence to the development of the thesis of the essay?

8. Explain the function of paragraph 10 in the essay. What rhetorical method is Epicurus using here?

9. Do you think living according to Epicurus's advice would lead to happiness? What ways of living do you think lead to happiness?

10. a. Write a paper detailing the three major requirements of the good life for you.
b. Write a paper in which you give advice to readers on dating, education, getting along with your parents, or getting along with friends.

EDITH HAMILTON

Roots of Freedom

Edith Hamilton (1867–1963), teacher, writer, and Grecophile, wrote her first book when she was 63. Her initial career was as headmistress of a private girl's school in Maryland. When she retired, she began to write about ancient civilizations, particularly Greek civilization. In 1930, *The Greek Way* was published. In later years, Hamilton also wrote *The Roman Way* (1932) and *The Prophets of Israel* (1936). She retold Greek, Roman, and Norse myths in *Mythology* (1942). At the age of 90, Hamilton visited Greece and was made an honorary citizen. The following essay makes clear why she admired Greek civilization.

Freedom's challenge in the Atomic Age is a sobering topic. We are facing today a strange new world and we are all wondering what we are going to do with it. What are we going to do with one of our most precious possessions, freedom? The world we know, our Western world, began with something as new as the conquest of space. 1

Some 2,500 years ago Greece discovered freedom. Before that there was no freedom. There were great civilizations, splendid empires, but no freedom anywhere. Egypt, Babylon, Nineveh, were all tyrannies, one immensely powerful man ruling over helpless masses. In Greece, in Athens, a little city in a little country, there were no helpless masses, and a time came when the Athenians were led by a great man who did not want to be powerful. Absolute 2 obedience to the ruler was what the leaders of the empires insisted on. Athens said no, there must never be absolute obedience to a man except in war. There must be willing obedience to what is good for all. Pericles, the great Athenian statesman, said: "We are a free government, but we obey the laws, more especially those which protect the oppressed, and the unwritten laws which, if broken, bring shame."

3 Athenians willingly obeyed the written laws which they themselves passed, and the unwritten, which must be obeyed if free men live together. They must show each other kindness and pity and the many qualities without which life would be intolerable except to a hermit in the desert. The Athenians never thought that a man was free if he could do what he wanted. A man was free if he was self-controlled. To make yourself obey what you approved was freedom. They were saved from looking at their lives as their own private affair. Each one felt responsible for the welfare of Athens, not because it was imposed on him from the outside, but because the city was his pride and his safety. The creed of the first free government in the world was liberty for all men who could control themselves and would take responsibility for the state. This was the conception that underlay the lofty reach of Greek genius.

4 But discovering freedom is not like discovering atomic bombs. It cannot be discovered once for all. If people do not prize it, and work for it, it will depart. Eternal vigilance is its price. Athens changed. It was a change that took place unnoticed though it was of the utmost importance, a spiritual change which penetrated the whole state. It had been the Athenians' pride and joy to give to their city. That they could get material benefits from her never entered their minds. There had to be a complete change of attitude before they could look at the city as an employer who paid her citizens for doing her work. Now instead of men giving to the state, the state was to give to them. What the people wanted was a government which would provide a comfortable life for them; and with this as the foremost object, ideas of freedom and self-reliance and responsibility were obscured to the point of disappearing. Athens was more and more looked on as a cooperative business possessed of great wealth in which all citizens had a right to share.

5 She reached the point when the freedom she really wanted was freedom from responsibility. There could be only one result. If men insisted on being free from the burden of self-dependence and responsibility for the common good, they would cease to be free. Responsibility is the price every man must pay for freedom. It is to be had on no other terms. Athens, the Athens of Ancient Greece, refused responsibility; she reached the end of freedom and was never to have it again.

But, "the excellent becomes the permanent," Aristotle said. Athens lost freedom forever, but freedom was not lost forever for the world. A great American statesman, James Madison, in or near the year 1776 A.D. referred to: "The capacity of mankind for self-government." No doubt he had not an idea that he was speaking Greek. Athens was not in the farthest background of his mind, but once a great and good idea has dawned upon man, it is never completely lost. The Atomic Age cannot destroy it. Somehow in this or that man's thought such an idea lives though unconsidered by the world of action. One can never be sure that it is not on the point of breaking out into action only sure that it will do so sometime. 6

QUESTIONS

1. What were the Greeks' conceptions of freedom? Why, according to Hamilton, did they lose their freedom?

2. What similarities does Hamilton see between Athens and America?

3. Explain the allusions to Pericles in paragraph 2 and James Madison in paragraph 6.

4. Is Hamilton's tone hopeful or pessimistic? What evidence can you give to support your opinion?

5. Narrative is an important rhetorical device in this essay. How is chronology developed in this essay? What transition words are used to mark the progress of the narrative? What paragraphs contain elements of narrative?

6. Where does Hamilton make explicit her comparison between America and Athens? Why does she defer this idea until so late in her essay? What evidence can you find that she intends us to note this comparison before this point?

7. In paragraph 5 how much of the paragraph is narrative? What other rhetorical methods appear here?

8. What is the purpose of paragraph 1? How do paragraphs 1 and 6 frame the essay?

9. Do you think our present ideas of freedom and country are similar to those of the early or the late Greeks? What can we do to maintain or improve the situation?

10. Narrate a personal experience that can illustrate an abstraction such as freedom—for example, tyranny, honesty, or ambition.

PLATO

The Allegory of the Cave

Plato (427?–347 B.C.), pupil and friend of Socrates, was one of the greatest philosophers of the ancient world. Plato's surviving works are all dialogues, many of them purporting to be conversations of Socrates and his disciples. Two key aspects of his philosophy are the dialectical method, represented by the questioning, probing of the particular event to reveal the general truth; and the existence of Forms. Plato's best-known works include *Phaedo, Symposium, Phaedrus,* and *Timaeus.* The following selection, from *The Republic,* is an early description of the nature of Forms.

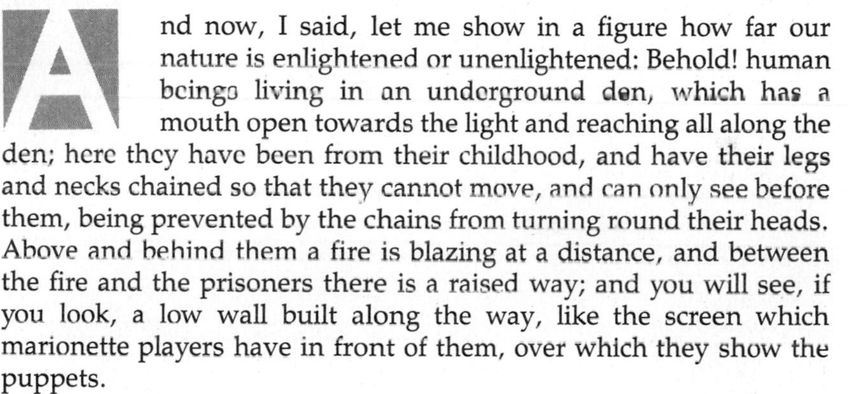

And now, I said, let me show in a figure how far our 1
nature is enlightened or unenlightened: Behold! human beings living in an underground den, which has a mouth open towards the light and reaching all along the den; here they have been from their childhood, and have their legs and necks chained so that they cannot move, and can only see before them, being prevented by the chains from turning round their heads. Above and behind them a fire is blazing at a distance, and between the fire and the prisoners there is a raised way; and you will see, if you look, a low wall built along the way, like the screen which marionette players have in front of them, over which they show the puppets.

I see. 2

And do you see, I said, men passing along the wall carrying 3
all sorts of vessels, and statues and figures of animals made of wood and stone and various materials, which appear over the wall? Some of them are talking, others silent.

You have shown me a strange image, and they are strange 4
prisoners.

Like ourselves, I replied; and they see only their own shad- 5
ows, or the shadows of one another, which the fire throws on the opposite wall of the cave?

True, he said; how could they see anything but the shadows if 6
they were never allowed to move their heads?

And of the objects which are being carried in like manner 7
they would only see the shadows?

Yes, he said. 8

And if they were able to converse with one another, would 9

they not suppose that they were naming what was actually before them?

Very true. 10

And suppose further that the prison had an echo which came 11
from the other side, would they not be sure to fancy when one of the passers-by spoke that the voice which they heard came from the passing shadow?

No question, he replied. 12

To them, I said, the truth would be literally nothing but the 13
shadows of the images.

That is certain. 14

And now look again, and see what will naturally follow if the 15
prisoners are released and disabused of their error. At first, when any of them is liberated and compelled suddenly to stand up and turn his neck round and walk and look towards the light, he will suffer sharp pains; the glare will distress him and he will be unable to see the realities of which in his former state he had seen the shadows; and then conceive some one saying to him, that what he saw before was an illusion, but that now, when he is approaching nearer to being and his eye is turned towards more real existence, he has a clearer vision—what will be his reply? And you may further imagine that his instructor is pointing to the objects as they pass and requiring him to name them—will he not be perplexed? Will he not fancy that the shadows which he formerly saw are truer than the objects which are now shown to him?

Far truer. 16

And if he is compelled to look straight at the light, will he not 17
have a pain in his eyes which will make him turn away to take refuge in the objects of vision which he can see, and which he will conceive to be in reality clearer than the things which are now being shown to him?

True, he said. 18

And suppose once more, that he is reluctantly dragged up a 19
steep and rugged ascent, and held fast until he is forced into the presence of the sun himself, is he not likely to be pained and irritated? When he approaches the light his eyes will be dazzled and he will not be able to see anything at all of what are now called realities.

Not all in a moment, he said. 20

He will require to grow accustomed to the sight of the upper 21
world. And first he will see the shadows best, next the reflections of men and other objects in the water, and then the objects themselves; then he will gaze upon the light of the moon and the stars and the spangled heaven; and he will see the sky and the stars by night better than the sun or the light of the sun by day?

Certainly. 22

Last of all he will be able to see the sun, and not mere 23
reflections of him in the water, but he will see him in his own proper place, and not in another; and he will contemplate him as he is.

Certainly. 24

He will then proceed to argue that this is he who gives the 25
season and the years, and is the guardian of all that is in the visible world, and in a certain way the cause of all things which he and his fellows have been accustomed to behold?

Clearly, he said, he would first see the sun and then reason 26
about him.

And when he remembered his old habitation, and the wis- 27
dom of the den and his fellow-prisoners, do you not suppose that he would felicitate himself on the change, and pity them?

Certainly, he would. 28

And if they were in the habit of conferring honors among 29
themselves on those who were quickest to observe the passing shadows and to remark which of them went before, and which followed after, and which were together; and who were therefore best able to draw conclusions as to the future, do you think that he would care for such honors and glories, or envy the possessors of them? Would he not say with Homer,

Better to be the poor servant of a poor master,

and to endure anything, rather than think as they do and live after their manner?

Yes, he said, I think that he would rather suffer anything than 30
entertain these false notions and live in this miserable manner.

Imagine once more, I said, such an one coming suddenly out 31
of the sun to be replaced in his old situation; would he not be certain to have his eyes full of darkness?

To be sure, he said. 32

And if there were a contest, and he had to compete in 33
measuring the shadows with the prisoners who had never moved out of the den, while his sight was still weak, and before his eyes had become steady (and the time which would be needed to acquire this new habit of sight might be very considerable) would he not be ridiculous? Men would say of him that up he went and down he came without his eyes; and that it was better not even to think of ascending; and if any one tried to loose another and lead him up to the light, let them only catch the offender, and they would put him to death.

No question, he said. 34

This entire allegory, I said, you may now append, dear Glaucon, to the previous argument; the prison-house is the world of sight, the light of fire is the sun, and you will not misapprehend me if you interpret the journey upwards to be the ascent of the soul into the intellectual world according to my poor belief, which, at your desire, I have expressed—whether rightly or wrongly God knows. But, whether true or false, my opinion is that in the world of knowledge the idea of good appears last of all, and is seen only with an effort; and, when seen, is also inferred to be the universal author of all things beautiful and right, parent of light and of the lord of light in this visible world, and the immediate source of reason and truth in the intellectual; and that this is the power upon which he who would act rationally either in public or private life must have his eye fixed. 35

I agree, he said, as far as I am able to understand you. 36

Moreover, I said, you must not wonder that those who attain to this beatific vision are unwilling to descend to human affairs; for their souls are ever hastening into the upper world where they desire to dwell; which desire of theirs is very natural, if our allegory may be trusted. 37

Yes, very natural. 38

And is there anything surprising in one who passes from divine contemplations to the evil state of man, misbehaving himself in a ridiculous manner; if, while his eyes are blinking and before he has become accustomed to the surrounding darkness, he is compelled to fight in courts of law, or in other places, about the images or the shadows of images of justice, and is endeavouring to meet the conceptions of those who have never yet seen absolute justice? 39

Anything but surprising, he replied. 40

Any one who has common sense will remember that the bewilderments of the eyes are of two kinds, and arise from two causes, either from coming out of the light or from going into the light, which is true of the mind's eye, quite as much as of the bodily eye; and he who remembers this when he sees any one whose vision is perplexed and weak, will not be too ready to laugh; he will first ask whether that soul of man has come out of the brighter life, and is unable to see because unaccustomed to the dark, or having turned from darkness to the day is dazzled by excess of light. And he will count the one happy in his condition and state of being, and he will pity the other; or, if he have a mind to laugh at the soul which comes from below into the light, there will be more reason in this than in the laugh which greets him who returns from above out of the light into the den. 41

That, he said, is a very just distinction. 42

QUESTIONS

1. According to Plato, do human beings typically perceive reality? To what does he compare the world?

2. According to Plato, what often happens to people who develop a true idea of reality? How well do they compete with others? Who is usually considered superior? Why?

3. Is the conversation portrayed here realistic? How effective is this conversational style at conveying information?

4. How do you interpret such details of this allegory as the chains, the cave, and the fire? What connotations do such symbols have?

5. How does Plato use conversation to develop his argument? What is Glaucon's role in the conversation?

6. Note examples of transition words that mark contrasts between the real and the shadow world. How does Plato use contrast to develop his idea of the true real world?

7. Plato uses syllogistic reasoning to derive human behavior from his allegory. Trace his line of reasoning, noting transitional devices and the development of idea in paragraphs 5 to 14. Find and describe a similar line of reasoning.

8. In what paragraph does Plato explain his allegory? Why do you think he locates his explanation where he does?

9. Are Plato's ideas still influencing contemporary society? How do his ideas affect our evaluation of materialism, sensuality, sex, and love?

10. Write an allegory based upon a sport, business, or space flight to explain how we act in the world.

JOSEPH WOOD KRUTCH

The New Immorality

Joseph Wood Krutch (1893–1970), American journalist, naturalist, and literary critic, is best known for *The Desert Year* (1952) and *The Modern Temper* (1956). The following essay, first published in 1960, reflects Krutch's concern for the contemporary condition. In it, he argues against an immoral society and criticizes what he terms "the paradox of our age."

he provost of one of our largest and most honored 1
institutions told me not long ago that a questionnaire was distributed to his undergraduates and that 40 percent refused to acknowledge that they believed cheating on examinations to be reprehensible.

Recently a reporter for a New York newspaper stopped six 2
people on the street and asked them if they would consent to take part in a rigged television quiz for money. He reported that five of the six said yes. Yet most of these five, like most of the college cheaters, would probably profess a strong social consciousness. They may cheat, but they vote for foreign aid and for enlightened social measures.

These two examples exhibit a paradox of our age. It is often 3
said, and my observation leads me to believe it true, that our seemingly great growth in social morality has oddly enough taken place in a world where private morality—a sense of the supreme importance of purely personal honor, honesty, and integrity—seems to be declining. Beneficent and benevolent social institutions are administered by men who all too frequently turn out to be accepting "gifts." The world of popular entertainment is rocked by scandals. College students put on their honor, cheat on examinations. Candidates for the Ph.D. hire ghost writers to prepare their theses.

But, one may object, haven't all these things always been 4
true? Is there really any evidence that personal dishonesty is more prevalent than it always was?

I have no way of making a historical measurement. Perhaps 5
these things are not actually more prevalent. What I do know is that there is an increasing tendency to accept and take for granted such personal dishonesty. The bureaucrat and disk jockey say, "Well, yes, I took presents, but I assure you that I made just decisions anyway." The college student caught cheating does not even blush. He shrugs his shoulders and comments: "Everybody does it, and besides, I can't see that it really hurts anybody."

Jonathan Swift once said: "I have never been surprised to find 6
men wicked, but I have often been surprised to find them not ashamed." It is my conviction that though men may be no more wicked than they always have been, they seem less likely to be ashamed. If anybody does it, it must be right. Honest, moral, decent mean only what is usual. This is not really a wicked world, because morality means mores or manners and usual conduct is the only standard.

The second part of the defense, "it really doesn't hurt 7
anybody," is equally revealing. "It doesn't hurt anybody" means it doesn't do that abstraction called society any harm. The harm it did

the bribe-taker and the cheater isn't important; it is purely personal. And personal as opposed to social decency doesn't count for much. Sometimes I am inclined to blame sociology for part of this paradox. Sociology has tended to lay exclusive stress upon social morality, and tended too often to define good and evil as merely the "socially useful" or its reverse.

What social morality and social conscience leave out is the narrower but very significant concept of honor—as opposed to what is sometimes called merely "socially desirable conduct." The man of honor is not content to ask merely whether this or that will hurt society, or whether it is what most people would permit themselves to do. He asks, and he asks first of all, would it hurt him and his self-respect? Would it dishonor him personally? 8

It was a favorite and no doubt sound argument among early twentieth-century reformers that "playing the game" as the gentleman was supposed to play it was not enough to make a decent society. They were right: it is not enough. But the time has come to add that it is indeed inevitable that the so-called social conscience unsupported by the concept of personal honor will create a corrupt society. But suppose that it doesn't? Suppose that no one except the individual suffers from the fact that he sees nothing wrong in doing what everybody else does? Even so, I still insist that for the individual himself nothing is more important than this personal, interior sense of right and wrong and his determination to follow that rather than to be guided by what everybody does or merely the criterion of "social usefulness." It is impossible for me to imagine a good society composed of men without honor. 9

We hear it said frequently that what present-day men most desire is security. If that is so, then they have a wrong notion of what the real, the ultimate, security is. No one who is dependent on anything outside himself, upon money, power, fame, or whatnot, is or ever can be secure. Only he who possesses himself and is content with himself is actually secure. Too much is being said about the importance of adjustment and "participation in the group." Even cooperation, to give this thing its most favorable designation, is no more important than the ability to stand alone when the choice must be made between the sacrifice of one's own integrity and adjustment to or participation in group activity. 10

No matter how bad the world may become, no matter how much the mass man of the future may lose such of the virtues as he still has, one fact remains. If one person alone refuses to go along with him, if one person alone asserts his individual and inner right to believe in and be loyal to what his fellow men seem to have given up, then at least he will still retain what is perhaps the most important part of humanity. 11

QUESTIONS

1. According to Krutch, what is the paradox of our age? What is unique about this paradox in terms of history?

2. What are the standard defenses and assumptions concerning the new immorality? How does Krutch respond to them?

3. Krutch employs highly connotative language in this essay. What are some of these words? How does the author both control and exploit connotative language in advancing his analysis and argument?

4. Why is the allusion to Jonathan Swift especially appropriate?

5. Explain the patterns of development in paragraphs 1 to 4, 5 to 7, and 8 to 11.

6. Does Krutch present an inductive or deductive argument in this essay? Explain your answer by reference to the text.

7. In what ways do causal analysis and extended definition enter into the development of the essay?

8. Analyze the last paragraph of the essay and evaluate its effectiveness.

9. Do you accept Krutch's premise that a good society depends on people of honor? Why or why not? Cite examples to support your contention.

10. Write an argumentative essay on personal immorality and the condition of modern American society.

MICHAEL NOVAK

Sports: A Sense of Evil

Michael Novak (1933–) is an author and educator. His interests, though principally in religion, also touch upon politics, sports, and popular culture. Novak's books include *The Tiber Was Silver* (1961), *The Open Church* (1964), *The Rise of the Unmeltable Ethnics* (1972), and *Choosing Our King* (1976). The following essay, which perceptively reveals America's schizoid view of sports, appeared in *The Joy of Sports* (1976).

The mythic tissue surrounding sports has always suggested that sports are "clean" and "All-American." This mythic world owes much both to Great Britain and to the Anglo-American spiritual sensitivity. The "fair play" of the playing fields of Eton, but also the scouting movement, the Temperance Leagues, the Chatauqua camps, and other American movements of individualism, self-improvement, and progressive thinking—these sanctified certain ideal types as truly American, compared to others. In the stories of Frank Merriwell, Garry Grayson, Tom Swift, and other heroes for red-blooded American boys, the most highly prized qualities were wit, pluck, clean-living, and implacable enmity against ever-present "bullies." Sports were imagined to be a realm of muscular Christianity—of maleness on the one hand and purity of heart on the other. If in other climes a certain shiftiness, sensuality, sheer physical aggression, duplicity, and trickiness were deemed appropriate, the true American hero was pure of heart, candid, straight, true, plucky, modest, and full of boyish charm and manly courage. 1

These traditions were not, be it noted, precisely British. The British are an older, wiser culture, given to a certain matter-of-fact toughness and pragmatic amorality. By contrast, those of the British who came to New England tended to be enthusiasts, dissidents, saints, passionately religious. The Anglo-American is quite different from the Briton: more democratic, more active, rougher, less formal. "Phlegmatic" would not be an apt description of his national character. "Moral" would be closer. 2

In a peculiar way, as a result, the American mythology of sports has moved on two separate levels. On the higher plane march Frank Merriwell and all the legions of straight-shooters and Christian athletes, self-effacing, gutsy, and victorious: the clean-living, true-blue gentlemen athletes. On the lower plane carouse the avaricious, sexy, aggressive, hedonistic Texans of *North Dallas Forty* and *Semi-tough*—the heavy-drinking, womanizing, masculine hell-raisers of the early days of baseball history, and of today: men like Max McGee, Paul Hornung, Joe Namath, and the horny hero-villains of contemporary sports fiction. In Babe Ruth, the high road and the low road ran as parallel as a modern urban street with elevated highway overhead: Babe Ruth visiting the orphans in a tuberculosis asylum in the newspaper story, and carousing late at night with the prostitutes in the parlor car, unknown to the public. 3

The moral pretenses of Anglo-American civilization demand a public standard of rectitude, while permitting a private standard of individual choice. Attacks upon "hypocrisy" are one of the most consistent patterns of our cultural life. "Muckraking" is possible only 4 because the public rectitude is prescriptive rather than descriptive, and the gap between the two is never closed. We are not even sure we want it closed. We hate Puritans. Yet our allergies inflict on us Puritan itches.

Liberal, radical, and (in general) progressive thinkers commonly undertake a double mission. First, they engage with gusto in the unmasking of hypocrisies. They attempt to reduce the gap between public myth and private practise by a stream of steamy exposés. Thus, they scratch the itch. Second, they hold aloft new standards of moral progress, idealism, and moral striving. "See," they say, "many athletes are horny, vulgar, racist, sexist hedonists. Frankness and candor are required of a truthful generation. Debunk the myths. For our society must *not* be racist, sexist, or nihilist. It must be just, egalitarian, brave, self-sacrificing, generous and truthful. It must live up to its ideals." Our muckrakers are not immoralists. On the contrary, they are busy setting up a new mythology which their children, carrying the endless project forward, will then debunk. Whatever we are allergic to, they inject into the nation's system. Saintly to the bitter end. 5

But the true practice of sport goes on, beneath the moralistic mythology of virtue and clean-living. Basketball without deception could not survive. Football without aggression, holding, slugging, and other violations—only a few of which the referees actually will censure—could not be played. Baseball without cunning, trickery, and pressing for advantage would scarcely be a contest. Our sports are lively with the sense of evil. The evil in them is, to be certain, ritualized, controlled, and channeled. But it is silly to deny that the disciplines of sport include learning how to cope with the illegal aggressions and unbounded passions of one's opponent and oneself. Sports provide an almost deliberate exercise in pushing the psyche to cheat and take advantage, to be ruthless, cruel, deceitful, vengeful, and aggressive. It is "good sportsmanship" not to let such passions dominate; it is naïve not to see them operate in others and oneself. 6

In football, defensive players hold, illegally, on almost every play. In basketball, a "non-contact game," the violence under the boards is fierce. In baseball, intimidation by pitchers, baserunners, and defensive players is straightforward and expectable. Morality on the athletic field is not a Pollyanna morality. It is controlled by more rules and referees than is any other part of life. Coaches devise ways to get around the rules (players change jerseys; feign injuries to stop the clock; call signals to draw the other team offsides, etc.). The many roles of bluff, feint, intimidation and trickery are so important in sports that they are codified and rendered classical. (There are similar 7 codes and classic moves in scholarship, journalism, politics, and every other field.)

Sports, then, are no escape from evil and immorality. They are designed to teach us how to live in a world that is less than moral. That, too, is one of sport's pleasures. To be an American is to be obliged to indulge in certain moral pretenses. The "American way" is to be decent, moral, trustworthy, law-abiding, tolerant, just, egalitarian, and so forth. Which is fairly heavy. To give a fellow an elbow when the referee isn't looking, just before the ball comes off the rim, is profoundly satisfying to the un-American, unregenerate, unsaintly self. 8

It is "good sportsmanship" to see to it that the basic structure and procedures of the contest are fair. A good contest, by its nature, requires fairness. The outcome should hang uncertainly between evenly matched opponents, playing under similar rules. A false conception of good sportsmanship, however, prevents many players from giving themselves fully to the competition. Instead of concentrating on the excellence of their own performance, many amateurs, in particular, begin to worry about the psyche of their opponents; they hold back. They lack the instinct for the jugular. They don't want to "humiliate" their opponents. Their condescension toward the frail ego (as they imagine it) of their opponents prevents them from playing as well as they might. They "let up." When they do, commitment and fire leave the contest. The true morality of sport is absent. 9

It is necessary to be objective about games—to play every one as thought it were one's last, seriously, with purpose, at full alert. The point of games is to propel oneself into a more intense mode of being. Not to play hard is to kill time, but not to transcend it. To concentrate on the game is, in a sense, to be indifferent about one's opponent or oneself. It is to refuse to be distracted by wayward passions. If an opponent plays unfairly, the sweetest revenge is not revenge but victory; one avoids striking back in kind in order to concentrate on the one thing necessary: perfect execution. Concentration on the game itself is the best safeguard against indulgence in ugly, errant passions. It is the highest form of sportsmanship. It is not so much a moral as an ontological attitude. One isn't trying to "be good," but to act perfectly. 10

Recently, the moralistic impulse has uncovered homosexuality in sports. Muckrakers have informed us that homosexuals appear in professional sports at about the same frequency as elsewhere in our society. Writers used to leer about fanny-patting, celibate training camps, nudity and team showering, and wrestling matches on the soapy floor. The new muckrakers seem to want to give a double 11

message: "See, the world of sports is corrupt and hollow, a world of fake machismo, infested by gays. But it's all right to be gay, it's great, it's fine." They want it both ways. In the pagan world, in Greece and in Nazi Germany, athleticism and homosexuality went (so to speak) hand-in-hand. As did art and homosexuality. Machismo and homosexuality are not opposites. Sport favors neither one.

Sports are natural religions. All things human are proper to them. In pushing humans to extremities, they push virtues and vices to extremities, too. The world of sports is no escape from virtue, excellence, and grace. In sports, we meet our humanity. Assuming one begins with limited hopes, there is more to admire in sports—and in our humanity, and in our nation—than to despise. 12

QUESTIONS

1. Explain what Novak means when he says, "Sports are natural religions."

2. Why does Novak believe that hypocrisy and muckraking are American obsessions?

3. Give examples of Novak's use of philosophical vocabulary.

4. How does the use of slang affect the tone of the essay? How does it complement the use of philosophical terms?

5. How does Novak's comparison in paragraph 2 contribute to the development of the essay?

6. Give examples of Novak's use of deduction in this essay.

7. Explain the organization of paragraphs 5 and 6. What rhetorical techniques are used in each paragraph? How are the two paragraphs related?

8. Novak uses examples frequently in the essay. Examine their use in paragraphs 1 and 10. How do these kinds of examples differ? How do they contribute to the development of the essay?

9. Novak says that the contrast between high and low planes in American sports exists elsewhere. Discuss how the contrast appears in politics, college life, and literature.

10. a. Write an essay about your own experience as a player or spectator in sports when you confronted the conflict between ideals and reality.
b. Write an essay analyzing other ambiguities in American life, such as the image of politicians, astronauts, or business people.

ALBERT CAMUS

The Myth of Sisyphus

Albert Camus (1913–1960), French author and philosopher, was one of the most important thinkers of the twentieth century. During World War II, he joined the French underground movement against the Germans and was the principal editor of the underground newspaper *Combat.* After the war, he became well known for his theories on the absurdity of life. Camus believed that men and women should respond to absurdity with courage and decency, not with despair. His theories are dramatized in *The Stranger* (1942) and in such later works as *The Plague* (1948) and the plays *Caligula* (1944), *State of Siege* (1948), and *The Just Assassins* (1950). Camus was awarded the 1957 Nobel Prize in Literature. *The Myth of Sisyphus* (1942), from which this essay is taken, is often considered the foundation of his absurdist philosophy.

1 The gods had condemned Sisyphus to ceaselessly rolling a rock to the top of a mountain, whence the stone would fall back of its own weight. They had thought with some reason that there is no more dreadful punishment than futile and hopeless labor.

2 If one believes Homer, Sisyphus was the wisest and most prudent of mortals. According to another tradition, however, he was disposed to practice the profession of highwayman. I see no contradiction in this. Opinions differ as to the reasons why he became the futile laborer of the underworld. To begin with, he is accused of a certain levity in regard to the gods. He stole their secrets. Aegina, the daughter of Aesopus, was carried off by Jupiter. The father was shocked by that disappearance and complained to Sisyphus. He, who knew of the abduction, offered to tell about it on condition that Aesopus would give water to the citadel of Corinth. To the celestial thunderbolts he preferred the benediction of water. He was punished for this in the underworld. Homer tells us also that Sisyphus had put Death in chains. Pluto could not endure the sight of his deserted, silent empire. He dispatched the god of War, who liberated Death from the hands of her conqueror.

3 It is said also that Sisyphus, being near to death, rashly wanted to test his wife's love. He ordered her to cast his unburied body into the middle of the public square. Sisyphus woke up in the underworld. And there, annoyed by an obedience so contrary to human love, he obtained from Pluto permission to return to earth in order to chastise his wife. But when he had seen again the face of this

world, enjoyed water and sun, warm stones and the sea, he no longer wanted to go back to the infernal darkness. Recalls, signs of anger, warnings were of no avail. Many years more he lived facing the curve of the gulf, the sparkling sea, and the smiles of earth. A decree of the gods was necessary. Mercury came and seized the impudent man by the collar and, snatching him from his joys, led him forcibly back to the underworld, where his rock was ready for him.

You have already grasped that Sisyphus is the absurd hero. 4
He *is*, as much through his passions as through his torture. His scorn of the gods, his hatred of death, and his passion for life won him that unspeakable penalty in which the whole being is exerted toward accomplishing nothing. This is the price that must be paid for the passions of this earth. Nothing is told us about Sisyphus in the underworld. Myths are made for the imagination to breathe life into them. As for this myth, one sees merely the whole effort of a body straining to raise the huge stone, to roll it and push it up a slope a hundred times over; one sees the face screwed up, the cheek tight against the stone, the shoulder bracing the claycovered mass, the foot wedging it, the fresh start with arms outstretched, the wholly human security of two earth-clotted hands. At the very end of this long effort measured by skyless space and time without depth, the purpose is achieved. Then Sisyphus watches the stone rush down in a few moments toward that lower world whence he will have to push it up again toward the summit. He goes back down to the plain.

It is during that return, that pause, that Sisyphus interests 5
me. A face that toils so close to stones is already stone itself! I see that man going back down with a heavy yet measured step toward the torment of which he will never know the end. That hour like a breathing-space which returns as surely as his suffering, that is the hour of consciousness. At each of those moments when he leaves the heights and gradually sinks toward the lairs of the gods, he is superior to his fate. He is stronger than his rock.

If this myth is tragic, that is because its hero is conscious. 6
Where would his torture be, indeed, if at every step the hope of succeeding upheld him? The workman of today works every day in his life at the same tasks, and this fate is no less absurd. But it is tragic only at the rare moments when it becomes conscious. Sisyphus, proletarian of the gods, powerless and rebellious, knows the whole extent of his wretched condition: it is what he thinks of during his descent. The lucidity that was to constitute his torture at the same time crowns his victory. There is no fate that cannot be surmounted by scorn.

If the descent is thus sometimes performed in sorrow, it can 7
also take place in joy. This word is not too much. Again I fancy

Sisyphus returning toward his rock, and the sorrow was in the beginning. When the images of earth cling too tightly to memory, when the call of happiness becomes too insistent, it happens that melancholy rises in man's heart: this is the rock's victory, this is the rock itself. The boundless grief is too heavy to bear. These are our nights of Gethsemane. But crushing truths perish from being acknowledged. Thus, Oedipus at the outset obeys fate without knowing it. But from the moment he knows, his tragedy begins. Yet at the same moment, blind and desperate, he realizes that the only bond linking him to the world is the cool hand of a girl. Then a tremendous remark rings out: "Despite so many ordeals, my advanced age and the nobility of my soul make me conclude that all is well." Sophocles' Oedipus, like Dostoevsky's Kirilov, thus gives the recipe for the absurd victory. Ancient wisdom confirms modern heroism.

One does not discover the absurd without being tempted to 8
write a manual of happiness. "What! by such narrow ways—?" There is but one world, however. Happiness and the absurd are two sons of the same earth. They are inseparable. It would be a mistake to say that happiness necessarily springs from the absurd discovery. It happens as well that the feeling of the absurd springs from happiness. "I conclude that all is well," says Oedipus, and that remark is sacred. It echoes in the wild and limited universe of man. It teaches that all is not, has not been, exhausted. It drives out of this world a god who had come into it with dissatisfaction and a preference for futile sufferings. It makes of fate a human matter, which must be settled among men.

All Sisyphus' silent joy is contained therein. His fate belongs 9
to him. His rock is his thing. Likewise, the absurd man, when he contemplates his torment, silences all the idols. In the universe suddenly restored to its silence, the myriad wondering little voices of the earth rise up. Unconscious, secret calls, invitations from all the faces, they are the necessary reverse and price of victory. There is no sun without shadow, and it is essential to know the night. The absurd man says yes and his effort will henceforth be unceasing. If there is a personal fate, there is no higher destiny, or at least there is but one which he concludes is inevitable and despicable. For the rest, he knows himself to be the master of his days. At that subtle moment when man glances backward over his life, Sisyphus returning toward his rock, in that slight pivoting he contemplates that series of unrelated actions which becomes his fate, created by him, combined under his memory's eye and soon sealed by his death. Thus, convinced of the wholly human origin of all that is human, a blind man eager to see who knows that the night has no end, he is still on the go. The rock is still rolling.

I leave Sisyphus at the foot of the mountain! One always 10
finds one's burden again. But Sisyphus teaches the higher fidelity that negates the gods and raises rocks. He too concludes that all is well. This universe henceforth without a master seems to him neither sterile nor futile. Each atom of that stone, each mineral flake of that night-filled mountain, in itself forms a world. The struggle itself toward the heights is enough to fill a man's heart. One must imagine Sisyphus happy.

QUESTIONS

1. What does Camus mean when he says, "Myths are made for the imagination to breathe life into them" (paragraph 4)?

2. Why does Camus think Sisyphus is such an appropriate symbol of people today?

3. Explain the style Camus uses to describe Sisyphus in paragraph 4. How does this narration differ in style from the preceding paragraphs?

4. Explain the connotations of such words as "tragic" (paragraph 6), "proletarian" (paragraph 6), "absurd" (paragraph 4), and "myth" (paragraph 4).

5. Why does Camus begin his essay with an analysis of the myth of Sisyphus?

6. Explain the organization of paragraph 4. Why does Camus end the narration where he does? How does this end lead to the next paragraph?

7. How does paragraph 8 differ from the paragraphs before it? How does it affect our sense of Sisyphus?

8. What crucial comparison is made in this essay? In what paragraphs does it appear? What transition words mark the development of the comparison?

9. Can you think of any other myths from the ancient world that help to explain our nature? Why do you think myths make such effective symbols of human nature?

10. a. Write an essay comparing yourself to a Greek hero such as Hercules, Jason, Medea, Odysseus, or Penelope. How do their histories relate to your own?
b. Write your own analysis of absurdity and the conditions of modern life.

BERTRAND RUSSELL

Can Religion Cure Our Troubles?

Bertrand Arthur William Russell (1872–1970) was one of the great philosophers, mathematicians, liberal political theorists, and authors of the twentieth century. His works are legion and range from abstruse explanations of mathematical theory to often bawdy memoirs. From the early *Principles of Mathematics* (1903) through *An Inquiry into Meaning and Truth* (1940), to his three-volume *Autobiography* (1967–1969), Russell demonstrated his multivarious talents as a writer and thinker. He was awarded the Nobel Prize in Literature in 1950. In the following essay, Russell scrutinizes the uses of religion and the relation of religion to morality.

I

Mankind is in mortal peril, and fear now, as in the past, is inclining men to seek refuge in God. Throughout the West there is a very general revival of religion. Nazis and Communists dismissed Christianity and did things which we deplore. . . . It is easy to conclude that the repudiation of Christianity by Hitler and the Soviet Government is at least in part the cause of our troubles and that if the world returned to Christianity, our international problems would be solved. I believe this to be a complete delusion born of terror. And I think it is a dangerous delusion because it misleads men whose thinking might otherwise be fruitful and thus stands in the way of a valid solution. 1

The question involved is not concerned only with the present state of the world. It is a much more general question, and one which has been debated for many centuries. It is the question whether societies can practise a sufficient modicum of morality if they are not helped by dogmatic religion. I do not myself think that the dependence of morals upon religion is nearly as close as religious people believe it to be. I even think that some very important virtues are more likely to be found among those who reject religious dogmas than among those who accept them. I think this applies especially to the virtue of truthfulness or intellectual integrity. I mean by intellectual integrity the habit of deciding vexed questions in accordance with the evidence, or the leaving them undecided where the evidence is inconclusive. This virtue, though it is underestimated by almost all adherents of any system of dogma, is to my mind of the very greatest social importance and far more likely to benefit the world than Christianity or any other system of organized beliefs. 2

Let us consider for a moment how moral rules have come to be accepted. Moral rules are broadly of two kinds: there are those which have no basis except in a religious creed; and there are those which have an obvious basis in social utility. In the Greek Orthodox Church, two godparents of the same child must not marry. For this rule, clearly, there is only a theological basis; and, if you think the rule important, you will be quite right in saying that the decay of religion is to be deprecated because it will lead to the rule being infringed. But it is not this kind of moral rule that is in question. The moral rules that are in question are those for which there is a social justification independently of theology. 3

Let us take theft, for example. A community in which everybody steals is inconvenient for everybody, and it is obvious that most people can get more of the sort of life they desire if they live in a community where theft is rare. But in the absence of laws and morals and religion a difficulty arises: for each individual, the ideal community would be one in which everybody else is honest and he alone is a thief. It follows that a social institution is necessary if the interest of the individual is to be reconciled with that of the community. This is effected more or less successfully by the criminal law and the police. But criminals are not always caught, and the police may be unduly lenient to the powerful. If people can be persuaded that there is a God who will punish theft, even when the police fail, it would seem likely that this belief would promote honesty. Given a population that already believes in God, it will readily believe that God has prohibited theft. The usefulness of religion in this respect is illustrated by the story of Naboth's vineyard where the thief is the king, who is above earthly justice. 4

I will not deny that among semi-civilized communities in the past such considerations may have helped to promote socially desirable conduct. But in the present day such good as may be done by imputing a theological origin to morals is inextricably bound up with such grave evils that the good becomes insignificant in comparison. As civilization progresses, the earthly sanctions become more secure and the divine sanctions less so. People see more and more reason to think that if they steal they will be caught and less and less reason to think that if they are not caught God will nevertheless punish them. Even highly religious people in the present day hardly expect to go to hell for stealing. They reflect that they can repent in time, and that in any case hell is neither so certain nor so hot as it used to be. Most people in civilized communities do not steal, and I think the usual motive is the great likelihood of punishment here on earth. This is borne out by the fact that in a mining camp during a gold rush, or in any such disorderly community, almost everybody does steal. 5

But, you may say, although the theological prohibition of 6

theft may no longer be very necessary, it at any rate does no harm since we all wish people not to steal. The trouble is, however, that as soon as men incline to doubt received theology it comes to be supported by odious and harmful means. If a theology is thought necessary to virtue and if candid inquirers see no reason to think the theology true, the authorities will set to work to discourage candid inquiry. In former centuries, they did so by burning the inquirers at the stake. In Russia they still have methods which are little better; but in Western countries the authorities have perfected somewhat milder forms of persuasion. Of these, schools are perhaps the most important: the young must be preserved from hearing the arguments in favour of the opinions which the authorities dislike, and those who nevertheless persist in showing an inquiring disposition will incur social displeasure and, if possible, be made to feel morally reprehensible. In this way, any system of morals which has a theological basis becomes one of the tolls by which the holders of power preserve their authority and impair the intellectual vigour of the young.

I find among many people at the present day an indifference to truth which I cannot but think extremely dangerous. When people argue, for example, in defence of Christianity, they do not, like Thomas Aquinas, give reasons for supposing that there is a God and that He has expressed His will in the Scriptures. They argue instead that, if people think this, they will act better than if they do not. We ought not therefore—so these people contend—to permit ourselves to speculate as to whether God exists. If, in an unguarded moment, doubt rears its head, we must suppress it vigorously. If candid thought is a cause of doubt we must eschew candid thought. If the official exponents of orthodoxy tell you that it is wicked to marry your deceased wife's sister, you must believe them lest morals collapse. If they tell you that birth control is sin, you must accept their dictum however obvious it may be to you that without birth control disaster is certain. As soon as it is held that any belief, no matter what, is important for some other reason than that it is true, a whole host of evils is ready to spring up. Discouragement of inquiry, which I spoke of before, is the first of these, but others are pretty sure to follow. Positions of authority will be open to the orthodox. Historical records must be falsified if they throw doubt on received opinions. Sooner or later unorthodoxy will come to be considered a crime to be dealt with by the stake, the purge, or the concentration camp. I can respect the men who argue that religion is true and therefore ought to be believed, but I can only feel profound moral reprobation for those who say that religion ought to be believed because it is useful, and that to ask whether it is true is a waste of time. 7

It is customary among Christian apologists to regard Communism as something very different from Christianity and to contrast 8

its evils with the supposed blessings enjoyed by Christian nations. This seems to me a profound mistake. The evils of Communism are the same as those that existed in Christianity during the Ages of Faith. The Ogpu differs only quantitatively from the Inquisition. Its cruelties are of the same sort, and the damage that it does to the intellectual and moral life of Russians is of the same sort as that which was done by the Inquisitors wherever they prevailed. The Communists falsify history, and the Church did the same until the Renaissance. If the Church is not now as bad as the Soviet Government, that is due to the influence of those who attacked the Church; from the Council of Trent to the present day whatever improvements it has effected have been due to its enemies. There are many who object to the Soviet Government because they dislike the Communist economic doctrine, but this the Kremlin shares with the early Christians, the Franciscans, and the majority of medieval Christian heretics. Nor was the Communist doctrine confined to heretics: Sir Thomas More, an orthodox martyr, speaks of Christianity as Communistic and says that this was the only aspect of the Christian religion which commended it to the Utopians. It is not Soviet doctrine in itself that can be justly regarded as a danger. It is the way in which the doctrine is held. It is held as sacred and inviolable truth, to doubt which is sin and deserving of the severest punishment. The Communist, like the Christian, believes that his doctrine is essential to salvation, and it is this belief which makes salvation possible for him. It is the similarities between Christianity and Communism that make them incompatible with each other. When two men of science disagree, they do not invoke the secular arm; they wait for further evidence to decide the issue, because as men of science, they know that neither is infallible. But when two theologians differ, since there are no criteria to which either can appeal, there is nothing for it but mutual hatred and an open or covert appeal to force. Christianity, I will admit, does less harm than it used to do; but that is because it is less fervently believed. Perhaps, in time, the same change will come over Communism; and, if it does, that creed will lose much of what now makes it obnoxious. But if in the West the view prevails that Christianity is essential to virtue and social stability, Christianity will once again acquire the vices which it had in the Middle Ages; and, in becoming more and more like Communism, will become more and more difficult to reconcile with it. It is not along this road that the world can be saved from disaster.

II

In my first article I was concerned with the evils resulting from any 9
system of dogmas presented for acceptance, not on the ground of
truth, but on the ground of social utility. What I had to say applies

equally to Christianity, Communism, Islam, Buddhism, Hinduism and all theological systems, except in so far as they rely upon grounds making a universal appeal of the sort that is made by men of science. There are, however, special arguments which are advanced in favour of Christianity on account of its supposed special merits. These have been set forth eloquently and with a show of erudition by Herbert Butterfield, Professor of Modern History in the University of Cambridge,[1] and I shall take him as spokesman of the large body of opinion to which he adheres.

Professor Butterfield seeks to secure certain controversial advantages by concessions that make him seem more open-minded than in fact he is. He admits that the Christian Church has relied upon persecution and that it is pressure from without that has led it to abandon this practice in so far as it has been abandoned. He admits that the present tension between Russia and the West is a result of power politics such as might have been expected even if the Government of Russia had continued to adhere to the Greek Orthodox Church. He admits that some of the virtues which he regards as distinctively Christian have been displayed by some free-thinkers and have been absent in the behaviour of many Christians. But, in spite of these concessions, he still holds that the evils from which the world is suffering are to be cured by adherence to Christian dogma, and he includes in the necessary minimum of Christian dogma not only belief in God and immortality, but also belief in the Incarnation. He emphasizes the connection of Christianity with certain historical events, and he accepts these events as historical on evidence which would certainly not convince him if it were not connected with his religion. I do not think the evidence for the Virgin Birth is such as would convince any impartial inquirer it it were presented outside the circle of theological beliefs he was accustomed to. There are innumerable such stories in Pagan mythology, but no one dreams of taking them seriously. Professor Butterfield, however, in spite of being an historian, appears to be quite uninterested in questions of historicity wherever the origins of Christianity are concerned. His argument, robbed of his urbanity and his deceptive air of broad-mindedness, may be stated crudely but accurately as follows: "It is not worth while to inquire whether Christ really was born of a Virgin and conceived of the Holy Ghost because, whether or not this was the case, the belief that it was the case offers the best hope of escape from the present troubles of the world." Nowhere in Professor Butterfield's work is there the faintest attempt to prove the truth of any Christian dogma. There is only the pragmatic argument that belief in Christian dogma is useful. There are many steps in Professor Butterfield's contention

[1]*Christianity and History* (London, 1950.)

which are not stated with as much clarity and precision as one could desire, and I fear the reason is that clarity and precision make them implausible. I think the contention, stripped of inessentials, is as follows: it would be a good thing if people loved their neighbours, but they do not show much inclination to do so; Christ said they ought to, and if they believe that Christ was God, they are more likely to pay attention to His teachings on this point than if they do not; therefore, men who wish people to love their neighbours will try to persuade them that Christ was God.

The objections to this kind of argumentation are so many that 11
it is difficult to know where to begin. In the first place, Professor Butterfield and all who think as he does are persuaded that it is a good thing to love your neighbour, and their reasons for holding this view are not derived from Christ's teaching. On the contrary, it is because they already hold this view that they regard Christ's teaching as evidence of His divinity. They have, that is to say, not an ethic based on theology, but a theology based upon their ethic. They apparently hold, however, that the non-theological grounds which make them think it a good thing to love your neighbour are not likely to make a wide appeal, and they therefore proceed to invent other arguments which they hope will be more effective. This is a very dangerous procedure. Many Protestants used to think it as wicked to break the Sabbath as to commit murder. If you persuaded them it was not wicked to break the Sabbath, they might infer that it was not wicked to commit murder. Every theological ethic is in part such as can be defended rationally, and in part a mere embodiment of superstitious taboos. The part which can be defended rationally should be so defended, since otherwise those who discover the irrationality of the other part may rashly reject the whole.

But has Christianity, in fact, stood for a better morality than 12
that of its rivals and opponents? I do not see how any honest student of history can maintain that this is the case. Christianity has been distinguished from other religions by its greater readiness for persecution. Buddhism has never been a persecuting religion. The Empire of the Caliphs was much kinder to Jews and Christians than Christian States were to Jews and Mohammedans. It left Jews and Christians unmolested, provided they paid tribute. Anti-Semitism was promoted by Christianity from the moment when the Roman Empire became Christian. The religious fervour of the Crusades led to pogroms in Western Europe. It was Christians who unjustly accused Dreyfus, and free-thinkers who secured his final rehabilitation. Abominations have in modern times been defended by Christians not only when Jews were the victims, but also in other connections. The abominations of King Leopold's government of the Congo were concealed or

minimized by the Church and were ended only by an agitation conducted mainly by free-thinkers. The whole contention that Christianity has had an elevating moral influence can only be maintained by wholesale ignoring or falsification of the historical evidence.

The habitual answer is that the Christians who did things 13
which we deplore were not *true* Christians in the sense that they did not follow the teachings of Christ. One might of course equally well argue that the Soviet Government does not consist of true Marxists, for Marx taught that Slavs are inferior to Germans and this doctrine is not accepted in the Kremlin. The followers of a teacher always depart in some respects from the doctrine of the master. Those who aim at founding a Church ought to remember this. Every church develops an instinct of self-preservation and minimizes those parts of the founder's doctrine which do not minister to that end. But in any case what modern apologists call 'true' Christianity is something depending upon a very selective process. It ignores much that is to be found in the Gospels: for example, the parable of the sheep and the goats, and the doctrine that the wicked will suffer eternal torment in hell-fire. It picks out certain parts of the Sermon on the Mount, though even these it often rejects in practice. It leaves the doctrine of non-resistance, for example, to be practised only by non-Christians such as Gandhi. The precepts that it particularly favours are held to embody such a lofty morality that they must have had a divine origin. And yet Professor Butterfield must know that these precepts were all uttered by Jews before the time of Christ. They are to be found, for example, in the teaching of Hillel and in the "Testaments of the Twelve Patriarchs", concerning which the Rev. Dr R. H. Charles, a leading authority in this matter, says: "The Sermon on the Mount reflects in several instances the spirit and even reproduces the very phrases of our text: many passages in the Gospels exhibit traces of the same, and St Paul seems to have used the book as a *vade-mecum*." Dr Charles is of the opinion that Christ must have been acquainted with this work. If, as we are sometimes told, the loftiness of the ethical teaching proves the divinity of its author, it is the unknown writer of these Testaments who must have been divine.

That the world is in a bad way is undeniable, but there is not 14
the faintest reason in history to suppose that Christianity offers a way out. Our troubles have sprung, with the inexorability of Greek tragedy, from the First World War, of which the Communists and the Nazis were products. The First World War was wholly Christian in origin. The three Emperors were devout, and so were the more warlike of the British Cabinet. Opposition to the war came, in Germany and Russia, from the Socialists, who were anti-Christian; in

France, from Juarès, whose assassin was applauded by earnest Christians; in England, from John Morley, a noted atheist. The most dangerous features of Communism are reminiscent of the medieval Church. They consist of fanatical acceptance of doctrines embodied in a Sacred Book, unwillingness to examine these doctrines critically, and savage persecution of those who reject them. It is not to a revival of fanaticism and bigotry in the West that we must look for a happy issue. Such a revival, if it occurs, will only mean that the hateful features of the Communist régime have become universal. What the world needs is reasonableness, tolerance, and a realization of the interdependence of the parts of the human family. This interdependence has been enormously increased by modern inventions, and the purely mundane arguments for a kindly attitude to one's neighbour are very much stronger than they were at any earlier time. It is to such considerations that we must look, and not to a return to obscurantist myths. Intelligence, it might be said, has caused our troubles; but it is not unintelligence that will cure them. Only more and wiser intelligence can make a happier world.

QUESTIONS

1. Russell divides religious moral rules into two categories. Which kind does he think are legitimate rules? Which kind are not? Why?

2. What similarities does Russell see between communism and Christianity?

3. How does word choice reflect Russell's attitude toward religion? Find evidence of words that reflect his attitude.

4. Explain the following allusions: Naboth's vineyard (paragraph 4), Thomas Aquinas (paragraph 7), the Inquisition (paragraph 8), and Sir Thomas More (paragraph 8).

5. Trace the line of reasoning from paragraph 4 through paragraph 7. What transition words mark the line Russell's reasoning takes?

6. How does the example given about mining camps at the end of paragraph 5 differ from the preceding examples in the paragraph? How does this kind of example help corroborate Russell's argument?

7. What is the subject of paragraphs 9 to 11? What purpose do they serve for the development of Russell's argument? How do they differ from paragraphs 12 and 13?

8. Explain how Russell uses paragraph 14 to conclude his essay.

9. How do you think Russell would respond to the resurgence of evangelical Protestant religion in America? Do you think such a movement threatens or supports morality?

10. a. Write an essay in which you refute the claims of an editorial in your local newspaper.
b. Write a paper explaining why religion can or cannot help you become a better person.

ROBERT LOUIS STEVENSON

Aes Triplex

Robert Louis Stevenson (1850–1894), poet, novelist, and journalist, was born in Scotland and spent a great part of his life traveling through Europe and the South Pacific. He is best known for his children's novel, *Treasure Island* (1881), his collection of children's poetry, *A Child's Garden of Verses* (1885), *Kidnapped* (1886), and *Dr. Jekyll and Mr. Hyde* (1886). Stevenson's love of adventure and his distaste for conventions influenced his opinions, as the following essay demonstrates.

1 The changes wrought by death are in themselves so sharp and final, and so terrible and melancholy in their consequences, that the thing stands alone in man's experience and has no parallel upon earth. It outdoes all other accidents because it is the last of them. Sometimes it leaps suddenly upon its victims, like a Thug; sometimes it lays a regular siege and creeps upon their citadel during a score of years. And when the business is done, there is sore havoc made in other people's lives, and a pin knocked out by which many subsidiary friendships hung together. There are empty chairs, solitary walks, and single beds at night. Again, in taking away our friends, death does not take them away utterly, but leaves behind a mocking, tragical, and soon intolerable residue, which must be hurriedly concealed. Hence a whole chapter of sights and customs striking to the mind, from the pyramids of Egypt to the gibbets and jule trees of medieval Europe. The poorest persons have a bit of pageant going towards the tomb; memorial stones are set up over the least memorable; and, in order to preserve some show of respect for what remains of our old loves and

friendships, we must accompany it with much grimly ludicrous ceremonial, and the hired undertaker parades before the door. All this, and much more of the same sort, accompanied by the eloquence of poets, has gone a great way to put humanity in error; nay, in many philosophies the error has been embodied and laid down with every circumstance of logic; although in real life the bustle and swiftness, in leaving people little time to think, have not left them time enough to go dangerously wrong in practice.

As a matter of fact, although few things are spoken of with 2
more fearful whisperings than this prospect of death, few have less influence on conduct under healthy circumstances. We have all heard of cities of South America built upon the side of fiery mountains, and how, even in this tremendous neighborhood, the inhabitants are not a jot more impressed by the solemnity of moral conditions than if they were delving gardens in the greenest corner of England. There are serenades and suppers and much gallantry among the myrtles overhead; and meanwhile the foundation shudders underfoot, the bowels of the mountain growl, and at any moment living ruin may leap sky-high into the moonlight, and tumble man and his merry-making in the dust. In the eyes of very young people, and very dull old ones, there is something indescribably reckless and desperate in such a picture. It seems not credible that respectable married people, with umbrellas, should find appetite for a bit of supper within quite a long distance of a fiery mountain; ordinary life begins to smell of high-handed debauch when it is carried on so close to a catastrophe; and even cheese and salad, it seems, could hardly be relished in such circumstances without something like a defiance of the Creator. It should be a place for nobody but hermits dwelling in prayer and maceration, or mere born-devils drowning care in a perpetual carouse.

And yet, when one comes to think upon it calmly, the 3
situation of these South American citizens forms only a very pale figure for the state of ordinary mankind. This world itself, traveling blindly and swiftly in overcrowded space, among a million other worlds traveling blindly and swiftly in contrary directions, may very well come by a knock that would set it into explosion like a penny squib. And what, pathologically looked at, is the human body with all its organs, but a mere bagful of petards? The least of these is as dangerous to the whole economy as the ship's powder-magazine to the ship; and with every breath we breathe, and every meal we eat, we are putting one more of them in peril. If we clung as devotedly as some philosophers pretend we do to the abstract idea of life, or were half as frightened as they make out we are, for the subversive accident that ends it all, the trumpets might sound by the hour and

no one would follow them into battle—the blue-peter might fly at the truck, but who would climb into a sea-going ship? Think (if these philosophers were right) with what a preparation of spirit we should affront the daily peril of the dinner-table: a deadlier spot than any battle-field in history, where the far greater proportion of our ancestors have miserably left their bones! What woman would ever be lured into marriage, so much more dangerous than the wildest sea? And what would it be to grow old? For, after a certain distance, every step we take in life we find the ice growing thinner below our feet, and all around us and behind us we see our contemporaries going through. By the time a man gets well into the seventies, his continued existence is a mere miracle; and when he lays his old bones in bed for the night, there is an overwhelming probability that he will never see the day. Do the old men mind it, as a matter of fact? Why, no. They were never merrier; they have their grog at night, and tell the raciest stories; they hear of the death of people about their own age, or even younger, not as if it was a grisly warning, but with a simple childlike pleasure at having outlived some one else; and when a draft might puff them out like a guttering candle, or a bit of a stumble shatter them like so much glass, their old hearts keep sound and unaffrighted, and they go on, bubbling with laughter, through years of man's age compared to which the valley at Balaklava was as safe and peaceful as a village cricket-green on Sunday. It may fairly be questioned (if we look at the peril only) whether it was a much more daring feat for Curtius to plunge into the gulf than for any old gentleman of ninety to doff his clothes and clamber into bed.

4 Indeed, it is a memorable subject for consideration, with what unconcern and gaiety mankind pricks on along the Valley of the Shadow of Death. The whole way is one wilderness of snares; and the end of it, for those who fear the last pinch, is irrevocable ruin. And yet we go spinning through it all, like a party for the Derby. Perhaps the reader remembers one of the humorous devices of the deified Caligula: how he encouraged a vast concourse of holiday-makers on to his bridge over Baiae bay, and, when they were in the height of their enjoyment, turned loose the Pretorian guards among the company, and had them tossed into the sea. This is no bad miniature of the dealings of nature with the transitory race of man. Only, what a checkered picnic we have of it, even while it lasts! and into what great waters, not to be crossed by any swimmer, God's pale Pretorian throws us over in the end!

5 We live the time that a match flickers; we pop the cork of a ginger-beer bottle, and the earthquake swallows us on the instant. Is it not odd, is it not incongruous, is it not in the highest sense of human speech, incredible, that we should think so highly of the

ginger-beer and regard so little the devouring earthquake? The love of Life and the fear of Death are two famous phrases that grow harder to understand the more we think about them. It is a well-known fact that an immense proportion of boat accidents would never happen if people held the sheet in their hands instead of making it fast; and yet, unless it be some martinet of a professional mariner or some landsman with shattered nerves, every one of God's creatures makes it fast. A strange instance of man's unconcern and brazen boldness in the face of death!

We confound ourselves with metaphysical phrases, which we 6
import into daily talk with noble inappropriateness. We have no idea of what death is, apart from its circumstances and some of its consequences to others; and although we have some experience of living, there is not a man on earth who has flown so high into abstraction as to have any practical guess at the meaning of the word *life*. All literature, from Job and Omar Khayam to Thomas Carlyle or Walt Whitman, is but an attempt to look upon the human state with such largeness of view as shall enable us to rise from the consideration of living to the Definition of Life. And our sages give us about the best satisfaction in their power when they say that it is a vapor, or a show, or made out of the same stuff with dreams. Philosophy, in its more rigid sense, has been at the same work for ages; and after a myriad bald heads have wagged over the problem, and piles of words have been heaped one upon another into dry and cloudy volumes without end, philosophy has the honor of laying before us, with modest pride, her contribution towards the subject: that life is a Permanent Possibility of Sensation. Truly a fine result! A man may very well love beef, or hunting, or a woman; but surely, surely, not a Permanent Possibility of Sensation! He may be afraid of a precipice, or a dentist, or a large enemy with a club, or even an undertaker's man; but not certainly of abstract death. We may trick with the word life in its dozen senses until we are weary of tricking; we may argue in terms of all the philosophies on earth; but one fact remains true throughout—that we do not love life, in the sense that we are greatly preoccupied about its conservation; that we do not, properly speaking, love life at all, but living. Into the views of the least careful there will enter some degree of providence; no man's eyes are fixed entirely on the passing hour; but although we have some anticipation of good health, good weather, wine, active employment, love, and self-approval, the sum of these anticipations does not amount to anything like a general view of life's possibilities and issues; nor are those who cherish them most vividly, at all the most scrupulous of their personal safety. To be deeply interested in the accidents of our existence, to enjoy keenly the mixed texture of human experience, rather leads a man to disregard precautions, and risk his neck against

a straw. For surely the love of living is stronger in an Alpine climber roping over a peril, or a hunter riding merrily at a stiff fence, than in a creature who lives upon a diet and walks a measured distance in the interest of his constitution.

There is a great deal of very vile nonsense talked upon both sides of the matter; tearing divines reducing life to the dimensions of a mere funeral procession, so short as to be hardly decent; and melancholy unbelievers yearning for the tomb as if it were a world too far away. Both sides must feel a little ashamed of their performances now and again, when they draw in their chairs to dinner. Indeed, a good meal and a bottle of wine is an answer to most standard works upon the question. When a man's heart warms to his viands, he forgets a great deal of sophistry, and soars into a rosy zone of contemplation. Death may be knocking at the door, like the Commander's statue; we have something else in hand, thank God, and let him knock. Passing bells are ringing the world over. All the world over, and every hour, some one is parting company with all his aches and ecstasies. For us also the trap is laid. But we are so fond of life that we have no leisure to entertain the terror of death. It is a honeymoon with us all through, and none of the longest. Small blame to us if we give our whole hearts to this glowing bride of ours—to the appetites, to honor, to the hungry curiosity of the mind, to the pleasure of the eyes in nature, and the pride of our own nimble bodies. 7

We all of us appreciate the sensations; but as for caring about the Permanence of the Possibility, a man's head is generally very bald, and his senses very dull, before he comes to that. Whether we regard life as a lane leading to a dead wall—a mere bag's end, as the French say—or whether we think of it as a vestibule or gymnasium, where we wait our turn and prepare our faculties for some more noble destiny; whether we thunder in a pulpit, or pule in little atheistic poetry-books, about its vanity and brevity; whether we look justly for years of health and vigor, or are about to mount into a bath-chair, as a step towards the hearse; in each and all of these views and situations there is but one conclusion possible: that a man should stop his ears against paralyzing terror, and run the race that is set before him with a single mind. No one surely could have recoiled with more heartache and terror from the thought of death than our respected lexicographer; and yet we know how little it affected his conduct, how wisely and boldly he walked, and in what a fresh and lively vein he spoke of life. Already an old man, he ventured on his Highland tour; and his heart, bound with triple brass, did not recoil before twenty-seven individual cups of tea. As courage and intelligence are the two qualities best worth a good man's cultivation, so it is the first part of intelligence to recognize our precarious estate in life, and the first part of courage to be not at all abashed before the 8

fact. A frank and somewhat headlong carriage, not looking too anxiously before, not dallying in maudlin regret over the past, stamps the man who is well armored for this world.

And not only well armored for himself, but a good friend and a good citizen to boot. We do not go to cowards for tender dealing; there is nothing so cruel as panic; the man who has least fear for his own carcase, has most time to consider others. That eminent chemist who took his walks abroad in tin shoes, and subsisted wholly upon tepid milk, had all his work cut out for him in considerate dealings with his own digestion. So soon as prudence has begun to grow up in the brain, like a dismal fungus, it finds its first expression in a paralysis of generous acts. The victim begins to shrink spiritually; he develops a fancy for parlors with a regulated temperature, and takes his morality on the principle of tin shoes and tepid milk. The care of one important body or soul becomes so engrossing that all the noises of the outer world begin to come thin and faint into the parlor with the regulated temperature; and the tin shoes go equably forward over blood and rain. To be otherwise is to ossify; and the scruple-monger ends by standing stock still. Now the man who has his heart on his sleeve, and a good whirling weathercock of a brain, who reckons his life as a thing to be dashingly used and cheerfully hazarded, makes a very different acquaintance of the world, keeps all his pulses going true and fast, and gathers impetus as he runs, until, if he be running towards anything better than wildfire, he may shoot up and become a constellation in the end. Lord look after his health, Lord have a care of his soul, says he; and he has at the key of the position, and swashes through incongruity and peril towards his aim. Death is on all sides of him with pointed batteries, as he is on all sides of all of us; unfortunate surprises gird him round; mim-mouthed friends and relations hold up their hands in quite a little elegiacal synod about his path: and what cares he for all this? Being a true lover of living, a fellow with something pushing and spontaneous in his inside, he must, like any other soldier, in any other stirring, deadly warfare, push on at his best pace until he touch the goal. "A peerage or Westminister Abbey!" cried Nelson in his bright, boyish, heroic manner. These are great incentives; not for any of these, but for the plain satisfaction of living, of being about their business in some sort or other, do the brave, serviceable men of every nation tread down the nettle danger, and pass flying over all the stumbling-blocks of prudence. Think of the heroism of Johnson, think of that superb indifference to mortal limitation that set him upon his dictionary, and carried him through triumphantly until the end! Who, if he were wisely considerate of things at large, would ever embark upon any work much more considerable than a halfpenny postcard? Who would project a serial novel, after Thackeray and Dickens had each

fallen in mid-course? Who would find heart enough to begin to live, if he dallied with the consideration of death?

10 And, after all, what sorry and pitiful quibbling all this is! To forgo all the issues of living, in a parlor with a regulated temperature—as if that were not to die a hundred times over, and for ten years at a stretch! As if it were not to die in one's own lifetime, and without even the sad immunities of death! As if it were not to die, and yet to be the patient spectators of our own pitiable change! The Permanent Possibility is preserved, but the sensations carefully held at arm's length, as if one kept a photographic plate in a dark chamber. It is better to lose health like a spendthrift than to waste it like a miser. It is better to live and be done with it, than to die daily in the sick room. By all means begin your folio; even if the doctor does not give you a year, even if he hesitates about a month, make one brave push and see what can be accomplished in a week. It is not only in finished undertakings that we ought to honor useful labor. A spirit goes out of the man who means execution, which outlives the most untimely ending. All who have meant good work with their whole hearts, have done good work, although they may die before they have the time to sign it. Every heart that has beat strong and cheerfully has left a hopeful impulse behind it in the world, and bettered the tradition of mankind. And even if death catch people, like an open pitfall, and in mid-career, laying out vast projects, and planning monstrous foundations, flushed with hope, and their mouths full of boastful language, they should be at once tripped up and silenced: is there not something brave and spirited in such a termination? and does not life go down with a better grace, foaming in full body over a precipice, than miserably straggling to an end in sandy deltas? When the Greeks made their fine saying that those whom the gods love die young, I cannot help believing they had this sort of death also in their eye. For surely, at whatever age it overtake the man, this is to die young. Death has not been suffered to take so much as an illusion from his heart. In the hot-fit of life, a-tiptoe on the highest point of being, he passes at a bound on to the other side. The noise of the mallet and chisel is scarcely quenched, the trumpets are hardly done blowing, when, trailing with him clouds of glory, this happy-starred, full-blooded spirit shoots into the spiritual land.

QUESTIONS

1. Why does Stevenson say, "The love of Life and the fear of Death are two famous phrases that grow harder to understand the more we think about them"?

2. For what kinds of people does Stevenson feel contempt? Why?

3. There are numerous instances of irony in this essay. Give five examples of Stevenson's use of hyperbole for ironic purposes.

4. Stevenson often uses allusions and expressions that no longer are common in our language. Explain the following: "the blue-peter might fly at the truck" (paragraph 3), "Curtius" (paragraph 3), "a party for the Derby" (paragraph 4), "the humorous devices of the deified Caligula" (paragraph 4), "like the Commander's statue" (paragraph 7), and "our respected lexicographer" (paragraph 8).

5. Stevenson says "A man may very well love beef, or hunting, or a woman; but surely, not a Permanent Possibility of Sensation!" How does Stevenson use this phrase as an organizing device? What is the difference between the two categories?

6. Explain the use of the analogy in paragraph 2. How is it interpreted? Give two other examples of extended analogies in this essay.

7. Most philosophers frequently use abstractions. Stevenson, of course, is critical of most philosophers. How does he use language to complement his thesis? Give examples of concrete language in this essay.

8. Divide this essay into three parts and explain why you divided it where you did. How are transitions used to mark the shifts you identified?

9. Stevenson believes that it is better to die bravely. Do you agree? Do you agree with his contempt for caution?

10. Write an essay using analogies and metaphors to describe love, beauty, life, or evil.

HANNAH ARENDT

The Human Condition

Hannah Arendt (1906–1975), scholar, political theorist, and writer, was born in Hanover, Germany, but was forced to flee because of the Nazi persecution of Jews in the 1930s. She came to the United States in 1940. Many of her works concern the nature of totalitarianism, such as *The Origins of Totalitarianism* (1951), *On Revolution* (1963), and *Eichmann in Jerusalem* (1963). Writing of Arendt, Mary McCarthy has said that she combines "tremendous intellectual power with great common sense." In the following selection, which is from *The Human Condition* (1958), Arendt analyzes three of the major qualities of human beings.

ith the term *vita activa,* I propose to designate three 1
fundamental human activities: labor, work, and action. They are fundamental because each corresponds to one of the basic conditions under which life on earth has been given to man.

Labor is the activity which corresponds to the biological 2
process of the human body, whose spontaneous growth, metabolism, and eventual decay are bound to the vital necessities produced and fed into the life process by labor. The human condition of labor is life itself.

Work is the activity which corresponds to the unnaturalness 3
of human existence, which is not imbedded in, and whose mortality is not compensated by, the species' ever-recurring life cycle. Work provides an "artificial" world of things, distinctly different from all natural surroundings. Within its borders each individual life is housed, while this world itself is meant to outlast and transcend them all. The human condition of work is worldliness.

Action, the only activity that goes on directly between men 4
without the intermediary of things or matter, corresponds to the human condition of plurality, to the fact that men, not Man, live on the earth and inhabit the world. While all aspects of the human condition are somehow related to politics, this plurality is specifically *the* condition—not only the *conditio sine qua non,* but the *conditio per quam*—of all political life. Thus the language of the Romans, perhaps the most political people we have known, used the words "to live" and "to be among men" (*inter homines esse*) or "to die" and "to cease to be among men" (*inter homines esse desinere*) as synonyms. But in its more elementary form, the human condition of action is implicit even in Genesis. ("Male and female created He *them*"), if we understand that this story of man's creation is distinguished in principle from the one according to which God originally created Man (*adam*), "him" and not "them," so that the multitude of human beings becomes the result of multiplication.[1] Action would be an unnecessary luxury, a capricious interference with general laws of behavior, if men were

[1]In the analysis of postclassical political thought, it is often quite illuminating to find out which of the two biblical versions of the creation story is cited. Thus it is highly characteristic of the difference between the teaching of Jesus of Nazareth and of Paul that Jesus, discussing the relationship between man and wife, refers to Genesis 1:27: "Have ye not read, that he which made *them* at the beginning made them male and female" (Matt. 19:4), whereas Paul on a similar occasion insists that the woman was created "of the man" and hence "for the man," even though he then somewhat attenuates the dependence: "neither is the man without the woman, neither the woman without the man" (I Cor. 11:8–12). The difference indicates much more than a different attitude to the role of woman. For Jesus, faith was closely related to action; for Paul, faith was primarily related to salvation. Especially interesting in this respect is Augustine (*De civitate Dei* xii. 21), who not only ignores Genesis 1:27 altogether but sees the difference between man and animal in that man was created *unum ac singulum,* whereas all animals were ordered "to come into being several at once" (*plura simul iussit exsistere*). To Augustine, the creation story offers a welcome opportunity to stress the species character of animal life as distinguished from the singularity of human existence.

endlessly reproducible repetitions of the same model, whose nature or essence was the same for all and as predictable as the nature or essence of any other thing. Plurality is the condition of human action because we are all the same, that is, human, in such a way that nobody is ever the same as anyone else who ever lived, lives, or will live.

All three activities and their corresponding conditions are 5
intimately connected with the most general condition of human existence: birth and death, natality and mortality. Labor assures not only individual survival, but the life of the species. Work and its product, the human artifact, bestow a measure of permanence and durability upon the futility of mortal life and the fleeting character of human time. Action, in so far as it engages in founding and preserving political bodies, creates the condition for remembrance, that is, for history. Labor and work, as well as action, are also rooted in natality in so far as they have the task to provide and preserve the world for, to foresee and reckon with, the constant influx of newcomers who are born into the world as strangers. However, of the three, action has the closest connection with the human condition of natality; the new beginning inherent in birth can make itself felt in the world only because the newcomer possesses the capacity of beginning something anew, that is, of acting. In this sense of initiative, an element of action, and therefore of natality, is inherent in all human activities. Moreover, since action is the political activity par excellence, natality, and not mortality, may be the central category of political, as distinguished from metaphysical, thought.

The human condition comprehends more than the conditions 6
under which life has been given to man. Men are conditioned beings because everything they come in contact with turns immediately into a condition of their existence. The world in which the *vita activa* spends itself consists of things produced by human activities; but the things that owe their existence exclusively to men nevertheless constantly condition their human makers. In addition to the conditions under which life is given to man on earth, and partly out of them, men constantly create their own, self-made conditions, which, their human origin and their variability notwithstanding, possess the same conditioning power as natural things. Whatever touches or enters into a sustained relationship with human life immediately assumes the character of a condition of human existence. This is why men, no matter what they do, are always conditioned beings. Whatever enters the human world of its own accord or is drawn into it by human effort becomes part of the human condition. The impact of the world's reality upon human existence is felt and received as a conditioning force. The objectivity of the world—its object- or thing-character—and the human condition supplement each other;

because human existence is conditioned existence, it would be impossible without things, and things would be a heap of unrelated articles, a non-world, if they were not the conditioners of human existence.

To avoid misunderstanding: the human condition is not the same as human nature, and the sum total of human activities and capabilities which correspond to the human condition does not constitute anything like human nature. For neither those we discuss here nor those we leave out, like thought and reason, and not even the most meticulous enumeration of them all, constitute essential characteristics of human existence in the sense that without them this existence would no longer be human. The most radical change in the human condition we can imagine would be an emigration of men from the earth to some other planet. Such an event, no longer totally impossible, would imply that man would have to live under man-made conditions, radically different from those the earth offers him. Neither labor nor work nor action nor, indeed, thought as we know it would then make sense any longer. Yet even these hypothetical wanderers from the earth would still be human; but the only statement we could make regarding their "nature" is that they still are conditioned beings, even though their condition is now self-made to a considerable extent. 7

The problem of human nature, the Augustinian *quaestio mihi factus sum* ("a question have I become for myself"), seems unanswerable in both its individual psychological sense and its general philosophical sense. It is highly unlikely that we, who can know, determine, and define the natural essences of all things surrounding us, which we are not, should ever be able to do the same for ourselves—this would be like jumping over our own shadows. Moreover, nothing entitles us to assume that man has a nature or essence in the same sense as other things. In other words, if we have a nature or essence, then surely only a god could know and define it, and the first prerequisite would be that he be able to speak about a "who" as though it were a "what."[2] The perplexity is that the modes of human 8

[2]Augustine, who is usually credited with having been the first to raise the so-called anthropological question in philosophy, knew this quite well. He distinguishes between the questions of "Who am I?" and "What am I?" the first being directed by man at himself ("And I directed myself at myself and said to me: You, who are you? And I answered: A man"—*tu, quis es?* [*Confessiones* x. 6]) and the second being addressed to God ("What then am I, my God? What is my nature?"—*Quid ergo sum, Deus meus? Quae natura sum?* [x. 17]). For in the "great mystery," the *grande profundum,* which man is (iv. 14), there is "something of man [*aliquid hominis*] which the spirit of man which is in him itself knoweth not. But Thou, Lord, who has made him [*fecisti eum*] knowest everything of him [*eius omnia*]" (x. 5). Thus, the most familiar of these phrases which I quoted in the text, the *quaestio mihi factus sum,* is a question raised in the presence of God, "in whose eyes I have become a question for myself" (x. 33). In brief, the answer to the question "Who am I?" is simply: "You are a man—whatever that may be"; and the answer to the question "What am I?" can be given only by God who made man. The question about the nature of man is no less a theological question than the question about the nature of God; both can be settled only within the framework of a divinely revealed answer.

cognition applicable to things with "natural" qualities, including ourselves to the limited extent that we are specimens of the most highly developed species of organic life, fail us when we raise the question: And *who* are we? This is why attempts to define human nature almost invariably end with some construction of a deity, that is, with the god of the philosophers, who, since Plato, has revealed himself upon closer inspection to be a kind of Platonic idea of man. Of course, to demask such philosophic concepts of the divine as conceptualizations of human capabilities and qualities is not a demonstration of, not even an argument for, the non-existence of God; but the fact that attempts to define the nature of man lead so easily into an idea which definitely strikes us as "superhuman" and therefore is identified with the divine may cast suspicion upon the very concept of "human nature."

On the other hand, the conditions of human existence—life itself, natality and mortality, worldliness, plurality, and the earth— can never "explain" what we are or answer the question of who we are for the simple reason that they never condition us absolutely. This has always been the opinion of philosophy, in distinction from the sciences—anthropology, psychology, biology, etc.—which also concern themselves with man. But today we may almost say that we have demonstrated even scientifically that, though we live now, and probably always will, under the earth's conditions, we are not mere earth-bound creatures. Modern natural science owes its great triumphs to having looked upon and treated earth-bound nature from a truly universal viewpoint, that is, from an Archimedean standpoint taken, wilfully and explicitly, outside the earth. 9

QUESTIONS

1. What does Arendt mean when she says, "The human condition is not the same as human nature"?

2. According to Arendt, why do people interpret their nature in terms of a deity? Does she agree with this idea? If so, why? If not, why not?

3. Explain the function of the allusions to Augustine, Plato, and the Bible. Why are references to such figures appropriate to Arendt's subject?

4. Does Arendt tend to write abstractly or concretely? Give examples of the style she uses most frequently.

5. Explain how Arendt uses classification to organize her essay. How many categories does Arendt give? What is the basis of her classification?

6. Definition is an important rhetorical device in this essay. Give five examples of definition and explain how they contribute to the development of the essay.

7. Explain the nature of the example in paragraph 7. How does it follow from the topic sentence of the paragraph?

8. Explain Arendt's syllogistic reasoning in paragraph 5. Give other examples of such reasoning elsewhere.

9. Arendt says we are "not mere earth-bound creatures" (paragraph 9). What does she mean by that? Do you agree? Do we, indeed, have souls?

10. Write an essay categorizing the three most important qualities of being one of the following—a parent, a student, or a teenager.

Mathematics, Science, and Technology

T. H. HUXLEY

We Are All Scientists

Thomas Henry Huxley (1825–1895) was one of the nineteenth century's most brilliant adventurers, educators, polemicists, and scientists. He defended Charles Darwin's theory of evolution to an often hostile English scientific community. He reformed the organization of the English elementary school. He labored incessantly to explain science to Britain's middle and working classes. Most of Huxley's works were republished in his *Collected Essays* (nine volumes, 1894–1908). In the following selection, Huxley dispels the popular belief that scientists think differently from the rest of us.

The method of scientific investigation is nothing but the 1
expression of the necessary mode of working of the human mind. It is simply the mode at which all phenomena are reasoned about, rendered precise and exact. There is no more difference, between the mental operations of a man of science and those of an ordinary person, than there is between the operations and methods of a baker or of a butcher weighing out his goods in common scales, and the operations of a

chemist in performing a difficult and complex analysis by means of his balance and finely graduated weights. It is not that the action of the scales in the one case, and the balance in the other, differ in the principles of their construction or manner of working; but the beam of one is set on an infinitely finer axis than the other, and of course turns by the addition of a much smaller weight.

You will understand this better, perhaps, if I give you some familiar example. You have all heard it repeated, I dare say, that men of science work by means of induction and deduction, and that by the help of these operations, they, in a sort of sense, wring from Nature certain other things, which are called natural laws, and causes, and that out of these, by some cunning skill of their own, they build up hypotheses and theories. And it is imagined by many that the operations of the common mind can be by no means compared with these processes, and that they have to be acquired by a sort of special apprenticeship to the craft. To hear all these large words, you would think that the mind of a man of science must be constituted differently from that of his fellow men; but if you will not be frightened by terms, you will discover that you are quite wrong, and that all these terrible apparatus are being used by yourselves every day and every hour of your lives. 2

There is a well known incident in one of Molière's plays, when the author makes the hero express unbounded delight on being told that he had been talking prose during the whole of his life. In the same way I trust that you will take comfort, and be delighted with yourselves, on the discovery that you have been acting on the principles of inductive and deductive philosophy during the same period. Probably there is not one here who has not in the course of the day had occasion to set in motion a complex train of reasoning, of the very same kind, though differing of course in degree, as that which a scientific man goes through in tracing the causes of natural phenomena. 3

A very trivial circumstance will serve to exemplify this. Suppose you go into a fruiterer's shop, wanting an apple—you take up one, and, on biting it, you find it is sour; you look at it, and see that it is hard and green. You take up another one, and that too is hard, green, and sour. The shopman offers you a third; but, before biting it, you examine it, and find that it is hard and green, and you immediately say that you will not have it, as it must be sour, like that you have already tried. 4

Nothing can be more simple than that, you think; but if you will take the trouble to analyze and trace out into its logical elements what has been done by the mind, you will be greatly surprised. In the first place, you have performed the operation of induction. You found that, in two experiences, hardness and greenness in apples went 5 together with sourness. It was so in the first case, and it was confirmed by the second. True, it is a very small basis, but still it is enough to make an induction from; you generalize the facts, and you expect to find sourness in apples where you get hardness and greenness. You found upon that a general law, that all hard and green apples are sour; and that, so far as it goes, is a perfect induction. Well, having got your natural law in this way, when you are offered another apple which you find is hard and green, you say, "All hard and green apples are sour; this apple is hard and green, therefore this apple is sour." That train of reasoning is what logicians call a syllogism, and has all its various parts and terms—its major premise, its minor premise, and its conclusion. And, by the help of further reasoning, which, if drawn out, would have to be exhibited in two or three other syllogisms, you arrive at your final determination, "I will not have that apple." So that, you see, you have, in the first place, established a law by induction, and upon that you have founded a deduction, and reasoned out the special conclusion of the particular case. Well now, suppose, having got your law, that at some time afterwards, you are discussing the qualities of apples with a friend: you will say to him, "It is a very curious thing but I find that all hard and green apples are sour!" Your friend says to you, "But how do you know that?" You at once reply, "Oh, because I have tried them over and over again, and have always found them to be so." Well, if we were talking science instead of common sense, we should call that an experimental verification. And, if still opposed, you go further, and say, "I have heard from the people in Somersetshire and Devonshire, where a large number of apples are grown, that they have observed the same thing. It is also found to be the case in Normandy, and in North America. In short, I find it to be the universal experience of mankind wherever attention has been directed to the subject." Whereupon, your friend, unless he is a very unreasonable man, agrees with you, and is convinced that you are quite right in the conclusion you have drawn. He believes, although perhaps he does not know he believes it, that the more extensive verifications are—that the more frequently experiments have been made, and results of the same kind arrived at—that the more varied the conditions under which the same results are attained, the more certain is the ultimate conclusion, and he disputes the question no further. He sees that the experiment has been tried under all sorts of conditions, as to time, place, and people, with the same result; and he says with you, therefore, that the law you have laid down must be a good one, and he must believe it.

In science we do the same thing; the philosopher exercises 6
precisely the same faculties, though in a much more delicate manner. In scientific inquiry it becomes a matter of duty to expose a supposed

law to every possible kind of verification, and to take care, moreover, that this is done intentionally, and not left to a mere accident, as in the case of the apples. And in science, as in common life, our confidence in a law is in exact proportion to the absence of variation in the result of our experimental verifications. For instance, if you let go your grasp of an article you may have in your hand, it will immediately fall to the ground. That is a very common verification of one of the best established laws of nature—that of gravitation. The method by which men of science establish the existence of that law is exactly the same as that by which we have established the trivial proposition about the sourness of hard and green apples. But we believe it in such an extensive, thorough, and unhesitating manner because the universal experience of mankind verifies it, and we can verify it ourselves at any time; and that is the strongest possible foundation on which any natural law can rest.

So much, then, by way of proof that the method of establishing laws in science is exactly the same as that pursued in common life. 7
Let us now turn to another matter (though really it is but another phase of the same question), and that is the method by which, from the relations of certain phenomena, we prove that some stand in the position of causes towards the others.

I want to put the case clearly before you, and I will therefore 8
show you what I mean by another familiar example. I will suppose that one of you, on coming down in the morning to the parlor of your house, finds that a teapot and some spoons which had been left in the room on the previous evening are gone—the window is open, and you observe the mark of a dirty hand on the window frame, and perhaps, in addition to that, you notice the impress of a hobnailed shoe on the gravel outside. All these phenomena have struck your attention instantly, and before two seconds have passed you say, "Oh, somebody has broken open the window, entered the room, and run off with the spoons and the teapot!" That speech is out of your mouth in a moment. And you will probably add, "I know he has; I am quite sure of it!" You mean to say exactly what you know; but in reality you are giving expression to what is, in all essential particulars, an hypothesis. You do not *know* it at all; it is nothing but an hypothesis rapidly framed in your own mind. And it is an hypothesis founded on a long train of inductions and deductions.

What are those inductions and deductions, and how have 9
you got at this hypothesis? You have observed, in the first place, that the window is open; but by a train of reasoning involving many inductions and deductions, you have probably arrived long before at the general law—and a very good one it is—that windows do not open of themselves; and you therefore conclude that something has opened the window. A second general law that you have arrived at in

the same way is, that teapots and spoons do not go out of a window spontaneously, and you are satisfied that, as they are not now where you left them, they have been removed. In the third place, you look at the marks on the window sill, and the shoe-marks outside, and you say that in all previous experience the former kind of mark has never been produced by anything else but the hand of a human being; and the same experience shows that no other animal but man at present wears shoes with hobnails in them such as would produce the marks in the gravel. I do not know, even if we could discover any of those "missing links" that are talked about,that they would help us to any other conclusion! At any rate the law which states our present experience is strong enough for my present purpose. You next reach the conclusion that as these kinds of marks have not been left by any other animals than men, or are liable to be formed in any other way than by a man's hand and shoe, the marks in question have been formed by a man in that way. You have, further, a general law, founded on observation and experience, and that, too is, I am sorry to say, a very universal and unimpeachable one—that some men are thieves; and you assume at once from all these premises—and that is what constitutes your hypothesis—that the man who made the marks outside and on the window sill, opened the window, got into the room, and stole your teapot and spoons. You have now arrived at a *vera causa;* you have assumed a cause, which it is plain, is competent to produce all the phenomena you have observed. You can explain all these phenomena only by the hypothesis of a thief. But that is a hypothetical conclusion, of the justice of which you have no absolute proof at all; it is only rendered highly probable by a series of inductive and deductive reasonings.

I suppose your first action, assuming that you are a man of 10
ordinary common sense, and that you have established this hypothesis to your own satisfaction, will very likely be to go off for the police, and set them on the track of the burglar, with the view to the recovery of your property. But just as you are starting with this object, some person comes in, and on learning what you are about, says, "My good friend, you are going on a great deal too fast. How do you know that the man who really made the marks took the spoons? It might have been a monkey that took them and the man may have merely looked in afterwards." You would probably reply, "Well, that is all very well, but you see it is contrary to all experience of the way teapots and spoons are abstracted; so that, at any rate, your hypothesis is less probable than mine." While you are talking the thing over in this way, another friend arrives, one of that good kind of people that I was talking of a little while ago. And he might say, "Oh, my dear sir, you are certainly going on a great deal too fast. You are most presumptuous. You admit that all these occurrences took place when

you were fast asleep, at a time when you could not possibly have known anything about what was taking place. How do you know that the laws of Nature are not suspended during the night? It may be that there has been some kind of supernatural interference in this case." In point of fact, he declares that your hypothesis is one of which you cannot at all demonstrate the truth, and that you are by no means sure that the laws of Nature are the same when you are asleep as when you are awake.

Well, now, you cannot at the moment answer that kind of 11
reasoning. You feel that your worthy friend has you somewhat at a disadvantage. You will feel perfectly convinced in your own mind, however, that you are quite right, and you say to him, "My good friend, I can only be guided by the natural probabilities of the case, and if you will be kind enough to stand aside and permit me to pass, I will go and fetch the police." Well, we will suppose that your journey is successful, and that by good luck you meet with a policeman; that eventually the burglar is found with your property on his person, and the marks correspond to his hand and to his boots. Probably any jury would consider those facts a very good experimental verification of your hypothesis, touching the cause of the abnormal phenomena observed in your parlor, and would act accordingly.

Now, in this suppositious case, I have taken phenomena of a 12
very common kind, in order that you might see what are the different steps in an ordinary process of reasoning, if you will only take the trouble to analyze it carefully. All the operations I have described, you will see, are involved in the mind of any man of sense in leading him to a conclusion as to the course he should take in order to make good a robbery and punish the offender. I say that you are led, in that case, to your conclusion by exactly the same train of reasoning as that which a man of science pursues when he is endeavoring to discover the origin and laws of the most occult phenomena. The process is, and always must be, the same; and precisely the same mode of reasoning was employed by Newton and Laplace in their endeavors to discover and define the causes of the movements of the heavenly bodies as you, with your own common sense, would employ to detect a burglar. The only difference is that the nature of the inquiry being more abstruse, every step has to be most carefully watched, so that there may not be a single crack or flaw in your hypothesis. A flaw or crack in many of the hypotheses of daily life may be of little or no moment as affecting the general correctness of the conclusions at which we may arrive; but, in a scientific inquiry, a fallacy, a great or small, is always of importance, and is sure to be in the long run constantly productive of mischievous, if not fatal results.

Do not allow yourselves to be misled by the common notion 13
that an hypothesis is untrustworthy simply because it is an hypothe

sis. It is often urged, in respect to some scientific conclusion, that, after all, it is only an hypothesis. But what more have we to guide us in nine-tenths of the most important affairs of daily life than hypotheses, and often very ill-based ones? So that in science, where the evidence of a hypothesis is subjected to the most rigid examination, we may rightly pursue the same course. You may have hypotheses and hypotheses. A man may say, if he likes, that the moon is made of green cheese: that is an hypothesis. But another man, who has devoted a great deal of time and attention to the subject, and availed himself of the most powerful telescopes and the results of the observations of others, declares that in his opinion it is probably composed of materials very similar to those of which our own earth is made up: and that is also only an hypothesis. But I need not tell you that there is an enormous difference in the value of the two hypotheses. That one which is based on sound scientific knowledge is sure to have a corresponding value; and that which is a mere hasty random guess is likely to have but little value. Every great step in our progress in discovering causes has been made in exactly the same way as that which I have detailed to you. A person observing the occurrence of certain facts and phenomena asks, naturally enough, what process, what kind of operation known to occur in Nature applied to the particular case, will unravel and explain the mystery? Hence you have the scientific hypothesis; and its value will be proportionate to the care and completeness with which its basis has been tested and verified. It is in these matters as in the commonest affairs of practical life: the guess of the fool will be folly, while the guess of the wise man will contain wisdom. In all cases, you see that the value of the result depends on the patience and faithfulness with which the investigator applies to his hypothesis every possible kind of verification.

QUESTIONS

1. Describe the process of reasoning that, according to Huxley, people use when they are deciding to eat green apples.

2. Why does Huxley reject the reasoning of "some person" in paragraph 10?

3. Huxley uses several "large words," particularly in paragraphs 2 and 5. What are these words and what do they mean?

4. Huxley uses both the second- and first-person pronouns in this essay. How does this affect the tone of the essay?

5. What is the thesis of this essay? Where is it expressed for the first time?

6. How does Huxley use coordinating conjunctions to maintain coherence?

7. Huxley employs two long examples to support and clarify his thesis. Identify these examples and show how Huxley relates them to his thesis.

8. How does paragraph 2 map out the structure of the essay?

9. Do you agree with Huxley's thesis? Why or why not?

10. Write a paper using examples to show how you use inductive and deductive reasoning in everyday life.

ALBERT EINSTEIN

The Common Language of Science

Albert Einstein (1879–1955), one of the greatest scientists who ever lived, was born in Germany. Einstein spent the early years of his career working in the Swiss patent office in Bern. In 1905, while working there, he published the first of many papers on the theory of relativity. These papers revolutionized physics. In 1933, with the advent of nazism, Einstein fled to the United States, where he continued his theoretical work and spoke out for peace in the world. His works range from the scientific *Relativity: The Special and General Theory* (1918), to the personal *The World as I See It* (1934). In the following essay, Einstein discusses the origin of scientific language.

the first step towards language was to link acoustically or otherwise commutable signs to sense-impressions. Most likely all sociable animals have arrived at this primitive kind of communication—at least to a certain degree. A higher development is reached when further signs are introduced and understood which establish relations between those other signs designating sense-impression. At this stage it is already possible to report somewhat complex series of impressions; we can say that language has come to existence. If language is to lead at all to understanding, there must be rules concerning the relations between the signs on the one hand and on the other hand there must be a stable correspondence between signs and impressions. In their childhood individuals connected by the same language grasp these rules 1 and relations mainly by intuition. When man becomes conscious of the rules concerning the relations between signs the so-called grammar of language is established.

In an early stage the words may correspond directly to 2
impressions. At a later stage this direct connection is lost insofar as some words convey relations to perceptions only if used in connection with other words (for instance such words as: "is," "or," "thing"). Then word-groups rather than single words refer to perceptions. When language becomes thus partially independent from the background of impressions a greater inner coherence is gained.

Only at this further development where frequent use is made 3
of so-called abstract concepts, language becomes an instrument of reasoning in the true sense of the word. But it is also this development which turns language into a dangerous source of error and deception. Everything depends on the degree to which words and word-combinations correspond to the world of impression.

What is it that brings about such an intimate connection 4
between language and thinking? Is there no thinking without the use of language, namely in concepts and concept-combinations for which words need not necessarily come to mind? Has not everyone of us struggled for words although the connection between "things" was already clear?

We might be inclined to attribute to the act of thinking 5
complete independence from language if the individual formed or were able to form his concepts without the verbal guidance of his environment. Yet most likely the mental shape of an individual, growing up under such conditions, would be very poor. Thus we may conclude that the mental development of the individual and his way of forming concepts depend to a high degree upon language. This makes us realize to what extent the same language means the same mentality. In this sense thinking and language are linked together.

What distinguishes the language of science from language as 6
we ordinarily understand the word? How is it that scientific language is international? What science strives for is an utmost acuteness and clarity of concepts as regards their mutual relation and their correspondence to sensory data. As an illustration let us take the language of Euclidian geometry and Algebra. They manipulate with a small number of independently introduced concepts, respectively symbols, such as the integral number, the straight line, the point, as well as with signs which designate the fundamental operations, that is the connections between those fundamental concepts. This is the basis for the construction, respectively definition of all other statements and concepts. The connection between concepts and statements on the one hand and the sensory data on the other hand is established

through acts of counting and measuring whose performance is sufficiently well determined.

The super-national character of scientific concepts and scientific language is due to the fact that they have been set up by the best brains of all countries and all times. In solitude and yet in cooperative effort as regards the final effect they created the spiritual tools for the technical revolutions which have transformed the life of mankind in the last centuries. Their system of concepts have served as a guide in the bewildering chaos of perceptions so that we learned to grasp general truths from particular observations. 7

What hopes and fears does the scientific method imply for mankind? I do not think that this is the right way to put the question. Whatever this tool in the hand of man will produce depends entirely on the nature of the goals alive in this mankind. Once these goals exist, the scientific method furnishes means to realize them. Yet it cannot furnish the very goals. The scientific method itself would not have led anywhere, it would not even have been born without a passionate striving for clear understanding. 8

Perfections of means and confusion of goals seem—in my opinion—to characterize our age. If we desire sincerely and passionately the safety, the welfare and the free development of the talents of all men, we shall not be in want of the means to approach such a state. Even if only a small part of mankind strives for such goals, their superiority will prove itself in the long run. 9

QUESTIONS

1. According to Einstein, when in the development of language does scientific language appear? How is it different from and similar to nonscientific language?

2. Why does Einstein say that language can "turn" into a dangerous source of error and deception?

3. Explain the use of rhetorical questions in this essay.

4. What is the point of view of this essay? How does this viewpoint complement the diction and tone of the essay?

5. What paragraphs use narrative? What words indicate the development of the narrative?

6. Give reasons and evidence for saying this essay uses extended definition.

7. Why is paragraph 6 important to the development of this essay? What rhetorical technique is used here?

8. Explain the relation of paragraphs 8 and 9 to the rest of the essay. What is the topic of paragraph 9?

9. If the language of science cannot define goals, what kinds of language can? Can we trust science to solve our problems? Explain.

10. a. Write an essay distinguishing means from goals in education, religion, or business.
b. Describe a particular kind of language—academic, political, or religious—and explain how it functions in relation to language in general.

LEWIS THOMAS

On Societies as Organisms

Lewis Thomas (1913–) has been the president of the Memorial Sloan-Kettering Cancer Center since 1973. He first came to public attention when his collection of essays, *Lives of a Cell* (1974), appeared. Because of his eloquent capacity to extract metaphors from the discoveries of modern biology and because of his optimism, Thomas's essays have attracted a large and enthusiastic following. Another collection of his essays, *The Medusa and the Snail,* was published in 1979. Thomas can discover an almost magical value in the most humble activities, as the essay below demonstrates.

Viewed from a suitable height, the aggregating clusters of medical scientists in the bright sunlight of the boardwalk at Atlantic City, swarmed there from everywhere for the annual meetings, have the look of assemblages of social insects. There is the same vibrating, ionic movement, interrupted by the darting back and forth of jerky individuals to touch antennae and exchange small bits of information; periodically, the mass casts out, like a trout-line, a long single file unerringly toward Child's. If the boards were not fastened down, it would not be a surprise to see them put together a nest of sorts. 1

It is permissible to say this sort of thing about humans. They do resemble, in their most compulsively social behavior, ants at a distance. It is, however, quite bad form in biological circles to put it the other way round, to imply that the operation of insect societies has any relation at all to human affairs. The writers of books on insect behavior generally take pains, in their prefaces, to caution that insects 2 are like creatures from another planet, that their behavior is absolutely foreign, totally unhuman, unearthly, almost unbiological. They are more like perfectly tooled but crazy little machines, and we violate science when we try to read human meanings in their arrangements.

It is hard for a bystander not to do so. Ants are so much like human beings as to be an embarrassment. They farm fungi, raise aphids as livestock, launch armies into wars, use chemical sprays to alarm and confuse enemies, capture slaves. The families of weaver ants engage in child labor, holding their larvae like shuttles to spin out the thread that sews the leaves together for their fungus gardens. They exchange information ceaselessly. They do everything but watch television. 3

What makes us most uncomfortable is that they, and the bees and termites and social wasps, seem to live two kinds of lives: they are individuals, going about the day's business without much evidence of thought for tomorrow, and they are at the same time component parts, cellular elements, in the huge, writhing, ruminating organism of the Hill, the nest, the hive. It is because of this aspect, I think, that we most wish for them to be something foreign. We do not like the notion that there can be collective societies with the capacity to behave like organisms. If such things exist, they can have nothing to do with us. 4

Still, there it is. A solitary ant, afield, cannot be considered to have much of anything on his mind; indeed, with only a few neurons strung together by fibers, he can't be imagined to have a mind at all, much less a thought. He is more like a ganglion on legs. Four ants together, or ten, encircling a dead moth on a path, begin to look more like an idea. They fumble and shove, gradually moving the food toward the Hill, but as though by blind chance. It is only when you watch the dense mass of thousands of ants, crowded together around the Hill, blackening the ground, that you begin to see the whole beast, and now you observe it thinking, planning, calculating. It is an intelligence, a kind of live computer, with crawling bits for its wits. 5

At a stage in the construction, twigs of a certain size are needed, and all the members forage obsessively for twigs of just this size. Later, when outer walls are to be finished, thatched, the size must change, and as though given new orders by telephone, all the workers shift the search to the new twigs. If you disturb the arrangement of a part of the Hill, hundreds of ants will set it vibrating, shifting, until it is put right again. Distant sources of food are somehow sensed, and long lines, like tentacles, reach out over the ground, up over walls, behind boulders, to fetch it in. 6

Termites are even more extraordinary in the way they seem to accumulate intelligence as they gather together. Two or three termites in a chamber will begin to pick up pellets and move them from place 7 to place, but nothing comes of it; nothing is built. As more join in, they seem to reach a critical mass, a quorum, and the thinking begins. They place pellets atop pellets, then throw up columns and beautiful, curving, symmetrical arches, and the crystalline architecture of vaulted chambers is created. It is not known how they communicate with each other, how the chains of termites building one column know when to turn toward the crew on the adjacent column, or how, when the time comes, they manage the flawless joining of the arches. The stimuli that set them off at the outset, building collectively instead of shifting things about, may be pheromones released when they reach committee size. They react as if alarmed. They become agitated, excited, and then they begin working, like artists.

Bees live lives of organisms, tissues, cells, organelles, all at 8
the same time. The single bee, out of the hive retrieving sugar (instructed by the dancer: "south-southeast for seven hundred meters, clover—mind you make corrections for the sundrift") is still as much a part of the hive as if attached by a filament. Building the hive, the workers have the look of embryonic cells organizing a developing tissue; from a distance they are like the viruses inside a cell, running off row after row of symmetrical polygons as though laying down crystals. When the time for swarming comes, and the old queen prepares to leave with her part of the population, it is as though the hive were involved in mitosis. There is an agitated moving of bees back and forth, like granules in cell sap. They distribute themselves in almost precisely equal parts, half to the departing queen, half to the new one. Thus, like an egg, the great, hairy, black and golden creature splits in two, each with an equal share of the family genome.

The phenomenon of separate animals joining up to form an 9
organism is not unique in insects. Slime-mold cells do it all the time, of course, in each life cycle. At first they are single amebocytes swimming around, eating bacteria, aloof from each other, untouching, voting straight Republican. Then, a bell sounds, and acrasin is released by special cells toward which the others converge in stellate ranks, touch, fuse together, and construct the slug, solid as a trout. A splendid stalk is raised, with a fruiting body on top, and out of this comes the next generation of amebocytes, ready to swim across the same moist ground, solitary and ambitious.

Herring and other fish in schools are at times so closely 10
integrated, their actions so coordinated, that they seem to be functionally a great multi-fish organism. Flocking birds, especially the seabirds nesting on the slopes of offshore islands in Newfoundland, are similarly attached, connected, synchronized.

Although we are by all odds the most social of all social 11
animals—more interdependent, more attached to each other, more

inseparable in our behavior than bees—we do not often feel our conjoined intelligence. Perhaps, however, we are linked in circuits for the storage, processing, and retrieval of information, since this appears to be the most basic and universal of all human enterprises. It may be our biological function to build a certain kind of Hill. We have access to all the information of the biosphere, arriving as elementary units in the stream of solar photons. When we have learned how these are rearranged against randomness, to make, say, springtails, quantum mechanics, and the late quartets, we may have a clearer notion how to proceed. The circuitry seems to be there, even if the current is not always on.

The system of communications used in science should provide a neat, workable model for studying mechanisms of information-building in human society. Ziman, in a recent *Nature* essay, points out, "the invention of a mechanism for the systematic publication of *fragments* of scientific work may well have been the key event in the history of modern science." He continues: 12

> A regular journal carries from one research worker to another the various . . . observations which are of common interest. . . . A typical scientific paper has never pretended to be more than another little piece in a larger jigsaw—not significant in itself but as an element in a grander scheme. *This technique, of soliciting many modest contributions to the store of human knowledge, has been the secret of Western science since the seventeenth century, for it achieves a corporate, collective power that is far greater than any one individual can exert.* [italics mine].

With some alteration of terms, some toning down, the passage could describe the building of a termite nest. 13

It is fascinating that the word "explore" does not apply to the searching aspect of the activity, but has its origins in the sounds we make while engaged in it. We like to think of exploring in science as a lonely, meditative business, and so it is in the first stages, but always, sooner or later, before the enterprise reaches completion, as we explore, we call to each other, communicate, publish, send letters to the editor, present papers, cry out on finding. 14

QUESTIONS

1. Describe the insects that Thomas says have humanlike behavior.

2. Why do writers of books about insects avoid using personification in their descriptions? Why does Thomas purposely use it?

3. Thomas tends to use words that are not generally used; therefore, define "genome," "ionic," "amebocytes," "mitosis," "acrasin," "ganglion," "stellate," and "organism."

4. Thomas uses metaphors frequently and imaginatively. List seven metaphors in the essay and describe how they are used.

5. Paragraph 4 is crucial to the organization of the essay. What two methods of classification does it introduce?

6. What is the difference between solitary and collective behavior among the social insects? Thomas compares this behavior to certain kinds of human behavior. What are the details of this comparison?

7. What is the etymology of the word "explore" according to your dictionary? How does Thomas use this etymology?

8. Thomas extends his discussion in paragraph 9 beyond insects. What effect does he achieve by doing this?

9. Do you find it reassuring or disturbing to compare human behavior to insect behavior? Do you find it difficult to consider human society an organism? Why do you think Thomas finds this encouraging?

10. a. Divide human behavior into groups (school, sports, business) and compare solitary and collective behavior within one or more groups.
b. Write an essay comparing your pet's behavior to human behavior.

LOREN EISELEY

How Natural Is Natural?

Loren Eiseley (1907–1977) was an educator, anthropologist, poet, and author. He is best known for his books *The Immense Journey* (1957), *Darwin's Century* (1958), *The Firmament of Time* (1960), and *The Night Country* (1971). His books wonderfully combine poetic imagination with scientific objectivity. In the following essay, Eiseley shows his capacity for seeing profoundly into the most common scenes.

In the more obscure scientific circles which I frequent there is a legend circulating about a late distinguished scientist who, in his declining years, persisted in wearing enormous padded boots much too large for him. He had developed, it seems, what to his fellows was a wholly irrational 1

fear of falling through the interstices of that largely empty molecular space which common men in their folly speak of as the world. A stroll across his living-room floor had become, for him, something as dizzily horrendous as the activities of a window washer on the Empire State Building. Indeed, with equal reason he could have passed a ghostly hand through his own ribs.

The quivering network of his nerves, the awe-inspiring movement of his thought had become a vague cloud of electrons interspersed with the light-year distances that obtain between us and the farther galaxies. This was the natural world which he had helped to create, and in which, at last, he had found himself a lonely and imprisoned occupant. All around him the ignorant rushed on their way over the illusion of substantial floors, leaping, though they did not see it, from particle to particle, over a bottomless abyss. There was even a question as to the reality of the particles which bore them up. It did not, however, keep insubstantial newspapers from being sold, or insubstantial love from being made. 2

Not long ago I became aware of another world perhaps equally natural and real, which man is beginning to forget. My thinking began in New England under a boat dock. The lake I speak of has been pre-empted and civilized by man. All day long in the vacation season high-speed motorboats, driven with the reckless abandon common to the young Apollos of our society, speed back and forth, carrying loads of equally attractive girls. The shores echo to the roar of powerful motors and the delighted screams of young Americans with uncounted horsepower surging under their hands. In truth, as I sat there under the boat dock, I had some desire to swim or to canoe in the older ways of the great forest which once lay about this region. Either notion would have been folly. I would have been gaily chopped to ribbons by teen-age youngsters whose eyes were always immutably fixed on the far horizons of space, or upon the dials which indicated the speed of their passing. There was another world, I was to discover, along the lake shallows and under the boat dock, where the motors could not come. 3

As I sat there one sunny morning when the water was peculiarly translucent, I saw a dark shadow moving swiftly over the bottom. It was the first sign of life I had seen in this lake, whose shores seemed to yield little but washed-in beer cans. By and by the gliding shadow ceased to scurry from stone to stone over the bottom. Unexpectedly, it headed almost directly for me. A furry nose with gray whiskers broke the surface. Below the whiskers green water foliage trailed out in an inverted V as long as his body. A muskrat still lived in the lake. He was bringing in his breakfast. 4

I sat very still in the strips of sunlight under the pier. To my 5 surprise the muskrat came almost to my feet with his little breakfast of greens. He was young, and it rapidly became obvious to me that he was laboring under an illusion of his own, and that he thought animals and men were still living in the Garden of Eden. He gave me a friendly glance from time to time as he nibbled his greens. Once, even, he went out into the lake again and returned to my feet with more greens. He had not, it seemed, heard very much about men. I shuddered. Only the evening before I had heard a man describe with triumphant enthusiasm how he had killed a rat in the garden because the creature had dared to nibble his petunias. He had even showed me the murder weapon, a sharp-edged brick.

On this pleasant shore a war existed and would go on until 6 nothing remained but man. Yet this creature with the gray, appealing face wanted very little: a strip of shore to coast up and down, sunlight and moonlight, some weeds from the deep water. He was an edge-of-the-world dweller, caught between a vanishing forest and a deep lake preempted by unpredictable machines full of chopping blades. He eyed me nearsightedly, a green leaf poised in his mouth. Plainly he had come with some poorly instructed memory about the lion and the lamb.

"You had better run away now," I said softly, making no 7 movement in the shafts of light. "You are in the wrong universe and must not make this mistake again. I am really a very terrible and cunning beast. I can throw stones." With this I dropped a little pebble at his feet.

He looked at me half blindly, with eyes much better adjusted 8 to the wavering shadows of his lake bottom than to sight in the open air. He made almost as if to take the pebble up into his forepaws. Then a thought seemed to cross his mind—a thought perhaps telepathically received, as Freud once hinted, in the dark world below and before man, a whisper of ancient disaster heard in the depths of a burrow. Perhaps after all this was not Eden. His nose twitched carefully; he edged toward the water.

As he vanished in an oncoming wave, there went with him a 9 natural world, distinct from the world of girls and motorboats, distinct from the world of the professor holding to reality by some great snowshoe effort in his study. My muskrat's shore-line universe was edged with the dark wall of hills on one side and the waspish drone of motors farther out, but it was a world of sunlight he had taken down into the water weeds. It hovered there, waiting for my disappearance. I walked away, obscurely pleased that darkness had not gained on life by any act of mine. In so many worlds, I thought, how natural is "natural"—and is there anything we can call a natural world at all?

QUESTIONS

1. Describe the three "worlds" mentioned in this essay by Eiseley.

2. Why is Eiseley surprised that a muskrat still lives in the lake? Cite specific details that might threaten a muskrat in the lake's world.

3. The phrases "sunlight world" and "darkness" (paragraph 9) are meant to be taken figuratively. What do they mean?

4. Explain the allusions to "Apollos" (paragraph 3); "the Garden of Eden" (paragraph 5); and Freud (paragraph 8).

5. Explain the relation between paragraphs 1 to 2 and 3 to 9. What rhetorical technique do both groups use?

6. How does Eiseley use narration and description in his essay? Cite examples of both.

7. What details does Eiseley use in contrasting the muskrat's world to the typical American's world?

8. Analyze the way Eiseley develops his concluding paragraph.

9. Why does Eiseley despair at the disappearance of the other world? Why should we protect wildlife and wilderness if it means limiting our own growth?

10. Write an essay in which you contrast aspects of the natural world with the artificial world. Use details to support your contrast. For example, you can describe the life of a bird in the city, of a raccoon in the suburbs, or a deer or bear in a state park.

RACHEL CARSON

The Changing Year

Rachel Carson (1907–1964) could write with eloquence and sensitivity even as she presented the reader with a rigorous, often demanding, scientific scrutiny of nature. Carson's most famous works are *The Sea around Us* (1951) and *The Silent Spring* (1962). The former book won her the National Book Award. The latter, an early study of the danger of pesticides to our environment, influenced President John Kennedy to appoint a commission to study her allegations. The following

essay, a chapter from *The Sea around Us,* illustrates her knowledge as a scientist and her skill as a writer.

Thus with the year seasons return.
MILTON

For the sea as a whole, the alternation of day and night, the passage of the seasons, the procession of the years, are lost in its vastness, obliterated in its own changeless eternity. But the surface waters are different. The face of the sea is always changing. Crossed by colors, lights, and moving shadows, sparkling in the sun, mysterious in the twilight, its aspects and its moods vary hour by hour. The surface waters move with the tides, stir to the breath of the winds, and rise and fall to the endless, hurrying forms of the waves. Most of all, they change with the advance of the seasons. Spring moves over the temperate lands of our Northern Hemisphere in a tide of new life, of pushing green shoots and unfolding buds, all its mysteries and meanings symbolized in the northward migration of the birds, the awakening of sluggish amphibian life as the chorus of frogs rises again from the wet lands, the different sound of the wind which stirs the young leaves where a month ago it rattled the bare branches. These things we associate with the land, and it is easy to suppose that at sea there could be no such feeling of advancing spring. But the signs are there, and seen with understanding eye, they bring the same magical sense of awakening. 1

In the sea, as on land, spring is a time for the renewal of life. During the long months of winter in the temperate zones the surface waters have been absorbing the cold. Now the heavy water begins to sink, slipping down and displacing the warmer layers below. Rich stores of minerals have been accumulating on the floor of the continental shelf—some freighted down the rivers from the lands; some derived from sea creatures that have died and whose remains have drifted down to the bottom; some from the shells that once encased a diatom, the streaming protoplasm of a radiolarian, or the transparent tissues of a pteropod. Nothing is wasted in the sea; every particle of material is used over and over again, first by one creature, then by another. And when in spring the waters are deeply stirred, the warm bottom water brings to the surface a rich supply of minerals, ready for use by new forms of life. 2

Just as land plants depend on minerals in the soil for their growth, every marine plant, even the smallest, is dependent upon the nutrient salts or minerals in the sea water. Diatoms must have silica, the element of which their fragile shells are fashioned. For 3 these and all other microplants, phosphorus is an indispensable mineral. Some of these elements are in short supply and in winter may be reduced below the minimum necessary for growth. The diatom population must tide itself over this season as best it can. It faces a stark problem of survival, with no opportunity to increase, a problem of keeping alive the spark of life by forming tough protective spores against the stringency of winter, a matter of existing in a dormant state in which no demands shall be made on an environment that already withholds all but the most meager necessities of life. So the diatoms hold their place in the winter sea, like seeds of wheat in a field under snow and ice, the seeds from which the spring growth will come.

These, then, are the elements of the vernal blooming of the 4
sea: the "seeds" of the dormant plants, the fertilizing chemicals, the warmth of the spring sun.

In a sudden awakening, incredible in its swiftness, the 5
simplest plants of the sea begin to multiply. Their increase is of astronomical proportions. The spring sea belongs at first to the diatoms and to all the other microscopic plant life of the plankton. In the fierce intensity of their growth they cover vast areas of ocean with a living blanket of their cells. Mile after mile of water may appear red or brown or green, the whole surface taking on the color of the infinitesimal grains of pigment contained in each of the plant cells.

The plants have undisputed sway in the sea for only a short 6
time. Almost at once their own burst of multiplication is matched by a similar increase in the small animals of the plankton. It is the spawning time of the copepod and the glassworm, the pelagic shrimp and the winged snail. Hungry swarms of these little beasts of the plankton roam through the waters, feeding on the abundant plants and themselves falling prey to larger creatures. Now in the spring the surface waters become a vast nursery. From the hills and valleys of the continent's edge lying far below, and from the scattered shoals and banks, the eggs or young of many of the bottom animals rise to the surface of the sea. Even those which, in their maturity, will sink down to a sedentary life on the bottom, spend the first weeks of life as freely swimming hunters of the plankton. So as spring progresses new batches of larvae rise into the surface each day, the young of fishes and crabs and mussels and tube worms, mingling for a time with the regular members of the plankton.

Under the steady and voracious grazing, the grasslands of 7
the surface are soon depleted. The diatoms become more and more scarce, and with them the other simple plants. Still there are brief explosions of one or another form, when in a sudden orgy of cell division it comes to claim whole areas of the sea for its own. So, for a

time each spring, the waters may become blotched with brown, jellylike masses, and the fishermen's nets come up dripping a brown slime and containing no fish, for the herring have turned away from these waters as though in loathing of the viscid, foul-smelling algae. But in less time than passes between the full moon and the new, the spring flowering of Phaeocystis is past and the waters have cleared again.

In the spring the sea is filled with migrating fishes, some of 8
them bound for the mouths of great rivers, which they will ascend to deposit their spawn. Such are the spring-run chinooks coming in from the deep Pacific feeding grounds to breast the rolling flood of the Columbia, the shad moving in to the Chesapeake and the Hudson and the Connecticut, the alewives seeking a hundred coastal streams of New England, the salmon feeling their way to the Penobscot and the Kennebec. For months or years these fish have known only the vast spaces of the ocean. Now the spring sea and the maturing of their own bodies lead them back to the rivers of their birth.

Other mysterious comings and goings are linked with the 9
advance of the year. Capelin gather in the deep, cold water of the Barents Sea, their shoals followed and preyed upon by flocks of auks, fulmars, and kittiwakes. Cod approach the banks of Lofoten, and gather off the shores of Iceland. Birds whose winter feeding territory may have encompassed the whole Atlantic or the whole Pacific converge upon some small island, the entire breeding population arriving within the space of a few days. Whales suddenly appear off the slopes of the coastal banks where the swarms of shrimplike krill are spawning, the whales having come from no one knows where, by no one knows what route.

With the subsiding of the diatoms and the completed spawn- 10
ing of many of the plankton animals and most of the fish, life in the surface waters slackens to the slower pace of midsummer. Along the meeting places of the currents the pale moon jelly Aurelia gathers in thousands, forming sinuous lines or windrows across miles of sea, and the birds see their pale forms shimmering deep down in the green water. By midsummer the large red jellyfish Cyanea may have grown from the size of a thimble to that of an umbrella. The great jellyfish moves through the sea with rhythmic pulsations, trailing long tentacles and as likely as not shepherding a little group of young cod or haddock, which find shelter under its bell and travel with it.

A hard, brilliant, coruscating phosphorescence often illumi- 11
nates the summer sea. In waters where the protozoa Noctiluca is abundant it is the chief source of this summer luminescence, causing fishes, squids, or dolphins to fill the water with racing flames and to clothe themselves in a ghostly radiance. Or again the summer sea

may glitter with a thousand thousand moving pinpricks of light, like an immense swarm of fireflies moving through a dark wood. Such an effect is produced by a shoal of the brilliantly phosphorescent shrimp Meganyctiphanes, a creature of cold and darkness and of the places where icy water rolls upward from the depths and bubbles with white ripplings at the surface.

Out over the plankton meadows of the North Atlantic the dry 12 twitter of the phalaropes, small brown birds, wheeling and turning, dipping and rising, is heard for the first time since early spring. The phalaropes have nested on the arctic tundras, reared their young, and now the first of them are returning to the sea. Most of them will continue south over the open water far from land, crossing the equator into the South Atlantic. Here they will follow where the great whales lead, for where the whales are, there also are the swarms of plankton on which these strange little birds grow fat.

As the fall advances, there are other movements, some in the 13 surface, some hidden in the green depths, that betoken the end of summer. In the fog-covered waters of Bering Sea, down through the treacherous passes between the islands of the Aleutian chain and southward into the open Pacific, the herds of fur seals are moving. Left behind are two small islands, treeless bits of volcanic soil thrust up into the waters of Bering Sea. The islands are silent now, but for the several months of summer they resounded with the roar of millions of seals come ashore to bear and rear their young—all the fur seals of the eastern Pacific crowded into a few square miles of bare rock and crumbling soil. Now once more the seals turn south, to roam down along the sheer underwater cliffs of the continent's edge, where the rocky foundations fall away steeply into the deep sea. Here, in a blackness more absolute than that of arctic winter, the seals will find rich feeding as they swim down to prey on the fishes of this region of darkness.

Autumn comes to the sea with a fresh blaze of phosphores- 14 cence, when every wave crest is aflame. Here and there the whole surface may glow with sheets of cold fire, while below schools of fish pour through the water like molten metal. Often the autumnal phosphorescence is caused by a fall flowering of the dinoflagellates, multiplying furiously in a short-lived repetition of their vernal blooming.

Sometimes the meaning of the glowing water is ominous. Off 15 the Pacific coast of North America, it may mean that the sea is filled with the dinoflagellate Gonyaulax, a minute plant that contains a poison of strange and terrible virulence. About four days after Gonyaulax comes to dominate the coastal plankton, some of the fishes and shellfish in the vicinity become toxic. This is because, in their normal feeding, they have strained the poisonous plankton out of the water. Mussels accumulate the Gonyaulax toxins in their livers, and the toxins react on the human nervous system with an effect similar to that of strychnine. Because of these facts, it is generally understood along the Pacific coast that it is unwise to eat shellfish taken from coasts exposed to the open sea where Gonyaulax may be abundant, in summer or early fall. For generations before the white men came, the Indians knew this. As soon as the red streaks appeared in the sea and the waves began to flicker at night with the mysterious blue-green fires, the tribal leaders forbade the taking of mussels until these warning signals should have passed. They even set guards at intervals along the beaches to warn inlanders who might come down for shellfish and be unable to read the language of the sea.

But usually the blaze and glitter of the sea, whatever its meaning for those who produce it, implies no menace to man. Seen from the deck of a vessel in open ocean, a tiny, man-made observation point in the vast world of sea and sky, it has an eerie and unearthly quality. Man, in his vanity, subconsciously attributes a human origin to any light not of moon or stars or sun. Lights on the shore, lights moving over the water, mean lights kindled and controlled by other men, serving purposes understandable to the human mind. Yet here are lights that flash and fade away, lights that come and go for reasons meaningless to man, lights that have been doing this very thing over the eons of time in which there were no men to stir in vague disquiet. 16

On such a night of phosphorescent display Charles Darwin stood on the deck of the *Beagle* as she plowed southward through the Atlantic off the coast of Brazil. 17

> The sea from its extreme luminousness presented a wonderful and most beautiful appearance [he wrote in his diary]. Every part of the water which by day is seen as foam, glowed with a pale light. The vessel drove before her bows two billows of liquid phosphorus, and in her wake was a milky train. As far as the eye reached the crest of every wave was bright; and from the reflected light, the sky just above the horizon was not so utterly dark as the rest of the Heavens. It was impossible to behold this plain of matter, as it were melted and consuming by heat, without being reminded of Milton's description of the regions of Chaos and Anarchy.*

Like the blazing colors of the autumn leaves before they 18

*From *Charles Darwin's Diary of the Voyage of H.M.S. Beagle*, edited by Nora Barlow, 1934 edition, Cambridge University Press, p. 107.

wither and fall, the autumnal phosphorescence betokens the approach of winter. After their brief renewal of life the flagellates and the other minute algae dwindle away to a scattered few; so do the shrimps and the copepods, the glassworms and the comb jellies. The larvae of the bottom fauna have long since completed their development and drifted away to take up whatever existence is their lot. Even the roving fish schools have deserted the surface waters and have migrated into warmer latitudes or have found equivalent warmth in the deep, quiet waters along the edge of the continental shelf. There the torpor of semi-hibernation descends upon them and will possess them during the months of winter.

The surface waters now become the plaything of the winter 19
gales. As the winds build up the giant storm waves and roar along their crests, lashing the water into foam and flying spray, it seems that life must forever have deserted this place.

For the mood of the winter sea, read Joseph Conrad's 20
description:

> The greyness of the whole immense surface, the wind furrows upon the faces of the waves, the great masses of foam, tossed about and waving, like matted white locks, give to the sea in a gale an appearance of hoary age, lustreless, dull, without gleams, as though it had been created before light itself.*

But the symbols of hope are not lacking even in the grayness 21
and bleakness of the winter sea. On land we know that the apparent lifelessness of winter is an illusion. Look closely at the bare branches of a tree, on which not the palest gleam of green can be discerned. Yet, spaced along each branch are the leaf buds, all the spring's magic of swelling green concealed and safely preserved under the insulating, overlapping layers. Pick off a piece of the rough bark of the trunk; there you will find hibernating insects. Dig down through the snow into the earth. There are the eggs of next summer's grasshoppers; there are the dormant seeds from which will come the grass, the herb, the oak tree.

So, too, the lifelessness, the hopelessness, the despair of the 22
winter sea are an illusion. Everywhere are the assurances that the cycle has come to the full, containing the means of its own renewal. There is the promise of a new spring in the very iciness of the winter sea, in the chilling of the water, which must, before many weeks, become so heavy that it will plunge downward, precipitating the overturn that is the first act in the drama of spring. There is the promise of new life in the small plantlike things that cling to the rocks

*From *The Mirror of the Sea*, Kent edition, 1925, Doubleday Page, p. 71.

of the underlying bottom, the almost formless polyps from which, in spring, a new generation of jellyfish will bud off and rise into the surface waters. There is unconscious purpose in the sluggish forms of the copepods hibernating on the bottom, safe from the surface storms, life sustained in their tiny bodies by the extra store of fat with which they went into this winter sleep.

Already, from the gray shapes of cod that have moved, unseen by man, through the cold sea to their spawning places, the glassy globules of eggs are rising into the surface waters. Even in the harsh world of the winter sea, these eggs will begin the swift divisions by which a granule of protoplasm becomes a living fishlet. 23

Most of all, perhaps, there is assurance in the fine dust of life that remains in the surface waters, the invisible spores of the diatoms, needing only the touch of warming sun and fertilizing chemicals to repeat the magic of spring. 24

QUESTIONS

1. What kinds of sea life appear in each season?

2. In her description, Carson indirectly describes the aquatic food chain. Describe that chain.

3. Carson frequently uses metaphors in this essay. Many of them concern human feelings, agriculture, and commerce. Identify them and explain their utility to the essay. Explain also the allusions to Joseph Conrad and Charles Darwin in paragraphs 17 and 20. Why are allusions to them especially appropriate?

4. Identify unfamiliar animals and places in the essay. What effect does Carson achieve by listing the names of unfamiliar creatures and places?

5. How does Carson develop her introductory paragraph?

6. In Carson's description of the cycle of the seasons, time is a crucial structural device. Identify temporal transitional devices in this essay.

7. How does the image of time presented in the essay contribute to Carson's conclusion?

8. How does Carson use analogies to explain the seasons?

9. Because the life of the sea has been deeply threatened by pollution in recent years, can you share Carson's view of the cycle of life in the sea? What can we do to protect the sea?

10. Our lives are full of cycles. Write an essay describing one of the following cycles: a college semester, a sports year, or a television season.

BERTRAND RUSSELL

The Study of Mathematics

Bertrand Arthur William Russell (1872–1970) was one of the great philosophers, mathematicians, liberal political theorists, and authors of the twentieth century. His works are legion. From the early *Principles of Mathematics* (1903) to his *An Inquiry into Meaning and Truth* (1940) and finally to his three-volume *Autobiography* (1967–1969), Russell demonstrated his multivarious talents as a writer and thinker. He was awarded the Nobel Prize in Literature in 1950. One aspect of Russell's career—his desire to explain science to lay people—is represented in the following essay.

in regard to every form of human activity it is necessary 1
that the question should be asked from time to time, What is its purpose and ideal? In what way does it contribute to the beauty of human existence? As respects those pursuits which contribute only remotely, by providing the mechanism of life, it is well to be reminded that not the mere fact of living is to be desired, but the art of living in the contemplation of great things. Still more in regard to those avocations which have no end outside themselves, which are to be justified, if at all, as actually adding to the sum of the world's permanent possessions, it is necessary to keep alive a knowledge of their aims, a clear prefiguring vision of the temple in which creative imagination is to be embodied.

Although tradition has decreed that the great bulk of educat- 2
ed men shall know at least the elements of the subject [of mathematics], the reasons for which the tradition arose are forgotten, buried beneath a great rubbish-heap of pedantries and trivialities. To those who inquire as to the purpose of mathematics, the usual answer will be that it facilitates the making of machines, the travelling from place to place, and the victory over foreign nations, whether in war or commerce. If it be objected that these ends—all of which are of doubtful value—are not furthered by the merely elementary study imposed upon those who do not become expert mathematicians, the reply, it is true, will probably be that mathematics trains the reasoning faculties. Yet the very men who make this reply are, for the most part, unwilling to abandon the teaching of definite fallacies, known to be such, and instinctively rejected by the unsophisticated mind of every intelligent learner. And the reasoning faculty itself is generally conceived, by those who urge its cultivation, as merely a means for the avoidance of pitfalls and a help in the discovery of rules for the guidance of practical life. All these are undeniably important achieve-

ments to the credit of mathematics; yet it is none of these that entitles mathematics to a place in every liberal education.

Mathematics, rightly viewed, possesses not only truth, but supreme beauty—a beauty cold and austere, like that of sculpture, without appeal to any part of our weaker nature, without the gorgeous trappings of painting or music, yet sublimely pure, and capable of a stern perfection such as only the greatest art can show. The true spirit of delight, the exaltation, the sense of being more than man, which is the touchstone of the highest excellence, is to be found in mathematics as surely as in poetry. What is best in mathematics deserves not merely to be learnt as a task, but to be assimilated as a part of daily thought, and brought again and again before the mind with ever-renewed encouragement. Real life is, to most men, a long second-best, a perpetual compromise between the ideal and the posssible; but the world of pure reason knows no compromise, no practical limitations, no barrier to the creative activity embodying in splendid edifices the passionate aspiration after the perfect from which all great work springs. Remote from human passions, remote even from the pitiful facts of nature, the generations have gradually created an ordered cosmos, where pure thought can dwell as in its natural home, and where one, at least, of our nobler impulses can escape from the dreary exile of the actual world. 3

So little, however, have mathematicians aimed at beauty, that hardly anything in their work has had this conscious purpose. Much, owing to irrepressible instincts, which were better than avowed beliefs, has been moulded by an unconscious taste; but much also has been spoilt by false notions of what was fitting. The characteristic excellence of mathematics is only to be found where the reasoning is rigidly logical: the rules of logic are to mathematics what those of structure are to architecture. In the most beautiful work, a chain of argument is presented in which every link is important on its own account, in which there is an air of ease and lucidity throughout, and the premises achieve more than would have been thought possible, by means which appear natural and inevitable. Literature embodies what is general in particular circumstances whose universal significance shines through their individual dress; but mathematics endeavours to present whatever is most general in its purity, without any irrelevant trappings. 4

QUESTIONS

1. In this essay, Russell compares and contrasts several disciplines or vocations to mathematics. Of which one does he approve? Of which ones does he disapprove?

2. According to Russell, what are the reasons for studying mathematics?

3. Identify examples of connotative language in this essay.

4. How many specific details appear in this essay? How does this affect the style of the essay?

5. Describe the structure of this four-paragraph essay.

6. Why does Russell compare mathematics to the arts? How is mathematics superior?

7. What assumptions about the world of nature and human beings and of the mind underlie the essay?

8. In paragraph 4, what method of definition does Russell use?

9. How would you define beauty, as Russell uses the word? Does your own idea of beauty differ from Russell's? How about your idea of mathematics?

10. Imitate the structure of this essay to organize your definition of engineering, literature, or medicine. Use specific details and examples from the field to clarify your extended definition.

J. B. S. HALDANE

On Being the Right Size

John Burdon Saunderson Haldane (1892–1964) was a geneticist, biologist, and writer of science books for the lay reader. His best-known work is *Animal Biology* (1927), written in collaboration with John S. Huxley. He also wrote *Adventures of a Biologist* (1940) and *Everything Has a History* (1951), a collection of essays. Haldane was famous for his ability to explain the abstract, often abstruse, ideas of modern science with concrete examples. "On Being the Right Size," which mixes mathematics and physics with insects and elephants, exemplifies Haldane's skill.

he most obvious differences between different animals are differences of size, but for some reason the zoologists have paid singularly little attention to them. In a large textbook of zoology before me I find no indication 1 that the eagle is larger than the sparrow, or the hippopotamus bigger than the hare, though some grudging admissions are made in the case of the mouse and the whale. But yet it is easy to show that a hare could not be as large as a hippopotamus, or a whale as small as a herring. For every type of animal there is a most convenient size, and a large change in size inevitably carries with it a change of form.

Let us take the most obvious of possible cases, and consider a 2
giant man sixty feet high—about the height of Giant Pope and Giant Pagan in the illustrated *Pilgrim's Progress* of my childhood. These monsters were not only ten times as high as Christian, but ten times as wide and ten times as thick, so that their total weight was a thousand times his, or about eighty to ninety tons. Unfortunately the cross sections of their bones were only a hundred times those of Christian, so that every square inch of giant bone had to support ten times the weight borne by a square inch of human bone. As the human thigh-bone breaks under about ten times the human weight, Pope and Pagan would have broken their thighs every time they took a step. This was doubtless why they were sitting down in the picture I remember. But it lessens one's respect for Christian and Jack the Giant Killer.

To turn to zoology, suppose that a gazelle, a graceful little 3
creature with long thin legs, is to become large, it will break its bones unless it does one of two things. It may make its legs short and thick, like the rhinoceros, so that every pound of weight has still about the same area of bone to support it. Or it can compress its body and stretch out its legs obliquely to gain stability, like the giraffe. I mention these two beasts because they happen to belong to the same order as the gazelle, and both are quite successful mechanically, being remarkably fast runners.

Gravity, a mere nuisance to Christian, was a terror to Pope, 4
Pagan, and Despair. To the mouse and any smaller animal it presents practically no dangers. You can drop a mouse down a thousand-yard mine shaft; and, on arriving at the bottom, it gets a slight shock and walks away, provided that the ground is fairly soft. A rat is killed, a man is broken, a horse splashes. For the resistance presented to movement by the air is proportional to the surface of the moving object. Divide an animal's length, breadth, and height each by ten; its weight is reduced to a thousandth, but its surface only to a hundredth. So the resistance to falling in the case of the small animal is relatively ten times greater than the driving force.

An insect, therefore, is not afraid of gravity; it can fall without 5
danger, and can cling to the ceiling with remarkably little trouble. It can go in for elegant and fantastic forms of support like that of the daddy-longlegs. But there is a force which is as formidable to an insect as gravitation to a mammal. This is surface tension. A man

coming out of a bath carries with him a film of water of about one-fiftieth of an inch in thickness. This weighs roughly a pound. A wet mouse has to carry about its own weight of water. A wet fly has to lift many times its own weight and, as everyone knows, a fly once wetted by water or any other liquid is in a very serious position indeed. An insect going for a drink is in as great danger as a man leaning out over a precipice in search of food. If it once falls into the grip of the surface tension of the water—that is to say, gets wet—it is likely to remain so until it drowns. A few insects, such as water-beetles, contrive to be unwettable; the majority keep well away from their drink by means of a long proboscis.

Of course tall land animals have other difficulties. They have 6
to pump their blood to greater heights than a man, and therefore, require a larger blood pressure and tougher blood-vessels. A great many men die from burst arteries, especially in the brain, and this danger is presumably still greater for an elephant or a giraffe. But animals of all kinds find difficulties in size for the following reason. A typical small animal, say a microscopic worm or rotifer, has a smooth skin through which all the oxygen it requires can soak in, a straight gut with sufficient surface to absorb its food, and a single kidney. Increase its dimensions tenfold in every direction, and its weight is increased a thousand times, so that if it is to use its muscles as efficiently as its miniature counterpart, it will need a thousand times as much food and oxygen per day and will excrete a thousand times as much of waste products.

Now if its shape is unaltered its surface will be increased only 7
a hundredfold, and ten times as much oxygen must enter per minute through each square millimetre of skin, ten times as much food through each square millimetre of intestine. When a limit is reached to their absorptive powers their surface has to be increased by some special device. For example, a part of the skin may be drawn out into tufts to make gills or pushed in to make lungs, thus increasing the oxygen-absorbing surface in proportion to the animal's bulk. A man, for example, has a hundred square yards of lung. Similarly, the gut, instead of being smooth and straight, becomes coiled and develops a velvety surface, and other organs increase in complication. The higher animals are not larger than the lower because they are more complicated. They are more complicated because they are larger. Just the same is true of plants. The simplest plants, such as the green algae growing in stagnant water or on the bark of trees, are mere round cells. The higher plants increase their surface by putting out leaves and roots. Comparative anatomy is largely the story of the struggle to increase surface in proportion to volume.

Some of the methods of increasing the surface are useful up 8
to a point, but not capable of a very wide adaptation. For example,

while vertebrates carry the oxygen from the gills or lungs all over the body in the blood, insects take air directly to every part of their body by tiny blind tubes called tracheae which open to the surface at many different points. Now, although by their breathing movements they can renew the air in the outer part of the tracheal system, the oxygen has to penetrate the finer branches by means of diffusion. Gases can diffuse easily through very small distances, not many times larger than the average length travelled by a gas molecule between collisions with other molecules. But when such vast journeys—from the point of view of a molecule—as a quarter of an inch have to be made, the process becomes slow. So the portions of an insect's body more than a quarter of an inch from the air would always be short of oxygen. In consequence hardly any insects are much more than half an inch thick. Land crabs are built on the same general plan as insects, but are much clumsier. Yet like ourselves they carry oxygen around in their blood, and are therefore able to grow far larger than any insects. If the insects had hit on a plan for driving air through their tissues instead of letting it soak in, they might well have become as large as lobsters, though other considerations would have prevented them from becoming as large as man.

Exactly the same difficulties attach to flying. It is an elemen- 9
tary principle of aeronautics that the minimum speed needed to keep an aeroplane of a given shape in the air varies as the square root of its length. If its linear dimensions are increased four times, it must fly twice as fast. Now the power needed for the minimum speed increases more rapidly than the weight of the machine. So the larger aeroplane, which weighs sixty-four times as much as the smaller, needs one hundred and twenty-eight times its horsepower to keep up. Applying the same principle to the birds, we find that the limit to their size is soon reached. An angel whose muscles developed no more power weight for weight than those of an eagle or a pigeon would require a breast projecting for about four feet to house the muscles engaged in working its wings, while to economize in weight, its legs would have to be reduced to mere stilts. Actually a large bird such as an eagle or kite does not keep in the air mainly by moving its wings. It is generally to be seen soaring, that is to say balanced on a rising column of air. And even soaring becomes more and more difficult with increasing size. Were this not the case eagles might be as large as tigers and as formidable to man as hostile aeroplanes.

But it is time that we pass to some of the advantages of size. 10
One of the most obvious is that it enables one to keep warm. All warm-blooded animals at rest lose the same amount of heat from a unit area of skin, for which purpose they need a food-supply proportional to their surface and not to their weight. Five thousand mice weigh as much as a man. Their combined surface and food or

oxygen consumption are about seventeen times a man's. In fact a mouse eats about one quarter its own weight of food every day, which is mainly used in keeping it warm. For the same reason small animals cannot live in cold countries. In the arctic regions there are no reptiles or amphibians, and no small mammals. The smallest mammal in Spitzbergen is the fox. The small birds fly away in winter, while the insects die, though their eggs can survive six months or more of frost. The most successful mammals are bears, seals, and walruses.

Similarly, the eye is a rather inefficient organ until it reaches a large size. The back of the human eye on which an image of the outside world is thrown, and which corresponds to the film of a camera, is composed of a mosaic of "rods and cones" whose diameter is little more than a length of an average light wave. Each eye has about a half a million, and for two objects to be distinguishable their images must fall on separate rods or cones. It is obvious that with fewer but larger rods and cones we should see less distinctly. If they were twice as broad two points would have to be twice as far apart before we could distinguish them at a given distance. But if their size were diminished and their number increased we should see no better. For it is impossible to form a definite image smaller than a wavelength of light. Hence a mouse's eye is not a small-scale model of a human eye. Its rods and cones are not much smaller than ours, and therefore there are far fewer of them. A mouse could not distinguish one human face from another six feet away. In order that they should be of any use at all the eyes of small animals have to be much larger in proportion to their bodies than our own. Large animals on the other hand only require relatively small eyes, and those of the whale and elephant are little larger than our own. 11

For rather more recondite reasons the same general principle holds true of the brain. If we compare the brain-weights of a set of very similar animals such as the cat, cheetah, leopard, and tiger, we find that as we quadruple the body-weight the brain-weight is only doubled. The larger animal with proportionately larger bones can economize on brain, eyes, and certain other organs. 12

Such are a very few of the considerations which show that for every type of animal there is an optimum size. Yet although Galileo demonstrated the contrary more than three hundred years ago, people still believe that if a flea were as large as a man it could jump a thousand feet into the air. As a matter of fact the height to which an animal can jump is more nearly independent of its size than proportional to it. A flea can jump about two feet, a man about five. To jump a given height, if we neglect the resistance of the air, requires an expenditure of energy proportional to the jumper's weight. But if the jumping muscles form a constant fraction of the animal's body, the 13 energy developed per ounce of muscle is independent of the size, provided it can be developed quickly enough in the small animal. As a matter of fact an insect's muscles, although they can contract more quickly than our own, appear to be less efficient; as otherwise a flea or grasshopper could rise six feet into the air.

QUESTIONS

1. List people's adaptations to the problems of their size.
2. What are the effects of size on insects and mice?
3. Cite examples of personification in the essay. Why does Haldane use them?
4. Haldane is an adept practitioner of parallel structure. Cite examples of parallel structure in paragraphs 4 and 5.
5. Describe the simple dichotomy Haldane uses to organize his essay.
6. Because Haldane is describing neither a scene nor an event, he cannot use temporal or spatial transitional devices to make his essay coherent. Identify the transitional devices he employs.
7. Many of Haldane's explanations involve mathematical formulas. Give specific examples of how he helps his reader understand his math.
8. Where does Haldane use hypothetical examples? Why are they effective?
9. Based on Haldane's discussion of size, speculate on how the size of a country, of a business, of a family, or of a college might have limits.
10. a. Write an essay on the effect of size on a human institution.
b. Although explaining mathematical and physical laws is difficult, Haldane is successful. Write an essay in which you try to explain a physical law.

STEPHEN JAY GOULD

Darwin at Sea

Stephen Jay Gould (1941–), an acclaimed contemporary science writer, teaches biology, geology, and the history of science at Harvard University. He writes a monthly column, "This View of Life," for *Natural History*, and is the author of *Ever*

Since Darwin (1977), *Ontogeny and Phylogeny* (1977), and *The Panda's Thumb* (1980). In this essay, which appeared originally in the September 1983 issue of *Natural History*, the author offers a revisionist interpretation of Darwin's discovery of evolution, the nature of scientific procedure, and the basis of scientific creativity.

Charles Darwin and Abraham Lincoln were born on the same day—February 12, 1809. They are also linked in another curious way—for both must simultaneously play, and for similar reasons, the role of man and legend. In a nation too young to have mythic heroes, men and women must substitute. Hence we have Honest Abe, who frees the slaves from a pure sense of the burning injustice of it all, and who, as a young man, trudges for miles to return a few cents to a woman he has inadvertently short-changed. We may have a national or psychological need for such a Lincoln, but it also behooves historians to rescue the real, and wondrously complex, man from this factually inaccurate role. Likewise, science has no gods, and ancient sages are in strictly short supply. Thus, historical figures again form the stuff of necessary legends. The apple beans Newton; Galileo drops his missiles from the Leaning Tower; and Darwin, alone at sea, transforms the intellectual world in splendid mental isolation. 1

The myth of the *Beagle*—that Darwin became an evolutionist by simple, unbiased observation of an entire world laid out before him during a five-year circumnavigation of the globe—fits all our romantic criteria for the best of legends: a young man, freed from the trammels of English society and its constraining presuppositions, face to face with nature, parrying his fresh and formidable mind with all the challenges provided by plants and animals and rocks throughout the world. He leaves England in 1831, planning to become a country parson upon his return. He lands in 1836, having seen evolution in the raw, understanding (albeit dimly) its implications and committed to a scientific life as revolutionary thinker. The chief catalyst: the Galápagos Islands. The main actors: tortoises, mockingbirds, and above all, the thirteen species of Darwin's finches that form the finest evolutionary laboratory offered to us anywhere in nature. 2

We may need such legends for that peculiar genre of literature known as the textbook. But it also behooves historians to rescue human beings from their legends in science—if only so that we may understand the process of scientific thought aright. Darwin, to begin, did not become an evolutionist until several months after his return to London—probably not until March 1837 (the *Beagle* docked in October 1836). He did not appreciate the evolutionary significance of the Galápagos while he was there, and he originally misunderstood the 3 finches so thoroughly that he was barely able to reconstruct the story later from his sadly inadequate records. The legend of the finches may persist, but it has been splendidly debunked in two recent articles by historian of science Frank Sulloway. His arguments form the basis of this essay. (For full details, see F. Sulloway, "Darwin and His Finches: The Evolution of a Legend," *Journal of the History of Biology*, Spring 1982, pp. 1-53; and "Darwin's Conversion: The Beagle Voyage and Its Aftermath," same journal, Fall 1982, pp. 325-96.)

The thirteen species of Darwin's finches form a closely knit genealogical group of widely divergent adaptations—a classic case of adaptive radiation into a series of roles and niches that would be filled by members of several bird families in more conventional, and crowded, continental situations. We get our major clues about the adaptive strategies of these species from the shapes of their bills. Three species of ground finches have large, medium, and small beaks, while a fourth has a sharp, pointed bill. All are adapted to eating differing seeds of appropriate size and hardness. Two species feed on cactus and another on mangroves. Four inhabit trees—of these, one is a vegetarian, while the other three eat large, medium, and small insects, respectively. A twelfth species closely resembles warblers in form and habits; while the thirteenth, the most curious of all, uses twigs and cactus spines as tools to extract insects from crevices in three trunks. 4

The fine work of the great British ornithologist David Lack has taught us that the thirteen species evolved and became more distinct through a four-stage process of colonization, isolation and speciation, reinvasion, and perfecting of adaptation in competition. Lack also gave the birds their felicitous name of "Darwin's finches," in his 1947 book of the same title. But, contrary to anachronistic legend, this classic description of speciation is not a story that Darwin ever knew. 5

Darwin visited the Galápagos in September and October 1835, landing on only four of the islands. At sea, sometime during the middle of 1836, he penned a famous statement in his *Ornithological Notes*, a major source for the legend that his Galápagos experiences directly converted him to evolution and that the finches were instrumental in this process: 6

> When I recollect, the fact from the form of the body, shape of scales and general size, the Spaniards can at once pronounce, from which Island any Tortoise may have been brought. When I see these Islands in sight of each other, and possessed of but a scanty stock of animals, tenanted by these

birds, but slightly differing in structure and filling the same place in Nature, I must suspect that they are only varieties. The only fact of a similar kind of which I am aware, is the constant asserted difference—between the wolf-like Fox of East and West Falkland Islds.—If there is the slightest foundation for these remarks the zoology of Archipelagos—will be well worth examining; for such facts would undermine the stability of Species.

First of all, the "birds" of this passage are Galápagos mockingbirds, not finches. Darwin did notice that three of the four islands he visited contained distinctly different mockingbirds. At face value, this statement seems to display a strong bias for evolution; it certainly raises the possibility. But a familiarity with nineteenth-century zoological terminology suggests an alternate interpretation. All creationists admitted that species often differentiated into mildly distinct forms in situations, as on island chains and archipelagoes, where populations could become isolated in differing circumstances of ecology and climate. These local races were called varieties, and they did not threaten the created and immutable character of a species' essence. Darwin is actually saying in this famous statement that either the tortoises and mockingbirds are merely varieties—in which case they do not threaten his creationist views—or they have become separate species, in which case they do. He briefly considered evolution by admitting the second possibility, but he ultimately rejected it while still at sea by tentatively deciding (incorrectly, for the mockingbirds at least) that the island forms were only varieties. Darwin's memories as an old man confirm this view that he only briefly flirted with, and then rejected, evolution while on the *Beagle*. He wrote to the German naturalist Otto Zacharias in 1877: "When I was on board the *Beagle* I believed in the permanence of species, but, as far as I can remember, vague doubts occasionally flitted across my mind." 7

A second statement, taken in conjunction with a misreading of the *Ornithological Notes*, might also be considered as a confirmation that Darwin became an evolutionist at sea in 1836. He wrote in his pocket journal: "In July opened first notebook on 'Transmutation of Species'—Had been greatly struck from about Month of previous March on character of S. American fossils—and species on Galapagos Archipelago. These facts origin (especially latter) of all my views." We know that he started the first Transmutation notebook in July 1837, and we might therefore interpret the "previous March" as 1836, about the time that he penned the *Ornithological Notes* at sea. But the 8 previous March might as well be 1837 when, as we shall soon see, he was in London learning from specialists at the Zoological Society about the true character of his Galápagos collections—a set of phenomena that he had failed to observe during his own visit.

What, then, did Darwin see on the Galápagos, and what did 9
he miss? Three groups of animals have come down through history as the most famous evolutionary laboratories of the Galápagos: mockingbirds, tortoises, and finches. Only for the mockingbirds did Darwin make the key observation that underlies the evolutionary tale later supplied (although, as we have seen, Darwin first explicitly rejected the evolutionary reading for a different interpretation). In short, he noticed that varying forms (later recognized as true species, although Darwin originally labeled them varieties) inhabited the different islands he visited. He landed first at Chatham Island, then at Charles, and he realized that he could distinguish the Charles Island mockingbird from the form he had previously collected at Chatham. Thus, he collected more mockingbirds wherever he landed and he carefully kept the separate island collections well labeled and distinct. He could not distinguish the Albermarle mockingbird, on the third island he visited, from the Chatham form, but the James Island bird represented a third, distinct variety (as he interpreted it).

Galápagos tortoises are all of one species, but virtually each 10
island has its own recognizable subspecies. These span an impressive range of form, from smooth, dome-shaped carapaces to the peculiar saddlebacks, with a pronounced hump in the carapace just above the head. Darwin missed this story completely. He never even noted the saddlebacks. His concept of this species virtually guaranteed that he would not be able to make the key observation.

Nicholas Lawson, the vice-governor, told Darwin that "the 11
tortoises differed from the different islands, and that he could with certainty tell from which island any one was brought" (although distinctions abound, this statement is overly optimistic and modern experts cannot always distinguish each island). But Darwin, by his own admission, made little of this information, writing in the 1845 edition of the *Beagle Voyage:*

> I did not for some time pay sufficient attention to this statement, and I had already partially mingled together the collections from two of the islands. I never dreamed that islands, about fifty or sixty miles apart, and most of them in sight of each other, formed of precisely the same rocks, placed under quite similar climate, rising to a nearly equal height, would have been differently tenanted.

As the result of an error in classification widely current at the time, Darwin was ill-disposed to consider the differences between islands as evolutionarily (or even taxonomically) meaningful. Darwin accepted the general view that the Galápagos tortoise was not taxonomically distinct but was the same creature as *Testudo indicus*, the giant land tortoise of the Aldabra Islands in the Indian Ocean. It had only recently been brought, so the false story continued, to the Galápagos by buccaneers. Hence, differences among islands, if they existed at all, could only represent immediate and superficial varietal distinctions inspired by harsh climates at the time of introduction. Moreover, Darwin never saw live saddleback tortoises. He only observed living tortoises on James and Chatham islands, and both contain nearly indistinguishable versions of the dome-shaped form. 12

Still, Darwin cannot be entirely excused from a charge of some carelessness in observation. He did have an opportunity to observe the saddleback form but either failed to do so or recorded no impression. The Charles Island race was extinct when Darwin landed, but carapaces were abundant at the settlement there, where they were commonly used as flowerpots. Moreover, Darwin showed singularly little interest in preserving specimens for comparison among islands, a sure sign that he did not regard Lawson's statement as significant (much to his later regret). Captain Fitzroy took thirty large Chatham tortoises on board to beef up the *Beagle's* supply of fresh meat during the long Pacific crossing. Sulloway remarks: 13

> But Darwin and the other crew members gradually ate their way through the evidence that eventually, in the form of hearsay, was to revolutionize the biological sciences. Regrettably, not one of the thirty Chatham Island carapaces reached England, having all been thrown overboard with the other inedible remains.

Darwin's reaction to the Galápagos finches was even more replete with error and misunderstanding. Again, he showed no appreciation of the importance of differences between islands. In fact, he didn't even bother to record or label the islands from which he had procured his specimens. Only three of his thirty-one finches are identified by island in the *Ornithological Notes*, all members of a highly distinctive species that Darwin remembered seeing only on James Island. He later wrote with regret in the *Voyage of the Beagle:* "Unfortunately most of the specimens of the finch tribe were mingled together." Secondly, he failed completely to collect any finches on one of the islands he visited—Albemarle. True, he was there for only 14 part of a day, but his own diary records an abundance of easily collectable finches at a spring they visited near Bank's Cove: "To our disappointment the little pits in the Sandstone contained scarcely a gallon of water and that not good. It was however sufficient to draw together all the little birds in the country; Doves and Finches swarmed around its margin."

Third, with the exception of cactus and warbler finches, 15
Darwin failed to observe any distinction in diet among the species and believed erroneously that they all ate the same kinds of food. Thus, he could not have reconstructed our modern story, even if he had been inclined to evolutionary views.

Fourth, Darwin's entire style of collection on the Galápagos 16
strongly reflected his creationist presuppositions. Evolutionists see variation as fundamental, as the raw material of evolutionary change. Species can only be well characterized by collecting many specimens and defining the spectrum of variation. Creationists believe that each species is endowed with a fixed essence. Variation is a mere nuisance, a confusing array of environmentally induced departures from an ideal form. Creationists tend to gather a limited number of specimens from each species and to concentrate on procuring individuals closest to the essential form. Darwin collected very few specimens, generally only a male and female of each species. In all, he procured but thirty-one finches from the Galápagos. By contrast, a 1905-06 California Academy of Sciences expedition, sent out to study evolution explicity, brought back more than 8,000 specimens.

Fifth, and most importantly, the finches tell no evolutionary 17
tale unless you recognize that, despite their outward differences in form and behavior, all form a tightly knit genealogical group. But Darwin, while on the Galápagos, was fooled by the stunning diversity and failed to recognize Darwin's finches as a taxonomic entity. He referred the cactus finch to a family of birds that includes orioles and meadowlarks, and he misclassified the warbler finch as either a wren or warbler. Those that he recognized as finches, he divided into two distantly related groups within the family. Sulloway remarks: "As for Darwin's supposed insight into evolution by adaptive radiation while he was still in the Galápagos, the more the various species of finch exhibited this remarkable phenomenon, the more Darwin mistook them at the time for the forms they were mimicking."

The theoretical source of Darwin's error lies in a fairly arcane 18
principle of the creationist style of taxonomy that he followed. If animals are created according to a rational and general plan in the Deity's mind, then certain "key" characters might be clues to taxonomic structure at different levels. For example, variation in such "superficial" characters as size and shape might define different

species, while variation in such "fundamental" traits as the form of essential organs might record the more important differences between genera and families. Ideally, a hierarchy of key characters should define taxonomic levels. Darwin tried to follow such a system in his preliminary *Beagle* classifications. Species within a bird genus should differ in plumage, while genera should be separated by such characters as the form of the beak. Darwin's finches are all similar in plumage, but differ greatly in their styles of feeding and, consequently, in the shapes of their beaks. By Darwin's creationist key character hierarchy, they belonged to different genera or families.

The key character hierarchy makes no sense in an evolutionary context. Characters that define genera in one situation might vary widely among species within another group. Bills may define feeding types, and feeding types may usually distinguish genera on continents. But if only one kind of small bird manages to reach an oceanic archipelago and then radiates, in the absence of competitors, into a wide range of niches and feeding types, then this usual criterion for genera will now differ among closely related species. In the blooming and buzzing confusion of evolution, as opposed to the order of a creator's mind, it all depends upon what part of the body becomes subject to adaptive modification. Behavior and plumage in one place; feeding and beak shape in another. There is no such thing as an invariably "specific" or "generic" character. 19

In summary, then, Darwin entered and left the Galápagos as a creationist, and his style of collection throughout the visit reflected his theoretical stance. Several months later, compiling his notes at sea during the long hours of a Pacific crossing, he briefly flirted with evolution while thinking about tortoises and mockingbirds, not finches. But he rejected this heresy and docked in England, October 2, 1836, still a creationist although with nascent doubts. 20

This retelling of the finch story should be welcome because it squares so much better than the legend with Darwin's use of the Galápagos finches throughout his later writing. He never mentioned them in any of the four *Transmutation Notebooks,* which he kept from 1837 to 1839 and which form the foundation for his later work. They receive only passing notice in the first (1839) edition of the *Voyage of the Beagle.* To be sure, the second edition (1845) does contain this prophetic statement, written after Darwin had learned that the finches form a closely knit genealogical group. 21

> Seeing this gradation and diversity of structure in one small, intimately related group of birds, one might really fancy that from an original paucity of birds in this archipelago, one species had been taken and modified for different ends.

But if the finches made such a belated impression, the impact didn't seem to last. Darwin's finches are not mentioned at all in the *Origin of Species* (1859); the ornithological star of that great book is the domesticated pigeon. Sulloway concludes, rightly I think: 22

> Contrary to the legend, Darwin's finches do not appear to have inspired his earliest theoretical views on evolution, even after he finally became an evolutionist in 1837; rather it was his evolutionary views that allowed him, retrospectively, to understand the complex case of the finches.

Darwin returned to England in 1836 as an ambitious young man, anxious to make his mark in science; his later, courtly modesty as an old man should not be allowed to mask this youthful vigor. He knew that the key to his reputation lay in the valuable specimens he had collected on the *Beagle,* and thus he made determined and successful efforts to farm them out to the best specialists and to procure funds for publication of the results. In March 1837 he moved to London to be near the various experts who were studying his specimens. He began a series of meetings with these men, finally learned the true character of his material, and emerged within a month or two as an evolutionist. 23

He wrote, in the famous entry in his pocket journal cited earlier, that the character of South American fossils and species of the Galápagos had been the primary catalysts of his evolutionary conversion. Richard Owen, Britain's most eminent vertebrate paleontologist, had agreed to study the fossils and informed Darwin that they represented different, usually larger versions of distinctive animals that still inhabit South America. Darwin recognized that the best interpretation of this "law of succession" cast the ancient forms as evolutionary ancestors of altered modern animals. 24

The famous ornithologist John Gould (no relation) had taken charge of the *Beagle*'s birds. Darwin met with him toward the middle of March and learned that the three forms of mockingbirds were clearly distinct at the species level, not mere and superficial varieties of a single, created form. Darwin had already proclaimed that such a conclusion (which he had previously rejected) "would undermine the stability of species." Moreover, Gould informed him that twenty-five of his twenty-six Galápagos land birds were new species, but clearly allied to related forms on the South American mainland. Darwin integrated this spatial information with the temporal data that Owen had supplied, and he wavered further toward evolution. The distinct Galápagos birds must be evolutionary descendants of mainland 25 colonists from South America. Darwin was now fully primed for an evolutionary reading of the finches, and Gould's correction of Darwin's errors furnished this piece of the puzzle as well (although it never drove Gould himself to adopt evolutionary views).

Although a creationist in taxonomy, Gould saw right away that bills could not be used as a key character to separate genera of Galápagos finches. He recognized that these birds were not, as Darwin had thought, a heterogeneous assemblage of divergent finches with an unrelated warbler and oriole thrown in, but a peculiar group of thirteen closely related species, which he placed in a single genus with three subgenera. "The bill appears to form only a secondary character," Gould proclaimed. Darwin finally had the basis of an evolutionary story. 26

Darwin was exhilarated as he converted to evolution and prepared to reread his entire voyage in this new light. But he was also acutely embarrassed because he now realized that his failure to separate finches by islands, no particular problem in a creationist context, had been a serious and lamentable lapse. He couldn't do much with his own collection, beyond calling upon a faulty and fading memory; but fortunately, three of his shipmates had also collected finches—and since they (ironically) had not collected with any particular theory in mind that suggested an irrelevancy for locality data, they had recorded the islands of collection. As a further irony, one of these collections had been made by Captain Fitzroy himself, later Darwin's implacable foe and the man who stalked around the British Association meeting where Huxley creamed Wilberforce, holding a Bible above his head and exclaiming, "the Book, the Book." (Fitzroy's collection included twenty-one finches, all labeled by island. Darwin also had access to the smaller collections of his servant Syms Covington and of Harry Fuller, who had spent a week collecting with him on James Island.) 27

Darwin therefore tried to reconstruct the localities of his own specimens by comparing them with the accurately labeled collections of his shipmates and, unfortunately as it turned out, by assuming that the finch story would resemble that of the mockingbirds—with certain species confined to definite islands. But since most of the finch species inhabit several islands, this procedure led to a large number of errors. Sulloway reports that substantial doubt still exists about the accuracy of locality information for eight of fifteen among Darwin's "type" (or name bearing) specimens of finches. No wonder he was never able to make a clear and coherent story of Darwin's finches. No wonder, perhaps, that they never even appeared in the *Origin of Species.* 28

Why, in conclusion, is this correction of the finch legend of 29 any great importance? Are the two stories really all that different? Darwin, in either case, was greatly influenced by evidence from the Galápagos. In the first, and false, version he sees it for himself while on the visit. In the second, modified account he requires a nudge (and some substantial corrections) from his friends when he returns to London.

I find a world of difference between the tales for what they 30
imply about the nature of creativity. The first (false) version upholds the romantic and empirical view that genius attains its status from an ability to see nature through eyes unclouded by the prejudices of surrounding culture and philosophical presupposition. The idea that such a thing is even possible has nurtured most legends in the history of science and purveys seriously false views about the process of scientific thought. Human beings cannot escape their presuppositions and see "purely"; Darwin functioned as an active creationist all through the *Beagle* voyage. Creativity is not an escape from culture but a unique use of its opportunities combined with a clever end run around its constraints. Scientific accomplishment is also a community activity, not a hermit's achievement. Where would Darwin have been in 1837 without Gould, Owen, and the active scientific life of London and Cambridge?

Once we abandon the alluring, but fallacious, image of 31
Darwin winning his intellectual battle utterly alone at sea, we can ask the really interesting question that begins to probe Darwin's particular genius. Gould was the expert. Gould saw the story right. Gould, a staunch creationist in taxonomy, nonetheless recognized that he had to abandon beaks as key characters. Darwin was able to accomplish none of this. But Darwin, not Gould, saw that all the pieces required a stunningly new explanation—evolution—to make a coherent story. The amateur triumphed when the stakes were highest, while the professional got the details right and missed the organizing theme.

Darwin functioned this way all his life. Somehow, as an 32
amateur, he could cut through older patterns of thought to glimpse new modes of explanation that might better fit an emerging, detailed story constructed by experts who, somehow, could not take the big and final step. But Darwin worked with his culture and with his colleagues. Science is a collective endeavor, but some individuals operate with an enlarged vision—and we would like to know how and why. This is one of the hardest questions we can ask, and I propose no general solution. But we do need to clear away heroic legends before we can begin.

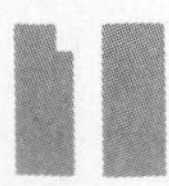

QUESTIONS

1. Summarize the "myth" and "reality" of Darwin's trip to the Galápagos. How did he hit on the idea of evolution? Where did he go badly astray? What, according to Gould, apparently saved this "amateur"?

2. What is creationism? What does the author say about the conflict between creationist and evolutionary theories as it affected Darwin's career as a scientist?

3. Using context clues, a dictionary, or scientific textbooks, explain the following terms: *adaptation, adaptive radiation, species* (paragraph 4), *colonization, isolation* and *speciation, reinvasion* (paragraph 5), *ecology* (paragraph 7), *classification, taxonimically* (paragraph 12), *variation* (paragraph 16), *genus* (paragraph 18), and *vertebrate paleontologist* (paragraph 24). To what branch of science do most of these terms refer? How does the use of these terms affect the tone of the essay? What do they presuppose of the essay's audience?

4. How does Gould's word choice reflect style and tone? Does the language tend to be general or specific, abstract or concrete?

5. What paragraphs constitute Gould's introduction? What is the thesis? Identify three unique aspects of this introduction. What paragraphs comprise the ending? What conclusions does the author draw from the evidence?

6. What varieties of evidence does Gould use? Why is the cumulative weight of this evidence especially effective?

7. Does Gould use inductive or deductive reasoning in this essay? Explain.

8. This essay is rich in a variety of major rhetorical strategies. Identify five of them, and point out notably successful examples of the method.

9. Gould declares, "Creativity is not an escape from culture but a unique use of its opportunities combined with a clever end run around its constraints" (paragraph 30). Do you agree with this definition or a more "romantic" one? Explain.

10. a. Gould accumulates different kinds of evidence to relate particular causes to a specific effect. Write an essay on some topic in science in which you cite evidence you have gathered to relate causes and effects.
b. Research a notable man or woman of science and write a paper on the myths and realities surrounding the scientist's theories.
c. Write a brief biography of a scientist, focusing on the time in that individual's life when a key creative moment led to a notable discovery.
d. Define the nature of scientific creativity. Evaluate whether scientific creativity differs from other forms of creativity.

ALDOUS HUXLEY

Time and the Machine

Aldous Leonard Huxley (1894–1963) was a grandson of T. H. Huxley. He is most famous as the author of *Point Counter Point* (1928) and *Brave New World* (1932). Unlike his grandfather, Aldous Huxley felt that science could threaten human individuality and dignity. In "Time and the Machine," Huxley shows, indeed, how modern technology has transformed our view of time.

ime, as we know it, is a very recent invention. The 1
modern time-sense is hardly older than the United States. It is a by-product of industrialism—a sort of psychological analogue of synthetic perfumes and aniline dyes.

Time is our tyrant. We are chronically aware of the moving 2
minute hand, even of the moving second hand. We have to be. There are trains to be caught, clocks to be punched, tasks to be done in specified periods, records to be broken by fractions of a second, machines that set the pace and have to be kept up with. Our consciousness of the smallest units of time is now acute. To us, for example, the moment 8.17 A.M. means something—something very important, if it happens to be the starting time of our daily train. To our ancestors, such an odd eccentric instant was without significance—did not even exist. In inventing the locomotive, Watt and Stevenson were part inventors of time.

Another time-emphasizing entity is the factory and its depen- 3
dent, the office. Factories exist for the purpose of getting certain quantities of goods made in a certain time. The old artisan worked as it suited him with the result that consumers generally had to wait for the goods they had ordered from him. The factory is a device for making workmen hurry. The machine revolves so often each minute; so many movements have to be made, so many pieces produced each hour. Result: the factory worker (and the same is true, *mutatis mutandis,* of the office worker) is compelled to know time in its smallest fractions. In the hand-work age there was no such compulsion to be aware of minutes and seconds.

Our awareness of time has reached such a pitch of intensity 4
that we suffer acutely whenever our travels take us into some corner of the world where people are not interested in minutes and seconds. The unpunctuality of the Orient, for example, is appalling to those who come freshly from a land of fixed meal-times and regular train services. For a modern American or Englishman, waiting is a psychological torture. An Indian accepts the blank hours with resignation,

even with satisfaction. He has not lost the fine art of doing nothing. Our notion of time as a collection of minutes, each of which must be filled with some business or amusement, is wholly alien to the Oriental, just as it was wholly alien to the Greek. For the man who lives in a pre-industrial world, time moves at a slow and easy pace; he does not care about each minute, for the good reason that he has not been made conscious of the existence of minutes.

5 This brings us to a seeming paradox. Acutely aware of the smallest constituent particles of time—of time, as measured by clock-work and train arrivals and the revolutions of machines—industrialized man has to a great extent lost the old awareness of time in its larger divisions. The time of which we have knowledge is artificial, machine-made time. Of natural, cosmic time, as it is measured out by sun and moon, we are for the most part almost wholly unconscious. Pre-industrial people know time in its daily, monthly and seasonal rhythms. They are aware of sunrise, noon and sunset of the full moon and the new; of equinox and solstice; of spring and summer, autumn and winter. All the old religions, including Catholic Christianity, have insisted on this daily and seasonal rhythm. Pre-industrial man was never allowed to forget the majestic movement of cosmic time.

6 Industrialism and urbanism have changed all this. One can live and work in a town without being aware of the daily march of the sun across the sky; without ever seeing the moon and stars. Broadway and Piccadilly are our Milky Way; our constellations are outlined in neon tubes. Even changes of season affect the townsman very little. He is the inhabitant of an artificial universe that is, to a great extent, walled off from the world of nature. Outside the walls, time is cosmic and moves with the motion of sun and stars. Within, it is an affair of revolving wheels and is measured in seconds and minutes—at its longest, in eight-hour days and six-day weeks. We have a new consciousness; but it has been purchased at the expense of the old consciousness.

QUESTIONS

1. According to Huxley, what lengths of time were most important to our ancestors? What lengths of time are most important to us? Why does Huxley say that Watt and Stevenson were "part inventors of time" (paragraph 2)?

2. Identify the time-emphasizing machines Huxley mentions.

3. Explain the analogy in paragraph 1, and the metaphor in paragraph 6.

4. Huxley calls time "our tyrant" (paragraph 1), "machine made" (paragraph 5), "artificial" (paragraph 6), and waiting "a psychological torture"

(paragraph 4). He calls time for preindustrial people "majestic" and "natural" (paragraph 5). Explain the connotations of these words, and explain how they contribute to Huxley's thesis.

5. What is the thesis of the essay? Where is it stated?

6. How does Huxley organize his contrast of types of time?

7. How does the example of time in the Orient differ from Huxley's other examples? How does this example complement Huxley's theme?

8. Explain the pattern of causal analysis in paragraphs 2 to 6.

9. How much of your life is determined by schedules? How would you feel living in a world in which cosmic time predominates?

10. Write an essay describing how you are a victim of the tyrant, time.

ARTHUR C. CLARKE

The Planets Are Not Enough

Arthur Charles Clarke (1917–), astronomer, science fiction novelist, and essayist, has been a full-time writer since 1951. Since then, over 5 million copies of his books have appeared in twenty languages. His most famous science fiction novels are *Childhood's End* (1953), *2001 Space Odyssey* (1972, with Stanley Kubrick), and *Rendezvous with Rama* (1978). His most recent collection of essays is *The View from Serendip* (1978). In fiction and essays, Clarke has considered humanity's possibly humble status in the cosmos. In the following essay, published in *Report from Planet 3* (1972), he speculates on ways of exploring the universe.

Altogether apart from its scientific value, space travel has one justification that transcends all others. It is probably the only way we can hope to answer one of the supreme questions of philosophy: Is Man alone in the Universe? It seems incredible that ours should be the only inhabited planet among the millions of worlds that must exist among the stars, but we cannot solve this problem by speculating about it. If it can be solved at all, it will be by visiting other planets to see for ourselves. 1

The Solar System, comprising the nine known worlds of our Sun and their numerous satellites, is a relatively compact structure, a snug little celestial oasis in an endless desert. It is true that millions of miles separate Earth from its neighbors, but such distances are 2 cosmically trivial. They will even be trivial in terms of human engineering before another hundred years—a mere moment in historical time—have elapsed. However, the distances that sunder us from the possible worlds of other stars are of a totally different order of magnitude, and there are fundamental reasons for thinking that nothing—no scientific discovery or technical achievement—will ever make *them* trivial.

When today's chemical fuels have been developed to the ultimate, and such tricks as refueling in space have been fully exploited, we will have spaceships which can attain speeds of about ten miles a second. That means that the Moon will be reached in two or three days and the nearer planets in about half a year. (I am deliberately rounding these numbers off, and anyone who tries to check my arithmetic had better remember that spaceships will never travel in straight lines or at uniform speeds.) The remoter planets, such as Jupiter and Saturn, could be reached only after many years of travel, and so the trio Moon-Mars-Venus marks the practical limit of exploration for chemically propelled spaceships. Even for these cases, it is all too easy to demonstrate that hundreds of tons of fuel would be needed for each ton of payload that would make the round trip. 3

This situation, which used to depress the pre-atomic-energy astronauts, will not last for long. Since we are not concerned here with engineering details, we can take it for granted that eventually nuclear power, in some form or other, will be harnessed for the purposes of space flight. With energies a millionfold greater than those available from chemical fuels, speeds of hundreds, and ultimately thousands of miles a second will be attainable. Against such speeds, the Solar System will shrink until the inner planets are no more than a few hours apart, and even Pluto will be only a week or two from Earth. Moreover, there should be no reasonable limit to the amount of equipment and material that could be taken on an interplanetary expedition. Anyone who doubts this may ponder the fact that the energy released by a single H-bomb is sufficient to carry about a million tons to Mars. It is true that we cannot as yet tap even a fraction of that energy for such a purpose, but there are already hints of how this may be done. 4

The short-lived Uranium Age will see the dawn of space flight; the succeeding era of fusion power will witness its fulfillment. But even when we can travel among the planets as freely as we now travel over this Earth, it seems that we will be no nearer to solving the problem of man's place in the Universe. That is a secret that will still lie hidden in the stars. 5

All the evidence indicates that we are alone in the Solar System. True, there is almost certainly some kind of life on Mars, and 6 possibly on Venus—perhaps even on the Moon. (The slight evidence for lunar vegetation comes from the amateur observers who actually *look* at the Moon, and is regarded skeptically by professional astronomers, who could hardly care less about a small slag heap little more than a light-second away.) Vegetation, however, can provide little intellectual companionship. Mars may be a paradise for the botanist, but it may have little to interest the zoologist—and nothing at all to lure the anthropologist and his colleagues across some scores of millions of miles of space.

This is likely to disappoint a great many people and to take 7
much of the zest out of space travel. Yet it would be unreasonable to expect anything else; the planets have been in existence for several billion years, and only during the last .0001 per cent of that time has the human race been slightly civilized. Even if Mars and Venus have been (or will be) suitable for higher forms of life, the chances are wildly against our encountering beings anywhere near our cultural or intellectual level at this particular moment of time. If rational creatures exist on the planets, they will be millions of years ahead of us in development—or millions of years behind us. We may expect to meet apes or angels, but never men.

The angels can probably be ruled out at once. If they existed, 8
then surely they would already have come here to have a look at us. Some people, of course, think that this is just what they are doing. I can only say that they are going about it in a very odd manner.

We had better assume, therefore, that neither on Mars nor 9
Venus, nor on any other of the planets, will explorers from Earth encounter intelligent life. We are the only castaways upon the tiny raft of the Solar System, as it drifts forever along the Gulf Streams of the Galaxy.

This, then, is the challenge that sooner or later the human 10
spirit must face, when the planets have been conquered and all their secrets brought home to Earth. The nearest of the stars is a million times farther away than the closest of the planets. The spaceships we may expect to see a generation from now would take about a hundred thousand years to reach Proxima Centauri, our nearest stellar neighbor. Even the hypothetical nuclear-powered spaceships which a full century of atomic engineering may produce could hardly make the journey in less than a thousand years.

The expressive term "God's quarantine regulations" has been 11
used to describe this state of affairs. At first sight, it appears that they are rigorously enforced. There may be millions of inhabited worlds circling other suns, harboring beings who to us would seem godlike, with civilizations and cultures beyond our wildest dreams. But we shall never meet them, and they for their part will never know of our existence.

So run the conclusions of most astronomers, even those who 12
are quite convinced that mere common or garden interplanetary flight is just around the corner. But it is always dangerous to make negative predictions, and though the difficulties of *interstellar* travel are stupendous, they are not insuperable. It is by no means certain that man must remain trapped in the Solar System for eternity, never to know if he is a lonely freak of no cosmic significance.

There are two ways in which we might gain direct knowledge 13
of other stellar systems without ever leaving our own. Rather surprisingly, it can be shown that radio communication would be perfectly feasible across interstellar space, if very slow-speed telegraphy were employed. However, we can hardly assume that anyone would be listening in at the precise frequency with a receiver tuned to the extremely narrow band that would have to be employed. And even if they were, it would be extremely tedious learning to talk to them with no initial knowledge of their language—and having to wait many years for any acknowledgment of our own signals, as the radio waves came limping back across the light-years. If we sent a question to Proxima Centauri, it would be almost nine years before any answer could reach Earth.

A more practical, though at first sight more startling, solution 14
would be to send a survey ship—unmanned. This would be a gigantic extrapolation of existing techniques, but it would not involve anything fundamentally new. Imagine an automatic vessel, crammed with every type of recording instrument and controlled by an electronic brain with preset instructions. It would be launched out across space, aimed at a target it might not reach for a thousand years. But at last one of the stars ahead would begin to dominate the sky, and a century or so later, it would have grown into a sun, perhaps with planets circling around it. Sleeping instruments would wake, the tiny ship would check its speed, and its sense organs would start to record their impressions. It would circle world after world, following a program set up to cover all possible contingencies by men who had died a thousand years before. Then, with the priceless knowledge it had gained, it would begin the long voyage home.

This type of proxy exploration of the universe would be slow 15
and uncertain and would demand long-range planning beyond the capacity of our age. Yet if there is no other way of contacting the stars, this is how it might be done. One millennium would make the investment in technical skill so that the next would reap the benefit. It would be as if Archimedes were to start a research project which could produce no results before the time of Einstein.

If men, and not merely their machines, are ever to reach the 16
planets of other suns, problems of much greater difficulty will have to be solved. Stated in its simplest form, the question is this: How can

men survive a journey which may last for several thousand years? It is rather surprising to find that there are at least five different answers which must be regarded as theoretical possibilities—however far they may be beyond the scope of today's science.

Medicine may provide two rather obvious solutions. There appears to be no fundamental reason why men should die when they do. It is certainly not a matter of the body "wearing out" in the sense that an inanimate piece of machinery does, for in the course of a single year almost the entire fabric of the body is replaced by new material. When we have discovered the details of this process, it may be possible to extend the life span indefinitely if so desired. Whether a crew of immortals, however well balanced and psychologically adjusted, could tolerate each other's company for several centuries in rather cramped quarters is an interesting subject for speculation. 17

Perhaps a better answer is that suggested by the story of Rip Van Winkle. Suspended animation (or, more accurately, a drastic slowing down of the body's metabolism) for periods of a few hours is now, of course, a medical commonplace. It requires no great stretch of the imagination to suppose that, with the aid of low temperatures and drugs, men may be able to hibernate for virtually unlimited periods. We can picture an automatic ship with its oblivious crew making the long journey across the interstellar night until, when a new sun was looming up, the signal was sent out to trigger the mechanisms which would revive the sleepers. When their survey was completed, they would head back to Earth and slumber again until the time came to awake once more, and to greet a world which would regard them as survivors from the distant past. 18

The third solution was, to the best of my knowledge, suggested over thirty years ago by Professor J. D. Bernal in a long out-of-print essay, *The World, the Flesh, and the Devil,* which must rank as one of the most outstanding feats of scientific imagination in literature. Even today, many of the ideas propounded in this little book have never been fully developed, either in or out of science fiction. (Any requests from fellow authors to borrow my copy will be flatly ignored.) 19

Bernal imagined entire societies launched across space, in gigantic arks which would be closed, ecologically balanced systems. They would, in fact, be miniature planets, upon which generations of men would live and die so that one day their remote descendants would return to Earth with the record of their celestial Odyssey. 20

The engineering, biological and sociological problems involved in such an enterprise would be of fascinating complexity. The artificial planets (at least several miles in diameter) would have to be completely self-contained and self-supporting, and no material of any kind could be wasted. Commenting on the implications of such closed systems, *Time* magazine's able, erudite science editor Jonathan 21

Leonard once hinted that cannibalism would be compulsory among interstellar travelers. This would be a matter of definition; we crew members of the two-billion-man spaceship Earth do not consider ourselves cannibals despite the fact that every one of us must have absorbed atoms which once formed part of Caesar and Socrates, Shakespeare and Solomon.

One cannot help feeling that the interstellar ark on its thousand-year voyages would be a cumbersome way of solving the problem, even if all the social and psychological difficulties could be overcome. (Would the fiftieth generation still share the aspirations of their Pilgrim Fathers who set out from Earth so long ago?) There are, however, more sophisticated ways of getting men to the stars than the crude, brute-force methods outlined above. After the hardheaded engineering of the last few paragraphs, what follows may appear to verge upon fantasy. It involves, in the most fundamental sense of the word, the storage of human beings. And by that I do not mean anything as naïve as suspended animation. 22

A few months ago, in an Australian laboratory, I was watching what appeared to be perfectly normal spermatozoa wriggling across the microscope field. They *were* perfectly normal, but their history was not. For three years, they had been utterly immobile in a deep freeze, and there seemed little doubt that they could be kept fertile for centuries by the same technique. What was still more surprising, there had been enough successes with the far larger and more delicate ova to indicate that they too might survive the same treatment. If this proves to be the case, reproduction will eventually become independent of time. 23

The social implications of this make anything in *Brave New World* seem like child's play, but I am not concerned here with the interesting results which might have been obtained by, for example, uniting the genes of Cleopatra and Newton, had this technique been available earlier in history. (When such experiments are started, however, it would be as well to remember Shaw's famous rejection of a similar proposal: "But suppose, my dear, it turns out to have my beauty and your brains?")* 24

The cumbersome interstellar ark, with its generations of travelers doomed to spend their entire lives in empty space, was merely a device to carry germ cells, knowledge, and culture from one sun to another. How much more efficient to send only the cells, to fertilize them automatically some twenty years before the voyage was due to end, to carry the embryos through to birth by techniques already foreshadowed in today's biology labs, and to bring up the 25

*We have Shaw's word for it that the would-be geneticist was a complete stranger and not, as frequently stated, Isadora Duncan.

babies under the tutelage of cybernetic nurses who would teach them their inheritance and their destiny when they were capable of understanding it.

These children, knowing no parents, or indeed anyone of a different age from themselves, would grow up in the strange artificial world of their speeding ship, reaching maturity in time to explore the planets ahead of them—perhaps to be the ambassadors of humanity among alien races, or perhaps to find, too late, that there was no home for them there. If their mission succeeded, it would be their duty (or that of their descendants, if the first generation could not complete the task) to see that the knowledge they had gained was someday carried back to Earth. 26

Would any society be morally justified, we may well ask, in planning so onerous and uncertain a future for its unborn—indeed unconceived—children? That is a question which different ages may answer in different ways. What to one era would seem a cold-blooded sacrifice might to another appear a great and glorious adventure. There are complex problems here which cannot be settled by instinctive, emotional answers. 27

So far, we have assumed that all interstellar voyages must of necessity last for many hundreds or even thousands of years. The nearest star is more than four light-years away; the Galaxy itself—the island Universe of which our Sun is one insignificant member—is hundreds of thousands of light-years across; and the distances *between* the galaxies are of the order of a million light-years. The speed of light appears to be a fundamental limit to velocity; in this sense it is quite different from the now outmoded "sound barrier," which is merely an attribute of the particular gases which happen to constitute our atmosphere. 28

Even if we could reach the speed of light, therefore, interstellar journeys would still require many years of travel, and only in the case of the very nearest stars would it appear possible for a voyager to make the round trip in a single lifetime, without resort to such techniques as suspended animation. However, as we shall see, the actual situation is a good deal more complex than this. 29

First of all, is it even theoretically possible to build spaceships capable of approaching the speed of light? (That is, 186,000 miles a second or 670,000,000 miles per hour.) The problem is that of finding a sufficient source of energy and applying it. Einstein's famous quotation $E = mc^2$ gives an answer—on paper—which a few centuries of technology may be able to realize in terms of engineering. If we can achieve the *total* annihilation of matter—not the conversion of a mere fraction of a per cent of it into energy—we can approach as near to the speed of light as we please. We can never reach it, but a journey at 99.9 per cent of the speed of light would, after all, take very little 30 longer than one at exactly the speed of light, so the difference would hardly seem of practical importance.

Complete annihilation of matter is still as much a dream as atomic energy itself was thirty years ago. However, the discovery of the anti-proton (which engages in mutual suicide on meeting a normal proton) may be the first step on the road to its realization. 31

Traveling at speeds approaching that of light, however, involves us at once in one of the most baffling paradoxes which spring from the theory of relativity—the so-called "time-dilation effect." It is impossible to explain *why* this effect occurs without delving into very elementary yet extremely subtle mathematics. (There is nothing difficult about basic relativity math: most of it is simple algebra. The difficulty lies in the underlying concepts.) Nevertheless, even if the explanation must be skipped, the results of the time-dilation effect can be stated readily enough in nontechnical language. 32

Time itself is a variable quantity; the rate at which it flows depends upon the speed of the observer. The difference is infinitesimal at the velocities of everyday life, and even at the velocities of normal astronomical bodies. It is all-important as we approach to within a few per cent of the speed of light. To put it crudely, the faster one travels, the more slowly time will pass. At the speed of light, time would cease to exist; the moment "Now" would last forever. 33

Let us take an extreme example to show what this implies. If a spaceship left Earth for Proxima Centauri at the speed of light, and came back at once at the same velocity, it would have been gone for some eight and one-half years according to all the clocks and calendars of Earth. *But the people in the ship, and all their clocks, would have recorded no lapsed time at all.* 34

At a physically attainable speed, say 95 per cent of the velocity of light, the inhabitants of the ship would think that the round trip had lasted about three years. At 99 per cent, it would have seemed little more than a year to them. In each case, however, they would return more than eight years—Earth time—after they had departed. (No allowance has been made here for stopping and starting, which would require additional time.) 35

If we imagine a more extensive trip, we get still more surprising results. The travelers might be gone for a thousand years, from the point of view of Earth, having set out for a star five hundred light-years away. If their ship had averaged 99.9 per cent of the speed of light, they would be fifty years older when they returned to an Earth—*where ten centuries had passed away!** 36

*The physical reality of the time-dilation effect has been the subject of unusually acrimonious debate in recent years. Very few scientists now have any doubt of its existence, but its magnitude may not have the values quoted above. My figures are based on special relativity, which is too unsophisticated to deal with the complexities of an actual flight.

It should be emphasized that this effect, incredible though it appears to be, is one of the natural consequences of Einstein's theory. The equation connecting mass and energy once appeared to be equally fantastic and remote from any practical application. It would be very unwise, therefore, to assume that the equation linking time and velocity will never be of more than theoretical interest. Anything which does not violate natural laws must be considered a possibility—and the events of the last few decades have shown clearly enough that things which are possible will always be achieved if the incentive is sufficiently great. 37

Whether the incentive will be sufficient here is a question which only the future can answer. The men of five hundred or a thousand years from now will have motivations very different from ours, but if they are men at all they will still burn with that restless curiosity which has driven us over this world and which is about to take us into space. Sooner or later we will come to the edge of the Solar System and will be looking out across the ultimate abyss. Then we must choose whether we reach the stars—or whether we wait until the stars reach us. 38

QUESTIONS

1. What are the three general means of propulsion? Which is the most advanced method?

2. What are the means of gathering information?

3. Clarke occasionally uses metaphors to enliven his prose. Identify such metaphors. Why would a popularizer of science want to use metaphors?

4. Clarke declares that he is writing in "nontechnical language" (paragraph 32). What evidence of this do you find?

5. Describe the different viewpoints from which Clarke looks at intervals of time and space.

6. How does Clarke utilize illustration in this essay?

7. Explain the structural importance of paragraphs 13, 16, and 29.

8. Analyze the relationship between the author's introductory and concluding paragraphs.

9. For what reasons do you agree or disagree with Clarke that space travel is of crucial importance? What other goals do you think humanity should achieve before space travel?

10. Arthur Clarke presumes that space travel is a critical goal for humanity, and he speculates on ways to achieve it. Write an essay describing another general goal for humanity and ways to achieve it.

12 Civilization

OLIVER GOLDSMITH

National Prejudices

Oliver Goldsmith (1730–1774), the son of an Anglican curate, was an Anglo-Irish essayist, poet, novelist, dramatist, and journalist. His reputation as an enduring figure in English literature is based on his novel, *The Vicar of Wakefield* (1766); his play *She Stoops to Conquer* (1773); his major poem, *The Deserted Village* (1770); and the essays and satiric letters collected in *The Bee* (1759) and *The Citizen of the World* (1762). In this essay, Goldsmith argues quietly for a new type of citizen who can transcend the xenophobia governing national behavior.

As I am one of that sauntering tribe of mortals, who spend the greatest part of their time in taverns, coffee-houses, and other places of public resort, I have thereby an opportunity of observing an infinite variety of characters, which, to a person of a contemplative turn, is a much higher entertainment than a view of all the curiosities of art or nature. In one of these, my late rambles, I accidentally fell into the company of half a dozen gentlemen, who were engaged in a warm dispute about some political affair; the decision of which, as they were equally divided in their sentiments, they thought proper to refer to me, which naturally drew me in for a share of the conversation. 1

Amongst a multiplicity of other topics, we took occasion to talk of the different characters of the several nations of Europe; when one of the gentlemen, cocking his hat, and assuming such an air of importance as if he had possessed all the merit of the English nation in his own person, declared that the Dutch were a parcel of avaricious wretches; the French a set of flattering sycophants; that the Germans were drunken sots, and beastly gluttons; and the Spaniards proud, haughty, and surly tyrants; but that in bravery, generosity, clemency, and in every other virtue, the English excelled all the rest of the world. 2

This very learned and judicious remark was received with a general smile of approbation by all the company—all, I mean, but your humble servant; who, endeavoring to keep my gravity as well as I could, and reclining my head upon my arm, continued for some time in a posture of affected thoughtfulness, as if I had been musing on something else, and did not seem to attend to the subject of conversation; hoping by these means to avoid the disagreeable necessity of explaining myself, and thereby depriving the gentleman of his imaginary happiness. 3

But my pseudo-patriot had no mind to let me escape so easily. Not satisfied that his opinion should pass without contradiction, he was determined to have it ratified by the suffrage of every one in the company; for which purpose addressing himself to me with an air of inexpressible confidence, he asked me if I was not of the same way of thinking. As I am never forward in giving my opinion, especially when I have reason to believe that it will not be agreeable; so, when I am obliged to give it, I always hold it for a maxim to speak my real sentiments. I therefore told him that, for my own part, I should not have ventured to talk in such a peremptory strain, unless I had made the tour of Europe, and examined the manners of these several nations with great care and accuracy: that, perhaps, a more impartial judge would not scruple to affirm that the Dutch were more frugal and industrious, the French more temperate and polite, the Germans more hardy and patient of labour and fatigue, and the Spaniards more staid and sedate, than the English; who, though undoubtedly brave and generous, were at the same time rash, headstrong, and impetuous; too apt to be elated with prosperity, and to despond in adversity. 4

I could easily perceive that all the company began to regard me with a jealous eye before I had finished my answer, which I had no sooner done, that the patriotic gentleman observed, with a contemptuous sneer, that he was greatly surprised how some people could have the conscience to live in a country which they did not love, and to enjoy the protection of a government, to which in their hearts they were inveterate enemies. Finding that by this modest 5 declaration of my sentiments I had forfeited the good opinion of my companions, and given them occasion to call my political principles in question, and well knowing that it was in vain to argue with men who were so very full of themselves, I threw down my reckoning and retired to my own lodgings, reflecting on the absurd and ridiculous nature of national prejudice and prepossession.

Among all the famous sayings of antiquity, there is none that 6
does greater honour to the author, or affords greater pleasure to the reader (at least if he be a person of a generous and benevolent heart), than that of the philosopher, who, being asked what "countryman he was," replied, that he was, "a citizen of the world."—How few are there to be found in modern times who can say the same, or whose conduct is consistent with such a profession!—We are now become so much Englishmen, Frenchmen, Dutchmen, Spaniards, or Germans, that we are no longer citizens of the world; so much the natives of one particular spot, or members of one petty society, that we no longer consider ourselves as the general inhabitants of the globe, or members of that grand society which comprehends the whole human kind.

Did these prejudices prevail only among the meanest and 7
lowest of the people, perhaps they might be excused, as they have few, if any, opportunities of correcting them by reading, travelling, or conversing with foreigners; but the misfortune is, that they infect the minds, and influence the conduct, even of our gentlemen; of those, I mean, who have every title to this appellation but an exemption from prejudice, which however, in my opinion, ought to be regarded as the characteristical mark of a gentleman; for let a man's birth be ever so high, his station ever so exalted, or his fortune ever so large, yet if he is not free from national and other prejudices, I should make bold to tell him, that he had a low and vulgar mind, and had no just claim to the character of a gentleman. And in fact, you will always find that those are most apt to boast of national merit, who have little or no merit of their own to depend on; than which, to be sure, nothing is more natural: the slender vine twists around the sturdy oak, for no other reason in the world but because it has not strength sufficient to support itself.

Should it be alleged in defence of national prejudice, that it is 8
the natural and necessary growth of love to our country, and that therefore the former cannot be destroyed without hurting the latter, I answer, that this is a gross fallacy and delusion. That it is the growth of love to our country, I will allow; but that it is the natural and necessary growth of it, I absolutely deny. Superstition and enthusiasm too are the growth of religion; but who ever took it in his head to affirm that they are the necessary growth of this noble principle? They are, if you will, the bastard sprouts of this heavenly plant, but

not its natural and genuine branches, and may safely enough be lopped off, without doing any harm to the parent stock: nay, perhaps, till once they are lopped off, this goodly tree can never flourish in perfect health and vigour.

Is it not very possible that I may love my own country, 9
without hating the natives of other countries? that I may exert the most heroic bravery, the most undaunted resolution, in defending its laws and liberty, without despising all the rest of the world as cowards and poltroons? Most certainly it is; and if it were not—But why need I suppose what is absolutely impossible?—But if it were not, I must own, I should prefer the title of the ancient philosopher, viz. a citizen of the world, to that of an Englishman, a Frenchman, a European, or to any other appellation whatever.

QUESTIONS

1. Why does Goldsmith maintain that he is "a citizen of the world"? According to the author, could such an individual also be a patriot? Explain.

2. What connection does Goldsmith establish between national prejudices and the conduct of gentlemen? Why does he allude to the manners of gentlemen?

3. Locate in the essay examples of the familiar style in writing. What is the relationship between this style and the tone and substance of the essay?

4. Explain the metaphors at the end of paragraphs 7 and 8.

5. What is the relevance of the introductory narrative, with its description of characters, to the author's declaration of thesis? Where does the author state his proposition concerning national prejudices?

6. Analyze the function of classification and contrast in paragraphs 2 to 5. How does the entire essay serve as a pattern of definition?

7. Examine the pattern of reasoning involved in the author's presentation of his argument in the essay, notably in paragraphs 6 to 8. What appeals to emotion and to reason does he make?

8. Assess the rhetorical effectiveness of Goldsmith's concluding paragraph.

9. Why has it been difficult to eliminate the problem that Goldsmith posed in 1765? Are we better able today to function as citizens of the world? In what ways? What role does the United Nations play in this issue? What factors contribute to a new world citizenry?

10. a. Write an argumentative essay on the desirability of world government, or on the need to be a citizen of the world.
b. Write a paper on contemporary national prejudices.

JOHN STEINBECK

Americans and the Land

John Steinbeck (1902–1968) was born in California, the setting for some of his best fiction. Steinbeck's fiction of the 1930s, including *The Pastures of Heaven* (1932), *Tortilla Flat* (1935), *In Dubious Battle* (1936), *Of Mice and Men* (1937), and the Pulitzer Prize–winning epic *The Grapes of Wrath* (1939), offers one of the best imaginative presentations of the American Depression. Steinbeck won the Nobel Prize in Literature in 1962, for "realistic and imaginative writings, distinguished as they are by a sympathetic humor and a social perception." In this section from *America and Americans* (1966), Steinbeck offers a probing, critical appraisal of American social development.

1 I have often wondered at the savagery and thoughtlessness with which our early settlers approached this rich continent. They came at it as though it were an enemy, which of course it was. They burned the forests and changed the rainfall; they swept the buffalo from the plains, blasted the streams, set fire to the grass, and ran a reckless scythe through the virgin and noble timber. Perhaps they felt that it was limitless and could never be exhausted and that a man could move on to new wonders endlessly. Certainly there are many examples to the contrary, but to a large extent the early people pillaged the country as though they hated it, as though they held it temporarily and might be driven off at any time.

2 This tendency toward irresponsibility persists in very many of us today; our rivers are poisoned by reckless dumping of sewage and toxic industrial wastes, the air of our cities is filthy and dangerous to breathe from the belching of uncontrolled products from combustion of coal, coke, oil, and gasoline. Our towns are girdled with wreckage and the debris of our toys—our automobiles and our packaged pleasures. Through uninhibited spraying against one enemy we have destroyed the natural balances our survival requires.

All these evils can and must be overcome if America and Americans are to survive; but many of us still conduct ourselves as our ancestors did, stealing from the future for our clear and present profit.

Since the river-polluters and the air-poisoners are not criminal or even bad people, we must presume that they are heirs to the early conviction that sky and water are unowned and that they are limitless. In the light of our practices here at home it is very interesting to me to read of the care taken with the carriers of our probes into space to make utterly sure that they are free of pollution of any kind. We would not think of doing to the moon what we do every day to our own dear country. 3

When the first settlers came to America and dug in on the coast, they huddled in defending villages hemmed in by the sea on one side and by endless forests on the other, by Red Indians and, most frightening, the mystery of an unknown land extending nobody knew how far. And for a time very few cared or dared to find out. Our first Americans organized themselves and lived in a state of military alertness; every community built its blockhouse for defense. By law the men went armed and were required to keep their weapons ready and available. Many of them wore armor, made here or imported; on the East Coast, they wore the cuirass and helmet, and the Spaniards on the West Coast wore both steel armor and heavy leather to turn arrows. 4

On the East Coast, and particularly in New England, the colonists farmed meager lands close to their communities and to safety. Every man was permanently on duty for the defense of his family and his village; even the hunting parties went into the forest in force, rather like raiders than hunters, and their subsequent quarrels with the Indians, resulting in forays and even massacres, remind us that the danger was very real. A man took his gun along when he worked the land, and the women stayed close to their thick-walled houses and listened day and night for the signal of alarm. The towns they settled were permanent, and most of them exist today with their records of Indian raids, of slaughter, of scalpings, and of punitive counter-raids. The military leader of the community became the chief authority in time of trouble, and it was a long time before danger receded and the mystery could be explored. 5

After a time, however, brave and forest-wise men drifted westward to hunt, to trap, and eventually to bargain for the furs which were the first precious negotiable wealth America produced for trade and export. Then trading posts were set up as centers of collection and the exploring men moved up and down the rivers and crossed the mountains, made friends for mutual profit with the Indians, learned the wilderness techniques, so that these explorer-traders soon dressed, ate, and generally acted like the indigenous 6

people around them. Suspicion lasted a long time, and was fed by clashes sometimes amounting to full-fledged warfare; but by now these Americans attacked and defended as the Indians did.

For a goodly time the Americans were travelers, moving 7
about the country collecting its valuables, but with little idea of permanence; their roots and their hearts were in the towns and the growing cities along the eastern edge. The few who stayed, who lived among the Indians, adopted their customs and some took Indian wives and were regarded as strange and somehow treasonable creatures. As for their half-breed children, while the tribe sometimes adopted them they were unacceptable as equals in the eastern settlements.

Then the trickle of immigrants became a stream, and the 8
population began to move westward—not to grab and leave but to settle and live, they thought. The newcomers were of peasant stock, and they had their roots in a Europe where they had been landless, for the possession of land was the requirement and the proof of a higher social class than they had known. In America they found beautiful and boundless land for the taking and they took it.

It is little wonder that they went land-mad, because there was 9
so much of it. They cut and burned the forests to make room for crops; they abandoned their knowledge of kindness to the land in order to maintain its usefulness. When they had cropped out a piece they moved on, raping the country like invaders. The topsoil, held by roots and freshened by leaf-fall, was left helpless to the spring freshets, stripped and eroded with the naked bones of clay and rock exposed. The destruction of the forests changed the rainfall, for the searching clouds could find no green and beckoning woods to draw them on and milk them. The merciless nineteenth century was like a hostile expedition for loot that seemed limitless. Uncountable buffalo were killed, stripped of their hides, and left to rot, a reservoir of permanent food supply eliminated. More than that, the land of the Great Plains was robbed of the manure of the herds. Then the plows went in and ripped off the protection of the buffalo grass and opened the helpless soil to quick water and slow drought and the mischievous winds that roamed through the Great Central Plains. There has always been more than enough desert in America; the new settlers, like overindulged children, created even more.

The railroads brought new hordes of land-crazy people, and 10
the new Americans moved like locusts across the continent until the western sea put a boundary to their movements. Coal and copper and gold drew them on; they savaged the land, gold-dredged the rivers to skeletons of pebbles and debris. An aroused and fearful government made laws for the distribution of public lands—a quarter section, one hundred and sixty acres, per person—and a claim had to be proved

and improved; but there were ways of getting around this, and legally. My own grandfather proved out a quarter section for himself, one for his wife, one for each of his children, and, I suspect, acreage for children he hoped and expected to have. Marginal lands, of course, suitable only for grazing, went in larger pieces. One of the largest land-holding families in California took its richest holdings by a trick: By law a man could take up all the swamp or water-covered land he wanted. The founder of this great holding mounted a scow on wheels and drove his horses over thousands of acres of the best bottom land, then reported that he had explored it in a boat, which was true, and confirmed his title. I need not mention his name; his descendants will remember.

Another joker with a name still remembered in the West worked out a scheme copied many times in after years. Proving a quarter section required a year of residence and some kind of improvement—a fence, a shack—but once the land was proved the owner was free to sell it. This particular princely character went to the stews and skid rows of the towns and found a small army of hopeless alcoholics who lived for whiskey and nothing else. He put these men on land he wanted to own, grubstaked them and kept them in cheap liquor until the acreage was proved, then went through the motions of buying it from his protégés and moved them and their one-room shacks on sled runners to new quarter sections. Bums of strong constitution might prove out five or six homesteads for this acquisitive hero before they died of drunkenness. 11

It was full late when we began to realize that the continent did not stretch out to infinity; that there were limits to the indignities to which we could subject it. Engines and heavy mechanical equipment were allowing us to ravage it even more effectively than we had with fire, dynamite, and gang plows. Conservation came to us slowly, and much of it hasn't arrived yet. Having killed the whales and wiped out the sea otters and most of the beavers, the market hunters went to work on game birds; ducks and quail were decimated, and the passenger pigeon eliminated. In my youth I remember seeing a market hunter's gun, a three-gauge shotgun bolted to a frame and loaded to the muzzle with shingle nails. Aimed at a lake and the trigger pulled with a string, it slaughtered every living thing on the lake. The Pacific Coast pilchards were once the raw material for a great and continuing industry. We hunted them with aircraft far at sea until they were gone and the canneries had to be closed. In some of the valleys of the West, where the climate makes several crops a year available, which the water supply will not justify, wells were driven deeper and deeper for irrigation, so that in one great valley a million acre feet more of water was taken out than rain and melting 12

snow could replace, and the water table went down and a few more years may give us a new desert.

The great redwood forests of the western mountains early attracted attention. These ancient trees, which once grew everywhere, now exist only where the last Ice Age did not wipe them out. And they were found to have value. The Sempervirens and the Gigantea, the two remaining species, make soft, straight-grained timber. They are easy to split into planks, shakes, fenceposts, and railroad ties, and they have a unique virtue: they resist decay, both wet and dry rot, and an inherent acid in them repels termites. The loggers went through the great groves like a barrage, toppling the trees—some of which were two thousand years old—and leaving no maidens, no seedlings or saplings on the denuded hills. 13

Quite a few years ago when I was living in my little town on the coast of California a stranger came in and bought a small valley where the Sempervirens redwoods grew, some of them three hundred feet high. We used to walk among these trees, and the light colored as though the great glass of the Cathedral at Chartres had strained and sanctified the sunlight. The emotion we felt in this grove was one of awe and humility and joy; and then one day it was gone, slaughtered, and the sad wreckage of boughs and broken saplings left like nonsensical spoilage of the battle-ruined countryside. And I remember that after our rage there was sadness, and when we passed the man who had done this we looked away, because we were ashamed for him. 14

From early times we were impressed and awed by the fantastic accidents of nature, like the Grand Canyon and Yosemite and Yellowstone Park. The Indians had revered them as holy places, visited by the gods, and all of us came to have somewhat the same feeling about them. Thus we set aside many areas of astonishment as publicly owned parks; and though this may to a certain extent have been because there was no other way to use them as the feeling of preciousness of the things we had been destroying grew in Americans, more and more areas were set aside as national and state parks, to be looked at but not injured. Many people loved and were in awe of the redwoods; societies and individuals bought groves of these wonderful trees and presented them to the state for preservation. 15

No longer do we Americans want to destroy wantonly, but our new-found sources of power—to take the burden of work from our shoulders, to warm us, and cool us, and give us light, to transport us quickly, and to make the things we use and wear and eat—these power sources spew pollution on our country, so that the rivers and streams are becoming poisonous and lifeless. The birds die for the lack of food; a noxious cloud hangs over our cities that 16 burns our lungs and reddens our eyes. Our ability to conserve has not grown with our power to create, but this slow and sullen poisoning is no longer ignored or justified. Almost daily, the pressure of outrage among Americans grows. We are no longer content to destroy our beloved country. We are slow to learn; but we learn. When a super-highway was proposed in California which would trample the redwood trees in its path, an outcry arose all over the land, so strident and fierce that the plan was put aside. And we no longer believe that a man, by owning a piece of America, is free to outrage it.

17 But we are an exuberant people, careless and destructive as active children. We make strong and potent tools and then have to use them to prove that they exist. Under the pressure of war we finally made the atom bomb, and for reasons which seemed justifiable at the time we dropped it on two Japanese cities—and I think we finally frightened ourselves. In such things, one must consult himself because there is no other point of reference. I did not know about the bomb, and certainly I had nothing to do with its use, but I am horrified and ashamed; and nearly everyone I know feels the same thing. And those who loudly and angrily justify Hiroshima and Nagasaki—why, they must be the most ashamed of all.

QUESTIONS

1. According to Steinbeck, how did the American attitude toward the land evolve?

2. Does Steinbeck think that the American attitude toward the land can be changed? Cite evidence from the essay to support your answer.

3. Analyze Steinbeck's use of figurative language in paragraphs 1, 2, 9, and 14.

4. Locate images and vocabulary relating to "rape" and destruction in the essay. What is the relevance of this motif to the development of Steinbeck's thesis?

5. How does Steinbeck use examples in paragraphs 1 and 2 to establish the subject and thesis of his essay?

6. Analyze the relationship between the patterns of description and example in the essay. What types of illustration does Steinbeck employ? How does he achieve concreteness through examples? Where does he employ extended example? Does he use examples subjectively or objectively? Explain.

7. How does Steinbeck employ process analysis to highlight his thesis?

8. Explain the relationship between paragraph 16 and paragraph 17 in the essay.

9. Compare and contrast Steinbeck's essay with "Wasteland" by Marya Mannes (see pages 132–133).

10. a. Write an essay entitled "Americans and the Land," using examples to support your thesis.
b. Write an essay on the relationship between ecology and the state of civilization.

JAMES BALDWIN

Stranger in the Village

James Baldwin (1924–), a major American essayist, novelist, short story writer, and playwright, was born and grew up in Harlem, winning a Eugene Saxon Fellowship, and living in Europe from 1948 to 1956. Always an activist in civil rights causes, Baldwin focuses in his essays and fiction on the black search for identity in modern America and on the myth of white superiority. Among his principal works are *Go Tell It on the Mountain* (1953), *Notes of a Native Son* (1955), *Giovanni's Room* (1958), *Nobody Knows My Name* (1960), *Another Country* (1962), and *If Beale Street Could Talk* (1975). One of the finest contemporary essayists, Baldwin has a rare talent for portraying the deepest concerns about civilization in an intensely personal style, as the following essay indicates.

From all available evidence no black man had ever set 1
foot in this tiny Swiss village before I came. I was told before arriving that I would probably be a "sight" for the village; I took this to mean that people of my complexion were rarely seen in Switzerland, and also that city people are always something of a "sight" outside of the city. It did not occur to me—possibly because I am an American—that there could be people anywhere who had never seen a Negro.

It is a fact that cannot be explained on the basis of the 2
inaccessibility of the village. The village is very high, but it is only four hours from Milan and three hours from Lausanne. It is true that

it is virtually unknown. Few people making plans for a holiday would elect to come here. On the other hand, the villagers are able, presumably, to come and go as they please—which they do: to another town at the foot of the mountain, with a population of approximately five thousand, the nearest place to see a movie or go to the bank. In the village there is no movie house, no bank, no library, no theater; very few radios, one jeep, one station wagon; and, at the moment, one typewriter, mine, an invention which the woman next door to me here had never seen. There are about six hundred people living here, all Catholic—I conclude this from the fact that the Catholic church is open all year round, whereas the Protestant chapel, set off on a hill a little removed from the village, is open only in the summertime when the tourists arrive. There are four or five hotels, all closed now, and four or five *bistros,* of which, however, only two do any business during the winter. These two do not do a great deal, for life in the village seems to end around nine or ten o'clock. There are a few stores, butcher, baker, *épicerie,* a hardware store, and a money-changer—who cannot change travelers' checks, but must send them down to the bank, an operation which takes two or three days. There is something called the *Ballet Haus,* closed in the winter and used for God knows what, certainly not ballet, during the summer. There seems to be only one schoolhouse in the village, and this for the quite young children; I suppose this to mean that their older brothers and sisters at some point descend from these mountains in order to complete their education—possibly, again, to the town just below. The landscape is absolutely forbidding, mountains towering on all four sides, ice and snow as far as the eye can reach. In this white wilderness, men and women and children move all day, carrying washing, wood, buckets of milk or water, sometimes skiing on Sunday afternoons. All week long boys and young men are to be seen shoveling snow off the rooftops, or dragging wood down from the forest in sleds.

The village's only real attraction, which explains the tourist 3
season, is the hot spring water. A disquietingly high proportion of these tourists are cripples, or semi-cripples, who come year after year—from other parts of Switzerland, usually—to take the waters. This lends the village, at the height of the season, a rather terrifying air of sanctity, as though it were a lesser Lourdes. There is often something beautiful, there is always something awful, in the spectacle of a person who has lost one of his faculties, a faculty he never questioned until it was gone, and who struggles to recover it. Yet people remain people, on crutches or indeed on deathbeds; and wherever I passed, the first summer I was here, among the native villagers or among the lame, a wind passed with me—of astonishment, curiosity, amusement, and outrage. That first summer I stayed

two weeks and never intended to return. But I did return in the winter, to work; the village offers, obviously, no distractions whatever and has the further advantage of being extremely cheap. Now it is winter again, a year later, and I am here again. Everyone in the village knows my name, though they scarcely ever use it, knows that I come from America—though, this, apparently they will never really believe: black men come from Africa—and everyone knows that I am the friend of the son of a woman who was born here, and that I am staying in their chalet. But I remain as much a stranger today as I was the first day I arrived, and the children shout *Neger! Neger!* as I walk along the streets.

4 It must be admitted that in the beginning I was far too shocked to have any real reaction. In so far as I reacted at all, I reacted by trying to be pleasant—it being a great part of the American Negro's education (long before he goes to school) that he must make people "like" him. This smile-and-the-world-smiles-with-you routine worked about as well in this situation as it had in the situation for which it was designed, which is to say that it did not work at all. No one, after all, can be liked whose human weight and complexity cannot be, or has not been, admitted. My smile was simply another unheard-of phenomenon which allowed them to see my teeth—they did not, really, see my smile and I began to think that, should I take to snarling, no one would notice any difference. All of the physical characteristics of the Negro which had caused me, in America, a very different and almost forgotten pain were nothing less than miraculous—or infernal—in the eyes of the village people. Some thought my hair was the color of tar, that it had the texture of wire, or the texture of cotton. It was jocularly suggested that I might let it all grow long and make myself a winter coat. If I sat in the sun for more than five minutes some daring creature was certain to come along and gingerly put his fingers on my hair, as though he were afraid of an electric shock, or put his hand on my hand, astonished that the color did not rub off. In all of this, in which it must be conceded there was the charm of genuine wonder and in which there was certainly no element of intentional unkindness, there was yet no suggestion that I was human: I was simply a living wonder.

5 I knew that they did not mean to be unkind, and I know it now; it is necessary, nevertheless, for me to repeat this to myself each time I walk out of the chalet. The children who shout *Neger!* have no way of knowing the echoes this sound raises in me. They are brimming with good humor and the more daring swell with pride when I stop to speak with them. Just the same, there are days when I cannot pause and smile, when I have no heart to play with them; when, indeed, I mutter sourly to myself, exactly as I muttered on the streets of a city these children have never seen, when I was no bigger

than these children are now: *Your* mother *was a nigger.* Joyce is right about history being a nightmare—but it may be the nightmare from which no one *can* awaken. People are trapped in history and history is trapped in them.

There is a custom in the village—I am told it is repeated in many villages—of "buying" African natives for the purpose of converting them to Christianity. There stands in the church all year round a small box with a slot for money, decorated with a black figurine, and into this box the villagers drop their francs. During the *carnaval* which precedes Lent, two village children have their faces blackened—out of which bloodless darkness their blue eyes shine like ice—and fantastic horsehair wigs are placed on their blond heads; thus disguised, they solicit among the villagers for money for the missionaries in Africa. Between the box in the church and the blackened children, the village "bought" last year six or eight African natives. This was reported to me with pride by the wife of one of the *bistro* owners and I was careful to express astonishment and pleasure at the solicitude shown by the village for the souls of black folk. The *bistro* owner's wife beamed with a pleasure far more genuine than my own and seemed to feel that I might now breathe more easily concerning the souls of at least six of my kinsmen. 6

I tried not to think of these so lately baptized kinsmen, of the price paid for them, or the peculiar price they themselves would pay, and said nothing about my father, who having taken his own conversion too literally never, at bottom, forgave the white world (which he described as heathen) for having saddled him with a Christ in whom, to judge at least from their treatment of him, they themselves no longer believed. I thought of white men arriving for the first time in an African village, strangers there, as I am a stranger here, and tried to imagine the astounded populace touching their hair and marveling at the color of their skin. But there is a great difference between being the first white man to be seen by Africans and being the first black man to be seen by whites. The white man takes the astonishment as tribute, for he arrives to conquer and to convert the natives, whose inferiority in relation to himself is not even to be questioned; whereas I, without a thought of conquest, find myself among a people whose culture controls me, has even, in a sense, created me, people who have cost me more in anguish and rage than they will ever know, who yet do not even know of my existence. The astonishment with which I might have greeted them, should they have stumbled into my African village a few hundred years ago, might have rejoiced their hearts. But the astonishment with which they greet me today can only poison mine. 7

And this is so despite everything I may do to feel differently, despite my friendly conversations with the *bistro* owner's wife, 8 despite their three-year-old son who has at last become my friend, despite the *saluts* and *bonsoirs* which I exchange with people as I walk, despite the fact that I know that no individual can be taken to task for what history is doing, or has done. I say that the culture of these people controls me—but they can scarcely be held responsible for European culture. America comes out of Europe, but these people have never seen America nor have most of them seen more of Europe than the hamlet at the foot of their mountain. Yet they move with an authority which I shall never have; and they regard me, quite rightly, not only as a stranger in their village but as a suspect latecomer, bearing no credentials, to everything they have—however unconsciously—inherited.

For this village, even were it incomparably more remote and incredibly more primitive, is the West, the West onto which I have been so strangely grafted. These people cannot be, from the point of view of power, strangers anywhere in the world; they have made the modern world, in effect, even if they do not know it. The most illiterate among them is related, in a way that I am not, to Dante, Shakespeare, Michelangelo, Aeschylus, Da Vinci, Rembrandt, and Racine; the cathedral at Chartres says something to them which it cannot say to me, as indeed would New York's Empire State Building, should anyone here ever see it. Out of their hymns and dances come Beethoven and Bach. Go back a few centuries and they are in their full glory—but I am in Africa, watching the conquerors arrive. 9

The rage of the disesteemed is personally fruitless, but it is also absolutely inevitable; this rage, so generally discounted, so little understood even among the people whose daily bread it is, is one of the things that makes history. Rage can only with difficulty, and never entirely, be brought under the domination of the intelligence and is therefore not susceptible to any arguments whatever. This is a fact which ordinary representatives of the *Herrenvolk*, having never felt this rage and being unable to imagine it, quite fail to understand. Also, rage cannot be hidden, it can only be dissembled. This dissembling deludes the thoughtless, and strengthens rage and adds, to rage, contempt. There are, no doubt, as many ways of coping with the resulting complex of tensions as there are black men in the world, but no black man can hope ever to be entirely liberated from this internal warfare—rage, dissembling, and contempt having inevitably accompanied his first realization of the power of white men. What is crucial here is that, since white men represent in the black man's world so heavy a weight, white men have for black men a reality which is far from being reciprocal; and hence all black men have toward all white men an attitude which is designed, really, either to rob the white man of the jewel of his naïveté, or else to make it cost him dear. 10

The black man insists, by whatever means he finds at his disposal, that the white man cease to regard him as an exotic rarity and recognize him as a human being. This is a very charged and difficult moment, for there is a great deal of will power involved in the white man's naïveté. Most people are not naturally reflective any more than they are naturally malicious, and the white man prefers to keep the black man at a certain human remove because it is easier for him thus to preserve his simplicity and avoid being called to account for crimes committed by his forefathers, or his neighbors. He is inescapably aware, nevertheless, that he is in a better position in the world than black men are, nor can he quite put to death the suspicion that he is hated by black men therefore. He does not wish to be hated, neither does he wish to change places, and at this point in his uneasiness he can scarcely avoid having recourse to those legends which white men have created about black men, the most usual effect of which is that the white man finds himself enmeshed, so to speak, in his own language which describes hell, as well as the attributes which lead one to hell, as being as black as night. 11

Every legend, moreover, contains its residuum of truth, and the root function of language is to control the universe by describing it. It is of quite considerable significance that black men remain, in the imagination, and in overwhelming numbers in fact, beyond the disciplines of salvation; and this despite the fact that the West has been "buying" African natives for centuries. There is, I should hazard, an instantaneous necessity to be divorced from this so visibly unsaved stranger, in whose heart, moreover, one cannot guess what dreams of vengeance are being nourished; and, at the same time, there are few things on earth more attractive than the idea of the unspeakable liberty which is allowed the unredeemed. When, beneath the black mask, a human being begins to make himself felt one cannot escape a certain awful wonder as to what kind of human being it is. What one's imagination makes of other people is dictated, of course, by the laws of one's own personality and it is one of the ironies of black-white relations that, by means of what the white man imagines the black man to be, the black man is enabled to know who the white man is. 12

I have said, for example, that I am as much a stranger in this village today as I was the first summer I arrived, but this is not quite true. The villagers wonder less about the texture of my hair than they did then, and wonder rather more about me. And the fact that their wonder now exists on another level is reflected in their attitudes and in their eyes. There are the children who make those delightful, hilarious, sometimes astonishingly grave overtures of friendship in the unpredictable fashion of children; other children, having been taught that the devil is a black man, scream in genuine anguish as I 13 approach. Some of the older women never pass without a friendly greeting, never pass, indeed, if it seems that they will be able to engage me in conversation; other women look down or look away or rather contemptuously smirk. Some of the men drink with me and suggest that I learn how to ski—partly, I gather, because they cannot imagine what I would look like on skis—and want to know if I am married, and ask questions about my *métier*. But some of the men have accused *le sale nègre*—behind my back—of stealing wood and there is already in the eyes of some of them that peculiar, intent, paranoiac malevolence which one sometimes surprises in the eyes of American white men when, out walking with their Sunday girl, they see a Negro male approach.

There is a dreadful abyss between the streets of this village and the streets of the city in which I was born, between the children who shout *Neger!* today and those who shouted *Nigger!* yesterday—the abyss is experience, the American experience. The syllable hurled behind me today expresses, above all, wonder: I am a stranger here. But I am not a stranger in America and the same syllable riding on the American air expresses the war my presence has occasioned in the American soul. 14

For this village brings home to me this fact: that there was a day, and not really a very distant day, when Americans were scarcely Americans at all but discontented Europeans, facing a great unconquered continent and strolling, say, into a marketplace and seeing black men for the first time. The shock this spectacle afforded is suggested, surely, by the promptness with which they decided that these black men were not really men but cattle. It is true that the necessity on the part of the settlers of the New World of reconciling their moral assumptions with the fact—and the necessity—of slavery enhanced immensely the charm of this idea, and it is also true that this idea expresses, with a truly American bluntness, the attitude which to varying extents all masters have had toward all slaves. 15

But between all former slaves and slave-owners and the drama which begins for Americans over three hundred years ago at Jamestown, there are at least two differences to be observed. The American Negro slave could not suppose, for one thing, as slaves in past epochs had supposed and often done, that he would ever be able to wrest the power from his master's hands. This was a supposition which the modern era, which was to bring about such vast changes in the aims and dimensions of power, put to death; it only begins, in unprecedented fashion, and with dreadful implications, to be resurrected today. But even had this supposition persisted with undiminished force, the American Negro slave could not have used it to lend his condition dignity, for the reason that this supposition rests on another: that the slave in exile yet remains 16 related to his past, has some means—if only in memory—of revering and sustaining the forms of his former life, is able, in short, to maintain his identity.

17 This was not the case with the American Negro slave. He is unique among the black men of the world in that his past was taken from him, almost literally, at one blow. One wonders what on earth the first slave found to say to the first dark child he bore. I am told that there are Haitians able to trace their ancestry back to African kings, but any American Negro wishing to go back so far will find his journey through time abruptly arrested by the signature on the bill of sale which served as the entrance paper for his ancestor. At the time—to say nothing of the circumstances—of the enslavement of the captive black man who was to become the American Negro, there was not the remotest possibility that he would ever take power from his master's hands. There was no reason to suppose that his situation would ever change, nor was there, shortly, anything to indicate that his situation had ever been different. It was his necessity, in the words of E. Franklin Frazier, to find a "motive for living under American culture or die." The identity of the American Negro comes out of this extreme situation, and the evolution of this identity was a source of the most intolerable anxiety in the minds and the lives of his masters.

18 For the history of the American Negro is unique also in this: that the question of his humanity, and of his rights therefore as a human being, became a burning one for several generations of Americans, so burning a question that it ultimately became one of those used to divide the nation. It is out of this argument that the venom of the epithet *Nigger!* is derived. It is an argument which Europe has never had, and hence Europe quite sincerely fails to understand how or why the argument arose in the first place, why its effects are so frequently disastrous and always so unpredictable, why it refuses until today to be entirely settled. Europe's black possessions remained—and do remain—in Europe's colonies, at which remove they represented no threat whatever to European identity. If they posed any problem at all for the European conscience, it was a problem which remained comfortingly abstract: in effect, the black man, *as a man*, did not exist for Europe. But in America, even as a slave, he was an inescapable part of the general social fabric and no American could escape having an attitude toward him. Americans attempt until today to make an abstraction of the Negro, but the very nature of these abstractions reveals the tremendous effects the presence of the Negro has had on the American character.

19 When one considers the history of the Negro in America it is of the greatest importance to recognize that the moral beliefs of a person, or a people, are never really as tenuous as life—which is not

moral—very often causes them to appear; these create for them a frame of reference and a necessary hope, the hope being that when life has done its worst they will be enabled to rise above themselves and to triumph over life. Life would scarcely be bearable if this hope did not exist. Again, even when the worst has been said, to betray a belief is not by any means to have put oneself beyond its power; the betrayal of a belief is not the same thing as ceasing to believe. If this were not so there would be no moral standards in the world at all. Yet one must also recognize that morality is based on ideas and that all ideas are dangerous—dangerous because ideas can only lead to action and where the action leads no man can say. And dangerous in this respect: that confronted with the impossibility of becoming free of them, one can be driven to the most inhuman excesses. The ideas on which American beliefs are based are not, though Americans often seem to think so, ideas which originated in America. They came out of Europe. And the establishment of democracy on the American continent was scarcely as radical a break with the past as was the necessity, which Americans faced, of broadening this concept to include black men.

This was, literally, a hard necessity. It was impossible, for 20
one thing, for Americans to abandon their beliefs, not only because these beliefs alone seemed able to justify the sacrifices they had endured and the blood that they had spilled, but also because these beliefs afforded them their only bulwark against a moral chaos as absolute as the physical chaos of the continent it was their destiny to conquer. But in the situation in which Americans found themselves, these beliefs threatened an idea which, whether or not one likes to think so, is the very warp and woof of the heritage of the West, the idea of white supremacy.

Americans have made themselves notorious by the shrillness 21
and the brutality with which they have insisted on this idea, but they did not invent it; and it has escaped the world's notice that those very excesses of which Americans have been guilty imply a certain, unprecedented uneasiness over the idea's life and power, if not, indeed, the idea's validity. The idea of white supremacy rests simply on the fact that white men are the creators of civilization (the present civilization, which is the only one that matters; all previous civilizations are simply "contributions" to our own) and are therefore civilization's guardians and defenders. Thus it was impossible for Americans to accept the black man as one of themselves, for to do so was to jeopardize their status as white men. But not so to accept him was to deny his human reality, his human weight and complexity, and the strain of denying the overwhelmingly undeniable forced Americans into rationalizations so fantastic that they approached the pathological.

At the root of the American Negro problem is the necessity of the American white man to find a way of living with the Negro in order to be able to live with himself. And the history of this problem can be reduced to the means used by Americans—lynch law and law, segregation and legal acceptance, terrorization and concession—either to come to terms with this necessity, or to find a way around it, or (most usually) to find a way of doing both these things at once. The resulting spectacle, at once foolish and dreadful, led someone to make the quite accurate observation that "the Negro-in-America is a form of insanity which overtakes white men." 22

In this long battle, a battle by no means finished, the unforeseeable effects of which will be felt by many future generations, the white man's motive was the protection of his identity; the black man was motivated by the need to establish an identity. And despite the terrorization which the Negro in America endured and endures sporadically until today, despite the cruel and totally inescapable ambivalence of his status in his country, the battle for his identity has long ago been won. He is not a visitor to the West, but a citizen there, an American; as American as the Americans who despise him, the Americans who fear him, the Americans who love him—the Americans who became less than themselves, or rose to be greater than themselves by virtue of the fact that the challenge he represented was inescapable. He is perhaps the only black man in the world whose relationship to white men is more terrible, more subtle, and more meaningful than the relationship of bitter possessed to uncertain possessor. His survival depended, and his development depends, on his ability to turn his peculiar status in the Western world to his own advantage and, it may be, to the very great advantage of that world. It remains for him to fashion out of his experience that which will give him sustenance, and a voice. 23

The cathedral at Chartres, I have said, says something to the people of this village which it cannot say to me; but it is important to understand that this cathedral says something to me which it cannot say to them. Perhaps they are struck by the power of the spires, the glory of the windows; but they have known God, after all, longer than I have known him, and in a different way, and I am terrified by the slippery bottomless well to be found in the crypt, down which heretics were hurled to death, and by the obscene, inescapable gargoyles jutting out of the stone and seeming to say that God and the devil can never be divorced. I doubt that the villagers think of the devil when they face a cathedral because they have never been identified with the devil. But I must accept the status which myth, if nothing else, gives me in the West before I can hope to change the myth. 24

Yet, if the American Negro has arrived at his identity by 25 virtue of the absoluteness of his estrangement from his past, American white men still nourish the illusion that there is some means of recovering the European innocence, of returning to a state in which black men do not exist. This is one of the greatest errors Americans can make. The identity they fought so hard to protect has, by virtue of that battle, undergone a change: Americans are as unlike any other white people in the world as it is possible to be. I do not think, for example, that it is too much to suggest that the American vision of the world—which allows so little reality, generally speaking, for any of the darker forces in human life, which tends until today to paint moral issues in glaring black and white—owes a great deal to the battle waged by Americans to maintain between themselves and black men a human separation which could not be bridged. It is only now beginning to be borne in on us—very faintly, it must be admitted, very slowly, and very much against our will—that this vision of the world is dangerously inaccurate, and perfectly useless. For it protects our moral high-mindedness at the terrible expense of weakening our grasp of reality. People who shut their eyes to reality simply invite their own destruction, and anyone who insists on remaining in a state of innocence long after that innocence is dead turns himself into a monster.

The time has come to realize that the interracial drama acted out on the American continent has not only created a new black man, it has created a new white man, too. No road whatever will lead Americans back to the simplicity of this European village where white men still have the luxury of looking on me as a stranger. I am not, really, a stranger any longer for any American alive. One of the things that distinguishes Americans from other people is that no other people has ever been so deeply involved in the lives of black men, and vice versa. This fact faced, with all its implications, it can be seen that the history of the American Negro problem is not merely shameful, it is also something of an achievement. For even when the worst has been said, it must also be added that the perpetual challenge posed by this problem was always, somehow, perpetually met. It is precisely this black-white experience which may prove of indispensable value to us in the world we face today. This world is white no longer, and it will never be white again. 26

QUESTIONS

1. What connections between Europe, Africa, and America emerge from this essay? What is the relevance of the Swiss village to this frame of reference?

2. In the context of the essay, explain what Baldwin means by his

statement, "People are trapped in history and history is trapped in them" (paragraph 5).

3. Analyze the effect of Baldwin's repetition of "there is" and "there are" constructions in paragraph 2. What does the parallelism at the start of paragraph 8 accomplish? Locate other examples of parallelism in the essay.

4. Analyze the figure of speech "wind" in paragraph 3 and its relation to the rest of the essay.

5. Where in the essay is Baldwin's complex thesis condensed for the reader? What does this placement of thesis reveal about the logical method of development in the essay?

6. How does Baldwin create his introduction? What is the focus? What key motifs does the author present that will inform the rest of the essay? What is the relationship of paragraph 5 to paragraph 6?

7. What paragraphs constitute the second section of the essay? What example serves to unify this section? What major shift in emphasis occurs in the third part of the essay? Explain the cathedral at Chartres as a controlling motif between these two sections.

8. What comparisons and contrasts help to structure and unify the essay?

9. Discuss the paradox implicit in Baldwin's statement in the last paragraph that the American Negro problem is "something of an achievement."

10. a. Write an essay on civilization based on the last sentence in Baldwin's essay.
b. Describe a time when you felt yourself a "stranger" in a certain culture.

WOODY ALLEN

My Speech to the Graduates

Allen Stewart Konigsberg (1935–), legally renamed Heywood Allen and known popularly as Woody Allen, is a comedian, actor, director, and writer for television, film, drama, and such national publications as *Playboy*, *New Yorker*, and *Esquire*. His notable screenplays include *What's New, Pussycat?* (1965), *Bananas* (1970), *Play It Again, Sam* (1972), *Sleeper* (1973), and *Annie Hall* (1977), a film that won the Academy Award, with Allen also taking honors for best director and, with Marshall Brickman, for best original screenplay. Allen's books, filled with the same comic genius as his best films, include *Getting Even* (1971), *Without Feathers* (1975), and *Side Effects* (1980). This essay from his latest collection is a parody of one graduation ritual as well as a satire on present civilization.

More than any other time in history, mankind faces a crossroads. One path leads to despair and utter hopelessness. The other, to total extinction. Let us pray we have the wisdom to choose correctly. I speak, by the way, not with any sense of futility, but with a panicky conviction of the absolute meaninglessness of existence which could easily be misinterpreted as pessimism. It is not. It is merely a healthy concern for the predicament of modern man. (Modern man is here defined as any person born after Nietzche's edict that "God is dead," but before the hit recording "I Wanna Hold Your Hand.") This "predicament" can be stated in one of two ways, though certain linguistic philosophers prefer to reduce it to a mathematical equation where it can be easily solved and even carried around in the wallet. 1

Put in its simplest form, the problem is: How is it possible to find meaning in a finite world given my waist and shirt size? This is a very difficult question when we realize that science has failed us. True, it has conquered many diseases, broken the genetic code, and even placed human beings on the moon, and yet when a man of 80 is left in a room with two 18-year-old cocktail waitresses nothing happens. Because the real problems never change. After all, can the human soul be glimpsed through a microscope? Maybe—but you'd definitely need one of those very good ones with two eyepieces. We know that the most advanced computer in the world does not have a brain as sophisticated as that of an ant. True, we could say that of many of our relatives but we only have to put up with them at weddings or special occasions. Science is something we depend on all the time. If I develop a pain in the chest I must take an X-ray. But what if the radiation from the X-ray causes me deeper problems? Before I know it, I'm in for surgery. Naturally, while they're giving me oxygen an intern decides to light up a cigarette. The next thing you know I'm rocketing over the World Trade Center in bedclothes. Is this science? True, science has taught us how to pasteurize cheese. And true, this can be fun in mixed company—but what of the H-bomb? Have you ever seen what happens when one of those things falls off a desk accidentally? And where is science when one ponders the eternal riddles? How did the cosmos originate? How long has it been around? Did matter begin with an explosion or by the 2 word of God? And if by the latter, could He not have begun it just two weeks earlier to take advantage of some of the warmer weather? Exactly what do we mean when we say man is mortal? Obviously it's not a compliment.

Religion, too, has unfortunately let us down. Miguel de Unamuno writes blithely of the "eternal persistence of consciousness," but that is no easy feat. Particularly when reading Thackeray. I often think how comforting life must have been for early man because he believed in a powerful, benevolent Creator who looked after all things. Imagine his disappointment when he saw his wife putting on weight. Contemporary man, of course, has no such peace of mind. He finds himself in the midst of a crisis of faith. He is what we fashionably call "alienated." He has seen the ravages of war, he has known natural catastrophes, he has been to singles bars. My good friend Jacques Monod spoke often of the randomness of the cosmos. He believed everything in existence occurred by pure chance with the possible exception of his breakfast, which he felt certain was made by his housekeeper. Naturally belief in a divine intelligence inspires tranquillity. But this does not free us from our human responsibilities. Am I my brother's keeper? Yes. Interestingly, in my case I share that honor with the Prospect Park Zoo. Feeling godless then, what we have done is made technology God. And yet can technology really be the answer when a brand new Buick, driven by my close associate, Nat Persky, winds up in the window of Chicken Delight causing hundreds of customers to scatter? My toaster has never once worked properly in four years. I follow the instructions and push two slices of bread down in the slots and seconds later they rifle upward. Once they broke the nose of a woman I loved very dearly. Are we counting on nuts and bolts and electricity to solve our problems? Yes, the telephone is a good thing—and the refrigerator—and the air conditioner. But not every air conditioner. Not my sister Henny's, for instance. Hers makes a loud noise and still doesn't cool. When the man comes over to fix it, it gets worse. Either that or he tells her she needs a new one. When she complains, he says not to bother him. This man is truly alienated. Not only is he alienated but he can't stop smiling. 3

The trouble is, our leaders have not adequately prepared us for a mechanized society. Unfortunately our politicians are either incompetent or corrupt. Sometimes both on the same day. The Government is unresponsive to the needs of the little man. Under five-seven, it is impossible to get your Congressman on the phone. I am not denying that democracy is still the finest form of government. In a democracy at least, civil liberties are upheld. No citizen can be wantonly tortured, imprisoned, or made to sit through certain 4

Broadway shows. And yet this is a far cry from what goes on in the Soviet Union. Under their form of totalitarianism, a person merely caught whistling is sentenced to 30 years in a labor camp. If, after 15 years, he still will not stop whistling they shoot him. Along with this brutal fascism we find its handmaiden, terrorism. At no other time in history has man been so afraid to cut into his veal chop for fear that it will explode. Violence breeds more violence and it is predicted that by 1990 kidnapping will be the dominant mode of social interaction. Overpopulation will exacerbate problems to the breaking point. Figures tell us there are already more people on earth than we need to move even the heaviest piano. If we do not call a halt to breeding, by the year 2000 there will be no room to serve dinner unless one is willing to set the table on the heads of strangers. Then they must not move for an hour while we eat. Of course energy will be in short supply and each car owner will be allowed only enough gasoline to back up a few inches.

Instead of facing these challenges we turn to distractions like 5
drugs and sex. We live in far too permissive a society. Never before has pornography been this rampant. And those films are lit so badly! We are a people who lack defined goals. We have never learned to love. We lack leaders and coherent programs. We have no spiritual center. We are adrift in the cosmos wreaking monstrous violence on one another out of frustration and pain. Fortunately, we have not lost our sense of proportion. Summing up, it is clear the future holds great opportunities. It also holds pitfalls. The trick will be to avoid the pitfalls, seize the opportunities, and get back home by six o'clock.

QUESTIONS

1. Explain the author's comic attitude toward science, religion, and politics. What specific subjects does he ridicule?

2. Beneath the surface of comedy in the essay, we can infer that Allen is concerned with the modern "predicament." Cite examples to support this judgment.

3. What purpose does the author's allusion to Nietzche, Unamuno, and Monod serve?

4. Does the author use understatement or overstatement in his ironic language? Explain by reference to the essay.

5. What is the relationship of the title to the substance of the essay? Does the author in his introduction give any appearance of writing seriously? How does the introduction echo standard speeches to graduates? How does Allen approach such standard speeches?

6. What role does logic, either inductive or deductive, play within the pattern of the essay?

7. In what manner does the pattern of cause and effect heighten the irony in the essay?

8. Examine the substance and structure of Allen's "summing up" in the last paragraph.

9. Does Allen's variety of humor seem too slapstick or strained? Explain.

10. a. Write your own comic speech to the graduates.
b. Satirize one aspect of the modern dilemma.

MARTIN LUTHER KING, JR.

The World House

Martin Luther King, Jr. (1929–1968) was born in Atlanta, Georgia and earned degrees from Morehouse College, Crozer Theological Seminary, Boston University, and Chicago Theological Seminary. As Baptist clergyman, civil rights leader, founder and president of the Southern Christian Leadership Council, and in 1964 Nobel Peace Prize winner, King was a celebrated advocate of nonviolent resistance to achieve equality and racial integration in the world. King was a gifted orator and a highly persuasive writer. His books include *Letter from Birmingham City Jail* (1963), *Why We Can't Wait* (1964), *Stride toward Freedom* (1958), *Strength to Love* (1963), and *Where Do We Go from Here: Chaos or Community?* (1967), a book published shortly before Reverend King was assassinated on April 4, 1968, in Memphis, Tennessee. In "The World House," a section from his last book, King uses analogy to promote his long-standing vision of a peaceful and united world civilization.

Some years ago a famous novelist died. Among his papers was found a list of suggested plots for future stories, the most prominently underscored being this one: "A widely separated family inherits a house in which they have to live together." This is the great new problem of mankind. We have inherited a large house, a great "world house" in which we have to live together—black and white, Easterner and Westerner, Gentile and Jew, Catholic and Protestant, Moslem and 1

Hindu—a family unduly separated in ideas, culture and interest, who, because we can never again live apart, must learn somehow to live with each other in peace.

However deeply American Negroes are caught in the struggle 2
to be at last at home in our homeland of the United States, we cannot ignore the larger world house in which we are also dwellers. Equality with whites will not solve the problems of either whites or Negroes if it means equality in a world society stricken by poverty and in a universe doomed to extinction by war.

All inhabitants of the globe are now neighbors. This world- 3
wide neighborhood has been brought into being largely as a result of the modern scientific and technological revolutions. The world of today is vastly different from the world of just one hundred years ago. A century ago Thomas Edison had not yet invented the incandescent lamp to bring light to many dark places of the earth. The Wright brothers had not yet invented that fascinating mechanical bird that would spread its gigantic wings across the skies and soon dwarf distance and place time in the service of man. Einstein had not yet challenged an axiom and the theory of relatively had not yet been posited.

Human beings, searching a century ago as now for better 4
understanding, had no television, no radios, no telephones and no motion pictures through which to communicate. Medical science had not yet discovered the wonder drugs to end many dread plagues and diseases. One hundred years ago military men had not yet developed the terrifying weapons of warfare that we know today—not the bomber, an airborne fortress raining down death; nor napalm, that burner of all things and flesh in its path. A century ago there were no skyscraping buildings to kiss the stars and no gargantuan bridges to span the waters. Science had not yet peered into the unfathomable ranges of interstellar space, nor had it penetrated oceanic depths. All these new inventions, these new ideas, these sometimes facinating and sometimes frightening developments came later. Most of them have come within the past sixty years, sometimes with agonizing slowness, more characteristically with bewildering speed, but always with enormous significance for our future.

The years ahead will see a continuation of the same dramatic 5
developments. Physical science will carve new highways through the stratosphere. In a few years astronauts and cosmonauts will probably walk comfortably across the uncertain pathways of the moon. In two or three years it will be possible, because of the new supersonic jets, to fly from New York to London in two and one-half hours. In the years ahead medical science will greatly prolong the lives of men by finding a cure for cancer and deadly heart ailments. Automation and cybernation will make it possible for working people to have

undreamed-of amounts of leisure time. All this is a dazzling picture of the furniture, the workshop, the spacious rooms, the new decorations and the architectural pattern of the large world house in which we are living.

Along with the scientific and technological revolution, we 6
have also witnessed a world-wide freedom revolution over the last few decades. The present upsurge of the Negro people of the United States grows out of a deep and passionate determination to make freedom and equality a reality "here" and "now." In one sense the civil rights movement in the United States is a special American phenomenon which must be understood in the light of American history and dealt with in terms of the American situation. But on another and more important level, what is happening in the United States today is a significant part of a world development.

We live in a day, said the philosopher Alfred North White- 7
head, "when civilization is shifting its basic outlook; a major turning point in history where the pre-suppositions on which society is structured are being analyzed, sharply challenged, and profoundly changed." What we are seeing now is a freedom explosion, the realization of "an idea whose time has come," to use Victor Hugo's phrase. The deep rumbling of discontent that we hear today is the thunder of disinherited masses, rising from dungeons of oppression to the bright hills of freedom. In one majestic chorus the rising masses are singing, in the words of our freedom song, "Ain't gonna let nobody turn us around." All over the world like a fever, freedom is spreading in the widest liberation movement in history. The great masses of people are determined to end the exploitation of their races and lands. They are awake and moving toward their goal like a tidal wave. You can hear them rumbling in every village street, on the docks, in the houses, among the students, in the churches and at political meetings. For several centuries the direction of history flowed from the nations and societies of Western Europe out into the rest of the world in "conquests" of various sorts. That period, the era of colonialism, is at an end. East is moving West. The earth is being redistributed. Yes, we are "shifting our basic outlooks."

These developments should not surprise any student of 8
history. Oppressed people cannot remain oppressed forever. The yearning for freedom eventually manifests itself. The Bible tells the thrilling story of how Moses stood in Pharaoh's court centuries ago and cried, "Let my people go." This was an opening chapter in a continuing story. The present struggle in the United States is a later chapter in the same story. Something within has reminded the Negro of his birthright of freedom, and something without has reminded him that it can be gained. Consciously or unconsciously, he has been caught up by the spirit of the times, and with his black brothers of

Africa and his brown and yellow brothers in Asia, South America and the Caribbean, the United States Negro is moving with a sense of great urgency toward the promised land of racial justice.

Nothing could be more tragic than for men to live in these revolutionary times and fail to achieve the new attitudes and the new mental outlooks that the new situation demands. In Washington Irving's familiar story of Rip Van Winkle, the one thing that we usually remember is that Rip slept twenty years. There is another important point, however, that is almost always overlooked. It was the sign on the inn in the little town on the Hudson from which Rip departed and scaled the mountain for his long sleep. When he went up, the sign had a picture of King George III of England. When he came down, twenty years later, the sign had a picture of George Washington. As he looked at the picture of the first President of the United States, Rip was confused, flustered and lost. He knew not who Washington was. The most striking thing about this story is not that Rip slept twenty years, but that he slept through a revolution that would alter the course of human history. 9

One of the great liabilities of history is that all too many people fail to remain awake through great periods of social change. Every society has its protectors of the status quo and its fraternities of the indifferent who are notorious for sleeping through revolutions. But today our very survival depends on our ability to stay awake, to adjust to new ideas, to remain vigilant and to face the challenge of change. The large house in which we live demands that we transform this world-wide neighborhood into a world-wide brotherhood. Together we must learn to live as brothers or together we will be forced to perish as fools. 10

We must work passionately and indefatigably to bridge the gulf between our scientific progress and our moral progress. One of the great problems of mankind is that we suffer from a poverty of the spirit which stands in glaring contrast to our scientific and technological abundance. The richer we have become materially, the poorer we have become morally and spiritually. 11

Every man lives in two realms, the internal and the external. The internal is that realm of spiritual ends expressed in art, literature, morals and religion. The external is that complex of devices, techniques, mechanisms and instrumentalities by means of which we live. Our problem today is that we have allowed the internal to become lost in the external. We have allowed the means by which we live to outdistance the ends for which we live. So much of modern life can be summarized in that suggestive phrase of Thoreau: "Improved means to an unimproved end." This is the serious predicament, the deep and haunting problem, confronting modern man. Enlarged material powers spell enlarged peril if there is not proportionate 12 growth of the soul. When the external of man's nature subjugates the internal, dark storm clouds begin to form.

Western civilization is particularly vulnerable at this moment, for our material abundance has brought us neither peace of mind nor serenity of spirit. An Asian writer has portrayed our dilemma in candid terms: 13

> You call your thousand material devices "labor-saving machinery," yet you are forever "busy." With the multiplying of your machinery you grow increasingly fatigued, anxious, nervous, dissatisfied. Whatever you have, you want more; and wherever you are you want to go somewhere else . . . your devices are neither time-saving nor soul-saving machinery. They are so many sharp spurs which urge you on to invent more machinery and to do more business.[1]

This tells us something about our civilization that cannot be cast aside as a prejudiced charge by an Eastern thinker who is jealous of Western prosperity. We cannot escape the indictment.

This does not mean that we must turn back the clock of scientific progress. No one can overlook the wonders that science has wrought for our lives. The automobile will not abdicate in favor of the horse and buggy, or the train in favor of the stagecoach, or the tractor in favor of the hand plow, or the scientific method in favor of ignorance and superstition. But our moral and spiritual "lag" must be redeemed. When scientific power outruns moral power, we end up with guided missiles and misguided men. When we foolishly minimize the internal of our lives and maximize the external, we sign the warrant for our own day of doom. 14

Our hope for creative living in this world house that we have inherited lies in our ability to re-establish the moral ends of our lives in personal character and social justice. Without this spiritual and moral reawakening we shall destroy ourselves in the misuse of our own instruments. 15

QUESTIONS

1. What does the author mean by the concept of a "world house"? Why is the modern era drawing the peoples of the world together? How does King explain the dangers confronting the world house? What is his proposal for "creative living"?

[1]Abraham Mitrie Rihbany, *Wise Men from the East and from the West,* Houghton, Mifflin, 1922.

2. Explain the connection that King draws between oppression, freedom, and revolution.

3. King, a compelling preacher and speaker (his "I Have a Dream" speech delivered in 1963 at the end of the March on Washington is a contemporary classic), often injected his prose with biblical and oratorical rhythms. Find three examples of rhythmical, carefully balanced cadences in this essay, and explain their effect.

4. A second characteristic of King's oratorical and literary style is his fondness for figurative language. Locate and identify five examples of figurative language.

5. What is King's thesis? How does the key rhetorical strategy of analogy help to advance it? What minor analogies exist in the essay?

6. Describe King's relationship with his reading audience. Identify words and phrases that clarify this relationship. Why, for example, does the author use the pronoun "we"?

7. How do the first and last paragraphs serve as a frame for this selection? How effective are they, and why?

8. What argumentative and persuasive techniques do you detect in this essay? How does King use illustration, comparison, and contrast to advance his proposition?

9. Comment on the relevance of King's analogy to the 1980s.

10. a. Write a paper on "the world house," using contemporary events, quotations from authorities, and your own ideas about today's conflicts to frame the analogy.
b. Using Whitehead's quotation (paragraph 7) as a guide, develop an argumentative essay on whether we are at a turning point in civilization.

ARNOLD TOYNBEE

Why I Dislike Western Civilization

Arnold Joseph Toynbee (1889–1975), noted English historian, posited in his twelve-volume *A Study of History* (1934–1961) a cyclical theory of the development and decline of civilizations that has elicited considerable contemporary controversy. A professor at the London School of Economics from 1925 until the time of his retirement in 1956, Toynbee was a prolific author of studies on history, international relations, contemporary wars, world religions, Western civilization, and travel. This essay reflects his main contention that the proper subject for the study of history is civilization itself.

When I say baldly that I dislike contemporary Western civilization, I am, of course, saying this partly to tease my fellow Westerners. The stand that I take is partly a joke, but it is also partly serious. 1

My dislike of the West, though genuine as far as it goes, cannot really be unmitigated. If it were, I should not feel lost—as I know that I should—if I did not have a *pied-à-terre* in London. I am a Londoner born and bred, but I have not reacted against my native city; and, though I dislike the congestion of the mechanized traffic there, I know that this pest is just as bad in all the other great cities of the postwar world. 2

If I were to be hounded out of London by some (nonexistent) British counterpart of the House Committee on Un-American Activities, I expect I could make myself at home in Edinburgh or Melbourne or Rome or Hamburg or Boston, Mass. (my great-grandfather's farm was in sight of Boston Stump, the tapering tower of St. Botolph's Church in Boston, England). I should not feel at home as a permanent resident in New York or Chicago or Pittsburgh or Glasgow or Manchester or Milan. And I do not suppose that I could strike root in Kyoto or in Damascus or in Istanbul or even in Athens, though I love and admire each of these beautiful non-Western cities. 3

In ancient Greece, the navel of the earth was marked by a monolith at Delphi. The navel of my earth is not in Greece (though my heart and mind reside there). My world-navel is the Albert Memorial in Kensington Gardens. This British monument may be comically ugly but, to me, it is reassuringly familiar. I used to play around its steps when I was a tiny child. Its frieze taught me the names of the great poets, artists and thinkers of the past; the group of figures at the four corners put the four continents on the map for me. 4

Yes, one is a prisoner of one's time and place. I belong to the presyncopation age. Classical Western music is music for my ears. When I hear jazz, I become uneasy and turn hostile. I feel my traditional world being victoriously invaded by tropical Africa. Politically, I am on the side of Africa against the Western colonial powers, but when it comes to music, Africa's cultural colonialism makes me cherish the West's pre-African musical past. 5

To be the prisoner of one's time and place is one of our human limitations. A human being has roots, like a tree, and these 6 roots tether him—though, unlike a tree's roots, they are emotional and intellectual roots. However, it is characteristic of our human nature that we rebel against our human limitations and try to transcend them. I myself, besides being human, happen to be a historian, and a historian's special form of human rebellion is to try to shake himself free of his own parochial blood and soil (to use Hitler's hateful but expressive words). A historian's métier is to move freely through time and space.

What a bore one's own native civilization is. It is dull just 7
because it is familiar. I had the good fortune to be educated in Greek and Latin. This education served me as a magic carpet on which I wafted myself from the twentieth century of the Christian era to the third century B.C., and from the North Atlantic to the Eastern Mediterranean. I hated having to learn the names and dates of the Kings of England. The kings of Israel and Judah were almost as bad, since the Old Testament in the King James version has become virtually part of English literature. But I enjoyed finding my way among the Ptolemies and the Seleucuses. English constitutional history? One glance at the syllabus of the Oxford school of medieval and modern history was enough to put me off reading for that. But the history of Islam, the history of Buddhism—these opened up fascinating new worlds.

Contemporary Western civilization annoys me, not because it 8
is Western, but because it is mine and because I am a historian. If I had happened to be born in 1889 in China instead of England, no doubt I should be annoyed today with the China of Pu Yi and Chiang Kai-shek and Chou En-lai. But being, as I am, a Western historian, I am inevitably annoyed by the contemporary West. It holds me fast entangled in its coils. It prevents me from getting back behind the machine age and from getting out into Russia, Dar-el-Islam, the Hindu world, Eastern Asia. My inescapable Westernness makes it impossible for me to become culturally acclimatized in any of these other contemporary civilizations. This is a limitation on my human freedom that I resent.

However, I have a more formidable reason for disliking the 9
West than any that I have mentioned so far. Since I have been grown-up (I am now turned 75), the West has produced two world wars; it has produced Communism, Fascism and National Socialism; it has produced Mussolini and Hitler and McCarthy. These Western enormities make me, as a Westerner, feel insecure. Now that my German fellow-Westerners have murdered six million Jews, how can I be certain that my English fellow-countrymen might not do something equally criminal? We did murder some thousands of defenseless civilians at Port Said in 1956. What might we not go on to do after

that? What might I not be capable of doing myself, if this contemporary Western criminal lunacy were to waylay me?

I shiver and shake. Old-fashioned Christian humility, please come to my rescue. Please save me from contemporary post-Christian Western self-complacent sinfulness. I should feel my spirits rise if, instead of being Hitler's fellow-Westerner—as I am—I could be Gandhi's fellow-Hindu. Yes, I believe I could even stomach Benares as the price of being liberated from Hitler's company. But I cannot escape Hitler. This fellow-Westerner of mine (of the same age to within a week) is going to haunt me for the rest of my West-bound life. 10

Apart from contemporary Western crimes, there are other blemishes on contemporary Western life that I find repulsive. Though I dislike the former enslavement of the individual to the community in Japan, I also dislike, and this perhaps even more, the lengths to which contemporary Western individualism has gone. The contemporary West is callous toward the aged. This is, I believe, the first civilization, so far, in which the aged have not had a place, as a matter of course, in their adult children's homes. Looking at this Western callousness with de-Westernized eyes, I find it shocking. 11

I also dislike the contemporary Western advertising business. It has made a fine art out of taking advantage of human silliness. It rams unwanted material goods down surfeited throats when two-thirds of all human beings now alive are in desperate need of the bare necessities of life. This is an ugly aspect of the affluent society; and, if I am told that advertising is the price of affluence, I reply without hesitation, that affluence has been bought too dear. Another item in the price of affluence is the standardization of mass-produced goods and services. This is, in itself, a deplorable impoverishment of the material side of human culture, and it brings spiritual standardization with it, which is still worse. 12

Looking back into the past history of the West—a past which was still present when I was a child—I admire the nineteenth-century West's success in postponing the age of sexual awakening, of sexual experience and sexual infatuation far beyond the age of physical puberty. You may tell me that this was against nature; but to be human consists precisely in transcending nature—in overcoming the biological limitations that we have inherited from our prehuman ancestors. 13

All human societies overcome death by creating and maintaining institutions that are handed on from one generation to another. Sex is a still more awkward feature of our biological inheritance than death, and our nineteenth-century Western society handled sex with relative success. By postponing the age of sexual awakening, it prolonged the length of the period of education. It is 14 this, together with the seventeenth-century Western achievement of learning to think for oneself instead of taking tradition on trust, that accounts for the West's preeminence in the world during the last few centuries.

Nineteenth-century Westerners condemned with justice the 15
Hindu institution of child-marriage, and they deplored, also with justice, the spectacle of an intellectually promising Moslem boy being allowed to commit intellectual suicide by sexual indulgence at the age of puberty. The twentieth-century West is now imitating the non-Western habits that the nineteenth-century West rightly—though perhaps self-righteously—condemned.

Our irrational contemporary Western impatience and our 16
blind adulation of speed for speed's sake are making havoc, today, of the education of our children. We force their growth as if they were chicks in a pullet factory. We drive them into a premature awareness of sex even before physical puberty has overtaken them. In fact, we deprive our children of the human right of having a childhood. This forcing of sex-consciousness started in the United States; it has spread to Britain, and who knows how many other Western countries this perverse system of miseducation is going to invade and demoralize?

Our whole present policy in the upbringing of the young is 17
paradoxical. While we are lowering the age of sexual awareness—and frequently the age of sexual experience, too—to a veritably Hindu degree, we are at the same time prolonging the length of education. We force our boys and girls to become sex-conscious at twelve or thirteen, and then we ask them to prolong their postgraduate studies till they are nearly thirty. How are they to be expected to give their minds to education during those last sixteen or seventeen sex-haunted years?

We are proud of ourselves for providing secondary educa- 18
tion, college education, postgraduate education for everybody. But we shall be plowing the sands if we do not simultaneously revert to our grandparents' practice of prolonging the age of sexual innocence. If we persist, in this vital matter, on our present Hindu course, our brand-new would-be institutions for higher education will become, in practice, little more than social clubs for sexual mating.

This relapse into precocious sexuality is one of the moral 19
blemishes of the contemporary Western civilization. One of its intellectual blemishes is its insistence on splitting up the universe into smaller and smaller splinters. It has split up the human race into a host of sovereign independent national states. It has split up knowledge and understanding into a host of separate watertight "disciplines." I dislike nationalism and I dislike specialization, and both are characteristically Western aberrations.

When I was about sixteen years old, I stayed with an uncle 20 who was a specialist on Dante, while his wife was a specialist on Horace Walpole. Their library was less specialized than they themselves were, and I browsed in it with excitement and delight. When I was due to leave, my uncle said to me: "Arnold, your aunt and I think you are allowing your interest to be too general. You ought to specialize." I said nothing, but I was instantaneously certain that I was not going to follow this advice; and, in fact, I have consistently done the opposite throughout the sixty years that have passed since then.

What a world to find oneself born into. Since as early as I first 21
became conscious of my native Western environment, Western technology has been inventing new and ever more complicated machines. I did learn to ride a bicycle. How can one be expected, in just one lifetime, to go on to learn to ride a motorcycle or to drive a car? I started shaving in the age of the cutthroat razor, and Mr. Gillette's invention came as a great relief to me. But how can I be expected to go on to use an electric razor? How could I know about volts and ohms and transformers? An American friend did give me an electric razor. This lies safely tucked away in a drawer, and whenever I unearth it, it alarms me.

I do now travel about the world in cars and airplanes. The 22
better these get at covering the distance, the worse they get at allowing an inquisitive passenger to see the view. I did my first traveling in Greece in 1911–12. I did it on foot with a rucksack on my back. I was as free as a bird. I could go where even mules could not go. I could see the world as I pleased. I have never traveled so satisfactorily as that since then.

The other day, I had a three-hour mule ride from an airstrip 23
to the rock-cut churches at Lalibela in Ethiopia. Once again I was seeing the real world, the unmechanized pre-Western world in which I feel truly at home. Machinery perplexes and dismays me, and I have been born into the Western machine age. Why was I not born in the third-century-B.C. Syria or seventh-century-A.D. China? I should not then have been harassed by machinery as I am in the contemporary West. I heartily dislike this side of contemporary Western life, and, in the eyes of the rest of the world, mechanization is what the contemporary West stands for.

Well, these are some of the reasons why I dislike the 24
contemporary Western civilization. But, as I have said at the beginning of this article, my dislike is not undiluted. My grandchildren, after all, are Westerners, and I certainly like them. Moreover, I want them, in their turn, to have grandchildren who will have grandchildren. I should be desolated if I believed that Western man was going to commit mass suicide by engaging in a third world war that, this time, would be fought with atomic weapons.

To discover the existence of the atom and to go on to discover how to split it has been the *chef d'oeuvre* of Western science and technology. I do not love Western science for having made these deadly inventions; but I have just enough faith in Western man's political commonsense to expect that he will not liquidate himself. So perhaps, after all, I do not rate my native Western civilization so low as I fancy that I do in my moments of acute exasperation at the West's more uncongenial vagaries. 25

QUESTIONS

1. List the reasons Toynbee dislikes Western civilization.

2. What are some of the features of non-Western civilization that appeal to Toynbee?

3. Identify the allusions in paragraphs 7 to 9. Why is the broad range of allusion throughout the essay an important aspect of Toynbee's subject and thesis?

4. Explain the following figures of speech: "world-navel" (paragraph 4); "A human being has roots, like a tree . . ." (paragraph 6); "This education served me as a magic carpet . . ." (paragraph 7); "It holds me fast entangled in its coils" (paragraph 8); "spiritual standardization" (paragraph 12); "to commit intellectual suicide by sexual indulgence . . ." (paragraph 15); ". . . the *chef d'oeuvre* of Western science and technology" (paragraph 25).

5. Analyze the way in which Toynbee moves from a defense of Western civilization to a preliminary criticism of it in paragraphs 1 to 8.

6. Examine the validity and authenticity of the premises upon which Toynbee bases his argument. What supporting evidence does he offer for his assumptions?

7. How does the essay employ the comparative method?

8. How does Toynbee inject appeals to emotion into the essay? What is the effect of this strategy on tone?

9. Toynbee writes that "it is characteristic of our human nature that we rebel against our human limitations and try to transcend them" (paragraph 6). How does this relate to his argument? Do you agree or disagree with his assertion? Explain.

10. a. Write an essay explaining why you like or dislike Western civilization.
b. Write an essay explaining why you like or dislike American civilization.

The Lessons of the Past

Edith Hamilton (1867–1963), teacher, writer, and Grecophile, wrote her first book when she was 63. Her initial career was as headmistress of a private girl's school in Maryland. When she retired, she began to write about ancient civilizations, particularly Greek civilization. In 1930, *The Greek Way* was published. In later years, Hamilton also wrote *The Roman Way* (1932) and *The Prophets of Israel* (1936). She retold Greek, Roman, and Norse myths in *Mythology* (1942). At the age of 90, Hamilton visited Greece and was made an honorary citizen. This essay focuses on Greek civilization in order to illuminate the problems confronting the modern era.

1 Is there an ever-present past? Are there permanent truths which are forever important for the present? Today we are facing a future more strange and untried than any other generation has faced. The new world Columbus opened seems small indeed beside the illimitable distances of space before us, and the possibilities of destruction are immeasurably greater than ever. In such a position can we afford to spend time on the past? That is the question I am often asked. Am I urging the study of the Greeks and Romans and their civilizations for the atomic age?

2 Yes; that is just what I am doing. I urge it without qualifications. We have a great civilization to save—or to lose. The greatest civilization before ours was the Greek. They challenge us and we need the challenge. They, too, lived in a dangerous world. They were a little, highly civilized people, the only civilized people in the west, surrounded by barbarous tribes and with the greatest Asiatic power, Persia, always threatening them. In the end they succumbed, but the reason they did was not that the enemies outside were so strong, but that their own strength, their spiritual strength, had given way. While they had it they kept Greece unconquered and they left behind a record in art and thought which in all the centuries of human effort since has not been surpassed.

3 The point which I want to make is not that their taste was superior to ours, not that the Parthenon was their idea of church architecture nor that Sophocles was the great drawing card in the theaters, nor any of the familiar comparisons between fifth-century Athens and twentieth-century America, but that Socrates found on every street corner and in every Athenian equivalent of the baseball field people who were caught up by his questions into the world of

thought. To be able to be caught up into the world of thought—that is to be educated.

How is that great aim to be reached? For years we have eagerly discussed ways and means of education, and the discussion still goes on. William James once said that there were two subjects which if mentioned made other conversation stop and directed all eyes to the speaker. Religion was one and education the other. Today Russia seems to come first, but education is still emphatically the second. In spite of all the articles we read and all the speeches we listen to about it, we want to know more; we feel deeply its importance. 4

There is today a clearly visible trend toward making it the aim of education to defeat the Russians. That would be a sure way to defeat education. Genuine education is possible only when people realize that it has to do with persons, not with movements. 5

When I read educational articles it often seems to me that this important side of the matter, the purely personal side, is not emphasized enough; that fact that it is so much more agreeable and interesting to be an educated person than not. The sheer pleasure of being educated does not seem to be stressed. Once long ago I was talking with Prof. Basil L. Gildersleeve of Johns Hopkins University, the greatest Greek scholar our country has produced. He was an old man and he had been honored everywhere, in Europe as well as in America. He was just back from a celebration held for him in Oxford. I asked him what compliment received in his long life had pleased him most. The question amused him and he laughed over it, but he thought too. Finally he said, "I believe it was when one of my students said, 'Professor, you have so much fun with your own mind.'" Robert Louis Stevenson said that a man ought to be able to spend two or three hours waiting for a train at a little country station when he was all alone and had nothing to read, and not be bored for a moment. 6

What is the education which can do this? What is the furniture which makes the only place belonging absolutely to each one of us, the world within, a place where we like to go? I wish I could answer that question. I wish I could produce a perfect decorator's design warranted to make any interior lovely and interesting and stimulating; but, even if I could, sooner or later we would certainly try different designs. My point is only that while we must and should change the furniture, we ought to throw away old furniture very cautiously. It may turn out to be irreplaceable. A great deal was thrown away in the last generation or so, long enough ago to show some of the results. Furniture which had for centuries been foremost, we lightly, in a few years, discarded. The classics almost vanished from our field of education. That was a great change. Along with it 7 came another. There is a marked difference between the writers of the past and the writers of today who have been educated without benefit of Greek and Latin. Is this a matter of cause and effect? People will decide for themselves, but I do not think anyone will question the statement that clear thinking is not the characteristic which distinguishes our literature today. We are more and more caught up by the unintelligible. People like it. This argues an inability to think, or, almost as bad, a disinclination to think.

Neither disposition marked the Greeks. They had a passion 8
for thinking things out, and they loved unclouded clarity of statement as well as of thought. The Romans did, too, in their degree. They were able to put an idea into an astonishingly small number of words without losing a particle of intelligibility. It is only of late, with a generation which has never had to deal with a Latin sentence, that we are being submerged in a flood of words, words, words. It has been said that Lincoln at Gettysburg today would have begun in some such fashion as this: "Eight and seven-tenths decades ago the pioneer workers in this continental area implemented a new group based on an ideology of free boundaries and initial equality," and might easily have ended, "That political supervision of the integrated units, for the integrated units, by the integrated units, shall not become null and void on the superficial area of this planet." Along with the banishment of the classics, gobbledegook has come upon us—and the appalling size of the Congressional Record, and the overburdened mail service.

Just what the teaching in the schools was which laid the 9
foundation of the Greek civilization we do not know in detail; the result we do know. Greek children were taught, Plato said, to "love what is beautiful and hate what is ugly." When they grew up their very pots and pans had to be pleasant to look at. It was part of their training to hate clumsiness and awkwardness; they loved grace and practiced it. "Our children," Plato said, "will be influenced for good by every sight and sound of beauty, breathing in, as it were, a pure breeze blowing to them from a good land."

All the same, the Athenians were not, as they showed 10
Socrates when he talked to them, preoccupied with enjoying lovely things. The children were taught to think. Plato demanded a stiff examination, especially in mathematics, for entrance to his Academy. The Athenians were a thinking people. Today the scientists are bearing away the prize for thought. Well, a Greek said that the earth went around the sun, sixteen centuries before Copernicus thought of it. A Greek said if you sailed out of Spain and kept to one latitude, you would come at last to land, seventeen hundred years before Columbus did it. Darwin said, "We are mere schoolboys in scientific thinking compared to old Aristotle." And the Greeks did not have a

great legacy from the past as our scientists have; they thought science out from the beginning.

The same is true of politics. They thought that out, too, from the beginning, and they gave all the boys a training to fit them to be thinking citizens of a free state that had come into being through thought. 11

Basic to all the Greek achievement was freedom. The Athenians were the only free people in the world. In the great empires of antiquity—Egypt, Babylon, Assyria, Persia—splendid though they were, with riches beyond reckoning and immense power, freedom was unknown. The idea of it never dawned in any of them. It was born in Greece, a poor little country, but with it able to remain unconquered no matter what manpower and what wealth were arrayed against her. At Marathon and at Salamis overwhelming numbers of Persians had been defeated by small Greek forces. It has been proved that one free man was superior to many submissively obedient subjects of a tyrant. Athens was the leader in that amazing victory, and to the Athenians freedom was their dearest possession. Demosthenes said that they would not think it worth their while to live if they could not do so as free men, and years later a great teacher said, "Athenians, if you deprive them of their liberty, will die." 12

Athens was not only the first democracy in the world, it was also at its height an almost perfect democracy—that is, for men. There was no part in it for women or foreigners or slaves, but as far as the men were concerned it was more democratic than we are. The governing body was the Assembly, of which all citizens over eighteen were members. The Council of Five Hundred which prepared business for the Assembly and, if requested, carried out what had been decided there, was made up of citizens who were chosen by lot. The same was true of the juries. Minor officials also were chosen by lot. The chief magistrates and the highest officers in the army were elected by the Assembly. Pericles was a general, very popular, who acted for a long time as if he were head of the state, but he had to be elected every year. Freedom of speech was the right the Athenians prized most and there has never been another state as free in that respect. When toward the end of the terrible Peloponnesian War the victorious Spartans were advancing upon Athens, Aristophanes caricatured in the theater the leading Athenian generals and showed them up as cowards, and even then as the Assembly opened, the herald asked, "Does anyone wish to speak?" 13

There was complete political equality. It was a government of the people, by the people, for the people. An unregenerate old aristocrat in the early fourth century, B.C., writes: "If you *must* have a democracy, Athens is the perfect example. I object to it because it is based on the welfare of the lower, not the better, classes. In Athens 14 the people who row the vessels and do the work have the advantage. It is their prosperity that is important." All the same, making the city beautiful was important too, as were also the great performances in the theater. If, as Plato says, the Assembly was chiefly made up of cobblers and carpenters and smiths and farmers and retail-business men, they approved the construction of the Parthenon and the other buildings on the Acropolis, and they crowded the theater when the great tragedies were played. Not only did all free men share in the government; the love of the beautiful and the desire to have a part in creating it were shared by the many, not by a mere chosen few. That has happened in no state except Athens.

But those free Greeks owned slaves. What kind of freedom 15
was that? The question would have been incomprehensible to the ancient world. There had always been slaves; they were a first necessity. The way of life everywhere was based upon them. They were taken for granted; no one ever gave them a thought. The very best Greek minds, the thinkers who discovered freedom and the solar system, had never an idea that slavery was evil. It is true that the greatest thinker of them all, Plato, was made uncomfortable by it. He said that slaves were often good, trustworthy, doing more for a man than his own family would, but he did not follow his thought through. The glory of being the first one to condemn it belongs to a man of the generation before Plato, the poet Euripides. He called it, "That thing of evil," and in several of his tragedies showed its evil for all to see. A few centuries later the great Greek school of the Stoics denounced it. Greece first saw it for what it is. But the world went on in the same way. The Bible accepts it without comment. Two thousand years after the Stoics, less than a hundred years ago, the American Republic accepted it.

Athens treated her slaves well. A visitor to the city in the 16
early fourth century, B.C., wrote: "It is illegal here to deal a slave a blow. In the street he won't step aside to let you pass. Indeed you can't tell a slave by his dress; he looks like all the rest. They can go to the theater too. Really, the Athenians have established a kind of equality between slaves and free men." They were never a possible source of danger to the state as they were in Rome. There were no terrible slave wars and uprisings in Athens. In Rome, crucifixion was called "the slave's punishment." The Athenians did not practice crucifixion, and had no so-called slave's punishment. They were not afraid of their slaves.

In Athens' great prime Athenians were free. No one told 17
them what they must do or what they should think—no church or political party or powerful private interests or labor unions. Greek schools had no donors of endowments they must pay attention to, no

government financial backing which must be made secure by acting as the government wanted. To be sure, the result was that they had to take full responsibility, but that is always the price for full freedom. The Athenians were a strong people, they could pay the price. They were a thinking people; they knew what freedom means. They knew—not that they were free because their country was free, but that their country was free because they were free.

A reflective Roman traveling in Greece in the second century 18
A.D. said, "None ever throve under democracy save the Athenians; *they* had sane self-control and were law-abiding." He spoke truly. That is what Athenian education aimed at, to produce men who would be able to maintain a self-governed state because they were themselves self-governed, self-controlled, self-reliant. Plato speaks of "the education in excellence which makes men long to be perfect citizens, knowing both how to rule and be ruled." "We are a free democracy," Pericles said. "We do not allow absorption in our own affairs to interfere with participation in the city's; we yield to none in independence of spirit and complete self-reliance, but we regard him who holds aloof from public affairs as useless." They called the useless man a "private" citizen, *idiotes,* from which our word "idiot" comes.

They had risen to freedom and to ennoblement from what 19
Gilbert Murray calls "effortless barbarism"; they saw it all around them; they hated its filth and fierceness; nothing effortless was among the good things they wanted. Plato said, "Hard is the good," and a poet hundreds of years before Plato said,

> Before the gates of Excellence the high gods have placed sweat.
> Long is the road thereto and steep and rough at the first,
> But when the height is won, then is there ease.

When or why the Greeks set themselves to travel on that road 20
we do not know, but it led them away from habits and customs accepted everywhere that kept men down to barbaric filth and fierceness. It led them far. One example is enough to show the way they took. It was the custom—during how many millenniums, who can say?—for a victor to erect a trophy, a monument of his victory. In Egypt, where stone was plentiful, it would be a slab engraved with his glories. Farther east, where the sand took over, it might be a great heap of severed heads, quite permanent objects; bones last a long time. But in Greece, though a man could erect a trophy, it must be made of wood and it could never be repaired. Even as the victor set it up he would see in his mind how soon it would decay and sink into

ruin, and there it must be left. The Greeks in their onward pressing along the steep and rough road had learned a great deal. They knew the victor might be the vanquished next time. There should be no permanent records of the manifestly impermanent. They had learned a great deal.

An old Greek inscription states that the aim of mankind should be "to tame the savageness of man and make gentle the life of the world." Aristotle said that the city was built first for safety, but then that men might discover the good life and lead it. So the Athenians did according to Pericles. Pericles said that Athens stood for freedom and for thought and for beauty, but in the Greek way, within limits, without exaggeration. The Athenians loved beauty, he said, but with simplicity; they did not like the extravagances of luxury. They loved the things of the mind, but they did not shrink from hardship. Thought did not cause them to hesitate, it clarified the road to action. If they had riches they did not make a show of them, and no one was ashamed of being poor if he was useful. They were free because of willing obedience to law, not only the written, but still more the unwritten, kindness and compassion and unselfishness and the many qualities which cannot be enforced, which depend on a man's free choice, but without which men cannot live together. 21

If ever there is to be a truly good and great and enduring republic it must be along these lines. We need the challenge of the city that thought them out, wherein for centuries one genius after another grew up. Geniuses are not produced by spending money. We need the challenge of the way the Greeks were educated. They fixed their eyes on the individual. We contemplate millions. What we have undertaken in this matter of education has dawned upon us only lately. We are trying to do what has never been attempted before, never in the history of the world—educate all the young in a nation of 170 millions; a magnificent idea, but we are beginning to realize what are the problems and what may be the results of mass production of education. So far, we do not seem appalled at the prospect of exactly the same kind of education being applied to all the school children from the Atlantic to the Pacific, but there is an uneasiness in the air, a realization that the individual is growing less easy to find; an idea, perhaps, of what standardization might become when the units are not machines, but human beings. 22

Here is where we can go back to the Greeks with profit. The Athenians in their dangerous world needed to be a nation of independent men who could take responsibility, and they taught their children accordingly. They thought about every boy. Someday he would be a citizen of Athens, responsible for her safety and her glory, "each one," Pericles said, "fitted to meet life's chances and 23 changes with the utmost versatility and grace." To them education was by its very nature an individual matter. To be properly educated a boy had to be taught music; he learned to play a musical instrument. He had to learn poetry, a great deal of it, and recite it—and there were a number of musical instruments and many poets; though, to be sure, Homer was the great textbook.

That kind of education is not geared to mass production. It does not produce people who instinctively go the same way. That is how Athenian children lived and learned while our millions learn the same lessons and spend hours before television sets looking at exactly the same thing at exactly the same time. For one reason and another we are more and more ignoring differences, if not trying to obliterate them. We seem headed toward a standardization of the mind, what Goethe called "the deadly commonplace that fetters us all." That was not the Greek way. 24

The picture of the Age of Pericles drawn by the historian Thucydides, one of the greatest historians the world has known, is of a state made up of people who are self-reliant individuals, not echoes or copies, who want to be let alone to do their own work, but who are also closely bound together by a great aim, the commonweal, each one so in love with his country—Pericles' own words—that he wants most of all to use himself in her service. Only an ideal? Ideals have enormous power. They stamp an age. They lift life up when they are lofty, they drag down and make decadent when they are low—and then, by that strange fact, the survival of the fittest, those that are low fade away and are forgotten. The Greek ideals have had a power of persistent life for twenty-five hundred years. 25

Is it rational that now when the young people may have to face problems harder than we face, is it reasonable that with the atomic age before them, at this time we are giving up the study of how the Greeks and Romans prevailed magnificently in a barbaric world; the study, too, of how that triumph ended, how a slackness and softness finally came over them to their ruin? In the end, more than they wanted freedom, they wanted security, a comfortable life, and they lost all—security and comfort and freedom. 26

Is not that a challenge to us? Is it not true that into our education have come a slackness and softness? Is hard effort prominent? The world of thought can be entered in no other way. Are we not growing slack and soft in our political life? When the Athenians finally wanted not to give to the state, but the state to give to them, when the freedom they wished most for was freedom from responsibility, then Athens ceased to be free and was never free again. Is not that a challenge? 27

Cicero said, "To be ignorant of the past is to remain a child." 28

Santayana said, "A nation that does not know history is fated to repeat it." The Greeks can help us, help us as no other people can, to see how freedom is won and how it is lost. Above all, to see in clearest light what freedom is. The first nation in the world to be free sends a ringing call down through the centuries to all who would be free. Greece rose to the very height, not because she was big, she was very small; not because she was rich, she was very poor; not even because she was wonderfully gifted. So doubtless were others in the great empires of the ancient world who have gone their way leaving little for us. She rose because there was in the Greeks the greatest spirit that moves in humanity, the spirit that sets men free.

Plato put into words what that spirit is. "Freedom" he says, "is no matter of laws and constitutions; only he is free who realizes the divine order within himself, the true standard by which a man can steer and measure himself." True standards, ideals that lift life up, marked the way of the Greeks. Therefore their light has never been extinguished. 29

"The time for extracting a lesson from history is ever at hand for them who are wise." Demosthenes. 30

QUESTIONS

1. According to Hamilton, what is the relationship between Greek civilization and the quality of American education?

2. How does the author seek to justify Greek democracy, even though, as she admits, slaves, women, and foreigners were not free or equal?

3. Explain the analogy in paragraph 7.

4. Analyze the elements of style in paragraph 28.

5. What is the author's thesis? How does the first paragraph prepare for it?

6. How does the author order her main topics in the essay?

7. What causal patterns of development appear in the essay? Where is comparison and contrast used as a rhetorical strategy? How does she use rhetorical questions as an argumentative tactic?

8. Explain the significance of definition as a pattern of development in Hamilton's essay.

9. Speaking of the Greeks, Hamilton writes: "In the end, more than they wanted freedom, they wanted security, a comfortable life, and they lost it all—security and comfort and freedom" (paragraph 26). What is the relevance of Hamilton's observation to the state of modern American

civilization? In this connection, do you believe that there is an ever-present past? Explain.

10. a. Write an essay on the lessons that modern nations can learn from the past.
b. Define freedom in terms of the American experience.
c. Analyze freedom in the modern world.

MARGARET MEAD

One Vote for This Age of Anxiety

Margaret Mead (1901–1979), famed American anthropologist, was curator of ethnology at the American Museum of Natural History and a professor at Columbia University. Her field expeditions to Samoa, New Guinea, and Bali in the 1920s and 1930s produced several major studies, notably *Coming of Age in Samoa* (1928), *Growing Up in New Guinea* (1930), and *Sex and Temperament in Three Primitive Societies* (1935). Her interest in contemporary society is evident in this essay.

When critics wish to repudiate the world in which we live 1
today, one of their familiar ways of doing it is to castigate modern man because anxiety is his chief problem. This, they say, in W. H. Auden's phrase, is the age of anxiety. That is what we have arrived at with all our vaunted progress, our great technological advances, our great wealth—everyone goes about with a burden of anxiety so enormous that, in the end, our stomachs and our arteries and our skins express the tension under which we live. Americans who have lived in Europe come back to comment on our favorite farewell which, instead of the old goodbye (God be with you), is now "Take it easy," each American admonishing the other not to break down from the tension and strain of modern life.

Whenever an age is characterized by a phrase, it is presum- 2
ably in contrast to other ages. If we are the age of anxiety, what were the other ages? And here the critics and carpers do a very amusing thing. First, they give us lists of the opposites of anxiety: security, trust, self-confidence, self-direction. Then, without much further discussion, they let us assume that other ages, other periods of history, were somehow the ages of trust or confident direction.

The savage who, on his South Sea island, simply sat and let breadfruit fall into his lap, the simple peasant, at one with the fields he ploughed and the beasts he tended, the craftsman busy with his tools and lost in the fulfillment of the instinct of workmanship—these are the counter-images conjured up by descriptions of the strain under which men live today. But no one who lived in those days has returned to testify how paradisiacal they really were. 3

Certainly if we observe and question the savages or simple peasants in the world today, we find something quite different. The untouched savage in the middle of New Guinea isn't anxious; he is seriously and continually *frightened*—of black magic, of enemies with spears who may kill him or his wives and children at any moment, while they stoop to drink from a spring, or climb a palm tree for a coconut. He goes warily, day and night, taut and fearful. 4

As for the peasant populations of a great part of the world, they aren't so much anxious as hungry. They aren't anxious about whether they will get a salary raise, or which of the three colleges of their choice they will be admitted to, or whether to buy a Ford or Cadillac, or whether the kind of TV set they want is too expensive. They are hungry, cold and, in many parts of the world, they dread that local warfare, bandits, political coups may endanger their homes, their meager livelihoods and their lives. But surely they are not anxious. 5

For anxiety, as we have come to use it to describe our characteristic state of mind, can be contrasted with the active fear of hunger, loss, violence and death. Anxiety is the appropriate emotion when the immediate personal terror—of a volcano, an arrow, the sorcerer's spell, a stab in the back and other calamities, all directed against one's self—disappears. 6

This is not to say that there isn't plenty to worry about in our world of today. The explosion of a bomb in the streets of a city whose name no one had ever heard before may set in motion forces which end up by ruining one's carefully planned education in law school, half a world away. But there is still not the personal, immediate, active sense of impending disaster that the savage knows. There is rather the vague anxiety, the sense that the future is unmanageable. 7

The kind of world that produces anxiety is actually a world of relative safety, a world in which no one feels that he himself is facing sudden death. Possibly sudden death may strike a certain number of unidentified other people—but not him. The anxiety exists as an uneasy state of mind, in which one has a feeling that something unspecified and undeterminable may go wrong. If the world seems to be going well, this produces anxiety—for good times may end. If the world is going badly—it may get worse. Anxiety tends to be without 8 locus; the anxious person doesn't know whether to blame himself or other people. He isn't sure whether it is the current year or the Administration or a change in climate or the atom bomb that is to blame for this undefined sense of unease.

It is clear that we have developed a society which depends on having the *right* amount of anxiety to make it work. Psychiatrists have been heard to say, "He didn't have enough anxiety to get well," indicating that, while we agree that too much anxiety is inimical to mental health, we have come to rely on anxiety to push and prod us into seeing a doctor about a symptom which may indicate cancer, into checking up on that old life-insurance policy which may have out-of-date clauses in it, into having a conference with Billy's teacher even though his report card looks all right. 9

People who are anxious enough keep their car insurance up, have the brakes checked, don't take a second drink when they have to drive, are careful where they go and with whom they drive on holidays. People who are too anxious either refuse to go into cars at all—and so complicate the ordinary course of life—or drive so tensely and overcautiously that they help cause accidents. People who aren't anxious enough take chance after chance, which increases the terrible death toll of the roads. 10

On balance, our age of anxiety represents a large advance over savage and peasant cultures. Out of a productive system of technology drawing upon enormous resources, we have created a nation in which anxiety has replaced terror and despair, for all except the severely disturbed. The specter of hunger means something only to those Americans who can identify themselves with the millions of hungry people on other continents. The specter of terror may still be roused in some by a knock at the door in a few parts of the South, or in those who have just escaped from a totalitarian regime or who have kin still behind the Curtains. 11

But in this twilight world which is neither at peace nor at war, and where there is insurance against certain immediate, downright, personal disasters, for most Americans there remains only anxiety over what may happen, might happen, could happen. 12

This is the world out of which grows the hope, for the first time in history, of a society where there will be freedom from want and freedom from fear. Our very anxiety is born of our knowledge of what is now possible for each and for all. The number of people who consult psychiatrists today is not, as is sometimes felt, a symptom of increasing mental ill health, but rather the precursor of a world in which the hope of genuine mental health will be open to everyone, a world in which no individual feels that he need be hopelessly brokenhearted, a failure, a menace to others or a traitor to himself. 13

But if, then, our anxieties are actually signs of hope, why is there such a voice of discontent abroad in the land? I think this comes perhaps because our anxiety exists without an accompanying recognition of the tragedy which will always be inherent in human life, however well we build our world. We may banish hunger, and fear of sorcery, violence or secret police; we may bring up children who have learned to trust life and who have the spontaneity and curiosity necessary to devise ways of making trips to the moon; we cannot—as we have tried to do—banish death itself. 14

Americans who stem from generations which left their old people behind and never closed their parents' eyelids in death, and who have experienced the additional distance from death provided by two world wars fought far from our shores are today pushing away from them both a recognition of death and a recognition of the tremendous significance—for the future—of the way we live our lives. Acceptance of the inevitability of death, which, when faced, can give dignity to life, and acceptance of our inescapable role in the modern world, might transmute our anxiety about making the right choices, taking the right precautions, and the right risks into the sterner stuff of responsibility, which ennobles the whole face rather than furrowing the forehead with the little anxious wrinkles of worry. 15

Worry in an empty context means that men die daily little deaths. But good anxiety—not about the things that were left undone long ago, but which return to haunt and harry men's minds, but active, vivid anxiety about what must be done and that quickly—binds men to life with an intense concern. 16

This is still a world in which too many of the wrong things happen somewhere. But this is a world in which we now have the means to make a great many more of the right things happen everywhere. For Americans, the generalization which a Swedish social scientist made about our attitudes on race relations is true in many other fields: anticipated change which we feel is right and necessary but difficult makes us unduly anxious and apprehensive, but such change, once consummated, brings a glow of relief. We are still a people who—in the literal sense—believe in making good. 17

QUESTIONS

1. What varieties of anxiety does Mead discuss in this essay? What distinguishes healthy anxiety from unhealthy anxiety? What are the causes of modern anxiety? Why does she give her vote to this age of anxiety?

2. What is Mead's vision of America and the world?

3. Analyze the parallelism in paragraphs 1, 10, and 14.

4. Discuss the connotations Mead develops for the core word "anxiety."

5. What is the function of Mead's opening paragraph?

6. Explain the purpose behind the author's use of contrast in paragraphs 3 to 6.

7. Examine the author's use of such conventional rhetorical techniques as illustration, definition, and causal analysis in the essay.

8. What pattern of logic does Mead employ in arriving at her conclusion? What are the stages in this pattern?

9. Mead wrote this essay in 1965. Are her observations still relevant? Explain. Are there new sources of anxiety today, and if so, what are the causes? Reread Woody Allen's essay in light of Mead's thesis on anxiety. How does anxiety work itself out in the world portrayed by Allen?

10. a. Write your own essay for or against this age of anxiety.
b. Analyze the cultural causes of anxiety in your own life.

HENRY ADAMS

The Dynamo and the Virgin

Henry Adams (1838–1918), American historian and author, the descendant of the United States presidents John Adams and John Quincy Adams, was one of the most important observers of the rapidly accelerating forces shaping modern life at *cation of Henry Adams* (1907), the uses of power in relationship to society. In this famous chapter from *The Education,* Adams contrasts medieval civilization, with its achievement of order, and the modern age, lacking the center that he so earnestly sought throughout his adult life.

Until the Great Exposition of 1900 closed its doors in November, Adams haunted it, aching to absorb knowledge, and helpless to find it. He would have liked to know how much of it could have been grasped by the best-informed man in the world. While he was thus meditating chaos, Langley came by, and showed it to him. At Langley's behest, the 1

Exhibition dropped its superfluous rags and stripped itself to the skin, for Langley knew what to study, and why, and how; while Adams might as well have stood outside in the night, staring at the Milky Way. Yet Langley said nothing new, and taught nothing that one might not have learned from Lord Bacon, three hundred years before; but though one should have known the "Advancement of Science" as well as one knew the "Comedy of Errors," the literary knowledge counted for nothing until some teacher should show how to apply it. Bacon took a vast deal of trouble in teaching King James I and his subjects, American or other, towards the year 1620, that true science was the development or economy of forces; yet an elderly American in 1900 knew neither the formula nor the forces; or even so much as to say to himself that his historical business in the exposition concerned only the economies or developments of force since 1893, when he began the study at Chicago.

Nothing in education is so astonishing as the amount of 2
ignorance it accumulates in the form of inert facts. Adams had looked at most of the accumulations of art in the storehouses called Art Museums; yet he did not know how to look at the art exhibits of 1900. He had studied Karl Marx and his doctrines of history with profound attention, yet he could not apply them at Paris. Langley, with the ease of a great master of experiment, threw out of the field every exhibit that did not reveal a new application of force, and naturally threw out, to begin with, almost the whole art exhibit. Equally, he ignored almost the whole industrial exhibit. He led his pupil directly to the forces. His chief interest was in new motors to make his airship feasible, and he taught Adams the astonishing complexities of the new Daimler motor, and of the automobile, which, since 1893, had become a nightmare at a hundred kilometres an hour, almost as destructive as the electric train which was only ten years older; and threatening to become as terrible as the locomotive steam-engine itself, which was almost exactly Adams's own age.

Then he showed his scholar the great hall of dynamos, and 3
explained how little he knew about electricity or force of any kind, even of his own special sun, which spouted heat in inconceivable volume, but which, as far as he knew, might spout less or more, at any time, for all the certainty he felt in it. To him, the dynamo itself was but an ingenious channel for conveying somewhere the heat latent in a few tons of poor coal hidden in a dirty engine-house carefully kept out of sight; but to Adams the dynamo became a symbol of infinity. As he grew accustomed to the great gallery of machines, he began to feel the forty-foot dynamos as a moral force, much as the early Christians felt the Cross. The planet itself seemed less impressive, in its old-fashioned, deliberate, annual or daily

revolution, than this huge wheel, revolving within arm's-length at some vertiginous speed, and barely murmuring—scarcely humming an audible warning to stand a hair's-breadth further for respect of power—while it would not wake the baby lying close against its frame. Before the end, one began to pray to it; inherited instinct taught the natural expression of man before silent and infinite force. Among the thousand symbols of ultimate energy, the dynamo was not so human as some, but it was the most expressive.

Yet the dynamo, next to the steam-engine, was the most 4
familiar of exhibits. For Adams's objects its value lay chiefly in its occult mechanism. Between the dynamo in the gallery of machines and the engine-house outside, the break of continuity amounted to abysmal fracture for a historian's objects. No more relation could he discover between the steam and the electric current than between the Cross and the cathedral. The forces were interchangeable if not reversible, but he could see only an absolute *fiat* in electricity as in faith. Langley could not help him. Indeed, Langley seemed to be worried by the same trouble, for he constantly repeated that the new forces were anarchical, and specially that he was not responsible for the new rays, that were little short of parricidal in their wicked spirit towards science. His own rays, with which he had doubled the solar spectrum, were altogether harmless and beneficent; but Radium denied its God—or, what was to Langley the same thing, denied the truths of his Science. The force was wholly new.

A historian who asked only to learn enough to be as futile as 5
Langley or Kelvin, made rapid progress under this teaching, and mixed himself up in the tangle of ideas until he achieved a sort of Paradise of ignorance vastly consoling to his fatigued senses. He wrapped himself in vibrations and rays which were new, and he would have hugged Marconi and Branly had he met them, as he hugged the dynamo; while he lost his arithmetic in trying to figure out the equation between the discoveries and the economies of force. The economies, like the discoveries, were absolute, supersensual, occult; incapable of expression in horse-power. What mathematical equivalent could he suggest as the value of a Branly coherer? Frozen air, or the electric furnace, had some scale of measurement, no doubt, if somebody could invent a thermometer adequate to the purpose; but X-rays had played no part whatever in man's consciousness, and the atom itself had figured only as a fiction of thought. In these seven years man had translated himself into a new universe which had no common scale of measurement with the old. He had entered a supersensual world, in which he could measure nothing except by chance collisions of movements imperceptible to his senses, perhaps even imperceptible to his instruments, but perceptible to each other,

and so to some known ray at the end of the scale. Langley seemed prepared for anything, even for an indeterminable number of universes interfused—physics stark mad in metaphysics.

Historians undertake to arrange sequences—called stories, or histories—assuming in silence a relation of cause and effect. These assumptions, hidden in the depths of dusty libraries, have been astounding, but commonly unconscious and childlike; so much so, that if any captious critic were to drag them to light, historians would probably reply, with one voice, that they had never supposed themselves required to know what they were talking about. Adams, for one, had toiled in vain to find out what he meant. He had even published a dozen volumes of American history for no other purpose than to satisfy himself whether, by the severest process of stating, with the least possible comment, such facts as seemed sure, in such order as seemed rigorously consequent, he could fix for a familiar moment a necessary sequence of human movement. The result had satisfied him as little as at Harvard College. Where he saw sequence, other men saw something quite different, and no one saw the same unit of measure. He cared little about his experiments and less about his statesmen, who seemed to him quite as ignorant as himself and, as a rule, no more honest; but he insisted on a relation of sequence, and if he could not reach it by one method, he would try as many methods as science knew. Satisfied that the sequence of men led to nothing and that the sequence of their society could lead no further, while the mere sequence of time was artificial, and the sequence of thought was chaos, he turned at last to the sequence of force; and thus it happened that, after ten years' pursuit, he found himself lying in the Gallery of Machines at the Great Exposition of 1900, his historical neck broken by the sudden irruption of forces totally new. 6

Since no one else showed much concern, an elderly person without other cares had no need to betray alarm. The year 1900 was not the first to upset schoolmasters. Copernicus and Galileo had broken many professorial necks about 1600; Columbus had stood the world on its head towards 1500; but the nearest approach to the revolution of 1900 was that of 310, when Constantine set up the Cross. The rays that Langley disowned, as well as those which he fathered, were occult, supersensual, irrational; they were a revelation of mysterious energy like that of the Cross; they were what, in terms of mediaeval science, were called immediate modes of the divine substance. 7

The historian was thus reduced to his last resources. Clearly if he was bound to reduce all these forces to a common value, this common value could have no measure but that of their attraction on his own mind. He must treat them as they had been felt; as 8 convertible, reversible, interchangeable attractions on thought. He made up his mind to venture it; he would risk translating rays into faith. Such a reversible process would vastly amuse a chemist, but the chemist could not deny that he, or some of his fellow physicists, could feel the force of both. When Adams was a boy in Boston, the best chemist in the place had probably never heard of Venus except by way of scandal, or of the Virgin except as idolatry; neither had he heard of dynamos or automobiles or radium; yet his mind was ready to feel the force of all, though the rays were unborn and the women were dead.

Here opened another totally new education, which promised 9
to be by far the most hazardous of all. The knife-edge along which he must crawl, like Sir Lancelot in the twelfth century, divided two kingdoms of force which had nothing in common but attraction. They were as different as a magnet is from gravitation, supposing one knew what a magnet was, or gravitation, or love. The force of the Virgin was still felt at Lourdes, and seemed to be as potent as X-rays: but in America neither Venus nor Virgin ever had value as force—at most as sentiment. No American had ever been truly afraid of either.

This problem in dynamics gravely perplexed an American 10
historian. The Woman had once been supreme; in France she still seemed potent, not merely as a sentiment, but as a force. Why was she unknown in America? For evidently America was ashamed of her, and she was ashamed of herself, otherwise they would not have strewn fig-leaves so profusely all over her. When she was a true force, she was ignorant of fig-leaves, but the monthly-magazine-made American female had not a feature that would have been recognized by Adam. The trait was notorious, and often humorous, but any one brought up among Puritans knew that sex was sin. In any previous age, sex was strength. Neither art nor beauty was needed. Every one, even among Puritans, knew that neither Diana of the Ephesians nor any of the Oriental goddesses was worshipped for her beauty. She was goddess because of her force; she was the animated dynamo; she was reproduction—the greatest and most mysterious of all energies; all she needed was to be fecund. Singularly enough, not one of Adams's many schools of education had ever drawn his attention to the opening lines of Lucretius, though they were perhaps the finest in all Latin literature, where the poet invoked Venus exactly as Dante invoked the Virgin:—

> "Quae quoniam rerum naturam *sola* gubernas."

The Venus of Epicurean philosophy survived in the Virgin of the Schools:—

"Donna, sei tanto grande, e tanto vali,
Che qual vuol grazia, e a te non ricorre,
Sua disianza vuol volar senz' ali."

All this was to American thought as though it had never existed. The true American knew something of the facts, but nothing of the feelings; he read the letter, but he never felt the law. Before this historical chasm, a mind like that of Adams felt itself helpless; he turned from the Virgin to the Dynamo as though he were a Branly coherer. On one side, at the Louvre and at Chartres, as he knew by the record of work actually done and still before his eyes, was the highest energy ever known to man, the creator of four-fifths of his noblest art, exercising vastly more attraction over the human mind than all the steam-engines and dynamos ever dreamed of; and yet this energy was unknown to the American mind. An American Virgin would never dare command; an American Venus would never dare exist.

The question, which to any plain American of the nineteenth 11
century seemed as remote as it did to Adams, drew him almost violently to study, once it was posed; and on this point Langleys were as useless as though they were Herbert Spencers or dynamos. The idea survived only as art. There one turned as naturally as though the artist were himself a woman. Adams began to ponder, asking himself whether he knew of any American artist who had ever insisted on the power of sex, as every classic had always done; but he could think only of Walt Whitman; Bret Harte, as far as the magazines would let him venture; and one or two painters, for the flesh-tones. All the rest had used sex for sentiment, never for force; to them, Eve was a tender flower, and Herodias an unfeminine horror. American art, like the American language and American education, was as far as possible sexless. Society regarded this victory over sex as its greatest triumph, and the historian readily admitted it, since the moral issue, for the moment, did not concern one who was studying the relations of unmoral force. He cared nothing for the sex of the dynamo until he could measure its energy.

Vaguely seeking a clue, he wandered through the art exhibit, 12
and, in his stroll, stopped almost every day before St. Gaudens's General Sherman, which had been given the central post of honor. St. Gaudens himself was in Paris, putting on the work his usual interminable last touches, and listening to the usual contradictory suggestions of brother sculptors. Of all the American artists who gave to American art whatever life it breathed in the seventies, St. Gaudens was perhaps the most sympathetic, but certainly the most inarticulate. General Grant or Don Cameron had scarcely less instinct of rhetoric than he. All the others—the Hunts, Richardson, John La

Farge, Stanford White—were exuberant; only St. Gaudens could never discuss or dilate on an emotion, or suggest artistic arguments for giving to his work the forms that he felt. He never laid down the law, or affected the despot, or became brutalized like Whistler by the brutalities of his world. He required no incense; he was no egoist; his simplicity of thought was excessive; he could not imitate, or give any form but his own to the creations of his hand. No one felt more strongly than he the strength of other men, but the idea that they could affect him never stirred an image in his mind.

This summer his health was poor and his spirits were low. For such a temper, Adams was not the best companion, since his own gaiety was not *folle;* but he risked going now and then to the studio on Mont Parnasse to draw him out for a stroll in the Bois de Boulogne, or dinner as pleased his moods, and in return St. Gaudens sometimes let Adams go about in his company. 13

Once St. Gaudens took him down to Amiens, with a party of Frenchmen, to see the cathedral. Not until they found themselves actually studying the sculpture of the western portal, did it dawn on Adams's mind that, for his purposes, St. Gaudens on that spot had more interest to him than the cathedral itself. Great men before great monuments express great truths, provided they are not taken too solemnly. Adams never tired of quoting the supreme phrase of his idol Gibbon, before the Gothic cathedrals: "I darted a contemptuous look on the stately monuments of superstition." Even in the footnotes of his history, Gibbon had never inserted a bit of humor more human than this, and one would have paid largely for a photograph of the fat little historian, on the background of Notre Dame of Amiens, trying to persuade his readers—perhaps himself—that he was darting a contemptuous look on the stately monument, for which he felt in fact the respect which every man of his vast study and active mind always feels before objects worthy of it; but besides the humor, one felt also the relation. Gibbon ignored the Virgin, because in 1789 religious monuments were out of fashion. In 1900 his remark sounded fresh and simple as the green fields to ears that had heard a hundred years of other remarks, mostly no more fresh and certainly less simple. Without malice, one might find it more instructive than a whole lecture of Ruskin. One sees what one brings, and at that moment Gibbon brought the French Revolution. Ruskin brought reaction against the Revolution. St. Gaudens had passed beyond all. He liked the stately monuments much more than he liked Gibbon or Ruskin; he loved their dignity; their unity; their scale; their lines; their lights and shadows; their decorative sculpture; but he was even less conscious than they of the force that created it all—the Virgin, the Woman—by whose genius "the stately monuments of superstition" were built, through which she was expressed. He would have seen 14 more meaning in Isis with the cow's horns, at Edfoo, who expressed the same thought. The art remained, but the energy was lost even upon the artist.

15 Yet in mind and person St. Gaudens was a survival of the 1500's; he bore the stamp of the Renaissance, and should have carried an image of the Virgin round his neck, or stuck in his hat, like Louis XI. In mere time he was a lost soul that had strayed by chance into the twentieth century, and forgotten where it came from. He writhed and cursed at his ignorance, much as Adams did at his own, but in the opposite sense. St. Gaudens was a child of Benvenuto Cellini, smothered in an American cradle. Adams was a quintessence of Boston, devoured by curiosity to think like Benvenuto. St. Gaudens's art was starved from birth, and Adams's instinct was blighted from babyhood. Each had but half of a nature, and when they came together before the Virgin of Amiens they ought both to have felt in her the force that made them one; but it was not so. To Adams she became more than ever a channel of force; to St. Gaudens she remained as before a channel of taste.

16 For a symbol of power, St. Gaudens instinctively preferred the horse, as was plain in his horse and Victory of the Sherman monument. Doubtless Sherman also felt it so. The attitude was so American that, for at least forty years, Adams had never realized that any other could be in sound taste. How many years had he taken to admit a notion of what Michael Angelo and Rubens were driving at? He could not say; but he knew that only since 1895 had he begun to feel the Virgin or Venus as force, and not everywhere even so. At Chartres—perhaps at Lourdes—possibly at Cnidos if one could still find there the divinely naked Aphrodite of Praxiteles—but otherwise one must look for force to the goddesses of Indian mythology. The idea died out long ago in the German and English stock. St. Gaudens at Amiens was hardly less sensitive to the force of the female energy than Matthew Arnold at the Grande Chartreuse. Neither of them felt goddesses as power—only as reflected emotion, human expression, beauty, purity, taste, scarcely even as sympathy. They felt a railway train as power; yet they, and all other artists, constantly complained that the power embodied in a railway train could never be embodied in art. All the steam in the world could not, like the Virgin, build Chartres.

17 Yet in mechanics, whatever the mechanicians might think, both energies acted as interchangeable forces on man, and by action on man all known force may be measured. Indeed, few men of science measured force in any other way. After once admitting that a straight line was the shortest distance between two points, no serious mathematician cared to deny anything that suited his convenience,

and rejected no symbol, unproved or unproveable, that helped him to accomplish work. The symbol was force, as a compass needle or a triangle was force, as the mechanist might prove by losing it, and nothing could be gained by ignoring their value. Symbol or energy, the Virgin had acted as the greatest force the Western world ever felt, and had drawn man's activities to herself more strongly than any other power, natural or supernatural, had ever done; the historian's business was to follow the track of the energy; to find where it came from and where it went to; its complex source and shifting channels; its values, equivalents, conversions. It could scarcely be more complex than radium; it could hardly be deflected, diverted, polarized, absorbed more perplexingly than other radiant matter. Adams knew nothing about any of them, but as a mathematical problem of influence on human progress, though all were occult, all reacted on his mind, and he rather inclined to think the Virgin easiest to handle.

The pursuit turned out to be long and tortuous, leading at last 18
into the vast forests of scholastic science. From Zeno to Descartes, hand in hand with Thomas Aquinas, Montaigne, and Pascal, one stumbled as stupidly as though one were still a German student of 1860. Only with the instinct of despair could one force one's self into this old thicket of ignorance after having been repulsed at a score of entrances more promising and more popular. Thus far, no path had led anywhere, unless perhaps to an exceedingly modest living. Forty-five years of study had proved to be quite futile for the pursuit of power; one controlled no more force in 1900 than in 1850, although the amount of force controlled by society had enormously increased. The secret of education still hid itself somewhere behind ignorance, and one fumbled over it as feebly as ever. In such labyrinths, the staff is a force almost more necessary than the legs; the pen becomes a sort of blind-man's dog, to keep him from falling into the gutters. The pen works for itself, and acts like a hand, modelling the plastic material over and over again to the form that suits it best. The form is never arbitrary, but is a sort of growth like crystallization, as any artist knows too well; for often the pencil or pen runs into side-paths and shapelessness, loses its relations, stops or is bogged. Then it has to return on its trail, and recover, if it can, its line of force. The result of a year's work depends more on what is struck out than on what is left in; on the sequence of the main lines of thought, than on their play or variety. Compelled once more to lean heavily on this support, Adams covered more thousands of pages with figures as formal as though they were algebra, laboriously striking out, altering, burning, experimenting, until the year had expired, the Exposition had long been closed, and winter drawing to its end, before he sailed from Cherbourg, on January 19, 1901, for home.

QUESTIONS

1. Explain Adams's philosophy of history and his attitude toward civilization. Why does he prefer medieval to modern times?

2. What does the author say about the process of his own education?

3. Adams develops many striking figures of speech to illuminate and reinforce abstract concepts and propositions in this essay. Locate examples of this interrelation of figurative and abstract language.

4. Identify the allusions to Langley (paragraph 1), Daimler (paragraph 2), Marconi and Branly (paragraph 5), and St. Gaudens (paragraph 12). What is the purpose of these allusions? What set of allusions is juxtaposed against them?

5. Explain the way the twin symbols of the Virgin and the dynamo create meaning, coherence, and unity in Adams's essay. What subject links these twin symbols? How do they dictate patterns of comparison and contrast?

6. Why does Adams, writing his autobiography, refer to himself in the third person? What is the effect? How does this strategy reinforce the overall tone of the essay?

7. Analyze the author's presentation of causal analysis in the essay.

8. Why does Adams emphasize St. Gaudens in paragraphs 12 through 16? How does this section prepare for the concluding two paragraphs?

9. Comment on Adams's declaration, "Nothing in education is so astonishing as the amount of ignorance it accumulates in the form of inert facts" (paragraph 2).

10. a. Write an essay investigating what you have learned about civilization from the process of your education.
b. Analyze the role of education in dealing with the forces of modern civilization.

KENNETH E. BOULDING

After Civilization, What?

Kenneth Ewart Boulding (1910–   ), born in England and a naturalized American citizen since 1948, was for many years a professor of economics at the University of Michigan and a

director of the Center for Research and Conflict Resolution. Currently he is director of the Institute of Behavioral Science at the University of Colorado. The author of *Economic Analysis* (1941), *The Organizational Revolution* (1953), *The Image* (1956), *Disarmament and the Economy* (1963), and other books, Boulding has been interested persistently in the problems of contemporary civilization. In this essay, he sets out to classify civilizations past, present, and future, and to analyze the problems and prospects inherent in all stages of civilization.

We are living in what I call the second great change in the state of man. The first is the change from pre-civilized to civilized societies. The first five hundred thousand years or so of man's existence on earth were relatively uneventful. Compared with his present condition, he puttered along in an astonishingly stationary state. There may have been changes in language and culture which are not reflected in the artifacts, but if there were, these changes are lost to us. The evidence of the artifacts, however, is conclusive. Whatever changes they were, they were almost unbelievably slow. About ten thousand years ago, we begin to perceive an acceleration in the rate of change. This becomes very noticeable five thousand years ago with the development of the first civilization. The details of this first great change are probably beyond our recovery. However, we do know that it depended on two phenomena: the development of agriculture and the development of exploitation. Agriculture, that is the domestication of crops and livestock and the planting of crops in fields, gave man a secure surplus of food from the food producer. In a hunting and fishing economy it seems to take the food producer all his time to produce enough food for himself and his family. The moment we have agriculture, with its superior productivity of this form of employment of human resources, the food producer can produce more food than he and his family can eat. In some societies in these happy conditions, the food producer has simply relaxed and indulged himself with leisure. As soon, however, as we get politics, that is exploitation, we begin to get cities and civilization. Civilization, it is clear from the origin of the word, is what happens in cities, and the city is dependent (in its early stages, at any rate) on the existence of a food surplus from the food producer and some organization which can take it away from him. With this food surplus, the political organization feeds kings, priests, armies, architects, and builders, and the city comes into being. Political science in its earliest form is the knowledge 1 of how to take the food surplus away from the food producer without giving him very much in return.

Now I argue that we are in the middle of the second great change in the state of man, which is as drastic and as dramatic, and certainly as large as, if not larger than, the change from pre-civilized to civilized society. This I call the change from civilization to post-civilization. It is a strange irony that just at the moment when civilization has almost completed the conquest of pre-civilized societies, post-civilization has been treading heavily upon its heels. The student of civilization may soon find himself in the unfortunate position of the anthropologist who studies pre-civilized societies. Both are like the student of ice on a hot day—the subject matter melts away almost before he can study it. 2

These great changes can be thought of as a change of gear in the evolutionary process, resulting in progressive acceleration of the rate of evolutionary change. Even before the appearance of man on the earth, we can detect earlier evolutionary gear-shiftings. The formation of life obviously represented one such transition, the movement from the water to the land another, the development of the vertebrates another, and so on. Man himself represents a very large acceleration of the evolutionary process. Whether he evolved from pre-existing forms or landed from a space ship and was not able to get back to where he came from, is immaterial. Once he had arrived on earth, the process of evolution could go on within the confines of the human nervous system at a greatly accelerated rate. The human mind is an enormous mutation-selection process. Instead of mutation-selection process being confined, as it were, to the flesh, it can take place within the image, and hence, very rapid changes are possible. Man seems to have been pretty slow to exploit this potentiality, but one suspects that even with primitive man, the rate of change in the biosphere was much larger than it had been before, because of the appearance of what Teilhard de Chardin calls the noosphere, or sphere of knowledge. 3

Civilization represents a further acceleration of the rate of change, mainly because one of the main products of civilization is history. With the food surplus from agriculture it became possible to feed specialized scribes. With the development of writing, man did not have to depend on the uncertain memories of the aged for his records, and a great process of accumulation of social knowledge began. The past could now communicate, at least in one direction, with the present, and this enormously increased the range and possibility of enlargements of the contents of the human mind. 4

Out of civilization, however, comes science, which is a superior way of organizing the evolution of knowledge. We trace the 5 first beginnings of science, of course, almost as far back as the beginning of civilization itself. Beginning about 1650, however, we begin to see the organization of science into a community of knowledge, and this leads again to an enormous acceleration of the rate of change. The world of 1650 is more remote to us than the world of ancient Egypt or Samaria would have been to the man of 1650. Already in the United States and Western Europe, in a smaller degree in Russia and in some other parts of the world, we see the beginnings of post-civilized society—a state of man as different from civilization as civilization is from savagery. What we really mean, therefore, by the anemic term "economic development" is the second great transition in the state of man. It is the movement from civilized to post-civilized society. It is nothing short of a major revolution in the human condition, and it does not represent a mere continuance and development of the old patterns of civilization.

As a dramatic illustration of the magnitude of the change, we 6
can contemplate Indonesia. This is a country which has about the same extent, population and per capita income as the Roman Empire at its height. For all I know it is producing a literature and an art at least comparable to that of the Augustan age. It is, therefore, a very good example of a country of high civilization. Because of this fact, it is one of the poorest countries in the world. It is desperately anxious to break out of its present condition. Jakarta is a city about the size of ancient Rome, though perhaps a little less splendid. All this points up the fact that the Roman Empire was a desperately poor and underdeveloped society. The Roman cities seem to have been always about three weeks away from starvation, and even at its height it is doubtful whether the Roman Empire ever had less than seventy-five to eighty per cent of its population in agriculture.

Civilization, that is, is a state of society in which techniques 7
are so poor that it takes about eighty per cent of the population to feed the hundred per cent. But we do have about twenty per cent of the people who can be spared from food-producing to build Parthenons and cathedrals, to write literature and poetry, and fight wars. By contrast, in the United States today we are rapidly getting to the point where we can produce all our food with only ten per cent of the population and still have large agricultural surpluses. But for the blessings of agricultural policy, we might soon be able to produce all our food with five per cent of the population. It may even be that agriculture is on its way out altogether and that within another generation or so we will produce our food in a totally different way. Perhaps both fields and cows are merely relics of civilization, the vestiges of a vanishing age. This means, however, that even in our society, which is at a very early stage of post-civilization, we can now

spare about ninety per cent of the people to produce bathtubs, automobiles, H-bombs and all the other conveniences of life. Western Europe and Japan are coming along behind the United States very fast. The Russians, likewise, are advancing toward post-civilization, although by a very different road. At the moment their ideology is a handicap to them in some places—especially in agriculture, which still occupies forty-five per cent of the people. And, if the Russians ever discover that super-peasants are a good deal more efficient than collective farms, they may cut away some of the ideology that hangs around their neck and move even more rapidly toward post-civilized society.

I'm not at all sure what post-civilization will look like but it 8
will certainly be a world-wide society. Until very recently, each civilized society was a little island in a sea of barbarism which constantly threatened to overwhelm it. Civilization is haunted by the spectre of decline and fall, though it is noteworthy that in spite of the rise and fall of particular civilizations, civilization itself expanded steadily in geographical coverage, from its very beginnings. We must face the fact, however, that post-civilized society will be world-wide, if only because of its ease of communication and transportation. I flew last year from Idlewild to Brussels, and on glimpsing the new Brussels Airport out of the corner of my eye, I thought for a moment that we had come back and landed at Idlewild again.

The characteristic institutions of civilization are, as we have 9
seen, first agriculture, then the city, then war, in the sense of clash of organized armed forces, and finally, inequality, the sharp contrast between the rich and the poor, between the city and the country, between the urbane and the rustic. The state is based very fundamentally on violence and exploitation, and the culture tends to be spiritually monolithic.

In post-civilization all these institutions suffer radical change. 10
Agriculture, as we have seen, diminishes until it is a small proportion of the society; the city, likewise, in the classical sense, disintegrates. Los Angeles is perhaps the first example of the post-civilization, post-urban agglomeration—under no stretch of the imagination could it be called a city. War, likewise, is an institution in process of disintegration. National defense as a social system has quite fundamentally broken down on a world scale. The ICBM and the nuclear warhead have made the nation-state as militarily obsolete as the city-state, for in no country now can the armed forces preserve an area of internal peace by pushing violence to the outskirts. Poverty and inequality, likewise, are tending to disappear, at least on their traditional scale. In civilized societies the king or the emperor could live in a Versailles and the peasant in a hovel. In post-civilized society,

it is almost impossible for the rich to consume on a scale which is more, let us say, than ten times that of the poor. There is no sense in having more than ten automobiles!

Another profound change in the passage from civilization to post-civilization is the change in the expectation of life. In civilized society, birth and death rates tend to be about forty per thousand and the expectation of life at birth is twenty-five years. In post-civilized society, the expectation of life at birth rises at least to seventy and perhaps beyond. It may be that we are on the edge of a biological revolution, just as dramatic and far-reaching as the discovery of atomic energy and that we may crack the problem of aging and prolong human life much beyond its present span. Whether or not, however, we go forward to Methuselah, the mere increase of the average age of death to seventy is a startling and far-reaching change. It means, for instance, that in an equilibrium population, the birth and death rate cannot be more than about fourteen per thousand. This unquestionably implies some form of conscious control of births. It means also that a much larger proportion of the population will be in later years. 11

It is perfectly possible to paint an anti-utopia in which a post-civilized society appears as universally vulgar or dull. On the whole, however, I welcome post-civilization and I have really very little affection for civilization. In most pre-civilized societies the fact that the life of man is for the most part nasty, brutish and short, does not prevent the poets and philosophers from sentimentalizing the noble savage. Similarly, we may expect the same kind of sentimentalizing of the noble Romans and civilized survivals like Winston Churchill. On the whole, though, I will not shed any tears over the grave of civilization any more than I will over pre-civilized society. The credit balance of post-civilization is large. It at least gives us a chance of a modest utopia, in which slavery, poverty, exploitation, gross inequality, war and disease—these prime costs of civilization—will fall to the vanishing point. 12

What we have at the moment is a chance to make a transition to this modest utopia—a chance which is probably unique in the history of this planet. If we fail, the chance will probably not be repeated in this part of the universe. Whatever experiments may be going on elsewhere, the present moment indeed is unique in the whole four billion years of the history of the planet. In my more pessimistic moments, I think the chance is a slim one, and it may be that man will be written off as an unsuccessful experiment. We must look at the traps which lie along the path of the transition, which might prevent us from making it altogether. 13

The most urgent trap is, of course, the trap of war. War, as I 14

have suggested, is an institution peculiarly characteristic of civilization. Pre-civilized societies have sporadic feuding and raiding, but they do not generally have permanent organized armed forces, and they do not generally develop conquest and empire; or if they do, they soon pass into a civilized form. An armed force is essentially a mobile city designed to throw things at another mobile or stationary city with presumably evil intent. As far as I know, not more than two or three civilizations have existed without war. The Mayans and the people of Mohenjodaro seem to have lived for fairly long periods without war, but this was an accident of their monopolistic situation and they unquestionably occupied themselves with other kinds of foolishness. If pre-civilized society, however, cannot afford war, post-civilized society can afford far too much of it, and hence will be forced to get rid of the institution because it is simply inappropriate to the technological age. The breakdown in the world social system of national defense really dates from about 1949, when the United States lost its monopoly of nuclear weapons. A system of national defense is only feasible if each nation is stronger at home than its enemies, so that it can preserve a relatively large area of peace within its critical boundaries. Such a system is only possible, however, if the range of the deadly missile is short and if the armed forces of each nation lose power rapidly as they move away from home. The technological developments of the twentieth century have destroyed these foundations of national defense, and have replaced it with another social system altogether, which is "deterrence."

"Deterrence" is a social system with properties very different 15
from that of national defense, which it replaced. Under national defense, for instance, it is possible to use the armed forces; under "deterrence" it is not—that is, if the deterring forces are ever used, the system will have broken down. We live in a society with a positive possibility of irretrievable disaster—a probability which grows every year. Herman Kahn recently said: "All we are doing is buying time, and we are doing nothing with the time that we buy." The armed forces of the world are caught in a technological process which not only destroys their own function, but threatens all of us. Even if a few of us do crawl out of the fallout shelters, it is by no means clear that we can put the world back together again. Even if the human race could survive one nuclear war, it is very doubtful that it could survive a second; and as the purpose of the first nuclear war would be to set up a political system which would produce the second, unless there is a radical change in attitude towards national defense, the prospects of the human race seem to be dim. Fortunately, "there is still time, brother" and evolution can still go on in the minds of men. The critical question is whether it can go on rapidly enough. The abolition

of national defense, which is what we must face, is going to be a painful process, as we have come to rely on it to preserve many of the values which we hold dear. If the task can be perceived, however, by a sufficient number of people, there is at least a chance that we may avoid this trap before it is too late.

Even if we avoid the war trap, we may still fall into the population trap. Population control is an unsolved problem even for the developed areas of the world, which have moved the furthest towards post-civilization. An equilibrium of population in a stable post-civilized society may represent a fairly radical interference with ancient human institutions and freedoms. In a stable post-civilized society, as I have suggested, the birth and death rates must be of the order of fourteen per thousand, and the average number of children per family cannot much exceed two. There are many social institutions which might accomplish this end. So far, however, the only really sure-fire method of controlling population is starvation and misery. 16

In many parts of the world—indeed, for most of the human race for the moment—the impact of certain post-civilized techniques on civilized society has produced a crisis of growth, which may easily be fatal. In the tropics especially, with DDT and a few simple public-health measures, it is easy to reduce the death rate to nine or ten per thousand while the birth rate stays at forty per thousand. This means an annual increase of population of three per cent *per annum*, almost all of it concentrated in the lower age groups. We see dramatic examples of this phenomenon in places like the West Indies, Ceylon, and Formosa; but thanks to the activity of the World Health Organization, it is taking place rapidly all over the tropical world. Perhaps the most important key to the transition to post-civilization is heavy investment in human resources—that is, in education. The conquest of disease and infant mortality, however, before the corresponding adjustment to the birth rate, produces enormous numbers of children in societies which do not have the resources to educate them—especially as those in the middle-age groups, who after all must do all the work of a society, come from the much smaller population of the pre-DDT era. 17

Even in the developed countries, population control presents a very serious problem. The United States, for instance, at the moment is increasing in population even more rapidly than India. The time when we thought that the mere increase in income would automatically solve the population problem has gone by. In the United States, and certain other societies, in the early stages of post-civilization, the child has become an object of conspicuous domestic consumption. The consumption patterns of the American 18 spending unit seem to follow a certain "*gestalt*" in which household capital accumulates in a certain order, such as the first car, the first child, the washer and dryer, the second child, the deep freeze, the third child, the second car, the fourth child, and so on. The richer we get, the more children we can afford to have and the more children we do have. We now seem to be able to afford an average of something like four children per family, and as, in a post-civilized society, these four children all survive, the population doubles every generation. A hundred years of this and even the United States is going to find itself uncomfortably crowded. It can be argued, indeed, that from the point of view of the amenities of life we are already well beyond the optimum population.

The third trap on the road to post-civilization is the techno- 19
logical trap. Our present technology is fundamentally suicidal. It is based on the extraction of concentrated deposits of fossil fuels and ores, which in the nature of things are exhaustible. Even at present rates of consumption, they will be exhausted in a time span which is not very long measured against human history and which is infinitesimally small on the geological time scale. If the rest of the world advances to American standards of consumption, these resources will disappear almost overnight. On this view economic development is the process of bringing closer the evil day when everything will be gone—all the oil, the coal, the ores—and we will have to go back to primitive agriculture and scratching in the woods.

There are indications, however, that suicidal technology is 20
not absolutely necessary and that a permanent high-level technology is possible. Beginning in the early part of the twentieth century, it is possible to detect an anti-entropic movement in technology. This begins perhaps with the Haber process for the fixation of nitrogen from the air. A development of similar significance is the Dow process for the extraction of magnesium from the sea. Both these processes take the diffuse and concentrate it, instead of taking the concentrated and diffusing it, as do most processes of mining and economic production. These anti-entropic processes foreshadow a technology in which we shall draw all the materials we need from the virtually inexhaustible reservoirs of the sea and the air and draw our energy from controlled fusion—either artificially produced on the earth or from the sun.

This is why I so much resent spending half the world's 21
income on armaments—because the more we do this, the less chance we have of making the transition to a stable, high-level society. The human race is in a precarious position on its planet and it should act accordingly. It has a chance, never to be repeated, of making its great transition, and if it fails, at least one good experiment in intelligence

will have gone to waste. I suppose there are similar experiments of this nature going on in other parts of the universe; but I must confess to a hopelessly anthropocentric prejudice in favor of planet earth. It's a nice planet, and I'm in favor of it and I have no desire to see its principal inhabitant blow it up or starve it out.

When we look at the nature of possible remedies for our immediate problems, it seems clear that we all are engulfed in a profound and appallingly dangerous misallocation of our intellectual resources. The misallocation lies in the fact that although all our major problems are in social systems, we persist in regarding them as if they were essentially problems in physical or biological systems. We persist in regarding agricultural problems, for instance, as one of crops, whereas it is clearly fundamentally a problem of farmers. We persist in regarding the flood-control problem as a problem of the river and we even turn it over to army engineers, who treat the river as an enemy. A flood, however, is no problem at all to a river. It is a perfectly normal part of its way of life. The flood, essentially, is a problem of people and of social institutions, of architecture and zoning. Professor Gilbert White, of the University of Chicago, suggests that after spending over four billion dollars on flood control in this country, we are more in danger of major disasters than we were before. What we really mean by flood control is the substitution of a major disaster every fifty or one hundred years for minor inconveniences every five or ten. 22

In national defense we have fallen into exactly the same trap. We regard this as a problem in physical systems and in hardware, whereas it is essentially a problem in social systems. Here again, we are building into our societies the eventual certainty of total disaster. In face of the fact that war and peace is the major problem of our age, we are putting practically nothing into peace research; even when we do put money into arms control and disarmament research we spend sixty million dollars for Project Vela, which deals wholly with physical systems, and one hundred and fifty thousand on Project Vulcan, which deals with social systems and with unanswerable questions at that. When we look at biological and medical research, and still more, research into population, the disparity is just as striking. We persist in regarding disease as a biological problem, whereas it is fundamentally a bio-social system. Yet the number of sociologists in our medical schools can be counted almost on the fingers of one hand. 23

Nevertheless, in spite of the dangers, it is a wonderful age to live in, and I would not wish to be born in any other time. The wonderful and precious thing about the present moment is that there is still time—the Bomb hasn't gone off, the population explosion may be caught, the technological problem can, perhaps, be solved. If the 24 human race is to survive, however, it will have to change more in its ways of thinking in the next twenty-five years than it has done in the last twenty-five thousand. There is hope, however, in the fact that we are very far from having exhausted the capacity of this extraordinary organism that we call man. I once calculated the capacity of the human nervous system in terms of the number of different states it might assume, which is a very rough measure. This comes to two to the ten billionth power, assuming that each of our ten billion neurons is capable of only two states. This is a very large number. It would take you ninety years to write it down at the rate of one digit a second. If you want a standard of comparison, the total number of neutrinos, which are the smallest known particles, which could be packed into the known astronomical universe (this is the largest physical number I could think of) could easily be written down in three minutes. I find it hard to believe, therefore, that the capacity of the human organism has been exhausted.

What we have to do now, however, is to develop almost a 25
new form of learning. We have to learn from rapidly changing systems. Ordinarily we learn from stable systems. It is because the world repeats itself that we catch on to the law of repetition. Learning from changing systems is perhaps another step in the acceleration of evolution that we have to take. I have been haunted by a remark which Norman Meier, the psychologist, made in a seminar a few months ago, when he said that a cat who jumps on a hot stove never jumps on a cold one. This seems precisely to describe the state we may be in today. We have jumped on a lot of hot stoves and now perhaps the cold stove is the only place on which to jump. In the rapidly changing system it is desperately easy to learn things which are no longer true. Perhaps the greatest task of applied social science at the moment is to study the conditions under which we learn from rapidly changing systems. If we can answer this question, there may still be hope for the human race.

QUESTIONS

1. According to Boulding, what distinguishes precivilization from civilization, and civilization from postcivilization?

2. Identify the main problems facing postcivilization.

3. What paradoxical language does the author employ in paragraph 2?

4. Would you label this essay as subjective or objective in writing style? Explain.

5. Analyze the patterns of classification that serve to organize the essay. Explain the divisions involved in the classification schemes.

6. Examine the relevance of definition and of comparison and contrast to the development of the essay.

7. Discuss the reasoning process by which Boulding arrives at his conclusion in paragraph 25 that "We have to learn from rapidly changing systems."

8. What is the thesis of the essay? Where is it stated most clearly?

9. Comment on Boulding's statement: "If the human race is to survive . . . it will have to change more in its ways of thinking in the next twenty-five years than it has done in the last twenty-five thousand" (paragraph 24).

10. a. Explain your vision of postcivilization.
b. Write a classification essay on the possible types of civilizations that might emerge in the future.

Glossary of Terms

Abstract/concrete patterns of language reflect an author's word choice. Abstract words (for example, "wisdom," "power," "beauty") refer to general ideas, qualities, or conditions. Concrete words name material objects and items associated with the five senses—words like "rock," "pizza," and "basketball." Both abstract and concrete language are useful in communicating ideas. Generally you should not be too abstract in writing. It is best to employ concrete words, naming things that can be seen, touched, smelled, heard, or tasted in order to support generalizations, topic sentences, or more abstract ideas.

Acronym is a word formed from the first or first few letters of several words, as in OPEC (Organization of Petroleum Exporting Countries).

Action in narrative writing is the sequence of happenings or events. This movement of events may occupy just a few minutes or extend over a period of years or centuries.

Alliteration is the repetition of initial consonant sounds in words placed closely next to each other, as in "what a *t*ale of *t*error now their *t*urbulency *t*ells." Prose that is highly rhythmical or "poetic" often makes use of this method.

Allusion is a literary, biographical, or historical reference, whether real or imaginary. It is a "figure of speech" (a fresh, useful comparison) employed to illuminate an idea. A writer's prose style can be made richer through this economical method of evoking an idea or emotion, as in E. M. Forster's biblical allusion in this sentence: "Property produces men of weight, and it was a man of weight who failed to get into the Kingdom of Heaven."

Analogy is a form of comparison that uses a clear illustration to explain a difficult idea or function. It is unlike a formal comparison in that its subjects of comparison are from different categories or areas. For example, an analogy likening "division of labor" to the activity of bees in a hive makes the first concept more concrete by showing it to the reader through the figurative comparison with the bees. Analogy in exposition can involve a few sentences, a paragraph or set of paragraphs, or an entire essay. Analogies can also be used in argumentation to heighten an appeal to emotion, but they cannot actually *prove* anything.

Analysis is a method of exposition in which a subject is broken up into its parts so as to explain their nature, function, proportion, or relationship. Analysis thus explores connections and processes within the context of a given subject. (See *Causal analysis* and *Process analysis*.)

Anecdote is a brief, engaging account of some happening, often historical, biographical, or personal. As a technique in writing, anecdote is especially effective in creating interesting essay introductions, and also in illuminating abstract concepts in the body of the essay.

Antecedent in grammar refers to the word, phrase, or clause to which a pronoun refers. In writing, antecedent also refers to any happening or thing that is prior to another, or to anything that logically precedes a subject.

Antithesis is the balancing of one idea or term against another for emphasis.

Antonym is a word whose meaning is opposite to that of another word.

Aphorism is a short, pointed statement expressing a general truism or idea in an original or imaginative way. Marshall McLuhan's statement that "the medium is the message" is a well-known contemporary aphorism.

Archaic language is vocabulary or usage that belongs to an early period and is old-fashioned today. A word like "thee" for "you" would be an archaism still in use in certain situations.

Archetypes are special images or symbols that, according to Carl Jung, appeal to the total racial or cultural understanding of a people. Such images or symbols as the mother archetype, the cowboy in American film, a sacred mountain, or spring as a time of renewal tend to trigger the "collective unconscious" of the human race.

Argumentation is a formal variety of writing that offers reasons for or against something. Its goal is to persuade or convince the reader through logical reasoning and carefully controlled emotional appeal. Argumentation as a formal mode of writing contains many properties that distinguish it from exposition. (See *Assumption, Deduction, Evidence, Induction, Logic, Persuasion, Proposition,* and *Refutation*.)

Assonance defined generally is likeness or rough similarity of sound. Its specific definition is a partial rhyme in which the stressed vowel sounds are alike but the consonant sounds are unlike, as in "late" and "make." Although more common to poetry, assonance can also be detected in highly rhythmic prose.

Assumption in argumentation is anything taken for granted or presumed to be accepted by the audience and therefore unstated. Assumptions in argumentative writing can be dangerous because the audience might not always accept the idea implicit in them. (See *Begging the question.*)

Audience is that readership toward which an author directs his or her essay. In composing essays, writers must acknowledge the nature of their expected readers—whether specialized or general, minimally educated or highly educated, sympathetic or unsympathetic toward the writer's opinions, and so forth. Failure to focus on the writer's true audience can lead to confusions in language and usage, presentation of inappropriate content, and failure to appeal to the expected reader.

Balance in sentence structure refers to the assignment of equal treatment in the arrangement of coordinate ideas. It is often used to heighten a contrast of ideas.

Begging the question is an error or fallacy in reasoning and argumentation in which the writer assumes as a truth something for which evidence or proof is actually needed.

Causal analysis is a form of writing that examines causes and effects of events or conditions as they relate to a specific subject. Writers can investigate the causes of a particular effect or the effects of a particular cause or combine both methods. Basically, however, causal analysis looks for connections between things and reasons behind them.

Characterization especially in narrative or descriptive writing, is the creation of people involved in the action. Authors use techniques of dialogue, description, reportage, and observation in attempting to present vivid and distinctive characters.

Chronology or chronological order is the arrangement of events in the order in which they happened. Chronological order can be used in such diverse narrative situations as history, biography, scientific process, and personal account. Essays that are ordered by chronology move from one step or point to the next in time.

Cinematic technique in narration, description, and occasionally exposition is the conscious application of film art to the development of the contemporary essay. Modern writers often are aware of such film techniques as montage (the process of cutting and arranging film so that short scenes are presented in rapid succession), zoom (intense enlargement of subject), and various forms of juxtaposition, using these methods to enhance the quality of their essays.

Classification is a form of exposition in which the writer divides a subject into categories and then groups elements in each of those categories according to their relationships to each other. Thus a writer using classification takes a topic, divides it into several major groups, and then often subdivides these groups, moving always from larger categories to smaller ones.

Cliché is an expression that once was fresh and original but has lost much of its vitality through overuse. Because terms like "as quick as a wink" and "blew her stack" are trite or common today, they should be avoided in writing.

Climactic ordering is the arrangement of a paragraph or essay so that the most important items are saved for last. The effect is to build slowly through a sequence of events or ideas to the most critical part of the composition.

Coherence is a quality in effective writing that results from the careful ordering of each sentence in a paragraph and each paragraph in the essay. If an essay is coherent, each part will grow naturally and logically from those parts that come before it. Following careful chronological, logical, spatial, or sequential order is the most natural way to achieve coherence in writing. The main devices used in achieving coherence are transitions, which help to connect one thought with another.

Colloquial language is conversational language used in certain types of informal and narrative writing, but rarely in essays, business writing, or research writing. Expressions like "cool," "pal," or "I can dig it" often have a place in conversational settings. However, they should be used sparingly in essay writing for special effects.

Comparison and contrast as an essay pattern treats similarities and differences between two subjects. Any useful comparison involves two items from the same class. Moreover, there must be a clear reason for the comparison or contrast. Finally, there must be a balanced treatment of the various comparative or contrasting points between the two subjects.

Conclusions are the endings of essays. Without a conclusion, an essay would be incomplete, leaving the reader with the feeling that something important has been left out. There are numerous strategies for conclusions available to writers: summarizing main points in the essay, restating the main idea, using an effective quotation to bring the essay to an end, offering the reader the climax to a series of events, returning to the beginning and echoing it, offering a solution to a problem, emphasizing the topic's significance, or setting a new frame of reference by generalizing from the main thesis. A conclusion should end the essay in a clear, convincing, or emphatic way.

Concrete (See *Abstract/concrete*.)

Conflict in narrative writing is the clash or opposition of events, characters, or ideas that makes the resolution of action necessary.

Connotation and denotation are terms specifying the way a word has meaning. Connotation refers to the "shades of meaning" that a word might have because of various emotional associations it calls up for writers and readers alike. Words like "patriotism," "pig," and "rose" have strong connotative overtones to them. Denotation refers to the "dictionary" definition of a word—its exact meaning. Good writers understand the connotative and denotative value of words, and must control the shades of meaning that many words possess.

Context is the situation surrounding a word, group of words, or sentence. Often the elements coming before or after a certain confusing or difficult construction will provide insight into the meaning or importance of that item.

Coordination in sentence structure refers to the grammatical arrangement of parts of the same order or equality in rank.

Declarative sentences make a statement or assertion.

Deduction is a form of logic that begins with a generally stated truth or principle and then offers details, examples, and reasoning to support the generalization. In other words, deduction is based on reasoning from a known principle to an unknown principle, from the general to the specific, or from a premise to a logical conclusion. (See *Syllogism.*)

Definition in exposition is the extension of a word's meaning through a paragraph or an entire essay. As an extended method of explaining a word, this type of definition relies on other rhetorical methods, including detail, illustration, comparison and contrast, and anecdote.

Denotation (See *Connotation.*)

Description in the prose essay is a variety of writing that uses details of sight, sound, color, smell, taste, and touch to create a word picture and to explain or illustrate an idea.

Development refers to the way a paragraph or essay elaborates or builds upon a topic or theme. Typical development proceeds either from general illustrations to specific ones or from one generalization to another. (See *Horizontal/vertical.*)

Dialogue is the reproduction of speech or conversation between two or more persons in writing. Dialogue can add concreteness and vividness to an essay, and can also help to reveal character. A writer who reproduces dialogue in an essay must use it for a purpose and not simply as a decorative device.

Diction is the manner of expression in words, choice of words, or wording. Writers must choose vocabulary carefully and precisely to communicate a message and also to address an intended audience effectively; this is good diction.

Digression is a temporary departure from the main subject in writing. Any digression in the essay must serve a purpose or be intended for a specific effect.

Discourse (Forms of) relates conventionally to the main categories of writing—narration, description, exposition, and argumentation. In practice, these forms of discourse often blend or overlap. Essayists seek the ideal fusion of forms of discourse in the treatment of their subject.

Division is that aspect of classification in which the writer divides some large subject into categories. Division helps writers to split large and potentially complicated subjects into parts for orderly presentation and discussion.

Dominant impression in description is the main impression or effect that writers attempt to create for their subject. It arises from an author's focus on a single subject and from the feelings the writer brings to that subject.

Editorialize is to express personal opinions about the subject of the essay. An editorial tone can have a useful effect in writing, but at other times an author might want to reduce editorializing in favor of a better balanced or more objective tone.

Effect is a term used in causal analysis to describe the outcome or expected result of a chain of happenings.

Emphasis indicates the placement of the most important ideas in key positions in the essay. As a major principle, emphasis relates to phrases, sentences, paragraphs—the construction of the entire essay. Emphasis can be achieved by repetition, subordination, careful positioning of thesis and topic sentences, climactic ordering, comparison and contrast, and a variety of other methods.

Episodic relates to that variety of narrative writing that develops through a series of incidents or events.

Essay is the name given to a short prose work on a limited topic. Essays take many forms, ranging from personal narratives to critical or argumentative treatments of a subject. Normally an essay will convey the writer's personal ideas about the subject.

Etymology is the origin and development of a word; tracing a word back as far as possible.

Evidence is material offered to support an argument or a proposition. Typical forms of evidence are facts, details, and expert testimony.

Example is a method of exposition in which the writer offers illustrations in order to explain a generalization or a whole thesis. (See *Illustration*.)

Exclamatory sentences in writing express surprise or strong emotion.

Expert testimony as employed in argumentative essays and in expository essays is the use of statements by authorities to support a writer's position or idea. This method often requires careful quotation and acknowledgment of sources.

Exposition is a major form of discourse that informs or explains. Exposition is the form of expression required in much college writing, for it provides facts and information, clarifies ideas, and establishes meaning. The primary methods of exposition are illustration, comparison and contrast, analogy, definition, classification, causal analysis, and process analysis (see entries).

Extended metaphor is a figurative comparison that is used to structure a significant part of the composition or the whole essay. (See *Figurative language* and *Metaphor*.)

Fable is a form of narrative containing a moral that normally appears clearly at the end.

Fallacy in argumentation is an error in logic or the reasoning process. Fallacies occur because of vague development of ideas, lack of awareness on the part of writers of the requirements of logical reasoning, or faulty assumptions about the proposition.

Figurative language, as opposed to literal language, is a special approach to writing that departs from what is typically a concrete, straightforward style. It is the use of vivid, imaginative statements to illuminate or illustrate an idea. Figurative language adds freshness, meaning, and originality to a writer's style. Major figures of speech include allusion, hyperbole, metaphor, personification, and simile (see entries).

Flashback is a narrative technique in which the writer begins at some point in the action and then moves into the past in order to provide crucial information about characters and events.

Foreshadowing is a technique that indicates beforehand what is to occur at a later point in the essay.

Frame in narration and description is the use of a key object or pattern—typically at the start and end of the essay—that serves as a border or structure to contain the substance of the composition.

Generalization is a broad idea or statement. All generalizations require particulars and illustrations to support them.

General/specific words are the basis of writing, although it is wise in college composition to keep vocabulary as specific as possible. General words refer to broad categories and groups, whereas specific words capture with force and clarity the nature of a term. General words refer to large classes, concepts, groups, and emotions; specific words are more particular in providing meanings. The distinction between general and specific language is always a matter of degree.

Genre is a type or form of literature—for example, short fiction, novel, poetry, drama.

Grammatical structure is a systematic description of language as it relates to the grammatical nature of a sentence.

Horizontal/vertical paragraph and essay development refers to the basic ways a writer moves from one generalization to another in a carefully related series of generalizations (horizontal), or conversely from a generalization to a series of specific supporting examples (vertical).

Hortatory style is a variety of writing designed to encourage, give advice, or urge to good deeds.

Hyperbole is a form of figurative language that uses exaggeration to overstate a position.

Hypothesis is an unproven theory or proposition that is tentatively accepted to explain certain facts. A working hypothesis provides the basis for further investigation or argumentation.

Hypothetical examples are illustrations in the form of assumptions that are based on the hypothesis. As such, they are conditional rather than absolute or certain facts.

Identification as a method of exposition refers to focusing on the main subject of the essay. It involves the clear location of the subject within the context or situation of the composition.

Idiomatic language is the language or dialect of a people, region, or class; the individual nature of a language.

Ignoring the question in argumentation is a fallacy that involves the avoidance of the main issue by developing an entirely different one.

Illustration is the use of one or more examples to support an idea. Illustration permits the writer to support a generalization through particulars or specifics.

Imagery is clear, vivid description that appeals to our sense of sight, smell, touch, sound, or taste. Much imagery exists for its own sake, adding descriptive flavor to an essay. However, imagery (especially when it involves a larger pattern) can also add meaning to an essay.

Induction is a method of logic consisting of the presentation of a series of facts, pieces of information, or instances in order to formulate or build a likely generalization. The key is to provide prior examples before reaching a logical conclusion. Consequently, as a pattern of organization in essay writing, the inductive method requires the careful presentation of relevant data and information before the conclusion is reached at the end of the paper.

Inference involves arriving at a decision or opinion by reasoning from known facts or evidence.

Interrogative sentences are sentences that ask or pose a question.

Introduction is the beginning or opening of an essay. The introduction should alert the reader to the subject by identifying it, set the limits of the essay, and indicate what the thesis (or main idea) will be. Moreover, it should arouse the reader's interest in the subject. Among the devices available in the creation of good introductions are making a simple statement of thesis; giving a clear, vivid description of an important setting; posing a question or series of questions; referring to a relevant historical event; telling an anecdote; using comparison and contrast to frame the subject; using several examples to reinforce the statement of the subject; and presenting a personal attitude about a controversial issue.

Irony is the use of language to suggest the opposite of what is stated. Writers use irony to reveal unpleasant or troublesome realities that exist in life, or to poke fun at human weaknesses and foolish attitudes. In an essay there may be verbal irony, in which the author says one thing but means another; or situational irony, in which the result of a sequence of ideas or events is the opposite of what normally would be expected. A key to the identification of irony in an essay is our ability to detect where the author is stating the opposite of what he or she actually believes.

Issue is the main question upon which an entire argument rests. It is the idea that the writer attempts to prove.

Jargon is the use of special words associated with a specific area of knowledge or a particular profession. Writers who employ jargon either assume that readers know specialized terms or take care to define terms for the benefit of the audience.

Juxtaposition as a technique in writing or essay organization is the placing of elements—either similar or contrasting—close together; positioning them side by side in order to illuminate the subject.

Levels of language refer to the kinds of language used in speaking and writing. Basically there are three main levels of language—formal, informal, and colloquial. Formal English, used in writing or speech, is the type of English employed to address special groups and professional people. Informal English is the sort of writing found in newspapers, magazines, books, and essays. It is popular English for an educated audience, but still more formal than conversational English. Finally, colloquial English is spoken (and occasionally written) English used in conversations with friends, employees, and peer group members; it is characterized by the use of slang, idioms, ordinary language, and loose sentence structure.

Linear order in paragraph development means the clear line of movement from one point to another.

Listing is a simple technique of illustration in which facts or examples are used in order to support a topic or generalization.

Logic as applied to essay writing is correct reasoning based on induction or deduction. The logical basis of an essay must offer reasonable criteria or principles of thought, present these principles in an orderly manner, avoid faults in reasoning, and result in a complete and satisfactory outcome in the reasoning process.

Metaphor is a type of figurative language in which an item from one category is compared briefly and imaginatively with an item from another area. Writers use such implied comparisons to assign meaning in a fresh, vivid, and concrete way.

Metonymy is a figure of language in which a thing is not designated by its own name but by another associated with or suggested by it, as in "The Supreme Court has decided" (meaning that the judges of the Supreme Court have decided).

Mood is the creation of atmosphere in descriptive writing.

Motif in an essay is any series of components that can be detected as a pattern. For example, a particular detail, idea, or image can be elaborated upon or designed so as to form a pattern or motif in the essay.

Myth in literature is a traditional story or series of events explaining some basic phenomenon of nature, the origin of humanity, or the customs, institutions, and religious rites of a people. Myth often relates to the exploits of gods, goddesses, and heroes.

Narration as a form of essay writing is the presentation of a story in order to illustrate an idea.

Non sequitur in argumentation is a conclusion or inference that does not follow from the premises or evidence on which it is based. The *non sequitur* thus is a type of logical fallacy.

Objective/subjective writing refers to the attitude that writers take toward their subject. When writers are objective, they try not to report their personal feelings about the subject; they attempt to be detached, impersonal, and unbiased. Conversely, subjective writing reveals an author's personal attitudes and emotions. For many varieties of college writing, such as business or laboratory reports, term papers, and literary analyses, it is best to be as objective as possible. But for many personal essays in composition courses, the subjective touch is fine. In the hands of skilled writers, the objective and subjective tones often blend.

Onomatopoeia is the formation of a word by imitating the natural sound associated with the object or action, as in "buzz" or "click."

Order is the arrangement of information or materials in an essay. The most common ordering techniques are *chronological order* (time in sequence); *spatial order* (the arrangement of descriptive details); *process order* (a step-by-step approach to an activity); *deductive order* (a thesis followed by information to support it); and *inductive order* (evidence and examples first, followed by the thesis in the form of a conclusion). Some rhetorical patterns such as comparison and contrast, classification, and argumentation require other ordering methods. Writers should select those ordering principles that permit them to present materials clearly.

Overstatement is an extravagant or exaggerated claim or statement.

Paradox is a statement that seems to be contradictory but actually contains an element of truth.

Paragraph is a unit in an essay that serves to present and examine one aspect of a topic. Composed normally of a group of sentences (one-sentence paragraphs can be used for emphasis or special effect), the paragraph elaborates an idea within the larger framework of the essay and the thesis unifying it.

Parallelism is a variety of sentence structure in which there is "balance" or coordination in the presentation of elements. "I came, I saw, I conquered" is a standard example of parallelism, presenting both pronouns and verbs in a coordinated manner. Parallelism can appear in a sentence, a group of sentences, or an entire paragraph.

Paraphrase as a literary method is the process of rewording the thought or meaning expressed in something that has been said or written before.

Parenthetical refers to giving qualifying information or explanation. This information normally is marked off or placed within parentheses.

Parody is ridiculing the language or style of another writer or composer. In parody, a serious subject tends to be treated in a nonsensical manner.

Periphrasis is the use of many words where one or a few would do; it is a roundabout way of speaking or writing.

Persona is the role or characterization that writers occasionally create for themselves in a personal narrative.

Personification is giving an object, thing, or idea lifelike or human characteristics, as in the common reference to a car as "she." Like all forms of figurative language, personification adds freshness to description, and makes ideas vivid by setting up striking comparisons.

Persuasion is a form of discourse, related to argumentation, that attempts basically to move a person to action or to influence an audience toward a particular belief.

Point of view is the angle from which a writer tells a story. Many personal and informal essays take the *first-person* (or "I") point of view, which is natural and fitting for essays in which the author wants to speak in a familiar way to the reader. On the other hand, the *third-person* point of view ("he," "she," "it," "they") distances the reader somewhat from the writer. The third-person point of view is useful in essays in which writers are not talking exclusively about themselves, but about other people, ideas, and events.

Post hoc, ergo, propter hoc in logic is the fallacy of thinking that a happening that follows another must be its result. It arises from a confusion about the logical causal relationship.

Process analysis is a pattern of writing that explains in a step-by-step way how something is done, how it is put together, how it works, or how it occurs. The subject can be a mechanical device, a product, an idea, a natural phenomenon, or a historical sequence. However, in all varieties of process analysis, the writer traces all important steps, from beginning to end.

Progression is the forward movement or succession of acts, events, or ideas presented in an essay.

Proportion refers to the relative emphasis and length given to an event, idea, item, or topic within the whole essay. Basically, in terms of proportion the writer gives more emphasis to a major element than to a minor one.

Proposition is the main point of an argumentative essay, the statement to be defended, proven, or upheld. It is like a *thesis* (see entry) except that it presents an idea that is debatable or can be disputed. The *major proposition* is the main argumentative point; *minor propositions* are the reasons given to support or prove the issue.

Purpose is what the writer wants to accomplish in an essay. Writers having a clear purpose will know the proper style, language, tone, and materials to utilize in designing an effective essay.

Refutation in argumentation is a method by which you recognize and deal effectively with the arguments of your opponents. Your own argument will be stronger if you refute—prove false or wrong—all opposing arguments.

Repetition is a simple method of achieving emphasis by repeating a word, phrase, or idea.

Rhetoric is the art of using words effectively in speaking or writing. It is also the art of literary composition, particularly in prose, including both figures of speech and such strategies as comparison and contrast, definition, and analysis.

Rhetorical question is a question asked only to emphasize a point, introduce a topic, or provoke thought, but not to elicit an answer.

Rhythm in prose writing is a regular recurrence of elements or features in sentences, creating a patterned emphasis, balance, or contrast.

Sarcasm is a sneering or taunting attitude in writing, designed to hurt by evaluating or criticizing. Basically, sarcasm is a heavy-handed form of irony (see entry). Writers should try to avoid sarcastic writing and to use more acceptable varieties of irony and satire to criticize their subject.

Satire is the humorous or critical treatment of a subject in order to expose the subject's vices, follies, stupidities, and so forth. The *intention* of much satire is to reform by exposing the subject to comedy or ridicule.

Sentimentality in prose writing is the excessive display of emotion, whether intended or unintended. Because sentimentality can distort the true nature of a situation or idea, writers should use it cautiously, or not at all.

Sensory language is language that appeals to any of the five senses—sight, sound, touch, taste, or feel.

Series as a technique in prose is the presentation of several items, often concrete details or similar parts of grammar like verbs or adjectives, in rapid sequence.

Setting in narrative and descriptive writing is the time, place, environment, background, or surroundings established by an author.

Simile is a figurative comparison using "like" or "as."

Slang is a kind of language that uses racy or colorful expressions associated more often with speech than with writing. It is colloquial English and should be used in essay writing only to reproduce dialogue or to create a special effect.

Spatial order in descriptive writing is the careful arrangement of details or materials in space—for example, from left to right, top to bottom, or near to far.

Specific words (See *General/specific words.*)

Statistics are facts or data of a numerical kind, assembled and tabulated to present significant information about a given subject. As a technique of illustration, statistics can be useful in analysis and argumentation.

Style is the specific or characteristic manner of expression, execution, construction, or design by an author. As a manner or mode of expression in language, it is the unique way each writer handles ideas. There are numerous stylistic categories—literary, formal, argumentative, satiric—but ultimately no two writers have the same style.

Subjective (See *Objective/subjective.*)

Subordination in sentence structure is the placing of a relatively less important idea in an inferior grammatical position to the main idea. It is the designation of a minor clause that is dependent upon a major clause.

Syllogism is an argument or form of reasoning in which two statements or premises are made and a logical conclusion drawn from them. As such, it is a form of deductive logic, reasoning from the general to the particular. The *major premise* presents a quality of class ("All writers are mortal."); the *minor premise* states that a particular subject is a member of that class ("Ernest Hemingway was a writer."); and the conclusion states that the qualities of the class and the member of the class are the same ("Hemingway was mortal.").

Symbol is something—normally a concrete image—that exists in itself but also stands for something else or has greater meaning. As a variety of figurative language, the symbol can be a strong feature in an essay, operating to add depth of meaning and even to unify the composition.

Synonym is a word that means roughly the same as another word. In practice, few words are exactly alike in meaning. Careful writers use synonyms to vary word choice, without ever moving too far from the shade of meaning intended.

Theme is the central idea in an essay; it is also termed the *thesis*. Everything in an essay should support the theme in one way or another.

Thesis is the main idea in an essay. The *thesis sentence*, appearing early in the essay (normally somewhere in the first paragraph) serves to convey the main idea to the reader in a clear and emphatic manner.

Tone is the writer's attitude toward his or her subject or material. An essay writer's tone may be objective, subjective, comic, ironic, nostalgic, critical, or a reflection of numerous other attitudes. Tone is the "voice" that writers give to an essay.

Topic sentence is the main idea that a paragraph develops. Not all paragraphs contain topic sentences; often the topic is implied.

Transition is the linking of ideas in sentences, paragraphs, and larger segments of an essay in order to achieve *coherence* (see entry). Among the most common techniques to achieve smooth transitions are: (1) repeating a key word or phrase; (2) using a pronoun to refer back to a key word or phrase; (3) relying on traditional connectives like "thus," "however," "moreover," "for example," "therefore," "finally," and "in conclusion"; (4) using parallel structure (see *Parallelism*); and (5) creating a sentence or paragraph that serves as a bridge from one part of an essay to another. Transition is best achieved when a writer presents ideas and details carefully and in logical order.

Understatement is a method of making a weaker statement than is warranted by truth, accuracy, or importance.

Unity is a feature in an essay whereby all material relates to a central concept and contributes to the meaning of the whole. To achieve a unified effect in an essay, the writer must design an effective introduction and conclusion, maintain consistent tone or point of view, develop middle paragraphs in a coherent manner, and above all stick to the subject, never permitting unimportant or irrelevant elements to enter.

Usage is the way in which a word, phrase, or sentence is used to express a particular idea; it is the customary manner of using a given language in speaking or writing.

Vertical (See *Horizontal/vertical*.)

Acknowledgments

Henry Adams, "The Dynamo and the Virgin," from *The Education of Henry Adams* by Henry Adams. Copyright 1918 by the Massachusetts Historical Society. Reprinted by permission.

Woody Allen, "My Speech to the Graduates," from *Side Effects* by Woody Allen. Copyright © 1980 by Woody Allen. Reprinted by permission of Random House, Inc.

Maya Angelou, "The Deterioration of My Marriage" (editor's title), from *Singin' and Swingin' and Gettin' Merry Like Christmas* by Maya Angelou. Copyright © 1976 by Maya Angelou. Reprinted by permission of Random House, Inc. "Graduation" (editor's title), from *I Know Why the Caged Bird Sings* by Maya Angelou. Copyright © 1969 by Maya Angelou. Reprinted by permission of Random House, Inc.

Hannah Arendt, "The Human Condition," from *The Human Condition* by Hannah Arendt. Copyright © 1958 by The University of Chicago Press. Reprinted by permission of the University of Chicago Press.

Russell Baker, "Little Red Riding Hood Revisited." Copyright © 1979 by The New York Times Company. Reprinted by permission. "Small Kicks in Superland." Copyright © 1980 by The New York Times Company. Reprinted by permission.

James Baldwin, "Stranger in the Village," from *Notes of a Native son* by James Baldwin. Copyright © 1955 by James Baldwin. Reprinted by permission of Beacon Press.

Amiri Baraka, "Expressive Language," from *Home: Social Essays* (1966) by LeRoi Jones. Copyright © 1963 by LeRoi Jones. By permission of William Morrow & Company. "Soul Food," from *Home: Social Essays* (1966) by LeRoi Jones. Copyright © 1962 by LeRoi Jones. By permission of William Morrow & Company.

Ruth Benedict, "Are Families Passé?" from *Saturday Review*. Copyright 1948 by *Saturday Review*, December 25, 1948. All rights reserved. Reprinted by permission.

Bruno Bettelheim, "Freud and Man's Soul," from *Freud and Man's Soul* by Bruno Bettelheim. Copyright © 1982 by Bruno Bettelheim. Reprinted by permission of Alfred A. Knopf, Inc.

Franz Boas, "The Diffusion of Cultural Traits," from *Social Research*, September 1937. Copyright by *Social Research*. Reprinted with permission.

Kenneth Boulding, "After Civilization, What?" from *Bulletin of the Atomic Scientists*, October 1962. Reprinted by permission of *The Bulletin of the Atomic Scientists*, a magazine of science and public affairs. Copyright © 1962 by the Educational Foundation for Nuclear Science, Chicago, IL.

Albert Camus, "The Myth of Sisyphus," from *The Myth of Sisyphus and Other Essays* by Albert Camus, translated by Justin O'Brien. Copyright © 1955 by Alfred A. Knopf, Inc. Reprinted by permission of the publisher.

Rachel Carson, "The Changing Year," from *The Sea Around Us* by Rachel L. Carson. Copyright © 1950, 1951, 1961 by Rachel L. Carson. Reprinted by permission of Oxford University Press, Inc.

Arthur C. Clarke, "The Planets Are Not Enough." Reprinted by permission of the author and the author's agents, Scott Meredith Literary Agency, Inc., 845 Third Avenue, New York, NY 10022.

Robert Coles, "I Listen to My Parents and I Wonder What They Believe," from *Redbook*, February 1980. Reprinted by permission of Dr. Robert Coles.

Harry Crews, "Why I Live Where I Live," from *Esquire*, September 1980. Copyright © 1980 by Harry Crews. Reprinted by permission of Paul R. Reynolds, Inc., 12 East 41 Street, New York, NY 10017.

John Dewey, "Education and Social Change," from *The Later Works of John Dewey, 1925-1953*, volume II, ed. Jo Ann Boydston. Carbondale and Edwardsville: Southern Illinois University Press, 1980. Quoted with permission of the Center for Dewey Studies, Southern Illinois University —Carbondale.

Joan Didion, "In Bed," from *The White Album* by Joan Didion. Copyright © 1979 by Joan Didion. Reprinted by permission of Simon & Schuster, Inc. "On Keeping a Notebook," from *Slouching towards Bethlehem* by Joan Didion. Copyright © 1966, 1968 by Joan Didion. Reprinted by permission of Farrar, Straus, & Giroux, Inc.

René Dubos, "A Family of Landscapes," from *The Wooing of Earth* by René Dubos. Copyright © 1980 René Dubos. Reprinted with the permission of Charles Scribner's Sons.

Albert Einstein, "The Common Language of Science," from *Out of My Later Years* by Albert Einstein. Reprinted by permission of the Estate of Albert Einstein.

Loren Eiseley, "How Natural Is Natural?" from *The Firmament of Time* by Loren Eiseley. Copyright © 1960 by Loren Eiseley; copyright © 1960 by the Trustees of the University of Pennsylvania. (New York: Atheneum, 1960.) Reprinted with permission of Atheneum Publishers.

Ralph Ellison, "On Becoming a Writer," from *Shadow and Act* by Ralph Ellison. Copyright © 1964 by Ralph Ellison. Reprinted by permission of Random House, Inc.

Frances Fitzgerald, "America Revised," from *America Revised* by Frances Fitzgerald. Copyright © 1979 by Frances Fitzgerald. First appeared in *The New Yorker*. By permission of Little, Brown and Company in association with the Atlantic Monthly Press.

E. M. Forster, "My Wood," from *Abinger Harvest* by E. M. Forster. Copyright 1936, 1964 by E. M. Forster. Reprinted by permission of Harcourt Brace Jovanovich, Inc., and Edward Arnold (Publishers), Ltd. "Not Looking at Pictures," from *Two Cheers for Democracy* by E. M. Forster, copyright 1951 by E. M. Forster; renewed 1979 by Donald Parry. Reprinted by permission of Harcourt Brace Jovanovich, Inc., and Edward Arnold (Publishers), Ltd.

Sigmund Freud, "Libidinal Types,"

from *International Journal of Psycho-Analysis,* 13:277-280. Reprinted by permission of *International Journal of Psycho-Analysis* and of Sigmund Freud copyrights, Ltd.

John Kenneth Galbraith, "The Higher Economic Status of Women," from *Annals of an Abiding Liberal* by John Kenneth Galbraith. Reprinted by permission of Houghton Mifflin Company.

Ellen Goodman, "Bamama Goes to College." Copyright © 1980, The Boston Globe Newspaper Company/Washington Post Writers Group. Reprinted with permission. "Being a Secretary Can Be Hazardous to Your Health," from *At Large* by Ellen Goodman. Copyright © 1981 by The Washington Post Company. Reprinted by permission of Summit Books, a division of Simon & Schuster, Inc.

Stephen Jay Gould, "Darwin at Sea," from *Natural History,* vol. 92, no. 9. Copyright © 1983 by the American Museum of Natural History. Reprinted with permission.

J. B. S. Haldane, "On Being the Right Size," from *Possible Worlds* by J. B. S. Haldane. Copyright © 1928 by Harper & Row, Publishers, Inc.; renewed © 1965 by J. B. S. Haldane. Reprinted by permission of Harper & Row, Publishers, Inc.; the author's Literary Estate; and Chatto & Windus.

Edith Hamilton, "The Lessons of the Past." Reprinted by permission of John D. Gray, Executor of the Estate of Doris Fielding Reid. "The Roots of Freedom," from *The Ever-Present Past* by Edith Hamilton. Copyright © 1964 by W. W. Norton & Company, Inc. Reprinted by permission of W. W. Norton & Company, Inc.

S. I. Hayakawa, "Words and Children," from *Through the Communication Barrier* by S. I. Hayakawa. Copyright © 1979 by S. I. Hayakawa. Reprinted by permission.

Langston Hughes, "Salvation," from *The Big Sea* by Langston Hughes. Copyright 1940 by Langston Hughes. Reprinted by permission of Farrar, Straus & Giroux, Inc.

Aldous Huxley, "Time and the Machine," from *The Olive Tree* by Aldous Huxley. Copyright 1937 by Aldous Huxley; renewed 1965 by Laura A. Huxley. Reprinted by permission of Harper & Row, Publishers, Inc.; Mrs. Laura Huxley; and Chatto & Windus.

Pauline Kael, "Rocky," from *When the Lights Go Down* by Pauline Kael. Copyright © 1975, 1976, 1977, 1978, 1979, 1980 by Pauline Kael. Reprinted by permission of Holt, Rinehart and Winston, Publishers.

Martin Luther King, Jr., "The World House," from *Where Do We Go from Here: Chaos or Community?* by Martin Luther King, Jr. Copyright © 1967 by Martin Luther King, Jr. Reprinted by permission of Harper & Row, Publishers, Inc.

Maxine Hong Kingston, "The Woman Warrior," from *The Woman Warrior: Memoirs of a Girlhood among Ghosts* by Maxine Hong Kingston. Copyright © 1975, 1976 by Maxine Hong Kingston. Reprinted by permission of Alfred A. Knopf, Inc.

Joseph Wood Krutch, "The New Immorality." Copyright © 1980 by *The Saturday Review.* All rights reserved. Reprinted by permission.

Katherine Kuh, "Break-up: The Core of Modern Art" from *Break Up: The Core of Modern Art* by Katherine Kuh. Copyright © 1965 by Cory, Adams and MacKay, Ltd., London, England. By permission of New York Graphic Society Books/Little, Brown and Company, Boston.

D. H. Lawrence, "Do Women Change?" from *Phoenix II: Uncollected Papers* by D. H. Lawrence. Copyright © 1959, 1963, 1968 by the Estate of Frieda Lawrence Ravagli. Reprinted by permission of Viking Penguin, Inc. "Why the Novel Matters," from *Phoenix: The Posthumous Papers of D. H. Lawrence.* Copyright 1936 by Frieda Lawrence, renewed 1964 by the Estate of Frieda Lawrence Ravagli. Reprinted by permission of Viking Penguin, Inc.

Doris Lessing, "Being Prohibited," from *A Small Personal Voice* by Doris Lessing. Copyright 1956 by Doris Lessing. Reprinted by permission of Jonathan Clowes, Ltd., on behalf of Doris Lessing.

Mary McCarthy, "Names," from *Memories of a Catholic Girlhood*, copyright © 1957 by Mary McCarthy. Reprinted by permission of Harcourt Brace Jovanovich, Inc.

Carson McCullers, "Home for Christmas," from *The Mortgaged Heart* by Carson McCullers. Copyright © 1963 by Carson McCullers. Copyright © 1971 by Floria V. Lasky. Reprinted by permission of Houghton Mifflin Company.

Marshall McLuhan, "Sight, Sound, and the Fury," from *Commonweal* magazine, April 9, 1954. Reprinted by permission of Commonweal Publishing Company, Inc.

Marya Mannes, "How Do You Know It's Good?" *Glamour* magazine, November 1962, copyright © 1962 by Marya Mannes. Reprinted by permission of David J. Blow. "The New Therapy," from *Last Rights* by Marya Mannes. Copyright © 1973 by Marya Mannes. By permission of William Morrow & Company. "Wasteland," from *More in Anger* by Marya Mannes. J. B. Lippincott Co., 1958, © 1958 by Marya Mannes. Reprinted by permission of David J. Blow.

Rollo May, "Powerlessness Corrupts," from *Power and Innocence* by Rollo May. Copyright © 1972 by Rollo May. Reprinted by permission of W. W. Norton & Company, Inc.

Margaret Mead, "A Day in Samoa," from *Coming of Age in Samoa* by Margaret Mead. Copyright © 1928, renewed 1955 by Margaret Mead. By permission of William Morrow & Company. "One Vote for This Age of Anxiety." Copyright © 1965 by The New York Times Company. Reprinted by permission.

A. G. Mojtabai, "Polygamy," from "Hers." Copyright © 1980 by The New York Times Company. Reprinted by permission.

N. Scott Momaday, "The Way to Rainy Mountain," first published in *The Reporter*, 26 January 1967. Reprinted from *The Way to Rainy Mountain*, copyright © 1969, The University of New Mexico Press.

Gunnar Myrdal, "The Direction of Aid," from *Beyond the Welfare State* by Gunnar Myrdal. Copyright © 1960 by Yale University Press, Inc. Reprinted by permission of Yale University Press.

Vladimir Nabokov, "Philistines and Philistinism," from *Lectures on Russian Literature* by Vladimir Nabokov, copyright © 1981 by the Estate of Vladimir Nabokov. Reprinted by permission of Harcourt Brace Jovanovich, Inc.

Pablo Neruda, "The Odors of Homecoming," from *Passions and Impressions* by Pablo Neruda. Copyright © 1978 by the Estate of Pablo Neruda. Translations copyright © 1980, 1981, 1983 by Farrar, Straus and Giroux, Inc. Reprinted by permission of Farrar, Straus and Giroux, Inc.

Anaïs Nin, "Morocco," from *The Diary of Anaïs Nin*, volume II, copyright © 1967 by Anaïs Nin. Reprinted by permission of Harcourt Brace Jovanovich, Inc. "Notes on Feminism," reprinted from *The Massachusetts Review*. Copyright © 1972 by The Massachusetts Review, Inc.

Michael Novak, "Sports: a Sense of Evil," from *The Joy of Sports* by Michael Novak. Copyright © 1976 by Michael Novak. Reprinted by permission of Basic Books, Inc., Publishers.

George Orwell, "Marrakech," from *Such, Such Were the Joys* by George Orwell, copyright 1945, 1952, 1953, 1980 by Sonia Brownell Orwell; copyright © 1973 by Sonia Pitt Rivers. Reprinted by permission of Harcourt Brace Jovanovich, Inc.; the Estate of the late Sonia Brownell Orwell; and Martin Secker & Warburg, Ltd. "Politics and the English Language," from *Shooting an Elephant and Other Essays* by George Orwell, copyright 1950 by Sonia Brownell Orwell; copyright © 1978 by Sonia Pitt Rivers. Reprinted by permission of Harcourt Brace Jovanovich, Inc.; the Estate of the late Sonia Brownell Orwell; and Martin Secker & Warburg, Ltd.

Sylvia Plath, "A Comparison," from *Johnny Panic and the Bible of Dreams* by Sylvia Plath. Copyright © 1962 by Sylvia Plath. Reprinted by permission of Harper & Row, Publishers, Inc., and of Olwyn Hughes Literary Agency.

J. B. Priestly, "Wrong Ism," from *Essays of Five Decades* by J. B. Priestley. Copyright © 1966 by J. B. Priestley. Reprinted by permission of J. B. Priestley.

Santha Rama Rau, "By Any Other Name," from *Gifts of Passage* by Santha Rama Rau. Copyright © 1951 by Vasanthi Rama Rau Bowers. Originally appeared in *The New Yorker*. Reprinted by permission of Harper & Row, Publishers, Inc.

Bertrand Russell, "Can Religion Cure Our Troubles," from *Why I Am Not a Christian* by Bertrand Russell. Copyright © 1957 by Allen & Unwin. Reprinted by permission of Simon & Schuster, Inc. "Knowledge and Wisdom," from *Portraits from Memory* by Bertrand Russell. Copyright © 1951, 1952, 1953, 1956 by Bertrand Russell. Reprinted by permission of Simon & Schuster, Inc., and of George Allen & Unwin, Publishers. "The Study of Mathematics," from *Mysticism and Logic* by Bertrand Russell. Copyright 1929 by Allen & Unwin, Ltd. Reprinted by permission of George Allen & Unwin, Publishers.

Jean-Paul Sartre, "American Cities," from *Literary and Philosophical Essays* by Jean-Paul Sartre. Copyright © 1955 by S. G. Phillips Inc. Reprinted by permission.

Isaac Bashevis Singer, "Why the Geese Shrieked," from *A Day of Pleasure* by Isaac Bashevis Singer. Copyright © 1963, 1965, 1966, 1969 by Isaac Bashevis Singer. Reprinted by permission of Farrar, Straus & Giroux, Inc.

Adam Smith, "You Keep Bringing Up Exogenous Variables," from *Paper Money* by Adam Smith. Copyright © 1981 by George J. W. Goodman. Reprinted by permission of Summit Books, a division of Simon & Schuster, Inc.

John Steinbeck, "Americans and the Land," from *America and Americans* by John Steinbeck. Copyright © 1966 by John Steinbeck. Reprinted by permission of Viking Penguin, Inc.

Gloria Steinem, "Erotica vs. Pornography," from *Outrageous Acts and Everyday Rebellions* by Gloria Steinem. Copyright © 1983 by Gloria Steinem. Reprinted by permission of Holt, Rinehart and Winston, Publishers. "Why Do Women Work?" from *Ms.* magazine, March 1979. Reprinted by permission of *Ms.* magazine.

Dylan Thomas, "A Visit to Grandpa's," from *Portrait of the Artist as a Young Dog* by Dylan Thomas. Copyright 1940 by New Directions Publishing Corporation. Reprinted by permission of New Directions and of David Higham Associates, Ltd., agents for J. M. Dent, Publishers.

Lewis Thomas, "On Societies as Organisms," from *The Lives of a Cell* by Lewis Thomas. Copyright © 1971 by the Massachusetts Medical Society. Originally appeared in the *New England Journal of Medicine*. Reprinted by permission of Viking Penguin, Inc.

Virgil Thomson, "Taste in Music," originally published in the New York *Herald Tribune*, July 16, 1944. Copyright 1944 and 1971 by Virgil Thomson. Reprinted with the permission of the copyright owner.

James Thurber, "The Night the Bed Fell." Copyright 1933, 1961 by James Thurber. From *My Life and Hard Times* published by Harper & Row. Reprinted by permission of Mrs. James Thurber.

Alexis de Tocqueville, "Some Reflections on American Manners," from *Democracy in America* by Alexis de Tocqueville, translated by George

Lawrence; J. P. Mayer and Max Lerner, editors. Translation copyright © 1966 by Harper & Row, Publishers, Inc. Reprinted by permission of Harper & Row, Publishers, Inc.

Arnold Toynbee, "Why I Dislike Western Civilization." Copyright © 1964 by The New York Times Company. Reprinted by permission.

Barbara Tuchman, "An Inquiry into the Persistance of Unwisdom in Government," from *Esquire*, 1980. Copyright © 1980 by Barbara Tuchman. Reprinted by permission of Russell & Volkening, Inc. as agents for the author.

Mark Twain, "The Mesmerist," from *Mark Twain in Eruption* by Mark Twain, edited by Bernard DeVoto. Copyright 1922 by Harper & Row, Publishers, Inc.; renewed 1940 by The Mark Twain Company. Reprinted by permission of Harper & Row, Publishers, Inc.

Judith Viorst, "How Books Helped Shape My Life." Copyright © 1980 by Judith Viorst. Originally appeared in *Redbook*. Reprinted by permission of Lescher & Lescher, Ltd.

Alice Walker, "Saving the Life That Is Your Own: The Importance of Models in the Artist's Life," from *In Search of Our Mothers' Gardens* by Alice Walker. Copyright © 1976 by Alice Walker. Reprinted by permission of Harcourt Brace Jovanovich, Inc.

E. B. White, "Education," from *One Man's Meat* by E. B. White. Copyright 1939, 1967 by E. B. White. Reprinted by permission of Harper & Row, Publishers, Inc. "Once More to the Lake," from *Essays of E. B. White*. Copyright 1939, 1967 by E. B. White. Reprinted by permission of Harper & Row, Publishers, Inc.

Virginia Woolf, "The Death of the Moth," from *The Death of the Moth and Other Essays* by Virginia Woolf, copyright 1942 by Harcourt Brace Jovanovich, Inc.; copyright 1970 by Marjorie T. Parsons, Executrix. Reprinted by permission of the publisher, of the author's Literary Estate, and of The Hogarth Press. "Professions for Women," from *The Death of the Moth and Other Essays* by Virginia Woolf, copyright 1942 by Harcourt Brace Jovanovich, Inc.; renewed 1970 by Marjorie T. Parsons, Executrix. Reprinted by permission of the publisher, of the author's Literary Estate, and of The Hogarth Press.

Richard Wright, "The Psychological Reactions of Oppressed People," from *White Man, Listen!* by Richard Wright. Copyright © 1957 by Richard Wright. Reprinted by permission of Doubleday & Company, Inc.

Index